SYLVIA PORTER'S YOUR OWN MONEY

Other Avon Books by
Sylvia Porter

SYLVIA PORTER'S INCOME TAX BOOK

SYLVIA PORTER'S NEW MONEY BOOK FOR THE 80'S

SYLVIA PORTER'S YOUR OWN MONEY

Earning It, Spending It,
Saving It, Investing It
And Living on It
In Your First Independent Years

 AVON
PUBLISHERS OF BARD, CAMELOT, DISCUS AND FLARE BOOKS

SYLVIA PORTER'S YOUR OWN MONEY is an original publication of Avon Books. This work has never before appeared in book form.

AVON BOOKS
A division of
The Hearst Corporation
959 Eighth Avenue
New York, New York 10019

Book design by Sheldon Winicour
Copyeditor: Trumbull Rogers

Library of Congress Cataloging in Publication Data
Porter, Sylvia Field, 1913–
  Sylvia Porter's Your own money.

  Includes index.
  Summary: Suggests ways to earn money from babysitting, hobbies, and part-time or summer jobs, and gives advice on saving, spending, and enjoying money, and on preparing for a career.
    1. Finance, Personal. 2. Young adults—Finance, Personal. 3. Vocational guidance.
[1. Finance, Personal. 2. Moneymaking projects.
3. Job hunting. 4. Vocational guidance]
I. Title
HG179.P5725   1983   332.024   82-24479
ISBN 0-380-83527-4

First Avon Printing, May, 1983

Printed in the U. S. A.

COM 10 9 8 7 6 5 4 3 2 1

To
JAMES F. FOX
My Husband

ACKNOWLEDGMENTS

As it always must be, books of this sort represent the learning and experience of thousands of individuals, specialized organizations, and a cross section of federal, state, and local government agencies. For me to claim credit for whatever it adds to your own knowledge would be presumptuous. My contribution is that I distilled the expert information of these thousands of resources into this book. To the extent that I have succeeded in making the book useful as well as readable, I owe these thousands my gratitude. To the extent that I have failed, the shortcomings are mine alone.

My special gratitude goes to:

Patricia Estess, for whom my respect has grown as the book has taken shape to the point where she now has been appointed editor of my new magazine.

Ellen Hermanson, my one-and-only "staff," for whom my respect also has developed, as she has devoted full time to research and drafting its chapters.

Paul Martin, who concentrated on "Computers"; Janice Kirkel who worked on "Wheels;" and Michael Buxbaum who documented "Investments."

Carole Matera, who typed the entire manuscript and guarded it with such caution.

Nellie Sabin, who edited the book with meticulous care and love.

My teen-age board of experts whose criticisms were so helpful: Luke Meade, Andrea, Peter and Jennifer Wohl, Noah Estess.

And Jim Fox to whom this book is dedicated and whose astonished admiration as the book raced to its conclusion was my special inspiration.

Also my thanks belong to:

Gaspar Anastasi, M.D.; Carol Brandt; Richard R. Brookman,

M.D.; Richard C. Brown, M.D.; Gary Cialfi; Charlotte Crenson; Ed Dean; Ray Elliott, M.D.; John Fleck; James Fullam; Eugene Galanter; Daniel Gensler; Richard A. Givens; Joyce Gober; William Gold; Alan Goldstein; Norman Goldstein, M.D.; Richard Hofacker; Michael Hudak; David Kaminer; Vilma Lieberman; Iris F. Litt, M.D.; Chip Lovitt; W.C. Madden; H. Lynn Martin; John McMeel; Claire D. McMullen; Harlene Mehr; Harold I. Meyerson; Hugo Moreno; Stephen Moss, D.D.S.; Eric Murphy; Jennifer Niebyl, M.D.; Arthur Norins, M.D.; Thomas O'Dwyer; H. William Porterfield, M.D.; Stanley Rosenbloom; David Saffer; S. Kenneth Schonberg, M.D.; Melvin Spira, M.D.; Martin Toscano.

ORGANIZATIONS

Allstate Insurance Companies; American Academy of Dermatology; American Academy of Facial Plastic and Reconstructive Surgery; American Anorexia Nervosa Association, Inc.; American Association of Orthodontists; American Automobile Association; American Bankers Association; American Bar Association; American Camping Association; American Cancer Society; American College of Obstetricians and Gynecologists; American Civil Liberties Union; American Dental Association; American Express; American Health Foundation; American Medical Association; American Optometric Association; American Red Cross; American Society of Plastic and Reconstructive Surgeons; American Stock Exchange; American Youth Hostels; Anorexia Nervosa and Associated Disorders, Inc.; Apple Computers, Inc.; Arthritis Foundation; Asthma and Allergy Foundation of America; Atari; Atlantis II; Automotive Information Council.

Bell Laboratories; Better Business Bureau of Detroit, Inc.; Better Business Bureau of Los Angeles-Orange County, Inc.; Better Business Bureau of Metropolitan New York, Inc.; Better Hearing Institute; Better Vision Institute; Bikecentennial; Blind Brook-Rye School District; Blue Cross, Blue Shield Association; Boy Scouts of America; Burroughs Corporation; Business and Professional Women's Foundation; Byram Hills High School.

Citicorp; College Board; Commodity Futures Trading Commission; Commodore Computer; Computer Sciences Corporation; Consolidated Edison; Control Data; Chrysler Corporation.

Data General Corporation; Eastman Kodak Co.; Emory University; Epilepsy Foundation of America.

Family Service Association; Footwear Council; Ford Motor Company; Fram/Autolite; Friends of Animals; Furniture Rental Association.

Gallup Youth Survey; General Motors Corporation; Girl Scouts of the U.S.A.

Health Insurance Institute; Hertz Corporation; Honeywell.

IBM; Investment Company Institute; International Fabricare Institute; Jewelry Industry Council; Juvenile Diabetes Foundation International.

Medic Alert Foundation; Money Management Institute/Household International; Moore School of Electrical Engineering—University of Pennsylvania; Multimedia Program Productions, Inc.

National Association of Mental Health; National Coalition against Shoplifting; National Education Association; National 4-H Council; National Golf Foundation; National Hearing Aid Society; National Migraine Foundation; National Runaway Switchboard/Metro-Help; National Safety Council; New York City Advisory Task Force on Rape; New York City Department of Consumer Affairs; New York State Association of Service Stations; New York State Department of Motor Vehicles; No-Load Mutual Fund Association; North Eastern Auto Lease Corporation.

Paulding's Cycle Store; Planned Parenthood Federation of America, Inc.; Proprietary Association; Putney Student Travel.

Radio Shack; Recreational Vehicle Industry Association; *Runners World* Magazine.

Samaritans; Scholastic, Inc.; Sears Roebuck and Co.; *Seventeen* Magazine; Shell Oil Company; Sperry Univac; Student Camp and Trip Advisors, Inc.; Sunglass Association of America; Systems Development Corporation.

Tampax, Inc.; Televideo Systems; *Tennis Industry* Magazine.

Wang Laboratories; Weight Watchers International; Xerox Corporation.

United States Departments of: Agriculture; Energy; Labor; and State.

Bureau of Apprenticeship and Training; Bureau of Labor Statistics; Centers for Disease Control; Customs Service; Food and Drug Administration; Internal Revenue Service; National Academy of Science; National Center for Health Statistics; National Institutes of

Health; National Highway Traffic Safety Administration; Office of Health Maintenance Organizations; Passport Office; Social Security Administration; Women's Bureau.

CONTENTS

SYLVIA PORTER'S YOUR OWN MONEY

INTRODUCTION
Why This Book

You, who are now opening these pages, are a member of the most intelligent and educated generation this or any other nation in world history has ever produced. Yet, obvious though your accomplishments already are, or inspiring though your potentials shape up to be, you are extraordinarily unprepared for the financial pitfalls waiting to trap you wherever and whenever you turn—hidden in deceptively simple pricing structures, concealed under accepted ways of identifying styles or models, obscured by deliberate mislabeling of products ranging from cosmetics to cassettes.

While you can figure out dazzlingly new ways to use a computer, you are lost when asked the difference between an interest rate and a finance charge. While you can make astoundingly complex computations with a calculator that fits easily into your shirt pocket, you are embarrassingly ignorant of your rights as the buyer of that calculating machine.

It's not your fault alone! In fact, at every age level, starting with preteen elementary school, you are demanding more education in economics and particularly in consumer education than your parents ever did. But this education cannot be provided to you by the stroke of a legislator's pen in Washington or your state capital.

The reason: few of your classroom teachers have taken even a single course in advanced economics or a subject related to economics! There are few "out there," therefore, to teach you the often bewildering economic concepts in terms that you will find palatable—because first the teachers must be taught economics so they can help themselves understand why the cost of coffee is rising (or falling) or why the local clothing store must borrow money (or go bankrupt). It will take time for the teachers to learn before

1

they can help you learn how you earn money; how you can spend what you earn wisely; and how the great, basic economic trends in our nation and in the world affect your parents, your communities, and your own lives, now and in the future.

It has begun. Under the supervision of the Joint Council on Economic Education (JCEE), students in a small town in Georgia are studying the impact of a professional football team's move into their small, rural hometown. The students are trying to decide on their own whether the team's new football stadium will be an asset or a liability to their community. In other areas, students are learning how to take out loans and start their own businesses, ranging from selling cookies to building vending machines that dispense grab bags filled with favors. Another finding of a recent JCEE survey is that finally economics is a required course in 48 percent of the nation's junior/senior high schools—against only 24 percent who took an economics course as recently as 1969.

But by the time this learning process has progressed to the point where it can help you, you will be way beyond your first independent years—and that is why I have written this book. In these pages, you will find my best efforts to give you the fundamental economic–financial facts of life, facts essential to any aspirations you may have for an improvement in your way of living as well as for basic survival in what I have long called the jungle of the marketplace.

I have tried to talk straight to you—not up, not down—just as I wish you would talk to me, and as many of you already have while I prepared the contents of these pages.

This book is for *you*. And this book is for *your parents*. If I achieve only a tiny fraction of what I am dreaming for you as I write these words, the winner will be triumphantly me.

In the following pages when the male gender is used, it is used for convenience and simplicity. It refers to either the male or female gender.

1

WHERE DOES YOUR MONEY COME FROM?

CONTENTS

ALLOWANCES

How do you get your pocket money? Do your parents regularly give you an allowance, or do you have to ask for money every time you want to go to the movies or need supplies for school? If you don't get an allowance, you probably have to ask for frequent handouts—which becomes tedious and irritating for all of you.

There are many reasons why some parents don't give allowances. They believe they should approve all expenses; they can't decide which expenses an allowance should cover; they think children will fritter away their money; they haven't budgeted for an allowance in their own spending or feel they simply can't afford it. Whatever the reason, if your parents don't yet give you an allowance, try to persuade them that you will all be more comfortable if they change their minds.

An allowance helps you manage your own money and gain experience in handling larger sums as you grow older. It's a tool to teach you about finances—to help you learn about money and develop good attitudes about it. You learn to plan your expenses and to make your own choices about what to buy and what to save for. You choose between going to the movies and saving for that record you've wanted for weeks; or you find a really terrific belt, buy it, and discover a week later that you can't stand it and give it away. With an allowance, you take responsibility for what you buy and what you decide to do—and that means learning to live with your own mistakes as well as doing without some things you think you desperately need right now.

But allowances aren't all grim and serious. An allowance gives you freedom, too. You don't have to second-guess when your parents might be in a good mood and you can touch them for another handout. You don't have to account to them for every pack of gum or can of soda. It's your own money!

How Much Is Enough and What's It for, Anyway?

Your parents and you are persuaded that an allowance will teach you about money and free them from constant entreaties for a dollar here, five bucks there. Now you all must decide on a reasonable amount. Or perhaps you currently get an allowance, but you are confused about its use, and your parents have never quite explained it to you. The solution? Plan a family conference to discuss it. You will be surprised at how much you and your folks will learn about each other.

Prepare for this discussion—not to be subversive but clearly to express your thoughts about what you need and want. Make a list of all the things for which you now need money. Divide the list into necessities (lunch, carfare, club dues, recreation) and luxuries (records, tapes, magazines, more recreation). Your lists will most likely be comparatively long, and they will differ from those of your friends (as well as from your parents' expectations).

Discuss with your parents which items they want you to pay for with your allowance. They may decide to give you a separate amount for school lunches and supplies, or they may determine it's time for you to buy your own clothes and include money for that in your allowance. As your talk progresses, make sure everyone is in agreement so no one gets confused later on.

As an aid for you and your parents, here are rough guidelines on what teenagers might be expected to pay for with their allowances:

- *Everything preteens buy:* including fees for skating rinks, pools, etc.; club dues; hobby and craft materials; sports equipment and repairs; games; special events; carfare and school lunches; gifts for birthdays and holidays; contributions; school supplies; trips; and clothing.
- *Ages 12–18:* all of the above, plus money for dates; grooming; cosmetics; jewelry; clothing; school activities; and saving for special purposes, such as travel and education.

Your first allowance conference will be only your *first*. Discuss your finances with your parents every couple of months, or at least every fall when school begins.

Chores and Jobs

Are you expected to perform certain jobs such as washing the dishes, doing the laundry, or collecting the trash in exchange for your allowance? If you don't do your chores well or on time, do you lose it? In that case, your allowance is really a wage, which probably doesn't seem fair to you. However, receiving an allowance does not mean you're free of responsibilities to your family: as a family member, you should take on extra chores around the house, especially as you grow older and if both your parents work outside your home. You'll feel better about yourself and will be rewarded by good feelings and self-respect.

If you have another source of income—a job—urge your parents to continue your allowance, if they can afford it. You can't count on your earnings to cover all your needs, particularly if you have an irregular job such as babysitting or shoveling snow. And as you grow older, you'll need more money for your social life and extracurricular activities. Finally, your allowance should not be docked because you're industrious enough to find work—and that's what it will seem like if your allowance is discontinued. Talk this over with your parents and explain your side calmly and reasonably. Suggest that your allowance be used for necessities, and that the money you earn go toward savings, special activities and purchases.

Budgets

Now that you and your parents have agreed on your allowance, you have money to spend exactly as you like, right? Well, yes and no. What about those expenses that your allowance is supposed to cover every week? Those are fixed costs—expenses you expect to have, week in, week out. You must always reserve enough money for them. If you foresee that this can get complicated, you won't need much persuasion to keep track of your outflow and income. In short, you need a budget and records. (For more on recordkeeping, see Chapter 2, *Document Your Life*.)

Tracking income and outflow must not be an elaborate, time-consuming chore—or you won't do it! It's an excellent habit to develop early, though; you'll find it's essential as you grow older and have more money to manage and greater demands on your cash.

To start your initial records, buy a pocket notebook. In one column, note all your income from your allowance, jobs, and gifts. In other columns, start jotting down every item you buy—even cups of coffee. Break down your entries into categories such as ''school expenses,'' ''snacks,'' ''transportation,'' etc.—whatever categories are meaningful to you. At the end of the week, add up each column. If your allowance was sufficient to cover all your expenses, lucky you! More likely, however, you started to run short and maybe your allowance vanished by midweek.

After you keep this notebook for a few weeks, you will see patterns develop. Then you can cut back spending in some categories and increase it in others. You will know when to choose between having a hamburger and fries or saving for a concert ticket.

Some Hints on Budgeting

• Discuss your budget with your parents. Keep your plans realistic, and listen to their advice.

• Never plan your budget down to the last penny. Always have something left over for unplanned expenses and emergencies. The goal of a budget is not to account for every cent but to curb your spending on things you neither need nor enjoy.

• Keep your records simple. A pocket notebook should be sufficient for the time being. If you devise an elaborate procedure, you'll become bored and ignore it completely.

• Once you develop your system, stick to it. If you make random notes on napkins and matchbooks, you'll confuse yourself and defeat the whole purpose.

Renegotiating Your Allowance

You've tried, but you find you simply can't manage. What's the best way to handle your new financial crisis? Since you've kept track of your income and expenses, you are ready to explain the situation to your parents and build a case for an increase in your allowance. Don't announce that you're broke. They probably know that already, since you've been buttering them up regularly for handouts. But if you can document your case and present a reasonable defense (no, you're not on trial, but you do have to prove your side), your parents will listen. Keep in mind that they have to decide whether you've justified your request and, if so, decide whether they can afford an increase. Even though it's critical to you, your allowance is only a small portion of the family finances, and your parents most likely are trying to stretch the overall family budget in a number of directions.

Allowances and Budgets in Boarding School and College

You're struggling to live on an allowance in boarding school or college and you're convinced it can't be done. While it's probably not true, everyone else seems to have more money than you do and is spending it more lavishly. By midweek or midmonth, you're broke or close to it, and you're trying to find a friend to hit for a loan, or you're turning down a date because you can't pay your way. Whether you live at home and receive your allowance weekly or you have checks mailed to you at regular intervals, your problem is this: you are fighting a losing battle to make ends meet. Convince yourself that to manage your money and still enjoy yourself *is* possible, if you plan and make the effort.

Think of your allowance as a paycheck. It is to be treated with the same respect and care you will give a formal paycheck when you have a paying job. If you learn this now and live by certain financial rules, you will be a lot less frantic and a lot more fun to be around.

Whatever your financial background, the following rules apply:

• Discuss your expenses with your parents before you start school and decide what your allowance should pay for. (Sound familiar?) Once you get to school, keep this agreement in mind!

• Don't accept $40 a week when you know perfectly well it won't do at all. Plan realistically, and when actually at school, work out your day-to-day budget to cover both your necessities and luxuries. Be honest. Include routine expenses such as gum, coffee, and cigarettes (yes, you're trying to quit, but meanwhile that money does go somewhere). If your allowance is supposed to cover such items as shaving cream, dry cleaning, gas, car maintenance, etc., don't overlook these expenses in your budget.

• Open a bank account and deposit your allowance when you receive it. (For more on bank accounts, see Chapter 3, *Money*.) You can then draw on the money as you need it. If you carry a wad of cash with you, you may feel so flush that you are tempted to unload it immediately. Besides, you'll be a tempting target for muggers. You're better off with a checkbook. If your school has banking facilities or a check-cashing window, use them. Wherever you open your checking account, learn how to make deposits, write checks and, especially, balance your checkbook every month.

• If you and your parents can afford it, start a savings account or try to build one yourself out of your allowance. Depend on it, you will face unforeseen expenses—a crisis, a great weekend trip—for which you'll want, or need, to spend money.

• Don't figure down to pennies, allowing yourself no leeway. No money plan should be that precise, even when you're dealing with small sums. For your relief and protection, give yourself a margin of safety.

• Keep your income and outflow records to show where your allowance is going and why.

• Shop wisely. Your allowance will stretch further if you buy necessities during special sales or in economy sizes. (More about this later.)

• If your records indicate that your funds are too limited, renegotiate. You're supposed to live with an allowance, not suffer from it.

More Deep-Meaning Words on Budgets

You think that keeping track of your income and outflow sounds easy, so you've decided to give it a try. Besides, you're curious to see where all those nickles and dimes disappear each week, and you have a hunch they vanish into video games and cans of soda. Now you'll know for sure.

Keeping a budget also will encourage you to develop your goals and philosophy of living. Does that sound absurd? Think about it: right now your income is not enough to finance everything you want, a fact likely to remain constant. You probably have a fantasy purchase or dream trip you crave—a home computer, a jaunt to the South Seas—and you wonder how you'll ever afford such luxuries, even though you look forward to a good job and a much larger income eventually. If you accept the idea that when you have a larger income you will have greater desires and bigger responsibilities (sound logical?), it appears that you will forever chase your dreams and never catch up to them. With a budget, you are forced to make choices, plan ahead, and control your spending. This means that you must think about your goals, your ambitions and choose what's best or most enticing.

What's really important to you? If it's a safari in Kenya or a college degree, you will start to save for it, no matter how small the sums you stash away. When you control your spending, you make progress toward the kind of life that means the most to you. That is a decision only you can make.

OTHER WAYS TO MAKE MONEY

Babysitting

Did you babysit this week? If so, you are among an estimated 1 million young adults who did. Most sitters work about three hours each week, which, multiplied by the going rate in your neighborhood, totals big money being spent nationwide for babysitters. If you don't already cash in on this source of income, perhaps you have thought about it but aren't sure whether you'd like it. Or perhaps you're a boy who thinks it's weird to take care of small children. You might want to give it a try—good babysitters are always in demand.

A survey reported in *Seventeen* magazine asked mothers to rank their top ten requirements for babysitters. The mothers ranked common sense as most important, followed by personal warmth, patience, experience, promptness, age, tidiness, pleasant physical appearance, education, and, at the bottom, pay requirements.

If you've not had much experience as a sitter, take heart.

How to Get Sitting Jobs and What to Charge

If you plan to make babysitting a regular activity, invest in one of the "how-to" books now available, or check them out of your local library. These books help steer you through a day of babysitting, advise you how to amuse children of different ages, and tell you how to handle any situation that might arise—with children *and* their parents. Among the books to consult are:

Benton, Barbara, *The Babysitter's Handbook*. William Morrow & Company, Inc., 1981.

Barkin, Carol, and James, Elizabeth, *The Complete Babysitter's Handbook*. Julian Messner, 1980.

You can let people know you want babysitting jobs using the

techniques listed later in this section. Once you start getting customers, you will make your reputation by the way you treat the children, and you will enhance it by being businesslike with the parents. Be sensible; be reliable; be honest. Common sense will help you. Always be on time; let your customers know well in advance if you absolutely have to cancel—and try to find a replacement; know before they leave what they expect of you; don't bring friends with you unless you have prior permission. You will learn quickly what different customers expect, but *you* should always be the same—that is, responsible.

Now that you're an established sitter, what to charge? Your hourly rate should be based on the going rate in your town or neighborhood. If there is a range of rates according to age and experience, decide where you fit in. As you gain experience, you can charge more.

Suppose parents ask you to do additional chores, such as tutor their child or sit for children of friends. You can rightfully ask for more money in these situations. Feeding lunch or changing diapers goes with the job, however. Your duties are to care for the child or children, not to serve as a maid, so let that guide you. Set your rates in advance so you won't be disappointed—the time to set your rates is *before* you get paid.

But What Can I Do? Use Your Imagination . . .

You can't think of a thing to do to earn money. You aren't able to take a part-time job after school, you don't like to babysit, and you live in a climate where there's never any snow. You have—you think—no marketable skills.

Wrong! Just think of all the things you know how to do, let alone things you do well: change storm windows, wax a car, polish silverware, mow a lawn, weed a garden. Any one of these—and dozens of other abilities—is a potential moneymaker. Apply your imagination and energy. In fact, energy is a key selling point for any skill you wish to market. As a young person, you have both energy and time to sell, and you will find many buyers.

Chances are that in many families you know, both adults work all day; or perhaps some of your neighbors are elderly and can't get around easily. Busy people will appreciate offers to water their gardens, walk their dog, clean their garage, wash their car. Adults who have trouble going places will welcome a shopping service: they provide you with money and a list of groceries or other items to be purchased, and then you do the work. Think about the tasks you and your parents perform at home and decide which ones you would enjoy doing for pay. There are lots of possibilities not mentioned here—the choice is yours!

Once you decide to "create" your kind of job, you will have to let potential customers know you are available and eager to work. Community bulletin boards, local newspapers, and word of mouth are good advertising methods. You can write your own brochure and leave copies in mailboxes in your neighborhood or apartment building, too.

Once you start lining up jobs, you must be prepared to do them well, since your client will be counting on you to be reliable and thorough, whatever the task. To help keep you organized, get a calendar, preferably one that allows you to see a full week or month at a time. Write down your appointments, being careful not to double up or schedule so many that your schoolwork suffers. In order to avoid any conflicts, don't forget to jot down music lessons, baseball tryouts, and other activities you want to attend.

You are performing these services for pay, of course, and you should negotiate your rates ahead of time. Sometimes your clients will offer you a sum of money. If you think it's a fair amount, accept it, but if you don't think it's enough, say so. Sometimes adults remember what *they* earned at your age—and pay accordingly.

Always be prepared to say what you wish to be paid. You can charge a flat amount for a particular job or you can charge by the hour. Before you choose, think about how long the job will take to do and how much labor is involved. Weeding a garden is more difficult than watering plants; cleaning a garage requires heavy physical work. Your parents and friends can offer suggestions and advice. You want to be fair to your customers and fair to yourself: If you charge too much, you might lose future jobs and recommendations; if you don't ask for enough you might resent the job and do sloppy work. In a successful business negotiation, both sides feel they are coming out ahead.

Your Hobbies and Money

Transform your hobbies into a moneymaking adventure—start your own (small) empire and learn about business at the same time! Leisure-time activities *can* pay off. Some examples:

• Suppose you play an instrument such as the piano or guitar. Learn some popular tunes and children's songs and you can provide entertainment at birthday parties. Advertise your services by posting brochures on community bulletin boards, sending the brochures to local churches, synagogues and day-care centers, and stuffing mailboxes in your apartment building or neighborhood.

• You have studied photography and never go anywhere without your camera. Why not photograph parties, family reunions, and other functions that occur in your town? Before you advertise your services, put together a portfolio of your work to show prospective clients. They will want to see samples before they agree to hire you. If you do get jobs for these events, charge for supplies—film, darkroom chemicals, etc.—in addition to charging for your time and the finished prints.

• You crochet beautifully and have made presents for everyone in your family and all your friends. Crochet for money! Investigate local craft fairs, church bazaars, and flea markets. Find out how to participate. If you practice another craft, the same guidance applies. You will need to have a supply of your wares on hand—macramé plant holders, leather wallets, handmade beads, ceramic pots, whatever your specialty is—or be prepared to take orders from customers. Craft fairs are a great way to learn about a small business and the efforts needed to make it successful.

• You've always enjoyed cooking. Why not expand your interest into a catering business? You can earn substantial amounts of money preparing food, serving, and cleaning up at neighborhood parties.

(For more information about selecting and pursuing a hobby, see Chapter 13, *Leisure in Your Life*.)

YOUR FIRST JOB

You want a job. No matter how carefully you budget your money, there's never enough for all the things you want to do. You can't afford to go to the movies with your friends, buy clothes for a special date, or get tickets to a concert. Or perhaps you now want to save for big purchases: a trip abroad, a motorcycle, your college education. These and similar reasons contribute to your decision to work after school, on weekends, or during the summer. But you don't know how to begin or where to look, and you've heard that it's very tough for teenagers to get jobs at all. You are discouraged even before you start. However, you have more resources and opportunities than you might think.

First things first. Before you even start to look for a job, you must make certain decisions and obtain a few important items.

Your search will be easier for you—and your prospective employers will be helped—if you know in advance:

• What hours are you free to work? Just because school ends at 2:30 doesn't mean you're free to work at 2:45. In addition to allowing time to get to your job, don't overlook extracurricular activities such as drama club, sports, and band practice.

• Can you work weekends and holidays, and during school vacations? Perhaps religious observance prevents you from working on Saturday, Sunday, or additional holidays, or you have regularly scheduled obligations on weekends. Maybe your family always takes trips during your vacations. Let an employer know even before you start working that you simply can't work at certain times. You may eventually arrange absences with your employer, but you shouldn't accept a job knowing you can't work when you're expected to.

• What kinds of work are you willing—or not willing—to do? If you are a vegetarian, you won't want to work at a hamburger palace; if you're allergic to animals, it would be foolish to clerk at a pet shop.

• Why do you want a job—simply for the cash, or for the experience you will gain? There's no right or wrong answer to this question: if experience in a certain business is more important to you than earnings, you will restrict your applications to that business, but if you are more concerned with earning money, you will apply for many different kinds of jobs.

Requirements

You probably already know that you won't be eligible for some jobs simply because you are too young. In addition to federal labor laws, each state has laws that prevent people under a mandated age from working at jobs that are considered dangerous or difficult, such as operating heavy machinery or mining. Additionally, you will not yet be old enough for most government and civil service jobs. If you have your heart set on working right now as a welder or a bartender, relax: you will outgrow this problem.

Now that you've made some elementary decisions about work—when to work and what kind of job to pursue—you must provide yourself with the documents you'll need to show a prospective employer. By now you might have a Social Security card, even if you've never held a job. If you don't yet have a card, apply for it now because you will certainly need one sooner or later. (For more on Social Security cards, see Chapter 2, *Document Your Life*.)

Almost every state and the District of Columbia require work permits or proof-of-age certificates for young workers. Depending on the state in which you live, the cutoff age will be sixteen, seventeen, or eighteen, after which you are considered an adult worker and do not need these papers. Some states have two or more types of permits that cover different age groups or times of year, and a few states require medical examinations before you can get your permit. A school guidance counselor can explain local requirements to you, and applications generally are available at your high school, school board office, or a branch of your state Labor or Industrial Relations Department.

Each state's rules on work permits vary (some states do not require them at all). Often you will have to have a promise of a job before you can get a work permit. Become familiar with the rules in your state, and have the necessary papers (such as a copy of your birth certificate and your Social Security card) ready so that you can apply promptly after you win your job.

Who Can Help You and Where to Look

How do you find out what jobs are open to you? If you limit yourself to newspaper ads or asking your friends, you may easily overlook good sources of jobs. Many helpful people and resources surround you (see also "Job Sources," later in this chapter):

1. Your parents, relatives, and their friends—people who own businesses or know the local business community.

2. Your high school counseling office. Local businesspeople phone in job descriptions; also, your guidance counselor has suggestions for you, if you ask.

3. Friends who already have jobs: they know first when someone quits or is fired.

4. Community bulletin boards and announcements in town halls, shopping areas, day-care centers, social agencies. Also, don't ignore churches and synagogues as resources.

5. Newspaper ads: everyone's stand-by and a good indication of the overall employment picture. The classified ads section can mislead you, however, since many part-time jobs are never advertised.

6. State employment offices.

7. Phone directories, especially the Yellow Pages. If you know you want to work in a flower shop, you can make a list of all the florists in your area—a much more efficient way to look for work than hiking from one shopping mall to another looking for ferns.

You may feel strong enough and mature enough to work on a road gang or in a Turkish bath. Can you handle the situation, the people you'll be working with? Better let your parents or an adult adviser know what you plan: they may have better judgment than you on the conditions you'll be getting into.

You already have a sense that some businesses are more apt to hire inexperienced workers than others, and you're right. But with a little resourcefulness you should not have any trouble finding an entry-level position. Offices always require clerks, receptionists, typists, and mail-room personnel, and stores hire cashiers, salespersons, stock clerks, and workers to make deliveries. Here are some possibilities:

- Fast-food restaurants: food preparer, counter help, cashier, cleanup.
- Restaurants and delicatessens: waiter/waitress, cashier, delivery.
- Supermarkets: stock clerk, cashier, delivery.

- Gas stations: attendant, mechanic.
- Parking garages: attendant, cashier.
- Hardware stores: stock clerk, sales clerk, cashier.
- Boutiques: sales clerk, cashier.
- Dry cleaners: counter help, launderer.
- Car washes: car-washer, cashier.
- Record shops: stock clerk, sales clerk, cashier.
- Farms, stables, ranches: chores.
- Theaters: ticket sales, usher, vendor.
- Recreation areas (playgrounds, parks, pools, gyms): supervisor, guide, guard, instructor.

In the summer, this list expands to include summer camps, resorts, and amusement parks. (See "Summer Jobs," later in this chapter.)

Basic Strategies for Finding a Job

How do you ensure that you get one of the scarce part-time jobs in your area? You have a vague idea that you should present yourself well, behave a certain way, and say the right things to convince employers to hire you instead of someone else. Your success depends a lot on your common sense as well as some familiarity with the strategies and time-tested rules of job-hunting. Later in this chapter you'll find more information about actually landing a job, but in the meantime here are four basic ways to apply for—or indicate your interest in—a job:

1. *By telephone:* Call a prospective employer only if you are responding to an ad in the paper or on a bulletin board. You may be asked a few preliminary questions over the telephone before being told to mail in your resume or come in and complete an application.

2. *By letter:* When an ad instructs you to respond by letter, type one out immediately. You will have so much competition that you must not waste an hour. You can also write unsolicited letters to businesses for which you want to work explaining your interests and the skills you offer.

3. *By making the rounds:* An effective way of uncovering jobs is to go from store to store or from one business to the next in a shop-

ping center or business district. You may show up just when an employer needs a new worker, or you may be hired because your appearance and qualifications fill an anticipated need. If no jobs are currently open, ask if you may fill out an application so that when an opening occurs, you will leap to mind. When you try this approach, always bring copies of your resume with you and be prepared for an interview. Dress appropriately, and carry proof of your age and your Social Security card.

4. *By referral:* One of the best ways to "get your foot in the door" of a particular business is to know somebody who already works there. Your contact can refer you to the person you should see, and can also put in a word on your behalf. Sometimes your contact will not be a direct acquaintance of your own, but rather the friend of a friend, or somebody who knows somebody who knows somebody. Your contact's knowledge and recommendation can still be helpful to you. Be creative when cultivating your contacts—this is part of "networking."

SUMMER JOBS

You know that February, with the fewest days, is the longest month of the year—the time when winter is so entrenched you believe summer will never come again. But February is when to start looking for a summer job. By the time you get spring fever, it might easily be too late—the good jobs will be long gone. If you're already in college, use your winter vacation and intersession to visit employers, write letters, schedule interviews.

Many seasonal jobs open up each summer, and in addition all sorts of businesses need temporary help while permanent staff goes on vacation. Don't start your search with the negative thinking that there are no jobs for you: this will only blind you to all your opportunities. Think instead about all the possibilities within the following broad categories.

Resorts and Hotels

How does a summer at the beach or in the mountains appeal to you? People by the thousands flock to these areas on their vacations, and hotels and resorts that cater to them hire extra workers to fill a multitude of jobs. Resort staffs include waiters, receptionists, chambermaids, gardeners, and kitchen assistants. These places need salespeople, too, for their pro shops, gift stores, and concession stands.

Outdoor resort activities are another source of jobs. Are you qualified to be a lifeguard or to teach swimming? How about golf or tennis? Can you drive a golf cart or carry a set of clubs?

To find out about resort facilities in an area near you or in an area where you'd like to spend the summer, write to the local chamber of commerce or state department of tourism. You can go to the library and consult such travel books as *Fodor's Guide to America* for names, addresses, and capsule descriptions of many hotels and resorts. A terrific source for resort, hotel, and camp jobs is *The Summer Employment Directory*, published annually by Writer's Digest Books (9933 Alliance Road, Cincinnati, OH 45242). You can order it from your bookstore, if it's not in the library.

What should you expect from a job at a hotel or resort? Most places provide free room and board for their workers, but some deduct these expenses from your salary. Ask about living arrangements *before* you agree to take a job. Also find out whether laundry and linen services are available and what your accommodations will be like. What is management's policy regarding free time? And, most important, what will you earn as a cash salary? Depending on the state's wage laws, your salary might be lower than minimum wage if your job will yield tips from customers (if you're a chambermaid or waiter, for example). Make sure you understand in advance what you can expect to earn.

Summer Camps

You've outgrown summer camp—as a camper—but you have many opportunities to return to camp as a counselor, instructor, or other staff assistant. The thousands of camps in this country provide tens of thousands of jobs for high school and college students every summer, and you can be among them.

It may help to apply to camps where you have spent a few summers as a camper, but you do have much broader choices. Many camps now specialize in music, dance, tennis, riding, sailing, weight loss, or other activities (such as computers!), so if you have a special talent or skill, apply to a camp that can use it and pay for it.

You won't get rich working as a counselor—your salary may be as low as $350 for eight weeks—but your room and board are usually included, you spend the summer outdoors, and you will meet many new people.

For information about camps and staff requirements, write to the following: American Camping Association, Bradford Woods, Martinsville, Indiana 46151; the Association of Independent Camps (covers the Northeast United States), 157 West 57th Street, New York, NY 10019; the Association of Jewish Sponsored Camps, 130 East 59th Street, New York, NY 10022. The New York and Boston regional offices of the ACA help place counselors in jobs in the Northeast.

Amusement Parks

Hundreds of amusement and theme parks open their gates to crowds of eager visitors each summer. High school and college students assist year-round park workers in accommodating vacationers from all over the world. You can be hired to sell tickets, serve ice cream and hot dogs, run concession stands, and clean up after the crowds go home. Most amusement parks do not provide living accommodations, so you probably will want a job close to home. To apply for a job at a theme or amusement park, write to the personnel office of the parks where you want to work and request an application. If you're not sure where the parks are located, write to the appropriate chamber of commerce and state tourist agency.

Office Work

Your parents or guidance counselor told you to learn to type. Now you can make those lessons pay off—literally. If you can type at least forty-five words per minute (accurately, please), you are on your way to an office job. A good starting point might be an agency that specializes in temporary help, such as Manpower, Inc., or Kelly Services, Inc., where your office skills will be tested and you will be interviewed. When you work as a temp, you fill in for employees who are sick or on vacation, or help a company whisk through stacked-up paperwork. Temporary agencies assign you to jobs that can last a few days or several weeks, and they collect a percentage of your hourly wage. You will get exposure to many kinds of businesses, and if you don't like one office, you know you'll soon be moving on.

Also check the "help wanted" ads in your local newspaper if you're interested in office work. Many employers do not want to hire workers just for the summer; don't try to fool them. Inform your guidance counselor or placement office, too, that you are seeking an office job so they can let you know if and when they learn of one.

Retail Stores

Many sales jobs are seasonal, and your chances of finding a selling job improve in the summer (and again at Christmas). If you spend the summer in a resort area, such as Cape Cod, you know that some stores are open for the vacation months only, and others that are open year 'round add to their staffs to handle the increased number of customers. Closer to home, local stores need replacements for vacationing workers, so you don't have to be in a summer resort area to find a job. Scout out local businesses and apply early. Good prospects include garden supply stores, drugstores, supermarkets, and hardware stores. Boutiques and other fancy stores usually want experienced salespeople, but, of course, it won't hurt to try those places. At most sales jobs, be prepared to work for the minimum wage and perhaps during the evening or on weekends.

Restaurants

Having spent a small fortune at fast-food restaurants, you would now like to recover some of it. Here's your chance. In recent summers, McDonald's alone has hired almost 5,000 teenagers nationwide. As a patron of similar restaurants, you're familiar with the tasks their workers perform: taking orders, working at the cash register, sweeping the floor, frying the fries. To apply for a job, go to the restaurant where you want to work, ask to speak to the manager, and fill out an application.

Other restaurants need summer help, too—waiters, kitchen assistants, dishwashers, and cashiers. You may be too young to work in restaurants that serve liquor, but you will find many family restaurants where you can apply.

Farm and Ranch Jobs

Ranching and farming depend on seasonal labor, and summer is a busy time for the nation's agribusinesses. Your state departments of agriculture and labor can direct you to employment centers and areas that need workers; county extension agents have the most detailed and current knowledge of employment trends in their territories. Check regularly the classified ads in local papers and shoppers' weeklies, and inquire, too, at farm equipment outlets. Keep up to date with publications such as *The Drovers Journal* which, although pitched toward a readership in livestock businesses, includes an extensive classifieds section.

During the harvest, you may get work as a day laborer simply by showing up early at orchards and farms and offering your muscles. You can't depend on a steady income this way, but you can earn some needed cash.

Government Programs

Summer employment programs run by government agencies change so regularly that one year's facts are next year's memories. All levels of government provide summer jobs and special programs for teenagers, disadvantaged youth, and other "categories" —governments love categories—that yield for the worker experience, training, and income. Since these initiatives depend on federal and state budgets which, in turn, rest on legislative wranglings, start your search early and keep at it. Be civic-minded, if needed, and write your representatives to lobby for a program you heard about that became stalled in some committee. High school guidance counselors are your first resource, since their job includes keeping up with employment prospects. They can best advise you on the steps to take in signing up and interviewing for programs in your area.

Internships

Most internships do not pay, so you might not consider them a possibility. However, an internship gives you a wonderful opportunity to learn about a field you might want to pursue as a career, and, as a bonus, you might receive school credit. If you're lucky, an internship can lead to a summer or part-time job in the future, too. Places that might offer internships include your local historical society, museums, theaters, newspapers, and television and radio stations. (Don't ignore cable TV!) Others will covet an internship for the same reasons you do—experience and contacts—so you must start looking early.

Be realistic in your expectations from an internship and know before you start what you will be doing. If you are placed at a radio station, for example, you almost certainly won't be broadcasting the news, and if that's what you expect, you will be disappointed. On the other hand, you don't want to pour coffee for visitors all day long, or be sequestered in the mail room. Usually, you will be assigned to interesting projects, and that's what you want. Talk frankly with your supervisor about what you hope to learn and, along with telling them what skills you can already offer, ask what you can expect to be taught.

Your guidance counselor or school placement office should have information about internships. Turn to *The Student Guide to Fellowships and Internships* (Amherst Students, E.P. Dutton Publishing Co., New York, 1980) for a thorough introduction.

This list by no means exhausts the possibilities for summer jobs. Have you forgotten child-care? A regular babysitting job can expand into day-care work or into a job as a parent's helper. Reread the suggestions for neighborhood jobs earlier in this chapter, then get to work and think up more!

It's *work* to find work—you have to seek out opportunities, apply and interview for jobs, and convince prospective employers to hire you instead of someone else. But you will gain more than money.

Part-time and summer jobs are only the first of many jobs you will have in your lifetime, and the skills and techniques you learn now will help you find good jobs in the future.

PREPARING FOR WORK

Steps You Can Take

It may be years before you're ready for a full-time job, but it is never too soon to start thinking about a job or a career. You don't have to make career decisions now, but the more information you have—

the more awareness you develop of your choices—the better your options and decisions will be. Since work involves about one-third of your adult life, it would be silly to be completely casual about it!

You've already thought about the kind of lifestyle you enjoy and some of the interests you want to pursue. But you can take additional steps ahead of time to prepare yourself for choosing a career.

One of your first stops should be the public or high school library. It may have a special "employment opportunities" or "career counseling" section. There you will find books about career planning, files of pamphlets from local businesses, and other resource materials from local, state, and federal agencies. Don't overlook librarians as a resource—they can direct you to materials you might not even know to ask about. (See "Resources," later in this chapter.)

The library should have copies of the job-hunter's bible, the *Occupational Outlook Handbook*, published every two years by the U.S. Labor Department. This book describes hundreds of occupations along with their education and training requirements, projected salary levels, and employment prospects for the coming decade. In its pages, you will find dozens of jobs of which you've never even heard, some of which may interest you. Also, the library should have a copy of the *Dictionary of Occupational Titles*, also published by the Labor Department. The most recent edition listed more than 20,000 job titles, many of which are explained more fully in the *Occupational Outlook Handbook*. Finally, the library probably subscribes to the *Occupational Outlook Quarterly*, a magazine published by the Labor Department that updates information from the *OOH*. (A more detailed description of these publications is included under "Resources," later in this chapter.)

There are many ways to find out even more.

• Talk to people. Neighbors, friends, strangers, relatives are all potential sources of information. If you are interested in historical preservation, for example, someone you know might already work in this field or be acquainted with someone who does. Or you can contact the local preservation society and arrange to speak with a staff member. Whatever the field, most people will be happy to spend some time with you if you explain what you want to know and are well prepared.

Questions you might ask include: How did they decide upon

their careers? Do they enjoy them? How much variety is there in their tasks? What is required for success? What are the most boring and the most interesting aspects of their jobs? Are there many opportunities for young people? And, finally: how should you get started? Most people like to talk about themselves and will be flattered by your interest.

Keep a list of people you speak with and note who introduced you to whom. This is how to develop your own "network" of contacts, and you will be rewarded by learning about your chosen field(s) of work.

• Study your studies. If you want to teach art but never enjoy art classes, figure out what really appeals to you in this plan. Look for clues in the subject in which you excel or, conversely, barely endure, and try to understand the reasons why. You might come up with hints about career interests—for example, you dislike working with your hands or you love anything to do with numbers.

• If your school doesn't have courses or programs in subjects that intrigue you, sign up for classes at community organizations, YMCAs, Scouting groups, and other local outlets. You can explore an interest at no academic or financial risk this way.

• Perhaps you've zeroed in on a career possibility. Find out more about it! Most professions and occupations have associations that represent their interests to the public at large. Go back to the library and look in a directory of associations for the occupations you want to investigate. (For more on professional associations, see "Resources," later in this chapter.)

• Try out your job interests. Look for a summer or part-time job or an internship in an occupation you want to explore. This will be easier for some of you than others. If you want to teach, for example, apply to day-care centers, camps, and religious schools. If you despair of finding a paying job, think about volunteer work. Many organizations—hospitals, local government agencies, schools—will be happy to accept you as a volunteer. Are you interested in police work? Maybe your local police department has an internship program. Some places will be unable to accept volunteers: they may be too busy to guide a volunteer worker, or union or government rules prevent them from accepting volunteers. Keep trying. Volunteer work can be an asset in many ways. For a start, you don't have to worry about your earnings, so you can concentrate on whether the tasks really interest you and whether you like the work people do farther down the line. Consequently, volunteer experience may confirm your career choice or convince you to look elsewhere. Finally, schools and future employers will be impressed when you can back up your interests with experience.

• The Boy Scouts of America has developed the Exploring Program to match your interests with adult experts and program resources in organizations within many communities. The program includes both young men and women, aged fourteen through twenty. Almost every Explorer post specializes in a certain field—more than 100 different specialties have been organized, ranging from accounting to zoology. As an example, the American Medical Association and other national health organizations support the organization of Explorer posts in hospitals, clinics, medical centers, and other health-care organizations. These posts render valuable community service and provide members with an insight into a variety of career opportunities.

Note: The research leading to the development of the Explorer program revealed that 83 percent of teenagers have a specific career or hobby interest, that 94 percent want to work with an adult having this hobby or interest, and that the majority want to belong to a co-ed organization! As of the start of this decade, 447,469 young adults belonged to Explorer posts. To find out more about opportunities in your vicinity, call your local Boy Scouts of America council, or write to Exploring (Boy Scouts of America, 1325 Walnut Hill Lane, Irving, TX 75062-1296).

• Keep your options open. You can afford to be flexible early in your working life, so don't feel only one position can possibly be of any help to you. Very often one thing leads to another, and if an unexpected opportunity presents itself, you will want to be ready for it.

What to Do if You're Still in High School

"Training is everything. The peach was once a bitter almond; cauliflower is nothing but cabbage with a college education."
                                                              —Mark Twain

Even though you may not yet have joined the job market, you probably spend a lot of time wondering what you will do someday to earn your living. If you are now in high school, you can take steps immediately that will enhance your chances for success later. You can make school pay off.

Take courses that teach high-paying skills. You may have decided that you want to be a television newscaster. Fine—but do you have extra skills that will make you a good candidate in this highly competitive and overcrowded field? Do you have alternative skills, in case you fail to land your chosen job? If you have experience in typing, shorthand (men as well as women), accounting, and, especially, computer programming, your value as an employee will soar, and you will find these skills in demand anywhere in the country.

- *Typing and shorthand*. You've heard it before, but it's absolutely true that these skills will be useful throughout your life. If you're going on to college, you will need to type your term papers (and you can earn extra money typing papers for other students who ignored this advice). You can highlight these skills on your resume and during interviews. Many entry-level jobs require basic office skills, and the better yours are, the better your chances.
- *Accounting and business*. Does your school offer any accounting and business courses? These are among the most practical subjects you can study. Economics courses will introduce you to the principles of how business works in this country, and accounting will teach you a skill that translates into employment and a possible career.
- *Computer programming*. Computers are everywhere. Rapid access to information is ever more important, and computer "literacy" will soon be as crucial as your ability to read and write. Does your high school offer at least a beginner's course in computer programming? Take it now—you will almost certainly need it later. Computer occupations wil be *the most rapidly* growing fields in the next decade.
- *Learn a foreign language*. What's the fourth largest Spanish-speaking country in the world? Guess again if you thought Mexico, Venezuela, Argentina, Colombia, or even Spain, and bull's-eye if you thought of the United States. You go to the head of the class and while you're there, sign up for language lessons.

Spanish is not the only useful language for an American to know. Increasingly, important languages for American business and foreign relations include Arabic, Chinese, and Japanese. Fluency in a foreign language paired with your technical skills and education can assist you in getting high-paying jobs overseas or jobs with foreign companies that have offices in the United States. And, of course, many American businesses have important international divisions. Or do you envision an academic or research-oriented career? Chances are, you will need to know at least one other language. Similarly, if you plan a career in journalism, you'll boost your chances by knowing another language. And if you're lucky enough to be bilingual, you have a head start your friends will envy.

- *Focus on your extracurricular activities.* Do they relate to the kind of jobs you're interested in? Almost every school activity has a professional counterpart. Do you love music and hope to play in an orchestra or teach? Play in the band or tutor other students. Is journalism your passion? Work on the school paper or yearbook. It's not essential that your after-school activities correspond to your career choice, though. Choose activities that you enjoy and care about, because employers prize enthusiasm and dedication, too.

Simple Communications Skills Are a Top Job Requirement

"It is the responsibility of each and every department head to properly arrange the affairs of this organization in such manner that each salaried employee, including himself, will receive the full vacation to which he is duly entitled."

Translation: Each department head must make sure that he and each salaried employee under him gets his full vacation.

"We solicit any recommendations that you wish to make and you may be assured that such recommendations will be given our careful consideration."

Translation: Please give us your suggestions. We shall consider them carefully.

Compare these two examples of "bafflegab" with the simple, clear writing that delivers a message so it can be easily understood. As a corporate executive employing a June college graduate, which writer would you hire?

The answer is, in a way, unexpected: Companies single out

"communications skills" ahead of production, financial, or marketing abilities as their most important requirement. Thus, being able to write simply and clearly actually can be the key to getting a desired job as well as being essential to steady promotion.

It's not only time and energy that may be wasted by those to whom the bafflegab messages are directed. Big sums of money can be involved, also, because of errors made by those who fail to grasp the meaning of letters, reports, and memoranda.

The Case of the Missing Hyphen

Consider the case of the missing hyphen. A written order called for radioactive rods to be cut in "ten foot long pieces." (Notice the absence of any hyphen.)

Did this order mean "ten foot-long pieces"? Or did it mean "ten-foot-long pieces"? The cutter interpreted the order—minus the hyphen—to mean ten pieces each a foot long, and the misunderstanding cost the company involved a bundle of money.

How can you begin to learn how to write simply and clearly? Here are ten principles developed by the Gunning-Mueller Clear Writing Institute in Santa Barbara, California:

- Keep sentences short.
- Be simple, not complex.
- Develop your vocabulary.
- Avoid extra words.
- Use active, not passive verbs.
- Use terms your reader can picture.
- Tie in with your reader's experience.
- Write the way you talk. A conversational tone is one of the best avenues to good writing.
- Make full use of variety.
- Write to express, not to impress.
- (Vital!) Present your ideas simply and directly.

A Fog Index and Readability Yardstick to test clear writing was developed by the late Robert Gunning. The index is calculated by averaging the number of words per sentence in a selected passage and then counting the number of words with three or more syllables in every 100 words. Add the two figures together and multiply by 0.4. The resulting figure is the same as the number of years of education, up to seventeen, that a reader needs to understand the passage.

Try applying the Fog Index to the material and instructions you read as well as to your own writing. It will tell you how clearly you express *yourself* when writing.

A tip: in business, it's a good idea to get right to the point. When your boss picks up your written report on any subject, assigned or not, he wants to know: "What is this all about?" He doesn't want your resume or details of your research. He doesn't want to be argued into a conclusion.

Put your conclusions first. Then follow with the details to document your conclusions. Then your boss will have both your view and the facts upon which you based your conclusions, and he will reach his own decision.

As a lifetime enemy of "professional" complicated theories of economics written in lingo with which one writer tries to impress his peers rather than to inform you and me, and as a devoted disciple of explaining the most obscure subject in words any reader can understand, I submit this advice with delight. If you take it seriously, it may help you more in your career than other skills and tools which seem far more complicated.

CHOOSING A CAREER

Your Parents and Your Career: A Brief Guide

You may feel that your parents are meddling in your plans for what is, after all, *your* future. They may urge you to make decisions, take special classes, stay in school, follow their advice. Your career choice is a subject important to all of you, so it's important to talk calmly about it, if you can.

Research indicates that your family will exert the strongest influence on your choice of career. That influence can show up in different ways—your family may steer you toward careers they admire and away from those they look down on. They may prod you to go into the family business or do what your father (mother) does. They may suggest that you shouldn't, or can't, attempt a particular activity or career.

Try with utmost care to trace where your ideas about careers originated, so that when you make your decision, it will truly belong to you. Think:

- What have your parents advised? Is this advice based on your interests and values or on theirs?
- Are you making your choice with the idea of pleasing them? Does this choice please you, too? You have to live with it.
- Are you accepting or rejecting their advice? Why?
- Have you explained your options to them as you see them?

More Than One Career in Your Life

You've spent untold hours thinking about how you'll earn your living and otherwise make your mark in life. You can see your future unfold: finish school, get your job training, start working, perhaps change employers a few times. Then what? Does the picture go blank? Don't be discouraged or disappointed if that's the case. Stop worrying if you can't envision your future fifteen or twenty years from now. Relax. Your career will not evolve from a single choice you make now in one big, heaving decision. It will be, rather, a continuous process.

Your career will consist of all the individual job choices you will make during your working life, combined with whatever education and training you get. You build, brick by brick, your career and future from these and other choices. You can expect to have more than one career and perhaps as many as three careers in your lifetime. Increasing numbers of people do.

You can look forward to a productive lifetime of forty or fifty years. Education and training can continue throughout that span, and you may move from job to job within one area or field, or may move from one field to another. If you make all your choices within one field (say communications, the military, or health), generally it would be said you have a career in that field. But you may choose among fields or may create distinct but related careers within a field—as a paralegal first studies to become a lawyer and then is appointed a judge.

The job market changes rapidly and your possibilities multiply as fast. A variety of factors over which you have no control will affect your career choices. But, ultimately, you make your own decisions. You can take charge of your one, or two, or many careers.

Lifestyle and Goals

No one has yet developed a magical formula for choosing careers. You will have to do the work yourself—so think long and hard. Assess your abilities, interests, and goals. There are no right or wrong answers to the questions you should ask yourself. No teacher will grade you and you won't pass or fail.

You have many aids at your disposal to help you in your choices, from library resources to career counselors to people already working in the field. And you are not chained to a job for life—you can choose (and I repeat, most of you probably will) and have more than one career in your life.

You will boost your chances of enjoying your work and will gain satisfaction from your choices if you evaluate all the elements that go into them. Following are key issues to assess, honestly and carefully, because each will affect your choice of occupation and, in turn, will be affected by what you do.

• How important are personal relationships to you? What kind? Do you like being around people or are you a loner?

• How important is status to you? To a great extent, your status depends on your income, and that will determine where you live and even with whom. Income shapes your leisure time and activities, so when you choose a career and its attendant income, you begin to choose a lifestyle.

• What are the rewards you expect from a job? For some of you, a paycheck will be enough for your hard work. Others will want to see a project completed or a goal achieved. You might want to help other people in some fashion. For those of you whose job is so absorbing that you can't wait to get to work, the size of your paycheck may be less important. For all of you, your rewards will be a blend of personal, emotional, and financial factors.

• How do your educational plans and choice of career fit together? Are you planning to go to school after high school? Will it be a technical school, a four-year college, or a community or junior college? Your post–high school education will definitely shape your career and job choices.

• Not least to consider, you will want to derive satisfaction from the work you do. Once you've assessed your needs and expectations, you can more wisely explore career clusters and find the job with the six best ingredients for your personal career recipe.

• Your goals and needs will change over time as you accumulate experience and test your options. Don't hesitate to reevaluate any of these keys in the years ahead.

Elements of Choice

Every job can be classified as "blue collar" or "white collar." The terms originated when most people worked with their hands in factories and wore work clothes that were usually blue. In contrast, white-collar workers were those who worked with their minds and wore a shirt, suit, and tie. If you think about the distinction, though, it gets more complicated. Don't dentists and word processors work with their hands? The differences between blue-collar and white-collar workers involve more than clothes. They concern educational level, tasks performed, opportunities for advancement, and income.

White-collar jobs include professional, managerial, clerical, and sales jobs. Examples: office administrators, lawyers, teachers, scientists, securities traders, journalists. The job outlook for white-collar workers in the coming decade varies widely according to occupation. For more about specific fields, look in the *Occupational Outlook Handbook.* Some white-collar jobs have bright futures; others cloudy. For example, the use of word processing equipment may eliminate many secretarial jobs in coming years as workers are expected to type their own letters and manuscripts routinely and edit them on video screens. But the demand for science and math teachers will grow more quickly than the supply.

Blue-collar workers hold jobs as skilled craftsworkers, such as mechanics, plumbers, machine operators, assembly-line workers, and construction workers.

Some Characteristics of White-Collar Workers

- Generally receive monthly or weekly wages for their work.
- Generally, white-collar jobs require a higher education level—a minimum of a high school diploma, and a college degree is almost always necessary for advancement.
- Competition for jobs can be stiff, and seniority is no guarantee of promotion within an organization.
- Few white-collar occupations are covered under contracts negotiated by unions.
- Work responsibilities for white-collar workers tend to be varied within a job and many workers attain some measure of independence from their supervisors. They are allowed to make decisions and delegate work.
- Most significantly, income ceilings for white-collar workers are higher than for most blue-collar jobs, and overall lifetime earnings are higher. However, many white-collar workers, particularly early in their careers, earn less than those in blue-collar jobs.

Some Characteristics of Blue-Collar Workers

- Specialized training, which can be gained on the job or at a technical school, is usually required.
- Blue-collar workers are usually supervised by managers.
- Many blue-collar workers see the immediate results of their work—a welded joint, a repaired air conditioner.
- Many blue-collar jobs take place outdoors and require heavy physical labor.
- Skilled trade workers often belong to unions and their wages and benefits are arranged by contract.
- Job salary and advancement often are protected by union membership.
- Blue-collar workers may have fewer opportunities to advance because breaking into management requires a level of education and experience they often lack.
- Hourly earnings for skilled workers are high, but the income ceiling is reached relatively early. That is, the earnings peak while a worker is in midcareer. As a skilled worker, your lifetime earnings are likely to be lower than those of many white collar employees.

However a skilled trade pays much more than a traditional "woman's" white-collar job and requires more skills and training.

• Blue-collar workers are more likely to be laid off in a business downturn. Even the annual incomes of those who earn high hourly wages may be reduced because of seasonal layoffs, strikes, and plant closings.

• Unionization has given some blue-collar trades more job security than the security of low-skilled white-collar workers.

• A blue-collar worker is more likely than a white-collar counterpart to retire early because of occupational injuries or disease.

The outlook for blue-collar occupations varies according to the field. To decide among occupations or trades, you will have to investigate thoroughly all aspects: job training required, earnings potential, employment outlook in your locality. Automation, competition from abroad, and many other economic forces affect the outlook for jobs in a wide variety of trades.

Skilled trades can offer you a comfortable life and lasting personal satisfaction. If you're not inclined to go to college, you like to work with your hands, you enjoy physical tasks, and you appreciate seeing the results of your work, you owe it to yourself to investigate these occupations.

Early/Late Entry

Another piece to insert in your job mosaic is time of entry. Careers can be divided into early- and late-entry or delayed-entry types. Where do your choices fit in?

In early entry careers, you can begin work right out of high school or college and develop skills and knowledge on the job. Among these jobs are: clerical work, bank teller, insurance sales, many service and technical jobs.

Other early-entry jobs fall into a gray zone in which you start your work right out of college but remain in low-level slots until you accumulate years of experience or postgraduate training. If you major in science, for example, you might work as a lab technician, but you must have additional training to design experiments, teach at a university, or hold an administrative job at the lab. In sum, as an occupation gets more technical or skilled, you will need advanced training to qualify for higher positions.

Some occupations are clearly late-entry fields: law, medicine, university professor, most clergy, scientific research. Late-entry careers require extensive postcollege training and education. When considering a late-entry career, you should factor in the extra years and added money required to finance this training and your living expenses. In the short run, your finances will suffer, but your lifetime earnings and self-fulfillment will more than compensate for any temporary deprivation.

The time you enter your chosen career is part of your overall job planning. Tailor your educational needs and planning to your preliminary choices or ideas about early- and late-entry careers.

APPRENTICESHIP

Apprenticeship—one of the oldest ways to learn a trade—is a prescribed time period during which you learn all aspects of a trade through on-the-job training and related lessons. Instructions can take place in a classroom or at home with additional study materials, and includes detailed information about how each task is performed, the theory behind the trade, and safety precautions to observe in the shop. Usually experienced craftsworkers teach the classes, using such texts as trade manuals and books. Coursework can be scheduled during the day or in the evening, depending on the apprentice's work schedule. One year of apprenticeship equals roughly 2,000 hours of on-the-job training (supplemented by related instruction).

Apprenticeships usually last about four years, but some may last as long as six or as few as one. As an apprentice during this time, you will work under the supervision of a journeyworker—the state you will attain when you successfully complete your training. Under his or her guidance, you will learn the mechanics of your chosen trade and gradually perform the different tasks under less and less supervision.

As an apprentice you will be a paid, full-time employee of the company where you work. Generally, apprentices earn about one half of what a journeyworker gets paid, but you can expect raises every six months or so until your salary is about 95 percent of the journeyworker rate.

Most registered apprentice programs are sponsored jointly by labor unions and employers. In such joint programs, the administrative body is called a Joint Apprenticeship Committee (JAC) and comprises representatives from the union, management, and the public. The JAC receives applications and interviews candidates, and consults with state and federal offices concerned with apprenticeship.

Many apprentice programs are registered with the federal government or a federally approved state apprenticeship agency. Apprentices who complete such programs receive a certificate from the U.S. Department of Labor which can be a valuable asset when looking for a job.

Standards

Registered and certified apprentice programs meet federal standards regarding planned related instruction (minimum of 144 hours a year), wages, safety and health conditions; and standards relating to job tasks. If you are a graduate of a registered program, you may have an easier time finding new jobs or changing employers because your certificate is a kind of job passport—all employers understand the significance of the Department of Labor stamp and the quality of training it represents. However, many employers with fine programs don't want the aggravation of paperwork or have special needs around which they structure their own programs, and consequently run programs not registered by the government. Usually these programs are operated by very large companies. panies. Most of them have similar standards, and many companies award certificates to successful apprentices at the completion of their training. Don't rule out an unregistered program but, like everything else, investigate it carefully before you sign up.

Every apprentice program operates under written standards which establish minimum qualifications, describe the work, and prescribe the wage rates, working conditions, number of hours, and length of training. You will sign a written aggreement with the employer or the Joint Apprenticeship Committee when you are accepted. (See example on page 42.)

The Federal Bureau of Apprenticeship and Training has established standards to ensure uniform and thorough training for apprentices within each craft. Among the standards:

- Minimum age of sixteen.
- Full and fair opportunity to apply.
- Proper supervision of on-the-job training.
- Progress evaluated periodically and adequate records maintained.
- Employer-employee cooperation.
- No discrimination in any phase of selection, employment, or training.

Considerations for Apprentices

Opportunities for apprenticeship have been expanding to new industries and occupations, and training and apprentice programs have been devised for jobs formerly taught informally through trial and error. Particularly in booming industries, such as the health-care and environmental fields, apprentice programs are providing many newly trained workers.

Here are some factors to consider when selecting a trade and deciding whether to become an apprentice:

- You must be at least sixteen years old before you can start, and some industries will require that you be eighteen for insurance purposes. But the process of becoming an apprentice can take several years, so your early teens is not too soon to start thinking about it and selecting a trade.
- When you think about a trade, consider your own qualifications and needs, and also the demand for jobs in different trades in your area. Additional factors are requirements for physical strength, overtime work, nightshift work, and travel. Many trades with opportunities for apprentices are not found in all areas of the country.
- Look into the working conditions of different trades. Does the work require physical strength? Will you have to move frequently? Does it require special clothing? Are there health hazards associated with this work? Are overall working conditions safe and pleasant?
- Explore the different programs within a trade and see what training facilities are available to you. What sort of related instruction is provided? Will you have to purchase books, tools, and special clothing, and how much will this cost you? Do you have to join

U.S. DEPARTMENT OF LABOR • Employment and Training Administration
Bureau of Apprenticeship and Training

APPRENTICESHIP AGREEMENT BETWEEN APPRENTICE AND JOINT APPRENTICESHIP COMMITTEE

CHECK APPROPRIATE BOX

☐ Vietnam-era Veteran   ☐ Other Veteran   ☐ Nonveteran

PRIVACY ACT STATEMENT

The information requested herein is used for apprenticeship program statistical purposes and may not be otherwise disclosed without the express permission of the undersigned apprentice.

Privacy Act of 1974 - P.L. 93-579

THIS AGREEMENT, entered into this *(date)* .... day of .... 19 ....

between the parties to *(Name of local apprenticeship standards)* ....

....

represented by the Joint Apprenticeship Committee, hereinafter referred to as the COMMITTEE, and

(Name of Apprentice) ...., born *(Month, Day, Year)* ....

.... hereinafter referred to as the APPRENTICE, and (if a minor) *(Name of parent*

or guardian) .... hereinafter referred to

as the GUARDIAN.

WITNESSETH THAT:

The Committee agrees to be responsible for the selection, placement, and training of said apprentice in the trade of ....
....
as work is available, and in consideration said apprentice agrees diligently and faithfully to perform the work of said trade during the period of apprenticeship, in accordance with the regulations of the Committee. The apprenticeship standards referred to herein are hereby incorporated in and made a part of this agreement.

This AGREEMENT may be terminated by mutual consent of the signatory parties, upon proper notification to the registration agency.

SIGNATURE OF APPRENTICE

ADDRESS *(Number, Street, City, State, ZIP Code)*

SIGNATURE OF PARENT OR GUARDIAN

SIGNATURE OF JOINT APPRENTICESHIP COMMITTEE, CHAIRPERSON

SIGNATURE OF JOINT APPRENTICESHIP COMMITTEE, SECRETARY

NAME OF REGISTRATION AGENCY

SIGNATURE AND TITLE OF AUTHORIZED OFFICIAL

TRAINING DATA	
APPRENTICESHIP TERM	PROBATIONARY PERIOD
CREDIT *(By previous trade experience)*	TERM REMAINING

TO BE COMPLETED BY THE APPRENTICE

SEX ➤ *(Check one)*
☐ Male
☐ Female

RACE/ ETHNIC GROUP ➤ *(Check one)*
☐ Caucasian/White
☐ Negro/Black
☐ Oriental
☐ American Indian
☐ Spanish American
☐ Information Not Available
☐ Not Elsewhere Classified

HIGHEST EDUCATION ➤ LEVEL *(Check one)*
☐ 8th grade or less
☐ 9th grade or more
☐ 12th grade or more

DATE *(Month, Day, Year)*

GPO 900-664

ETA 6-111
Jan. 1976

the union? When? Will your dues be reduced? Does the training program offer dual-enrollment with a community college in which you earn an associate degree? In increasing numbers, apprentice programs, in cooperation with post-secondary schools, offer college credit for classroom study, and you can earn the degree if you complete the school's other requirements.

• Look into yourself. Think carefully about what you like to do and how you like to live. Are you willing to commit yourself to working, studying, and completing the terms of an apprenticeship agreement? If and when you decide you are, you will find many resources to guide you.

Sources of Information

As you explore apprenticeable careers, begin with the *Occupational Outlook Handbook*. You will find descriptions of job duties, educational and training requirements, employment outlooks, and salary ranges for most apprenticeable trades.

Employer associations and unions can provide you with details about application procedures and training programs. You will find their names and addresses in the *OOH*. Write to them and request their career literature.

The Bureau of Apprenticeship and Training of the Department of Labor (BAT) publishes booklets describing the standards for different trades. You can learn a great deal about job duties and activities to expect by reading about the courses in a program. The booklets are available from BAT regional offices. Regional and area BAT offices can also give you information about apprentice programs in your area and can refer you to state agencies.

The Women's Bureau of the Department of Labor publishes *A Woman's Guide to Apprenticeship,* a comprehensive introduction that describes both opportunities and difficulties for women in the trades. Also available is *Sources of Assistance for Recruiting Women for Apprenticeship Programs and Skilled Non-Traditional Blue Collar Work.* Request your copies from the Women's Bureau (U.S. Department of Labor, Washington, DC 20013), or any of the regional offices. (A list of regional offices, as well as further description of the Women's Bureau, is included later in this chapter.)

Apprenticeship Information Centers (AICs) operate in more than 40 states as part of the U.S. Employment Service. The staff in these centers can assist you with counseling, arrange for you to take an aptitude test in the craft that interests you, and provide you with details about apprenticeships in your area, including information regarding entrance requirements and application dates. For a list of AICs, write to the Apprenticeship Information Center Program (U.S. Department of Labor/USES, Room 8118, 601 D Street, N.W., Washington, DC 20013).

The following organizations operate national outreach programs to recruit and prepare apprentices, and make special efforts to attract minorities and women to different jobs. You can find their addresses in the phone book, or write to the national office if you can't find a local listing.

Human Resources Development Institute (HRDI)
AFL-CIO
815 16th Street, N.W.,
Washington, DC 20006

HRDI, the employment and training arm of the AFL-CIO, operates apprenticeship outreach programs for minorities and women. Programs are sponsored by local building trades councils.

National Urban League
Labor Education Advancement Program (LEAP)
500 East 62nd Street
New York, NY 10021.

LEAP recruits and places women and minorities in apprenticeships and skilled jobs around the country.

Recruitment and Training Program (RTP, Inc.)
162 Fifth Avenue
New York, NY 10010

RTP operates local outreach and placement programs for minorities and women in skilled nontraditional jobs and apprenticeships.

Range of Apprenticed Trades

The Department of Labor recognizes more than 700 apprenticeable trades, about 95 percent of which are divided among three basic industries: construction, manufacturing, and service. The following list represents the range of apprenticed trades and the numbers of years you can expect to train for them:

Aircraft fabricator (3–4)
Airplane mechanic (3–4)
Automobile body builder and repairer (4)
Automotive mechanic (4)
Baker (3)
Barber (2)
Beekeeper (4)
Biomedical equipment technician (4)
Blacksmith (4)
Bricklayer (3–4)
Building maintenance service repairer (2)
Cabinetmaker/machinist, wood (4)
Cable television line worker (1)
Candymaker (3–4)
Carpenter (4)
Chef (3)
Computer programmer (2)
Correction officer (1)
Data processing technician (1)
Dental assistant (1)
Designer/draftperson (5)
Electrician (4–5)
Embalmer (2)
Fabric cutter (3–4)
Farm equipment mechanic (3–4)
Floral designer (1)
Foundry worker (2–4)

Furrier (3–4)
Glass worker/glazier (2–4)
Ironworker (2–4)
Jeweler (3–4)
Laboratory technician (3–4)
Leather worker (3–4)
Legal secretary (1)
Machinist (4)
Medical secretary (1)
Meteorologist (3)
Musical instrument mechanic (3–4)
Nursing assistant (1)
Office machine repairer (4)
Orthopedic-prosthetic technician (3–4)
Painter and decorator (2–3)
Physical therapy technician (1)
Plasterer (3–4)
Plumbing and pipe fitter (4–5)
Production coordinator, TV and radio (3)
Sheet metal worker (3–4)
Silversmith (3–4)
Stoneworker (2–4)
Tailor (4)
Textile technician (2–4)
Tool-and-die maker (4–5)
Upholsterer (3–4)
Wallpaper craftworker (4–5)
Vending machine mechanic (3)

WIDER OPPORTUNITIES FOR WOMEN, NOW!

Just look at the world around you. From astronauts to zookeepers, women work at a spectrum of jobs and in a full range of careers to satisfy personal and financial goals. The options open to women have never been greater—and, perhaps, more confusing. It's nonsense even to dispute the fact that women have entered the workplace and are here to stay. Some facts:

• In 1880, almost 15 percent of all women and girls aged ten and over worked outside their homes. (No compulsory education and child labor laws back then!)

• More recently, the number of households in which one partner earned the salary and was the "breadwinner" declined from 49.6 percent in 1969 to 22.4 percent in 1980.

• At the same time, the percentage of married women in the work force soared from 32 to 51 percent.

• The number of children whose mothers work is now greater than the number of children whose mothers stay at home. (Those mothers who work at home may labor very hard, but they don't draw a salary.)

So how do you deal with the dazzling array of choices and the sometimes scary decisions? The best way to dive in never changes: know yourself. Discover what turns you on, challenges you, satisfies your interests, and complements your values. Don't fret that you don't know all the answers yet: What would you do now with a blueprint for the next fifty years of your life?

Women work chiefly to earn money to support themselves and their families, just as men do. Many factors contributed to the stampede of women into the workplace. Women are deferring marriage and child-rearing to pursue independent lives and careers outside the home—perhaps you've already decided to explore career options and live on your own before you "settle down." Meanwhile, because of divorce and separation, many women have to work to support their children and themselves. And a rising standard of living, plus a high rate of inflation, motivate—or compel—women to contribute to family incomes. You already may live with some of these circumstances and the idea of women working seems very ordinary to you. But it hasn't always been this way, and outmoded stereotypes and patterns about women workers linger on.

The Grim Facts

Did you know that, although the number of women working outside their homes has skyrocketed, they still perform the same kinds of jobs traditionally called "women's work"? Most women, even those who entered the labor market during the 1970s, work in a relatively small number of occupations: over half of all women workers are employed in just 20 of the 441 categories listed in the 1980 Census Occupational Job Classification system! What that means is that most jobs women hold are closely related to familiar roles: homemaking, and supporting other people's efforts. About 80 percent of women workers were concentrated in "pink collar" jobs—mainly clerical and service workers—at the start of the decade. The remainder were in professions—chiefly librarians, teachers, nurses, and social workers. True, increasing numbers of women study medicine, law, and engineering, and learn the skilled trades, and the percentage of women in these fields, although small, is growing. But the scarcity of women in traditionally male jobs, plus continuing discrimination to an incredible degree, clamp down on earnings.

Despite the 1963 Equal Pay Act and its amendments, women are not only a long way from achieving equality in earnings, but in fact wage disparities between men and women in many occupations are growing. In the late 1970s, the average male worker earned $17,427 per year; the average female worker earned $10,244. In some states, such as Louisiana, women earned a mere 49.8 cents for every dollar a man earned. Here is what the latest Department of Labor statistics show about specific occupations:

• *Bookkeeping:* Women held 90.6 percent of the bookkeeping jobs as this decade opened, but earned an average of $98 a week *less* than men holding the same position.

• *Elementary and secondary school administrators:* Men earned an average of $520 per week, compared with $363 for women.

• *Computer systems analysts:* Men received an average weekly salary of $546, while women averaged $420.

• *Health technicians:* Women held 68.5 percent of these jobs and averaged $273 per week, while men in comparable positions earned $324.

• *Elementary school teachers:* Women held 82.2 percent of the jobs, but earned an average of $68 a week *less* than men.

Myth: Progress in the upper end of the earnings scale has been notable.

Fact: As the 1980s began, only 2 percent of corporate directors were women. The number of women serving as corporation managers has crawled up from 5 percent in 1960 to 6 percent today. Women in 1960 held 1 percent of skilled crafts jobs; today that figure is a picayune 2 percent.

Myth: The reason for salary differences is that women remain in the work force only a short time.

Fact: Hardly. Married women work for pay an average of twenty-three years. Single women remain in paying jobs roughly forty-five years.

Myth: Most women who work outside the home do so because they're bored and want to get out.

Fact: Women who take outside employment for the "fun" of it are a rare exception. Of 44 million women in the work force in the early 1980s, 1.4 million held two or more jobs—hardly a "fun" way of life. Moreover, open discrimination forces women into jobs with low status as well as low pay. For example, 98.7 percent of receptionists, 97 percent of typists, and 86 percent of file clerks—the "pink collar" jobs—are women. Millions of women are working at these often monotonous occupations to maintain the family's standard of living, or to support themselves and their children after a divorce (the marriage of one in three women aged twenty-six to forty ends in divorce). The odds are against a woman receiving any support from her former husband.

Perhaps worst of all, our Social Security program, as the decade started, was based on the archaic assumptions that women are always homemakers, that men provide the family's sole economic support, that the housework performed by a wife has no monetary value, that marriages last for life.

These stereotypes were never true, of course. But although

women make up a huge proportion of the work force, they frequently leave it to have children, then return either because of divorce or when the children reach school age. A woman's absences from the paid work force mean there will be blanks in her Social Security record, thereby reducing her future benefits. In addition, since a woman's salary is about two-thirds that of a man's, her average workers' benefits on retiring are far less than a man's. Many married women who work, will, in fact, get benefits no higher than they would have received if they'd never worked for pay, never paid a penny in Social Security taxes. And a married working couple can end up with *smaller* combined retirement benefits than if the husband alone had earned the equivalent of their combined salaries. Moreover, a marriage must last at least ten years for a woman to qualify for dependent's benefits in her old age.

Our entrance into the work force in such vast numbers is one of the most important developments of the twentieth century. It has forever changed the economic face of our nation as well as the basic relationship between the sexes. Of the significance of this phenomenon, I am proud—and, I trust, justifiably so.

But the discriminations continue. They are, at times, encouraged by women themselves, and for this I can find no excuse. And thus I swear to continue the fight of the suffragettes, who, in 1920, finally won the Nineteenth Amendment guaranteeing our right to vote, until true equality is achieved.

You can expect to hold a paying job at some point during your life, and whether you plan to postpone marriage in order to pursue an education and career, or you hope to marry after high school graduation and start a family, you may have no choice about working. Incidentally, don't think of your salary as a supplement to your husband's—not only do you downplay the importance and value of your job, it simply may not be true. Economic realities make it likely that two salaries will be required in your family.

The Women's Bureau of the U.S. Department of Labor has these cautionary words for young women: ''Occupational segregation by sex is primarily the result of sex-role stereotyping about appropriate jobs for women and men. While traditional roles may be satisfying, they sometimes have the effect of limiting a woman's options before she is ready to make important choices about her future. For example, some girls of junior high or high school age are encouraged to avoid difficult mathematics and science courses. . . .

Avoidance of these has the unfortunate effect of eliminating a great many job options and reducing possible employment opportunities to jobs which are, on the whole, lower paying than those which require mathematics, scientific, or technical skills.''*

Do you recognize yourself in that paragraph? Have you skipped out on classes you think might be too difficult or that your friends told you are boring? You might be closing doors to your own future, right now.

Your motivation, training, skills, and determination will mold your career choices. Do you want to work in construction or at a trade or craft? Has police work fascinated you all your life? Does your faith ordain women in its clergy? Can you see yourself as a forest ranger or biochemist? Go ahead. Find out all you can about these careers. Women are moving into nontraditional occupations such as these and hundreds of others that you might not even know about—yet.

Where to Start

As a potential or even current female worker, you can profit from a bountiful array of resources developed just for you, in addition to the general occupational guides. So get going!

• Start with the Women's Bureau (U.S. Department of Labor, Washington DC 20013), the only federal agency devoted exclusively to the concerns of women in the labor force. It takes note of the difficulties young and minority women face in getting good jobs. Read *Job Options for Women in the 80's,* and *A Working Woman's Guide to Her Job Rights.* While you're at it, request a list of its current publications and services. Following is a list of regional offices nationwide:

Region I
1700-C JFK Building
Boston, MA 02203
(Connecticut, Maine,
 Massachusetts, New Hampshire,
 Rhode Island, Vermont)

Region II
1515 Broadway, Room 3575
New York, NY 10036
(New Jersey, New York, Puerto
 Rico, Virgin Islands)

*From Women's Bureau—pamphlet #18 *Job Options for Women in the 80's.*

Region III
15230 Gateway Building
3535 Market St.
Philadelphia, PA 19104
(Delaware, District of Columbia,
   Maryland, Pennsylvania, West
   Virginia, Virginia)

Region IV
1371 Peachtree St., N.E.,
   Room 737
Atlanta, GA 30309
(Alabama, Florida, Georgia,
   Kentucky, Mississippi, North
   Carolina, South Carolina,
   Tennessee)

Region V
230 South Dearborn St.,
   8th Floor
Chicago, IL 60604
(Illinois, Indiana, Michigan,
   Minnesota, Ohio, Wisconsin)

Region VI
555 Griffin Square Building,
   Room 863
Griffin and Young Sts.
Dallas, TX 75202
(Arkansas, Louisiana, New Mexico,
   Oklahoma, Texas)

Region VII
2511 Federal Building
911 Walnut St.
Kansas City, MO 64106
(Iowa, Kansas, Missouri, Nebraska)

Region VIII
1432 Federal Building
1961 Stout St.
Denver, CO 80202
(Colorado, Montana, North
   Dakota, South Dakota, Utah,
   Wyoming)

Region IX
11411 Federal Building
450 Golden Gate Avenue
San Francisco, CA 94102
(Arizona, California, Hawaii,
   Nevada)

Region X
3032 Federal Office Building
909 First Avenue
Seattle, WA 98174
(Alaska, Idaho, Oregon,
   Washington)

• Call on your local chapter of the National Organization for Women (NOW). You'll find career-counseling guides and staff members who can help you locate details about job openings and training programs. If you can't find an office of NOW nearby, write to national headquarters (NOW, 425 13th Street, N.W., Suite 1048, Washington, DC 20004).

• Catalyst, a nonprofit national organization launched to help women choose, begin, and advance their careers, provides self-help materials and career information. Write for their listing, *National Network of Career Resource Centers* and *Publications List*. (Catalyst, 14 East 60th Street, New York, NY 10022.)

• Wider Opportunities for Women, Inc. (WOW) publishes *The National Directory of Women's Employment Programs,* a list of employment counseling and advocacy organizations for women, and *Suit Yourself: Shopping for a Job,* a handbook for women puzzling over career decisions. Write for a catalog and brochure. (WOW, 1511 K Street, N.W., Washington, DC 20005.)

• Many Young Women's Christian Associations are involved in outreach programs designed to introduce young women to various careers. Check with the YWCA in your vicinity, or write to the national office (Data Center, Young Women's Christian Association, 135 West 50th Street, New York, NY 10020).

• If you're active in the Girl Scouts of the U.S.A. (GSUSA), you already know that a career component is built into every badge and certificate you earn, and perhaps your troop leader has introduced you to the GSUSA's entertaining and informative career development materials, *From Dreams to Reality: Adventures in Careers.* If so, you've seen the activity book and played with the special packet of career cards. If your troop hasn't reached the cards yet, ask your leader, or the local council, to provide the materials. And did you know that the Girl Scout Career Education Program, which builds on these resources (and includes boys, too) is expanding into school systems around the country? For more information, write to the Program Department, Girl Scouts of the U.S.A. (830 Third Avenue, New York, NY 10022).

• The American Association of University Women (AAUW) publishes a list of professional groups that offer job information about each field. The guide, revised yearly, includes the names and addresses of specific people in those associations whom you can write or phone. (AAUW, 2401 Virginia Avenue, N.W., Washington, DC 20037.)

• The Association for Women in Science (AWIS) provides a number of services for women in the natural sciences (and the rest of us can benefit, too!). Request a copy of *Resources for Women in Science,* a leaflet which includes valuable references for all women, not only future biologists, chemists, and mathematicians. Also, *Encouraging Science Education and Careers,* an annotated bibliography of resources, is yours on request. Enclose a stamped, self-addressed envelope (SASE) (see below) when you write. Ask, too, about AWIS's educational foundation, which provides scholarship awards to predoctoral students in the sciences, and its registry of women in science and engineering. This is the largest talent bank of its kind; employers use it to find qualified women job candidates. (AWIS, 1346 Connecticut Avenue, N.W., Suite 1122, Washington, DC 20036.)

• Direct specific questions about careers and organizations to the Resource Center, Business and Professional Women's Foundation (2012 Massachusetts Avenue, N.W., Washington, DC 20036). You will receive a reply with a list of any references for your subject.

• Contact a local chapter of the Business and Professional Women's Club and ask about outreach programs for career development, or write to the National Federation of Business and Professional Women's Club at the above address.

• Many unions and professional associations have pamphlets and career guides written expressly for teenage girls. Write to those in the fields you want to explore; you'll find addresses in the *Encyclopedia of Associations* at your library.

• Networks in many professions have banded together and have formed their own groups. Among their goals: assisting younger women—*you*. Among them:

American Women's Society of
  Certified Public Accountants
P.O. Box 389
Marysville, OH 43040

American Society of Women
  Accountants
35 East Wacker Street, Suite 1036
Chicago, IL 60601

9 to 5
140 Clarendon Street
Boston, MA 02116

National Association of Women in
  Construction
2800 West Lancaster Avenue
Fort Worth, TX 76107

Society of Women Engineers
345 East 47th Street, Room 305
New York, NY 10017

American Medical Women's
  Association
1740 Broadway
New York, NY 10019

Association of American Women
  Dentists
435 North Michigan Avenue—
  17th Floor
Chicago, IL 69611

National Association of Insurance
  Women
1047 East 64th Place
Tulsa, OK 74136

Association for Women in Science
1346 Connecticut Avenue, N.W.
Washington, DC 20009

• Investigate nontraditional means of job training. The Women's Bureau can send you *A Woman's Guide to Apprenticeship* (mentioned earlier in this chapter), which will introduce you to this challenging world. And look for a copy of *Time for a Change: A Woman's Guide to Nontraditional Occupations*, published by the Women's Outreach Project in the Department of Education's Office of Vocational and Adult Education. It describes jobs you may not even have considered and discusses the rewards of such jobs, how to decide on them, which are most promising, and how to get training.

This list merely suggests the range of resources for you to explore; it can't possibly enumerate them all. As you define your career goals, you will uncover new guides—use them and share them with friends.

Is an M.B.A. a Woman's Golden Passkey to the Executive Suite?

Is a Master in Business Administration degree—an M.B.A.—the golden passkey to the executive suite for a woman? Increasing numbers of women seeking executive jobs obviously think so, for there has been a spectacular upsurge in the total number of women entering graduate schools of business administration.

During the last years of the 1970s, the number of women graduating with degrees in business and management jumped more than 400 percent. This is more than twice the increase in the total of female lawyers, and it won't be long before the upper educational schools in business attract more women than does law.

In the late 1970s, women made up less than 10 percent of business school classes. (When I went to New York University Graduate School of Business Administration, then down in the Wall Street area, I was the only woman, and my biggest "problem" was finding a ladies' room; the single one available to me was in the basement and it was the superintendent's. He graciously permitted me to use it when essential during my 5:15 P.M. to 9 P.M. classroom time.)

Today, women hold one-quarter to one-third of the seats at such major business schools as Harvard, Stanford, and Wharton.

Within the next several years, Yale University's School of Organization and Management may have as many female business students as male.

Whether the M.B.A. is the passkey so many women think it is has its doubters as well as supporters. Says one doubter: ''Women who perform well early in their careers are not hindered by the absence of an M.B.A. They have outstanding opportunities for advancement. Due to the deluge of graduates with M.B.A.s, the degrees are not as important as they once were, unless they come from one of the top six or eight schools.''

But this attitude is ignored by the upward-moving woman, eager for an M.B.A. for a variety of reasons: instant prestige, important skills, unusual career flexibility, vital self-confidence, and, of course, the promise of a better salary.

A survey of M.B.A. holders who graduated ten years ago was recently completed by the Association of MBA Executives. It showed:

• Women M.B.A.s 25 to 29 years old are earning average salaries of $22,500 to $25,000 a year (against the average family income in the United States of about $18,000 a year at the start of the 1980s).

• Women M.B.A.s between the ages of 30 and 34 are pulling down $27,500 to $30,000 a year, while women M.B.A.s between 35 and 39 are drawing salaries of $25,000 to $27,500. (The study does not explain why older female M.B.A. holders tend to earn less than their slightly younger peers, but I'll make a stab at it: They started from lower pay levels; they've been held back more by their older, more biased male superiors than the younger women, who now work in an era when discrimination practices may bring extremely costly penalties; and they've not fought so hard for equality nor complained so loudly. And this is just for starters.)

• Women in their early thirties who interrupted their careers to have children are earning considerably less than M.B.A. holders who did not take time out. (The familiar story.)

• Women M.B.A.s earn less than their male counterparts no matter what their age or child-rearing commitments. A possible explanation for this disparity in salaries, outside of discrimination: Men are more likely to enter business with technical training that enables them to command higher paychecks.

• The cost of attending any of the country's most prestigious business schools runs around $20,000 for two years of tuition, books, and standard living expenses.

• Most students are about twenty-six years old, but many schools admit women over thirty, some single mothers with children, some married women with families. Increasing numbers of female business school women students have had previous work experiences.

• And *yes*, the overwhelming majority sincerely believes the degree is the golden passkey to upper levels of management.

So, What Next?

Take charge of your career decisions. Unshackle your imagination and let your ambitions soar. Think about how to upgrade your goals within a field you know you like: become a systems analyst rather than a keypunch operator; a dentist rather than a dental technician. If you've decided to work as a secretary, choose a special high-paying skill, such as medical, legal, or bilingual work. More tips:

1. Don't restrict yourself to traditional "women's work." If you want to be an oceanographer or petroleum engineer, find out all you can about educational requirements and job opportunities.

2. Read biographies of women who work(ed) in your fields of interest; check your favorite magazines for interviews with women you admire.

3. Make a long-range plan to meet the requirements of the occupations you choose. Your goal right now probably is to complete your education and training. *If you're in school, stay put! Have you interrupted your education? Pick it up on a part-time or full-time basis just as soon as you can.*

4. If you're already working, ask your personnel representative about tuition assistance for continuing education, or about training for another job within the company. Educational funds from employers are a frequently overlooked—and invaluable—fringe benefit.

5. Find out where job opportunities will be in your community or in areas of the country where you want to live. Chances are, technical, medical service, and science- and math-related jobs will turn up on your list. Is there anything there that excites you? Find out more about it!

6. Know your rights. Familiarize yourself with questions interviewers cannot legally ask (but sometimes will, anyway). Often,

they simply don't know better, but whatever the motive, you will do well to plan your answer just in case. For example, it is illegal to ask you whether you plan to have a family, or, if you already have children, how you plan to take care of them while you work.

7. If you ever feel you've been discriminated against because of your sex, at work or during the hiring process, contact the U.S. Equal Employment Opportunities Commission (2401 E. Street, N.W., Washington, DC 20006) or its regional offices; a state or local human rights commission; or the American Civil Liberties Union (22 East 40th Street, New York, NY 10016). The law is on your side.

RESOURCES

Surely, by now you realize that choosing a career is serious business. But don't be overawed: you can enjoy the search and seize this time to learn about different jobs, ways of life, and even more about yourself in the process.

The following list of resources will launch your career investigation.

Publications to Help You

Occupational Outlook Handbook

Every two years the Bureau of Labor Statistics of the U.S. Department of Labor issues this essential career guide. It summarizes information on over 450 occupations, including job descriptions, working conditions, employment statistics, training and educational requirements, earnings, employment outlook, related occupations, and sources of additional information. If your library does not have a copy of the current edition, it's worth investing in a copy yourself. Write the the Superintendent of Documents, U.S. Government Printing Office, Washington, DC 20402.

The *OOH* is divided into twenty occupational clusters that guide you in focusing on an area of related jobs. Within that area you will find a multitude of job listings, many of which may be just right for you.

The career clusters are:

1. Administrative and Managerial Occupations
2. Engineers, Surveyors, and Architects
3. Natural Scientists and Mathematicians
4. Social Scientists, Social Workers, Religious Workers, and Lawyers
5. Teachers, Librarians, and Counselors
6. Health Diagnosing and Treating Practitioners
7. Registered Nurses, Pharmacists, Dieticians, Therapists, and Physician Assistants
8. Health Technologists and Technicians
9. Writers, Artists, and Entertainers
10. Technologists and Technicians (except health)
11. Marketing and Sales Occupations
12. Administrative Support Occupations, including clerical
13. Service Occupations
14. Agriculture and Forestry Occupations
15. Mechanics and Repairers
16. Construction and Extractive Occupations
17. Production Occupations
18. Transportation and Material Moving Occupations
19. Helpers, Handlers, Equipment Cleaners, and Laborers
20. Military Occupations

Occupational Outlook Quarterly

The *OOQ*, also published by the Department of Labor, updates employment projections contained in the *OOH* and features special job-related articles. Its wealth of information and projection of job openings in different fields make it worth a subscription or regular trips to the library.

Dictionary of Occupational Titles

Known as *DOT*, this Department of Labor publication lists more than 20,000 separate jobs. The *OOH* is based on these job titles. The *DOT* will open your eyes to the vast range of possible jobs in this country.

Directory of Post-Secondary Schools With Occupational Programs

Copies are available for sale from the Superintendent of Documents (U.S. Government Printing Office, Washington, DC 20402). (Also see information on trade and technical schools, later in this chapter.)

Job Openings

The Employment and Training Administration of the U.S. Department of Labor publishes this monthly bulletin which highlights occupations with large numbers of job openings at Public Service Job Banks the previous month. It gives you information on local areas with large numbers of job openings, industries in need of workers, pay ranges, and the average number of jobs available. Look for this bulletin in your library or local career counseling agency, or request a copy from the Consumer Information Center, Department G, Pueblo, CO 81009.

Professional Associations

Interested in a career in aquaculture or harness racing? How about interior design or fashion, or stained glass making? You can get details on these and hundreds of other careers in your library. Moreover, just about any occupation you can name has a society or professional wing. These organizations usually mail career guides to those energetic enough to request them. You can obtain pamphlets from many professional groups that will introduce you to the basic information about that career. (Read the pamphlets carefully; some brochures may gloss over employment difficulties, make the occupation sound more glamorous or professional than it really is, or exaggerate salary levels.) In addition, many associations publish journals and newsletters for their members. Association journals contain articles, research reports, book reviews, job announcements, and news of special programs and awards. Try to locate current issues of some of these journals, even if you have to go to a nearby college or university library. You might not understand a lot of what you read, since you're not yet familiar with the field, but these journals can give you an insight into the kinds of work people do and what you can expect to study to keep abreast of the field. Many occupations and professions have more than one journal or bulletin, and looking at different examples will broaden your understanding of the many possibilities within your chosen field.

You can find the names and addresses of professional associations in directories at your local library. Start with the *Directory of Associations*, published by Gale Research, and *The National Trade and Professional Association Directory*.

Career Series

Several series of books are aimed at you, the young person considering the smorgasbord of career options. Your library will probably carry some, or all, of them, and they make good reading:

- *The Opportunities In . . .* series is published by Vocational Guidance Manuals, written by career practitioners.
- *Your Future In . . .* series is published by Richards Rosen Press, Inc., in New York. Among its popular titles is *Your Future in Exotic Occupations*, published in 1978.
- *Arco's Career Guidance Series* gives you titles according to job-related clusters. You might also look into *College, Yes or No*, by William F. Shanahan. (Arco Publishing Co., Inc., 219 Park Avenue South, New York, NY 10003)

All series include in each book a list of associations offering further information, lists of state and local agencies and, when appropriate, vocational schools and courses.

Sources of Engineering Career Information

This resource lists career data in engineering, including jobs and salaries. (Engineering Manpower Commission of Engineers Joint Council, 345 E. 47th Street, New York, NY 10017).

B'nai Brith Occupational Brief Series

The B'nai Brith writes these brief guides for high school students. Each contains information on job outlook, duties, required preparation, entry qualifications, earnings, and opportunities for advancement. The series is revised frequently. (B'nai Brith Vocational Service, 1640 Rhode Island Avenue, N.W., Washington, DC 20036).

Exploring Careers

The Bureau of Labor Statistics publishes *Exploring Careers*, a career education resource designed and written for junior high and high school students. In a lively, varied format, the book presents you with workers' stories about their jobs, questions designed to evaluate your interests, and suggested games and activities. The illustrated volume emphasizes how people feel about their work, and what they actually do while on the job.

Newspapers

Many big-city newspapers regularly run special supplements about the local job market and employment trends. You'll find a wealth of current details and suggestions for career guidance, local resources, and training programs. The *New York Times* publishes a national employment report each fall; the *Washington Post, Los Angeles Times, Dallas Morning News*, and *Houston Chronicle* are among the other papers that feature special employment surveys.

The American Almanac of Jobs and Salaries

No matter what career you choose, you want to know how much you will be paid. *The American Almanac of Jobs and Salaries*, by John W. Wright (Avon Books, 1982), will satisfy your curiosity about how much people earn, and let you judge whether a salary offer is fair. Additional tables detail careers with great potential (computers, you know that) and gloomy prospects (would you believe lawyers?).

The National Job-Finding Guide

When you perfect your resume and plan your campaign to blitz every business in your field, check out a copy of *The National Job-Finding Guide*, by Heinz Ulrich and J. Robert O'Connor (Doubleday, 1981), which, in a cross-indexed format, lists types of companies, locations, and names of business and contacts.

The Metropolitan Job Bank

If you've narrowed your sites (geographically, that is) study a copy of *The Metropolitan Job Bank*. Editions covering New York, Chicago, Los Angeles, and Boston are available and provide much the same information as the above listing.

There exist career guides too numerous to mention. Your library and bookstore shelves are crammed with books on every imaginable career and every possible angle of looking for and securing a job. Use them. This brief list should convince you of the wealth of resources out there for you. Just allow yourself enough time to read the resources carefully, profit from their advice, and follow through!

Trade and Technical Schools

You can continue your education and learn a trade at the same time at a trade, technical, or vocational school. Dozens of course programs are offered, from acting through X-ray technician training. Data processing and computer programming are currently very popular choices. These schools equip you with a skill or trade within a short time—the average length of instruction is forty weeks. Reputable schools receive accreditation from the National Association of Trade and Technical Schools (NATTS) or the Association of Independent Schools and Colleges. Details and directories are available from:

NATTS
2021 K Street, N.W.
Washington, DC 20006

Association of Independent
Colleges and Schools
1730 M Street, N.W.
Washington, DC 20036

Handbook of Trade and Technical Courses and Training

This handbook, published by NATTS and available on request, provides information on schools where career-related training can be obtained. Details, too, on school accreditation, steps on how to apply, and job placement and length-of-training specifics are included. Write to NATTS at the address above. Ask also for their brochure, *How to Choose a Career—And a Career School.*

Choosing a School and Program

Trade and technical schools can be expensive, and there is a racketeering fringe which will not deliver on its extravagant promises. Investigate! Write to several schools that offer the training you want, request their catalogs, and talk to current or former students. You will find the guidance you want on these schools in Chapter 4, *Financing Higher Education.* Beware the swindlers! Read and be warned!

Trade Associations List

Selecting a career is a baffling exercise; it is confusing to sort out all the variables—what you like to do, what you do well, the lifestyle you want to enjoy, and all the rest. But when you have done the chores, you will have given yourself an important boost.

It is vital to your future that you get as much information as possible about any occupation that intrigues you before you commit yourself—your time, energy, and money—to what could become an unsatisfactory career. The following list of trade and professional groups and other organizations will provide you with information about specific fields. While this list can start you on your way, not every occupation is included, so don't hesitate to look further.

Accountant
American Institute of Certified
   Public Accountants
1211 Avenue of the Americas
New York, NY 10036

Advertiser
American Association of
   Advertising Agencies
666 Third Ave.
New York, NY 10017

American Advertising Federation
1225 Connecticut Ave., N.W.
Washington, DC 20036

Aerospace Engineer
American Institute of Aeronautics
   and Astronautics, Inc.
1290 Avenue of the Americas
New York, NY 10019

**Agriculture and Agricultural
   Research**
Office of Personnel
United States Department
   of Agriculture
Washington, DC 20250

American Farm Bureau Federation
225 Touky Ave.
Park Ridge, IL 60068

Future Farmers of America
P.O. Box 15160
Alexandria, VA 22309

National 4-H Council
7100 Connecticut Ave.
Chevy Chase, MD 20815

**Air Conditioning and
   Refrigeration Mechanic**
Air Conditioning and Refrigeration
   Institute
1815 North Fort Myer Dr.
Arlington, VA 22209

Airplane Mechanic
Air Transport Association of
   America
1709 New York Ave., N.W.
Washington, DC 20006

Aviation Maintenance Foundation
P.O. Box 739
Basin, WY 82410

Anthropologist
American Anthropological
   Association
1703 New Hampshire Ave., N.W.
Washington, DC 20009

Apparel Industry
International Ladies Garment
   Workers' Union
1710 Broadway
New York, NY 10019

Amalgamated Clothing and Textile
   Workers Union (men's clothing)
15 Union Square West
New York, NY 10003

Apparel Manufacturers Association
1440 Broadway
New York, NY 10018

American Apparel Manufacturers
   Association
1611 N. Kent St., Suite 800
Arlington, VA 22209

Appliance Repairers
Association of Home Appliance
  Manufacturers
20 North Wacker Drive
Chicago, IL 60606

Architect
The American Institute of
  Architects
1735 New York Ave., N.W.
Washington, DC 20006

Archaeologist
Archaeological Institute of America
53 Park Place
New York, NY 10007

Astronomer
American Astronomical Society
Education Office
University of Delaware
Newark, DE 19711

Auto Mechanic and Body Repair
Automotive Service Industry
  Association
230 North Michigan Ave.
Chicago, IL 60611

Automotive Service Councils, Inc.
188 Industrial Drive, Suite 112
Elmhurst, IL 60126

National Automotive Dealers
  Association
8400 Westpark Drive
McLean, VA 22102

National Institute for Automotive
  Service Excellence
1825 K St., N.W.
Washington, DC 20006

Banker, Bank Teller
American Bankers Association
Bank Personnel Division
1120 Connecticut Ave., N.W.
Washington, DC 20036

National Bankers Association
499 S. Capitol St., S.W.
Washington, DC 20003

Biochemist
American Society of Biological
  Chemists
9650 Rockville Pike
Bethesda, MD 20014

Biologists
American Institute of Biological
  Sciences
1401 Wilson Boulevard
Arlington, VA 22209

Bricklayer and Stonemason
International Union of Bricklayers
  and Allied Craftsmen
815 15th St., N.W.
Washington, DC 20005

Business Management
American Management
  Associations
135 West 50th St.
New York, NY 10020

Carpenter
United Brotherhood of Carpenters
  and Joiners of America
101 Constitution Ave., N.W.
Washington, DC 20005

Associated General Contractors of
  America, Inc.
1957 E St., N.W.
Washington, DC 20006

Chemical Engineer
American Institute of Chemical
 Engineers
345 East 47th St.
New York, NY 10017

Chemist
American Chemical Society
1155 16th St., N.W.
Washington, DC 20036

Chemical Manufacturers
 Association, Inc.
2501 M St., N.W.
Washington, DC 20037

Child Welfare Worker
National Association of Social
 Workers
1425 H St., N.W., Suite 600
Washington, DC 20005

City Planner
American Planning Association
1776 Massachusetts Ave., N.W.
Washington, DC 20036

American Society of Planning
 Officials
1313 East 60th St.
Chicago, IL 60637

Clerical Worker
State Supervisor of Office
 Occupations
State Department of Education
State Capitol (Your state)

**Computer Operator, Programmer,
 Systems Analyst, Service**
American Federation of
 Information Processing
 Societies
1815 North Lynn St.
Arlington, VA 22209

Association for Computing
 Machinery
11 West 42nd St.
New York, NY 10036

Association for Systems
 Management
24587 Bagley Rd.
Cleveland, OH 44138

Business Equipment Manufacturers
 Association
1828 L St.,N.W.
Washington, DC 20036

Data Processing Management
 Association
505 Busse Highway
Park Ridge, IL 60068

Institute for Certification of
 Computer Professionals
35 East Wacker Dr., Suite 2828
Chicago, IL 60601

Conservationist
The Conservation Foundation, Inc.
1717 Massachusetts Ave., N.W.
Washington, DC 20036

The Nature Conservancy
1800 North Kent St.
Arlington, VA 22209

The Wilderness Society
1901 Pennsylvania Ave., N.W.
Washington, DC 20006

National Wildlife Federation
1412 16th St., N.W.
Washington, DC 20036

National Parks and Conservation
 Association
1701 18th St., N.W.
Washington, DC 20009

National Audubon Society
950 Third Ave.
New York, NY 10022

Cook, Chef
American Culinary Federation
P.O. Box 3466
St. Augustine, FL 32084

Culinary Institute of America
P.O. Box 53
Hyde Park, NY 12538

National Institute for the Food and
Service Industry
20 North Wacker Dr., Suite 2620
Chicago, IL 60606

Credit Manager
National Retail Merchants
Association
100 West 31st St.
New York, NY 10001

National Association of Credit
Management
475 Park Ave. South
New York, NY 10016

Data Processor
American Federation of Information
Processing Societies
1815 North Lynn St.
Arlington, VA 22209

Day-Care Worker
Day Care and Child Development
Council of America, Inc.
711 14th St., N.W.
Washington, DC 20005

Dentist
American Dental Association
Council on Dental Education
211 East Chicago Ave.
Chicago, IL 60611

American Association of Dental
Schools
1625 Massachusetts Ave., N.W.
Washington, DC 20036

Dental Assistants
American Dental Assistants
Association
666 N. Lake Shore Dr., Suite 1130
Chicago, IL 60611

Commission on Dental
Accreditation
211 E. Chicago Ave.
Chicago, IL 60611

Dental Assisting National Board,
Inc.
666 N. Lake Shore Drive, Suite 1136
Chicago, IL 60611

Dental Hygienists
Division of Professional
Development
American Dental Hygienists'
Association
444 N. Michigan Ave., Suite 3400
Chicago, IL 60611

Diesel Mechanic
International Association of
Machinists and Aerospace
Workers
1300 Connecticut Ave., N.W.
Washington, DC 20036

Dietician
American Dietetic Association
430 North Michigan Ave., 10th Fl.
Chicago, IL 60611

Direct Selling
Direct Selling Association
1730 M St., N.W.
Washington, DC 20036

Economist
American Economic Association
1313 21st Ave. South
Nashville, TN 37212

National Association of Business
　Economists
28349 Chagrin Blvd., Suite 201
Cleveland, OH 44122

Educator
National Education Association
1201 16th St., N.W.
Washington, DC 20036

American Council on Education
One Dupont Circle, N.W.
Washington, DC 20036

American Association of University
　Professors
One Dupont Circle, N.W.,
　Suite 500
Washington, DC 20036

Electrical Contracting
National Electrical Contractors
　Association
7315 Wisconsin Ave.
Bethesda, MD 20814

**Electrical-Electronic Technician
(Radio and T.V.)**
National Association of Television
　and Electronic Servicers of
　America
5930 S. Pulaski St.
Chicago, IL 60629

Electronics Industries Association
2001 Eye St., N.W.
Washington, DC 20006

Electrician
International Brotherhood of
　Electrical Workers
1125 15th St., N.W.
Washington, DC 20005

Edison Electric Institute
1111 19th St., N.W.
Washington, DC 20036

National Joint Apprenticeship and
　Training Committee for the
　Electrical Industry
9700-E George Palmer Highway
Lanham, MD 20706

Engineer
National Society of Professional
　Engineers
2029 K St., N.W.
Washington, DC 20006

Engineering Manpower
　Commission
American Association of
　Engineering Societies
345 East 47th St.
New York, NY 10017

Society of Women Engineers
345 East 47th St.
New York, NY 10017

**Family and Home Economists,
　Nutritionists**
American Home Economics
　Association
2010 Massachusetts Ave., N.W.
Washington, DC 20036

Farmer, Agricultural Research
Future Farmers of America
P.O. Box 15160
Alexandria, VA 22309

Fire Fighter
International Association of Fire
 Fighters
1750 New York Ave., N.W.
Washington, DC 20006

Flight Attendants
Air Transport Association of
 America
1709 New York Ave., N.W.
Washington, DC 20006

Food Scientist
Institute of Food Technologists
221 North LaSalle St., Suite 2120
Chicago, IL 60610

Foreign Service
Board of Examiners
Foreign Service
Box 9317 Rosslyn Station
Arlington, VA 22209

Forester
Society of American Foresters
5400 Grosvenor Lane
Bethesda, MD 20814

U.S. Forest Service
U.S. Department of Agriculture
P.O. Box 2417
Washington, DC 20250

American Forestry Association
1319 18th St., N.W.
Washington, DC 20036

Geographer
Association of American
 Geographers
1710 16th St., N.W.
Washington, DC 20009

Geologist
American Geological Institute
5205 Leesburg Pike
Falls Church, VA 22041

Geophysicist
American Geophysical Union
2000 Florida Ave., N.W.
Washington, DC 20009

Society of Exploration
 Geophysicists
P.O. Box 3098
Tulsa, OK 74101

Government Jobs (federal)
U.S. Civil Service Commission
Bureau of Recruiting and
 Examining
Room 1416A
1900 E St., N.W.
Washington, DC 20415

Health
Division of Careers and
 Recruitment
American College of Hospital
 Administrators
840 North Lake Shore Drive
Chicago, IL 60611

National Health Council
Health Careers Program
70 West 40th St.
New York, NY 10019

Program Services Department
American Medical Association
535 North Dearborn St.
Chicago, IL 60610

Hospital Administrator
American College of Hospital
  Administrators
840 North Lake Shore Drive
Chicago, IL 60611

Association of University Programs
  in Health Administration
One Dupont Circle, N.W.
Washington, DC 20036

American Public Health
  Association
Division of Program Services
1015 15th St., N.W.
Washington, DC 20036

Hotel-Motel Worker
American Hotel and Motel
  Association
888 Seventh Ave.
New York, NY 10019

Council on Hotel, Restaurant and
  Institutional Education
Human Development Building,
  Room 118
University Park, PA 16802

**Insurance Underwriter or
  Claim Examiner**
American Council of Life Insurance
1850 K St., N.W.
Washington, DC 20006

Insurance Information Institute
110 William St.
New York, NY 10038

Alliance of American Insurers
20 North Wacker Drive
Chicago, IL 60606

Interior Design
American Society of Interior
  Designers
1430 Broadway
New York, NY 10018

Institute of Business Designers
National Headquarters
1155 Merchandise Mart
Chicago, IL 60654

Jewelers
Jewelers of America
Time-Life Building, Suite 650
1271 Avenue of the Americas
New York, NY 10020

Journalism
Association for Education in
  Journalism
University of South Carolina
School of Journalism
Columbia, SC 29208

American Newspaper Publishers
  Association Foundation
Box 17407
Dulles International Airport
Washington, DC 20041

The Society of Professional
  Journalists
Sigma Delta Chi
35 East Wacker St.
Chicago, IL 60601

Women in Communications, Inc.
P.O. Box 9561
Austin, TX 78766

Lawyer and Legal Assistant

Association of American Law
  Schools
One Dupont Circle, N.W.,
  Suite 370
Washington, DC 20036

The American Bar Association
Standing Committee on Legal
  Assistants
1155 East 60th St.
Chicago, IL 60637

National Federation of Paralegal
  Associations
P.O. Box 1410
Ben Franklin Station
Washington, DC 20044

Librarian

American Library Association
50 East Huron St.
Chicago, IL 60611

American Society for Information
  Science
1010 16th St., N.W.
Washington, DC 20036

Licensed Practical Nurse

National League for Nursing, Inc.
10 Columbus Circle
New York, NY 10019

National Association for Practical
  Nurse Education and Service,
  Inc.
254 West 31st St.
New York, NY 10001

Life Insurance Sales Worker

American Council of
  Life Insurance
1850 K St., N.W.
Washington, DC 20006

Machinists

The National Machine Tool
  Builders Association
7901 Westpark Drive
McLean, VA 22102

National Tool, Die, and Precision
  Machining Association
9300 Livingston Rd.
Washington, DC 20022

Mathematicians

American Mathematical Society
P.O. Box 6248
Providence, RI 02940

Society for Industrial and Applied
  Mathematics
1405 Architects Building
117 S. 17th St.
Philadelphia, PA 19103

Medical Laboratory Workers

American Society for Medical
  Technology
330 Meadowfern Drive
Houston, TX 77067

American Medical Technologists
710 Higgins Rd.
Park Ridge, IL 60068

Accrediting Bureau of Medical
  Laboratory Schools
Oak Manor Office
29089 U.S. 20 West
Elkhart, IN 46514

Medical Record Librarian

American Medical Record
  Association
875 North Michigan Ave.,
  Suite 1850
John Hancock Center
Chicago, IL 60611

**Medical Technologist and
   Medical Technician**
American Medical Association
Department of Health Education
   and Accreditation
535 North Dearborn St.
Chicago, IL 60610

American Society for Medical
   Technology
330 Meadowfern Drive
Houston, TX 77067

Meteorologist
American Meteorological Society
45 Beacon St.
Boston, MA 02108

**Mineral Industry Worker and
   Mining**
Bureau of Mines
U.S. Department of the Interior
18th and C Sts., N.W.
Washington, DC 20240

Models
World Modeling Association
P.O. Box 100
Croton-on-Hudson, NY 10520

Museum Worker
American Association of Museums
1055 Thomas Jefferson St., N.W.
Washington, DC 20007

Music Teachers
Music Educators National
   Conference
1902 Association Drive
Reston, VA 22091

Music Teachers National
   Association
2113 Carew Tower
Cincinnati, OH 45202

Music Therapy
National Association for Music
   Therapy, Inc.
P.O. Box 610
Lawrence, KS 66044

National Park Service Worker
National Recreation and Park
   Association
Division of Professional Services
1601 North Kent St.
Arlington, VA 22209

Nurse's Aide
Division of Careers and
   Recruitment
American Hospital Association
840 Lake Shore Drive
Chicago, IL 60611

Occupational Therapist
American Occupational Therapy
   Association
1383 Piccard Drive
Rockville, MD 20850

Nursing
Department of Nursing Education
American Nurses' Association
2420 Pershing Rd.
Kansas City, MO 64108

Oceanographer
International Oceanographic
   Foundation
3979 Rickenbacker Causeway
Virginia Key
Miami, FL 33149

American Society for Limnology
and Oceanography
I.S.T. Building
Great Lakes Research Division
University of Michigan
Ann Arbor, MI 48109

Oil Industry
American Petroleum Institute
2101 L St., N.W.
Washington, DC 20037

Opticians
Opticians Institute of America
1250 Connecticut Ave., N.W.
Washington, DC 20036

Chairperson, Optical Council
IUE-AFL-CIO-CLC
200 Park Avenue South
New York, NY 10003

Optometrists
American Optometric Association
243 North Lindbergh Boulevard
St. Louis, MO 63141

Painters
International Brotherhood of
Painters and Allied Trades
1750 New York Avenue, N.W.
Washington, DC 20006

Painting and Decorating
Contractors Association
of America
7223 Lee Highway
Falls Church, VA 22046

National Joint Painting,
Decorating, and
Drywall Finishing
Apprenticeship and
Training Committee
1709 New York Ave., N.W.,
Suite 110
Washington, DC 20006

Paper Industry
American Paper Institute
260 Madison Ave.
New York, NY 10016

Pathologists
American Society of Clinical
Pathologists
P.O. Box 12270
Chicago, IL 60612

Pharmacist
American Pharmaceutical
Association
2215 Constitution Ave., N.W.
Washington, DC 20037

American Association of Colleges
of Pharmacy
Office of Student Affairs
4630 Montgomery Ave., Suite 201
Bethesda, MD 20014

Photography
Professional Photographers of
America, Inc.
1090 Executive Way
Des Plaines, IL 60018

Physician
Association of American Medical
Colleges
One Dupont Circle, Suite 200
Washington, DC 20036

Council on Medical Education
American Medical Association
535 North Dearborn St.
Chicago, IL 60610

Physician's Assistant
Association of Physician Assistant
  Programs
2341 Jefferson Davis Highway,
  Suite 700
Arlington, VA 22202

American Medical Association
Department of Allied Medical
  Professions
535 North Dearborn St.
Chicago, IL 60610

Physical Therapy
American Physical Therapy
  Association
1156 15th St., N.W.
Washington, DC 20005

Physicist
American Institute of Physics
335 East 45th St.
New York, NY 10017

Plasterer
International Union of Bricklayers
  and Allied Craftsmen
815 15th St., N.W.
Washington, DC 20005

Operative Plasterers and Cement
  Masons International
  Association
1125 17th St., N.W.
Washington, DC 20036

Plumber, Pipefitter
National Association of Plumbing-
  Heating-Cooling Contractors
1016 20th St., N.W.
Washington, DC 20036

United Association of Journeymen
  and Apprentices of the Plumbing
  and Pipefitting Industry
901 Massachusetts Ave., N.W.
Washington, DC 20001

Police Officer
International Brotherhood of Police
  Officers
2139 Wisconsin Ave., N.W.
Washington, DC 20007

Pollution Control
Water Pollution Control Federation
2626 Pennsylvania Ave., N.W.
Washington, DC 20036

Printing and Publishing Trades
Graphic Arts Technical Foundation
4615 Forbes Ave.
Pittsburgh, PA 15213

Printing Industries of America, Inc.
1730 North Lynn St.
Arlington, VA 22209

Psychiatrist
American Psychiatric Association
1700 16th St., N.W.
Washington, DC 20009

National Association for Mental
  Health
1800 North Kent St.
Arlington, VA 22209

Public Health Worker
American Public Health
  Association, Inc.
1015 15th St., N.W.
Washington, DC 20036

Public Relations Worker
Public Relations Society of America
Career Information
845 Third Ave.
New York, NY 10022

Radio and Television
Broadcast Education Association
1771 N St., N.W.
Washington, DC 20036

Real Estate Agents and Brokers
National Association of Realtors
430 North Michigan Ave.
Chicago, IL 60611

Recreation Worker, Therapist
National Recreation and Park
  Association
1601 North Kent St.
Arlington, VA 22209

Registered Nurses
Career Information Services
National League for Nursing
10 Columbus Circle
New York, NY 10009

Respiratory Therapist
American Association for
  Respiratory Therapy
1720 Regal Row, Suite 112
Dallas, TX 75235

The National Board for Respiratory
  Therapy, Inc.
11015 West 75th Terrace
Shawnee Mission, KS 66214

Scientist
Scientific Manpower Commission
1776 Massachusetts Ave., N.W.
Washington, DC 20036

Secretary
Professional Secretaries
  International
2440 Pershing Road, Suite G10
Kansas City, MO 64108

Social Worker
The National Association of Social
  Workers
1425 H St., N.W., Suite 600
Washington, DC 20005

Council on Social Work Education
111 Eighth Ave.
New York, NY 10011

Sociologist
The American Sociological
  Association
1722 N St., N.W.
Washington, DC 20002

Speech Pathologist
American Speech-Language-
  Hearing Association
10801 Rockville Pike
Rockville, MD 20852

Statistician
American Statistical Association
806 15th St., N.W.
Washington, DC 20005

Systems Analyst
American Federation of
 Information Processing
 Societies
1815 North Lynn St.
Arlington, VA 22209

Tax Work
Chief, Recruitment Section
Internal Revenue Service
1111 Constitution Ave., N.W.
Washington, DC 20226

Technician
Engineer's Council for Professional
 Development
345 East 47th St.
New York, NY 10017

Television-Radio Servicers
National Alliance of Television and
 Electronic Service Associations
5908 South Troy St.
Chicago, IL 60629

Tilesetter
International Union of Bricklayers
 and Allied Craftsmen
International Masonry
 Apprenticeship Trust
815 15th St., N.W.
Washington, DC 20005

Tile, Marble and Terrazzo Finishers
 and Shopment International
 Union
Suite 116, 801 N. Pitt St.
Alexandria, VA 22314

Travel Agents
American Society of Travel Agents
711 Fifth Ave.
New York, NY 10022

Tool and Die Maker
International Association of
 Machinists and Aerospace
 Workers
1300 Connecticut Ave., N.W.
Washington, DC 20036

Skilled Trades Department
United Automobile Workers of
 America
8000 East Jefferson Ave.
Detroit, MI 48214

Veterinarian
American Veterinary Medical
 Association
930 N. Meacham Rd.
Schaumburg, IL 60196

Vocational Counseling
American Personnel and Guidance
 Association
2 Skyline Place
5203 Leesburg Pike, Suite 400
Falls Church, VA 22041

Vocational Rehabilitation
American Rehabilitation
 Counseling Association
2 Skyline Place
5203 Leesburg Pike, Suite 400
Falls Church, VA 22041

National Rehabilitation Counseling
 Association
Cary Building, Suite B-110
8136 Old Keene Mill Rd.
Springfield, VA 22152

National Council on Rehabilitation
 Education
2210 Massachusetts Ave., N.W.
Washington, DC 20008

Welder
The American Welding Society
2501 Northwest 7th St.
Miami, FL 33125

X-Ray Technician
The American Society of Radiologic
  Technologists
55 East Jackson Boulevard
Chicago, IL 60604

A LOOK TO THE FUTURE

How the Teenage Job Market Shapes Up

The teenage population will decline from 16.4 million in 1979 to 13.1 million by 1990, the Census Bureau projects. Consequently, the teenage labor force is projected to decline, too, from 9.5 million in 1979 to 7.6 million in 1990, and teens will represent only 6.7 percent of the total U.S. labor force, down from 9.2 percent in 1979. Roughly half of all teenagers were in the labor market in 1980, and that percentage stays about the same over time.

What these numbers mean to you is that you will have *less competition* for scarce part-time jobs in the decade ahead. Most of you will enter the job market as part-time and summer workers, and these jobs will not necessarily lead to careers. For most of you, the transition from school to full-time work will occur gradually as school attendance ends and you move into the full-time labor force. Others of you might make this transition abruptly by dropping out of school. Be forewarned: This may have a short-term appeal, but in the end, you and your earnings will lose. As a dropout, one of the main problems you will have is that you will choose a job before you are eligible for most career jobs. You will compete with your peers for "youth" jobs—sales clerks, waiters, stock clerks, and the like—and you will stay there. Eventually you will find that you lack the expert knowledge required for more complicated work, and in many cases you will remain ineligible for a number of career jobs because you lack the necessary educational credentials.

You've heard it all before and it's true: stay in school! If you possibly can, hang in there just a while longer. It will be worth it in the long run. Don't condemn yourself to a lifetime of reduced earnings and limited horizons.

Where Will the Jobs Be in the 1980s?

True or False?

• The demand for elementary school teachers, after a prolonged period of decline, is entering a new upturn. The whole pattern in the education field will change dramatically as the babies born to the babies of the post–World War II "baby boom" generation reach school age.

• The service fields will be prime areas for jobs—particularly in banking, communications, and health care. Jobs in the health care and food-related spheres will grow rapidly during the 1980s.

• Women will be seeking paying jobs in the marketplace because the types of service jobs they often fill—nurses and nurses aides, child-care attendants, waitresses, hairdressers—are increasing.

• Benefiting from basic economic trends in the United States will be *skilled* blue-collar workers. As our society grows more automated and moves toward higher levels of technology, skilled blue-collar workers will be essential to manage and repair our increasingly complicated machines and computers. Benefiting, too, from higher military spending will be skilled machinists and specialists in high technology industries.

• On the outside looking in will be the unskilled or semiskilled. There will be fewer and fewer jobs for the unskilled human in a workplace in which machines created to be robots continue to displace a laborer who can't compete on any scale.

Every one of these above five statements is *true*.

Learn a Skill, and Make Sure It's Needed

Every one of the above five statements telegraphs to you a message about your future in the U.S. work force. For decades, the U.S. economy has been shifting away from an industrial society concentrating on producing autos, steel, shoes. These industries are being phased out, and as this occurs the tasks of the unskilled and semi-skilled American disappear. By the year 2000, some experts predict that a full 25 percent of the world's manufactured goods will be produced by third world countries.

Meanwhile, the fundamental movement in our advanced society

toward white-collar occupations is slated to continue. Among occupations in major growth trends are health professionals, managers, and sales and clerical workers. Reinforcing this movement are two factors: the rising educational level of workers and the unrelenting flow of women into jobs.

The two-earner family has become the norm and women everywhere—not just in the developed countries—are seeking work outside the home. The only exceptions are countries in which religion or custom prevent women from taking paying jobs (Saudi Arabia, Iraq). A side effect of this fundamental trend is that the housekeeper will be an ever tougher person to find. Not until there are great (and essential) changes in the traditionally low-paying, low-status household job will the workers return.

In the early 1980s, the construction trades were crushed by the almost unbelievably steep cost of mortgage money—but this, in turn, means the normal demand for new homes has been pent up. With interest rates at more tolerable levels, there should be an explosion of jobs for blue-collar workers in the construction fields.

Also due for a major expansion are the ranks of the self-employed and owners of small businesses. "Being your own boss" is, as it always has been, the American dream, for women now as well as men.

During this decade, teenage unemployment rates will, I repeat and stress, drift downward as the proportion of young people in our population declines—but white teenagers will be favored for employment more than blacks.

As for cutbacks in federal spending, if these, in turn, lead to cutbacks in state and local spending, the targets will be minorities (including women), the young, and the poorly trained.

The messages couldn't be clearer: go where the jobs are! Get out of the occupations that are declining and into those on the upswing. Learn a skill. Black or white, move to the regions where you are needed and get the training that is in demand.

FOCUS: COMPUTER OCCUPATIONS

Millions of workers routinely use computers. Ticketing agents, bank clerks, engineers, sales workers, machinists—the list encompasses hundreds of occupations. If you get one of these jobs, you probably will find yourself working with computers before too long. Computer use is growing so rapidly and reaches into so many areas of life that there is a shortage of skilled, available workers, and employment in computer occupations is expected to almost double between 1980 and 1990. Most computer operators—excluding those in the kinds of jobs mentioned above—fall into one of five categories: systems analyst, programmer, computer and peripheral equipment operator, keypunch operator, and computer service technician. All have glowing futures, with the exception of keypunch operators.

Projected average annual job openings in computer occupations, 1980–90

Occupation	Total average annual openings, 1980–90	Employment change	Replacement needs[1]
Total	93,700	68,500	25,200
Systems analysts	19,000	15,700	3,300
Programmers	20,550	15,900	4,650
Computer and peripheral equipment operators	41,800	32,800	9,000
Keypunch operators	3,900	−3,600	7,500
Computer service technicians	8,450	7,700	750

[1]Separations from the labor force due to deaths and retirements.
SOURCE: Bureau of Labor Statistics.

Systems Analyst

Systems analysts plan efficient methods of processing data and handling the results. For example, if a new inventory system is needed for a business, a systems analyst determines what new data must be collected, the equipment needed, and the steps to be followed in processing the information. Analysts use various techniques such as cost accounting, sampling, and mathematical model-building to analyze a problem and devise a new system.

Once a system has been developed, they prepare charts and diagrams that describe its operation in terms that the system's users can understand. Because the work is so varied and complex, systems analysts usually specialize in either business or scientific engineering applications.

College graduates are generally sought for these jobs and graduate training is required for more complicated positions. Experience with computers is vital, and the more preparation you have, the better.

The job outlook for systems analysts is excellent: employment is expected to increase 65 percent from 243,000 in 1980 to 400,000 in 1990.

Programmer

Computer programmers write detailed instructions called programs that list in logical order the steps a computer must follow in order to organize data, solve a problem, or perform other tasks. Programmers usually work from descriptions prepared by systems analysts. A programmer writes the program by breaking down each step into a series of coded instructions using one of the languages developed especially for computers (such as COBOL or FORTRAN). Next, the programmer debugs the program by testing its operation to be sure the instructions are correct and the desired information is produced. The programmer tries a sample of the data with the program and reviews the results. Finally, he or she prepares an instruction sheet for the computer operator who will actually run the program. Programs can take many months to develop.

Most programmers are college graduates; others have taken special courses in programming to supplement their experience in such fields as accounting or inventory control.

Computer programmer employment will increase as less expensive and more sophisticated computer hardware and software attract new computer users and increase the number and type of uses for the machines. Computer programmer employment is expected to grow 47 percent from 341,000 in 1980 to 500,000 in 1990.

Computer and Peripheral Equipment Operators

All data systems require specialized workers to enter data and instructions, operate the computer, and retrieve the results. The data to be processed and the instructions are called "input"; the results are called "output." Computer operators monitor and operate the control console of a computer to process data according to the operating instructions. They set control switches on the equipment, select and load the input and output units with materials, such as tapes and printout forms, and then clear the system and start the equipment. During the run, they observe the machines and control panel for error signals. Peripheral equipment operators operate on-line or off-line peripheral machines according to instructions, transfer data from one form to another, print output, and read data into and out of the computer.

Usually a high school diploma is a minimum requirement, and computer experience can help you here. The employment of computer and peripheral equipment operators is expected to increase 63 percent from 522,000 in 1980 to 850,000 in 1990. The major cause of this growth is the increasing use of computer hardware. Particularly as small businesses acquire computer systems, they will need workers to operate the equipment.

Keypunch Operators

Keypunch operators prepare input by punching patterns of holes in computer cards to represent specific letters, numbers, and special characters, using a machine similar to a typewriter. The Bureau of Labor Statistics expects that, alone among computer occupations, employment of keypunch operators will decline 14 percent from 1980 to 1990, from 266,000 down to 230,000. The reason: more accurate and swift methods of coding data are being developed to replace the slower and cumbersome keypunch system.

Keypunch operators usually have a minimum of a high school education.

Computer Service Technicians

Computer service technicians routinely service systems to keep them operating efficiently. They adjust, oil, and clean mechanical and electromechanical parts, and check for loose connections and defective components or circuits. When computer equipment breaks down, technicians must quickly find the cause of the problem and make repairs. They often help install new equipment.

Besides knowing how to use specialized tools and test equipment, computer technicians must be familiar with technical and repair manuals for each piece of equipment and they must keep up with the technical information and revised maintenance procedures periodically issued by computer manufacturers.

If you are interested in a career as a computer service technician, start now by taking courses in mathematics, physics, electronics, and computer programming. Employers require a technician trainee to have one to two years post–high school training in basic electronics or electrical engineering. Mechanical aptitude is essential.

Of all the computer occupations, service technicians will experience the largest growth, from 83,000 in 1980 to 160,000 in 1990, an explosion of 93 percent.

Are you convinced of the vigor of computer occupations? A Bureau of Labor Statistics study in 1981 concluded that the computer occupations will be the most rapidly growing field in the economy for the next decade at least, increasing three times as fast as the expected rate of growth for all occupations.

Other conclusions and highlights of this study:

• The increasing sophistication and complexity of computer operations will require workers with more and better training. Already, education and training for computer operators have fallen behind demand.

• Most important, the shortage of computer personnel is expected to continue, resulting in higher wages, more job mobility, increased job security, and generally greater opportunities for these workers.

If you think there is the slightest possibility that you might be interested in a career with computers, *now*—NOW!—is when to start your investigation and training.

FOCUS: PARALEGALS, AN EXPLODING CAREER OPPORTUNITY

If you want to reach beyond the field of a legal secretary, your next step upward is as a paralegal or legal assistant. You're beyond the status of a legal secretary but are not yet qualified to be a lawyer.

The paralegal is a development of the post–World War II era. Legal assistants were first extensively employed in the probate field; generally, they were legal secretaries who worked for lawyers on wills and probate cases. Eventually, the secretary became as qualified as the lawyer to carry out certain administrative chores. As the lawyer's time was saved, the secretary's value to the firm increased—and the secretary's pay reflected it.

Later, paralegals were used in real estate law, corporate law, litigation, and antitrust law. Today, such fields of law as bankruptcy, admiralty, criminal law, and labor relations depend heavily on paralegals.

What a paralegal may do varies widely from office to office. In brief, you work under a lawyer's supervision and take care of many of the duties in a law office short of what the lawyer must do. You may not set fees, represent a client in court or give legal advice, accept clients, or present a case.

The National Association of Legal Assistants (NALA) outlines some of the duties of a legal assistant, but its outline is by no means all-inclusive. The NALA merely says that a legal assistant, under the supervision of a lawyer, "shall apply knowledge of law and legal procedures in rendering direct assistance to lawyers, clients, and courts." The legal assistant can "design, develop and modify procedures . . . prepare and interpret legal documents . . . research, assess, compile and use information from the law library and other references; and analyze and handle procedural problems that involve independent decisions."

In some offices, a paralegal actually can draft briefs, perform detailed legal research, conduct client interviews, draft wills, deeds, mortgages, separation agreements, and contracts, and even supervise and manage office staff and keep financial records.

The American Bar Association has issued only general guidelines on a paralegal's duties. No state has either passed legislation defining what a paralegal is or set performance standards. However, the NALA has established a Certified Legal Assistance Program that involves completing a two-day comprehensive examination which is administered each year at several regional testing centers. When you pass, you can use the designation "Certified Legal Assistant (CLA)."

If you choose to pursue a career as a paralegal, you can follow one of several directions. As a legal secretary, you can ask to be assigned work projects within the firm that will lead to a paralegal career. You also may watch the kinds of work done by paralegals in your office and become familiar with the job's duties—and then offer to assist in your spare time. A good bet is to find out about paralegal training programs that are offered at universities and community colleges throughout the country. Several of these programs meet the American Bar Association's requirements. Most legal assistance programs are completed in two years, but some require four years of study. One plus to many programs: an internship in which students gain practical experience by working in a law office, corporate legal department, or government agency. Depending on the course of study, graduates receive a certificate, associate degree or, in some cases, a bachelor's degree in legal assistance.

Note, too, that other occupations call for a detailed understanding of the legal system but not the intensive training (and expensive education) of a lawyer—including claims examiners, health and regulation inspectors, legal investigators, occupational safety and health workers, patent agents, police officers, and title examiners.

For more information on careers and a list of legal assistant schools approved by the American Bar Association, write to the ABA, Standing Committee on Legal Assistants (1155 East 60th Street, Chicago, IL 60637). And, for information on certification, write to the National Association of Legal Assistants, Inc., (3005 East Skelly Drive, Suite 120, Tulsa, OK 74105).

If you're blocked from a full law career by financial considerations or ability, this is a way to jump over barriers. But be warned: competent and experienced legal secretaries are a vanishing species, while experienced paralegals are multiplying quickly. Still, career prospects are bright through the 1980s.

It may well be that in coming years, you may find it harder to get employment as a paralegal than as a legal secretary—a twist hard to imagine. But right now, as you plan your career, law firms are in hot pursuit of both. And, future paralegals, FYI: the pay is superior.

FOCUS: LEGAL SECRETARIES

You are developing excellent office skills and the ability to work closely with highly trained professionals in a complex organization. And you are looking for a career that offers salaries above the national average and opportunities for advancement. In addition, you are working toward a degree from a business college or two-year community college. Consider becoming a legal secretary—among the most highly respected of any specialty in the secretarial field.

Legal secretaries are in great demand. The average starting salary in the early 1980s was well over $250 per week; $350 to $400 for those with experience. Overtime pay, rapid advancement, and movement into the paralegal field can boost those figures higher.

Why is the demand so high and why are the opportunities so broad? The National Association of Legal Secretaries estimates that there are more than 300,000 practicing attorneys in the United States, and the tendency is toward ever-larger law firms and increasing specialization.

According to *Webster's Legal Secretaries Handbook*, the law field has been marked "by enormous specialization since the 1930s, requiring more lawyers and more legal secretaries.

"A vast range of legal specialties has developed in such areas as corporate law, antitrust, criminal, family, aviation, probate, medical malpractice, personal injury, and others. Now energy, environmental, and public interest law have also emerged."

All these fields require the services of lawyers and their assistants. The legal secretary has a chance to climb the corporate ladder and move into either paralegal work or administrative functions. Many larger firms employ former legal secretaries in positions such as director of administration, director of personnel services, or director of finance or computer services.

As a legal secretary, you can expect to prepare legal papers, correspondence such as summonses, complaints, motions, and subpoenas. In some offices, you might assist with legal research and review law journals.

The National Association of Legal Secretaries (NALS) offers a certification program which, when successfully completed, designates you as a Professional Legal Secretary (PLS). The two-day exam is given in March and October each year. Application to take the exam may be made after five years' experience as a legal secretary. For a study guide and copy of *So You Want to Be a Legal Secretary*, write to the NALS headquarters (3005 East Skelly Drive, Tulsa, OK 74105).

You'll find jobs advertised in the classified section of your newspaper. Employment agencies often have many listings for legal secretaries. Local legal secretarial associations can offer leads, as can local bar associations and chambers of commerce. You also can write directly to the personnel departments of law firms in your community. Many large firms establish in-house training programs for secretaries who possess only basic dictation and typing skills—check with larger firms about this.

The group interview is an unusual gimmick used when a law firm is suddenly faced with an extraordinary amount of work. This involves a blind ad for applicants with only fundamental office skills. A resume is requested. You take a written test and get a group interview and a private interview. If hired, you have a good chance of staying and becoming a qualified legal secretary.

Private law firms offer the widest variety of work and the greatest opportunity for individual initiative. Law departments of large organizations provide well-defined work and regular hours. You decide which you like best. As a legal secretary, you're a key link in a lawyer's chain and you can just about create your own career.

FOCUS: NURSING

Count a nursing license among the hottest career tickets of the 1980s.

Although there has been a nursing shortage as long as there have been nurses, the shortage has reached crisis proportions due to three chief factors: a drop in nursing school enrollments of 1 percent a year since the late 1970s, a backlog of 100,000 unfilled jobs, and our rapidly aging population.

By 1985, 240,000 registered nurses and 165,000 practical nurses will be needed to fill the available jobs.

Price wars have broken out among hospitals for the dwindling supply of nurses in the face of soaring demand. Bounties are even awarded to successful headhunters (read recruiters!). And perquisites—such as use of a car, day-care for children, convenient working hours, special courses, and generous benefits—sweeten many job offers.

As a career, nursing is virtually recession-proof. Nationwide, the unemployment rate is consistently less than 2 percent, and 70 percent of today's nursing school students line up jobs before they graduate.

And yet . . . the field is still dominated by women (97 percent of all nurses are females); overwork and stress are commonplace; pay is still noncompetitive with other professions.

When considering a nursing career, let these key facts guide you:

Registered Nurses

After high school, there are three ways to become a registered nurse, all of which prepare you for the state exam that is required for a license.

* *Associate degree* (held by 50 percent of registered nurses). This takes two years, usually in a junior or community college. Costs in 1982 were about $700 (public) and $3,000 (private) per year.
* *Diploma* (held by 20 percent of registered nurses). This is a three-year program, usually in a hospital setting.
* *Baccalaureate degree* (held by 30 percent of registered nurses). You receive this degree after completing four years at a college or university program, and you will need a baccalaureate degree for graduate work if you want to teach, do research, or do administrative work.

Despite the differences in the three routes to becoming an RN, the license you receive is the same, as are starting salaries. In 1982, salaries began at $10,500 and ranged to as high as $15,000, depending on the community and type of hospital.

Licensed Practical Nurses

Licensed practical nurses (called Vocational Nurses in California and Texas) work in hospitals and nursing homes. In fact, in 1981, about 1,105,000 LPNs were employed, and two out of three worked in hospitals. That year, salaries averaged $12,500 for hospital-based LPNs, and $11,400 for nursing home-based workers. A one-year program prepares high school graduates for the state exam required for a license; students are based in hospitals, concentrating on "learning by doing" rather than classroom instruction.

For a list of free or low-cost publications on registered nursing, send a self-addressed stamped envelope to National League for Nursing (10 Columbus Circle, New York, NY 10019). For one dollar you can obtain a directory of programs and financial aid for licensed practical nurses from National Association for Practical Nurse Education and Service, Inc. (254 West 31st Street, New York, NY 10001).

GETTING A CAREER JOB

Job Sources

Your search for a full-time career job is not unlike the search for your first job (earlier in this chapter), but now the stakes are higher. Select your job leads from among the following:

• Newspaper ads. The best jobs usually are not listed in newspapers, but thousands of interesting jobs are, and the ads are an essential tool for the job-hunter. Help wanted ads are usually found in the back of your daily paper or in a separate section on Sunday. Ads generally are listed alphabetically by job category.

Read through the ads and circle those that intrigue you. Since ads can be misleading, study them carefully and make sure you understand what each means. Vague ads should leap out at you: they may lead to door-to-door selling, and may even require that you first buy merchandise you're expected to sell (a sign of a scam?). Be wary of jobs that promise terrific money with no experience needed. They're con jobs.

• Local offices of the state and federal employment service. These offices list private-sector jobs for most areas. Since state employment services operate computerized job banks in all major cities and many smaller ones, you have access to the latest information on job openings in any area of the country. These agencies can assist you further with job counseling, with special programs for women and minority youths, and will provide aptitude and proficiency testing. Best of all, these services and more are provided free.

• Your career counseling office at school. This office can match you with known jobs and put you in touch with local companies. When recruiters come to your campus, you will sign up for interviews at this office. Watch school bulletin boards and campus newspapers closely so you'll know of important activities and services at this primary job source.

• Large corporations, which usually maintain management training programs. Locate the largest employers in your area and contact their personnel offices for further information.

• Journals, magazines, and newspapers in your special field of interest. Job leads may appear in these publications.

• A temporary employment agency. Temp jobs can lead to full-time employment, but even if they don't, you gain experience in a variety of offices and learn about different companies and work situations. This experience can help you better define your career objectives.

• Family and friends—a resource, but try to avoid working directly for family or friends. You lose some independence even before you start to work. You can sell yourself on your own merits and, since you will have to sooner or later, it won't hurt to start now.

• Your school's alumni office. Previous graduates may well work in industries and for companies that you want to enter. The "old-boy" and, increasingly, "old-girl" network of school ties can assist you at all stages of your career.

After you inventory your job prospects, keep records. A 3-by-5-inch card system will do well. Note on each card the name of the firm, its address and phone number, the name of your contact there, and the job you applied for. Other useful tidbits are worth recording too, along with the date you wrote or phoned.

Job Applications

You almost surely are not accustomed to filling out applications, so before you start applying for jobs in earnest, try to get one or two applications for practice. Perhaps your guidance counselor has some samples for you to use.

When you get the application, study it thoroughly so you understand what information is requested and where to put it down. As you fill in the spaces, write or print neatly and spell everything correctly. After you finish, make sure you've provided all the information asked for, and then have someone check it over for neatness and accuracy. You will be more confident when you have to complete a real application.

Any standard application form will include the following information:

- Name, address, and telephone number. Also, Social Security number and date and place of birth.
- Names, addresses, and telephone numbers of previous employers.
- Names and dates of schools you attended.
- Names, addresses, and phone numbers of people who will give references on your behalf. Your references should not be family members or personal friends. They can be teachers, guidance counselors, tutors, clergy, babysitting clients. These people will be asked about your reliability, honesty, and other character traits, so choose people who can truthfully tell a prospective employer good things about you.

Are You a Good Job Candidate? Test Yourself

If you're in the market for a job, do not take a single step without first testing yourself with a realistic assessment designed to answer the basic question: Am I a good job candidate?

Study the following test, answer each question as honestly as you can. Write down your answers, and force yourself to a candid appraisal of yourself. Then, search for the right fit, where you're the best candidate for a specific job.

1. What is your motivation? Is it just a paycheck or do you genuinely believe that you're ready to take on responsibilities and can manage them?

2. What are your academic credentials? What school did (do) you attend and what degrees do you have (or are you in line for)? Do you have any special training or abilities that might set you apart

from your peers (languages, oral or written communications skills, a talent for transferring different disciplines)?

3. What kind of company are you working for now (or have you worked for)? Is it a company well regarded within its own industry? Is it profitable? Has it demonstrated growth in terms of market share? Is it in the public eye? How is it regarded in the stock markets?

4. How long have you been with your present company? Too short a time to make a definite contribution or long enough to do so? Even if your rise hasn't been meteoric, have you enjoyed steady upward movement in your responsibilities and kept the momentum going?

5. What is your pay? Better than average for your peers in your profession, industry, or company? If your age/salary ratio is better than average, you're obviously a better than average job candidate.

After answering these basic questions—which will reveal far more than you expected if you answered honestly—you should also set your sights realistically in terms of your abilities and experience in relation to the kinds of companies you would like to work for and the potential growth and salary they might offer. The trick is not to set your sights too high or too low.

You don't have to be the best candidate in the world for a job. A multinational company based in a large city might be looking for one kind of candidate and a $25 million company in the midwest might be looking for another kind.

When this self-examination has satisfied you that you are a good job candidate, you could generate your own job-seeking campaign. Carefully scrutinize all ''help wanted'' ads and use the personal contacts you've made in your own industry. Check the numerous corporate reference books for industry, product lines, location, and growth potential. Then write to, say, 100 suitable companies (using proper names, addresses, etc.), detailing why you are indeed a good job candidate.

Your Resume

You are about to look for a job—part-time, summer, or full-time—and you're paralyzed. Calm down! Learn the sound methods employed by generations of job-hunters: contemplate yourself and your goals, write a resume, compose cover letters, make phone calls, and prepare to endure many interviews.

As you sample any of the hundreds of books available to help you in your job hunt, you will discover quickly that although some authorities say interviews are more important than resumes, or that clever cover letters add little to your chances of success, these are actually the three key elements to winning a good, satisfying job.

Before you actually write your resume, look hard and honestly at yourself. Here are the basic areas to explore, when you are alone with a pad and pen:

- *Your abilities, skills, and talents.* What do you most enjoy? What are you good at? What personal qualities—patience, perseverence, leadership, imagination, organization—do you have? Note them all. And what about special abilities? Do you have an analytical mind? Are you precise with details, adept with your hands?
- *Your work history.* List every job you've had. That includes neighborhood chores, summer jobs, and *volunteer* work (don't overlook!), along with a description of your duties at each. What aspects of each did you like, dislike? Were any of these jobs in potential career fields that intrigue you?
- *Your education.* Make a chronological list of all the schools and special training programs you've attended, along with addresses and dates of attendance. Which were your most important or most satisfying courses, and which the least? Why? Did you earn any special prizes, awards, or scholarships? What extracurricular activities do you participate in? Are they job-related?
- *Your hobbies.* What hobbies do you enjoy that might relate to a job? Don't dismiss them—hobbies can serve as valuable clues to your real interests. For example, do you excel at drawing, or caring for children? Do you have musical training? Can you speak and read a second language?
- *Your physical condition.* Are you healthy? Strong? Do you have any physical problems that limit your mobility or reduce your stamina? If you're a girl, do you assume you can't perform certain jobs because you're not strong enough?
- *Your career goals.* Whether you've even thought about your career at this stage, try to put your goals in perspective. Can you imagine what you'd like to be doing five years from now? How about

ten years from now? Does a goal this long-range require additional education or training? Is it realistic? Do you have the determination and ability to get there, and will there be jobs once you arrive? Don't write off possible career choices because employment prospects are dim now, but be alert to this fact and keep your options open by acquiring other skills. Write a "dream" resume for that future. Tinkering with what you want to be able to list in the future can be a good way to start accomplishing it now.

• *Your values and personal (as opposed to professional) goals.* Note the kind of lifestyle you hope to achieve, the activities you enjoy, and the kind of family and community roles you want.

All the consideration you give to your interests and desired lifestyle will help you put together your resume, which is the lure that will lead an employer to reel you in for an interview. A resume summarizes and highlights, *on one page*, your education, work experience, activities, awards, special skills, and so on. No matter what resume style and layout you use, it must display the absolute best you have to offer. Remember that when you send out a copy, you are making an impression on a stranger. Impressive credentials will mean nothing if your resume is sloppy and disorganized—an employer will focus on those qualities instead of your varsity letters and award-winning graphic designs.

Your resume should be as perfect as you can make it. Show it to a teacher or friendly adult and ask for advice. Don't be satisfied until you've written and rewritten it several times. For formats and other tips, consult books in your library, and study *Merchandising Your Job Talents,* available for sale ($2 in 1982) from the Consumer Information Center, Department G, Pueblo, CO 81009. You'll find samples of effective resumes and hints on how to spice up your own.

A resume should strike a fine balance between detail and brevity. You want to give a busy employer as much pertinent data in as few words as possible. In your education history, for example, the sentence, "I was graduated first in my class and was chosen valedictorian," can be reduced to "graduated first in class, chosen valedictorian." Use a telegraphic style.

Another tip: think of all the best things you can say about yourself. A resume does not have to tell the whole, unvarnished truth—select the facts that highlight your special skills, talents, and achievements. Don't lie. It is wrong, and, if detected, you can deservedly lose your job and tarnish your record for years to come.

First you need a basic resume, which should include the following:

• *Personal data:* name, address, and telephone number. If you are away at school, note that mail should be sent to you there only until the end of term. Your date of birth, state of health, and marital status are optional.

• *Employment objective:* optional, too, but helpful to an employer. Indicate your objective in one sentence: ''Seek entry-level position as bookkeeper.''

• *Education:* list your formal education, starting with your most recent degree or diploma. Include names and locations of schools, years attended, major and minor, honors and awards, and extracurricular activities *if* they are relevant to your job goal.

• *Work history:* List each job starting with your most recent (or current) one. Include dates of employment, names and addresses of each employer, your position, and a brief description of your duties. Be concise and be precise. Did you supervise other employees? How many? Did you use special equipment? What kind?

You can organize your work history in another style, which is by function. Choose one style only for your resume, however. For a functional resume, list the functions of previous jobs that relate to your present objective. Describe the type of work in each area without breaking it down to individual jobs. This format can be tricky; consult manuals on resume style.

• *Military experience:* include branch and length of service, major duties, special training, and awards and citations.

• *Miscellany:* include any information that, while pertinent, doesn't fit into any other category. For example, foreign languages, special skills, publications, awards.

• *References:* names and addresses of three people who can speak knowledgeably about you and your abilities. Ask for their permission first—you don't want to be surprised if someone can't, or won't, give you a good recommendation, and you don't want your references to be surprised when they are contacted.

Eventually you may want to prepare a resume for more specific job objectives. This tailored resume should be targeted to a specific job; make sure the employment goal matches the job opening.

When you finish, double-check for consistency, neatness, spelling, and punctuation. Type your resume carefully (handwritten resumes, except in extreme cases, are unacceptable). Have yours reproduced on a photocopying machine that makes clean, crisp copies on good quality bond paper. Your resume's appearance should match the clear, bright image you project of yourself.

Your Cover Letter

Equipped with your resume, you're ready to continue the campaign to find yourself a job. You have before you a list of prospective employers, culled from newspaper ads and school referrals. Now you must sit down and compose a cover letter for each prospective job. One all-purpose cover letter will not do.

The cover letter demonstrates your interest in a job, and it entices the reader to study your enclosed resume. It should be snappy, clear, and to the point. Keep in mind the following guides as you write your letters:

1. For each company, find out the name of a person to write to rather than simply a title. For example, "Mr. Samuel Green," rather than "Personnel Director," or "Ms. Lily Smith," instead of "Vice-President for Finance." Double-check the spelling of the person's name.
2. Apply for a specific job, not for "any openings in your company."
3. Keep your letter to one page. Don't repeat your resume.
4. State your qualifications and be clear, concise, and enthusiastic. Avoid jargon, gushy language, and gimmicks.
5. After you have written a draft, edit it. Cut out unnecessary words and correct any spelling errors. Retype it neatly on 8½-by-11-inch bond paper, or cajole a friend into doing it for you if you can't type.
6. Do not *ever* send photocopied letters to several employers. No one wants to read a letter addressed to Dear Sir/Madam.
7. Include an accurate return address (with zip code) and current

telephone number, even though that information is on your resume.

8. Make a photocopy or carbon of each letter you write for reference in case you receive a positive response.

9. Keep in mind that your cover letter will be seen first. Make sure it's neat, clear, and reflects your personal flair.

The following model can assist your efforts:

10101 Hibiscus Drive
Carefree Happyland, 12345
U.S.A.
March 5, 1982

Ms. Meredith Sands, Editor
Community Pride Weekly
Flower Ridge, 67891
U.S.A.

Dear Ms. Sands:

Thank you for taking the time to talk to me on the phone this morning. I am sending you the resume and writing samples you requested. As you recall, I am applying for the summer opening at your paper, and since I am planning a career in journalism I am very excited at the prospect of working for a newspaper.

My writing samples are articles I wrote for my college paper this year. As you will see, my editors assigned me to features most often. I covered some sports events, too. In addition to writing, I can do layouts, paste-up, and proofreading. I am eager to contribute in any way I can.

The semester ends on May 20 and I will be available for work on May 25. My spring vacation is in two weeks, and I will call you next week to arrange an interview during that time.

Thank you for your consideration.

Sincerely yours,

How to Avoid Job-Counseling Traps

The job career counselors who charge you heartbreaking sums for what often is no more than the preparation of a resume are emerging from their sleazy backgrounds to "take you" for whatever they can.

To avoid the traps:

• Steer clear of any job-counseling firm that leads you to believe it also is an employment agency or makes extravagant claims or promises. This is the time for informed skepticism of any easy offer.

• Check out the reputations of any firms you are considering; ask for and follow through on references from former clients in situations similar to yours.

• Get the definitions and facts straight on this befuddling subject of job assistance so you know what to expect. First confirm exactly what services the firm intends to provide and for what price.

• Shop for job advice. Compare the claims in the ads, promotional literature, and the sales pitch with the contract. The ads may refer to "placement, jobs, success, earnings," while the contract will mention only "consult, advise, attempt, prepare," and usually will state in the fine print, "We are not an employment agency and cannot guarantee employment or placement." Quite a difference in meaning.

• In investigating any of these firms, ask for the names of those with skills and backgrounds similar to yours that the firm has placed. See what you get. Ask for the number of clients from whom the firm has collected advance fees in the past year and the number the firm has directly helped. If the firm claims "confidential information," run.

• Never sign a "fine print" contract before you have read it several times at your leisure and have checked it out with a lawyer, accountant, or person you trust who is on your side. Note the phases of the program and the cutoff points for a partial refund, if any. What functions must the counseling service carry out before each phase is completed and you lose the right to a refund of that portion of the fee?

You may learn more about selling yourself by studying these warnings than you learn from the counseling service. And you will protect yourself even more against the swindlers in career counseling by getting satisfactory answers to the following key questions:

1. What obligation am I incurring? What is the cost? When must I pay and precisely for what service?
2. How long has this firm been active in this business under the current management?
3. How competent is its staff in executive guidance—and what are the qualifications? What are the firm's resumes like?
4. What is the firm's record of success in placement and what are the names of satisfied clients? Can I check them myself? How soon did they get jobs? What jobs did they get?
5. What are the names of satisfied employers with whom this firm has placed personnel? Can I verify this? How?
6. Has the firm's advertising accurately described services offered? Is the promotional literature different from the contract?
7. Does the contract cover all aspects of the agreement? Have I read this contract several times and double-checked it with experts?
8. Are additional promises in writing signed by an officer of the firm? Does this officer have authority to obligate the firm?
9. What provisions are there, if any, for a refund? Are there phases of service tied to a partial refund?
10. What service period is covered by the contract? Can I wait that long to get a job and paycheck?

The key protection: be on guard against job counseling firms that charge in advance, and don't sign any contracts hastily.

The Interview

"Leaning forward in her seat, listening intently to the senators' sometimes rambling questions, she gave the impression of having researched every conceivable query and deciding in advance how specific she wanted to be in responding."

That was how a leading newspaper described Judge Sandra Day O'Connor as she faced the Senate interviewers who stood between her and the job she wanted: Associate Justice of the U.S. Supreme Court.

The job interview can be a traumatic experience for even the most self-assured individual. Yet 99 percent of American companies use the interview as a selection tool in making hiring decisions. Polishing your interview techniques is essential for you as you launch your career—and later.

A successful approach to an employer creates interest in your qualifications and leads to an interview. Either the employer contacts you or, more likely, you call a week after you send your letter and set up an appointment. (Have a calendar at hand and schedule your date and time to suit the prospective employer.)

The interview is your big chance to sell yourself. Show your qualifications and enthusiasm for the job. Evaluate both your prospective employer and the job itself: interviews work both ways. Give yourself every possible advantage. Prepare yourself thoroughly before the interview, thus gaining the self-confidence which will free you to present yourself in the very best way you can.

Before Your Interview

• Know the exact location of the office and how to get there.
• Do your homework on the company. Know its product(s), size, income, reputation, image, goals, problems, competition, history, philosophy, *and* which aspects of its operations fit your particular interests or talents. Get whatever literature you can from the company's information department; check the public library; consult financial references—whatever applies. Don't be caught unaware of a fact you should know.
• Investigate the job. Learn what duties to expect, hours, approximate salary, working conditions, travel opportunities, and potential. Will the job lead anywhere or is it a dead end?
• Be ready to tell why you want this particular job.
• Prepare a short, well-organized outline of your past experience and future goals. At some point during most interviews, you will be asked to "say something about yourself." This is no time to blush or stammer! Rehearse your brief speech before your family or friends.
• Know in advance how you will handle difficult questions. It's a good idea to list the common "problem questions" that may trip you up and to practice your answers. Nearly all difficult job interview questions are variations on these seven: (1) Tell me about yourself. (2) What can you offer us? (3) What are your strengths?

(4) What have you accomplished? (5) What are your limitations? (6) How much are you worth? (7) What do you want?

• Of course, interviewers know it's discriminatory to ask directly about your marital status, religion, child-rearing plans, etc., and they will be cautious about opening their company to a lawsuit on the basis of discrimination. But some may ask the forbidden questions in a roundabout way and talk you into a corner. The best way to handle this delicate situation is to try to find out what is behind the awkward questions.

• Be ready to demonstrate the relationship between this job and your previous experience.

• Know which of your skills, abilities, and interests you want to stress, and be able to explain what you can contribute to the company.

• Don't overlook your appearance. The day before the interview, organize your clothes and make sure they are clean, neat, pressed, and mended. Dress for the job you want. Employers scrutinize your appearance and if you're dressed in sloppy, unkempt clothes—jeans, a T-shirt, and rubber thongs, for example—he or she will conclude that you're not serious about work and you lack respect for yourself and your interviewer. And elaborate, trendy clothes, plus jangling accessories and heavy makeup for girls, are *out*. You're not on your way to a disco. Concentrate on being neat, clean, and comfortable. Take a shower and brush your teeth that day! Poor hygiene will lose you a job faster than you can say "chili with onions."

• Have another copy of your resume to take along—employers misplace things, too. You might bring a copy of your school transcript and letters of recommendation, and definitely include any materials specifically related to the job. If you're applying as a photographer's assistant, have with you a portfolio of your best work.

• Arrive early for the interview and be ready to fill out an application. Have a pen with you.

• Be prepared to take any required placement tests, such as typing or shorthand. Find out in advance whether you will be asked to take any aptitude, personality, intelligence, or other tests at the interview and how long each will take. Leave yourself plenty of time, in case you plan another interview for that day.

• When you actually start any test, carefully listen to or read the instructions. Don't be in a hurry and blow your chances!

The interview itself is your chance to shine and is a key factor in your getting (or losing) a job offer. It also gives you a glimpse of what it might be like to work for that particular company and whether the atmosphere, work, and personnel appeal to you. The interviewer was selected for this job because the company feels this person represents it well. If you don't like him—or her—then you probably won't like working for the company, either.

Heed These Interview "Dos and Don'ts"

• Never take anyone to the interview with you. Leave your parents or friends at home or in a restaurant nearby where you can meet them later. Your interviewer wants to get to know *you*—and the company wants to hire an independent young adult.

• Don't chew gum or munch candy, even if offered.

• Do not smoke. Smoking irritates many people and, even if it helps you relax, it can cloud your image—fast.

• Be aware of the interviewer as a person. Notice the office surroundings, the desk arrangements, the mannerisms of the individual across the desk. Try to take stock of the interviewer's style and respond to questions appropriately. Use your instincts and intuition to read the signals your interviewer transmits.

• Strive from the outset for a natural dialogue with your interviewer. But allow the interviewer to set the tone and pace—don't take control of the conversation. ("Natural?" you gasp. "How can I be natural with all these things to keep in mind?" With practice and experience, that's how!)

• Avoid using key material in the first few questions. Save your big hits for later when momentum has been established.

• Don't bad-mouth any former employer or confide domestic and financial problems. Also avoid mention of politics, sex, religion, and other controversial—if fascinating—subjects.

• Respond briskly and concisely to questions. If you're not sure you've answered in sufficient detail, ask if you should elaborate. Be sure you understand each question. Ask for clarification rather than take a chance on a guess.

• Keep your answers relevant. Don't volunteer information unless it is positive and pertinent.

• Avoid the use of negative terms and phrases in your answers.

Instead of "problem," for instance, say "challenge," or "opportunity."

• Seek to discover, as naturally as possible, all key details about the position. You'll need to know as much as you can, since first, you'll want to address your comments about how your education, possible past experience, and accomplishments will meet the company's needs; and second, you'll need the information to decide whether or not you're seriously interested.

• Don't prolong the interview. Your would-be employer has other things to do besides chat with you.

• Don't make up answers on the assumption that they are what the interviewer wants to hear. Sooner or later, you'll trip up.

• Ask questions about the company and the job. Your questions may elicit interesting answers, and will also give your interviewer clues to your interest, enthusiasm, knowledge—all qualities in demand.

• Rely on good manners. That means, shake hands when you enter and leave, know the interviewer's name and title, listen carefully, and don't interrupt. Sit down when you are asked to and, when you leave, thank the interviewer for his or her time.

• If you don't get an immediate job offer or indication of when you will know, ask when to call about the decision.

• If you are asked to return for a follow-up interview, jot down the time, date, and address.

• Let the interviewer raise the subject of money. You should have a good idea of what salary you expect to earn, but be realistic. (Don't be coy about money. No one expects you to work for free.) Be as flexible as you can when you discuss salary, particularly if your expectations exceed the prevailing rates in your area, or if you have overestimated your skills and experience. Ask about fringe benefits, such as health insurance and tuition assistance for job-related education. These two vital benefits can be worth thousands of dollars and easily compensate for a salary lower than your hopes.

• If you are offered the job, tell the employer you want a day or so to think it over. This is not merely a tactic—you really need the time to evaluate fully all your impressions. An employer should understand and grant you the time.

As you weigh the offer, ask yourself if the job is as exciting to you now as before the interview. Will you gain valuable work experience? Does the job lead in the direction you want? Are the people friendly and the environment pleasant? Do you think you will be happy, enthusiastic, and cooperative in the company and at this specific job?

• After the interview, send the employer a thank-you note. This little, courteous detail can nail down a job you want because it gives you a chance to restate your interest and, additionally, confirm the favorable impression you made. The note should be brief.

• Learn from each interview. When you get home, quiz yourself and explore ways you can improve for the next one. Ask yourself: What points did I make that seemed to interest the employer? Did I present my qualifications well? Did I pass up any clues as to the best way to sell myself? Did I learn all I need to know about the job? Did I talk too much or not enough? Was I tense, too aggressive, or too passive? How can I help myself do better next time?

• Study the reasons employers reject applicants. Poor appearance, inability to express yourself clearly, indifferent attitude, and inflated expectations count heavily against you.

• It is estimated that it takes an average of ten interviews to secure one job offer. Ideally, you want to choose among two or three offers, which multiplies to twenty or thirty interviews. That's all the reason you need to sharpen your basic interview skills.

• Finally, don't panic. Your world won't collapse if you lose out on any one particular job. Millions of happy, successful people experience this disappointment in their lives and overcome it. You will get a job. Hold fast to that conviction.

Fringe Benefits: A Menu of Choices

As you weigh every aspect of a job offer, don't discount the importance of fringe benefits. Fringes or perquisites can be as important to you as salary and regular raises, and they sweeten many a deal. The reason? Our convoluted tax structure: if your employer simply increases your pay so you can purchase your own health and life insurance, pension plan, and the rest, you will be booted into a higher tax bracket by this fatter check. But when your employer pays for those same benefits, you get the coverage without the taxes, and the company gets a good buy on group rates *and* tax relief from the IRS. Think of your fringe benefits as a key to your standard of living: American workers received a record $400 billion in fringes a year as the decade began, and employers spent approximately 37 cents in fringes for every dollar paid out in wages. Put another way, fringes can be worth between 35 and 40 percent of your cash pay.

The following rundown will familiarize you with the major benefits to keep in mind—and ask about—as you compare prospective options and offers:

• *Paid vacation and holidays*. Typically, to start, expect a two-week vacation plus six to eight days of paid holidays. This can escalate to three weeks and ten to twelve paid holidays after a few years with a company. Personal days—days to spend on errands you can't accomplish on weekends—are another common feature.

• *Sick leave*. Most companies have a policy allowing a specified number of sick days per year.

• *Group insurance*. Nearly all American companies make a contribution toward some form of insurance for their employees. You can expect to join health and life insurance plans. In fact, you might be allowed to choose between enrolling in a Health Maintenance Organization (HMO) or signing up with a conventional health plan that, increasingly, includes dental coverage, too. As a rule, your policies will be canceled when you change jobs, but often you can convert group coverage to an individual policy if you do so within a period of time set by the insurance company. Ask about this before you leave a job!

• *Education and training benefits*. Look on this as a gold mine. Many employers today will bear the full cost of further education and training, or will assume at least a major percentage, especially if it is job-related. You gain in two ways: your educational costs are slashed and your earnings potential leaps forward as you prepare for another step in your career.

• *Time off to vote*. Most firms make some arrangement so you can take time to vote on Election Day. Incidentally, many states now have laws mandating time off with pay.

• *Use of company recreation and vacation facilities*. These are often available to employees at minimal cost.

• *Day-care services for preschool children*. Ideally day-care is provided free or at low cost.

• *Profit-sharing plans*. Millions of workers in all occupations participate in private profit-sharing plans—often set up as alternatives to private pension plans. Although the idea of a pension may seem far off now, it means money for you when you can no longer work. In some plans, profits are distributed as periodic bonuses to employees, but usually funds are retained until you quit or retire. A key advantage of typical "deferred" profit-sharing plans is that you pay no taxes on your share until you withdraw it from the profit pool. Before you can claim your full entitlement under these plans, you will be expected to work a prescribed number of years.

Fringe benefits are changing fast, and on the increase are those that enhance an employee's health and quality of home life. Companies have had to respond to the dramatic shifts in American life in the past few decades. Traditional employee benefits were tailored to the needs of the stereotypical family: the married man who was the sole financial support for one or more dependents. How many families do you know that fit that description? Definitely a minority. Today, new benefit programs are designed to appeal to the vast majority: working couples, often with duplicated benefits, and single people, with special needs of their own.

Learn these new trends. Your company may incorporate some of them soon—or you may enjoy them now.

• *Flexitime.* Perhaps the quickest of the new fringes to catch on, flexitime means flexible work hours whereby companies let employees rearrange their normal nine-to-five routine to meet needs at home. Early in the 1980s, a full 16 percent of the labor force was on flexitime! Here's how it works: the total workday is known as *bandwidth,* and can run from 7:30 A.M. to 6:30 P.M. (of course, this varies from company to company). Inside this bandwidth are core times when you have to be on the job—say, 9:30 to 11:30 A.M. and 2 to 2:30 P.M.—and the rest is flexitime, with the requirement that you put in your quota of work hours. Flexitime adapts well to office environments but, as yet, there are few blue-collar flexible hours programs in the U.S.

• *Paternity leave and adoption benefits.* A new era of offbeat fringes is before us. Many, although they appeal to relatively few employees, are inexpensive for companies to provide. Among them: paternity leave and adoption benefits. You may not care now, but it's fascinating (and possibly important for your future) that about thirty companies, including Hallmark, Xerox, Pitney Bowes, and IBM, grant adoption benefits. Some pay a fixed allowance; others reimburse such expenses as agency fees, court and legal costs, and even such extras as medical exams for the adopted child.

• *Group automobile and homeowners insurance.* Increasing numbers of employers are assuming the cost of both auto and homeowners insurance, and now several insurance companies offer these packages.

• *Health clubs.* Reasoning that healthy employees are happy, productive, and infrequently absent, many companies include fitness centers on their premises or subsidize memberships in health clubs as part of fringe packages. A few companies, such as IBM, have introduced programs in health education; classes in exercise, diet, and first aid; and courses in quitting smoking.

• *Cafeteria plans.* These plans provide flexible, individualized benefits to workers. Typically, employees can trade off one benefit for another—an extra week of vacation for increased health insurance or a cash payment. The plans allow workers to select among a menu of benefits they need and to reduce, or skip entirely, benefits that mean less to them at this stage in their lives and careers. Since these programs can be quite complicated to understand (let alone supervise—one reason they are not found in more companies), employers introduce them with special brochures and introductory material. And, while they are not widely popular now, benefit consultants predict that these plans are the wave of the future.

Wherever you work, and however many times you change jobs in the future, you owe it to yourself to understand fully the fringe benefits to which you're entitled—you're earning them!

Does Your Job Have a Future?

Have you taken a dead-end job—without realizing it? Are you ignoring the early warning signals that are telling you that you have advanced about as far as you are likely to go in this firm and in your area? Are you still counting on your untapped abilities to take you to heights you won't reach?

These may be uncomfortable questions to many of you who have begun to read this. But the more unpleasant the answers may be, the more essential it is that you ask the questions—and now!

The time to face the corporate clues that may emphasize you're in a rut is before the fact becomes obvious to all around you. The time to search for and find the objective answers to the fundamental forces shaping your future career is when you retain control of your future and can shift it from a negative bias to a new, productive outlook.

What are the early warning signals? Here is a list of basic questions relating both to your job and to the corporation for which you work that, when honestly answered, will reveal the traps (if any) around you. Each of these questions will pull out answers that point the way to your own future—whether the disclosures please or depress, even terrify, you.

• To whom do you report? Is your supervisor well-regarded in your company and slated to move up? How much time does he/she spend with you in developing your skills?

• How long have you been in your present position? Are you still really learning? Have your responsibilities expanded so that you're making a significant contribution to the profitability of your company?

• Have you been passed over for promotion at least once or even more times than you can identify? How long have you been in this same job in comparison with other persons in similar jobs? How does your age compare with the ages of other people with the same job title in your company and in other companies?

• What is your pay level? How does your pay level compare with others in your profession and in relation to others within your company in your age and experience range?

• Are you listened to? Do your superiors—or workers in your category—seek you out to ask your opinion? Ever?

• Are you being moved around into other functional areas? In simple words, is your job narrow and specifically defined, perhaps too much so? Or do you have real leeway for creativity in both your own area and in other areas, a flexibility which allows you to demonstrate your individual approach to achieving your own goals and advancing the objectives of your company as a whole?

• Are you challenged by problems presented to you for solution, and are your abilities being used by these challenges? Are the goals measurable? Are you stretched to your capacity?

• How do you feel about yourself in relation to your job and your employer? Do you have the self-esteem and self-confidence you want? How strong are your aspirations, how determined is your drive? In all honesty, do you really want to advance?

And what about your company and its future?

• Does the industry in which your company operates have a future? (Buggy whips against computers, for instance.)

• What's the situation within your own company? Is the rate of growth of your company rapid, are new opportunities for promotion being created?

• What about sales and return on investment? Are sales on a solid upswing, or in a continued decline? Is your company's share of its market rising or falling?

• What about new products? Is your company holding with established products, or does it have an active program of research and new product development?

• What about the corporate mentality? Is it resting on past performance, or actively dedicated to creating new areas of growth in which you can find a rewarding future as well?

Signals, indeed! Look. Interpret. And act in time.

How to Quit a Job and Not Hurt Your Future

True tale: A middle-aged man resigned and went to a new marketing company. He left under the most pleasant circumstances, with good wishes all around. Only six months later, his previous boss, a vice-president, was brought in by his new company, so that his old boss became his new boss. Since he had left with dignity and style, there were no problems and the arrival of his former superior at his new work place worked out fine.

True tale: A young executive in another marketing firm stormed out of his corporation headquarters in a nasty anger. He already had been hired by another company and felt safe in telling how he really felt. But a final check of references still had to be made (without his knowledge), and the new personnel chief found out about the way he had quit. After learning the details, the new company withdrew its job offer—and the young executive was left unemployed.

True tale: A woman executive in a chemical company left her management job on the best of terms, explaining that she had received an offer of advancement and it seemed just too good to turn down. Her corporate superiors agreed and asked her to stay in touch. She did so. After fourteen months, her old company called her back because it had an unexpected opening four slots higher than she would have achieved if she had stayed on her old job. She was told: "You now have the credentials for this higher post. Welcome home."

How you resign from a job can be almost as important as how you obtain a job. If you leave a position graciously and with dignity, you stand a good chance of being invited back to the company someday in a more important post, or at least remaining on good terms with those who knew you. If you leave without style and poise, entirely unanticipated repercussions can result.

What, then, are the guidelines for you, a teenager and new in the job market, for resigning a position properly, so you do not slam the door behind your present career—and perhaps also slam the door on your future?

- Make it clear that your resignation is precipitated by a firm offer from another corporation.
- Don't express dissatisfaction with the firm you are leaving or any of the work you did.
- If there is a farewell interview with a higher echelon corporate officer—a key step in your friendly exit—be sure you don't say anything derogatory about your immediate superior.
- Up to the last minute of employment, provide cooperative and intelligent workmanship.
- In breaking in the person who might be succeeding you, offer as much genuine assistance as you can.
- Say nice things about the company and personnel, and indicate you learned many things while there and enjoyed your tenure.

- Don't breach any confidences you have held.
- Clear up any financial debts you might have, and return all company property you might be holding.
- While standard procedure is two weeks' notice, if you can—and the situation warrants it—give the company additional notice.
- Stress that you have made some good friends at the company and that you hope to stay in touch with them.
- Don't bad-mouth the company you are leaving to your new organization, and in resigning, see your immediate superior and explain your move verbally. Then submit a cordial letter outlining your reasons.
- In the same way, acknowledge your acceptance of your new position in writing to your new company, expressing your pleasure at the prospect of joining them.
- Don't brag to your peer group about your new job. It may create bad feelings with upper management, and may make your peers feel inadequate.

If you resign and leave a negative impression, this one unfortunate memory may hamper your future success for years to come. Be forewarned; and simple as this advice may seem, accept it as among the most valuable guides you'll get in job-hunting and job-quitting.

2

DOCUMENT YOUR LIFE

CONTENTS

These are the years—when you've really not had time enough to accumulate mounds of paper and to develop bad habits—to learn how to maintain your personal records so the job of recordkeeping will be easy, won't irritate you, and will be of extraordinary help to you in countless ways throughout your entire life.

Once you organize your own filing system, even tackling tax returns in the future will be a snap. No groping around for paycheck stubs and dividend statements—you will always be able to locate any scrap of paper you need. You do not need a compulsion to be revoltingly neat in order to be well organized. You will be amazed at how much aggravation you can save yourself merely by careful planning.

Throwing things away can be one of life's great pleasures—or it can clash with an equally enjoyable activity: hoarding. As your canceled checks, insurance policies, and tax records mount up, you'll know that you don't even want to try to save every scrap.

You need to set up your own recordkeeping system as soon as possible, and you can establish a filing system efficiently, economically, and quickly. First, just get an inexpensive cardboard filing box, plus a box of manila file folders. You can purchase these at any store that sells stationery supplies. If your desk has a file drawer, buy only the box of folders. Collect all the papers you think you want to keep and sit down to sort through them all. Also purchase a box that locks, for valuable documents.

As you assemble your system, you will discover that you have three types of files: *personal documents*, *current materials*, and *past records*. Label your files clearly and insert your papers into the appropriate folders. That's all. Now you are organized, *painlessly*.

Recommended Records

Personal Documents

In one folder, keep copies of all items that prove your name, age, birthplace, and achievements: birth certificate, baptismal certificate, Social Security card, passport, and diplomas. These documents are valuable: keep them locked in a safe place. Don't leave them lying around.

Current Materials

You will want to subdivide this pile and make individual folders for each category that applies to you:

1. *Bank statements.* Canceled checks, passbooks, money order receipts, statements of interest earnings.
2. *Bills.* Credit card bills (and a record of your account numbers), car payments, magazine subscriptions.
3. *Insurance policies.* If you have a car or motorcycle, you have an insurance policy. Keep old policies around for a few years in case an old claim should be activated.
4. *Warranties.* When you buy an appliance such as a television, stereo, or hairdryer, you receive a warranty card from the manufacturer. Fill it out and return the company's portion. (That way, if the product is recalled, the company can let you know.) Keep your stub and jot down the date and place of purchase. Pay attention to the expiration date—when the warranty expires, toss out the card.
5. *Scholarship agreements, financial aid.* Keep your copies of any notices of financial awards for your education.
6. *Employment and career records.* As you develop career plans, accumulate all data you will need in order to write a resume or fill out a job application. Keep these records current: as soon as you get a new job, update your old resume.
7. *Salary statements.* Save your paycheck stubs until tax time. Then, after you match them against your wage and tax statement, throw them out.
8. *Benefits.* If your employer gives you any papers explaining health, vacation, and other fringe benefits, save them.
9. *Household goods.* Keep a complete inventory of your most valued possessions so you can recover an insured or guaranteed loss in full if you get ripped off. Record serial numbers, proof of ownership, dates and places of purchase, proof of sale, and a brief description. This is essential if you live in a dormitory or apartment open to strangers who covet your typewriter, stereo, watch, etc.
10. *Special investments.* You may not think you have any special investments yet. But the jewelry you receive for birthdays and

graduations, the stamp collection you've built up since you were young, your cache of silver dollars—any possession which increases in value—counts as an investment.

Back Records

You may decide to organize your back records and then store them separately since you won't need them often. Minimize the amount of paper that mounts up over the years by regular pruning of your files. Before you consign anything to a folder, ask yourself, "Will I really need this?" Often, the answer is *no.* So out it goes.

You can dispose of your tax records after six years. Even if you pay no taxes, hold on to copies of your income tax return in the event that the Internal Revenue Service calls on you.

Health Records

Your filing system reflects your interests, activities, and special needs. But it will be incomplete if you fail to include a personal health record which, updated regularly, maintains your accurate and full medical history. As you change doctors and consult with different specialists for specific health problems throughout your life, your doctors' health records will almost surely not keep up with you. Make the effort to keep your own and, eventually, those of your family.

The following guidelines will help you:

• Your health records begin with basics: your name, date of birth, and blood type. Also, any chronic diseases or allergies.

• Record any and all serious illnesses in your family background, since heredity plays a crucial role in many diseases. Include illnesses of your parents, brothers and sisters, and grandparents, if possible. List the histories of serious or chronic diseases in your family, such as diabetes, epilepsy, cancer, tuberculosis, heart conditions, and birth defects.

• If any close relatives have died, record the cause and age at the time of death.

• Histories of good health are medically useful, too. If your mother has never been sick a day in her life, make a note of that.

• Record any injuries you've suffered in accidents. These injuries may result in disabling conditions—possibly years after you've forgotten the incident.

• Write down which immunizations you've received, and when. Not all vaccinations against preventable diseases are permanent, so you may need a new one for a specific illness. The dates of previous vaccinations become crucially important.

• Note the date when you start to menstruate and keep tabs on your monthly cycle.

SOCIAL SECURITY

By now you almost surely have a Social Security number. Perhaps your parents got the card for you and asked you to sign it. Or maybe you filled out the application, collected the necessary documents, and sent in the form yourself. Yet you might not know what Social Security is all about, or why you need a card in the first place.

Essentially, Social Security replaces part of the earnings lost by an individual or family when a worker retires, is disabled, or dies. You are entitled to retirement, disability, death, and other benefits if you register with the Social Security Administration (SSA) and receive a number for indentification. The SSA gets its money from workers, employers, and self-employed people who pay a percentage of their annual income in contributions. Congress regulates the flat percentage at which you pay Social Security contributions, or FICA (Federal Insurance Contributions Act) as it appears on your paycheck. The money collected each year is used to pay Social Security checks to people currently receiving a variety of benefits. When you are eligible for Social Security—a long time away from these, your teen years—people who are contributing to the system then will pay for your benefits.

Social Security protection is lifelong: no matter where you move or how many times you change jobs, your Social Security number remains the same. Although the United States doesn't have a national identification system, Social Security numbers come close. When you file a return on your annual income, the Internal Revenue Service refers to you by your Social Security number. Banks need it to report your interest earnings to the Internal Revenue Service each spring, and employers must have it so they can report your FICA earnings to the Social Security Administration. Many states ask you to supply the number to use on your driver's license, and, if you enter the military, you will use it as your identification number. School and work identification cards are often embossed with those familiar nine digits. In short, sooner or later, you will want and need to have your own, unique number.

Social Security covers almost every kind of employment, including military service. Almost any payroll check you receive will list FICA deductions along with other taxes. A rare exception is made at some state institutions for college work-study student employees. If that applies to you, in your state, check with your school about FICA deductions, since you do not have to pay for the duration of your job.

When to Get a Card and How to Apply

Even before you apply for your first job, you should obtain a Social Security card. Usually, employers won't hire you unless you can produce your number for their employment records.

The procedure for obtaining a Social Security card is not as simple today as it was earlier. Time was when you could walk into any Social Security office, say that you had never applied for a number previously, and walk out, card in hand. Mainly out of concern over the growing number of illegal aliens, Congress changed the law in the 1970s to require that an applicant furnish evidence of age, identity, United States citizenship, or lawful admission to the United States.

In an average year, Social Security numbers are issued to about 5.5 million persons—primarily young people reaching working age, but also to babies for whom bank accounts are being set up, and legally admitted immigrants.

If you are a U.S. citizen applying for a number for the first time, you will need two documents, including one which proves your identity. The best proof of age and citizenship is a birth certificate (or church record showing the date and place of birth). Other acceptable documents include certificates of naturalization and U.S. passports. To prove your identity—that you are who you and the documents say you are—you need a document that shows your name along with your signature, photograph, or other identifying information. This could be a passport, marriage license, driver's license, or school record.

You must submit original documents, not photocopies. The documents will be returned to you. If you need any help in getting such documents, get in touch with any Social Security office for assistance. It's a good idea to check with the Social Security office by phone before you go there, since the documents needed are specific and you don't want to arrive and find you have forgotten something or taken the wrong proof. If you're under the age of eighteen you can apply for a Social Security card by mail—not true if you're older.

If you lose your card or need a new one because you are changing your name—for instance, in case of marriage—you must be ready to present evidence showing your identity under your old name and under the new one. Sufficient documents are: a marriage certificate showing both names; an old and new driver's license; utility bills and bank statements showing both names.

If you were born outside the United States and are not a citizen, you need evidence that you are here legally to get a Social Security number. Any document issued by the U.S. Immigration and Naturalization Service will serve. But those who want the cards in order to work while in the United States must show evidence that they have been authorized for employment by the Immigration and Naturalization Service.

If lawfully admitted to the United States, but not permitted to work here, foreigners can be issued numbers to set up a bank account, for instance, but the Social Security Administration flags their records. If they go to work and give the Social Security number to an employer, the Immigration and Naturalization Service will be notified.

Note: If you are working, ask your Social Security office for a preaddressed postcard form on which to request a statement of earnings. Mail it. It will take up to two months to get a reply, probably showing your earnings up to a few years ago. You will then know what records to keep until the agency has caught up on its recordkeeping in the mid-1980s. Then keep sending in requests for earnings to find out what progress the agency has made on your credits.

TAXES

You already pay some taxes, yet you might not know about them. For example, you pay taxes every time you buy a gallon of gas or a pack of cigarettes. And, if you live in a state that charges a sales tax on goods and services, you pay taxes almost every time you go to a store.

Taxes are classified in two important ways: according to the type of tax and according to the ability of the taxpayer—you—to pay it.

Direct and Indirect Taxes

"Direct" and "indirect" refer to the way taxes are paid. You remit direct taxes to a government. The best example of this kind is the federal individual income tax.

You often pay indirect taxes—those on goods and services—without realizing it. Excise taxes, such as those on cigarettes and liquor, are included in the sales price. The federal government charges excise taxes on gasoline and tires, and these funds help build and maintain the interstate highway system. And when you buy products imported from abroad, such as French perfume and Japanese video recorders, you usually pay a duty, or import tax, "hidden" within the purchase price.

Sales taxes, another indirect form of taxation, are levied by most states and a few cities. A sales tax is a percentage of the total price of the merchandise and is tacked onto your bill at the close of a sale. You pay the tax to the store or business, and the merchant, in turn, passes it along to the state or city government.

Progressive and Regressive Taxes

"Progressive" and "regressive" taxes refer to the taxpayer's ability to pay. Sales taxes, excise taxes, and import duties are all regressive taxes—meaning they hit everyone equally regardless of income and ability to afford the tax. In particular, for poor people, sales taxes can be a real hardship. Whether you earn $20,000 or $10,000, the percentage or amount of a regressive tax remains the same.

Progressive taxes, in contrast, are based on ability to pay—people with higher incomes pay greater percentages of their overall income as tax. The federal income tax is the most notable example of a progressive tax. All things being equal, if you earn $20,000 and your friend earns $10,000, you not only pay more in total dollars as income tax, you pay a greater percentage of your income, too.

Income Taxes

Income taxes are a fact of American life. You probably have often watched your parents or older brothers and sisters hunker down with pads of paper, calculators or adding machines, and stacks of checks, bills, and receipts. This annual ritual occurs every spring and culminates on April 15 when, with certain exceptions, all individual tax returns are due.

In special circumstances, you may have to file, too, although your tax return will most likely be quite simple to figure out. In fact, the government probably will owe you money (a refund on taxes you've already paid).

Taxable Income

The number of teenagers working in either full-time or part-time jobs and the total of their earnings—and thus, their spending power—may stun you. I know I did not expect to learn that three out of five teens between the ages of twelve and nineteen are holding full- or part-time jobs (according to a 1981 survey of teenage consumers in this age bracket by Simmons Market Research Bureau). Nor did I expect the Simmons estimate that the weekly earnings of U.S. teenagers reached $600 million—a clout at the cash register totaling billions of dollars annually and explaining without any additional elaboration from me why so many products widely used by teens are such spectacular successes (cosmetics, record albums, pimple creams, diet drinks, etc.).

All these subjects (and more) are covered later in this book. Meanwhile, what about you and your taxes?

You will have to pay taxes, or at least file a tax return, if you meet any of these criteria:

- You have a job for which you receive a salary and taxes are withheld from your paycheck.

- Your taxable income meets the minimum established by the federal government.
- Your parents claim you as a dependent on their tax return(s), but you have taxable dividends, interest, or other unearned income that equals or exceeds a minimum amount determined by the government.

Chances are, you won't owe any taxes. For most of you, the amount you earn from an after-school or summer job will be less than the federal (taxable) minimum.

You can request that your employer not withhold taxes from your paycheck. Ask the company personnel manager to report your earnings to the government on a W-4 form instead of on a W-2 form. If you paid no income taxes last year and you don't expect to earn enough to pay taxes this year, there will be no problem: you will have a larger total left in your paycheck and can skip the process of filing a tax return entirely.

Note that Social Security (FICA) will still be deducted from your check—you can't ask the government to give it back to you.

Nontaxable Income

You may have received certain kinds of income, gifts of cash, or financial awards that are nontaxable. Among them:

- Social Security benefits
- Gifts
- Previous income tax refunds
- Prizes from school, such as cash awards for scholastic achievements
- Most kinds of post–secondary school financial aid: scholarships, grants, loans, work-study jobs

Note to College Students

While you are in college, your parents probably will continue to claim you as a tax deduction on their return(s), as long as they provide more than half your support. The amount of scholarship aid you receive is not counted in calculating your parents' support, and, even if you earned enough to pay taxes this year, your parents can still take you as a deduction. You may jeopardize their deduction, however, in many ways that careful planning together could easily avoid. Urge your parents to study along with you the following money-saving tips!

Parents: Nail Down Maximum Family Deductions When Your Child Goes to College

Parents: you can get a $1,000 dependency deduction for your child in college as long as you provide more than half of his or her support. You may be among the many parents who miss out on dependency deductions to which you are legally entitled. Because of some common misconceptions, you figure that when your children leave home, so do your deductions. Here are four examples to help set you straight.

"My daughter won a big college scholarship, so I won't be able to claim her as a tax dependent."

Wrong! In fact, if your daughter wins a scholarship, you win a grade-A tax break. First, the scholarship money is tax-free to you and her. Second, you can still get a dependency deduction for her no matter how big the scholarship. If you do a little homework on the tax laws, you'll learn that money isn't considered "support." So it doesn't count either for or against you in meeting the more-than-half-support test.

Let's say you pay $2,500 toward your daughter's college costs. She gets a $2,800 scholarship. Result: She's still your dependent for tax purposes. Since the scholarship doesn't enter the picture, you, in effect, have provided all of her support—$2,500 out of $2,500.

"My son has found a job for this summer and will earn around $2,000 to pay for his college expenses. That means his income will be too high for me to claim him as a dependent."

Wrong! There is a general income limit—a dependent must have less than $1,000 in gross income—but it doesn't apply to your situation. The income limit does not apply to a child who is (a) under nineteen, or (b) a full-time student. So, for your child in college, all you, the parent, have to do is meet the more-than-half-support test to get a dependency deduction.

"My daughter will earn around $2,600 this summer. I expect to provide another $2,400 in support this year, so I flunk the more-than-half-support test and lose her as a deduction."

Wrong! You may save your dependency deduction because of an often-overlooked tax rule. Money your daughter *earns* doesn't necessarily all count as support she provides for herself. It's what she actually *spends* on support that's crucial. For instance, say you have your daughter put $150 of her earnings in the bank. You pick up the tab for an extra $150 of her expenses. Your daughter can use the bank savings for future expenses—and you get a dependency deduction for her. Her earnings—what she has available for support—do not count against you unless she actually uses it for support. If you have your daughter bank her earnings and you take up the slack, you provide more than half of her support—$2,550 versus $2,450.

"My son will earn around $3,500 this year. I provide $2,500 for his support. So, if I'm not able to come up with more than $500, the banking idea won't work. He has provided more than half his support, and I can't claim him as a dependent."

Not necessarily right! Yes, he has provided more than half the money for his college expenses, but that doesn't necessarily mean you lose him as a dependent. There's a lot more to "support" than just the outlay for college expenses. Counted as support you provide for him is the "fair rental value" of his lodging while he's at home. If he's at home for four months, this amount added to what you spend for college expenses could put you well over the more-than-half mark.

If you provide a car, arrange the financing yourself, and make a small down payment, but note that this capital expenditure may count as support for your child. Make a gift of the car and have your son register it in his name.

By providing more than half your child's support, you're also entitled to deduct any medical expenses for him or her. Many colleges include a charge for medical care in their tuition fees, even though it may not be broken down as such. Ask the college for an itemized statement of the charges and then get a deduction for the charge of the medical care.

Note to Working Teens

*Parents: Hire Your Teenagers Yourself
for Summer Jobs*

If you're among the hundreds of thousands of parents whose teenagers are looking for summer jobs and *not* finding any jobs available, and if you happen to be among the large proportion who own your own business, how about solving the problem by hiring your child or children yourself? You'll achieve twin goals: giving your children employment, plus spending money and gaining major tax advantages.

But you must know the rules on hiring children—and violations of our wage-hour law can be expensive, no matter how innocent your errors may be. Federal and state laws do differ, too. Here are some significant guides on hiring your own children or the children of friends this summer:

• If you own the business, there is no minimum age on hiring your own child (under fourteen, let's say). There also are no minimum age restrictions on children who deliver newspapers or advertising handbills. The general minimum age for nonhazardous factory work is sixteen, but for a job other than in a factory (in an office or in sales), you could hire a fourteen-year-old.

"Hazardous" work would include operating a motor vehicle or other types of machinery; work in a mine; or a job that would expose the child to radioactive material. For instance, a child under sixteen could not work in a boiler or an engine room; could not use grease pits, racks, or lifting equipment in a service station; could not work in a freezer, or cook, or bake; could not operate power-driven machines, load or unload trucks, or do warehouse work.

A teenager under sixteen, though, could help in sales or clerical work. This minor could pack purchases in a store, run errands, make deliveries, do cleanup work, mark prices. This minor could prepare and serve food even though prohibited under the law from cooking it.

And while an under-sixteen-year-old is prohibited from operating many types of machinery, this minor could handle such equipment as milk shake blenders, coffee grinders, toasters, dishwashers, and dumbwaiters.

• You are forbidden, under the federal and state antidiscrimination laws, from asking for birth certificates, baptismal papers, or similar documents when hiring young people. Children can prove age by presenting age certificates or working papers, available from the schools they attend during the school year.

• There are advantages to hiring a sixteen-year-old as opposed to hiring a fourteen-year-old (unless this is your own child and the age is therefore a subsidiary issue). The sixteen-year-old can work in or about manufacturing plants and can work in all occupations not open to under-sixteen-year-olds (unless the occupation itself is listed as "hazardous" by the Secretary of Labor, and there are only about seventeen occupations so listed).

The sixteen-year-old (or older) also is not so limited by the strict regulations on total of hours worked as the younger minor. The child under sixteen is strictly prohibited from working more than eight hours any day, whether the worker is your own child or not. When school is open, the under-sixteen-year-old cannot work more than eighteen hours a week—or more than three hours in any day. Nor can this minor begin working before 7 A.M. or work beyond 7 P.M.

As of June 1, however, the evening curfew hour becomes 9 P.M., and this curfew applies until Labor Day. The maximum workweek while school is closed is forty hours.

• On taxes, the regulations are fairly lax. With the possible exception of federal income tax withholding, the law applies as usual. You *do not* withhold federal income taxes *if* the minor fills out and files a W-4 form stating that he/she had no income tax liability for last year and if the child expects to incur no tax liability for this current year.

What parents achieve by hiring their own child now becomes clear. With this move, you supply your child or the child of a close friend with productive work; the child earns money that can be saved for college or spent as the minor desires; your own tax advantages are clear and can be repeated in coming summers. Why not? It's all plus!

Paying Taxes: Timing

The tax season begins every January. By the end of that month, you should receive statements of earnings from your employer, any bank where you have an interest-bearing account, and any company which pays you dividends on stock you own. The form you receive from your employer, the W-2, details your wage and tax statements for the preceding calendar year. Specifically, the form will tell you how much you earned; how much was withheld in federal, state, and local income tax; and your total Social Security contributions. You receive three copies of this form: you will attach one to your federal return, the second to your state return, and keep the third for your records. Expect to receive one copy of each Form 1099, or the form detailing other sources of income. The U.S. Treasury receives its own copies from banks and other institutions, so the Treasury has current information about these sources of income.

If you plan to file a tax return, collect these slips of paper and set them aside. You will need tax forms and an instruction booklet, which you can request from the nearest IRS office. Write or phone your state tax office and get a copy of your state tax return and instruction booklet, too.

Tax returns must be filed by April 15, unless you get an extension.

Preparing Your Tax Return

Put aside at least a few afternoons or evenings to prepare your tax return.

• Assemble all your tax records: wage and tax statements, dividend and interest statements. Your recordkeeping system should have done this for you through the year.

• Prepare your federal return first; the information on state returns is usually the same and may be based on your federal return.

• Read through the instruction booklet carefully. The instructions are vague, so don't be dismayed if you are confused. Reread what you don't understand or ask an experienced taxpayer for help.

• You will be provided with two tax return forms. One is your copy. Following the instructions, and using a pencil, fill out your copy and check it carefully for errors. When you are satisfied that it is correct, fill out the second copy, in ink.

- Sign and date the return.
- Proofread your tax form, making sure you filled in every blank you should have.
- Remember to glue a stamp on the envelope. Send it in prior to the April 15 deadline, unless you get an extension for one reason or another.
- To learn more about taxes, request a copy of *Your Federal Income Tax*, also known as Publication 17, from the Internal Revenue Service.

The Invisible Economy That Visibly Hurts

A veiled economy more vast in scope than the individual economies of most other countries lies underneath the in-the-open economy in which tens of millions of us in the United States live. An immense proportion of all transactions that occur in our country take place in this underground—but they are untraced in any fashion and, thus, uncounted, unreported, and—most significant—untaxed. The dollar estimates are enormous and unprovable—one-half trillion dollars of goods and services may be changing hands. Perhaps the total is $700 billion, possibly it's lower—who knows?

No matter what the amount, individuals and corporations are paying zero taxes on the income, zero taxes on dividends, zero taxes on interest. Estimates of the unofficial dollar total *not* collected in taxes range to as much as half the official amount collected!

What is being discussed here is not the filthy underground of the drug peddlers, prostitutes and pimps, illegal gamblers, etc. This half-trillion dollars (plus or minus) of uncounted money represents legal transactions: barter deals mounting to a huge total of income that never changes hands, is never recorded, reported, or taxed; cash tips or cash fees never recorded, reported, or taxed; and capital gains, interest, and dividends received but never recorded, reported, or taxed.

Several of your relatives, friends, neighbors, and casual acquaintances may be comparatively active members of this underground without realizing that they are participants. Certainly, they are unaware that they are doing anything to hurt the United States. And you, too, may well be a part of it, completely unaware.

No matter how sophisticated you are, the odds are that you have only a hazy notion of the pervasiveness of this thriving underground. For example:

• *Legal barter.* A tax accountant agrees to take care of the books and fill out the annual tax return of a dentist in exchange for extensive dental work. The two arrange (orally) how many dollars of tax work is worth how many dollars of dental work and that's that. No money changes hands. No papers are signed. No records are kept. No income is reported by either beneficiary and no taxes acknowledged as owed or paid. Gainers: the accountant and dentist. Losers: the IRS and us, the millions of other taxpayers who are not in barter deals and who must fill the gaps created by their tax avoidance. And there are hundreds of variations on barter deals, all with similar gainers and losers.

• *Individual tax cheaters.* A taxi driver reports just enough in tips to keep the IRS examiners quiet. The balance—easily $500 or more a week in big cities—goes into his wallet. No income reported, no taxes paid. There are also hundreds of variations on this theme, involving self-employed professionals, "mom and pop" stores, and so forth.

• There are huge totals of capital gains from sales of real property, securities, etc., that are neither reported nor taxed.

• There are equally enormous totals of rental and royalty income that are not reported and not taxed.

• Astounding totals of interest and dividend income disappear behind this invisible veil.

• As for free-lance writers and artists—they think they have enough trouble existing without paying taxes owed.

• Beneficiaries of tax shelters? They're escaping, not paying.

Oddly enough, immense as this underground economy of legal deals is, it was scarcely mentioned a few years ago. Even tax experts rarely referred to it and failed to weigh the extent to which escapees from federal taxes were unduly draining spendable funds from honest taxpayers. Even imaginative economists did not take into consideration the extent to which the never-ending boom in the unofficial, uncharted underground was backing up the strength in the official, carefully charted economy.

What happened? Why did the underground suddenly stir out of the mud, expand to reach our awareness, and now hit the headlines?

• The relentless rise of inflation from the early 1960s to the early 1980s must be the number one explanation. The squeeze became intolerable for millions of Americans hit on one side by endless price hikes and on the other by the tax creep (the lift into higher and higher tax brackets as wages/salaries increase, thereby erasing an apparent rise in living standards). Resentment against the burden of income, Social Security, and other taxes has frozen into a determination to wiggle out of the bind, somehow, some way. Minor tax evasion is commonplace; major tax evasion is spreading rapidly.

• A widespread disgust with the integrity of our leadership in Washington—and with that disgust, a deeper and deeper inclination to try to "get away with it, too." The Watergate scandals left a profound blotch on our society, and although most Americans don't talk much about that era—and you may scarcely remember it—the impact has not been wiped out. The resulting distrust easily translates into an individual willingness to cheat more often and on a bigger scale than before.

• An awareness of the extremely limited capabilities of the IRS to audit average tax returns and to enforce IRS regulations. The percentage of tax returns reviewed by IRS examiners is now around a picayune 2 percent—and not improving. The IRS has about 19,000 revenue agents and auditors to handle about 140 million returns—a ridiculous ratio that actually encourages cheating.

• The recurrence of federal budget deficit piled on top of budget deficit year after year has been a red flag of rebellion to taxpayers. To a pinched, honest taxpayer, this has seemed an invitation to duck underground (at least now and then).

• Similarly, the complexities of our tax laws and tax forms have aggravated the situation. In view of the record, the yearly promises of simplification have been ludicrous.

How can the IRS collect on the hundreds of billions in taxes owed each year but not paid by the 20 million Americans (or more) involved in the underground economy today?

Right now, the approach is to clamp down on unreported barter deals, unreported cash fees and tips, unreported capital gains, interest, dividends, rent, royalties, etc. The IRS, for instance, has instructed its agents to examine all noncash exchanges when verifying how much income you really receive. If you were the accountant cited above, the IRS says your tax work for the dentist is of dollar value, should be reported as income, and should be subject to income taxes. And if you were the dentist doing the dental work for the tax accountant, the IRS says your work is also of dollar value, should be reported as income, and should be subject to income taxes.

But how many people in the huge barter world will the IRS nab with that approach? Not many, most likely. And what effect will clamping down have on our fundamental system of voluntary compliance with our tax laws? It's virtually certain to help undermine it, I'll wager.

All the new, tougher approaches being applied or studied by the IRS raise similar questions.

There is no disagreement among present or past IRS officials about the need for a balanced criminal enforcement program to underpin the voluntary compliance system. There is clear recognition that if our compliance falters, our nation is in dreadful, even unspeakable financial trouble. Here lies the foundation of our economy.

At the same time, there is full agreement that enforcement officials cannot and should not haunt every restaurant, barber shop, and office of a self-employed professional dealing mainly in cash. There is wide recognition, too, that it would be self-defeating for any government agency at any level to pry into the books of U.S. citizens operating in fields where tax evasion is believed to be high and pervasive.

But, as a former IRS commissioner puts it, "participants in the underground economy are placing an overwhelming and brutally unfair burden on the majority of honest American taxpayers."

YOUR LEGAL RIGHTS: A FEW BASICS

Each of us has legal rights and obligations that we take so much for granted, we never bother to identify them.

Until you reach the age of majority, as established by your state (when you acquire most, if not all, the legal rights of an adult), you remain the responsibility of your parents or guardians. The law requires that they feed, clothe, shelter you; send you to school; see that you receive medical care; provide for your basic needs until you are old enough to do so yourself. Parents and guardians exercise many rights where you're concerned. They decide where you live, for example, and they have the right to discipline you (without excessive force), and give you your name, among many others. In turn, because of your special status as a child under the law, you are granted certain rights, including the right to an education and to support, which adults over the age of majority do not automatically have.

When you reach the age of majority, you may not necessarily acquire all the rights of an adult at once. The state can set different ages of qualifications for different activities. You may be able to drive and work for wages, yet you may not be old enough to buy or consume alcohol; inherit money; serve on a jury.

Below the age of majority, you are considered a minor. In general, the laws that deal with minors are established by the fifty states; few federal laws and Supreme Court decisions apply to all minors everywhere. The draft is one law that does.

One term you might encounter is "emancipation." This is a legalism that describes the condition in which a child—you, perhaps—receives the rights and duties of an adult even before reaching the age of majority. At the same time, the parents are freed of their rights and duties, including the charge to support and educate their child.

Emancipation usually takes place when you reach the age of majority. Before then, it occurs when a minor marries, joins the armed forces, or meets other conditions, as established by state law, or is declared emancipated by a court of law. Some states have written laws that provide emancipation at a particular age for certain purposes only. Your state may have such a law: for example, a law that emancipates children at a certain age to permit them to receive medical treatment without parental consent.

More basics:

• *Contracts.* A topic of special interest to you is a contract—an agreement between two or more people. A contract can be written and, in certain circumstances, can be a spoken, or verbal, agreement, too. Most contracts entered by minors cannot be enforced and, in many cases, minors can back out of contracts they make. As a result, a large percentage of adults and businesses balk at entering into contracts with minors. If, for instance, you buy something on credit from a merchant and decide later that you don't want it, the store has to accept your return and refund your money.

There are exceptions. As any first-year law student knows, there are a variety of contracts. Some are void from the moment they are made—that is, they cannot be enforced at all. *Example:* minors cannot sign a lease. If you sign one, and you are below the age of majority, it is a void contract. In contrast, some contracts made by minors are fully binding. If you enlist in the armed forces, you can't change your mind and back out. When you receive your driver's license, you have the same obligations—and liabilities—as an adult driver. Marriage, too, is a contract. The only way to break a legally contracted marriage is via a divorce.

• *Real estate.* As a minor, you have the right to own real estate, but you can't manage it, until you reach the age of majority (whatever that age is in your state). If you own property—land, a house, apartment building, farm—you can't rent or sell it until you are of age. If you do own property, a trustee or guardian almost surely manages it for you.

• *Inheritance.* You can definitely inherit property from someone who has died. However, although the property belongs to you, if you are a minor, you can't dispose of it as you please until you reach the age of majority. Either the person's will appoints a guardian or trustee to manage the property or money for you, or the court appoints someone to perform this duty.

• *Wills.* As a minor, you cannot make a valid will. The state sets the age at which you can do so; usually, it is the age of majority.

• *Working.* You have rights in the workplace. For example, you have a right to work, but each state has a number of laws that define and restrict the kinds of work that children can perform, the age at which they can get jobs, and that stipulate what hours they can work. You can get a copy of your state's child labor laws from a state employment office and probably at your high school. Exceptions are made to many laws that enable minors to work on farms, around the house, and for their parents, and in other carefully described circumstances (see earlier in this chapter).

Most states require that minors obtain work permits or certificates before starting a job. In most states, not only is it illegal for a minor to work without a permit, it also is illegal for the employer to hire a minor without one.

• *Workers' compensation* is a protection for you as well as adults. If you are injured on the job, report the accident to your supervisor or employer right away. Your employer must then report it to the Workers' Compensation Board. You are entitled to workers' compensation if you are injured in an on-the-job accident sustained during work.

• *Equal pay laws* apply to minors, too. Employers cannot pay higher wages to boys than to girls (or vice versa). If you think, or know, that you are not receiving a fair wage, or that your employer is discriminating against you, contact the state and federal departments of labor. If the discrimination is on the basis of sex, contact the Equal Employment Opportunity Commission (EEOC) of the federal government.

• *Education*. The law requires that you attend school. And you have a right to attend school. The state is required, by law, to provide you with a free education.

This sketchy introduction can only touch on legal areas of special interest to you. Learn more about your legal rights—and obligations, too—by visiting your library or bookstore and reading up on the subject. The American Civil Liberties Union has published a handbook on this subject: *The Rights of Young People: The Basic ACLU Guide to a Young Person's Rights,* by Alan Sussman (Avon Books, 1977). Also see: *Your Legal Rights,* by Linda Atkinson (Franklin Watts, 1982), which includes charts and lists that show varying laws in each state.

3

MONEY: WHEN TO SAVE IT, CHECK IT, BORROW IT

CONTENTS

When to Bank

Your parents cashed in the savings bonds you received as gifts when you were born and have just given you the money—$250.

Your summer job netted you $700.

After you sort and roll the change you saved over the year from your allowance and lunch money, you find you have accumulated $58.

You just started an after-school job at the supermarket.

Your grandparents, aunts, and uncles decided you are getting too old for clothes as a birthday present and sent you money instead: $120.

These are just examples of how your banking experiences are triggered—either by a lump sum accumulation or the start of a job, full- or part-time. Of course, if you are living on your own, banking should begin immediately. Once you make your first banking connection, you will build on it throughout the years.

What Is Banking?

In its simplest form, banking is a business which deals in money— yours and other people's. A bank or financial institution gets money from its depositors and lends that money to borrowers, who are expected to return the money, plus interest, to the financial institution.

To stay in business, banks must show a profit, so they pay their depositors less money in interest than they receive from their borrowers. That spread—the difference between the interest a financial institution pays depositors on its money and the interest it charges borrowers—is expected to cover the institution's expenses and also generate a profit.

Bankers have an image: austere, intimidating men in pinstripe suits. While both men *and women* bankers may have pinstripe suits and wear them occasionally, they remember when they were teens and went to their local banks to open accounts. They understand that this new experience can be confusing. They expect questions.

Don't be any more afraid of asking them than you would be of asking your pharmacist what's the best salve for poison ivy or your sporting goods salesperson how to determine which running shoes are best for you.

What Each Financial Institution Is

First, here is what each isn't.

Each institution does not offer separate and distinct services. That's the way it was several years ago.

Today, the differences lie in:

- The *names* of the services, even though they perform the same function
- The emphasis of the services offered
- The *rates, incentives,* and *options* of the services
- To whom the financial institution wants *to appeal*—large groups or corporations, small businesses, or individuals

Even though the services offered are similar—all the institutions offer various savings programs, checking accounts (by different names), credit cards, mortgages, and loan programs—there are variations on the theme.

Commercial Banks

Commercial banks offer just about every service and convenience you need. The only area in which traditionally they have been weak is savings—but that's changing. In October, 1982, the government took its first step toward deregulating financial institutions, making it possible for banks and savings and loan associations to offer you higher interest on your savings. Deregulation of deposit interest rates by the government is scheduled to be completed by 1986, and at that time there will be free market competition among all the institutions for *your* money.

Savings and Loan Associations

Savings and loan (S&L) customers generally use the S&Ls for savings because these institutions have been allowed by law to pay slightly more interest than banks. This too is changing. By 1986 all financial institutions should be on a par. When people borrow money from S&Ls, they usually seek long-term mortgage loans.

S&Ls can offer what are essentially interest-bearing checking accounts, known as NOW or Negotiable Order of Withdrawal accounts. Most of these are free checking accounts, provided you maintain a minimum balance. If you drop below the minimum, the NOW account has charges attached to it.

Mutual Savings Banks

Though found in only a minority of states, mutuals are virtual duplicates of commercial banks. The services vary from bank to bank, though.

Credit Unions

A credit union (CU)—and there were over 21,000 of them in this country as the decade began—is a nonprofit savings and loan cooperative consisting of people with something in common: their place of employment, their union, their religion, profession, and so on. Over 46½ million people belonged to credit unions in the early 1980s. Credit unions are governed and run by their own members.

Traditionally, CUs have offered reasonably priced credit and often higher interest on savings than other financial institutions. In some instances, a few of the services of the credit union are extended to children of members—savings accounts, for example—but this is not uniformly true.

While continuing to emphasize consumer loans and some financial counseling, CUs also offer a service which they are not permitted to call "checking," but which really is. It's called "share draft accounts," and you use the share drafts as you would checks. Most of these share draft accounts are free. Some allow share draft accounts to draw interest, the amount of which depends on your minimum balance. Services vary from credit union to credit union depending on government regulations and on the decisions made by the directors of each CU.

A large percentage of commercial banks, savings and loan associations, mutual banks, and credit unions are insured. Each account under a different name (David Smith; Susan Smith in trust for David Smith; Gene Smith as custodian for David Smith) was insured up to $100,000 early in the decade. If you have any doubts about your institution's federal insurance, ask! On this, you should have *no* doubts whatsoever.

Your Savings Account

Why Have One?

We all like to have a little money on hand at home for everyday or spur-of-the-moment spending. But when those few dollars grow to many, then it is unsafe and unwise to keep them at home—piggybank or not. You're tempting others outside and inside the house with the cash, and more important, you're tempting yourself. Money in your hands, jeans, or house will be spent—usually frittered away. Also, money at home doesn't earn interest. So start shopping for the right financial savings institution for yourself. The savings habit will serve you well throughout life.

What Kinds of Accounts Are Available to You?

• *A Passbook Savings Account.* In this kind of account your money is always instantly available to you—a real plus. Because of this liquidity (the ability to withdraw money as you need it), people don't object vigorously to the low interest rates these accounts pay you. Interest usually is compounded annually, semiannually, quarterly, or in some cases, daily. (More about that in a moment.)

Having a passbook account in the past has meant that you had to bring this little book into the institution each time you made a transaction so it could be recorded in the passbook. The physical transporting of the passbook from home to institution is being phased out, and more and more of the banks and institutions are sending out computerized statements and scrapping the passbook.

• *Time Deposit Accounts.* A variety of these are available. Time deposit means that you are required to keep your money (usually a set sum) on deposit for a minimum time period. It could be as short as thirty days; it could be years. Because the institution is almost completely assured of the use of your money for a defined period, it will pay you a higher rate of interest on a time deposit account than on a passbook savings account. The minimum amount of money for a time deposit program varies from $100 to $500.

If you need your money before the time period is up, you pay a heavy penalty—usually a reduction of interest. Time deposit accounts (certificates of deposit—CDs—are the most common) shouldn't be considered unless you have a substantial sum (over $500) that you are reasonably certain you won't need for a given period of time.

How Can Accounts Be Set Up?

At this time in your life, there are usually only three types of accounts which you would have to consider:

1. *An individual account.* You open this account. It's yours alone; you're the person who makes the deposits and the withdrawals. Some institutions require a substantial deposit of up to $500. This is the type of account you probably would want to open for yourself.

2. *A trust account.* A parent usually opens this type of account for a child, or one spouse for another. In the case of parent for child (you), the money is deposited by the parent and belongs to and is controlled by the parent. You, the child, are the trust beneficiary, a designation which can be changed at any time by your parent.

3. *A custodial account.* This is opened by a parent as your custodian. The money is your property and must be used for your benefit.

Comparison Shop for Savings Accounts

Go to the New Accounts Department of several nearby institutions. If you're planning to open an account at the same time you're doing your "shopping," bring with you not only your list of questions, but also your money (in the form of a check or cash) plus your Social Security number. Speak to the person in charge and ask these questions:

What are the institution's business hours?

If they're not convenient to your schedule, are there automatic teller machines which at least would let you do your basic banking?

Will there be a person available to talk to if I have a question or a problem?

If all the banking is electronically operated and the institution is never open on Saturdays or evenings, then this institution might not be for you.

What is the interest rate on savings?

Don't stop with this question—5½ percent in one bank may mean less in real dollars earned than 5½ percent in another bank. Ask on.

How often is the interest compounded (computed)?

Daily compounding gives you the most interest on your dollar because as each day's interest is calculated, it is calculated on a slightly higher base. When you have hundreds of dollars in your account which sit undisturbed for quite a while, daily compounding becomes significant.

How soon after I deposit money in a savings account will this institution start to pay interest on it?

Look for "day of deposit to day of withdrawal." That's what is best for you. Also important: the institution which pays interest on all funds in your account during the interest period, and not just on the smallest balance you have had in your account during that period.

What happens if I withdraw funds before the stated interest payment date? Will I lose all the interest owed to me on these funds for the interest period?

If that's the case, hold off withdrawing the funds until after the crediting date—assuming that's possible. If you're shopping for a time deposit savings account, check whether a fixed or variable (fluctuating) interest rate would be best for you. In some cases, institutions might let you have access to part of your money without penalty, and they'll let you make additional payments to your account during the period. These are good features. In the case of variable interest rates, check whether the bank offers a guaranteed minimum on your rate of interest.

Is there a "grace period" around the interest payment date so that I can withdraw funds a little early and still get the interest? If so, how many grace days?

For instance, superior would be a grace period after each interest payment date that would allow you to deposit funds and have the funds earn interest as if the money had been there from the start of the payment date.

Is there a minimum balance I must maintain in order to draw interest?

Some institutions say ''yes.'' You must have $50 in the account or they won't pay any interest. If that's not a problem you expect, fine. If you think it might be, continue shopping.

Are there penalties for frequent withdrawals? If so, what are they? On the flip side, do I get any bonus interest if I don't make any withdrawals for a year?

Are there any penalties involved in closing an account?

Some institutions have a service charge for closing an account if the account has been open less than a year. If and when you do close an account, check when the next interest crediting date is. You may want to keep a minimal amount in your account so that you can earn interest, or you might want to postpone the closing for a few days.

These questions are all valid. If you get the brush-off or if anyone makes you feel uncomfortable while you're asking, go to another institution. You may not be a big customer now, but the good institutions know you have the potential. They should handle your questions courteously and openly.

In addition to savings accounts, money market funds have become an important savings vehicle. (See Chapter 5, *Investment Options for Today's Teenagers.*)

Saving Is Not Easy

Ten Tricks to Help You

1. Gather up all your loose change from the week's allowance and lunch money and faithfully deposit it at week's end.
2. Put two-thirds of all the money you get from birthday and holiday gifts into a savings account.
3. If you have a part-time job, put one paycheck out of two or three into your account.

4. Have a "nothing week" once in a while. Don't go out to the movies or spend any money on snacks. Put the money you would have spent into your account.
5. Give up something. Cigarettes would be sensational. Did you know that if you smoke one pack a day, you could save at least $350 a year by giving it up? Candy bars are also a good give-up item.
6. Get up an extra ten or fifteen minutes earlier to make your lunch instead of buying it. Save the difference.
7. Buy records, clothes, cosmetics, sports equipment, etc., on sale. Save the difference between sale and regular prices.
8. Have your employer automatically deposit part of your paycheck into your savings account. Such services can be worked out.
9. Get into the exercise habit. Walk to a friend's house, the library, school, the store. Save the gas money and transportation costs.
10. Make sure your employer deducts enough withholding tax from your paycheck so that you will not owe taxes at the end of the year. You could even get a refund.

Savings Grow Slowly, but With Certainty

Suppose you want to accumulate $2,000 for a car. Or $4,000 by the time you start college. Or $10,000 before you get married. How much money would you have to set aside monthly, and for how long, at institutions paying interest rates of 5 and 5¾ percent, to reach your goal?

Note: if you can get a higher interest rate, it will mean less money to save per month or less time needed to accumulate the amount you want.

Savings Timetable

If you want this amount	It will take:	Saving this much each month at the interest rate of:	
		5%	5¾%
$2,000	1 year	$162.20	$161.53
	3 years	$ 51.39	$ 50.78
	5 years	$ 29.28	$ 28.70
$4,000	1 year	$324.40	$323.06
	3 years	$102.78	$101.56
	5 years	$ 58.56	$ 57.40
$6,000	1 year	$486.60	$484.59
	3 years	$154.17	$152.34
	5 years	$ 87.84	$ 86.10
$8,000	5 years	$117.12	$114.80
	10 years	$ 51.28	$ 49.21
$10,000	5 years	$146.40	$143.50
	10 years	$ 64.10	$ 61.51

Your Checking Account

When Do You Need One?

You should have your own checking account:

- When you're away from home most of the year at a college, boarding school, or vocational school.
- When you're working and living on your own. Often a checking account is necessary if you have a full-time job even when you are still living at home.
- If you are operating your own small business (gardening or flea market booth, for example), that would mean there is a flow of money to and from you. In this case, it doesn't matter if you're living at home or not.

If you live at home and have minimal expenses which require you to send out a check a month, for example, it probably makes more sense to keep your money in a savings account and have a periodic cashier's check drawn than to open a checking account. (More about cashier's checks later in this chapter.)

Can You Get One?

Institutions vary in their requirements. Some say no checking accounts if you're under eighteen years of age (but they do bend rules, especially if your parents have an active account at the institution); some say yes to checking if you also have a substantial savings account with them; some say yes if you maintain a large minimum balance (if you fall below the minimum you pay a monthly penalty charge); some say yes only if you can prove you have a steady monthly income.

Find out what the institution's requirements are by comparison shopping. Start at the institution where you have your savings account. It should be most amenable because you are already a customer.

Financial institutions around colleges, universities, and vocational schools are accustomed to having students open checking accounts, even when they are under eighteen. As long as you can prove you're a student at a particular school, you shouldn't have a problem opening an account.

Checking Accounts Cost Money

Financial institutions are beginning to retreat from the practice of providing free or below-cost checking to attract customers. That's because the cost of processing a check has been increasing from the early 1980s, when processing cost between 10 and 30 cents a check.

The trend actually is to charge for all services. One prototype system of fees expected to be widely accepted throughout the country soon is to give the customer a monthly credit allowance, dependent upon the size of the average balance in the account. If the average balance is $500, for example, the credit is $5.50. With each transaction you (the customer) make, you are charged against that credit. A check costs 30 cents; withdrawal from an automatic teller machine is 10 cents; a bounced check costs you $30. If at the end of the month you go beyond your $5.50 credit, you pay a service charge. If you haven't used all your credit, there is no service charge. (No refund either.)

Regular Checking Accounts

Regular checking accounts require you to maintain a certain minimum balance. As long as you maintain the balance (and it could be as little as $100, though it is often more), some banks will permit you to write as many checks and make as many deposits as you please without paying additional charges. Once you fall below the minimum, though, you are hit with a service charge. In the early 1980s, some banks offered ''free'' checking while requiring you to tie up a certain minimum amount of money in a savings account at the same institution. It's worth their while to give you certain services as long as they can hold onto your money.

A regular checking account is a good choice if you write over five or six checks each month and can maintain the required minimum balance in your account.

Special Checking Accounts

Special checking accounts do not require you to keep a minimum balance. Instead you pay a small fee (fifteen to twenty cents) for each item that is processed—a check or a deposit. And you also pay a flat monthly service charge.

Not So Traditional Checking Accounts

Alternatives to traditional checking accounts include:

• *Use of the automatic teller machines.* Now available for customers at most financial institutions, these ATMs (as they are affectionately known by those in the business) let you make deposits, make withdrawals, move money from one account to another, and even pay off loans. You must be issued a transaction card by the institution before the ATM is operable for you. (More about this technical tidal wave later in this chapter.)

• *Bill-paying services.* If you make official arrangements with the institution—generally in writing—you can have funds automatically transferred from your savings to cover your regular monthly bills.

• *Overdraft accounts.* These are also called automatic lines of credit, which means you can write checks for more money than you have in the bank (overdraft) up to a set limit. Once you do, however, it is equivalent to taking out a loan from the bank and you must pay interest on the overdraft amount.

• *Checking with interest.* Share drafts and NOW accounts are both interest-bearing checking accounts. Share drafts are offered by credit unions; NOW accounts by savings and loan associations. There are usually no fees on share drafts; not so on NOW accounts, which you must check out carefully because it makes no sense to pay big dollars in service charges to get pennies in interest. Some commercial banks, too, are now offering interest on checking accounts, but not without special requirements which you should investigate carefully.

• *Telephone transfers.* If you can move money from your savings to your checking account merely by making a telephone call, you are, in effect, creating your own interest-bearing checking account. Some institutions allow you to do this, sometimes for a fee.

Rules for Writing and Endorsing Checks

It's strange that so many older adults do not know how to write, endorse, or deposit a check. Don't be one of them. Here are the basic rules.

1. Date your checks properly.
2. Don't leave any spaces on a check. Look how easy it is to turn $8.00 into $98.00 because of the space between the dollar sign and the sum. If in spelling out the amount there is a space between the written amount and the word "dollars" at the end of the line, draw a line through to "dollars." (See the example check at the end of this list.)
3. Number each check properly so that you will know what goes where when it's checkbook balancing time. Better yet, get checks with numbers preprinted on them.
4. Sign your checks the same way each time—not "Pete Green" one time and "Peter Noah Green" the next.
5. "Mr.," "Ms.," "Miss," or "Mrs." are not part of your signature. Don't use them.
6. Fill out the middle line ending with the word "dollars" this way. For $9.83, write: "Nine and ———83/100." For $650, write: "Six hundred and fifty and ———no/100." If you write a check for less than $1, write "Only 95 cents" and cross out the word "dollars."
7. Don't use somebody else's check, and don't lend anyone one of your checks unless you punch a hole in the lower left-hand corner of the check where the numbers appear for a special magnetic code—otherwise the face amount of the check may well be taken out of the wrong account. (An interesting sidelight: Technically checks can be written on any surface from an envelope to a square of toilet paper. But you'd have a difficult time convincing anyone your check was valid with this kind of eccentricity.)

8. Endorse a check payable to you on the back left-hand side exactly as it has been made out to you—even if your name is misspelled. If the endorsement is not your usual signature, sign again on the next imaginary line.

9. Your endorsement is important. It means you transfer the ownership of the check to the person or firm holding it at the time. There are different ways to make the endorsement:

"Pay to the order of" a person or organization is an endorsement in full, or special endorsement. Only that person or organization can cash it.

"For deposit only" over your signature means that you're making a restrictive endorsement. You should do this when you make a deposit by mail or when you give a check to someone to deposit for you.

10. Deposit all checks immediately. If you wait too long—two or three months—banks may refuse to honor them without reauthorization by the payer.

11. Be cautious when you write a check to "cash," because if you drop it, it is negotiable by any bearer and can be cashed. It's similar to dropping money.

12. Don't write a check in pencil. It's legal but dumb. Someone can erase the amount you entered and fill in a more pleasing sum (ten thousand dollars instead of ten dollars).

13. Record your check and all the key facts about it. Do fill out the stub fully before you write the check so that you don't forget.

14. Never, never give a signed blank check to anyone (except someone in whom you have absolute trust—and then only on an emergency basis) because the person can fill in any amount that appears reasonable.

This is how a check should look:

Check These Questions

How long do your deposited checks take to clear before you can safely write your own checks against the amount(s)?

It depends on where the check is from. If the check is drawn on a bank in your city, allow at least three business days for the funds to be collected. Out-of-town and out-of-state banks take longer. Allow five to fifteen business days for them. Make certain the check you deposit in your account has cleared before you write checks against it. Otherwise your checks will be returned (bounced), and you'll be charged a fee by the bank . . . and embarrassed.

Can a check be dated on Saturday, Sunday, or a holiday?

Yes. Forget anything to the contrary you might have heard.

Suppose that when you're making out a check, you mistakenly write one amount in words and another amount in figures. What happens?

Two things might occur. The bank might pay the written amount or it might return the check.

What happens if you make a mistake on a check?

Rip it up and start again. (Make a note of that in your checkbook.) Since banks will often refuse to honor an altered check even if you've initialed the change, don't give a check that way and don't accept one.

How long is a check good for?

Technically, six years. But most banks will not honor a check that is more than six months old without first getting an okay from the payer.

How do you stop payment on a check?

Telephone your bank's stop-payment department immediately. Tell them the date, amount, name of payee, check number, and the reason for stopping the payment. Follow up by sending a written statement confirming your call. The bank will send you a stop-payment form to complete and return. Generally banks will not issue a stop-payment order if you don't have sufficient funds in your account to cover the payment since they believe, in that case, that you had no intention of paying the check in the first place.

When you stop payment, be sure to notify the person or company who was to have received the check.

Outsmarting Forgers

Forgery is big business. The best way not to be an unwitting accomplice is to know how a forger operates and outsmart him.

Forgers will try to find or steal checks of yours. Then they loot your mailbox around the date your bank mails out monthly statements, study samples of your signature, and learn how much money you generally keep in your account. Now they're ready to go to work. You may not discover the damage until strange canceled checks start being returned to you.

Or forgers simply change the numbers on carelessly written checks.

Protect yourself by:

- Guarding your checks. If you notice the checkbook or any of your checks missing, inform the bank at once.
- Notifying the bank if your statement is more than a couple of days late.
- Going over your bank statement promptly each month. Also examine the returned checks for evidence of tampering or forgery.
- Reporting any suspicious evidence to the bank immediately.
- Writing checks out properly and clearly signing your name.
- Keeping old checks in a safe place, and destroying checks before throwing them away.

How to Balance Your Checkbook

Few people look forward to sitting down each month to compare their checkbook balance with the balance shown on the bank statement. Yet it has to be done for two good reasons:

1. If you've made a mistake in your tally, you must know it as soon as possible to avoid compounding your error.

Suppose you think you have $400 in your checking account. Feeling secure, you send away for an $80 stereo component. The check is returned to you because, in fact, you have only $40 as a balance (''insufficient funds'' is the official term). You don't get your component. You certainly don't appear to be a good credit risk from the merchant's point of view. Furthermore, the bank slaps a hefty service charge on your account to cover the processing of this uncovered check.

There is always the possibility that you think you have $40 in your account, but you really have $400. (This happens about as frequently as going through life without a pimple.) However, finding a windfall in your account after four years isn't necessarily cause for joy. There are so many goods or services you could have bought and enjoyed over the period of time. And even if you hadn't spent the money, you could have saved it and collected some interest.

2. If the bank has made the error, it wants to know as soon as possible—say within ten days after you receive the statement—for the same reasons you would want to know if you had made the error.

Here are key steps to follow to balance your statement:

1. Your own checkbook balance	_____
2. Minus service charges appearing on your bank statement	_____
3. Your own new checkbook balance	_____
4. Balance in the bank's statement	_____
5. Plus recent deposits not yet recorded in bank statement	_____
6. Minus value of all outstanding checks (those not appearing on bank statement)	_____
7. New bank statement balance	_____

After you have gone through these preliminary steps, item 7 and item 3 should be the same. If they are not, your work continues.

• Check off each canceled check with the amount appearing in the bank statement.

• Now stack the checks in number order and check them off against the entries in your checkbook. Compare the amount of the checks and the amounts on your stubs to be sure they are in agreement.

- Make a note of which checks are outstanding.
- See if the deposits you recorded in your checkbook coincide with those on the bank statement.
- Don't forget deposits and withdrawals made at the automatic teller machines.
- Add up the amounts of all the checks you have written which don't appear on your statement. Subtract this total from the balance appearing at the end of your bank statement.
- Figure the total of all the deposits you have made to your account which do not appear on the bank statement and add this total to the bank statement's balance.
- Subtract any bank service charges which appear on your statement from the balance which you have in your checkbook.

Now—do you have a statement which balances with your checkbook?

If not, keep working.

- Recheck the math in your checkbook. The problem may lie in this simple solution.
- Recheck the balances you carried forward from page to page in your checkbook.
- Recheck to see that you have subtracted all outstanding checks from your bank statement balance—even those still missing from previous statements.
- Recheck to be certain that you haven't forgotten to enter any automatic teller machine transfers or telephone transfers you may have made during the period of the statement.

If the two records still don't agree and you're befuddled, go to the bank and ask for help. You'll probably be given the help without charge. But do reconcile the two balances. If there is a mistake—yours or the bank's—or if there is any foul play, the sooner you find out the better.

And Then There Are More Kinds of Checks

In addition to your personal checks, there are other types of checks you will see or use.

Certified Check

A certified check is your own personal check made out to a specific party, which is signed and stamped by a bank officer. What this certification means is that you have X dollars (the amount of the check) in your account and the bank has set that money aside so that the person to whom you're giving the check is certain to receive the amount. If you have an interest-bearing checking account or a NOW account, that amount stops drawing interest as soon as the check is certified.

Unless a certified check is lost or stolen, stopping payment on it is difficult. There will probably be a fee involved and you may have to post a surety bond to indemnify the bank against any lawsuits.

Since certified checks are as good as cash, you may well be asked for a certified check when, for example, you're buying a used car from another person or a new car from a dealer.

Cashier's Check

A cashier's check has many aliases—teller's check, bank check, official check. It's the financial institution's check to you or a third party. Suppose, for example, you want to send $300 to State University as a deposit toward next year's tuition. You withdraw that sum from your savings account and ask the teller to make the check payable to the university, because you certainly are not about to send cash through the mail. There might be a minimal charge for this service. If the check is made out to you, you endorse it "Pay to the order of State U."

The trouble with the cashier's check is in the recordkeeping. Since the check is returned to the bank, you really have no way of knowing who received that $300 withdrawal which will show up on your passbook or balance statement. Therefore, keep the receipt the bank gives you.

Money Order

If you don't have a checking account or a savings account and you must send money somewhere, get a U.S. Post Office Money Order. *Never send cash through the mail.* The fee is small and the person or company to whom you're sending the money order can cash it at any U.S. Post Office.

While there are bank money orders (use insured banks only), cashing these can be difficult if the receiver doesn't have a savings or checking account at a bank.

Traveler's Checks

Traveler's checks can be very helpful if you're . . . traveling. There is always the possibility that money (and you usually carry large sums when you are on vacation) can be lost or stolen. Traveler's checks protect you against being stranded penniless. You can buy the checks at most financial institutions.

To determine which kind to get (for some there is a small fee; for others, none), make sure the place or area at which you're vacationing will cash the kind you're buying. Some traveler's checks are internationally known. Others are not known outside a region. While they are all valid, if you can't cash them, they're useless.

For traveler's checks to be meaningful in case of an emergency or loss, you must:

• Be near an office which deals in the traveler's checks you're carrying.

• Have a record of your traveler's check numbers. The record must be kept separate and apart from the traveler's checks themselves. If you carry the checks in your pocket, for example, keep the record of the numbers in your toiletry bag. Before you even leave your home, you leave another record of the numbers there. To get quick replacement of the lost checks, you must have the numbers at hand.

Automatic Teller Machines

These polite little devils, nicknamed ATMs, which are being installed around the country are a boon to the financial institution's customer—you—in terms of convenience. Any time—day or night, weekday or weekend, holiday or workday—you can get cash, make deposits, transfer money from one account to another, and make balance entries. Because the ATMs are not set up for complicated banking services at this time, you can be fairly certain that the line for the ATM will move faster than the one in front of a teller's window.

It is generally standard practice for the institution to issue a transaction card (a plastic card resembling a credit card) to anyone with an account. But there are dangers!

Dangers

To avoid any electronic mishaps:

- Request a personal demonstration and explanation of how the ATM works from the bank personnel.
- Do not write your personal identification number or code on your transaction card or anywhere else where it might be observed, stolen, or misplaced.
- The panel will resemble that of a pushbutton phone with lettered and numbered buttons. Choose a number you won't forget, but one which wouldn't be obvious—such as your address, social security or phone number—should someone be using your card illegally. Good choices might be your favorite food (bacon would be 22266), the last four digits of a friend's phone number, or your lucky numbers. Once you've selected the number, memorize it. In some systems, you're the only one who knows your code or number. If you forget it, you must choose another.
- Be extremely careful about lending your transaction card or telling your personal identification code number *to anyone!* It's a hazardous thing to do unless the person is absolutely (and I do mean *absolutely*) trustworthy.
- Make certain you get the receipt of the transaction you have made. Before you leave the ATM, check the receipt. You could have switched money into your checking account from your savings account when you wanted to do the opposite. Then hold these receipts so that you can compare them with your monthly statements.
- Be sure that the machine has finished the transaction and that you have your card before you walk away.
- Be certain you enter each transaction into your checkbook—a chore you could easily forget.
- Don't use cash-dispensing machines which are in low-traffic

areas if it's late at night or an offbeat hour. And once you enter the area where many of these machines are located, walk out immediately if there is anyone there who looks suspicious. Don't set yourself up for foul play.

• If you have a problem with the ATM, use the phone located near it to speak to a bank official who, at the other end of the line, is there to help.

Legal Protection for You, the Electronic Banking Customer

If you lose your card or think it has been stolen, contact the financial institution within two business days after learning of the loss. Then you are liable for no more than $50.

The only time you are liable for more—up to $500—is when you don't notify the institution within two days *and* it can prove that it could have prevented the loss if you had informed it.

What if there is a discrepancy between the bank statement and your balance as a result of electronic fund transfers? Then you must notify the bank within 60 days after your statement is mailed. If you don't, *and* the institution can show that had you contacted it, it would have prevented the loss, you may be out the money withdrawn from your account by an unauthorized transfer.

Obviously, the pitfalls of electronic banking lie directly under your feet—in all directions. Be warned! Use with care!

If you have any problems or complaints about an electronic fund transfer or the service, try to resolve it first with the institution with which you're dealing. If you can't, get in touch with The Division of Consumer & Community Affairs (Board of Governors of the Federal Reserve System, Washington, DC 20551).

Looking Ahead

The ATMs are the babes in this new era of electronic fund transfers. Soon sophisticated technology should allow you to:

• Pay for your groceries, your doctor's bill, your appliance repair, and the like on the spot without cash or a check. By inserting your electronic transfer card into a point of sale terminal and punching out the amount you want taken from your account and credited to the merchants, you make the transfer. This type of transfer has its problems. What to do if you are unhappy with the purchase or the service? Will merchants or service people be willing to refund or repair when they already have your money in their accounts? More "bewares!"

• Bank at home by means of a personal computer. Through a telephone hookup you can pay bills, transfer funds, and keep financial records.

• Bank nationwide. Either through a network of individual institutions or by larger financial institutions expanding across state lines (all of which already has happened), you'll be able to travel across country, for example, with a minimum amount of money. You will stop at ATMs at participating institutions along your route to get cash when you need it.

Laws are also changing. Regulations are being lifted. Financial institutions are rapidly of becoming financial supermarkets—offering everything from the traditional banking services to stock exchange and real estate services.

TO YOUR CREDIT

Consumer Credit: What It Is and When to Use It

You've heard of "buy now, pay later." That's what credit is all about. It's a financial arrangement that gives you the right to defer the payment on merchandise or services. While you may use credit occasionally now to charge gas on your parents' card, take out a student loan, or have your doctor send you a bill after you have had treatment, one thing is certain: You *will* use credit in the future. The sooner you get started establishing a good credit rating for yourself, the better.

Right and Wrong Reasons for Borrowing

There are right and wrong reasons for being a borrower. Test yourself.

	Right reason to borrow	*Wrong reason to borrow*

1. You are faced with a major dental problem. As a young adult you haven't had an opportunity to accumulate enough money in an emergency fund.

2. You always have wanted a waterbed and you saw one that's a dandy. Even though you don't have a job yet and your funds are dwindling, you want it.

3. You must have a refrigerator. The 25-year-old one you inherited from your grandmother gave out three weeks ago. There's a half-price sale at the local store, but you haven't saved up enough money even for that.

4. The appliance store is offering a large-screen TV for $100 down with three years to pay off the rest. You like its looks.

5. You know a public speaking course would be valuable to you in your job, but you don't have tuition money.

6. Although the digital stereo only plays digital recordings, you are anxious to buy one because it sure will impress your friends.

If you said that number one was the right reason to borrow and alternated thereafter with "wrong," you're a credit pro. Let's see why.

1. *Right.* Borrowing to meet emergency needs such as health is about as valid as a reason can be.

2. *Wrong.* Waterbeds are fine, but not if you don't have a reasonable prospect of repaying the loan at this time. Wait.

3. *Right*. If you buy the refrigerator now—at this attractive sale price—and charge it, putting it on a time-payment plan or getting a low-cost loan, you'll be playing it smart. You need a refrigerator. Get the best price and enjoy it.

4. *Wrong*. Don't be lured into buying something you don't need by payment terms which seem so "easy."

5. *Right*. A top-notch reason to borrow is for education—the value of which cannot be measured by the usual yardsticks. If that education will help you in a career as well as in your everyday existence—hurrah!

6. *Wrong*. Never use credit to increase your status or boost your morale. Buying items you can't afford and can't maintain won't impress anyone—especially when they are repossessed because you can't meet the payments.

Credit Costs Money

Buying something on credit will cost you *more* than paying cash for it.

Shop for credit carefully. Get it on terms that are most advantageous to you. Generally it will be less expensive, for example, to borrow from a bank or credit union than from the retailer, the dealer, or a small loan firm. You have the *right* and the *responsibility* to ask lots of questions about the credit deal you are being offered.

• Don't sign any paper you don't understand fully.

• Keep a copy of the contract and receipts of your payments in a safe place.

• Understand that you can't get out of an installment debt simply by returning the merchandise or reselling it, because in most instances you sign two contracts: one for the actual merchandise, and one for the money to finance the purchase.

• Check the seller's reputation; reaffirm your belief that you're dealing with a responsible businessperson.

• Do buy what you want or need, but don't let anyone lean on you with high pressure sales techniques.

• Learn the difference between the annual percentage rate (the simple annual rate which relates the finance charge to the amount of credit you get and to the amount of time you have to pay back the money) and the finance charge (the total of all the charges—interest, loan fees, finder's fee, service charge, and so on, that you are asked to pay to get credit). A handy pocket-size guide which will help you in your comparative shopping for credit is put out by the Federal Trade Commission: *Credit Shopping Guide* can be bought for $2.75 from the Superintendent of Documents, U.S. Government Printing Office, Washington, DC 20402.

• Do have the courage to say no to an installment deal if you have any doubts about it.

The Catch-22 of Credit and How to Get Started

You can't get credit unless you have a credit record.

You can't get a credit record unless you have already obtained credit.

(A *credit record* is a file on your credit history kept at a credit bureau. You can request a copy of it—and so can a licensed lender. More about this in a moment.)

Now what, Matilda?

There are ways to get an "in" into a credit rating.

First you must be of legal age to sign a contract (eighteen years of age in most states).

Then you have a variety of routes which can lead to a credit record. Obviously they all mean starting small, for no institution or person is going to lend even $1,000 to an eighteen-year-old on good looks. You have to have a tested ability to repay debt if you're to get substantial credit. For starters, try one of the following to establish a credit rating.

Borrowing Cash

• *Personal Installment Loan.* Take out a small personal installment loan. Not all institutions use the same standards to judge the creditworthiness of young adults, so shop around.

The usual term of such a loan is one to three years. If you don't need the money, put the loan principle into some savings vehicle and let it collect interest as you pay it off. It takes time to build a credit rating, but when you do, it will be solid (assuming you pay the loan back on schedule).

If this is your first loan, the institution might require you to have a cosigner, such as your parent, who agrees to make payments in the event you can't.

Obviously it is easier to get a loan if you are employed full time than if you're a student, but check around. There are institutions—mainly around colleges and universities—which count parental support or grants as part of student income and grant loans on that basis.

• *Borrow against Savings.* A savings account indicates you are not spending everything you make or get. It tells the lender something about you. You're disciplined; you have a respect for money. So it puts the lender in the right frame of mind when you ask for a loan.

Rather than take the money you've saved from your account to pay for a used car, for example, borrow against the account. Not only will you keep your savings intact, you'll also be establishing a credit rating.

• *Take Out a Student Loan.* Student loans are made by financial institutions on the contractual promise that after you have completed your education, you will be in the position to repay your loan—and you'll do so. (For more information on student loans, see Chapter 4, *Financing Higher Education.*)

• *Family Loans.* These will not help you establish a credit rating, but they can be helpful if you are in need of money and your family is in a position to lend it and wants to. Yours could be a no-interest loan or you could insist on paying the same interest you would pay another lender. I opt strongly for paying an interest rate, but this is *your* loan negotiation.

The One, Two, Three of Where to Go for Loans

Where to start in your search for a loan when you need it is based simply on where you think you will get the most willing reception and where you can get the most favorable annual interest charge. There are other sources than those listed below, but they are generally reserved for the more established wage earner.

• *Relatives:* Sometimes. Can be uncomfortable. If your need is for a credit rating and not money, don't use relatives. They have no input into the credit system.

- *Credit unions:* If you belong.
- *Employer:* If the corporation you work for provides this kind of service.
- *Banks and savings institutions:* There are no industry regulations as to who is creditworthy. Shop around.
- *Licensed small loan companies:* You pay high interest rates because they take more risky creditors than banks do.
- *Tuition loan specialists:* Very high interest rates in exchange for a relatively easy-to-obtain loan.
- *Pawnbroker:* One of the worst loan sources because you can't borrow much money and what you can borrow is at interest rates three to four times higher than most major lending institutions. You also must turn over your assets until you repay.
- *Loan shark: Don't.* You'd be dealing with a dangerous racketeer.

Using the Plastic Cards

What Are Credit Cards?

Credit cards are identification cards (usually plastic) which allow you to pay for dental work, driving lessons, and dogs; savings bonds, stereos, and skis; TVs, telephones, and telescopes; in short, just about everything—by signing your name. You, the credit card holder, agree to pay for your purchases, either once a month or over an extended period. If you pay only part of the charges, the unpaid balance is treated as a loan and interest is charged.

Credit cards can be a tremendous convenience. They:

- can allow you to charge the costs of travel and entertainment anywhere in the world.
- can simplify your bookkeeping by allowing you to pay for many purchases with a single check at the end of a billing period.
- allow you to buy items you need on sale, even if you don't have the cash on hand.
- can help you order goods easily by mail or phone.

What can be wrong with an arrangement that gives you the use of large amounts of cash for as long as twenty-five days from the date of billing—often without asking you to pay interest on this "advance"?

Their great potential danger is in overspending, in lulling you into a false sense of security—until you get the bill. You must always be on guard against charging more than you can afford!

For Credit Starters, Get a Bank Credit Card

Bank credit cards, of which Visa and MasterCard are the best known, are "everything" cards. They can be used for shopping, eating out, all types of services. They charge an annual rate, and if you pay the end-of-the-month bill within the time specified, there is no finance charge. If you don't pay within the time specified, there is a service charge of about 1½ percent a month levied against the balance.

Credit requirements vary. Some banks and credit unions will grant bank cards to young adults without asking for a cosigner; others require that you have had a job for at least a year; still others, that you meet their income requirements.

Search for banks that offer cards, using your savings as collateral. Thus if you don't pay your credit balance, the lenders can get the money from your savings.

If you're a student, find out whether your local banks offer credit card "starter" programs in conjunction with your college or university. Some banks will offer cards with very low credit limits (often as low as $100 to $300) as long as you have a student I.D. Your credit limit can then be raised once you prove yourself responsible. (Your *credit limit* is the dollar amount which you are not permitted to exceed on your charge card.)

Bank credit cards usually open the door to department store and oil company cards. Once you have a MasterCard or Visa, you will find it much easier to get special-purpose and multipurpose credit cards (Diners Club, Carte Blanche, and American Express), which are mostly used by businesspeople.

If a credit card is lost or stolen, notify the credit card issuer *immediately*. Most have toll-free numbers which you are given when you get your card. If you notify the issuer before an unauthorized purchase is made, you are not responsible for its payment. In any case, the limit of your liability on each credit card is $50.

Establishing Credit Experience without Cards or Loans

• If you live away from home, even if you're at college, sign up for utilities in your own name—though often that means making a sizable deposit.

• Check whether local retailers with which you do business regularly (pharmacies, ma and pa corner stores, cleaners, gas stations) will set up charge accounts so you can pay all your bills at the end of the month.

• Be sure to pay your bills on time!

• Layaway plans vary from store to store. You see something you need and love for the winter, such as a sheepskin jacket, but you don't have the money now to pay for it. Give the storeowner a percentage of the selling price (say 25 percent) and set up a schedule of payments with the store, a schedule you'll be expected to meet. The jacket is put away for you. Get a written agreement for this layaway plan.

Some places tack on a service charge for this service; others do not. You are expected to complete payments within the given time frame. If you can't, you forfeit the money you put down *and* the storekeeper retains the merchandise. Layaways are often used by young persons who haven't had time to build a savings account and haven't yet obtained a credit card. It's basically an enforced savings plan rather than a credit plan.

Know the Rights of Your Creditor . . . and Your Own Rights

You are legally and morally expected to meet the credit obligations for which you sign. But at times, for reasons beyond your control, you will find you can't meet a payment or series of payments.

Contact your creditors immediately so they don't lose faith in you. Explain the situation to them. They generally will help you work out new payment plans.

You might need to speak to a reputable nonprofit consumer credit-counseling organization, affiliated with or working in cooperation with a merchant's group. Its suggestions might be helpful. (For severe debt problems, see Chapter 17, *Times of Trouble and Feeling Bad.*)

If your creditors cannot or will not rework your payment schedule, they have the right to:

- Repossess the merchandise, since you don't own items until all the payments are made.
- Collect the collateral.
- Garnish your wages (put a lien on up to 10 percent of what you earn).
- Furnish negative information about you to the credit bureau—such as you are a "slow pay" or "delinquent." This information is passed on to other lenders.

What are your rights in the area of credit?

Different credit bureaus will begin to track your credit history as soon as you become active in credit arrangements. Your credit record will be extremely important to you as credit assumes a larger part in your life. Under the Fair Credit Reporting Act, if you are denied credit on the basis of your credit bureau file, you have a right to:

- See the file and to know who else has seen it for credit purposes in the last six months
- Have any inaccurate information reinvestigated and deleted, with notification of that happening and a new report furnished to all creditors who have received the incorrect information
- Enter a written statement into your file concerning information you consider unfair

Adverse information in a credit file can legally be kept there for seven years. It's a good idea to monitor your credit profile by periodically writing to credit bureaus and requesting a copy of your credit report. (They will charge a fee for this service unless you have recently been denied credit on the basis of their report.) There may be inaccurate information included in your credit profile, inaccuracies you will want to clear up right away.

THE VOCABULARY OF FINANCE

Don't be baffled by the terms you hear. Most of them you already know from the reading you have just done. Here's a glossary of terms, to which others that are commonly used have been added.

Annual percentage rate: The total cost of credit in relative terms. For example, the annual percentage rate of 1½ percent monthly is 18 percent.

Balance: The amount you owe on an account or loan; the amount you have in the bank.

Borrower: The person who borrows cash or who buys something on time.

Collateral: Possession of value against which you may borrow money. Examples are a car, passbook savings account, home furnishings.

Cosigner: Another person who signs a credit contract with you. That person is responsible for payment if you default.

Credit rating: An evaluation of your qualifications to receive credit based, in large part, on your past record of responsible (or irresponsible) repayment of loans.

Creditor: A person or firm that extends credit to you and to which you are indebted.

Default: Failure to make a payment specified in a contract on the due date or to meet other contractual obligations.

Down payment: Cash required by the creditor from you prior to an installment-sale credit transaction.

Face amount: The total amount of your loan before finance charges.

Finance charge: In dollars and cents, the amount you are paying for use of credit. You don't have to pay this charge when you pay cash.

Forfeit: Giving something up to a creditor after you, the borrower, have failed to meet a contractual obligation.

Installment: One of a series of payments to pay off a debt.

Licensed lender: A lending organization licensed to do business in the state in which it is located.

Maturity date: Date on which final payment on loan or installment purchase is due.

Principal: Amount of money you borrow; the amount of money you invest in a savings plan.

Repossession: Forced or voluntary surrender of merchandise as a result of your inability to pay as contracted.

Term: Time within which you must make installment or other payments under your loan or credit contract.

Terms: Details and conditions of a loan or other contract—such as cash price, payment schedule, maturity date, penalty clause, and more.

Trade in: Practice of trading in an old product for a new one (often used in automobile buying), using the amount of money allowed for the article traded in against the total purchase price of the article being bought.

Truth in Lending: A familiar name for the Consumer Credit Protection Act of 1969—an historic law which applies to virtually all individual consumer borrowing transactions up to $25,000.

Wage garnishment: Court order requiring that a certain amount of the credit user's wages be paid by the employer directly to the creditor.

4

FINANCING HIGHER EDUCATION

CONTENTS

THE ABCD (ABOUT BIG COLLEGE DOLLARS) QUIZ

True or False?

Let's think about education, for now, in terms of money.

1. If your parents had banked $30 a month for your education since the day you were born (say fifteen years ago), they would have accumulated at least enough money to send you to a private college for two years.
2. There is no financial help available for those who go to vocational or technical schools.
3. A high school senior whose family income is $25,000 will be entitled to more financial aid than one whose family income is $40,000.
4. It is possible to earn over $5,000 a year and still be a full-time college student living on campus.
5. A college diploma assures you of a high-paying job in the field of your choice when you graduate.

After you have finished reading this chapter, you will know the answers to the ABCD Quiz. But if patience is not your virtue, the answers follow. Read the answers; then, at the end of the chapter, come back to this quiz which, by then, should have new meaning for you.

The Answers

1. *False.* Fifteen years ago the average yearly expenses at a private college were $2,600. If your parents had been able to put $30 a month into the bank (then a great deal of money for young adults just getting started in their careers) at an average rate of interest of 6 percent (it was 4½ percent in 1967; 5¼ percent in 1973), they could reasonably have expected that the accumulated total—approximately $9,300—would have covered at least two years worth of expenses at a private college. Not so. To the horror of all of us, the price tag for education has skyrocketed and is still soaring. For example, at Middlebury College in Vermont, Williams College in

Massachusetts, and Yale University in Connecticut, an estimate of total tuition and fees alone for one academic year in the early 1980s was around $12,000.

2. *False.* If you go to an *accredited* technical or vocational school, there is federal aid available based on need. Individual schools also have scholarships.

3. *True.* Most of the time. But not always. If you are from a family with an income of $40,000, have two siblings—one in college and another at home with a serious eye problem requiring constant medical attention—and you want to go to a private college in another state, your *need* for financial aid may be greater than an only child from a family whose income is $25,000. Many circumstances go into the determination of need. So *don't prejudge your own eligibility.* Fill out a financial aid form and let the experts apply the formulas.

4. *True.* Cooperative education (co-oping) has become a way of life in over a third of the colleges and universities in this country. With the help of the college, an alternating work-study program is set up tailored to meet your needs. (More information about work-study programs later in this chapter.)

5. *False.* While it is true that over a lifetime the average college graduate earns more money than someone who did not go to college, a college diploma does not guarantee a high-paying job (or a job at all!) in your field upon graduation. The job market operates on the theory of supply and demand. Right now—and for the next ten years—it is expected that the demand for technically educated people will outstrip the supply. So if you study engineering, computer technology, mathematics, or an allied field, your chances of getting a high-paying job in your field are excellent. But if you're a philosophy or history major, career opportunities in your field with a B.A. degree are limited—and so is the pay.

THINKING ABOUT HIGHER EDUCATION

Education for Its Own Sake

Has it ever happened to you?

You've been studying a vocabulary list. ''Gregarious means friendly, sociable.'' Then you hear someone describe you as gregarious. It rings a bell. You're pleased you know what the word means. (You're also pleased that that's how you were described. Better than misanthropic.)

Your friend is buying a used car and calls to ask you if you would go along with him to check it out because you're so good with all things mechanical, especially since you took that two-year auto mechanic course. You're flattered.

Before you usurped the stereo, your mom had classical music playing all the time. At a record store one day you hear Beethoven's Ninth Symphony. You stop. Listen. Even hum. And then you realize how nice it was to hear that familiar swell of music.

You're faced with a problem you've never experienced before. After an initial moment of panic, you settle down, decide what has to be done first, what next, and so on. In short order you've solved the problem with your logical thinking.

Education, whether formal or informal, has an inherent value which is even more precious than the dollars it can provide. Knowing skills, subject areas, concepts, and ways of thinking helps us enjoy the richness of life's offerings and meet its challenges with confidence and pride.

Whether you continue your formal education after high school or postpone it until later, your informal education never stops. Be thankful. It may be that a little learning is a dangerous thing—but think about the perils and emptiness of none.

No Such Thing as the Right Way

Even though it may have been the "thing to do" in the 1950s to go directly into college from high school, there never was a "right way" to get an education. And there isn't today.

Because each individual is different, and because there are so many places to learn the skills and the information you will need for jobs and careers, consider all the options instead of assuming your next step after high school will be onto the granite steps of a college building.

Is College for You?

Consider three vital points about yourself.

"What Do I Want to Be When I Grow Up?"

The last time I heard the question, it was being asked by a woman of 48 who thus far had had successful careers in teaching, business, and writing, so don't be anxious if you don't have the answer at your fingertips. While some people know early in life what they want to do (Dr. David Baltimore, 1975 Nobel Prize winner in medicine, knew in high school he was going to work on a cure for cancer), most teens are not that focused. They have leanings. They're good at certain things. They hate certain subjects. But they don't know exactly how that fits into their life's plans.

That's perfectly okay. You might get help finding a direction by taking one of the vocational interest tests for career decision-making which are administered regularly in many high schools. (If not in yours, ask your guidance counselor for one.) From the result you'll be able to see clearly where your interests lie (though not necessarily your aptitude). If you score low in the scientific areas, don't plan for a career in medicine. You won't be happy with it, even if the idea of doctoring is appealing now.

Once you know where your interests lie, you have to assess whether college or vocational school is the right place to pursue them.

"Why Am I Thinking about College Immediately after High School?"

Is it because your parents want this for you? Do they assume that a diploma is the key to a successful job and career? Are you going because that's what all your friends are doing? Are you going because you want to go?

If you're not sure college is the right path now, talk to your parents. Explore your doubts with them; research other possibilities (the rest of this chapter will help). Keep in mind that how you present the alternatives is important to getting your parents' approval and cooperation.

"Am I Mature Enough to Handle the Commitments of College?"

A college education has always been valuable in what it *affords* students; now its value has been vastly increased because of what it *costs* them. If you're not ready to put in the studying commitment (it's figured you will have two hours of study for each class hour, sometimes more), there are less expensive places to have a good time than on a college campus.

Deferring College

The Advantages of Waiting

• Gives you an opportunity to zero in on your interests, to decide on what area of study you'd like to concentrate.

• Gives you an opportunity to work for a year or more and put money aside for your higher education.

• Gives you breathing space between the academic pressures of high school and college.

• Gives you time to mature, to set goals for yourself, to build up your confidence. Returning to school, you won't be the oldest in the class because if today's trend continues, at the end of this decade there will be almost as many students twenty-five and over as between the ages of eighteen and twenty-four.

The Drawbacks of Waiting

• You lose the study rhythm and might even lose interest in pursuing a higher education.

• You might assume familial responsibilities in the interim which make it harder (financially and physically) to go back to school.

• You might incur parental displeasure.

• You will spend more for your education the longer you wait.

Whatever the advantages and disadvantages of deferring higher education may be, it's happening more and more.

Not wanting to run the risk of losing the good students who, for a variety of reasons, are waiting before continuing their education, many colleges and universities are formalizing the practice with a "deferred admission" policy. So if you're thinking about taking off a year before starting college, apply anyway in your senior year of high school; just be sure the college knows for what year you're applying for freshman status. Then if you're accepted in the school, you go in the deferred year.

CHOOSING A COLLEGE

If You're Going to College, Where?

With over 3,000 colleges and universities in the United States to choose from, narrowing the choice down to one may seem nearly impossible. But your choices shrink as you begin to make decisions.

Your Interests

If you are fascinated by robots and want to be a robotics specialist, you want to go where there are fine programs in the discipline and not to a small school in Oklahoma. The more unusual your interests, the more quickly your choices narrow. If you want to major in English, that's another story, since almost every college in the country offers an English major. Your choice in that case will be influenced by the fact that the strength of English departments in colleges varies.

Size of the College

Would you feel lost in a university ten times the size of your home town, or would you thrive on the excitement of the hundreds of courses to choose from and activities to participate in? Would you benefit from the attention offered on a campus of 800 undergraduates, or would you feel smothered?

Location of the College

Do you want to live at home and commute? Live away but be close enough to come back for weekends? Fly back during big breaks such as Christmas and end of semester?

Do you want a rural setting; a city school; a college close to, but not in, a big city?

Your Chance of Getting In

It's commendable that now, when you're a junior, you decide to really hit the books. But with straight Cs for two and a half years, realistically what are your chances of getting into Princeton or Stanford? Since high school guidance counselors have a handle on this knowledge, they will know (assessing your grades, test scores, extracurricular activities, special talents, and class rank) with a fair degree of accuracy whether a school is one you can get into easily, one you should be able to get into, one that's a stretch for you but not impossible, and one that's a pipe dream. Don't, however, aim too low and possibly sell yourself short. Colleges do need a mix of personalities—you may do better than you think.

The Cost

The cost is often a key factor in determining where you eventually wind up, so it's important to know where colleges fit in the hierarchy of dollars expended.

	Least Expensive
Public two-year or state college in your own state	living at home
State college in your own state	living at home
State college in another state	living at school
Private two-year college	living at home
Private four-year college	living at home
Private college	living at school
	Most Expensive

Contrary to what most people think, you do not save massive sums by living at home. Dormitory living is relatively inexpensive; you can't eat for much less at home. Also you must figure in the cost of commuting to and from college. So while you will save money living at home instead of on campus, the difference generally will not be more than $600 a year for students attending the same school.

If finances are a major consideration in your choice of college, choose schools in different categories of the hierarchy when working out the college/technical school expense worksheet later in this chapter.

The Law of Supply and Demand Reinterpreted

As financial aid gets tighter, public or state colleges (lower in cost) become more attractive and therefore more competitive. When there is more financial aid available and the economy is booming, private colleges are more attractive and more competitive. Your most important hedge against massive competition for admission to the college of your choice (public or private, since you really can't predict what will be the state of the economy—yours included—when you're ready to apply) is to absorb all you can in high school and have your school record reflect that knowledge.

CHOOSING A VOCATIONAL OR TRADE SCHOOL

As a result of an act passed probably before you were born (the Vocational Education Act of 1963), there has been a tremendous improvement in the quality and quantity of vocational education—public and private. That's because our rapidly changing society (government, industries, businesses) has an ever-growing need for a highly skilled labor force. In fact, the U.S. Labor Department predicts that some trade or technical training will be required for over 50 percent of all jobs by 1985. Responding to that need are over 10,000 vocational or training schools—and more spring up daily.

What Are These Schools?

Vocational and trade schools provide education and training in specific areas, with courses designed to help you on the job. Not all deal in the technical trades. In fact, they run the whole range—from art, music, drama, and dance to pet grooming, kennel management, and civil engineering technology. You must have a high school diploma or its equivalent to enroll in most of the programs.

The length of courses varies from a few months to four years. At the end, a certificate or degree is usually awarded.

An especially important function of the vocational schools has been in the education of paraprofessionals. These workers handle the aspects of a professional's work that do not require full professional training. Paraprofessionals in law, medicine, accounting, engineering, education, and library work, for example, generally can complete their formal training in one or two years.

Is Vocational School What You Want?

Before you decide to enroll in a single-course career education program, make sure you've asked yourself:

• *Am I fairly certain I know what I want to do for a living?* It is folly to enroll in a data processing school only to find out that you're more people oriented than technically oriented.

• *Have I decided that I don't want to take liberal arts courses in addition to the technical training?* It is difficult, though not impossible, to transfer technical or vocational school credits to a four-year college if you decide later on that you want a B.A. or B.S. degree.

• *Am I ready for more practical and less theoretical education?* If you want more hands-on training and less time in the classroom, maybe a technical or vocational school is for you.

• *Have I investigated and made sure there will be jobs available in this field when I finish the schooling?* Best to know if welding is a craft of the past or if it has a hot future *before* you spend the time and the money being trained as a welder.

What to Look For in Choosing a School

Once you've chosen two or three schools which would offer you the vocational training you want, find out:

• *Is the school licensed?* Does it have state authorization to operate as a business? If it doesn't, stop right here. It's a sham.

• *Is the school accredited?* This is a very important factor for two reasons. First, it refers to the quality of the school. If it has received accreditation by the U.S. Office of Education, it means it has met the standards of competency as decided by educators.

Equally important, *only accredited schools can participate in federal aid programs.* Generally, the school's catalogue will prominently display the fact that it is accredited, but if you have any doubt, check your library or write for directories from the National Association of Trade and Technical Schools and the Association of Independent Colleges and Schools (see "Trade and Technical Schools" in Chapter 1).

• *What kinds of courses are available?* They must be up-to-date and of high quality, taught by instructors with professional experience in the career.

• *What equipment and facilities are used?* Again, up-to-date is a key factor. You must be prepared to compete in the job market after you graduate.

• *Does the school help its graduates find jobs?* And, equally important, how successful are the school's graduates? Beware if any school makes excessive claims, such as guaranteeing you a job. Most states have enacted laws prohibiting schools from making job guarantees because this has been an area of widespread abuse. To learn about a school's job placement success, contact recent graduates of the school you're examining. Ask the school for a list of names and addresses of graduates in the field you think will include your future occupation. Get in touch with these graduates. Probe into the training they received and find out how they got their present jobs. If at all possible, speak to their employer(s) to find out if the graduates had been trained with the skills the employer(s) needed. Did the vocational school graduates start with a better salary than that of an on-the-job trainee? Which route does the employer feel provides the best means for advancement?

Avoid Being Taken

Be alert to two areas of abuse which less reputable vocational schools have been known to engage in: downplaying their dropout rates and omitting information about their tuition refund policies.

To be on the safe side:

• Ask the admissions officer how many students actually finished the courses in which you're interested. Be suspicious if the officer hedges, and follow up your inquiry by asking students what their estimates are.

• Be sure you understand the school's refund policy. If you quit after completing only half of the prescribed classes, will you owe the full tuition? (Yes, even if you drop out, if that's what the contract you signed reads.) Or will you get half your money back? If less, how much less?

• Study the school's catalogue closely to see how it compares with the offerings of your nearby community college, adult education programs, public high schools, state vocational training programs, and on-the-job training programs offered by business and industry. Tax-supported educational institutions may offer similar courses of training which are equal to or of even better quality than those of vocational schools.

• Your state's Department of Education will tell you if the schools you are interested in are licensed, and this agency is likely to know if there have been any complaints against these schools. (A list of state agencies for vocational schools follows.)

• Write to the National Association of Trade and Technical Schools (2021 K Street, N.W., Washington, DC 20006), for its directory of accredited schools. Also ask for its brochure *How to Choose a Career—And a Career School,* as well as the *Handbook of Trade and Technical Courses and Training.*

State Agencies for Vocational Schools

Following are the names, addresses, and telephone numbers of the statewide agencies responsible for postsecondary institutions that offer vocational-technical training in forty-eight states and the District of Columbia.

Governing boards are indicated by (G), coordinating boards by (C).

Alabama
Alabama State Department of
  Education
Postsecondary Division
817 South Court Street
Montgomery 36104
(205) 832-3340 (G)

Alaska
Board of Regents
University of Alaska Statewide
  System
Fairbanks 99701
(907) 479-7312 (G)

Arkansas
Department of Education
Division of Vocational, Technical,
  and Adult Education
Arch Ford Education Building
Little Rock 72201
(501) 371-2165 (G)

California
California Advisory Council on
  Vocational Education
708 Tenth Street
Sacramento 95814
(916) 445-0698 (C)

Colorado
State Board for Community
  Colleges and Occupational
  Education
State Services Building
1525 Sherman Street
Denver 80203
(303) 839-3071 (G)

Connecticut
Board of Trustees for State
  Technical College
165 Capitol Avenue
Hartford 06115
(203) 566-3976 (G)

Delaware
Delaware Technical and
  Community College
P.O. Box 897
Dover 19901
(302) 678-4621 (G)

District of Columbia
District of Columbia Commission
  on Postsecondary Education
1329 E Street, N.W.
Washington, DC 20004
(202) 347-5905 (C)

Florida
Florida Department of Education
Division of Vocational Education
Knott Building
Tallahassee 32304
(904) 488-8961 (C)

Georgia
Georgia Department of Education
Office of Vocational Education
237 State Office Building
Atlanta 30334
(404) 656-6711 (C)

Hawaii
University of Hawaii
State Director for Vocational
  Education
Bachman Hall
2444 Dole Street
Honolulu 96822
(808) 948-7461 (C)

Idaho
State Board of Education and Board
  of Regents of the University of
  Idaho
650 West State Street
Boise 98720
(208) 384-3216 (G)

Illinois
Illinois Community College Board
518 Iles Park Place
Springfield 62718
(217) 782-2495 (C)

Indiana
State Board of Vocational and
  Technical Education
401 Illinois Building
17 West Market Street
Indianapolis 46204
(317) 633-7673 (C)

Iowa
Department of Public Instruction
Grimes State Office Building
Des Moines 50319
(515) 281-5331 (C)

Kansas
State Department of Education
Vocational Education
120 East Tenth Street
Topeka 66612
(913) 296-3951 (C)

Kentucky
State Department of Education
Bureau of Vocational Education
Capital Plaza Tower
Frankfort 40601
(502) 564-4286 (G)

Louisiana
State Department of Education
Division of Vocational Education
Department of Education Building
P. O. Box 44064
Baton Rouge 70804
(504) 389-2312 (G)

Maine
Department of Educational and
  Cultural Services
Bureau of Vocational Education
Education Building
Augusta 04333
(207) 289-2621 (G)

Maryland
State Department of Education
Division of Vocational-Technical
  Education
P. O. Box 8717
Baltimore-Washington
  International Airport
Baltimore 21240
(301) 796-8300 (G)

Massachusetts
Board of Education
Bureau of Postsecondary
  Occupational-Technical
  Education
182 Tremont Street
Boston 02111
(617) 727-5738 (G)

Michigan
State Board of Education
P.O. Box 30008
Lansing 48909
(517) 373-3373 (C)

Minnesota
State Department of Education
State Board for Vocational
  Education
Capitol Square Building
550 Cedar Street
St. Paul 55101
(612) 296-3994 (G)

Mississippi
State Department of Education
Division of Junior Colleges
P. O. Box 771
Jackson 39205
(601) 354-6962 (C)

Missouri
Co-ordinating Board for Higher
    Education
Department of Higher Education
600 Clark Avenue
Jefferson City 65101
(314) 751-2361 (C)

Montana
Board of Public Education
State Capitol
Helena 59601
(406) 449-3126 (G)

Nebraska
Nebraska Co-ordinating
    Commission for Postsecondary
    Education
301 Centennial Mall South
Lincoln 68509
(402) 471-2332 (C)

New Hampshire
State Department of Education
Division of Postsecondary
    Education
163 Loudon Road
Concord 03301
(603) 271-2722 (G)

New Jersey
Department of Education
Division of Vocational Education
225 West State Street
Trenton 08625
(609) 292-6340 (C)

New Mexico
Board of Educational Finance
Legislative Executive Building
Santa Fe 87503
(505) 827-2115 (C)

New York
Regents of the University of the
    State of New York
State Education Department
Albany 12234
(518) 474-5880 (G)

North Carolina
State Board of Education
Department of Community
    Colleges
Education Building
Raleigh 27611
(919) 733-7051 (G)

North Dakota
North Dakota State Board of Higher
    Education
State Capitol Building
Bismarck 58505
(701) 224-2960 (G)

Ohio
Ohio Board of Regents
30 East Broad Street
Columbus 43215
(614) 466-5810 (C)

Oklahoma
Oklahoma State Regents for Higher
    Education
500 Education Building
State Capitol Complex
Oklahoma City 73105
(405) 521-2444 (C)

Oregon
Oregon Department of Education
Division of Community Colleges
942 Lancaster Drive, N.E.
Salem 97310
(503) 378-8609 (C)

Pennsylvania
State Board of Education
Box 911
Harrisburg 17126
(717) 787-5530 (G)

Rhode Island
Rhode Island Junior College State
    System
400 East Avenue
Warwick 02886
(401) 825-2188 (C)

South Carolina
State Board for Technical and
    Comprehensive Education
Rutledge Building
1429 Senate Street
Columbia 29201
(803) 758-6915 (G)

South Dakota
State Board of Vocational Education
State Office Building #3
Pierre 57501
(605) 224-3423 (G)

Tennessee
Department of Education
Division of Vocational-Technical
    Education
200 Cordell Hull Building
Nashville 37219
(615) 741-1716 (G)

Texas
State Department of Education
Department of Occupational
    Education
201 East Eleventh Street
Austin 78701
(512) 475-2585 (G)

Utah
State Board of Regents
807 East South Temple Street
Salt Lake City 84102
(801) 533-5617 (G)

Vermont
Vermont State Colleges Board of
    Trustees
322 South Prospect Street
Burlington 05401
(802) 864-0241 (G)

Virginia
Community College System
P. O. Box 1558
Richmond 23212
(804) 786-2231 (G)

Washington
Commission for Vocational
    Education
Airdustrial Park
Olympia 98504
(206) 753-5662 (G)

West Virginia
State Department of Education
Bureau of Vocational, Technical,
    and Adult Education
B221 State Capitol Complex,
    Building 6
Charleston 25305
(304) 348-2346 (C)

Wisconsin
Wisconsin Board of Vocational,
   Technical, and Adult Education
4802 Sheboygan Avenue
Madison 53703
(608) 266-1207 (G)

Wyoming
Community College Commission
New Boyd Building
1720 Carey Avenue
Cheyenne 82002
(307) 777-7764 (C)

HOW TO COMPARE COLLEGE AND
TECHNICAL SCHOOL COSTS

After you have made the basic choice of what type of college or
school you want to attend, write to the institution for details. Ask
each for catalogues and all available material on local living costs,
financial aid programs, and the like.

Sample Letter

                                             Date

Dean of Admissions
Voyagers School
Drake, New Hampshire 12345

Dear Dean:

I am a junior at Oakridge High School and will graduate in 1985.
Please send me a catalogue, an application for admission, and
any other material about your school which I might find helpful
in making my post-high school graduation plans.

If a representative of your school will be visiting in this area in
the near future, please notify me and tell me how I can make arrangements for an interview.

                                             Sincerely,

Now, using the material that the school sends you plus the estimates of other costs that you and your parents make, fill out the fol-

lowing financial worksheet to give yourself an idea of what a year's total expenses will be.

Three tips: Add 10 percent a year for the second year, 10 percent a year for the third year, and 10 percent for the fourth year to take inflation and other price-boosting factors into account. If this percentage is an exaggeration, fine. Don't underestimate and be surprised later on. Remember your eligibility for assistance is greater at schools with higher costs.

College/Technical School Expense Worksheet

Use the following expense worksheet to estimate and compare college/technical school costs.

Annual Expense Item	School A	School B	School C
Tuition			
All fees (student activity, library application, breakage, etc.)			
Room and board			
Books			
Equipment and supplies			
Laboratory charges			
Travel to and from school			
All other travel			
Recreation and entertainment			
Clothing			
Laundry, dry cleaning, etc.			
Dues for fraternity or sorority			
Grooming (cosmetics, haircuts, etc.)			
Health expenditures (include insurance premiums)			
Snacks, cigarettes, etc.			
Church and charity contributions			
Your capital expenditures, prorated annually (car, bicycle, record player and records, musical instruments, sports equipment, etc.)			
Miscellaneous current expenses			
Total annual estimate			

WHO NEEDS FINANCIAL ASSISTANCE?

Just about everyone who goes to college or vocational school after high school could use a little financial help; some need substantial amounts. Don't feel embarrassed about that need or allow your parents to feel guilty that they couldn't save enough for your education. At most colleges at least *50 percent* of the students are getting some financial help; at a few that proportion is as high as 80 percent.

Need was never more acute than at the beginning of the 1980s when college costs shot up an average of 14 percent annually and federal assistance programs, which had been growing yearly, were sharply curtailed. I suspect that as in most instances when there is radical change, the pendulum will swing back. Government leaders will once again understand that this country's future is dependent on a well-educated populace and not just a well-educated elite, and federal assistance programs will be viewed as a necessary expenditure and not a budgetary frill.

How much assistance you can get from the government (the single largest supplier of financial aid to students) depends on where we are in the swing, and our position changes yearly. It also depends on how great your need for money is. (Need is not only dependent on what your family and you earn and have in assets; it also is dependent upon the costs of the school you want to attend.)

It is true, though, in this as in other financial matters, that middle-income families feel the cost of higher education most painfully.

A Word about Forms—Before You Start to Fill Them Out

For most of us, filling out forms provides more opportunity for error than trying to solve Rubik's Cube.

Did you ever:

- Put your last name where your first should be?
- Fill in your address only to realize later you wrote it on the wrong line?
- Feel confused because the application asked for your age and your next birthday was in twelve days?

And that's just the simple material! When applications call for calculation, written data, or thoughtful expository, they're even more forbidding.

How can you conquer the natural fear of forms?

• Set aside sufficient quiet time to read through the form point by point in its entirety before you begin to write anything.

• Read directions carefully. Don't be embarrassed about reading them aloud. Often hearing something helps to understand it better.

• Ask a parent to sit down with you—especially when you're filling out a financial aid form. But no matter what the form, if you feel skittish, it's a good idea to have another person with you in the beginning.

• Have at least *two* forms available. The first is for pencil practice. The other is the real thing. Don't think you're doubling the time spent by doing the form twice. You're not. With apologies to Einstein, in the case of forms $E = (MP)^2$—Energy put into filling out forms = $(Mistakes in Pen)^2$.

About Acronyms and Abbreviations

Just for fun, I underlined the acronyms and abbreviations mentioned on the first two pages of the Financial Aid Form for 1982–83: FAF, CSS, ACR, ED, SEOG, CWS, NDSL, GSL, SAR, SAI, CFR —11 in all. How can anyone short of a financial aid officer remember what these stand for?

For sanity, I used a gimmick similar to one you probably have used when trying to sort out characters in a Russian novel. I listed each acronym and abbreviation and its meaning in alphabetical order for quick reference. It saved much frustration and time as I read on.

How Do You Know if You Qualify for Financial Aid?

There are agencies which help you determine how much you and your family are expected to contribute to your schooling. The American College Testing Program's Family Financial Statement (FFS) and the College Scholarship Service's Financial Aid Form (FAF) are two of the best known. Others include the U.S. Department of Education's Application for Federal Student Aid (AFSA); the Pennsylvania Higher Education Assistance Application (PHEAA), and the Student Aid Application for California (SAAC).

If you use a form other than the AFSA and you want to be considered for federal aid, you have to check a box to have your data sent to the Department of Education. Do it. In addition to providing you with an estimate of what you and your family are expected to contribute to your education, the agency will send its calculations to the schools of your choice.

Warning: Though the agencies determine your family contribution, they have no control over whether your need is met. (Need is the difference between what your family can pay and cost of attendance at a particular institution.) The schools and the predetermined formulas make this determination. *But the needs analysis form is the basis for all federal and most state and college determinations, so it is very important.*

Here's how it works.

Filling Out the Needs Analysis Form

1. After you know which schools you're applying to, go to your high school guidance office and pick up *two* aid forms. (Remember that one is for penciling; one for real.)

2. Gather the following personal and family records for the past year before you begin the chore.

- U.S. income tax return
- State and local tax returns
- Records of nontaxable income, such as veterans, Social Security, or welfare benefits
- W-2 and other records of money earned last year
- Current bank statements
- Current mortgage information
- Records of medical and dental bills
- Business and farm records

3. Do not worry in advance that your personal situation is so unusual that you won't be able to fill out the form. The form has clear instructions about what to do if your parents are separated, divorced, remarried; if one of your parents is dead; if you are consid-

ered an independent student (not dependent on parents for support or lodging).

4. Make certain you include all the special conditions which have a bearing on your family's ability to pay because of their drain on family resources.

- Number of children in the family
- Number of children in post–high school institutions
- Family illnesses
- Family disabilities
- Unemployment
- Changes in employment for working parents (such as loss of overtime, loss of full-time job)
- Extra dependents
- Debts

5. Assure your parents of two things:

a. The form is confidential and will be sent only to those schools you authorize. However, the U.S. Department of Education can check the information on it through a validation process, which means you might have to show a financial aid administrator the income tax returns and other material on which you based your calculations. So make certain the information provided is accurate.

b. Up to $25,000 of home equity is not counted in the formula used to compute a family's contribution to costs, so your parents shouldn't feel that just because they own a house, you'll never get aid (or that they might have to sell it if you are to continue your education).

The sooner you mail in the needs analysis form, the sooner you'll know how much you need, how much the schools of your choice can provide for you, and finally (whew!), you'll know where you'll be going to school after your senior year.

If you're not yet a senior, you might want to do some early planning. The Early Financial Aid Planning Service can give you a computerized *estimate* of your eligibility for aid from several different sources, plus a comprehensive picture of your family's financial situation in relation to costs and aid funds. It is *not* sent to colleges. It also outlines some steps to help you develop your own personal financing strategy. Ask your guidance counselor for more information, or write to Early Financial Aid Planning (Department 1978,

Box 2843, Princeton, NJ 08541). Repeat: this service is *not* for seniors.

A Cause for Your Discontent—An Important One to Voice

Until the early 1980s, a candidate's need for financial aid was never part of the admissions process of a school. You applied to a college, university, or vocational school, were accepted on your merits, and then, separate and apart, the financial aid administrator of the school would work out an assistance plan which might (or might not) cover your needs.

But as federal aid to education began shrinking in the early 1980s, some private schools admitted they were looking not only at a student's record when they were choosing people for admission; they were also looking at the student's ability to pay. With schooling costs going up and a government policy shifting away from grants and low-interest loans, there was less money to distribute even though there was greater need. The private colleges were in a bind. High school counselors reported that admissions patterns shifted in these troubled educational times. A talented young person who needed a tremendous amount of financial aid would either be rejected immediately by a school which, during a different economic time, he/she could get into easily, or the student would be accepted and then get no financial aid—the theory being that with $10,000 to distribute, it was better to give $1,000 to each of ten less needy people than to give $10,000 to one very needy student.

The tying of admissions to aid may be a necessary evil for colleges in some instances. The *reason* they may have to do this isn't a necessary evil, though.

It is shameful that this country would allow such massive cutbacks in the field of educational aid. If you're looking for a cause worthy of support which directly affects you, make yourself heard on this one.

WHERE DO YOU GET FINANCIAL AID?

What Is Available?

Financial aid comes from four main sources:

The largest resource

The federal government
The state governments
The college or vocational school
Community or private groups

The smallest resource

And it comes in four basic forms:

- *Grants.* Based on *need* and *do not have to be repaid.*
- *Scholarships.* Based on *talent, ability,* or *need* and *do not have to be repaid.*
- *Loans.* Interest rates and starting dates for repayment vary depending on the loan program under which you are borrowing, but one certainty is loans *must be repaid.*
- *Jobs.* Work and earn while going to school.

Chances are that when you apply to the college or school for financial aid (because the college or school administers most of the financial aid that is available), and you need more than a few hundred dollars, you will get an aid *package.* This will be a combination of two or more of the basic forms possibly from two or more of the basic sources.

It's similar to ordering from a menu in a Chinese restaurant. As much as everyone would like all financial aid in grants or scholarships (the Column A selections), chances are a loan and/or a job (Column B choices) will also be included in the package. That's because financial aid administrators like to present a "balanced package." Many administrators feel that it is important for a student to assume the responsibility of a little work and/or a loan in addition to the "free" grant aid.

What might a balanced package look like?

Financial Aid Package

Consider a four-person family, one earner with two children, one in college. The breadwinner earns $35,000 a year and the family has limited assets.

The college-age child is accepted and wants to go to a private university where total expenses are expected to run $12,000 yearly.

Yearly college expenses		$12,000
The family's expected contribution as defined in the needs analysis	$3,200	
The student's expected contribution	$ 900	
	$4,100	$ 4,100
	Need	$ 7,900
Loan (interest free during in-school period)	$2,000	
Job (requires 12–15 hours a week)	$1,400	
Grants (from university, state, and federal sources)	$4,000	
	Total Aid	$ 7,400
	Unmet Need	
(could be met by other loans or other cost-cutting strategies)		$ 500

Federal Government Programs

The U. S. Government can be fickle. Programs change yearly. So does the funding for these programs. So does the eligibility requirement. What that means is that while the following are the five major federal programs in the early 1980s, they may not be current when you read this book. Check with your guidance counselor.

While it is important to know what is available and what each of these programs means, you don't really have a choice (except for loans). Financial aid packages are put together by the school and depend on your need, the amount of money the school has to distribute, and how much it wants you as a student.

Pell Grants

The largest of all the federal student aid programs ($2.2 billion spent in 1982–83), Pell Grants provide the basis of financial aid for millions of students. There is no subjective judgment attached to these. The Department of Education uses a standard formula to evaluate the information on your student aid (needs analysis) application. Need is the key to this grant. Even though the formula might become more restrictive if there is less money appropriated for Pell Grants, it nonetheless guarantees equal treatment for all applicants, so, except for a few special cases, no exceptions are made for unique financial circumstances. How much you are awarded is based on your need, how much funding the program has, and whether you are a full- or part-time student.

Supplemental Educational Opportunity Grants (SEOG)

Like the Pell, the SEOG is also a grant dependent on need. But here's the difference: the Pell Grant is an entitlement. If you qualify for it, you get it. Depending upon the criteria the government sets for itself, it can award two dozen or two billion. Not so with SEOG —there are no guarantees. Each year, a school gets an amount of money from the Department of Education to use for SEOGs. Once that money has been spent, that's it.

College Work-Study Programs

A work-study program provides you with a job in the public interest so you can earn money to pay for part of your schooling expenses. The number of hours you work depends upon your financial need, how much money the school has for the program, and what sort of package the financial aid administrator has developed for you. The government provides up to 80 percent of the salaries of those students who qualify for jobs. Many of the jobs are right on campus, but even those that are not are still for a public or private nonprofit agency and in the public interest.

National Direct Student Loans (NDSL)

The NDSL program has the lowest interest rate around. (In the early 1980s, it was 5 percent.) The loan is made through the financial aid office at your school. Need is the key factor in determining who is eligible for a NDSL.

Of course, the loan must be paid back. But payment does not begin until six months after you graduate, leave school, or drop below half-time status, and then you have ten years in which to repay.

How much you can borrow, when to apply, when payment can be postponed (and even in certain circumstances canceled) are all questions you should ask the financial aid administrator at your school.

Guaranteed Student Loans (GSL)

This is a low-interest loan made to you through a bank or credit union. It's insured by either the federal government or the guarantee agency in your state. The interest at the start of the 1980s was 9 percent, but it can change. If your family income is over $30,000, you have to show need. Also there is a 5 percent origination fee added to the cost of the loan, and talk about raising the fee to 10 percent.

You cannot borrow more than the cost of attendance minus any other financial aid you receive. The maximum you can borrow as an undergraduate is $2,500 per year; and as a graduate student, $5,000 per year (some states have lower totals.) As an undergraduate the total debt you can have outstanding is $12,500; as a graduate student, $25,000, which includes any loans made as an undergraduate.

Since banks and other lenders voluntarily take part in GSL, they might restrict or limit the amount of money in GSL because the administration of the program is cumbersome and costly (but don't worry about the banks losing money on this: they don't!). They cannot, however, discriminate to whom they lend money on the basis of an applicant's race, religion, national origin, sex, age, marital status, or because the applicant is receiving public assistance or has exercised certain consumer rights.

For sources of information on Guaranteed Student Loans, see the list after the following state aid section.

PLUS Loans (Parent Loans for Undergraduate Students)

PLUS loans provide additional funds for educational costs. Like GSLs, they are made by a lender such as a bank, credit union, or savings and loan association. Early in the decade, the interest rate was 12 percent.

PLUS loans are available to students at all income levels. Parents of dependent undergraduates can borrow up to $3,000 each year, and graduate students themselves can borrow up to the same amount. Independent undergraduates can borrow only up to $2,500 per year, and the PLUS loan, combined with any GSL, cannot exceed the yearly and total GSL limits.

Note that borrowers must begin repaying a PLUS loan within 60 days of receiving the loan. If, however, you are a full-time student or on active military duty, you are entitled to a deferment of principal payments; parent borrowers do not get a deferment based on their child's educational status. And all borrowers must begin paying the interest within 60 days unless the lender agrees to allow the interest to accrue until the deferment ends.

Participation in the PLUS program varies from state to state, so contact your guidance counselor, financial aid office, or state guarantee agency to find out whether you might obtain one.

State Programs

Our fifty states collectively administer about $1 billion in student aid a year, so whether or not you qualify for financial aid from federal programs, apply for help from your home state.

Most of the time state aid is available only to resident students going to schools within the state. However, before you count yourself out of the state picture, check this. Some states make exceptions and have programs which help state residents going to other states or non-state residents who are educated within their boundaries.

The State Student Incentive Grant Program (SSIG)

The SSIG, through which the federal government matches the state grant to students, has become an increasingly important source of help since 1972. It makes up about 8 percent of the state aid available. In the early 1980s, all states shared over $75 million in SSIG funds yearly.

This money is also distributed on the basis of need. To save time and to reduce the number of forms you fill out, ask the state scholarship agency, your guidance counselor, or the college financial aid administrator if you can use the same form that you used to apply for federal and college money.

Since each state is fairly autonomous in the way it distributes its SSIG money, when you contact the state scholarship agency in the capital of your state, ask at least the following questions:

- Can part-time and half-time students get awards?
- Can the money be used at both private and public colleges?
- Can the money be used for vocational schooling?

- Can grants be used at colleges out of my home state?
- When is the application deadline?
- What are the requirements for eligibility?

The Folks in the Know

Of all people, two of the wisest to consult about financial aid are your high school guidance counselor (before you decide where you want to go to continue your education) and then the financial aid administrator at the school you finally select. These are experts; they must keep with up changing legislation (that's their job), and they're problem-solvers, especially the financial aid administrator, who knows how to develop the best (and most tempting, if the school wants to woo you) package for you. They are "people people," so don't be shy about sharing your concerns and problems with them.

Sources of Information on Guaranteed Student Loans and State Student Aid*

Alabama
ALABAMA COMMISSION ON
  HIGHER EDUCATION
1 Court Square, Suite 221
Montgomery, Alabama 36197
GSL and State Aid
(205) 832-3790

Alaska
ALASKA COMMISSION ON
  POSTSECONDARY
  EDUCATION
400 Willoughby Avenue
Pouch FP
Juneau, Alaska 99801
GSL and State Aid
(907) 465-2962

Arizona
GSL: ARIZONA EDUCATIONAL
  LOAN PROGRAM
301 East Virginia Avenue
Phoenix, Arizona 85004
(602) 252-5793

State Aid: ARIZONA
COMMISSION FOR POST-
  SECONDARY EDUCATION
1937 West Jefferson
Phoenix, Arizona 85009
(602) 255-3109

Arkansas
GSL: STUDENT LOAN
  GUARANTEE FOUNDATIONS
  OF ARKANSAS
1515 West 7th Street—Suite 515
Little Rock, Arkansas 72202
(501) 371-2634

*Government Publication No. E-81-15001

State Aid: DEPARTMENT OF
HIGHER EDUCATION
1301 West Seventh Street
Little Rock, Arkansas 72201
(501) 371-1441 Ext. 56

California
CALIFORNIA STUDENT AID
COMMISSION
1410 Fifth Street
Sacramento, California 95814
GSL (916) 322-0435
State Aid (916) 445-0880

Colorado
GSL: COLORADO
GUARANTEED STUDENT
LOAN PROGRAM
7000 N. Broadway, Suite 100
Denver, Colorado 80221
(303) 427-0259

State Aid: COLORADO
COMMISSION ON HIGHER
EDUCATION
1550 Lincoln Street, Room 210
Denver, Colorado 80203
(303) 866-2748

Connecticut
GSL: CONNECTICUT STUDENT
LOAN FOUNDATION
25 Pratt Street
Hartford, Connecticut 06103
(203) 547-1510

State Aid: CONNECTICUT
BOARD OF HIGHER
EDUCATION
61 Woodland Street
Hartford, Connecticut 06105
(203) 566-6218

Delaware
GSL: DELAWARE HIGHER
EDUCATION LOAN
PROGRAM
c/o Brandywine College
Post Office Box 7139
Wilmington, Delaware 19803
(302) 478-3000 Ext. 201

State Aid: DELAWARE
POSTSECONDARY EDUCATION
COMMISSION
Carvel State Office Building
220 French Street
Wilmington, Delaware 19801
(302) 571-3240

District of Columbia
GSL: HIGHER EDUCATION
ASSISTANCE FOUNDATION
HIGHER EDUCATION LOAN
PROGRAM (HELP) OF D.C.,
INC.
1001 Connecticut Avenue, N.W.
Suite 825
Washington, D.C. 20036
(202) 861-0701

State Aid: OFFICE OF STATE
EDUCATION AFFAIRS
614 H Street, N.W.
8th Floor, Room 817
Washington, D.C. 20001
(207) 727-3688

Florida
FLORIDA STUDENT FINANCIAL
ASSISTANCE COMMISSION
Knott Building
Tallahassee, Florida 32301
GSL and State Aid:
(904) 487-1800

Georgia
GEORGIA HIGHER EDUCATION
　ASSISTANCE CORPORATION
9 LaVista Perimeter Park
2187 Northlake Parkway
Suite 110
Tucker, Georgia 30084
GSL: (404) 393-7241
State Aid: (404) 393-7253

Hawaii
GSL: HAWAII EDUCATION
　LOAN PROGRAM
1314 South King Street, Suite 603
Honolulu, Hawaii 96814
(808) 536-3731

State Aid: STATE
POSTSECONDARY EDUCATION
　COMMISSION
124F Bachman Hall, University of
　Hawaii
2444 Dole Street
Honolulu, Hawaii 96822
(808) 948-6862

Idaho
GSL: STUDENT LOAN FUND OF
　IDAHO, INC.
Processing Center
Route 2, North Whitley Drive
Fruitland, Idaho 83619
(208) 452-4058

State Aid: OFFICE OF STATE
　BOARD OF EDUCATION
650 West State Street, Room 307
Boise, Idaho 83720
(208) 334-2270

Illinois
GSL: ILLINOIS GUARANTEED
　LOAN PROGRAM
102 Wilmot Road
Deerfield, Illinois 60015
(312) 945-7040

State Aid: ILLINOIS STATE
　SCHOLARSHIP COMMISSION
102 Wilmot Road
Deerfield, Illinois 60015
(312) 948-8550

Indiana
STATE STUDENT ASSISTANCE
　COMMISSION OF INDIANA
219 North Senate Avenue
1st Floor
Indianapolis, Indiana 46202
GSL: (317) 232-2366
State Aid: (317) 232-2351

Iowa
IOWA COLLEGE AND COMMIS-
　SION
201 Jewett Building
9th and Grand
Des Moines, Iowa 50309
GSL: (515) 281-8537
State Aid: (515) 281-3501

Kansas
GSL: HIGHER EDUCATION AS-
　SISTANCE FOUNDATION
34 Corporate Woods
10950 Grand View Drive
Overland Park, Kansas 66210
(913) 648-4255

State Aid: BOARD OF REGENTS—
　STATE OF KANSAS
1416 Merchants National Bank
Topeka, Kansas 66612
(913) 296-3421

Kentucky
KENTUCKY HIGHER EDUCA-
　TION ASSISTANCE
　AUTHORITY
1050 U.S. 127 South
West Frankfort Office Complex
Frankfort, Kentucky 40601
GSL and State Aid:
(502) 564-7990

Louisiana
GOVERNOR'S SPECIAL COM-
MISSION ON EDUCATION
SERVICES
4637 Jamestown Street
Post Office Box 44127
Baton Rouge, Louisiana 70804
GSL and State Aid:
(504) 925-3630

Maine
STATE DEPARTMENT OF
EDUCATIONAL AND
CULTURAL SERVICES
Division of Higher Education
Services
State House Station 23
Augusta, Maine 04333
GSL and State Aid:
(207) 289-2183

Maryland
GSL: MARYLAND HIGHER
EDUCATION LOAN
CORPORATION
2100 Guilford Avenue
Baltimore, Maryland 21218
(301) 659-6555

State Aid: MARYLAND STATE
SCHOLARSHIP BOARD
2100 Guilford Avenue
Baltimore, Maryland 21218
(301) 659-6420

Massachusetts
GSL: MASSACHUSETTS
HIGHER EDUCATION ASSIS-
TANCE CORPORATION
330 Stuart Street
Boston, Massachusetts 02116
(617) 426-9796

State Aid: MASSACHUSETTS
BOARD OF REGENTS OF
HIGHER EDUCATION
Scholarship Office
330 Stuart Street
Boston, Massachusetts 02116
(617) 727-9420

Michigan
GSL: MICHIGAN DEPARTMENT
OF EDUCATION
Guaranteed Student Loan
Program
Box 30047
Lansing, Michigan 48909
(517) 373-0760

State Aid: MICHIGAN
DEPARTMENT OF EDUCA-
TION
Post Office Box 30008
Lansing, Michigan 48909
(517) 373-3394

Minnesota
GSL: HIGHER EDUCATION AS-
SISTANCE FOUNDATION
900 American National Park Build-
ing
Fifth and Minnesota Streets
St. Paul, Minnesota 55101
(612) 227-7661

State Aid: MINNESOTA HIGHER
EDUCATION COORDINATING
BOARD
400 Capitol Square
550 Cedar Street
St. Paul, Minnesota 55101
(612) 296-3074

Mississippi
GSL: STUDENT FINANCIAL
ASSISTANCE
U.S. DEPARTMENT OF
EDUCATION
101 Marietta Tower—Suite 423
Atlanta, Georgia 30323
(404) 221-5658

State Aid: MISSISSIPPI POST-
SECONDARY EDUCATION
FINANCIAL ASSISTANCE
BOARD
Post Office Box 2336
Jackson, Mississippi 39205
(601) 982-6168

Missouri
GSL: MISSOURI DEPARTMENT
  OF HIGHER EDUCATION
Post Office Box 1437
Jefferson City, Missouri 65102
(314) 751-3940

State Aid: MISSOURI
  DEPARTMENT OF HIGHER
  EDUCATION
P.O. Box 1437
Jefferson City, Missouri 65102
(601) 751-3940

Montana
GSL and State Aid: MONTANA
  UNIVERSITY SYSTEM
33 South Last Chance Gulch
Helena, Montana 59601
(406) 449-3024

Nebraska
HIGHER EDUCATION
  ASISTANCE FOUNDATION
Cornhusker Bank Building
11th and Cornhusker Highway
Suite 304
Lincoln, Nebraska 68521
(402) 476-9129

State Aid: NEBRASKA COORDI-
  NATING COMMISSION FOR
  POSTSECONDARY EDUCA-
  TION
301 Centennial Mall South
Post Office Box 95005
Lincoln, Nebraska 68509
(402) 471-2647

Nevada
GSL: NEVADA STATE DEPART-
  MENT OF EDUCATION
400 West King Street
Carson City, Nevada 89710
(702) 885-3107

State Aid: UNIVERSITY OF
  NEVADA SYSTEM
405 Marsh Avenue
Reno, Nevada 89509
(702) 784-4666

New Hampshire
GSL: NEW HAMPSHIRE HIGHER
  EDUCATION ASSISTANCE
  FOUNDATION
143 North Main Street
P.O. Box 677
Concord, New Hampshire 03301
(603) 225-6612

State Aid: NEW HAMPSHIRE
  POSTSECONDARY EDUCA-
  TION COMMISSION
61 South Spring Street
Concord, New Hampshire 03301
(603) 271-2555

New Jersey
GSL: NEW JERSEY HIGHER
  EDUCATION ASSISTANCE
  AUTHORITY
C. N. 00538
Trenton, New Jersey 08638
(609) 292-3906

State Aid: DEPARTMENT OF
  HIGHER EDUCATION
Office of Student Assistance
Number 4 Quakerbridge Plaza
C. N. 540
Trenton, New Jersey 08625
(609) 292-4646

New Mexico
GSL: NEW MEXICO
  EDUCATIONAL ASSISTANCE
  FOUNDATION
2301 Yale S.E., Building F
Albuquerque, New Mexico 87106
(505) 277-6304

State Aid: BOARD OF
EDUCATION FINANCE
1068 Cerrillos Road
Santa Fe, New Mexico 87503
(505) 827-5017

New York
NEW YORK STATE HIGHER
EDUCATION SERVICES
CORPORATION
99 Washington Ave.
Albany, New York 12255
GSL: (518) 473-1574
State Aid: (518) 474-5642

North Carolina
NORTH CAROLINA STATE
EDUCATION ASSISTANCE
AUTHORITY
Post Office Box 2688
Chapel Hill, North Carolina 27514
GSL and State Aid: (919) 473-1688

North Dakota
GSL: STUDENT FINANCIAL
ASSISTANCE DEPARTMENT
OF EDUCATION
11037 Federal Office Building
19th and Stout Streets
Denver, Colorado 80294
(303) 837-3676

State Aid: NORTH DAKOTA
STUDENT FINANCIAL
ASSISTANCE PROGRAM
10th Floor, State Capitol
Bismarck, North Dakota 58505
(701) 224-4114

Ohio
GSL: OHIO STUDENT LOAN
COMMISSION
P.O. Box 16610
Columbus, Ohio 43216
(614) 466-3091

State Aid: OHIO BOARD OF RE-
GENTS
3600 State Office Tower
30 East Broad Street
Columbus, Ohio 43215
(614) 466-7420

Oklahoma
OKLAHOMA STATE REGENTS
FOR HIGHER EDUCATION
500 Education Building
State Capitol Complex
Oklahoma City, Oklahoma 73105
GSL and State Aid: (405) 521-8262

Oregon
OREGON STATE SCHOLARSHIP
COMMISSION
1445 Willamette Street
Eugene, Oregon 97401
GSL: (800) 452-8807 (within OR),
(503) 686-3200
State Aid: (503) 686-4166

Pennsylvania
PENNSYLVANIA HIGHER
EDUCATION ASSISTANCE
AGENCY
660 Boas Street
Harrisburg, Pennsylvania 17102
GSL: (800) 692-7392 (within PA),
(717) 787-1932
State Aid: (800) 692-7435 (within
PA), (717) 787-1937

Rhode Island
RHODE ISLAND HIGHER
EDUCATION ASSISTANCE
AUTHORITY
274 Weybosset Street
Providence, Rhode Island 02903
GSL and State Aid: (401) 277-2050

South Carolina
GSL: SOUTH CAROLINA
    STUDENT LOAN
    CORPORATION
Interstate Center, Suite 210
P.O. Box 21337
Columbia, South Carolina 29221
(803) 798-0916

State Aid: HIGHER EDUCATION
    TUITION GRANTS AGENCY
411 Keenan Building, Box 11638
Columbia, South Carolina 29211
(803) 758-7070

South Dakota
GSL: SOUTH DAKOTA
    EDUCATION ASSISTANCE
    CORPORATION
105 First Ave. SW
Aberdeen, South Dakota 57401
(605) 225-6423

State Aid: DEPARTMENT OF ED-
    UCATION AND CULTURAL
    AFFAIRS
Richard F. Kneip Building
Pierre, South Dakota 57501
(605) 773-3134

Tennessee
TENNESSEE STUDENT ASSIS-
    TANCE CORPORATION
B-3 Capitol Towers—Suite 9
Nashville, Tennessee 37219
GSL and State Aid:
    (800) 342-1663 (within TN),
    (615) 741-1346

Texas
GSL: TEXAS GUARANTEED STU-
    DENT LOAN CORPORATION
Champion Tower, Suite 510
Austin, Texas 78752
(512) 835-1900

State Aid: COORDINATING
    BOARD TEXAS COLLEGE AND
    UNIVERSITY SYSTEM
P.O. Box 12788, Capitol Station
Austin, Texas 78711
(512) 475-8169

Utah
GSL: UTAH EDUCATION LOAN
    SERVICE
1800 South West Temple
Suite 101
Salt Lake City, Utah 84108
(801) 486-5921

State Aid: UTAH STATE BOARD
    OF REGENTS
807 East South Temple
Suite 204
Salt Lake City, Utah 84102
(801) 533-5617

Vermont
VERMONT STUDENT
    ASSISTANCE CORPORATION
5 Burlington Square
Burlington, Vermont 05401
GSL and State Aid:
    (800) 642-3177 (within VT)
    (802) 658-4530

Virginia
GSL: VIRGINIA STATE
    EDUCATION ASSISTANCE
    AUTHORITY
6 North Sixth Street
Suite 400
Richmond, Virginia 23219
(804) 786-2035

State Aid: STATE COUNCIL OF
    HIGHER EDUCATION FOR
    VIRGINIA
James Monroe Building
101 N. 14th Street
Richmond, Virginia 23219
(804) 225-2141

Washington

GSL: WASHINGTON STUDENT LOAN GUARANTY ASSOCIATION
100 South King Street, Suite 560
Westland Building
Seattle, Washington 98104
(206) 625-1030

State Aid: COUNCIL FOR POST-SECONDARY EDUCATION
908 East Fifth Avenue
Olympia, Washington 98504
(206) 753-3571

West Virginia

GSL: HIGHER EDUCATION ASSISTANCE FOUNDATION
HIGHER EDUCATION LOAN PROGRAM OF WEST VIRGINIA INC.
P.O. Box 591
Union Building, Suite 900
723 Kanawha Boulevard East
Charleston, West Virginia 25322
(304) 345-7211

State Aid: WEST VIRGINIA BOARD OF REGENTS
950 Kanawha Boulevard East
Charleston, West Virginia 25301
(304) 348-0112

Wisconsin

GSL: WISCONSIN HIGHER EDUCATION CORPORATION
137 East Wilson Street
Madison, Wisconsin 53702
(608) 266-1653

State Aid: WISCONSIN HIGHER EDUCATIONAL AIDS BOARD
P.O. Box 7858
Madison, Wisconsin 53707
(608) 266-2897

Wyoming

GSL: HIGHER EDUCATION ASSISTANCE FOUNDATION
American National Bank Building
20 Street at Capitol, Suite 320
Cheyenne, Wyoming 82001
(307) 635-3259

State Aid: WYOMING COMMUNITY COLLEGE COMMISSION
1720 Carey Avenue
Boyd Building, Fifth Floor
Cheyenne, Wyoming 82002
(307) 777-7763

American Samoa

GSL: STUDENT FINANCIAL ASSISTANCE
U.S. DEPARTMENT OF EDUCATION
50 United Nations Plaza, Rm. 250
San Francisco, California
(415) 556-0137

State Aid: DEPARTMENT OF EDUCATION, GOVERNMENT OF AMERICAN SAMOA
Pago Pago, American Samoa 96799
(Overseas) 633-4256

Commonwealth of the Northern Mariana Islands

GSL: See American Samoa

State Aid: DEPARTMENT OF EDUCATION, COMMONWEALTH OF THE NORTHERN MARIANA ISLANDS
Saipan, Mariana Islands 96950
(Saipan) 9812/9311

Guam

GSL: See American Samoa

State Aid: UNIVERSITY OF GUAM
Post Office Box EK
Agana, Guam 96910
(734) 2177

Puerto Rico
GSL: STUDENT FINANCIAL
 ASSISTANCE
U.S. DEPARTMENT OF
 EDUCATION
26 Federal Plaza
New York, New York 10007
(212) 264-4022

State Aid: COUNCIL ON HIGHER
 EDUCATION
BOX F-UPR Station
Rio Piedras, Puerto Rico 00931
(809) 751-5082/1136

Trust Territory of the Pacific Islands and Wake Island
GSL: See American Samoa

State Aid: OFFICE OF THE HIGH
 COMMISSIONER, TRUST
 TERRITORY OF THE
 PACIFIC ISLANDS
Saipan, Mariana Islands 96950
(Saipan) 9870

Virgin Islands
BOARD OF EDUCATION
P.O. Box 9128
St. Thomas, Virgin Islands 00801
GSL and State Aid:
 (809) 774-4546

USAF, INC.
California only: (800) 227-3037
Alaska and Hawaii: (800) 428-5390
Indiana: (800) 382-4506
All other states: (800) 428-9250
UNITED STUDENT AID FUNDS
 PROCESSING CENTER
P.O. Box 50827
Indianapolis, Indiana 46250

Scholarships and Grants from Private Sources

The major public programs provide you with the single largest source for grants and scholarships. But that doesn't mean you shouldn't seek out private sources. You should!

You might fit into one of the many specialized scholarships around, for future home economics majors with abilities in writing, leaders of church youth groups, would-be marine biologists, students of Syrian descent, and hundreds of others.

The problem is that only a minuscule percentage of those who need money ever qualify for these grants—and those who do find the amounts involved are so small that the grant hardly makes a dent in their overall needs.

Don't believe that large amounts of scholarship or grant money go begging each year. They don't. Because the need for money to finance higher education is so acute, students themselves have become expert scholarship sleuths. And there are computerized scholarship matching services which, for a fee, search for scholarships to meet a student's particular status, needs, interests, and background.

Where should you start your search for scholarships and grants from private sources?

Private Scholarship Shopping List

• Colleges themselves are a major source of scholarship money. They set aside certain sums to use for student aid, and those sums have been increasing as federal aid shrinks. Also check the college's catalogue to see whether you are eligible for an award because of your special talent, interest, or ability. Sometimes a college awards a scholarship based on need, and sometimes on excellence. Find out what the situation is at your college by asking the financial aid administrator.

• The National Merit Scholarship Corporation is the largest, best known, and most widely sought private scholarship source in the United States today. Awards are made based on your PSAT/NMSQT scores. But only about 5,000 outstanding students each year ever get a Merit Scholarship, which can range in value from $250 to $1,500 a year for four years, with financial need the yardstick determining who gets the $1,500. Some winners simply get one-shot stipends of $1,000. About 18,000 high schools in the country give the test, so you might give it a try. See your guidance counselor.

Even if you're not one of the lucky winners, you could be one of the 50,000 who receive special commendations and citations because of your test scores. These are prestigious on your record and might help you when you look for financial help elsewhere.

• Labor unions award large numbers of scholarships. Check the union your parents belong to.

• Corporation scholarships are a worthwhile source of funds. Many businesses offer scholarships for children of employees. Some companies award scholarships to students who have no connection with the company. Among the best known are Scholastic's Art, Photography, and Writing Awards; Westinghouse's Talent Search for scientists; and Shell's awards to student leaders.

• Trade associations often have their own scholarships for children of members.

• Civic and fraternal organizations sponsor scholarships. In most instances, scholarships are for students living in the community in which the organization is located.

- Other sponsors include the Boy Scouts of America, the Girl Scouts of the U.S.A., 4-H, PTAs, Chambers of Commerce, Jaycees, Junior Achievement, and a wide range of religious organizations.
- National minority organizations offer scholarships and/or special counseling and referral services. A few are: Aspira of America, Inc. (Aspira Educational Opportunity Center, 205 Lexington Avenue, New York, NY 10016) (Puerto Rican); Bureau of Indian Affairs (Higher Education Program, Box 8327, Albuquerque, NM 87108); League of United Latin American Citizens (National Education Service Centers, 400 First Street, N.W., Washington, DC 20001); National Association for the Advancement of Colored People (1790 Broadway, New York, NY 10019); National Urban League (500 E. 62nd Street, New York, NY 10021).
- Women, too, have additional opportunities for scholarships and grants. Athletic scholarships for women are increasing. The Business and Professional Women's Foundation in Washington, DC, has programs for women only, and some foundations award grants to colleges and universities, which then select the women to receive the awards.
- Handicapped students should check with the department of vocational rehabilitation in their states.
- Many professional associations encourage students to enter their fields through scholarships and grants. Check with the professional associations in your future specialty to find out what financial aid they may offer.

Check your library and guidance office for up-to-date materials listing available scholarships and grants.

Suggested References

For current information regarding federal government grant and loan programs, call the Student Information Center, toll-free:
1-800-638-6700 (except Alaska and Hawaii)
1-800-492-6602 (Maryland)

Reading

The College Blue Book: Scholarships, Fellowships, Grants and Loans, 19th edition, Volume I, Lorraine M. Mathies, editor, and Elizabeth Dixon, associate editor. Macmillan Information, 1981.

The College Cost Book: Your Step-by-Step Guide to Paying for College, 1982–83. College Entrance Examination Board, 1982.

Financial Aids for Higher Education, 10th edition. Oreon Keeslar (Dubuque, Iowa), 1982.

Paying for Your Education: A Guide for Adult Learners. College Entrance Examination Board, 1983. (Includes helpful deadline calendars and checklists as well as month-by-month strategies in looking for financial aid.)

The Student Guide: Five Federal Financial Aid Programs. U.S. Department of Education. (Available free from Pell Grants, P.O. Box 84, Washington, DC 20044.)

The following pamphlets are also helpful:

Don't Miss Out: The Ambitious Student's Guide to Scholarships and Loans, 1981–83, 6th edition, by Robert Leider. Octameron Association (P.O. Box 3437, Alexandria, VA 22302). Available for $2.50.

Financial Aid for College Students: Sources of Information. American Chemical Society (Education Department, 1155 16th Street, N.W., Washington, DC 20036). Available for 10 cents.

Financial Aid to Education. Knights of Columbus Supreme Council (Columbus Plaza, P.O. Drawer 1670, New Haven, CT 06507). Available free.

Need a Lift? Educational Opportunities, Careers, Loans, Scholarships, Employment. American Legion Education and Scholarship Program (National Headquarters, P.O. Box 1055, Indianapolis, IN 46206). (Updated every September.) Available for $1.

Above All Else, Remember . . .

* *Ask your school for all their information on financial aid.*
* *Do not prejudge your eligibility for financial aid.* (Unless you file a form, you'll never know whether or not you're eligible.)
* *File all the forms requested, using the most accurate data you can provide.* (The object is to do it right the first time.)
* *Make sure you meet the deadlines.* (If you're late, you are the loser. And in the case of financial aid, the "early bird" theory holds. The sooner you file, the more likely you are to get some discretionary funding.)
* *In a separate folder for each school, keep a record of the school's deadlines and when you sent what.* (It is easy to become confused and think you sent something to one school when you sent it to another.)

• *Reapply for financial aid every year.* (Don't forget this. You will not get aid this year just because you did last year. And even if you were turned down last year, circumstances—yours, the school's, the government's—may have changed enough this year to make you eligible.)

• *Respond to all requests made by the financial aid office.* (If you make a mistake and forget to include something, you've made a mistake. Everyone does. Don't compound it by delaying its correction.)

• *There is a way to finance your higher education. Don't give up!*

Let's Talk about Loans

I overheard two students talking about the loans they had taken out for their schooling.

"I start to worry about it when I get into bed each night," Andrea said of her loan from the local PTA. "I wonder if I'll ever be able to pay it back. Will I get a good job when I graduate? I wish I hadn't taken it out. Is my education really worth sleepless nights?"

"You're kidding," Eric replied. "I never even think of my Guaranteed Student Loan. I'm hoping the bank will forget I even owe them money. But if they remember, let them wait. Don't they have more money than I do?"

Two attitudes. One fearful. One irresponsible.

Both are dangerous. But both of these attitudes are prevalent among the millions of students applying for and getting loans.

Be straight about it. Loans are the last resort because *you do have to repay them.* You shop for them *after* you have explored other cost-cutting strategies. But often loans are vital, especially when you aren't considered needy enough by federal, state, or university standards to qualify for a scholarship.

To answer our two students:

• Yes, Andrea. If the only way you can go to college is by taking out a loan, consider it among the best investments you'll ever make.

• Yes, Eric. The banks do have more money than you. But that's irrelevant. When you sign a loan agreement, you have a moral and legal responsibility to live up to its terms. And that means repaying it.

Loans Available to You

The best terms on loans are offered by National Direct Student Loans, Guaranteed Student Loans and PLUS loans (discussed earlier in this chapter).

But if those are not available to you, other loan possibilities, starting with the least expensive, are:

1. A college loan involving low interest on the loan, which is repayable starting sometime after graduation
2. A low-interest loan through a civic or religious group
3. A deferred-tuition plan offered by a number of schools
4. A loan from a credit union, if you're a member
5. A bank or insurance company loan
6. As a last resort, a finance company loan

Questions to Ask Each Lender

Before the details of each of the possibilities are presented, here are the questions you should ask each lender:

- What is the simple interest rate on the loan? (By law, this rate must be disclosed.)
- What extra charges are involved?
- Can you (the lender) terminate the plan? Under what conditions? Do you have to give me (the borrower) notice before cancellation?
- Can I pay off the loan before the expiration of the contract? How much notice am I required to give? Are there any prepayment penalties involved?
- Are there any other restrictions?

Loans from Colleges

Most colleges and universities offer long-term loan programs of their own for students. Consider yourself lucky if you borrow through the school's own programs because almost all these loans are bargains in terms of low interest rates and reasonable repayment schedules.

Loans made to:	Students.
Loans made by:	College itself. May be short-term, emergency loan; or may be in cooperation with federal government for long-term; or may be a long-term loan under a postponed tuition plan.
Amount of loans:	Varies widely. Can be small, if short-term, emergency loan, or can run into thousands of dollars, depending on your need.
Interest rates:	Also vary widely. No fixed rate, but always compare very favorably with rates charged by commercial lenders.
Repayment:	Starts at graduation or a year thereafter if ordinary college loan; can be stretched over a very long period. Repayment is likely to be deferred for as long as you are in graduate school.
How to apply:	Check with the financial aid administrator at your college.

Loans from Civic and Other Organizations

There is not an abundant amount of college loan money available through local civic, labor, and church groups, but there is some. Check into these sources before you turn to a commercial lender.

Loans made to:	Students.
Loans made by:	Organizations sponsoring the loan program: Rotary, Lions, Kiwanis, PTA, labor unions, churches, religious organizations, employers, etc.
Amount of loans:	Vary, depending on the financial resources of the organization and your need.
Interest rates:	Comparatively low against the money market at the time of loan.
Repayment:	Varies according to the agreement between you and the lender.
How to apply:	Consult your high school guidance counselor, your community center, your church or synagogue, and similar likely sources of information.

Loans from Private Financial Institutions

If you can't develop other alternatives to finance your education and must borrow from a private institution, go ahead. But understand that interest rates and repayment terms are least favorable to you when you go this route.

Loans made to:	Parents, guardians, or students—usually the adults or students of legal age of majority.
Loans made by:	Commercial banks, savings institutions, finance companies, credit unions, other financial sources.
Amount of loans:	Not specifically limited, if borrower has demonstrated ability to repay or has satisfactory collateral (an item or items of value which you pledge to secure your loan in case of default). This is, in short, an ordinary personal loan for educational purposes.
Interest rates:	Vary depending on state of money market, area of country, caliber of borrower, and term of loan. Rates are high, and a minimum service charge may be added.
Repayment:	Terms vary and depend on deal agreed upon, but a period of six to eight years is fairly typical and repayment often starts at end of the first month of the loan's life.

"Special" College Loan Sources

Private lending companies also specialize in education loans. Some offer special arrangements—"budget" plans, revolving credit accounts under which the borrower may repay loans in installments and prepay whenever possible. The plans might involve a fee for joining, a monthly service charge, insurance premium, and possibly a cancellation charge.

How to Shop for an Educational Loan

1. Determine the extent of your unmet need. After you've figured out what your expenses will be, subtract what you and your family can contribute, and what you are getting in financial aid. What is left is unmet need.

2. Decide how big a debt you think you can handle (either actually or psychologically) and don't exceed your limit.

3. Figure out (honestly) how long you think you would need to repay the loan.

4. Speak to at least two or three different lenders before deciding on one.

5. Compare bids. The lowest monthly charge will be most favorable to you—assuming equal repayment periods, equal loan amounts, and equal insurance charges (if there are any).

A Helpful Source of Information

The largest private grantor of student loans today is the nonprofit United Student Aid Funds (USAF). Basically it is a servicing agent for the federal government's Guaranteed Student Loan Program, and for a number of state and college programs. It is not in the business of making personal loans to students or their parents. But the USAF is a valuable source of information to students—undergraduate and graduate—and parents by directing them to the proper starting point in their search for financial aid information. The USAF encourages questions. Their toll-free numbers follow.

- California only: (800) 227-3037
- Alaska and Hawaii: (800) 428-5390
- Indiana only: (800) 382-4506
- All other states: (800) 428-9250

OTHER COST-CUTTING STRATEGIES

Special Payment Plans

These vary with each school. The plans can range from paying monthly tuition payments to the school to deferring tuition until after graduation when you're working and can pay back the cost plus interest. Ask about the plans available at your school.

Turning Assets into Cash

This might mean taking your electric guitar and amp (assets) and selling them. Or it might mean taking your ability to play the electrical guitar (an asset) and using it to make money playing at high school dances.

Stretching Dollars

You may have to turn yourself into:

- A do-it-yourselfer (hemming pants instead of sending them to the tailor).
- A coupon saver (ask everyone you know to help you save shampoo, detergent, lotion, etc., coupons, and redeem them at stores which give you double the face amount).
- A bargain hunter (thrift shops, flea markets, garage sales).
- A do-withouter (saving the pizza and beer for special treats since the dorm food is what you paid for and eating in is considerably less expensive than eating out).

In subsequent chapters, you'll read the wisest advice I know on saving and making the most of your money.

ALTERNATIVE KINDS OF HIGHER EDUCATION

The Armed Forces

Uncle Sam wants you—enough to pay for all or part of your education, if you join the armed forces.

Why? What's behind all the educational opportunities?

From the services' point of view:

- They have and employ technically sophisticated equipment. They need people with enough education and training to be able to handle the rapidly changing technology.
- There is more to the armed forces than arms. There is broad strategic planning requiring people with excellent abstract reasoning abilities. There is a wide range of support services that require the talents of photographers, chefs, doctors, computer programmers, dentists, teachers, air traffic controllers, radio operators, lawyers, cartographers, etc. In other words, the talents of all the peo-

ple who make any community function properly are needed in the military community, too.

• They have to attract and keep people who can fulfill their needs. The best way to do that is to offer a host of educational opportunities for men and women, so that is what they are doing. In an era when the federal government is decreasing support for those pursuing higher education outside the military, it is increasing its support for higher education within the military.

The Academies

There are five military academies:

- U.S. Military Academy at West Point, New York
- U.S. Naval Academy at Annapolis, Maryland
- U.S. Air Force Academy at Colorado Springs, Colorado
- U.S. Coast Guard Academy at New London, Connecticut
- U.S. Merchant Marine Academy at Kings Point, New York

The price is right. They're free—from tuition to living expenses —so they're highly competitive. Some also require your congressional representative's recommendation.

In return for the generous gift of a four-year education, you are required to make a postgraduate commitment to the service. The length of that commitment varies depending on the service, but the minimum is four years.

Reserve Officer Training Corps (ROTC)

If you're interested in pursuing a career as an officer in the military service, but don't want to go to or can't get into the academies, think about the Reserve Officer Training Corps (ROTC) of the branch of service you're interested in.

ROTC provides a limited number of highly competitive scholarships yearly, which cover tuition, books, fees, and a monthly allowance for living expenses. Even if you don't qualify for a scholarship, ROTC does pay up to $1,000 a year during your last two years of college, plus six weeks of summer pay for the training required each year.

Not all colleges have ROTC programs. So check that out *before* you apply to a school. As is true with the academies, ROTC requires a time commitment of service following graduation.

Inducement Programs

To induce enlistees who have academic potential (and thus will function better in today's services), but who might not have the funds to continue their education immediately after high school, the services hold out this carrot: you defer your education for a certain number of years and join the service. When your tour is up, the service will help you pick up your tuition tab.

One of the newest programs is the Army College Fund, which is a savings plan. Soldiers who participate designate from $25 to $100 of their pay each month to be put into the fund. The government will match their savings five-to-one. The total amount (including the matched funds) that can be saved for those who put aside the maximum is $15,200 after two years of service; $20,100 after three or four years. The money can be used for college, university, and vocational and technical training.

For further information about all the tuition assistance and training programs the armed forces offer, see your local recruiting officer.

College Credits without College Classrooms

Acceleration

If you are academically gifted or if experience outside the classroom has taught you a measurable amount, there are ways to speed up your college education, thereby cutting costs. Not only does it make sense financially, it is also intellectually wise. Why would you want to waste brain time taking a course in something you already know?

There are two ways to accelerate:

• *Advanced Placement (AP) Courses.* About 25 percent of the high schools in the country offer some AP courses, with the average school offering three to four. The form of the courses can differ. In some high schools they can be honors classes; in others, strong regular courses, tutorials, or independent study programs. All the courses are challenging, require more work, and go into greater depth than the average high school courses. They are on a college level.

You are expected to do reasonably well on the nationwide exam given in May for the course you have taken. If you do, chances are you will get college credit and/or advanced placement.

Generally AP courses are offered to highly qualified students in their senior year of high school. Speak to your guidance counselor to see if your school offers the program and if you qualify.

There is a fee in the mid-40-dollar range for each exam taken. But think of the value—if you earn the required grade on an AP exam. You may receive the equivalent of three to eight semester hours, which is probably worth between $300 and $1,000 of tuition. That's a good investment.

• *College Level Examination Program (CLEP).* You are an avid reader of the classics. You have spent countless hours in the company of other avid readers, talking about the literature, its philosophy, its relevance to life today, its structure.

You love plants. By the time you are a junior in high school you have a nursery business which is extremely successful because of your green thumb and your knowledge of marketing acquired by reading every book in the library on the subject.

Your mother is a hematologist and you are fascinated by her work. You spend every afternoon and every summer in her lab working alongside of her, learning the complexities of her field.

In any one of these cases you may be a candidate for the College Level Examination Program (CLEP) of the College Board. It's a way of earning college credit without enrolling in a college course, by demonstrating your knowledge of a subject in an examination.

CLEP exams are given monthly at 1,000 locations throughout the United States and more than 1,800 colleges and universities grant credit toward degrees to those who score high enough on the tests. Before you decide to take CLEP exams for college credit, check with your college on its CLEP policy.

To find out whether or not you're ready to take a CLEP exam, the College Board suggests you send for the *CLEP General and Subject Examinations* which describes each test and provides sample questions. There is a small fee for it. For more information, write CLEP

(College Board Publication Orders, Box 2815, Princeton, NJ 08540).

External Degree Program

This is a unique form of low-cost education with particular appeal if you must maintain a job. You do your regular college studies off campus.

One large program of this kind is New York State's Empire State College, which is a nontraditional individualized degree program. You work with tutors and attend group study sessions. Your tuition costs are the same as the State University's. In the early 1980s, you would have spent about $1,600 per semester if you were a full-time student (who also had a full-time job).

Another nontraditional program is the New York Regents External Degree Program, which is unique in its willingness to grant a degree to an applicant who has not followed any prescribed program of study—*if* he/she can demonstrate ability in a field through exams.

The degree you get through one of these external degree programs is equivalent to a university degree. Despite the fact that these programs are not traditional, they offer you great potential, if you are capable of studying independently.

College Co-op Programs

Cooperative education programs (which could rightly be called "learn and earn") allow students to alternate periods of study with periods of work *in their fields of study*. They're very different from "earning money to put yourself through school" jobs because they are supervised by your school and designed to help you reach specific educational goals. In other words, no soda jerking for the potential electrical engineer.

Not only is this type of education relevant in that it combines hands-on experience with book learning, it is an excellent way of dealing with the growing financial crises students face. Here's how it works:

In most four-year colleges, the work and the study periods alternate with each quarter or semester. Two-year colleges are more apt to parallel the two experiences. That means you would work half a day and go to classes half a day, or you would work three days a week and attend classes two.

Work means getting paid. In the beginning you might earn the minimum wage since your skills are untested. But jobs do not remain static. As you gain more experience and more knowledge through study, your job should get more challenging and your pay should get better. It is not unusual for a co-op student to earn $5,000 a year.

Naturally you get credit for your work experiences, but you also pay the college tuition for the time you're working (though sometimes at a lower rate).

Except for five-year programs, co-oping does not take any more than the usual four years of college. But you do not have summers off.

Over 1,100 colleges and universities offer co-op programs in almost all courses of study. At some schools, such as Antioch College and Northeastern University (one of the pioneers in the co-op movement), participation in the program is mandatory.

Co-oping is a wonderful way to help assume a large chunk of the financial obligations of your schooling. And you graduate with priceless experience (could be vital in the job market).

If you're interested in co-oping, make certain the school of your choice offers it in your field.

Since a program which is closely supervised and which plans your work experiences will be more valuable to you than one which does not, ask the following questions:

- Is there a full-time person in charge of the co-op program to whom I can speak?
- Am I given individual counseling before, during, and after each work experience?
- Is there any follow-up on the work experience—such as papers, seminars?
- Does someone from the college visit me on the job? Maintain contact with my employer?
- How do I get placed? Do I have interviews with a number of employers? Do the employers have a say in who they are are going to hire? Do I have a say in who I am going to work for? (Both you and the employer should have a choice.)
- Are jobs in the area of the school or must I go to another city,

state? (That might be a plus or a minus, depending on your preferences.)

- Is everyone who wants it able to co-op in meaningful jobs?
- If I drop out of the co-op program, do I lose college credit?

For more details on co-oping write to The National Commission for Cooperative Education (360 Huntington Avenue, Boston, MA 02115) for their free pamphlet *The Undergraduate Program of Cooperative Education in the United States and Canada.*

Education Does Not Begin or End in the Classroom

The exciting part about education is that it never stops. You learn even when you're unaware of it. And if you want to increase your rate and kind of learning, you can, by taking advantage of a variety of opportunities.

Industry Training Programs

Many large corporations have extensive training programs. Companies vary on how they recruit for these training programs. They might take you directly from school—high school or college, depending on the program—to train you for a specific area. Or, they might draw on employees whose work habits and abilities they already know. Employees have to show a sincere interest in the program and a potential for success to get their supervisor's approval.

Though the military was listed as a source of tuition earlier in this chapter, it is also a rich source of training, especially in technical areas.

Industry Tuition Aid

As part of their benefits packages, many corporations offer some sort of financial assistance to employees who want to take courses (toward a degree or not) and who have been with them a certain length of time. It could cover the whole tuition; most of the time it's a percentage. If you are going into industry immediately after high school, check whether the company in which you are interested has some tuition aid—even if, at this time, you don't think you'll ever go to college. The fact that the aid is available can often be magnetic in drawing you into using it.

Travel

You've probably heard some classmate say, "I'm going to take the next year to travel and work." That's wonderful. You can learn from seeing, touching, feeling, and experiencing what you can never learn from a textbook.

Travel can give you the time you need to grow and mature before you direct yourself to more definite goals. But, be aware of its drawbacks. Unless you know exactly why and for what purpose you're traveling, you have no direction. No permanence. And it is hard to ascertain measurable growth in yourself.

Home Study Courses

The thousands of worthwhile home study courses have been a boon to all of you who are interested in upgrading your skills and your educational-economic status. But because you are operating without personal contact when you sign up for a home study course, you leave yourself open to trouble from the racketeering fringe.

Therefore, *beware!* Use the same guidelines for selecting home study courses as for choosing a trade or technical school.

• If you have any doubt whatsoever about the value of a home study or extension course you have seen advertised, check its reputation with your local Better Business Bureau, Chamber of Commerce, or state Department of Education.

• To find out what legitimate courses are available to you in the field in which you are interested, check with your guidance counselor.

• For a free list of accredited, reputable home study schools, write to: the National Home Study Council (1601 Eighteenth Street, N.W., Washington, DC 20009).

• On correspondence courses offered by accredited colleges and universities, a similar list entitled *Guide to Independent Study through Correspondence Instruction* is available for sale from National

University Extension Association (Book Order Department, P.O. Box 2123, Princeton, NJ 08540).

• You'll also find useful information on choosing a correspondence school in *Tips on Home Study Schools*, a pamphlet available from the Council of Better Business Bureaus, Inc., 1515 Wilson Blvd., Arlington, VA 22209. (Single copies cost 25 cents. Enclose a self-addressed, stamped envelope.)

Continuing Education

All around us, courses are being given—free seminars by stock brokerage firms on investments; assertiveness training at the public library; adult education courses in woodworking. And on and on.

An interesting continuing education form is the vacation college which gives people a chance to couple their annual summer holiday with an intellectually refreshing course or two at college. It's fun. You mix all the facilities of a university campus—a nicely furnished dorm room, swimming, golf, tennis—with noncompetitive courses, often led by some of America's leading intellectuals, teachers, authors, etc. If this concept of a vacation intrigues you, go about selecting this college differently from the way you would any other. Decide in what region you'd like to spend your holiday weeks and then write the surrounding schools to see if they offer a summer program.

"DEAR SYLVIA"

Dear Sylvia,
   There is an SAT review course being given in my town. It costs $200. Is it worth it? How much should I expect my SAT scores to go up after taking it?
                    —**Scoring 900 and Wanting to Bat 1,000**

There is much controversy surrounding the value of Scholastic Aptitude Test (SAT) review courses. Comparative results of test score increases between those who take the review courses and those who don't are inconclusive. It would be nice if you could find out how successful the review course of which you're thinking has been in lifting scores. But you won't be able to because all the courses claim extraordinary success.

In my opinion, the greatest value in the courses is that they give you an acquaintance with the test so that you are not uncomfortable with the format when you finally take it.

Since the SAT is designed to test cumulative knowledge, it is unlikely that any cram course can raise your grades significantly. Read, read, read. Absorb all you can in school. Challenge your mind.

Those are the best ways to bat 1,000.

Dear Sylvia,

I heard that some states give you money just for going to a private school in your own state. Could that be true? Why would they do that?

—Georgia Peach

They would. And yours does.

Here's how they reason the gift: Of all those going to college in the United States, 78 percent are educated at a state institution. The state schools pay much more to educate each student than they are charging in tuition. So, many states figure that it is worth it to them to entice you with a small stipend to stay within the state boundaries (where you'll spend your money and help the economy) and attend a private school. Then, the states will *not* have to pick up the more expensive tab of educating you at a state university.

Dear Sylvia,

Why should I waste my money going to college or vocational school when I plan to get married and have children in a few years?

—Confused by Degrees

Here are the facts, ma'am.

- Women have an average work life of 25–45 years.
- One out of four households today is headed by a woman who supports the family.

- Women stay single longer.
- Women get divorced.
- Women work while they are married.
- Women work when they have children.

All this being the case, my advice to you is: go to school and develop every skill and talent you can. You never know when you might *need* them—or *want* them.

Dear Sylvia,
   My parents are very upset about the spiraling cost of education. Is there anything I can do to help them?
                                                        —Sharing Concerns

Do your best to dig out all the financial aid you can get. Assure your parents you won't spend money unnecessarily at school. (And don't.) Finally, ask your parents to check with their accountant, broker, or banker and to look into custodial accounts and special loans for parents.

Dear Sylvia,
   Is there ever a chance I'll be able to forget the forms and use a computer to tell my financial woes to?
                                                        —Had It with Forms

Maybe *you* won't have that luxury, but your younger brother or sister might.

The College Board is exploring a system, Project Transaction, which would use computer technology to simplify the whole process of applying for financial aid, having your needs analyzed, and communicating these needs to the appropriate postsecondary institutions. Perhaps the system will be in operation by the time you're ready to go to graduate school.

Dear Sylvia,
   I know I'm going to have to go on to get an M.A. and a Ph.D. if I want a challenging, well-paying career in my field.

But graduate school is very long and very costly. Is it worth the investment considering that I'm going to have to borrow substantial sums of money?

—Looking Ahead

That is a question only you can answer, because in this case "investment" is more than money received for money put in. It includes the sense of fulfillment you will get from your life's work.

Before you make any decision, though, find out:

• What the five-year projection is for career opportunities in your field. (See "A Look to the Future" in Chapter 1.)

• What the salary ranges are expected to be once you get your graduate degrees. (If you have to borrow money, you must know if you'll be in a financial position to repay it.)

• What financial aid is available. (See and speak to the financial aid administrator in your school, the United Student Aid Fund, and the national professional organizations which would be applicable to you.)

• What fellowships, corporate grants, etc., are available.

• If the programs you are interested in would allow you to work part time.

• If there is another way to earn your graduate degrees without going to school full time.

Best of luck whichever route you take.

WORDS OF CAUTION

Yes, higher education is costly. But don't let the mounting dollars scare you. You can and will find the money to finance it. For your own self-fulfillment (not to mention society's), seek and get the best and most meaningful education you can. Short of victims of gangland killings, I think no one has ever been hurt by "knowing too much."

5

INVESTMENT OPTIONS FOR TODAY'S TEENAGERS

CONTENTS

FORMING A PERSONAL INVESTMENT STRATEGY

The Power to Spend Money

Do you recall your first weekly allowance? What did you buy with it? Turn back to page 7. Honestly, did you spend all of it on a movie that week? Or did you set aside some or all of it for something really special you craved that required weeks, perhaps months, of disciplined saving? If the choices seemed endless, it was because a new source of financial power became available to you at that moment, a power you had never exercised before: the power to spend money.

Soon after you first experienced this financial power, however, you probably became accustomed to it. You may have found so many ways to make your weekly allowance disappear that your new source of financial power seemed to be suffering a power failure. You simply needed more money. So perhaps you asked your parents to raise your allowance. Or perhaps you took a part-time job to supplement what your parents were giving you. Whatever course you took, chances are your higher allowance or additional earnings once again didn't satisfy you very long. Day by day, as you grow older, you are finding that the amount of money you need is growing too—money for the clothes *you* want to wear, for the food *you* want to eat, for everything that you, an American teenager, want or need. Now, as you read this, it's almost a sure bet you're *still* not satisfied with what you're earning or receiving, even though you're living on amounts that would have been beyond your expectations—even your dreams—just a few years ago.

As a perceptive young person, you already probably have learned two vital economic lessons:

1. Your financial needs will rise steadily throughout your entire productive life, just as they have risen steadily in your life thus far.
2. Even more important: No matter how much you earn, it never seems to be quite enough.

So—what are you going to do?

You can, of course, do what so many other young people do as they enter adulthood and set out on the road to their careers: you can do absolutely nothing.

In that case, you will join the ranks of a modern, consumption-oriented American society that saves far less of its after-tax income than other industrialized nations, while eating one of every two meals away from home. You will spend freely on the latest electronic gadgetry, on entertainment, on fashions and cosmetics—leaving just enough in the checking account at the end of each month to pay the bills (you hope). When you shop for a car, you will suffer "sticker shock" when you realize you can't afford the prices dealers are demanding for new cars. And when an emergency strikes, you will be forced to scramble, then appeal to your family, friends, or even outside sources for money because you never thought about the future.

But you also can begin to plan for the future *now*. You can start formulating your own personalized investment strategy that will allow you to build for the future without serious hardship (although you will have to make some sacrifices). By beginning today to develop your own strategy—and it is *you* in the end who must carefully map out your personalized investment strategy—you will be taking a giant step toward conquering the otherwise perpetual dilemma of constantly increasing financial needs. And while you may never be satisfied with what *you* earn, what your investments earn *for you* can make the difference between a life of constant financial dissatisfaction and one of actual contentment.

What Is a Personalized Investment Strategy?

Exactly what it says it is. It is *personalized*, taking into account your unique needs and objectives. It involves *investment*, putting your money to work earning income that will beat the rate of inflation rather than just storing your money where inflation eventually will erode it. Most important, it demands *strategy* on your part, constant attention to your investments and to the world around you, as well as a readiness to take advantage of new opportunities or to abandon stale ideas.

If the world of investment brings to mind overweight, blue-suited executives thumbing through thick reports or scrutinizing ticker tapes, you have the wrong idea. Investing is for everyone—*especially* you, because as a teenager you are not yet burdened with the massive expenses of a home or family that would soak up most of your spendable income. In fact, *now* is one of the *best* times for you to invest because you can be bold, even gamble with the few dollars you can afford to risk in search of that truly worthwhile investment. You don't have to be rich to do it: as little as $100 will buy you a stake in certain mutual funds, for example. What you do need is the determination to think through your own needs, develop a strategy to meet those needs, and follow through on that strategy.

How Much Should You Invest?

The answer to this difficult question depends on you, since you are developing your own *personalized* strategy. Always set aside a certain portion of your spendable income in savings—whether in "liquid" bank accounts or in quickly cashed short-term securities—for future personal or educational needs, as well as for such emergencies as car breakdowns, a stolen wallet or purse. But don't let your savings program deter you from investing. After you've contributed adequately to your savings, whatever other spendable income you can scrape together may be considered available for investment. Saving and investing a total of 10 percent of your income is a fair goal to aim for. This may be too much for you at first, but learn the discipline of saving and investing together as soon as you can.

Why Not Put All Your Money in Savings?

Because you'll be *saving*, not *investing*. Bank accounts are just about the safest places to put your money; they're insured by an agency of the federal government for up to $100,000 per account. And U.S. savings bonds are effectively as safe; they're backed by the full faith and credit of the U.S. Treasury. But neither of these repositories offers you a chance to make your money really *grow*. History underlines that, in the long run, both financial institutions' savings accounts and U.S. savings bonds will pay you less than the inflation rate. In the short run, you're unlikely to come out a winner unless you lock yourself into a bond, note, or certificate yielding high interest rates the moment before interest rates tumble. Saving money *is* important for emergencies and for high-ticket necessities, and savings accounts and U.S. savings bonds are good places to store your money until you determine where you want to invest. But once you're ready to start investing, shift away from sluggish accounts and put the money you can afford to risk to work for you.

What Is a Good Return on Investments?

This is another difficult question, the answer to which depends not only on your own strategy but also on such market factors as the level of inflation and of interest rates. As a general rule, you want to: (1) stay ahead of the rate of inflation; (2) do better than the return on long-term savings accounts; and (3) do both (1) and (2) for long periods of time, not just for a month or two each year.

For most of the twentieth century, when both interest rates and inflation ran at single-digit rates, a return on investments of 10 percent a year was considered extremely productive. During the double-digit late 1970s and early 1980s, however, anything less than 15 percent might have been considered a foolish risk when insured savings certificates frequently could offer an equivalent return. The only way to keep on top of the situation is to monitor inflation and interest rates constantly on your own. Keep a notebook with monthly entries for the Consumer Price Index (the semiofficial inflation indicator) and the prime rate (the interest rate charged by major banks for loans to their best, biggest customers). When you get accustomed to these fluctuating rates, you'll have a much better sense of what you should be doing with your investment money.

Are There Any Rules to the Game?

There are several. As you work out your personalized investment strategy, keep these guidelines in mind:

Set Aside As Much As You Can for Investment Purposes

Without jeopardizing your savings program, try to discipline yourself to pass by some minor but costly pleasures for the sake of your investment program. If you can achieve the 10 percent combined savings-and-investment goal, that's admirable. If you can do more —that's ''wow!''

Whatever Your Goal Is, Stick to It

By far the most destructive blow to any investment program is dealt by the investor's lack of discipline. You have already learned that discipline is vital in the study hall, on the playing fields, in the study of a musical instrument. View this as a test of your character. When you are successful, you will have gained something in addition to financial strength: confidence in your ability to decide on a course of action and to follow it through. Make investment an essential item in your personal budget, and don't cheat. You're cheating only one—and the most important—person: yourself.

Don't Put All Your Eggs in One Basket

Since you are just starting out as an investor, it may be difficult at first to obey this rule. You may have enough available money for just one stock or mutual fund. That's a good initial move, but your investment strategy must not end there. As soon as you can, diversify. That way, you can take advantage of long-term upswings while minimizing the chance of being wiped out by a temporary but drastic downturn. Many different investments, you will find, will suit your individualized needs.

Don't Go Swinging Off with Several Baskets of Eggs, Either

Just because diversity is a good thing doesn't mean anything that's new or different is worthwhile. Some speculators (or just greedy, naive gamblers) will snap at any rumor or tip no matter how wacky—but not you, since you start out with limited resources. No matter how inviting an opportunity looks, be on guard: there are so many get-rich-quick schemes advertised in the media, every person who can read or see should be a millionaire-plus by now. You know better. A little skepticism won't hurt you. Few *investment* opportunities are so fleeting that you have to jump for them before thinking them through.

Nevertheless, Be Open to Change

Here is where you, the young investor, have a particular advantage. Don't be so hypnotized by your first investment that you hold on to it blindly when every market signal tells you to sell. On the other hand, don't be so overly cautious that you sit by as opportunity after opportunity approaches and then recedes. Take the same energy you devote to school and after-school recreation, devote it to investing, and you have a great chance of coming out a winner. Keep on your toes.

Now That You Know the Rules, What Are Your Goals?

Investors generally look for three distinct goals: (1) a steady flow of income; (2) long-term appreciation in value; and (3) short-term, rapid growth.

Of these three, you are not interested in a steady flow of income at all. Older Americans with large holdings often seek to live off the steady flow of interest or dividends paid on their investments, and often such income serves as their retirement income in whole or in large part. On the money I assume you can afford to invest right now, you can't possibly care about the few dollars of current income your investments could earn.

You are always interested in long-term appreciation in the value of your investments. Certainly you will be glad twenty or thirty years from now if your foresightedness yields investment gains that significantly improve your lifestyle in your middle, and later years. Keep long-term growth constantly in mind. But at your age, with your freedom, you can afford to let long-term growth be of minor importance.

What you really want, above all else, is strong, rapid growth over a period of five to ten years. Your investments, although thoughtful, should display an aggressive strategy that takes a few calculated risks. You are in a race, and if you spring ahead of the pack, you are at a tremendous advantage.

How do you achieve this growth? That is the most important, and most unanswerable, question. One rule is basic, though: *The greater the risk, the greater the potential return.*

Developing your strategy at this stage of your life, then, requires balancing the risk of investments against their potential for large profits. In the process of balancing, be bold at your age, but not silly. There is a fine line between boldness and foolhardiness—and you must learn to draw this line with increasing accuracy as you grow older.

But Am I Not Too Young to Invest?

Yes and no. If you are under age eighteen, you cannot walk into a broker's office with a wad of bills and begin speculating in commodities. In fact, persons under eighteen are not allowed to trade in any kind of securities in any established market in their own name. Being under age need not stop you, however, since the vast majority of states have enacted their own versions of the Uniform Gifts to Minors Act. Under this act, your parent does the actual buying and selling but, merely by filling out a short form (available at any broker's office), your parent transfers real ownership to you. In effect, your parent acts as your agent—buying and selling as you direct—while you are the ultimate winner or loser.

All this brings up one final and absolutely crucial point for those of you under age eighteen and for those of you who are legally adults but are still living with (or under the care of and with the financial support of) your parents: *Do not attempt to invest without your parents' knowledge!*

There is no reason why your parents should not applaud your desire to formulate an investment strategy as opposed to saving for a fast car, this year's clothes, or a week with your friends bumming around on your own. You are investing *after* you take care of all your legitimate needs, not before. The money you invest is money you normally would waste or fritter away if you did not put it to work.

If your parents are absolutely opposed, you are still one step ahead because you can begin as soon as you become financially independent. Then you can implement the strategy you already have developed while your friends are still trying to figure out why their money seems to disappear so quickly each week.

Following is your list of potential investments as you think about your own personalized investment strategy.

THE STOCK MARKET

As the 1980s opened, almost 20½ million Americans under age twenty-one owned stock in domestic corporations. It is no coincidence that stockholders as a group are better educated and wealthier than the general population. Whether you decide to make stocks a part of your investment strategy now, during your teenage years, is up to you. But here is what you need to know in order to decide whether, when, and how to invest in stocks—the cornerstone of American capitalism.

What Stocks Are and How They Earn Money for You

When you buy a *stock*, you buy a piece of a company. You become a part owner, your participation rising with the company's good fortunes, falling with its failures.

Companies issue stock in exchange for money—*capital*. They need to undertake projects too large to be accomplished without turning to outside investors for financing. A group of scientists may have a brilliant idea for a revolutionary new computer "chip" they want to market, or an existing company may need to finance a project as basic as a new plant. So the scientists form a company and issue stock, and the existing company issues still more of its stock—both to obtain capital. In exchange, stockholders get the right, in most instances, to share in their company's profits (when distributed to shareholders, called *dividends*), to vote in elections for company leaders, and other rights one might expect would go with company ownership.

There are thus two ways that you, the shareholder, can profit from a company's successes. If the scientists' new computer chip proves to be everything they said it would be, or if the established company with its new plant doubles its production or sales, company management can declare a dividend and you will get some of the profits—your share directly proportional to the amount of stock you own. But you do not want dividends primarily, because with prices of most stocks ranging from a few dollars to many hundreds of dollars a share, you will not own much stock in a company, even with a $5,000 investment (the average investment of America's 36 million shareholders in the early 1980s). And with dividends traditionally ranging from $1 to $5 per share annually—seldom more—the few dollars you earn, even from a highly productive company issuing dividends, would probably not beat the return you could achieve by putting your money in a savings account.

But there is another way you can gain from your stocks. The value of the shares themselves can grow. If your company succeeds, other investors will want to buy your stock in order to have a piece of the action as well. The price they are willing to give and the price you are willing to accept will be governed by the classic law of demand and supply; the more your company is worth, the more they will be willing to pay for your stock. This type of growth is what you, the young investor, are after. You want your company to achieve phenomenal growth so that the price of your stock doubles or triples in the time you own it. Your ultimate aim: Buy low, sell high.

Where to Buy Stocks

Stock Markets

The stock you purchase will almost certainly *not* be stock that was issued to you by a corporation in exchange for your capital. You will be buying stock from someone else, who bought his or her stock from someone else, and so on. This buying and selling occurs on *stock markets*.

The stocks of America's largest corporations are traded by the millions daily on the two "national" markets, the *New York Stock Exchange* and the *American Stock Exchange*. Smaller companies' stocks trade on "regional" exchanges located in Boston, Philadelphia, Cincinnati, Chicago, Salt Lake City, San Francisco, Los Angeles, and Spokane. Still other stocks trade on the "over the counter" market, which is not an exchange at a location at all but an invisible coast-to-coast telephone and telex network over which buyers and sellers negotiate sales.

Stock Brokers

In order to have access to any of these markets, you need a broker or dealer. Your stock broker executes your order to buy or sell and charges you a fee or *commission* for this service. Since commissions were deregulated in 1975, the over 300 brokers who will deal with you, the individual investor, charge widely varying fees. For instance, to buy or sell 300 shares of stock valued at $10 a share early in the decade, you could pay as much as $90 at a full-service broker or one-third of that at the least expensive "discount" brokers.

For a young investor, such as you, with a small portfolio, minimizing commissions is crucial. But since you probably are as inexperienced as your means are moderate, investment advice is crucial too. Full-service brokers put their experience, research staffs, and information services to work for you to earn their high commissions. Discount brokers offer virtually nothing except access to the market. You are therefore caught in a bind: to benefit from advice (good or bad) you must pay high commissions you probably cannot afford. To get a break on commissions, you must forgo the investment advice of men and women trained to help you. A solution: start out doing at least a little trading through a full-service broker. That way, you gain access to the resources and techniques your full-service broker has to offer. Then, disillusioned or not with that broker's help, do the rest of your investing through a discount broker. Perhaps you'll even use some of the information you gathered from your full-service broker.

Dividend Reinvestment

There is a way to avoid brokerage fees entirely once you have bought a stock. Over 700 companies on the New York Stock Exchange alone offered dividend reinvestment plans at the start of the 1980s, and the number of participating corporations has been growing steadily every year. Under a dividend reinvestment plan, you elect to have the company reinvest any or all dividends payable on your stock in additional stock of the company. You pay not one cent for this service. In fact, some companies will allow you to purchase stock at 85 to 95 percent of the value it is currently trading at on the market, giving you an instant profit margin.

You can get a list of all New York Stock Exchange companies offering these plans by writing to the Public Information Office (New York Stock Exchange, 11 Wall Street, New York, NY 10005).

Employee Purchase Plans

Still another solution to brokerage fees are employer purchase plans. When you are ready to enter the working world, or if you're already working steadily, look for a plan offered by your employer under which you can buy stock commission-free through regular payroll deductions. These employee stock purchase plans hold two advantages for you:

1. There are no commissions and there may even be discounts, as in the case of dividend reinvestment plans (above).
2. Because you are an "insider," you are in a better position to know how your company actually is making out than some of the most sophisticated brokerage firm research departments. Do not underestimate this advantage. Even the best of the full-service brokers cannot see the trash piling up in your wastebaskets every other day, indicating your company's cutback in maintenance services due to financial strains. Keep your eyes wide open around your place of work, and you will find fascinating clues to your company's financial situation.

The Financial Supermarket

An exciting prospect in the coming five to ten years is the emergence of the "financial supermarket" as a one-stop place for all your money matters: banking, investing, insurance, bill paying, etc. The impetus for this is twofold: The banking and financial industries are being deregulated by the federal government, while at the same time the miracle of computers and electronics is allowing these financial services to be carried on at any place and at any time.

More and more, you will be able to buy stock at your bank, insurance at your stock broker, and a savings certificate at a department store. Depending on the size and nature of your *portfolio* (your combined stock investments), you already may be able to maintain a checking account and have credit cards through your stock broker, although as a teenager you are probably not yet ready for these services.

Some of this wizardry baffles older Americans who are accustomed to banking in a building with marble pillars and then going to their broker, and only their broker, for investment advice. You are not nearly as uncomfortable with the innovations of electronics, putting you at a comparative advantage. Watch for: standardized stock portfolios being marketed by sources other than brokers (e.g., a "growth" portfolio, an "income" portfolio, etc.); consolidated banking and investing, where idle cash is constantly invested in the stocks and bonds of your choice; even at-home purchases and sales, without the aid of a broker, executed by you directly through your personal computer.

What Kinds of Stocks Are There?

There are two major *types* of stocks; then there is a wide variety of *grades* of stocks, ranging from the so-called "blue chip" to "cats and dogs" or "garbage" stocks.

Incidentally, it is commonplace for you not to hold stock certificates in your own possession but for your broker to have custody of them instead, in which case they are held in "street name," a reference to Wall Street. The two basic types of stock are:

Common Stock

These are the bread-and-butter shares of companies. They confer dividend rights, voting rights, etc. Think of them as a catchall as you read through the rest of this list.

Preferred Stock

Preferred stock normally carries no voting rights. Its right to dividends is usually limited to some percentage of its face value, say 5 or 7 percent, so its inherent profit potential and growth potential are both limited as well. What preferred stock does confer is a *preference* on dividends—"first divs" on profits if and when they are distributed. And many preferred stocks are so-called "cumulative" preferred, meaning that each year a dividend is not paid, the right to that amount is retained by preferred stockholders (who, for example, after four years of no dividends on 7 percent cumulative preferred, would get a 28 percent dividend before the common shareholders see a penny).

Preferred stock is for investors who want dividends, dividends, and more dividends and the safety implied. This is certainly not for you. You might recall preferred stocks when you're ready to retire in your beachfront condominium.

Now to name just a few of the many grades and categories of stocks.

Blue Chip Stocks

Named after the most valuable poker chip, these stocks are issued by the country's strongest, most reliable companies. Although ten brokers will give you ten different definitions of a blue chip, you should expect slow, reliable growth and regular dividends from a blue chip stock. Some blue chips have paid dividends every year for more than a century. A list of these dividend-paying stocks is available from the New York Stock Exchange. To find your own blue chips, ask yourself: does the company produce a product or render a service it is unlikely we could ever do without? Your local water company, if publicly owned, is likely to be a blue chip.

Because a blue chip promises so much security, much of its value consists of its dividend-paying potential and the probability it never will become worthless. It is not, therefore, growth oriented.

Growth Stocks

This is what you want at your age—stock with the potential for big increases in per-share volume. If you find it, you've won.

Some huge companies listed on the New York and American Stock Exchanges were once called "growth" companies. IBM was once a small company that believed businesses would someday need computers; the founder of Polaroid thought people would like instant film; and McDonald's thought it had found the secret of the perfect hamburger (you be the judge of that one).

Junior Growth Stocks

Rather than look for "miracle" growth companies, you are better off searching for the so-called "junior growths."

Junior growth companies are generally firms with annual sales of less than $100 million that have developed a unique technology or perform a special service, leading them to carve out a special niche in their industry. They often have above-average growth potential and give you an opportunity to see your capital appreciate more than it might in other investment media.

When looking for a junior growth, you should think in terms of a three- to five-year growth period and be prepared to ride out the short-term fluctuations in the stock market. Because the companies are small and obscure, you should also be patient and expect to see your stock fall during a ''bear'' or poorly performing market.

Areas to find these stocks:

Technology is the key during this decade. Genetic engineering, robots, security protection systems, scientific instruments, tele-communications, and medical technology are all ''hot'' areas and *you* are in an excellent position to outsmart other investors because of your age. You are far closer to the latest scientific advances than older Americans. You learn about them in school and perhaps even use them yourself (how many adults do you know who have access to a computer like the one in your school?). You can answer the question: what is sure to take off? Your own experience could make you a small fortune.

Penny Stocks

Some really far-out ventures—for instance, oil drilling projects in the Rocky Mountain states—issue stock for prices as low as a penny a share in order to attract as many investors as possible. If the venture strikes oil, the stock can multiply spectacularly in value. If not, it's hard to lose a lot of money at 1 cent a share.

In a way, penny stock is ''super growth'' stock. But the problem is that so very few companies issuing it ever succeed. It's a good bet you're throwing away your money when you invest in penny stock. When gamblers began to realize this in the early 1980s, the market in penny stocks suffered a disastrous decline.

Junk Stocks

From the name alone, you know what to do about this type of stock: steer clear.

''Cats and dogs,'' ''junk,'' or ''garbage'' stocks are issued by companies with erratic management, poor or no performance in the past, too much corporate debt, impending lawsuits, or any other combination of negative attributes which drive the price of the stock way down. Only the wildest gambler (not speculator) takes a chance on these stocks. If the company digs itself out of its hole, the gambler makes a huge profit. If not, as is almost invariably the case, the stock becomes worthless (at which point the certificates themselves may become collectors' items—more about that later in this chapter.) Gambling in these stocks is not for you, a new investor. Look for growth, not garbage.

How about Options?

When you buy an *option*, you buy the privilege of buying or selling stock at a fixed price in the future. For instance, you may buy an option contract to purchase 1,000 shares of your target company at $10 a share. There is no way you could have afforded the $10,000 to buy the shares outright on your beginner's budget, but the option costs only $400.

The stock rises from $10 to $15 a share, and the time to exercise your option arrives. You exercise your option, buy the shares at the bargain price of $10 a share (you will have to borrow the money for this), and then immediately resell the shares at $15 per share for a $5,000 profit before commissions and the $400 option fee. You just made a lot of money on a little investment. (You also can just sell the option without going through the motions of buying and selling the stock.)

Or, say the stock declines to $5 a share. You aren't forced to buy the stock at $10 and take a $5,000 loss. You just refuse to exercise your option and the $400 fee is lost. You have used an option to limit your losses.

Margins

Another way to speculate in stocks without paying the full price of the shares is *buying on margin*. More than 1 million investors had margin accounts at brokerage firms in the early 1980s. Briefly, the system works like this:

Using your own judgment or with the help of a broker, you select a stock listed on the NYSE and pay at least 50 percent of the purchase price. (This was the Federal Reserve Board rule in the early 1980s. It prohibited smaller down payments.) You borrow the other 50 percent from your broker, paying interest on the loan. You are able to buy twice as many shares this way as with an outright purchase.

Buying on margin is fine if your stock takes off, since you profit on more shares than you could have bought yourself with your own cash. But if your stock declines, you lose money fast, too. Also, your broker has the right to demand more money from you if your stock falls below a specified level. Under New York Stock Exchange rules, the cash you post with your broker (less the amount you owe the broker) can be no less than 25 percent of the stock's current value at any time; most brokers demand 30 percent as a safety cushion. Thus, if your stock goes down, you can be subject to a *margin call*.

Selling Short

Still another way to "play the market" is *selling short*. In brief, when you sell short you sell stock you don't yet own. Instead, you borrow shares from your broker and sell them, hoping that the price of the stock will then *decline*. If it does, you purchase the same amount of shares at their lower price and return these shares to your broker. The difference between the price of the shares you borrowed to sell and the price of the shares you bought back to return to the lender is your profit.

Options, buying on margin, selling short—all are very risky techniques even for you, a young investor eager to take risks. Each tactic involves *leveraged buying*—the purchase or option to purchase shares with money you don't put up. While in the case of some options all you stand to lose is your option *premium*, in others you may be forced to buy the stock you have optioned. The same can happen with margined stock, where a margin call means: Sell out (or be sold out) or put up more cash. And in the topsy-turvy world of selling short, you can lose big if the price of your target stock *increases*. All these techniques demand the talents of a fairly sophisticated investor, and that's not yet you. Keep options, margins, and short sales in mind for a few years down the road when you feel confident about the stock market.

Now That You Know What You Want— How Do You Find It?

To find a perfect investment would take perfect knowledge of the stock market. Your local library has shelf after shelf of books devoted to stocks, and you will never know all there is to know. The best you can do is follow a few general rules when shopping during the next several years.

Study the Market

Learn how to read stock tables. Follow a number of different stocks for several months to learn how they perform as interest rates move up and down, inflation accelerates or slows, etc. For a free "New Investors" packet that explains stock tables, among other things, write to the Public Information Office (New York Stock Exchange, 11 Wall Street, New York, NY 10005), or visit your local library.

Study Your Potential Target Companies

Send away for their annual reports, which tell you how the companies are and have been performing. Note the dividends paid in the last few years and the company's research budget. A good growth company should *not* use its profits to pay dividends but should instead invest in research projects. And, to decode the reports, obtain "How to Read a Financial Report," available free on request from Merrill Lynch Service Center (P.O. Box 2021, Jersey City, NJ 07303).

Don't Panic on Sharp, Sudden Declines

When you've selected one or more stocks, don't panic when the price of the shares goes down the next day. You are looking for growth over a period of years, not hours.

Keep Informed

News events shouldn't influence your day-to-day attitude toward your investments, but a major development such as a nationwide boycott of your company's products may have a substantial effect on your stock's value.

Try Dollar-Cost Averaging

If, after a while, you feel satisfied with one or more stocks, try dollar-cost averaging. This involves regular, consistent buying of dollar amounts of shares, such as $50 worth a month, rather than numbers of shares. For example, if in the first month the price of the stock is $50 a share, you would buy one share. If the price falls to $25 a share, next month you would buy two shares, and so on. Notice that you do not sell out when the market falls—you buy more, in the confident belief that the stock will climb back and make up your losses. Unless your stock is a real loser, you have an excellent chance of beating the market in the long run because in a falling market the average cost of your shares goes down, and you get more shares for the same total of dollars, and in a rising market, your shares are worth more.

You Are Buying a Few Stocks, Not the Averages

Always keep in mind that you are buying a few selected stocks, not the Dow Jones average. When the nightly news tells of a fall in the market, your stocks could have hit new highs. Don't miss your trees for the forest.

Be Faithful to Your Goals

Above all, be faithful to your goals. Be aggressive, be a skeptic, be attentive—but be disciplined!

WHAT ABOUT BONDS?

When you buy a *bond*, you do not buy ownership of part of the issuing company. You simply lend money to the company—money the company promises to pay back with interest. The company may pay that interest on an annual or other periodic basis (usually through coupons attached to the bond that the holder redeems regularly to receive payment), or at the end of the bond's term, when both principal and interest are repaid in one lump sum. If a bond was issued at less than the value stated on its face (a *discount bond*), the difference between the issue price and the face value due the lender at redemption constitutes interest. If the bond was issued at face (*par*) and interest was not paid regularly over time, the bond will be *redeemed* or closed out by a payment in excess of face value.

The value of bonds depends on interest rates. If a bond promises to pay its holder 8 percent a year for the next thirty years, and interest rates over that term average just 4 percent, clearly the holder of the bond has a valuable item indeed. If, though, the bond promises to pay 4 percent and interest rates over the thirty years average 8 percent, the bond will be worth only a fraction of its face value. Bonds of major corporations are regularly traded on a bond market much like a stock exchange. Rather than being affected mainly by corporate performance and the general business climate (except, of course, where the issuing company is so weak there's doubt the bonds will ever be redeemable), the value of bonds is affected by the level of interest rates.

Trading in bonds became an extremely popular investment activity during the 1970s when interest rates began to fluctuate rapidly and in extreme ranges. Under such circumstances, the value of bonds fluctuated too, and speculators tried to "buy low, sell high," just as you would want to do with your investments. If interest rates continue to range way up and down, bonds will continue to be a hot trading medium.

As a young investor, however, owning and trading bonds almost surely will be a bit too much for you right now. Bonds are commonly issued in denominations of $1,000, $5,000, or $10,000—out of your price range. Most important, bonds themselves are good *income* assets, many of them paying a solid 8 or 10 percent interest rate, but do not have the potential for *growth* that you, as a teenager looking for capital appreciation, seek.

The world of bonds, including U.S. Treasury securities, waits for you as you grow older. Meanwhile there is plenty of action for you in the stock market.

MUTUAL FUNDS

Even if you have diligently studied the stock market and have tentatively chosen one or more target companies for your initial investment, your youth and lack of experience may leave you frightened—understandably so—when you finally put your savings into investments. If you are taking a bold step into the market, you will feel worried that your modest stake has bought you a limited portfolio at best, which your studies underline is not nearly as safe or valuable as a diversified assortment of stocks.

Mutual funds are almost an ideal solution to the twin problems of inexperience and limited portfolio size that commonly confront the youthful investor. A mutual fund is a financial service organization run by investment managers that pools your modest investment with that of thousands of others like you to purchase a diverse portfolio of stocks, bonds, or other instruments. The advantages of a good mutual fund are obvious: diversity; informed management; market "clout." By the early 1980s, over 17 million Americans had invested $250 billion in the 750 mutual funds available to anyone who could come up with the minimum investment (which ranges from $500 to $2,500, with most in the $1,000 range; a handful even allow a $100 or "no minimum" first investment).

Types of Mutual Funds

The remarkable diversity of mutual funds allows you to choose a fund that suits your individual investment goals, which means that mutual funds fit nicely into the concept of a personalized investment strategy. Overall, however, there are three major types of mutual funds: *growth stock and bond funds, income stock and bond funds,* and *money market funds*.

Growth Funds

Also called *equity funds* or *capital appreciation funds*, the approximately 320 growth funds available in the early 1980s typically invested in 30 to 60 different issues at one time, although funds specializing in a handful of stocks were available, and funds with 100 or more different stocks or bonds were not uncommon. Depending on the temperament and commitment of fund management, the portfolio of a growth fund might undergo a 20 to 50 percent turnover in a year, meaning that this percentage range in the value of stocks might be sold and the same range bought to "freshen" the fund and maximize opportunities.

Growth funds invest, as you might suspect, in stocks and bonds that are expected to appreciate in value rather than pay dividends or interest. Within the general category of growth funds are several gradations:

• *Aggressive growth funds* seek maximum appreciation and are willing to take the risk necessary to achieve that goal. Leveraged purchases, options, short sales, even purchases of "junk" stocks are within the realm of these funds. While a 25 percent return in a single year is often cited as the goal of these funds, a big loss obviously is possible, too.

• *Growth funds* without the adjective "aggressive" usually restrict purchases to stocks pinpointed by the management as possible "growth," junior, or otherwise.

Growth-Income Funds

• *Growth-income funds* combine the possibility of growth holding stocks with regular income from dividends or even interest, in the case of mutual funds also owning bonds. Capital appreciation is naturally somewhat limited by this diluted purpose.

• *Balanced funds* strive not only for growth and income, but also for a balanced portfolio that is unlikely to waver if one or two companies' fortunes decline. These funds are conservative in their outlook, so there is a "cap" on both capital appreciation and income.

Income Funds

• *Income Funds* in their commonly known form invest in stocks that best promise strong, steady earnings: blue chips, preferred stock, high-grade bonds, etc.

• *Option-income funds* take somewhat greater chances to boost income by experimenting with options, often in conjunction with other income-magnifying devices.

• *Bond funds* invest in income-generating corporate bonds as opposed to aggressive growth funds that invest in bonds for capital appreciation.

• *Tax-exempt bond funds* invest in state and local bonds, which under federal law pay interest exempt from federal income taxes. Some states also exempt this type of bond interest from tax. For investors in ultrahigh tax brackets, the lower yields offered by these bonds are more than offset by their tax exemption. You surely don't have to think about these bonds unless you're a millionaire's son or daughter. The same applies to short-term municipal bond funds that are very much like tax-exempt money market funds.

Money Market Funds

This type of mutual fund demands special attention. There are over 220 of these funds with, as of the early 1980s, over $200 billion in assets. In 1981, when interest rates soared to nearly 20 percent, money market funds outperformed *every other investment available* to the benefit of 12 million fund holders.

Money market funds do not invest in stocks, bonds, or options. They buy a wide variety of interest-yielding securities and top-grade instruments such as short-term certificates of deposit (of large denominations and carrying higher rates than you can get at your bank), U.S. Treasury Bills, commercial paper, and other similar short-term assets. (For example, $10,000 face value Treasury Bills and $100,000 bank certificates of deposit are common money market investments.) Your investment in a money market mutual fund (MMMF) thus earns interest at the highest rates available.

When interest rates are rising, MMMFs can offer up to 17 percent or more on investments, as they did during the interest rate up-surge of 1981. At that rate of return, MMMFs are more attractive than common stocks, which usually pay 10 to 15 percent in appreciation plus dividends under superb conditions. This explains the overwhelming popularity of these funds. It also should serve as a warning that there must be a catch.

There is a catch. When interest rates are falling, MMMFs no longer can find high-interest investments and the value of the funds plummets. You'll still earn relatively high interest in a MMMF compared to other interest-bearing investments, such as personal bank deposits, but your principal will never grow in a money market fund.

Services You Can Get with Mutual Funds

A remarkable list of additional services comes with many mutual funds today, especially money market funds. The age of electronic banking actually has turned many of these funds into forerunners of the real "financial supermarket." A sampling of the features you can get:

- *Dividend reinvestment plans* that automatically plow your mutual fund earnings back into more shares.
- *Automatic withdrawal plans* that cash out your profits regularly (the opposite of dividend reinvestment).
- *Telephone transfer privileges* offered by some groups of funds run by the same investment management firm. This allows you to switch from, say, the group's MMMF to its aggressive growth fund, to its income fund, and back and forth as your perception of the market dictates.
- *Preauthorized check transactions* that allow you to make regular investment from your savings or bank account or your paycheck.
- *Free checking accounts* are offered by many MMMFs as long as you're willing to write checks only in even multiples of $500 (you also withdraw simply by writing yourself a check).
- *Credit cards* such as MasterCard and Visa, using your MMMF as a credit guarantee.
- And more. Pay attention: new fund benefits are appearing almost every day.

How to Invest in a Mutual Fund

First, decide on your investment goals. Because you're on the lookout for growth, mainly short-term growth in the five-to-ten year range, you probably will want to seek a growth fund. If you're leaning toward gambling, an aggressive growth fund might be worth a try. At the same time, however, look at the returns being offered by money market funds. If they are extremely high at the time, consider putting your money in a MMMF until interest rates fall and stocks again become an attractive investment.

Next, watch the progress of a few target funds in the financial section of your newspaper. See which ones are beating the market as a whole, measured by such leading market barometers as the Standard & Poor's index of 500 stocks and the Dow Jones average of thirty industrial stocks. Not all mutual funds are listed in the paper, but you're sure to find some good candidates from among the 250 or so that are.

Also, ask your parents, older friends, relatives, and peers what mutual funds they like most for performance. Get as much guidance as you can.

Now, order the prospectus of your favorite candidate. Read it carefully. How has the fund performed in the last five years? In the last year? Does it do better than similar funds in hard times? In good times? (Each year *Forbes* magazine publishes a list of mutual funds that rates performance in good and bad markets.) Who is the fund manager? Just one person, whose judgment you will have to trust, or a huge investment firm that uses complex computer analysis to develop its portfolio? What is the minimum investment required? And above all, what is the fund's philosophy? The prospectus will state and describe the fund's portfolio (perhaps even giving you a hint as to what stocks you might consider buying on your own).

Consider the fund charges. There are two general types of funds as far as service charges go: *load funds* that charge a standard 7½ percent to 8½ percent commission (mainly offered by major investment companies charging, in effect, for their advice), and *no-load funds* that do not charge a fee. Since there are over 200 no-load funds available, many of which are as big and as successful as (if not bigger and more successful than) the load funds, you will have no basic reason to choose a load fund (the commissions you save are substantial, the additional advice you get minimal). There will also be a management fee charged annually no matter what kind of fund you choose; a typical fee runs about ¾ percent to 1½ percent.

How to Tell How Your Fund Is Doing

Once you buy a share in a mutual fund, you cannot just sell it on the open market if your fund is a winner. There is only one purchaser of your shares: the fund itself.

A few mutual funds are *closed-end* funds that offer only a limited amount of shares. These shares *are* publicly traded. But there are so few that you can ignore them for your investment purposes.

Most funds are so-called *open end* funds that are indefinite in lifespan and that issue an unlimited number of shares to anyone who is willing to buy. On the day you purchase your shares, the price is determined by the net asset value of the fund's investments.

If the assets are worth $100 million and you invest $1,000, you will get 100 shares worth $10 each if the fund has sold a total of 10 million shares. If only 1 million shares have been sold, you will get 10 shares worth $100 each.

Now assume the net asset value of the fund's assets climbs to $200 million. The value of each share you own doubles, or perhaps you are credited with more shares instead. If no dividends have been paid (a likely event in your case as an investor in growth funds), you may sell back your shares to the fund at the then net asset value per share and take your profit. Or you can hold on.

This is an important service of a mutual fund: its liquidity, if you must sell your shares at any time. Your fund itself will buy back your shares, usually at net asset value at redemption; you need not seek a buyer. Another benefit with a no-load fund is privacy. You buy directly from the fund. There are no securities salesmen or other middlemen involved.

How Do Mutual Funds Fit into Your Personal Investment Strategy?

While it is up to you whether to buy into mutual funds and which one(s) to choose, these are the guidelines:

• You can afford to be aggressive at this point in your life, so aggressive growth funds are a choice.

• Growth over five to ten years is your major objective.

• Long-term growth is a hallmark of mutual funds. This is a guide as you grow older.

• Money market funds should be used as you would use bank accounts to store your money when interest rates are high. But most experts point to equities—stocks—as the eventual investment winner of the 1980s.

• If you want more information, contact any local broker or dealer in mutual funds, or write to the Investment Company Institute (1775 K Street, Washington, DC 20006). For information on no-load mutual funds, contact the No-Load Mutual Fund Association (Valley Forge, PA 19481). This association publishes a no-load directory.

COMMODITIES

Let's say you think the fast-food industry will continue growing in the 1980s at the same fast pace it achieved during the 1970s. You might seriously consider purchasing stock in a nationwide chain of hamburger restaurants, for example, if you believe Americans will gobble up increasing numbers of ever higher-priced burgers over the next five to ten years. Or you might go one step further and buy stock in a beef processing company, since booming burger joints will need continually increasing supplies of beef. You might buy into a beef processor if your educated teenage palate could not distinguish between one chain's burgers and another's (which is unlikely), or if you simply didn't have the foggiest idea which restaurant chains would show the most profit and which would show only sluggish growth. By purchasing stock of a supplier, you wouldn't care which restaurants succeeded more than others as long as the market, for hamburgers in general, remained strong.

But what if you weren't sure which beef processor would become the favorite of restaurant chains? Conceivably you could buy stock in cattle feedlot companies that sell their beef to the processors. But which of these feedlots is bound to succeed? Your inquiries could go on and on until you reached the level of the raw commodity itself: beef. If you bought beef of a certain grade, it would be like all other beef of the same grade. No one would prefer your beef over others' or vice versa. When the demand for beef increased, your beef would go up in value. The same with wheat sold to grain silos, then to processors who turn it into flour, then to bakers who turn the flour into hamburger buns, then finally to your neighborhood burger place.

Trading in raw commodities goes on daily at one of ten commodities exchanges located in New York (which has five), Chicago (which has two), Minneapolis, Kansas City, and New Orleans. Different exchanges specialize in different commodities: the Chicago Board of Trade handles most of the Farm Belt's crops and livestock, for example, while the Commodity Exchange in New York specializes in precious metals, such as gold, silver, and platinum. Other exchanges handle oil, plywood, cocoa, coffee, even Treasury Bills and foreign currency. Because the prices of commodities fluctuate broadly and almost continuously in response to production or harvest, current rates of interest and inflation, and even political crises, speculators in commodities can make or lose fortunes in just a few days (or even hours).

At the commodity exchanges, the raw goods themselves are not actually bought and sold on the trading floor. Instead, contracts to buy and sell at a future date—called *commodities futures*—are the linchpin of the market. For example, you could purchase a contract to buy 50,000 pounds of potatoes three months in the future at 7 cents a pound. If the price goes up to 10 cents a pound three months hence, you do not buy the potatoes at your (low) contract price and then immediately sell them for a profit. Instead, you merely buy an offsetting contract to sell the same amount of potatoes at the price offered when your contract matures. By exchange rules, these offsetting contracts cancel each other out and you are simply mailed a check for your profit of $1,500 (before commissions). Likewise, if the price of potatoes drops to 4 cents a pound, you don't have to fulfill your contract to buy potatoes. You simply buy an offsetting contract to sell at a higher price and take your loss. This way, you're never in danger that you'll be compelled to pay for twenty-five tons of potatoes that are dumped on your front lawn one morning.

Two factors make gambling in commodities attractive to some investors: (1) the price of commodities depends almost entirely on fundamental forces of supply and demand rather than company management, research, dividend history, and other attributes that influence the worth of corporate stock; and (2) more important, gamblers can take much more advantage of leverage.

Because commodities exchanges are not subject to the strict margin requirements of the stock exchanges (requiring in the early 1980s, as you read earlier in this chapter, that at least 50 percent of a stock's price be paid in cash at the moment of purchase), speculators can buy a substantial total of commodities futures with just a little cash. Typical margin requirements run 1 to 2 percent of the futures' prices. Where your $500 will buy you $1,000 of New York Stock Exchange listed shares, for instance, you may be able to purchase a $50,000 contract in pork futures (bacon) on a commodities exchange. A 10 percent rise in the value of the stock earns you $100; a similar rise in the price of pork nets you $5,000 before commissions.

All this makes speculating in commodities seem a fantastic investment opportunity for a young investor like you, right?

Wrong.

I never mentioned *investing* in commodities. One gambles or at most *speculates*. This implies tremendous risk. You're not investing, as emphasized in every line of this section; you're *gambling*—out-and-out gambling.

In the commodities market, the time-honored stockbrokers' advice that "you can never go wrong taking a profit" is not true. In commodities, *you always will go broke* taking small profits because you can win only if you take very large profits to offset the many small losses you invariably will sustain. This is true because of the tiny margin used to buy and sell commodities. When you put up just 2 percent to buy a futures contract, your profits are magnified, *but so are your losses.* And you don't have time to give your contracts a chance to rebound, since most futures contracts are *marked to market* daily. Marking to market is the same as a margin call—the commodities exchange will demand that you put up more cash to cover the falling futures prices immediately.

If you go into the commodities futures market with a stake of just $5,000—probably more than you possibly could afford right now—the odds are 60 percent you'll be wiped out almost at once. Just a slight drop in futures prices your first day in the market could easily result in a margin call requiring an extra $5,000 in cash or surrendering your original stake. In fact, you need at least $50,000 to have a 50-50 chance of winning.

With the odds so heavily stacked against you, it seems crazy to trade in commodities futures. Without recommending such gambling in the least, here are tips that wealthy speculators—who can afford to lose thousands in any particular day—often use:

• Don't use the stock market as a guide to the commodities market. Use commodities instead as a forecaster of the stock and other markets. The commodities market daily fluctuations average 25 percent of the investor's *equity* (margin), but the stock market fluctuations rarely reach 2 percent daily. Therefore, in the commodities market there are billions of dollars involved in a quick search for the "real price," which usually is reflected in the stock market much later.

• Don't watch gold; watch silver and copper. The silver market is made up mostly of silver users (such as Eastman Kodak and mining companies) and professional floor traders. Silver is a good indicator of where other commodities are going. Copper, too, is a leading indicator, because it is primarily an industrial metal, sensitive to economic changes.

• Organize a plan—when to get in and out—and stick with it. Too many speculators, when facing a loss, want to give it a bit more time.

• Limit your bullish bias. In commodities, it's as easy to sell short as it is to buy long. Many traders in commodities got stuck in gold in the early 1980s because they knew only how to buy and hold.

• Don't news-jerk. The commodities market is too smart and varied for teenagers, even smart ones, to make money by making decisions based on international rumors or on closing prices in Hong Kong or London.

• Never buy a commodity because the price is low. The longs—those expecting the commodity to rise—have lost all their capacity at these lows. They'll need a lot of time to build up again.

• Don't pyramid. This means adding to positions in your favor. You can be wiped out by a small move against you.

• Don't put too much of your capital on one side of the market—either too long or too short—and don't trade in markets that are illiquid, relative to the size of your position. You'll find yourself locked in.

• Don't trade during inactive periods, near the close on Fridays or before holidays. Markets often move against the next major trend.

• Don't focus on selling round numbers. The way floor traders manipulate stop orders—usually at round numbers—dictates against being able to sell at round numbers. Beware.

And after all this, you still want to play? Okay, play—it's your money and your losses!

COLLECTIBLES

What is a collectible?

It can be almost anything—a postage stamp or a car, an Oriental rug or a comic book, an autographed baseball or a baseball card, even an original Barbie doll (at the start of the 1980s, worth over a hundred times its initial retail price).

Most kinds of property grow old and wear out gradually until you discard them. A collectible is property that you preserve because you think its value will increase over the years. And you, an observant teenager, are in a unique position to spot a potential collectible when adults three times your age scoff and say: "Oh that? It's just a worthless piece of junk!"

You are young, open-minded, and willing to change. When a new fad arrives, whether it be in fashion, sports, or anything else, you are willing to give it a fighting chance. Most important, you have a certain feel for what is valuable and lasting in your generation, a feeling older investors wish they had. You also have a sixth sense about what is catchy and gimmicky.

Take, for example, the Beatles. When Americans first heard them, the older generation thought their music was a lot of static while younger people heard something there that was unique and lasting. Who turned out to be right? Today, unplayed copies of rare Beatle albums that initially sold for $2.98 command hundreds of dollars at auctions (where they're bought by older investors who have learned their lesson). You can hear the difference between audio "junk" and the real stuff, while your parents probably complain that it's all noise to their ears. And you can profit from your powers of discernment.

What Kinds of Collectibles Make Good Investments?

There are more traditional collectibles: stamps, coins, art, rare gems, antiques, and others with established markets. You can buy or sell coins, for instance, at coin or hobby shops throughout the country, or you can buy a painting at an art auction (although you probably can't afford to attend these black-tie affairs, even with the bottom falling out of the art market during the early 1980s). If you want to invest in such collectibles, the key to success is: become an expert.

You must specialize. Buying stamps—any stamps—is not good enough; you must study, say, pre–World War II German stamps or United States airmail stamps in order to learn what is really worthwhile and what is just trash. Catalogue values for these items are often wildly exaggerated; a coin worth $100 in an "official" price book may bring you offers of only $20 to $30 at reputable dealers.

Also, you can be easily fooled by collectibles and those selling them. If your interest is Chippendale antique furniture, for instance, you can purchase (1) authentic British Chippendale, (2) authentic American Chippendale, or (3) clever reproductions of both, worth very little. Investing in such valuable collectibles requires considerable experience and money—and you have far too little of either at this age.

But you do have a youthful flair for the more offbeat collectibles because of your perspective. If cars are your passion, you already sense that the following types of cars may someday be in great demand: convertibles, full-size sedans, sports cars with big engines, pre-EPA cars without pollution control equipment, and others that are no longer built in quantity (the hugely successful Checker is bound to become a collector's item someday, after having been driven out of production by high fuel costs).

If political campaign buttons are your specialty, you probably know that Nixon-Agnew buttons are a hot item, and you may also have your eye on a particular button for campaign 1984. Or you may be comic book fanatic, a Smurf collector, a yo-yo expert—no matter. Ask yourself this one question when you consider a potential collectible: does this item have the appeal—justified or not—to increase in value, and thus in demand, over the next five to ten years?

How to Estimate the Value of a Collectible

The value of any item you may decide to keep as an investment will be determined by three factors: (1) rarity; (2) intrinsic collectible worth; and (3) sentimental or "nostalgic" value.

Unless you begin immediately with the more traditional collectibles, the item or items you select to start your collection won't be rare. The first Superman comic book was widely available on the newsstands and worth only its cover price. Only after the vast majority of undiscerning readers threw their copies away did a perfectly preserved comic book become the $10,000 rarity it is in the 1980s. You don't want a rare item; it will be too expensive in the first place. You want something that is inexpensive now because it is easily available, but will be expensive as it becomes a rarity later.

Likewise, the intrinsic value of an item is not important to you as a beginning investor in collectibles. Gold or silver has intrinsic value; so does a car. But the price of gold or silver fluctuates so wildly it would be almost impossible for you to profit from an increase in gold or silver prices with so many seasoned "gold bugs" around. And the intrinsic value of a car is bound to decrease as the car deteriorates. Buying a collectible for the intrinsic worth of its makeup or parts is just like buying commodities (see above) where you're bound to lose.

Instead, look for an item that will be popular someday, in your opinion, because it will catch people's fancy, make them laugh, feel sentimental or nostalgic, make them want to have it. No one buys the bedsheets Elvis Presley slept on because they are custom-made or woven from the finest silk (although the King of Rock 'n' Roll may have had such luxuries). These bedsheets and other similar everyday possessions of the stars are auctioned off at high prices because of the story behind them. Use your imagination: if you see an item in a store that intrigues you—buy it. Then store it carefully, making sure to preserve it in as nearly new condition as possible. Who knows—in a decade or so, your imagination could make you rich!

The Phony Collectibles

Be careful, however, of the so-called "limited edition" items widely advertised in the print media. You've seen loads of them: commemorative medallions ("our Presidents"); porcelain ducks; a set of fifty silver spoons (plates) representing each of our fifty states. The advertisements lead you to believe that the merchandise offered is rare, of intrinsic worth, and in great demand. In fact, these "limited editions" are limited to precisely the number of people who order them—meaning that everyone who wants a porcelain duck for his/her fireplace mantel gets one. As for intrinsic worth, the value of the gold, silver, pewter or other ingredients of these phony collectibles rarely approaches 20 percent of the original purchase price, meaning you're certain to lose unless the prices of the commodities go through the roof. To allay your suspicions, some manufacturers of phony collectibles agree to repurchase the item at face value for a year or more after their sale. Those who actually make good on this promise expect most of you not to realize the item's true worth until it's too late. The only reason to buy these phony collectibles is your own personal taste.

NOW IT'S TIME TO THINK OF
YOUR RETIREMENT

Surely this must be a joke, you say to yourself, a healthy teenager half a century away from retirement.

It is not a joke. Changes in the tax laws as the decade opened make it simple common sense that you open an Individual Retirement Account, or IRA, as soon as you begin earning money on your own. You do not, repeat, *not* have to be eighteen or older to open an IRA as long as you have *earned income.* Even if you haven't yet begun your first job, learn now what to do about an IRA when you find employment.

IRA—The Best Tax Shelter Ever Designed
for U.S. Individuals

If you work for pay, you are eligible to open an Individual Retirement Account (IRA)—the best tax shelter ever designed for and available to U.S. individuals in any tax bracket.

You can contribute up to $2,000 a year tax-free to an IRA and then defer taxes on the interest, dividends, or gains earned on accumulated savings until retirement or age 70½.

Invest the maximum you are allowed in an IRA per year. Be conservative in your IRA investments, for this is retirement money. And maintain your contributions, for the advantages to you of tax-free investments compounding tax-free year after year are wondrous to behold.

No tax shelter ever devised for average taxpayers even approaches an IRA in its financial benefits and safety. (I've had one since the original law authorizing IRAs was passed.) But in the past, ownership of an IRA was restricted to those of us not protected by any other private pension plan and millions of eligible Americans simply ignored the opportunity to participate.

But the IRA is just too valuable a tax shelter to shrug off. Even though the total you can contribute is limited to a relatively small amount ($2,000 maximum a year, with a small extra for a spousal IRA), even this amount can multiply to startlingly high levels due to the compounding of earnings on contributions tax-deferred until retirement. And the permissible contribution will be increased in coming years. This has been the trend in such programs; it will be again.

How Should You Invest Your IRA?

Virtually all financial institutions (banks, insurance companies, mutual funds, securities dealers) are competing for your IRA funds. Most institutions can efficiently handle your IRA.

Whatever you do, keep in mind that an IRA is a tax shelter and all earnings of an IRA are treated alike when you finally withdraw your funds. Thus, municipal bonds are a ridiculous vehicle for an IRA, for you would be converting relatively low, current tax-free income into deferred taxable income.

Aim for the highest total return from your IRA, taking more risk now, when you are young, and switching to safer investments as you near retirement. You can manage switches easily.

When Should You Make Your Contributions?

Make your contributions as early in the calendar year as possible so that your money can start working under a tax shelter. You can, though, contribute at any time during the calendar year and into the next calendar year until you file your tax return. Try to start January 2, of any year.

What about Withdrawals and Taxes?

You can start to withdraw from your IRA after you are 59½ years old, at which time the money is taxed as ordinary income. You must start withdrawals at age 70½, but you can arrange for distributions to be paid over your life expectancy. (Life expectancy tables are provided by the IRS.)

Can Part-Time Workers Set Up IRAs, Too?

Yes. All working people under age 70½, whether or not covered under a qualified retirement plan, are eligible to contribute to an IRA. This includes the self-employed, government workers, and all workers in private industry—full-time and part-time workers and even students working summers.

Can Anyone Contribute up to $2,000 a Year?

You can contribute up to $2,000 a year as long as that is not more than 100 percent of your income. If you earn only $1,500 a year, your contribution is limited to $1,500 a year. If you earn more than $2,000, your contribution is limited to $2,000.

What Are the Benefits in Precise Dollar Terms?

You get the double benefit of a current tax deduction *and* tax-deferred compounding of earnings in the IRA.

To repeat: *do not shrug off this shelter!!!!*

Your Investment Choices—in Brief*

Investment Medium	Overall Degree of Risk	Approximate Flow Yield	Appreciation/ Depreciation of Capital	Liquidity	Maturity	Tax Aspects	Professional Assistance Required	Minimum Investment Required
Savings accounts (passbook, statement, club)	Very low	Low		Can be withdrawn at any time	N/A	Interest income is fully taxable subject to certain exclusions or deferrals	None	None
Time deposits and certificates	Very low	Generally moderate	Generally not possible	Can be withdrawn at any time but with penalty for early withdrawal	90 days to 10 years		None	Varies but usually $500
Common Stocks	Moderate to high	Varies	Possible	Varies depending if stock is publicly traded or closely held	N/A	First $100 of dividends not taxable ($200 if joint return is filed), capital gains on sale	Generally moderate to substantial	Varies with range of stock prices
Corporate Bond	Generally moderate	Generally moderate	Potential increases with the term of maturity	Varies depending on volume of trading and if issue is publicly traded	Up to 30 years	Income taxes payable on interest, capital gains on sale	Moderate	Usually $1,000

Municipal Bonds	Moderate	Low to moderate	Potential increases with the term of maturity	Varies with size of issue and market or region	Up to 30 years	Generally exempt from Federal and some state income taxes, capital gains on sale	Moderate	Usually $5,000 but sometimes as low as $100 or $500
Treasury Bills, Bonds, and notes	Very low to moderate	Moderate	Potential increases with the term of maturity	Less than 1 week, generally very liquid	90 days to 30 years	Federal income taxes payable on interest exempt from state taxes, capital gains on sale	Little to moderate	Generally $1,000 for notes and bonds, $10,000 for Treasury Bills
Money Market Funds	Low to moderate	Moderate to high	Generally not possible	Very liquid	N/A	Income taxes on interest, first $100 of dividends not taxable, capital gains on sale	None	Varies but usually $500-$1,000
Mutual Funds	Moderate to high	Low to moderate	Varies with type of fund	Generally very liquid	N/A	Taxation on income depends on types of assets held in the funds	Moderate	Varies
Real Estate	Moderate to high	Depends on nature of investment and its respective market	Quite possible	Generally limited	N/A	Some income sheltered by expenses, depreciation and tax credits, capital gains on sale	Generally moderate to substantial	Varies

*Adapted from the Maryland Association of CPAs, Inc., by Preston Publishing Company, a subsidiary of Prentice-Hall, Inc.

6

THE SOUND OF MUSIC

CONTENTS

CONCERTS

What's Happening and Where?

Rock and country fans have a hot line more ablaze than the Pentagon's. Before a concert is advertised on radio or in the newspapers, devotees are deciding whose turn it is to wait on the Ticketron line this time. Nobody quite knows where the information comes from ("John's sister's roommate has a friend who's the drummer's cousin and she says . . ."), but it's usually accurate. So believe it: the best way to find out what rock and country concerts are coming to your area is to know people who know people.

Your next best options include getting schedules from box offices and record companies or calling the "concert hot line" (if you have one near you). But do count on newspapers and radio for finding out about classical, jazz, and pop music concerts.

If you live near a college campus, you have the best deal of all. Musicians—from classical to punk rock—perform often at colleges. And tickets are usually much less expensive than at a public arena. Whether or not you get near a classroom, buy a subscription to the college newspaper and study it carefully.

Getting Tickets

Once you know when and where the concert will be, how do you go about getting tickets? The answer often depends upon your tolerance for sleeping in soggy clothes; your ability to find a stamp or drive a hard bargain; and your funds. Let's look at the alternatives.

Camping Out

Often the best way to get tickets (and also the most fun) is to wait on line, sometimes for as long as twelve hours before Ticketron or the concert hall opens. It's a way of meeting people who like your kind of music and sharing the camaraderie that goes with being together for hours with nothing planned. For the most part it's a practice your parents worry about but understand because they remember doing the same thing in their youth. But on nights when the thermometer plunges to the point where two pairs of thermal socks lift the temperature of your toes to the freezing level, or when it has been raining for six days and the governor has called for all inflatable rafts to be registered as part of the state's emergency rescue fleet, camping out loses its excitement.

Pluses:	Fun, possibility of choice seats (if you come early enough) at box office prices.
Minuses	A lot of wasted time, no control over the weather, danger of having bullies shove into line.
Keep in Mind:	Wear layers of warm clothing that you can peel off as desired; bring food, a blanket, a radio; help organize the line by giving people numbers.

Writing Away

There are two occasions when writing away may get you good seats:

1. When the performer(s) is so popular that promoters know it would be too dangerous for people to camp out waiting for ticket sales to start; and
2. When the performer(s) is not well-known and the only way to get a full house would be to offer tickets at the box office and through the mail.

In the first case, tickets are usually doled out through a lottery. Everyone sends in a self-addressed, stamped envelope (SASE) to a certain place by a certain day. Then the envelopes are selected at random. Promoters notify the lottery winners that they can get a certain number of tickets for box office price if a check is received by a certain date.

Pluses:	Fairest way to distribute tickets, especially for people who live a distance from the concert hall; box office prices; element of surprise.
Minuses:	No control over whether or not you can go or where you'll be sitting; element of disappointment.
Keep in Mind:	If it's a show you really want to see, the gamble is only a few minutes of your time and two stamps (one for your envelope and one for the SASE).

The second occasion is surely one of first come, first served. The earlier you get in your requests, the better your chances to see the performance from the seats you request.

Pluses:	Easier than standing on line; box office prices.
Minuses:	The mail can be slow and, these days, frequently undependable. Lost letters are not unusual.
Keep in Mind:	Be sure you tell the promoters where to send the tickets, how many you want, and the price you want to pay. Pay by check or money order; never send cash.

Getting Scalped

Scalping, a common practice—illegal in most states—takes place outside a concert hall the night of the event. Someone is trying to sell tickets to the performance at a price substantially above the box office's. The amount in excess of what is printed on the ticket depends upon how popular the performer(s) is and how many people want to buy the same tickets. (Reselling tickets at box office price is not illegal.)

Let's say you love the group performing and you're willing to spend $12.50 (ticket price) plus $5—the total of $17.50 that the scalper is asking. But while you're negotiating this price, someone else comes over and offers the scalper $12.50 plus $10. You now have a choice. Should you bid $12.50 plus $12.50 (for a total of $25.00)? Or should you walk away, try to find someone else to buy the tickets from, and, if unsuccessful, go home? What you do will depend upon how much you want to see the performance and how much money you have to spend.

Pluses:	It's a way to see the performance if you haven't obtained tickets in advance; sometimes good seats are offered.
Minuses:	It's costly (could be *five times* the box office price); it's dangerous (the ticket could be counterfeit and then you would be out the money *and* out of the concert hall); it's risky (unless you know the seating arrangement of the hall, you could spend a great deal of money and wind up in nosebleed country).

Keep in Mind: Be wary of counterfeit tickets. Before you buy, try to compare the scalper's tickets with a friend's legitimate tickets. (If the scalper doesn't want you to do a close examination, chances are the tickets are counterfeit.) All tickets should be identical except for seat number and perhaps color (often color indicates place of seat and therefore price of ticket). Check the date on the ticket. Shop the scalpers. Don't buy from the first one who approaches you. But don't be taken in by someone who appears to be giving the tickets away at an unbelievably low price—sure as you're standing there, something's phony.

Don't bid up just because someone is bidding against you. That someone might be a shill (a person in cahoots with the scalper to drive up the price of the ticket). Bid only what you have and can afford.

This form of buying cannot be recommended.

Going for Brokers

Ticket brokers are people or firms who buy blocks of tickets for a show and then resell them quite legitimately prior to the performance to anyone who is willing to pay more than box office price for a good seat. How much more depends upon state regulations and how much in demand the ticket is. Brokers usually advertise in the local newspapers when they have seats for a hot concert.

Pluses: Legal method of buying ticket; generally excellent seats available.

Minuses: Ouch! The cost.

Keep in Mind: You might be able to bargain with brokers, especially close to show time when ticket sales haven't been too good. There's nothing worth less to a broker (or to anyone, for that matter) than a front row seat to last night's show. On the other hand, if you wait too long before contacting the broker for tickets to a hot performance, there will be none left. Do not give a deposit to a ticket broker you have not dealt with before because there are many fly-by-night outfits which won't return deposit money if a concert is canceled.

General Admission, or Festival-Seating

On December 3, 1979, a terrible tragedy occurred in Cincinnati's Riverfront Coliseum. In a human stampede, eleven people died and twenty were injured. Why?

At that time the Coliseum sold general admission tickets. This meant that ticket holders did not have reserved seats. To get the best seats possible, you had to get to the stadium early. This particular concert featured the popular British rock group, The Who. Thousands of people holding general admission tickets lined up at the main gate of the Coliseum, which was not opened until fifty minutes before the group was scheduled to appear. When the gate was opened, these thousands, eager for good seats, surged forward, trampling people.

The Riverfront Coliseum no longer has unreserved seats; other stadiums also have given up that practice as a result of this and similar tragedies. But there still are some arenas and stadiums which have general admission or festival-seating. While these tickets are less expensive than reserved seats, there is a potential hazard in being part of a crushing crowd. Don't take the risks for a couple of dollars.

The Extras

Programs, shirts, buttons. They are the extras at a concert which have nothing to do with the music. But they're promoted fiercely, and they cost money. Whether or not you buy them depends on how important these items are to you. And because there is a flea market atmosphere surrounding the vendors, decide in advance whether you're a buyer. If not, stay away. You could get caught up in the excitement and wind up buying two shirts you'll never wear just because they seemed like such a bargain at two for $18.98.

If you really want to buy, however, know that the performer's authorized representatives have concessions *inside* the arena. The unauthorized sellers hawk *outside*. Generally the quality of the goods inside is better, but the prices are higher.

If overpriced foot-long hot dogs are your thing, eat in the arena or concert hall. But if you want to be kind to your pocketbook and stomach, either eat before you get inside or brown bag it. Be warned: you're not allowed to bring cans or bottles into most halls, so don't even try. They'll be confiscated and it will be a complete waste of money.

Fred Hit His Head, Can't Go to the Dead

What should you do when you're so sick that you have to miss the concert for which you've bought tickets, made all the preparations, and looked forward to for months?

1. Call all the people you were going with to see if they know anyone who would like to buy a ticket.
2. Be a sport. Give the ticket to your sister/mother/a friend.
3. Give the ticket to a friend who is going to the concert to sell there—at box office price only. Anything more is scalping and illegal.

Don't Get Taken

Concerts draw crowds. Crowds draw pickpockets, ticket snatchers, and drug dealers. Stay alert.

• Never flash money or a wallet.
• Don't carry a wallet in your back pocket or in the pocket of a jacket; use your front pockets. (For more anti-crime advice, see Chapter 11, *Teenagers on Guard!*)
• Don't stick your ticket up out of your shirt pocket because it's easier for you to get to. It's also easier for snatchers.
• Don't put your pocketbook on the floor or under your seat during the concert. Hang on to it! Best of all, don't bring one.
• Don't buy drugs. You don't know who the pushers are or what they're selling. You'll never see them again, so you have no recourse if you get cheated or hurt. Aside from the real physical dangers involved with drugs, remember they are illegal. If you're caught, at the very least they'll be confiscated and you'll be out every penny you spent. At worst, you could be liable for arrest and imprisonment.

INSTRUMENTS

Play It Again, Sam

At countless parties this night, friends will gather around the piano or organ to sing as an amateur among them pounds away at the old favorites. At other gatherings, younger people will form circles to make music on their guitars or harmonicas or ukuleles or just to hum along and harmonize.

The number of amateur musicians in the United States today is at an all-time high. And while pianos, guitars, and organs continue to be the most popular instruments with amateur musicians, sales of violins are also rising sharply.

If you were to ask high school students what their favorite activity is, more than one of every two probably would reply "music," with the piano played by almost six of every ten. The piano is also the most popular with the general musical population. The guitar—acoustic and electric—ranks next, followed by the organ and clarinet. Why this spectacular popularity and growth? Not career planning, but simply enjoyment and self-satisfaction.

While many students receive private lessons on their instruments, a surprising number are self-taught. Sales of self-instruction aids, including audiovisual cassettes, have been climbing steadily—with better than 70 percent of electric guitarists sharpening their musical skills on their own.

Heed these pointers to help you in pursuing your goal of playing music and to save you money as well:

• Since there are easy, average, and hard-to-learn instruments, decide in advance how big an investment of time and money you want and can afford to make. If you're not sure how much of an investment you want to make in time or money, rent an instrument from a reliable dealer and try it out before you buy. (More about this in a moment.)

• If you buy, your first instrument should be of high enough quality to give you a good tone, but it need not be expensive. You can always trade up.

• If you buy a second-hand instrument, get the counsel of a knowledgeable friend or teacher, and make sure you're trading with a reliable dealer.

• Use the instrument. All instruments perform better when they are in constant use than when left alone for long periods of time.

• Wipe your instrument after each use with a soft cloth to remove oils that might affect the finish.

• Other than keyboards, store your instruments in special cases, preferably with a hard or semihard shell.

• If you have fretted instruments, try to keep them in a room at about 72 degrees. Some guitar players put half a potato in their cases to maintain the needed moisture. Replace all strings at the same time when they begin to lose their brilliance, and when replacing strings, remove one at a time.

To guide you in selecting an instrument, here are the grades of ease of playing:

- *Easy:* autoharp, bongo drums, conga drums, chord organ, recorder, ukulele.
- *Fairly easy:* accordion, alto horn, banjo, concertina, drums, guitar, harmonica, mandolin.
- *Average:* baritone horn, clarinet, cornet, flute, marimba, organ, piano, saxophone, sousaphone, trombone, trumpet, tuba, vibraharp, xylophone.
- *Fairly difficult:* bass, cello, French horn, viola, violin.
- *Difficult:* bassoon, harp, oboe.

Questions to Ask before Starting

For the teenager who always has wanted to play the guitar, flute, trumpet, piano, or—? and who wants to know how to get started selecting an instrument, read on. If you already have made the commitment, you are, for my purposes, a pro, and you can skip or skim this section.

Before you, the prospective musician, buy or rent an instrument, you must talk to the pros—to the music teachers in your school, to the salespeople at the local music stores, to musicians you already know.

Here's What You *Want to Know*	*Here's What You* *Must Ask Yourself*
1. How difficult is this instrument to learn?	1. Am I willing to spend eight hours a week practicing? Will that mean I can't be on the baseball (football, hockey, etc.) team?
2. Are there people in my area who teach this instrument? If so, what's the going rate for a half-hour lesson?	2. Are my parents willing/able to give me the money for private lessons? Can I chip in or pay for the lessons myself by working after school?
3. Are group lessons less expensive? Are they available in my area?	3. If the local Y's lessons are good and much less expensive, how can I get there? Will my older sister/brother drive me?
4. Can I learn this instrument in school?	4. Will school instruction be best for me if I want to be a serious musician? What if I just want to have a good time and learn the basics?
5. What should I look for when choosing an instrument?	5. I'm 5'1" and weigh 93 pounds—maybe a tuba is the wrong instrument for me.
6. What are the brand names I should be aware of?	6. Do I need/can I afford the best? Will a beginner model do?
7. Should I think about renting?	7. What are the monthly charges? Who pays for repairs and part replacements? If I like the instrument and want to continue playing, can I buy it at the end of the rental period?
8. Should I buy a used instrument?	8. Do I know anyone who's selling, say, a French horn?
9. How will I know what I'm getting?	9. Who can I take with me to check out the instrument?
10. If I buy it new, what is the warranty on it?	10. What if I leave it out in the rain?

11. Is there a resale market for instruments?

11. Suppose it turns out I hate it? Suppose I don't have time to practice?

12. Should I expect to lose money on a resale?

12. Will this instrument be in vogue when I want to sell it? Is it considered a collectible (rare)? What is its quality? What kind of condition is it in?

13. What sort of care does this instrument require?

13. Seriously, will I take care of it the way I should?

What's the Right Instrument for You?

Pianist Stevie Wonder has been blind from birth.

Guitarist Jerry Garcia of the Grateful Dead is missing part of a finger.

What this proves is that there are *no hard and fast* rules connecting musical instruments and physical characteristics. Desire is the most important ingredient for success in learning and playing an instrument.

Keeping that in mind, here are some physical factors to *consider* when choosing an instrument, since they make the learning easier.

- Outstandingly buck teeth can cause problems for brass instruments (trumpet, trombone, French horn). Orthodontics helps.
- It's harder to play higher brass instruments (French horn, trumpet) with thick lips. Easier to play, in general, are the trombone, baritone horn, and tuba.
- If you cannot make a single opening with your lips for air to pass through (an embouchure problem), it's hard to play a flute.
- String instrumentalists should be able to discern pitch and they must be willing to develop their hand muscles.
- It's helpful for piano players to have large palms (for greater range).

But the most important physical characteristic of all is the *heart*. When that says "yes" to an instrument, you've made the right choice.

New, Used, or Rented?

Whichever choice you make, buying or renting, always listen to the instrument and play it yourself before you reach any decision.

New

On new instruments, you should not have to pay list price. The only time list price is even a slight possibility is when you live in a small town with only one music store. For a large purchase (and even a small instrument can be considered a large purchase because of the dollars involved), it would be worthwhile to make a trip to a metropolitan area. Competition in the cities drives prices down, and sales are rampant.

The one problem with buying an instrument at a place far from home lies with the warranty and service. Warranties which cover all repairs and parts for a year are worthless if to make use of them it costs you $100 and a day's time to lug your instrument back to the store.

When buying a new instrument (or a used one, for that matter), many stores will include, free of charge, a carrying case, some cleaning equipment, or some spare parts (like reeds for oboes or strings for guitars). If the store doesn't make you an offer gratuitously, don't hesitate to ask. The worst that can happen is that you'll be refused.

Used

The term "used" often evokes a negative feeling—as though you were buying something second-rate. Sometimes that's true. But in the case of instruments, it could be exactly the opposite.

Quality instruments that are kept in good condition often *appreciate* in price (get more valuable with age) as their sound to the trained ear becomes richer. It's hard for someone unschooled in the instrument to hear this, though, so you need to seek a pro's judgment before you buy. If possible, take a musician with you to see and test the instrument. If you're buying from an individual, ask the owner if you can have it on approval to check it out with a reputable music store. Don't be insulted if the instrument's owner insists on coming with you when you're going for an appraisal; an instrument is valuable, so you can understand why it's important to keep an eye on it. After the appraiser tells you about the instrument, ask him to step aside for a moment. Inquire in private what he thinks the instrument should sell for. Then you'll know if the price asked is reasonable.

Used instruments are sold in music stores and personally through ads in newspapers and notices on bulletin boards. One excellent way of tracking down the instrument of your choice is to run an ad in the classified section of your local newspaper under "Merchandise Wanted." Specify your needs. "A Gibson Les Paul Recording Guitar and Case in Excellent Condition." The number and variety of responses will surprise you. This kind of ad jogs into action someone who has been thinking about selling the guitar but out of inertia hasn't done anything about it yet.

Rented

Renting an instrument provides a relatively inexpensive test of whether or not you will enjoy playing it.

Rental contracts range from ten weeks to a year and generally require a deposit which you get back at the end of the contract period. If you rent an instrument through the store that supplies your school with instruments, the store might waive the deposit requirement.

Stores usually rent you a used instrument in good condition. Unless you take out an insurance policy—which some rental stores offer at a minimal fee—you will be expected to replace such damage as broken strings at your own expense. The insurance policy covers damage to the instrument through normal use, but does not cover you against loss.

Most music stores have a clause in the rental contract which allows you to apply 50 to 100 percent of the rental money toward the purchase of a new instrument (either the one you've been renting or another).

The Invaluables: Time and Service

Two factors not yet mentioned and which cannot be measured in terms of dollars are (1) your time, and (2) the service provided by stores.

One store tells you they will repair your guitar for $12. They do—six weeks later. Another says they'll charge you $14 and you'll be able to pick up the guitar the next day.

Which is more important to you, the money or the time?

Store #1's prices are about 10 percent lower than its competitors. As you walk in, the owner points to you and whispers to his assistant to follow you. When you ask a question about the resonance of a certain instrument, the clerk responds with ''Why do you want to know?'' When your friend asks to see the harmonica in the glass cabinet, nobody seems to hear her, even though you do and you're standing twenty-five feet away.

Store #2 is different. You've heard that it is a little more expensive than store #1, but when you and your friend walk in, a salesperson cheerfully asks you if you need help. You ask about the resonance of a certain instrument and the salesperson takes it out to show you and has you try it as you talk. Your friend asks to see the harmonica in the glass cabinet and the salesperson takes it out and explains how it differs from the one next to it. You explain you are saving up for your instrument and hope to have enough money to buy it by summer. The salesperson says, ''Terrific. If you need to talk about it more, stop by. I'd be happy to help.''

Which store would you come back to? What price do you place on congeniality and service?

Pianos

Because of their popularity, price, and size, pianos are a family affair. That's why a piano demands separate treatment.

If no one in your family now plays the piano, the experts say to start with a good used one. The joy of a new piano may be beyond the reach of all but the serious musicians, since new ones start in the four figures and range to $65,000.

When I asked a piano teacher friend how she would go about buying a used piano, she looked at me squarely and answered, ''I wouldn't do a thing without bringing my piano tuner. Technically, he's the expert.'' So before you say ''yes'' to any piano, have the instrument surveyed by a member of the Piano Technicians Guild who is a craftsperson in rebuilding as well as tuning procedures. For a fee this person should check the hammers, strings, pin block, plate, soundboard, bridges, the action, and the tune and give you a rundown of the piano's present condition and how much it will cost you to repair, replace, or rebuild the problem areas.

What you, the lay person, can do:

• Know what model you want:

Grands are the biggest and best, and on a horizontal measurement range from the baby (about 5½ feet) to the concert grand (eight to nine feet).

Full uprights have wonderfully rich tones and even though they are no longer made in the United States, there are still many used ones in existence. If they are technically sound, they're terrific bargains. They're at least fifty-one inches tall.

Consoles or studio uprights are thirty-nine inches or more in height and are fine for most piano students.

• Try to buy the piano privately or from a piano rebuilder. You'll get a better price than buying it through a piano dealer.

• Stick to name brands (found over the keyboard or inside). But keep in mind: a well-known name brand piano which has been poorly treated is not as good as a lesser piano in excellent condition. Also, the top names now may not have been well known or even in existence fifty years ago.

• Play the piano—one note at a time. Are all the keys playing? How does it sound to you? Sharp or dead? Mellow or brilliant? If you don't think it is in tune, ask if it has been tuned recently. Then let your expert consultant tell you how serious the tuning problem is.

• How do the keys feel under your touch? Too hard? Too slow in responding? Can the piano be played quite loud? Can it be played softly?

After you've found your piano, *be good to it*. Hire professional movers to bring it home. Have a qualified piano technician tune your piano four times during the first year and twice each year thereafter (after moving, yes; in humid weather, no). Try to keep the temperature of the room in which you have your piano constant, at about 72 degrees, and try to keep the humidity around 45 percent. Avoid placing the instrument in direct sunlight, against an outside wall, or near a heating vent—and leave ivory keys uncovered so they won't turn yellow.

Lessons

Musicians are funny people. They like to eat. And being a musician is not an outstandingly lucrative profession, so there are a multitude of good, sometimes great, musicians who give lessons. Some are students themselves; others are professionals. But because someone is a good musician, it doesn't necessarily follow that he/she is a good teacher.

To start your quest for a teacher who's right for you, ask around. Speak to others who play your instrument. Listen to *how* and *what* they play. Check the ads in the local papers.

Can you go to the teacher for your lesson, or must he/she come to you? House calls are generally more expensive. Does the teacher have a good reputation?

But the keys to selecting a good teacher are:

- How does the teacher teach? Is it how and what you want to learn?
- Will you be able to learn the fundamentals? Or is it just the latest song of the day you'll be concentrating on?
- Do you and the teacher like the same music? If the teacher thinks Chapin is Chopin misspelled, is this relationship going to work?

The Payoff

It takes many years of practice, but playing an instrument eventually pays off. The best way is in hours and hours of personal enjoyment, but occasionally the payoff also comes in dollars. Good teen bands are in demand for school dances and parties. Really fine groups or individuals can give concerts, play at weddings and other events, and go on tour. Many advanced students give lessons to beginners.

And once in a while, out of the vast blur of high school musicians, comes a true artist, one who will make music a career.

RECORDS AND TAPES

Buying Isn't the Only Way

Borrow

Very often the public library has an extensive record collection out of which you can borrow free if you hold a library card. If there's an album you think you might like to buy one day, listen to it first by borrowing it from the library. If you decide it's just okay, something you might like to listen to once in a while, but not something you need in your collection, fine. Borrow it occasionally.

Two factors: (1) library records are not maintained in top condition, and (2) overdue fees can be steep if you are late in returning the album.

Swap

At one time you were into punk rock. Now you're mellowing and would like to get into some other kind of music. It's possible and a good idea to swap albums. If you can get the school's permission to set up an area for ''Record/Tape Exchanges'' on the bulletin board, you create a wider range of swap possibilities. Some music stores have this kind of bulletin board as a service for patrons. Also, in many parts of the country you will find music and swap shops where you can sell your old records and pick up others at good prices. The key point in swapping is the condition of your records. Give the best; get the best.

Tape

Even though record companies cringe at their loss of profits from the practice, taping a borrowed record for *personal* use is legal. And blank tapes are less expensive than prerecorded ones (although there is a push on to superimpose fees on blank tapes which would increase their cost—making their cost equal to that of prerecorded ones).

In addition to saving you money (at this time), home taping allows you to tape only those selections you like. If you plan to tape from borrowed records, make your records available to friends for the same purpose. Fair is fair.

Buying Means Never Having to Pay List Price

Records and tapes vary in price. *List price* is the manufacturer's suggested retail price. But the existence of discount stores, price wars, and sales means you should rarely pay list price.

• *Discount Stores* generally provide you with a standard discount, and have deeper discounts during sales.

• *Music Stores* may have special items not found in the mass-market discount stores. Prices are usually higher than in discount stores, especially if there aren't many competing stores in the area. Watch for sales.

• In both discount and music stores, look for the bins which hold "close-outs" in excellent albums released a few years ago. The bins are there because record companies clean out their inventories regularly, and they encourage stores to offer jazz, rock, pop, and country albums at a mid-price range.

• Anytime you buy a record from a reputable dealer—discount or regular—you should get expert quality sound reproduction. Don't forgive warps, scratches, or poppings—return the record. Stores must give you a replacement for the damaged album (as long as you didn't do the damage). Make sure you save your receipt until you've tested the record. If the store refuses to replace the record, complain to your local Better Business Bureau. Also, tell the store owner you will tell your friends about the treatment you received and will urge them not to shop there (boycott). The smart merchant will replace the damaged album.

• Same holds true for tapes.

• *Flea Markets, Garage Sales, and Used Record Shops* can be excellent sources of good records if you can muster up enough patience to rummage through unclassified and unsorted bins of records. It is possible to come across the find of the century. It is also possible that the time spent will be wasted. Collector's items (those records which should increase in value throughout the years if they remain in good condition) are rare recordings and albums of disbanded groups (like the Beatles) or of people who have recently died. But, as is the case when you buy anything that is old, the condition is of paramount importance. A one-of-a-kind recording which sounds like a Chipmunk album is worthless to the ear and the pocketbook.

• *Mail Order* can be an excellent source of good records and tapes at reasonable prices (even with the postage charges), especially for people who live far from large cities, where the competition for sales keeps record prices down. If you have doubts about the mail-order firm's authenticity or reputation, call the Better Business Bureau nearest you and inquire before you send any money. The drawbacks to mail-order buying are the lapse between the time you send in the money and the date you get your order; and the annoyance plus additional time lost if you get a faulty recording and have to return it.

• *Record and Cassette Clubs* at first glance look too good to be true. And sometimes they are. Almost always they give you a good deal in the initial offer. But there are questions: Will the clubs send you an album a month of their choice, unless you notify them not to? How much choice do you have? What kind of tapes do they use? Are you committing yourself to spending more money than you have or want to? You must study the fine print to get the answers to these questions. Do so before you sign up.

Record Care

Over the years you will spend a lot of money for records. Here are basic tips for preserving them.

- Keep your sound equipment in good condition. Change your stylus regularly.
- Take the shrink-wrap off the album immediately when you get home. It pulls on the record and warps it.
- Store albums vertically—not so tight that they don't have breathing space; not so loose that they droop.
- Don't leave albums in the sunlight or on the turntable.
- Keep your albums dusted and clean for the best sound reproduction.

Questions for the ''Turntable Column''

''I want to give my friend a gift certificate to a music store for his birthday, but that seems so impersonal. What do you think?''

According to our informal survey, teenagers love getting gift certificates to music stores. It eliminates duplicate albums and the embarrassment of not liking a record received. Most teens feel it says,

"I think so much of you, I want you to have the fun of getting something special for yourself." If you want to make the gift a little more personal, go with your friend when he selects his present. And treat yourselves to pizza afterward.

"I have a cassette recorder and by mistake I got an eight-track tape. What can I do?"
Track back to the store and return it. Eight-track tapes are outdated, and anyway, you can't play them on your cassette recorder.

"I've been hinting that I need tape and record holders for my birthday (June), but it's now October and the records are falling out of my closet and I'm finding tapes under the bed. I need help in organizing—right away!"
Follow these hints and you'll be organized in record time:
• Shoeboxes, both cardboard and plastic, are great for holding cassettes when they stand on their side horizontally. Keep title side out for fast finding.
• Fruit crates and heavy cardboard boxes are perfect for albums. Pack them upright so that the spines show for easy selection.

"My friend and I were having an argument. She says, 'If you like the song, buy the album. You'll get to like the rest.' I say, 'Get singles. Why buy a whole album if you like only one song.' Who's right?"
You both are. It's a matter of personal preference and available money. Going single is less expensive initially. But if you like the group, go with the album.

"Here's one that has my head spinning. Which are better: tapes or records?"
This is tough—there's a lot to consider. Record quality is usually superior to that of tapes. Records are also collectibles and less expensive, too. On the flip side, there's the longevity, the compactness, and the easy care of a tape. This one's a fielder's choice.

"My friends are always talking about buying bootleg albums. What does that mean?"
There are three ways that people steal music in the recording business, all of which cause the artists and songwriters to lose royalties, reputable retailers to lose sales, and you to lose quality:
• *Counterfeits* are duplicated records or tapes in packaging that is

also duplicated. Counterfeits can seem like a real bargain, but their quality is inferior to the real thing.

- *Pirated* albums or tapes are those copied from originals and resold in a new wrapper. These also are of second-rate quality.
- *Bootleg* albums (what your friends are buying) are illicit recordings of live performances. These albums or tapes are costly.

"I want to buy blank tapes for recording and I figure the less I spend for them the better. Am I figuring right?"

Not necessarily. There are so many different tape configurations on the market that your best bet is to speak to a competent salesperson. Tell him/her what you plan to use the tape for and then get the best you can for the money you have. The experts say that the cheapest is not the best and that in tape quality especially, you get what you pay for.

"I'm sick. Seasick. My favorite record is in waves. What can I do for warping?"

Lay the record on a flat surface (such as a dresser top) and pile heavy books (such as telephone directories) on it. Let the record stay that way for a week or more. It should have straightened out by the time you desandwich it.

Give and Get Taken—It's Bound to Happen

If an adult says, "I've never been taken," don't believe it. We've all been duped, and it's a bummer. Everyone consoles you with "It's a learning experience," and after you get over the anger, the feeling of foolishness, and the lack of funds, it probably *can* be chalked up to experience. Not that it won't happen again (it might), but probably not in the same way.

Prevention: Follow the slogan a discount chain store has been using: "An educated consumer is our best customer."

Know Prices

Look, ask, read, and remember. That way when the ad reads "Today only, we're taking $3 off the list price of the Bruce Springsteen Album. Was $10.95; now $7.95," you'll know $7.95 isn't such a bargain because you've seen the album regularly in the stores for

$7.50. (By the way, retailers love to slash prices. It really looks like something has been reduced. The only way to be sure is to deal with a reputable dealer and know the going, not list, price.)

Know What You Want

If you're interested in buying a guitar and you've never played before, why would you need "the best"? And just because you're in the music store in response to an ad which said this store was selling "a limited quantity" of your favorite group's newest album at $1 (and it's "sold out"), doesn't mean you have to buy something else. Don't be hooked by the old "bait" trick.

SOUND EQUIPMENT

> There was a young lady from Grand Cedar
> Whose personality none could find sweeter
> Her one learning block
> Which all seemed to knock
> Was not knowing a woofer from tweeter*

And she was afraid to ask because everyone around her seemed to know the jargon.

Young friend from Grand Cedar, here are the facts—minus the electronicese.

Sound equipment can be bought four ways:

1. *A compact* is a single-cabinet stereo system which includes a turntable, a stereo receiver, possibly a tape deck, and a separate pair of speakers.
2. *Components* are units, often from different manufacturers, which when put together make a complete system.
3. *A prepackage system* is made up of components already chosen for you.
4. *Portable sound equipment* hooks on to your belt and fits in your

---

*In stereo speakers, the *woofer* reproduces bass sounds; the *tweeter* reproduces the treble (or high-pitched) sounds.

purse or pocket, and comes equipped with headphones for listening to taped or radio music.

Compacts

The compacts are popular as a first hi-fi because of their price, their easy availability, and, their compactness. For under $300 you can get equipment which gives you pleasant sound.

If this is your first hi-fi, look for:

- Two speeds on the phonograph
- Smooth turntable operation
- Easy-to-operate controls
- Automatic return and record changer
- Jack for headphones
- Automatic shutoff for the entire system
- Diamond stylus

Components

For those into fine sound, here's exciting news. There is a vast amount of excellent component equipment available in all price ranges. And because most of the components are now standardized, pieces from different manufacturers are usually compatible. For a complete set of good, midprice components, figure on spending about $1,000.

But how do you put the parts together?

Speakers

Choose speakers first because they will have a bearing on the selection of your other components. While it's a mistake to get cheap speakers, you don't have to have the most powerful ones to get distortion-free sound. Chances are you won't be able to go up to full range anyway because of the size of your room. Nor would you want to, because if your neighbors didn't evict you, your family would. Also, you might injure your hearing.

When you test the speakers in the store, use a good quality record, one you know well. Make sure each set of speakers is being played at the same volume and from the same receiver, so you can compare honestly.

However the speakers sound in the store, they will sound different in your room. Try moving them around and raising them off the floor until you get the sound you like.

Good speakers range from $250 to $500 a pair; some top-of-the-line models cost much more.

Receivers

The buzz words for receivers are "tuner," "phono-preamp," and "power amplifier."

Tuner means AM/FM radio.

The *phono-preamp* corrects the bass/treble imbalance.

The *power amplifier* delivers sound signals to the loudspeaker.

A *receiver* is the unit which combines all of these and is the nerve center of the stereo system. (Tuners can also be purchased separately and added later, in which case you buy the amplifier alone.)

About amps and power:

You want to have an amplifier that will produce the volume you like plus a little more (not a lot). Consider the size of your room and whether it is furnished with thick carpeting, drapes, and furniture, or is relatively bare. The heavily furnished room will absorb sound and needs more amplification. The bare one will reverberate and therefore needs less.

Give the dealers (that's plural—you should be shopping around) all your room information and solicit their suggestions. They can supply you with charts if you want to do your own figuring.

When assembling your component system, pay attention to how much power—watts per channel—your speakers require. More power means more watts and often a higher price, but not necessarily better quality sound.

The receiver you buy should have good FM reception, easy-to-read tuning controls, and jacks for microphones and/or headphones. Also helpful are tone and balance controls and a "loudness" control for better bass sound at low volumes. Electronic conveniences, such as digital tuners and scanners, add to the convenience and price of receivers, but not necessarily to the quality of sound. That's something for you, if you're a gadget-lover, to keep in mind.

Good midrange receivers sell from $200 to $400.

Turntables and Cartridges

In the old days, turntables were called "record changers" because they were designed to play a stack of "platters." Since they no longer do that, they are simply called turntables.

Buy the turntable and cartridge at the same time in the hope (and don't shy away from asking or bargaining) that the dealer will include the cartridge at a very sharp discount as part of the deal. A cartridge is a tiny device at the end of the tone arm which holds the stylus (like the old needle). Let the dealer do all the installation.

Keep an eye out for:

- Easy-to-operate controls.
- A dust cover to protect the turntable.
- An arm that is low and hugs the record for smoother playing.
- A cartridge with a diamond stylus.
- An automatic return arm.
- A mechanism which prevents the tone arm from skating over the record.

Midrange prices for turntables are between $120 and $300.

Cassette Player/Recorders

Sometimes the cassette recorder is part of your receiver, but if you're buying it as a separate component, listen carefully and avoid cassettes which flutter when the tape is played.

Basics to look for:

- Easy-to-read controls.
- Automatic search (for finding selections in the middle of the tape).
- A built-in Dolby noise reduction system to eliminate the hissing sounds.
- Jacks for microphones.
- A nice frill if you can afford it is a dual-mouth cassette deck which allows you to record one cassette while playing another.

Midrange prices for a cassette player/recorder range from $200 and $350.

Headphones

Plugged into your receiver, headphones allow you to listen to your music without having someone yelling, "Turn that down!" Get lightweight headphones (or you'll wind up with a headache); with padded earcups (for comfort); with a long enough cord so you don't feel confined (at least nine feet); and with adjustable parts.

Headphones range from $20 to $60 and make wonderful birthday gifts for grandparents to give their grandchildren. (That's a hint for any grandparents who may be sneaking a peek at this book.) Teen-agers really appreciate headphones and their parents are eternally grateful.

Note: Good headphones reproduce sound just as accurately as good speakers. You might consider this as an alternative to costly loudspeakers if you're on a tight budget. However, keep in mind that loud music over a long period of time can cause hearing loss.

The Personal Portable Walkarounds

Talk about being in your own little world! These gizmos put you there—whether you're on a noisy bus, a crowded street, or a tightly packed elevator. Public response to them has varied:

"They're antisocial and unrealistic. It's psychologically un-healthy to go through life plugging up life's real sounds. What happens to conversation?"

"They're dangerous. How can you hear the car horns warning you not to cross the street if you're glazed by the rhapsodies of Schubert or the volume of Led Zepplin?"

"They're practical. You can brush up on your Spanish or listen to the lecture you missed in biology while walking to school in the morning."

"They're wonderful. You can listen to your music any time you want. They're especially great when you're doing something routine (like jogging) or boring (like algebra)."

No matter what the response, these gadgets, introduced by the Sony Walkman in 1979, are now part of society, and they're being manufactured with many different functions and features. Your problem will be figuring out what you need and which machine has the features you want. No need to worry about the hi-fi sound reproduction, because on most of the walkarounds, it's good.

Before you go shopping, know what function you're looking for:

- *Cassette player only.* You can play tapes but you can't record them.
- *Radio only.*
- *Cassette player/radio.*
- *Cassette player/recorder.*
- *Cassette player/recorder/radio.*

General features to consider:

- *Weight.* In general, walkarounds weigh from fourteen to twenty-five ounces. The lighter the better, especially for joggers.
- *Carrying attachments.* Clips (convenient, versatile); belt loops (safe, but if you're not wearing a belt, you have a problem); shoulder straps.
- *Size.* The smaller the better. It's nice when they're unobtrusive and tuck away neatly into a pocket or purse.
- *Extra headphone jack.* A friend can listen with you.
- *Single volume control.* Better than separate volume controls for each ear—unless you have a hearing problem in one ear.
- *Talk line.* That's a button you press to turn down the volume to hear someone who speaks to you.
- *Auto-stop.* This stops the machine automatically when the tape ends.
- *Convenient control layout.* So you don't have to stop everything to see which button you have to press. It should be considerably easier to learn than touch-typing.
- *Comfortable headphones.*

Sound Equipment Is Expensive: *Beware!*

Even at the low end of the price scale, sound equipment means big-ticket items costing big dollars. So, to get the most out of your money:

- Know in advance what you want the equipment to do for you and how much you can afford to spend.

- Familiarize yourself with what's on the market. Seek the advice of dealers. Read consumer-oriented magazines, and keep up with those that rate stereo equipment.
- Familiarize yourself with prices. Discounts up to 30 percent off list price are offered widely; you should seldom have to pay list price.
- Find out who the reputable dealers are.

After you've done all that, *beware*. Even the most savvy buyer has been caught by:

- *Offbeat brands*. The dealer assures you that "Audiophool" makes the finest speakers on the market. You have never heard of this brand, but it is less expensive than the others and it doesn't sound too bad.

Beware. The store probably has been stuck with a truckload of Audiophools which it is trying to unload because the company went out of business.

- *High-pressure salespeople*. "Everybody who's in the know buys this brand." "Today only we're selling it at this price. Tomorrow it will be 50 percent more."

Beware. Don't be intimidated or pushed. Buy what and when you can.

- *Stores that won't let you listen to the system*. You wouldn't think of buying a pair of shoes without trying them on. Nor should you buy sound equipment without listening to it first.

Beware. Any dealer who opposes your listening is selling something not worth listening to.

- *Open boxes*. You have made your purchase assuming that you're buying a brand-new piece of equipment. Insist on a sealed box.

Beware: Open boxes indicate the item has been used—either by the store for demonstration, or by another buyer who has returned the equipment, perhaps because of a defect.

- *Closeouts and discontinued models*. No doubt closeouts and discontinued models are tempting because of the price, but they're being closed out for a reason. And once a model is closed out, repair parts might be difficult, if not impossible, to find.

Beware. Before jumping into a fantastic bargain, find out if the bargain model is being discontinued.

• *Exceptions in the warranty.* Generally, reputable manufacturers have a standard warranty. Check what's covered. Will your dealer repair? Or must you send it back to the manufacturer?

Beware. Mail in your warranty card. That's the only way to assure that the warranty is valid.

• *Being first.* It's exciting to have the first digital audio equipment, but it's also expensive and risky. New technology must be on the market for a while before the bugs are worked out. It also has to be expensive because in the beginning it is sold in such limited quantity.

Beware. Wait. Give technology time to work out the bugs and the price a chance to flatten out.

• *Model number confusion.* With all the numbers attached to the name of a piece of equipment (Technics SLB5/Technics SLD202; Shure M95ED/Shure M97ED), it's easy to get a case of "digit dizziness."

Beware: Write down the model number of the item you want. Purchase exactly that model.

Repair Reminders

A friend told me the spring on his tape recorder's stop button needed repair. To find that out, he paid $35 for a "consultation" and $1.30 for the part and labor—$36.30 in all. He learned.

Now before he does anything, he asks. He gets a reasonable written estimate of repairs which he pays for, but which is deductible from the cost of the repair if he chooses that shop to do the work. If the estimate seems too high, he takes the equipment somewhere else for another estimate. He uses only reputable repair people.

A Tantalizing Peek into the Future

Audio equipment is changing so rapidly that it is literally impossible to predict how you will be listening to music in 1990. But without even pretending to be an expert, I can confidently forecast it will be tantalizingly different from how you listen today. Just the addition of the computer to the complicated and vastly varied technology already available to you, the teenager of the early 1980s, makes that a certainty.

Will the extraneous noise and distortion you now hear on regular albums be eliminated because you'll be using digital recordings and digital home players?

Will a laser replace the stylus and "read" a "no-wear" disc to deliver superior hi-fi sound?

Will a cable TV network, via a communications satellite, be able to broadcast new albums directly into subscribers' homes, so that all they have to do is call a toll-free number and switch on their home tape recorders to record the album?

Will you be able to sit at a desk and with a hand-operated remote control box give commands to your record player, telling it when to start and stop and what to play next?

The answers to all these questions: probably *yes*.

7

COMPUTERS AND YOU

CONTENTS

YOU'RE LUCKY

You're lucky.

You're living in the computer age. And in the decade of the 1980s, you are seeing the full force of the computer revolution. (*Time* magazine even named the computer "Man of the Year.")

It is a force that already has changed and will continue to change every part of the way you live. It will make your life safer, easier, happier, more interesting, more challenging—longer, too.

It is helping the paralyzed move arms and legs that were helpless before. It is enabling some totally blind people to see. It has made possible the creation of different forms of life (new bacteria) which fight disease and could help solve the world's food problems.

How can a computer do all these things? Is there no limit to what remains to be discovered that it can do? Things we can't even begin to imagine?

Older people have an extremely hard time understanding the good that computers can do because they see them as threats to their jobs. Bookkeepers, for instance, who were happy to be working with figures, felt threatened when computers suddenly appeared that could digest and tabulate huge masses of numbers dozens, and eventually thousands, of times faster and more accurately than they could.

In newspaper composing rooms, operators of Linotype machines had been setting seven lines of type (about forty words) a minute for almost a hundred years. The Linotype machine was patented in 1884 and gets its name from its capacity to set a line of type on one metal slug, so that whole lines can be handled. Before that, each word was set one letter at a time.

The computer can set type at the rate of 1,500 words a minute, almost forty times as fast. In his book, *The Third Wave*, Alvin Toffler says computer-operated microprinters are capable of turning out 10,000 to 20,000 lines per minute, 200 times faster than anyone can read them.

Aside from its incredible speed, the computer can correct spelling and punctuate properly, because it has been programmed for many thousands of commonly used words. They are stored in its memory, and it couldn't spell them wrong if it tried. The Writer's Workbench at Bell Laboratories, in Piscataway, New Jersey, has twenty-three computer programs aimed at improving the quality of writing. They flag poor writing, including incorrect punctuation and spelling, split infinitives, overlong sentences, awkward phrases, and repetition. They can even be used to update data and, of course, they are marvelous training devices.

For example, at the command "double," it searches for repetition of words or phrases. The "diction" program may flag the phrase "the reason why" and suggest that "why" is unnecessary.

The Writer's Workbench is based on dictionaries and well-known usage guides. Although it doesn't claim to substitute for a live teacher, it is an excellent way to learn, especially if you don't have access to an editor or an instructor.

It is true that the computer replaced Linotype operators by the thousands. Some of them were older and simply retired. Others were given fairly large sums of money by their employers to leave their jobs and look for other kinds of work or train for new skills. Young as you are, do not minimize the hardship suffered by these men (there were almost no women in newspaper composing rooms). To see not only your job but the very kind of work you do taken over by a machine is, at the least, demoralizing.

But you can be sure that no Linotype operators in the last twenty years even thought of having their sons train to enter the same trade. Some of their sons and daughters probably became computer programmers.

Nobody and nothing can stand in the way of progress. If the telephone company had not gone to dial phones—which make it possible to call anywhere in the United States without human assistance—it would take every woman between the ages of twenty and fifty working as a telephone operator just to handle all the calls!

THE WONDERFUL, SHORT HISTORY OF COMPUTERS

To understand better where computers will take you, look carefully at where they've been and how they got started in the first place.

What are the roots of the word "compute"? It is a combination of the Latin verb *putare*, to think, and the preposition *cum*, meaning with. *Computer* literally means to think with, and has, of course, come to mean to reckon or count, or determine by calculation.

The very first machine that could do arithmetic was invented in the seventeenth century by a mathematical genius named Blaise Pascal. While still a very young man, he completed the design for the mathematical adder.

It was the world's first calculating machine, and it was called the Pascaline. It worked on the principle of a speedometer, by gears and wheels bearing the numbers 0 through 9 that rotated when you dialed in the number you wanted to add. And you could reverse it to make it count backward—that is, to subtract. It multiplied by a series of repeated additions and divided by repeated subtractions. The problem with Pascal's machine was that every single number from 0 to 9 had to be represented by a tooth on a cogwheel, so every cogwheel had to have ten teeth. Since there was a cogwheel for each "power" of ten—10s, 100s, 1000s, and so on—the higher you went in the machine's ability to count, the more cogwheels, the bigger the mass of interconnecting gears, with greater possibility for mechanical error. (A close look at the binary system, counting by two basic numbers, 0 and 1, shows how simple and easy binary numbers are for the computer to work with. More about this in a moment.)

The idea of zero is extremely important to our system of numbering, which we took from the Arabs in the Middle Ages. For example, before the European world started using Arabic numerals, it would have to write the number 1776 as MDCCLXXVI, literally 1000 + 500 + 100 + 100 + 50 + 10 + 10 + 5 + 1. It is because we all understand that the four numbers 1, 7, 7, 6, placed next to each other left to right represent a lot of zeros in place (1 is really 1,000, 7 is 700, 7 is 70) that we can easily represent the year our country was born with four Arabic instead of nine Roman numerals.

The Pascaline was improved on some thirty years later by another young genius. His name was Gottfried Wilhelm Leibniz. He was so bright that he was writing verses in Greek and Latin at the age of ten. In 1673, when he was twenty-seven years old, he exhibited the Leibniz wheel to the Academy of Science in Paris and the Royal Society of London.

The Leibniz wheel was a better machine than the Pascaline because it could not only add and subtract automatically, but could also multiply and divide. Leibniz contributed a great deal to computers, not only by his machine but also by his studies of what is now known as symbolic logic. Leibniz became fascinated with the idea of binary arithmetic, but for some reason never saw fit to apply it to his calculator.

It remained for Charles Babbage, an English mathematician, who was a friend and lover of Lord Byron's beautiful and wealthy daughter, Augusta Ada, to invent the computer. In his excellent, highly readable book, *The Micro Millenium*, the late Christopher Evans described Lord Byron's daughter as an intriguing woman who was an exceptional mathematician (a trait she inherited from her mother, and very rare for a woman of that time) and an unusually beautiful one as well. When she met Babbage and realized the significance of what he was trying to do, she set out to study his designs in depth. She published everything in a long series of "Notes" entitled *Observations on Mr. Babbage's Analytical Engine*.

Augusta Ada Byron (she later became the Countess of Lovelace) showed in her writing that she was fully aware of the philosophical problems posed by construction of such a machine. She wrote:

"The Analytical Engine has no pretensions whatever to originate anything. It can do whatever we know how to order it to perform. It can follow analysis but it has no power of anticipating any analytical relationships or truths."

Thus, Evans points out, Lady Lovelace was the very first to state that a computer can do only what you program it to do.

Babbage himself was wealthy. He had inherited 100,000 pounds, a tidy fortune in the early nineteenth century, but he spent it all building and designing his Difference Engine and later, his Analytical Engine. The latter was truly programmable and is recognizable as a computer. (In addition to publishing papers on mathematics, statistics, physics, and geology, Babbage also helped develop the penny post and invented the speedometer and the cowcatcher.)

Babbage took some ideas for his computer from a weaving machine invented in 1805 by a Frenchman, Joseph Jacquard. That device revolutionized the textile industry. By 1812, there were 11,000 Jacquard looms all over France, in spite of the fact that the weavers tried to destroy his machines and sometimes even beat up Jacquard himself.

Jacquard's ideas can be traced to two other men, Vaucanson

and Bouchon, both designers of looms. Vaucanson borrowed from Bouchon, and Bouchon, whose father was an organ maker, adapted the principle of the automated organ, which worked by a series of pegs on a cylinder. When the cylinder turned, the peg hit a note; if you changed the position of the pegs, you got a whole new piece of music.

Jacquard's loom worked by a series of cards with holes in them. The holes allowed hooks to come up and pull down threads so that when the shuttle passed through it went *over* certain predetermined threads and *under* others. Babbage was so excited by Jacquard's loom that he wrote:

"The Jacquard loom is capable of weaving any design that the imagination of man may conceive. Holes are punched in a set of pasteboard cards in such a manner that when they are placed in the loom, they will weave the exact pattern performed by the artist."

For over one hundred years, these cards had to be designed by hand, a very painstaking job. Then, in the mid 1960s, Janice R. Lourie of IBM, found a way of automating the whole process of making the cards with the help of the modern computer. But back to our story.

What Babbage saw in the punched cards for his Analytical Engine was the possibility of changing the cards so that his machine could do a different set of calculations. In other words, each set of cards was a program. The use of punched cards was also the basis of a music organ invented in 1852. It was programmable: when you changed the punched card, you changed the tune. That was followed by the player piano in 1879, which worked the same way, but with a roll of paper instead of a card. The pianist programmed the piano by playing a tune on it, thereby hitting the keys, which then punched a hole in the roll of paper for every note. When you ran the roll through again, the holes were read by small levers which activated the keys and played the tune.

Hollerith's "Punched Cards"

It was Herman Hollerith who brought the punched card into such visible use that it led to the formation of a commercial organization, the Tabulating Machine Company, which in turn gave birth in 1924 to International Business Machines, more widely known as IBM. Although IBM ranked eighth in sales on *Fortune* magazine's list of the 500 largest industrial organizations in the early 1980s, it was number two in both net income and stockholder's equity, second only to Exxon.

Hollerith's boss at the Census Office was a remarkable man named John Shaw Billings, who became Deputy Surgeon General of the Army, Director of the Hospital of the University of Pennsylvania, and eventually the founder of the New York Public Library. Billings was in charge of the work on vital statistics on both the 1880 and 1890 census.

While the returns of the 1880 census were being tabulated in Washington, Billings and Hollerith were walking through the office in which hundreds of clerks were laboriously and painstakingly transferring items of information by hand. Billings turned to Hollerith and said, "There ought to be some mechanical way of doing this job. Something on the principle of the Jacquard loom, whereby holes in a card regulate the pattern to be woven."

Hollerith did more than listen to that suggestion. When the 1880 census results were still being processed by hand in 1887, the Census office realized that the results, when completed, would be hopelessly out of date and that hand tabulation of the 1890 census would be even tougher. The country was growing very fast.

So the Census Office decided to hold a competition. In 1889, three finalists competed in a practical test, analyzing the data on 10,000 people in St. Louis, Missouri. William E. Hunt and his colored cards took 55 hours. Charles F. Pidgin and his color-coded tokens took 44 hours. Hollerith's punch cards won in 5 ½ hours and his system was selected for the 1890 census, even though a number of people opposed the idea of such data being entrusted to a machine.

Hollerith's cards were 6⅝ by 3¾ inches in size, with 288 locations at which holes could be made. He chose that size because it was the same as the dollar bill (at that time) and it saved making additional equipment. He built a machine for punching these cards and a simple sorter. This sorter had a box containing twenty-four bins, each with a lid held closed by an electromagnetic latch working against a spring. Normally all lids were closed, but when a hole was sensed, the electric current that flowed as a result turned off the latch and the spring opened the lid. The card was then dropped into the open bin by hand. This part of the operation wasn't automated until much later.

Did Hollerith's system work? And how! Just one month after all returns arrived in Washington, the Superintendent of the 1890 Census announced the total population count, 62,622,250 people. The results were tabulated not only by state, county, and city but also by 150,000 divisions.

A billion holes were punched just for one detail. And because Hollerith's electrical tabulating system permitted easy counting, it made it possible to ask more questions. For the first time, the census tabulated the number of children born, number of children living, number of families speaking English. Also counted were the ownership of homes and farms and the amount of mortgages secured by real estate.

Why was this so important, and what far-reaching effect did it have? It was the spark that actually set off the computer revolution, even though the computer as we know it wasn't created until almost sixty years later.

Hollerith proved that machines could sort data much faster and more accurately than human beings. In fact, the sheer capacity of the new mechanical system to process all those numbers so fast made those numbers more meaningful. The speed of tabulation made it possible to interpret them every which way and to see relationships among them that were not possible even to think of getting before. With a machine doing the sorting and making the tabulation, it was easy to do cross-tabulation. For example, how many families who had children born, had children still living? And how many families who spoke English had children who died? In 1890, medicine had not begun to conquer the childhood diseases that are virtually wiped out today. Mumps, chicken pox, diphtheria, scarlet fever, polio—all took their horrible toll. With Hollerith's card-sorter, it was possible to find out what section of the country suffered the highest rate of infant mortality and whether or not the family spoke English (meaning whether they were foreign-born). In those days, immigrants were coming to the United States by the millions.

And again, once Hollerith's system had proved itself, it was possible to include more and more–detailed questions in the census of other years and eventually to make historical comparisons between each base year.

Hollerith's system and its capacity to complete tabulations so quickly was consistent with the basic purpose of the census, as provided for in the Constitution. By counting the people and where they live, the House of Representatives is able to apportion its members among the states and the districts within each state, so that all the people of the United States have a more or less equal chance for representation.

Our emerging, fast-growing nation needed more information about its people if it was going to be able to plan for their well-being. In the 1870 census, only five subjects were covered. In 1880, 215 were included, but these took seven years to tabulate. In 1890, there were 235 subjects. One of its findings was how many survivors of the Civil War were in each age group.

In 1936, forty-six years later, Hollerith's methods and IBM, born out of the company he had started, made it possible to provide the machines and services for what has been called "the biggest accounting operation of all time"—the Social Security program. With punched cards, the Social Security Administration could locate and keep track of many millions of people once they had all been assigned individual numbers. Of course, by that time, the machines had improved a great deal. They had many more columns of information and could do full-scale accounting.

In July of 1982, the People's Republic of China conducted its third census and used computers for the first time in its history to count a billion people. More than 5 million workers were involved, and because of computers they were able to count and code 100 million people a day for ten days. (The two previous censuses, in 1953 and 1964, covered only a few basic subjects, and the results were manually tabulated with abacuses.)

But this is getting ahead of the story and you. Your part of the computer tale started at the Moore School of Electrical Engineering of the University of Pennsylvania in February, 1946, with ENIAC, the first electronic computer.

ENIAC and the Birth of the Computer Age

ENIAC, the Electronic Numerical Integrator and Computer, originally conceived as a top-secret military project to develop a machine that could rapidly calculate the ballistic tables for Army Ordnance, performed so spectacularly that in one stroke it gave birth to the computer age. It added 97,376 to itself 5,000 times in the then unbelievable time of one second.

It had taken two and a half years of twenty-four-hour workdays to put ENIAC together. It was 100 feet long, 10 feet high, and 3 feet deep. It contained 18,000 vacuum tubes, 70,000 resistors, 10,000 compacitors, and 6,000 switches. It drew enough electricity (140 kilowatts) to keep a small power station busy. And, of course, it had tremendous cooling problems.

But ENIAC had other, more serious limitations. As huge as it was—3,000 cubic feet—it had a tiny memory. And to change a program, you actually had to rewire part of it.

It was John von Neumann, the distinguished mathematician, who took the computer a giant step forward. He thought of treating programs as numbers and storing them in the computer that way.

That meant the computer could change programs when called on, switching from one to the other in a fraction of a second. It also meant that one program could call up another program. Von Neumann had given computer capability a potentially infinite horizon.

Von Neumann had a mind that, by itself, seemed to have the infinite capacity of the giant computers he was destined to help bring into being. Not only was he a superb logician, but he had total recall of anything and everything he had read just once. Once, when tested by being asked to recite how *A Tale of Two Cities* started, von Neumann immediately began to repeat the first chapter and continued without pause until he was begged to stop.

Of course, von Neumann's brain, like yours and the brains of all humans, could hold 10 trillion (10 million-million) bits of information. That's better than a million times the capacity of today's largest computer.

No one had any idea that within less than two human generations, computers, much smaller in size, much more sophisticated and capable, would be affordable by practically everyone and would be in millions of homes, probably including yours. The prediction is that by the end of 1985 there will be 18 million personal computers in homes and businesses throughout the United States. (*Note:* I write "human generations" because computer people speak of "computer generations," and the "micros" are the fourth.)

In the late 1940s, most observers thought that the world market for computers would be ten at the most. They couldn't visualize computers as anything smaller than the giant installations they were. The transistor and the microchip hadn't been invented.

It is far from a digression to examine now the binary system of numbering which was used for the first time in the EDVAC (Electronic Discrete Variable Computer), which von Neumann designed in 1949.

There is nothing mysterious about the binary system, a method of counting by twos. It's just that we are accustomed to the decimal system. We have ten fingers and ten toes, and we like to think we were born to count 1, 2, 3, 4, etc.

But were we really? Suppose we didn't have fingers and toes, just two arms and two legs. Wouldn't it be natural to count by twos? There's a tribe in Australia which expresses numbers in terms of a wild dog's legs. The number eight, for example, is expressed as "two dogs."

The Binary System

But why the binary system? Because it is linked to the way the computer works, and, by its sheer simplicity, it makes the computer's job that much easier.

The table below tells you how. A computer is really a system of switches, many thousands, even millions of them in microscopic size. Two switches in a series have three possibilities for anything to be happening—that is, any computation to be going on. Either switch can be on, or they can both be on. (If they're both off, there's simply no activity.)

Here's how that applies to the binary system. Imagine a series of switches as shown below. Each switch represents double the numerical value of the switch to the right of it, starting with 1.

ON/OFF ON/OFF ON/OFF ON/OFF ON/OFF ON/OFF ON/OFF ON/OFF

| 128 | 64 | 32 | 16 | 8 | 4 | 2 | 1 |

Let us assume that a line under the number indicates the switch is on. No line means it's off.

To get the number 5, our diagram will look like this:

| 128 | 64 | 32 | 16 | 8 | <u>4</u> | 2 | <u>1</u> |

We get the number five by turning on switches 4 and 1.

And here are other numbers we can get simply by turning on the proper switches.

| 128 | <u>64</u> | 32 | 16 | 8 | <u>4</u> | <u>2</u> | <u>1</u> |

The above number is 71, the total of 64, 4, 2, and 1.

Possibly it has occurred to you by this time that the binary series shown above can total to a maximum of only 255, one less than the double of 128. To get that number, all switches in this series would have to be on as shown. ("Zero" means all switches are off.)

| <u>128</u> | <u>64</u> | <u>32</u> | <u>16</u> | <u>8</u> | <u>4</u> | <u>2</u> | <u>1</u> |

The sum of all the above numbers is 255. Thus with only eight switches, you can get the computer to "read" up to 255. With the decimal system it would take thirty different digits, three "wheels" with zero to nine on each wheel.

By adding one more switch on the left, the double of 128, you can then, with only nine switches, derive every number between 1 and 511.

But the "ninth" switch is for purposes of illustrating the logic and expandability of the binary system. In actual computer language the "on" and "off" are shown by 1 or 0, and that's a *binary digit*, a *bit*, the smallest unit of information. It takes eight bits to make a *byte*, which is a computer character.

Once you went to the ninth switch, you would be in the second group of eight binary digits or on byte number two. In that case, the binary digit on the extreme left of the second set would be 32,768 (2^{15}). With that set of only sixteen switches you could derive every number up to 65,535, one less than the double of 32,768. With the decimal system you'd need fifty digits, five sets of ten each.

But you are not restricted to numbers. The binary code is simply a way of indicating which combinations of the computer switches are off and on. The binary code can represent not only a number, but also a letter of the alphabet, a punctuation mark, or a special symbol. You are accustomed to the letters of our alphabet and our punctuation marks. You are so familiar with them that they're not symbols to you as much as a picture might be. One of the difficulties American businesspeople have in selling American computers in Japan is that the alphabet in that country has more than three thousand symbols.

In BCD (Binary Coded Decimal), one of the early computer languages used back in the 1950s, the binary alphabet code looked like this:

A = 110001	J = 100001	S = 010010
B = 110010	K = 100010	T = 010011
C = 110011	L = 100011	U = 010100
D = 110100	M = 100100	V = 010101
E = 110101	N = 100101	W = 010110
F = 110110	O = 100110	X = 010111
G = 110111	P = 100111	Y = 011000
H = 111000	Q = 101000	Z = 011001
I = 111001	R = 101001	

If you analyze this code, it becomes apparent that the *four* binary digits on the *right* of A through I and J through R represent the numbers one through nine, and that the letters S through Z represent the numbers 2 through 9. To differentiate these letters from each other (the four right-hand digits appear in triplicate among the 26 letters of the alphabet), the first set of nine is preceded by binary 11, the second set by binary 10, and the remaining eight by binary 01.

So, say you wanted to spell out Ada Byron in a love letter using BCD, the Binary Coded Decimal. Your romantic effort would look like this:

A 110001	B 110010
D 110100	Y 011000
A 110001	R 101001
	O 100110
	N 100101

Romance!

But by now, bit codes for the alphabet, numbers, and punctuation marks have been standardized among most manufacturers of computers so that their equipment can communicate with each other. There's no need to reproduce the whole code here, but seven bits of another system show the letter A (upper case) as 1000001 and a (lower case) as 1100001. The eighth bit is used for checking between computers. This particular code is called ASCII ("askey"), or American Standard Code for Information Interchange.

Computers have lots of switches. A tiny microchip, one-tenth the size of a postage stamp, can hold as many as 30,000, all too small to be seen by the naked eye. Microchips are getting smaller and smaller all the time. Very soon they may be no bigger than the head of a pin.

And that brings us to the transistor, which more than any other invention brought the computer into your home, as well as countless millions of us into the information age.

If not for the transistor and the silicon wafer, computers would have remained huge, expensive machines of very limited use, perhaps with a world market of only ten as most experts thought when they first appeared.

The Transistor and the Silicon Wafer

The transistor is the single most important invention in the whole complex of computer inventions.

Tubes, or "valves" as they were called in the early computer days, amplify through a heater electrode, which pumps electrons through a vacuum. The electrode has to be made out of metal and, if it's made smaller than a certain size, it can't produce enough heat to activate the electrons.

But an electron, the basic unit of electricity, is only one five-billionth of an inch in diameter. Silicon is normally an insulator, which means electrons cannot flow through it. But, by a chemical process called *doping*, silicon can be turned into a semiconductor. A transistor is made by literally sandwiching one type of silicon between two layers of the opposite type. That arrangement allows a free flow of electrical current.

The development of the transistor, and the subsequent rapid reduction in its size, was given great impetus by the U.S. space program, which made it necessary to squeeze as many transistors as possible onto a single piece of silicon.

That miniaturization has been going on for well over twenty years. With the reduction in size has come vastly reduced cost. In 1952 the cost of making 100,000 computer calculations was $1.26. Only twenty years later, that cost was less than half a cent and shrinking, and the speed of computation was 6,000 to 7,000 times faster.

A startling comparison: If the automobile industry had developed at the same rate as computers and over the same period, you would have been able to buy (in 1979) a Rolls-Royce for $1.35, wrote the late Christopher Evans in his book, *The Mighty Micro*. It would deliver 3 million miles to the gallon, produce enough energy to drive the Queen Elizabeth II, and six of them would fit on the head of a pin!

We have become accustomed to the incredible speed of computers. We who are not computer specialists hear talk about their ability to perform in *nanoseconds, billionths of seconds,* and glibly make the transition in our own mind from *millionths of seconds* without having any conception of the huge difference of degree between them.

Put it this way. A million seconds is about 11½ days. A billion seconds is approximately 11,500 days. So a nanosecond has the same relationship to a full second as a second has to 31½ years.

The nanosecond measure is not just theoretical. There are silicon switches, a millionth of a meter wide, which can turn on and off about 1 billion to 10 billion times a second. Hundreds of thousands of them can be put on a single silicon chip about as big as your thumbnail. They even could be made four times faster and four times smaller, but that's their limit, says a prominent authority in technology development, Richard Pashley.

Gallium arsenide is also a semiconductor and it can switch on and off three or four times faster than silicon. Gallium arsenide is used now in certain microwave communications systems. As I write this, the prediction is that in the mid-1980s, gallium arsenide will indeed be manufactured and marketed for computer circuits. But it has drawbacks: it's more expensive and not as adaptable as silicon—which happens to be the most available substance on the face of the earth.

But 40 billion times a second, even if achieved with gallium arsenide, might not be fast enough. Some problems, such as forecasting the weather, need trillions of calculations.

Computer scientists are experimenting with light pulses as a means of transmitting data, since light is faster than electricity. But there's a catch. Switches that use light can't be as small as their silicon counterparts. Thousands of them won't fit on a single chip, and besides, they use more power.

Another possibility, and scientists are working on this, is single molecules which exist in nature in one of two states and could be made to work like switches, one state for "on," the other for "off." But still to be figured out is how to get wires (they would have to be infinitesimal) into and out of the molecules and how to put them all together into a computer.

Still another idea for increasing the speed of computers is to stick with silicon, but build parallel circuits that can do as many as 16,384 additions at the same time, 6 billion additions a second. Such a machine is now being created by the Goodyear Aerospace Corporation and at the Massachusetts Institute of Technology. NASA scientists need a computer of that capability to interpret satellite photographs of earth. Six billion additions a second.

That possibility may seem like science fiction, but already Cray Research, Inc., and Control Data Corporation, both of Minneapolis, are producing supercomputers capable of 100 million arithmetic operations a second. They are used in defense, fusion research, and weather forecasting; by oil companies, universities, and in the space program.

Japan is bending every effort to overtake the United States in this capability. It has begun a project to develop a supercomputer by 1990 which will be 100 times faster than our fastest machine, capable of 10 billion additions a second. That's 2 million times as fast as the ENIAC, which startled the world as being "faster than thought" in 1946.

The most ingenious idea is to change bacteria by genetic engineering and coax the bacteria into producing a protein skeleton. The molecule switches would then adhere to specific parts of the skeleton to form computer circuitry.

But at this point, even as far as you, an imaginative, bold teenager, are concerned, that's really science fiction. It's certainly beyond my horizon and my imagination, the high technology of a brave new world.

COMPUTERS IN THE WORKPLACE

You've just examined briefly the interesting and challenging things scientists are doing to improve the computer. Now look at what the computer is doing and can do for you.

The computer takes jobs and the computer makes jobs.

Millions of jobs in manufacturing, automobile, steel, and other industries will disappear because of automation, and the laid-off auto or steel workers will not have up-to-date skills. The new jobs, having to do with the computer in all its phases, will pay well and will be looking for young workers with the skills to fill them.

In the early 1980s, the U.S. Labor Department predicted 17 to 26 million new job opportunities by 1990, with large increases in the computer field. (See "Focus: Computer Occupations," in Chapter 1.) Many of the new jobs will be for computer service technicians, which will go from 83,000 in 1980 to almost double that in 1990. The number of computer programmer jobs is expected to dramatically increase, as will systems analysts jobs. The Labor Department predicts that by 1985 the computer industry will need more programmers than are expected to be available. Part of the demand now is for software engineers who are really programmer's programmers; they have broader training and are more highly skilled.

But the biggest percentage of growth by far will be in the number of robots. The few thousand robots in operation as the decade opened will grow to 100,000, according to Professor Wickam Skinner of the Harvard Business School. He also predicts that the number of electronic work stations will grow from a total of 4 million to six or seven times that many.

Shoshanah Zuboff, also of the Harvard Business School, says that when a computer takes over part of the production process, it changes the very relationship between the worker and work. Arthur Luehrmann, founder of the Computer Literacy Company, says that by 1986, 50 percent of all jobs will require interaction with computer-based information. If you become a plant foreman or a bank auditor, you won't make the rounds anymore. You will sit in front of a computer, watch the display terminal, and make judgments about information that shows how well the work is going right at the moment it's being done. The computer will watch and record the work of many people at one time, something you, a human being, can't do. But you, as a supervisor or manager, will sit at the computer terminal and be on-line with what's going on, and be able to ask questions right on the terminal if the computer shows the work isn't going right.

The computer is changing the very nature of work itself. The Boston Consulting Group reports that with computer controls, setups for tool and die arrangements that once required several hours and several people now take only minutes as a result of more sophisticated equipment and microprocessor control. Today, machines can switch rapidly from one setup to another without wasting time on a trial run or making an adjustment or having people go to the toolroom. Result: minimum downtime of the equipment and far less inventory cost.

If different segments of the market—whether it's automobiles or appliances, or whatever—want different models, it pays to manufacture only as many as can be sold quickly. It just costs too much to keep a lot of stock. If the business borrows money to meet the huge cost of payroll and materials, and the products stay in the warehouse, interest rates plus the cost of storage will eat up the profits.

Toyota pioneered this strategy in the 1970s when it doubled the number of models and wanted to avoid increased cost. But now it has plenty of company.

Thomas M. Hout and George Stalk, Jr., of the Boston Consulting Group, report that one large engine manufacturer, over a five-year period, tripled the number of different models it was making, reduced the work-in-process inventory by half, doubled the output per factory worker, and cut waste of materials and make-good work by 40 percent.

By this time you are familiar with the supermarket checkout scanner which uses laser beams to read the automatic universal product code (the set of bars printed on the product). In an instant the whole transaction is recorded right on the customer's tape—the name of the product and the price. Of course, it's a great laborsaving device. It makes checkouts faster and error-free. You, a customer, can see on a screen exactly what the scanner is recording.

But it really tells the supermarket chain what's selling, how fast it's selling, and how much more of it to stock in answer to demand. It also shows how much better it sells as a result of an ad or a money-saving coupon and, just as important, what's not selling and can therefore be taken off the shelves to put that expensive space to better use.

Not only is the computer doing a much better job of recording sales, it's actually doing selling on the floor, in place of human salespeople. Manning Mills, Inc., of Salem, New Jersey, maker of vinyl floor covering, installed more than a hundred computerized store displays and early in the 1980s planned 2,000 more at a cost of

$10,000 each. Mannington Compu-Flor consists of a small computer programmed to digest the answers to eight questions about the decor of a customer's room. Compu-Flor then can display from three to ten appropriate Mannington patterns so the customer doesn't have to sort through 225 samples.

After giving out the fast answers, the electronic salesman puts a human salesman on the screen—Ed McMahon, one of television's best-known personalities. After he's through, the computer goes back into its act and comes up with specific suggestions.

As you might expect, a computer manufacturer, Atari, is trying the same thing. Its Electronic Retail Information Center (ERIC) is a computer programmed to sell computers.

If this works as expected, everybody will get into the act. But as of the start of the decade, it's so novel, that, as one floor covering dealer said, "Customers find it very hard to say no to a computer." Whether the sales computer or sales robot can ever totally replace the human salesperson who completes the order and gives the customer personal assurance is a big question. There's even news of a robot that will listen for suspicious sounds, frighten intruders, and summon police.

One industrial robot displaces 1.7 workers in an assembly plant and 2.7 workers in a manufacturing plant. Of course, the robots themselves have to be told what to do, but the men and women who will do that will be engineers, both in hardware and software. Robots can be programmed to do work of unbelievable precision and to keep doing it until told to stop—no coffee breaks, lunch hours, or days off.

James O'Toole, professor at the University of Southern California's Graduate School of Business, who has made a study of how the computer will affect jobs, has put it very well: "Those who will succeed in the work force will be those who have learned to learn. The unthinking jobs will all be done by machines."

YOUR EDUCATION IN THE COMPUTER AGE

Computer education starts with the young, the very young. You almost certainly have learned to work with a computer and you are not as uncomfortable with it as, say, your parents, are.

There are increasing numbers of schools, on both sides of the Atlantic, that teach children how to use computers. In September 1982, about forty-five youngsters in several kindergarten and first grade classes in New York City schools were scheduled to start learning to use computers. Every child in the program had constant access to a terminal.

Several colleges have taken decisive steps to bring their students into the computer world. Stevens Institute of Technology in New Jersey now requires every freshman studying science or systems planning and management to buy an Atari microcomputer system at a cost of about $750.

Beginning in the fall of 1982, freshmen and transfer students at Rochester Institute of Technology in New York must prove that they have working familiarity with computers (computer literacy) in order to earn a degree—even if they are majoring in fine arts.

And in October of 1982, Drexel University in Philadelphia announced that starting in 1983 it would require all freshman students, including those in liberal arts and the humanities, to purchase their own computers.

Clarkson College in Potsdam, New York, started in 1982 handing out personal computers to all incoming freshmen for use while at college.

What often happens, as educators have observed, is that some children don't do well in basic subjects because traditional instruction doesn't begin to convince them they really need to learn what they're being taught, but these same children often can't get enough of those subjects once they get a crack at working with them on the computer.

Take geometry. It is a "dead" subject, difficult to grasp. But if children can sit in front of a computer and program a square or a circle or a triangle or any other shape by a series of simple commands, geometry soon belongs to them. When children discover that they can create a shape on the screen that is a duplicate of the way they move, that concept is theirs forever.

Or, if you're a Latin student, the computer can show you in just a few minutes how the same word was used differently throughout Virgil's *Aeneid*. You'll quickly get a good idea of the various shades of meaning of the word and the subtleties of that Latin masterpiece. There is no more resentment, no more rebellion at being forced to memorize material students can't really understand or see the need for, because through the computer, *learning becomes doing*.

But you don't have to wait until you're old enough to use the computer for geometry or Latin. Between the ages of five and eight children become infatuated with the computer. By age fourteen they're experts.

The reasons young children take so readily to the computer has to do with their emotional health, according to Dr. Eugene Galanter, professor of psychology and psychophysics at Columbia University. Dr. Galanter is founder of the Children's Computer School and author of *Kids and Computers, the Parents' Microcomputer Handbook.*

Dr. Galanter believes that a computer should not be substituted for a teacher or used merely as an audiovisual aid. Rather, interacting with a computer is an opportunity for children to explore their own thought processes. When a small child gets control over an enormously complex machine, it has, as Dr. Galanter points out, "a spellbinding capability."

The computer treats the child like an adult, and a capable one at that. It won't tolerate ambiguity or foolishness. As Dr. Galanter emphasizes, "The computer makes demands that are serious, clear, unforgiving, and, very important, fair." Moreover, interestingly enough, there's a human need for trust. According to this computer education pioneer, the computer is the one thing you can trust in today's world.

Children as young as five can learn simple computer programs that enable them to form interesting patterns on the screen with their own name as a design. They can set blocks of their name in all sorts of different shapes and sizes. That sort of thing is pleasing to a child because children have the patience to play around. Even children who are severely handicapped can do this—a computer input device can be set up that can be operated with a pointer held in the mouth or even operated by eye blinks.

But the importance of Dr. Galanter's approach is that it gets away from computer-aided instruction, which in many schools means making the computer teach the child. The importance of this distinction is emphasized by Seymour Papert, who holds two professorships at the Massachusetts Institute of Technology, one in mathematics and the other in education. In his book, *Mindstorms,* which is about children and computers, Papert says that computer-aided instruction is in fact using the computer to program the child. Papert's new computer language, LOGO, which he developed with his colleagues at M.I.T., now makes it possible for the child to program the computer. "In doing so," writes Papert, "the child both acquires a sense of mastery over a piece of the most modern and powerful technology and establishes an intimate contact with some of the deepest ideas from science, and from mathematics."

"Learning in our schools today," Papert's book continues, "is not significantly participatory—and doing sums is not an imitation of an exciting recognizable activity of adult life. But writing programs for computer graphics or music and flying a simulated spaceship do share very much with the real activities of adults, *even with the kind of adult who could be a hero and a role model for an ambitious child* [emphasis added]."

One of the strongest reasons that children take to computers as enthusiastically as they do is that they've been watching television from the time they were babies. But television is a one-way street. The computer is a two-way street with both ways completely controlled on a television screen by a child.

It's not unusual for children introduced to the computer as early as kindergarten to develop more computer skills than their teachers have. It is also a fairly common sight to see a seminar on computer programming attended by adults in their thirties, forties, and fifties listening attentively to a fourteen-year-old computer expert.

In "Here Come the Microkids," published in 1982, *TIME* magazine reported about Lewis Stewart, a fourteen-year-old ninth grader at Manhattan's P.S. 118, who can read at only a fifth grade level. But he's the best computer programmer at his school and works after school for a computer consulting firm. He went to Chicago to address a meeting of educators.

Jonathan Dubman, 14, and Kay Borzsony, 13, have formed a company to sell their own computer games and graphics programs. Borzsony says that in the computer business there is no bias against children. Computer magazines often run articles by twelve- and thirteen-year-olds.

The computer in the classroom is so important that in the early 1980s Apple Computer wanted to give one to each of the more than 83,000 elementary and secondary public schools in the country. It would have amounted to a $200-million-dollar giveaway and Apple asked for a special tax allowance from the federal government. Legislation was introduced into Congress to amend the Internal Revenue Code of 1954 and encourage contributions of computers and other sophisticated technological equipment to elementary and secondary schools. The legislation would have tripled the corporate charitable deduction limit for contributions of scientific equipment. The reason: the United States is losing its lead in technology. With Japan graduating twice as many electrical engineers per capita, the United States will fall hopelessly behind unless major actions are taken by our government.

The need for computer specialists is growing fast, but in 1982 we graduated fewer doctorates in computer science than we did five years before.

COMPUTERS AND MEDICINE—A REVOLUTION

By 1985, according to medical scientists, doctors will be able to make electronic house calls. With TV and special devices, they'll be able to monitor pulse, blood pressure, and the other vital signs and check them against computer records.

The *New England Journal of Medicine* says a computer program, Internist I, is about as good a medical diagnostician as the physicians at Massachusetts General Hospital. Another goal is to enable people with spinal injuries to walk again with the aid of computers. Two physiologists, Jerrold Petrofsky and Roger Glaser, and a physician, Chandler Phillips, are the team working on this goal.

They have rigged a computer as a substitute brain. It's programmed to generate the same pattern of electrical signals that are sent by the brain to the muscles when a person wants to move. Just one step calls on scores of muscles and thousands of nerve cells. And the computer has to react too: receive signals returning from the legs, know that the foot has touched the ground, and change commands.

The eventual goal of Petrofsky, Glaser, and Phillips is to make it possible for the paralyzed to walk. The medical benefits of the tiny microprocessor are incalculable.

PERSONAL COMPUTERS—
ANOTHER REVOLUTION

The number of personal computers in schools is growing at a tremendous rate. By the end of 1985, there should be more than

1 million in use in schools alone, compared to just over 50,000 prior to 1980. One explanation is the shrinking cost of computer power. Personal computers cost 40 cents per student hour compared to $2 an hour for the time-share systems built around large mainframe computers. (They're called "mainframe" because they have a central processing unit for many terminals.)

Personal computers have revolutionized the very nature of communication. They are becoming as universal as the telephone. Technologists forecast that they will be in 80 percent of all homes in the United States by 1990 to assist with everything from office- and school-work to the family budget. By that year, some experts think computers won't have to be programmed anymore. They will respond to the human voice.

By this time I have either piqued your curiosity and made you impatient to get your hands on a computer; told you more about it than you wanted to know; or put you in awe of it because its possibilities seem so far out of reach for the ordinary person. But the computer's potential is within the reach of everyone. And that's my whole point. You don't have to be a genius to work a computer. You do have to be a genius to invent it and all the improvements that are making it work even close to the speed of light, and approaching the point where it will think on its own—use "artificial intelligence," as the computer experts like to call it.

Of all man's tools, the computer, and only the computer, is an extension of the brain. Therefore it will continue to develop as far as the imagination of the human mind can take it, limited only by the laws of physics.

Of course, as advanced as the computer is, it has a long, long way to go before it *even approaches* the capacity of the human brain. According to RCA's Advanced Technology Laboratories, your brain has ten times the storage capacity of the entire National Archives, ten thousand times the capacity of the *Encyclopedia Britannica*. The 125 trillion characters your brain can store would fill about a hundred million average-size books.

But your brain has one huge shortcoming. It is a tremendous storehouse, but it is so big that it can't quite remember where everything is—whereas the computer can call up everything in its memory in an instant. That's why Caduceus, an advanced medical system developed at the University of Pittsburgh, can diagnose unrelated diseases. The system uses sophisticated reasoning, keeps zeroing in on the solution, and also keeps getting more information as it needs it. Dr. John D. Myers, who developed Caduceus with Harry E. Pople, Jr., described its use this way: "The human brain is not capable of entertaining an adequate number of simultaneous hypotheses. So the physician has to have a crutch."

There are computers that are fluent in ordinary English, that can read your mail and tell you what's important, that read newspapers and correlate the articles by subject. More and more public libraries are now able to offer a Machine-Assisted Retrieval System (MARS), which can give you a complete readout, at very little cost, of the titles that have been published on a given subject up to the last ten days or so. No more poring over those cumbersome indexes that are months behind and can't list nearly as many sources as the computer.

With a personal computer you can take a giant step beyond that. The world of published information about any subject can be on your screen or run off on your printer in the time it takes to make a local phone call. With a low-price *modem* (telephone attachment to receive and send information from one computer to another—Commodore put one on the market in early 1982 for a little over $100), you can have access to a large central computer service such as Compu-Serve and get the latest news stories about any subject. Once you've seen on the screen what has been published about that subject within the last three days, or a week, or a month, you can take your choice and get the hard copy or a printout of the actual article.

So, as a student with a computer you have a distinct advantage. You don't have to wait in line for a book or a magazine that other students are using. As long as they have a computer and a modem, many students can get the same information from the same computer at the same time. The home computer has made information instantaneous, accessible, and universal.

How will artificial intelligence affect this process? The Japanese are investing many millions in research to develop the so-called fifth generation of computers that they think will give them world leadership in the field by the 1990s. The first generation used vacuum tubes; the second generation, transistors; the third generation, integrated circuits; and the fourth generation uses microprocessors.

Computers now convert raw data to information. And because

they can process so much raw data so fast, they give us more information about practically everything than we've ever had before. The next step—and this is where artificial intelligence comes in—is to get the computer to convert information to knowledge, which systems like Caduceus are starting to do. And the final step is to convert knowledge to wisdom. To paraphrase John von Neumann's amusing definition of a computer with artificial intelligence ("If you give it $300, can it get to Cleveland?"), the computer that has true intelligence might ask why it should go there in the first place.

A good way of looking at it is this: artificial intelligence is concerned with making computers do things that are said to require intelligence when people do them—in other words, solve problems on their own.

Earl C. Joseph at Sperry Univac predicts that by 1990 a computer no bigger than a calculator will be "a mind amplifier" for architects and attorneys. He says that it will be like an encyclopedia with which you can have a conversation. You talk to it, and it will talk back to you. And, if it doesn't have the answer, it will plug itself into another data base and get the information.

But in spite of the fact that computers can do very complicated tasks with such incredible speed, they can't even touch a five-year-old child when it comes to understanding speech or identifying a three-dimensional object.

If the computer has to compete with the young, it is quite understandable, because the young singlehandedly took the computer out of its forbidding and expensive ivory tower, away from the elitists and technocrats, and put it in homes on the street where you live.

In 1975, Steve Jobs, a nineteen-year-old designer of video games at Atari, and his friend Steve Wozniak, electronics designer at Hewlett Packard, decided they would build their own computer. They had bought a microprocessor for $25. A year later they had their product, the Apple I. It was smaller than a portable typewriter, but it could do the work of a much larger computer. They took it to a computer store—a very new kind of store at that time—and the owner ordered fifty. So, Steve Jobs sold his VW van, Wozniak pawned his calculator, and they went into business with the $2,500 they raised. By the start of the decade, Apple was a 600-million-dollar company. Jobs had once tried to convince his boss, Nolan Bushnell (who had started Atari after he invented PONG, the first video game) that personal computers had an even better future than video games. Bushnell didn't believe him. But he did recommend Jobs to Don Valentine, a venture capital investor.

When Valentine met the young genius, he looked at Jobs's cutoff jeans, sandals, shoulder-length hair, and Ho Chi Minh beard and asked, ''Why did you send me this renegade from the human race?'' But he invested nevertheless, and Apple grew from sales of $2.7 million in 1977 to over two hundred times that in the early 1980s—even faster than the computer itself.

What Kind of Computer for You?

What kind to get? That depends on what you want it to do.

If you want to learn what the computer can do for you and want to ''rein it in'' one horse at a time, it makes sense to start looking at the lowest-priced ones.

Timex Computer Corporation, part of the company that introduced the world's first inexpensive wristwatch, put the Sinclair 1000 on sale in the early 1980s for $99.95. It weighed only twelve ounces and measured 6 by 6½ by 1½ inches and could communicate with other large-scale computers.

At the other end of the personal computer scale are the ''Porsches,'' so to speak, such as the Compass, which at the start of the decade fit into half a briefcase, had a high resolution pop-up flat screen and bubble memory the size of a matchbook. The price: over $8,000. It was strictly for the high-level executive who wanted to be able to carry a computer anywhere.

Before you buy or even make up your mind that you want to buy, shop around and find out what different equipment can do. Ask questions about everything. Read some of the magazines and books listed at the end of this chapter. If your community has a computer club, go to a couple of meetings.

No doubt computers are changing, becoming easier to use—more ''user friendly''—every day, giving more bang for the buck with each new improvement. That will continue at a faster and faster pace.

Do you want to develop your mind? Should you learn to use it to its maximum and have fun with it—the way you use your arms and legs and body in running, skiing, surfing, playing football, basket-ball, tennis?

Should you find out what you may be missing by seeing what you can do with a mind that has never been tested to limits you might not even suspect?

Should you learn to think? Not to memorize, but to discover your own brain's fantastic capacity to give you control over and enjoy-ment through an infinitely powerful information machine—a ma-chine that is constantly learning how to do hundreds of new things as fast as the brain can figure out how to program the machine to do them.

At the very beginning of this chapter I wrote that you are lucky to have been born in the computer generation.

I hope I have shown you why. Oh, if I were your age!

Books You Can Use

Most computer stores have dozens of technical books about the ac-tual workings of computers, in general, and computer languages such as BASIC, COBOL, and FORTRAN.

The following is a list of books about computers and their place in society. They will help you make up your mind about the computer and help you find your way through the maze of what's available.

General Books

Austrian, Geoffrey D., *Herman Hollerith*. Columbia University Press, 1982.
Burke, James, *Connections*. Little Brown and Co., 1979.
Carron, Peter L., Jr., *Computers—How to Break into the Field*. Liberty Pub-lishing, 1982.
Ditlea, Steve, *A Simple Guide to Home Computers*. A & W Visual Library, 1978.
Dowling, Colette, *The Techno/Peasant Survival Manual*. Bantam Books, 1980.
Evans, Christopher, *The Making of the Micro*. Van Nostrand Reinhold, 1981.
Evans, Christopher, *The Micro Millenium*. Washington Square Press, 1981.
Frank, Mark, *Discovering Computers*. Time Life Books, 1982.
Goldstine, Herman H., *The Computer from Pascal to von Neumann*. Princeton University Press, 1980.
Hyman, Anthony, *Charles Babbage, Pioneer of the Computer*. Princeton Uni-versity Press, 1982.
Kidder, Tracy, *The Soul of a New Machine*. Avon Books, 1981.

McWilliams, Peter A., *The Personal Computer Book*. Prelude Press, 1982. (Includes a buying guide.)

McWilliams, Peter A., *The Word Processing Book*. Prelude Press, 1982.

Nora, Simon, and Minc, Alain, *The Computerization of Society*. M.I.T. Press, 1981.

Papert, Seymour, *Mindstorms*. Harper Colophon Books, 1980.

Porter, Kent, *Computers Made Really Simple*. Thomas Y. Crowell, 1976.

Technical Books

Ashley, Ruth, *Background Math for a Computer World: A Self-Teaching Guide*. John Wiley & Sons, 1980.

Frenzel, Louis E., Jr., *Crash Course in Microcomputers*. Howard W. Sams & Co., 1980 and 1982.

Gilman, Charles M., *Beginners Guide to Micro Processors*. Tab Books, Inc., 1977.

Hollerbach, Lew, *A 60-Minute Guide to Microcomputers*. Prentice-Hall, 1982.

Hutchinson, David, *Fundamentals of Computer Logic*. Halsted Press, 1981.

Jeffries, Ron, and Fisher, Glen, *Pet Fun & Games*. Osborne/McGraw Hill, 1982.

Lawson, Harold W., Jr., *Understanding Computer Systems*. Computer Science Press, 1982.

Lewis, T. G., *How to Profit from Your Personal Computer*. Hayden Book Co., 1978.

Osborne, Adam, with Cook, Steven, *A Business Systems Buyer's Guide*. Osborne-McGraw, 1981.

Sessions, Laura S., *How to Break into Data Processing*. Prentice-Hall, 1982.

Sippl, Charles J. and Roger J., *Computer Dictionary & Handbook*. Howard W. Sams & Co., Inc., 1982.

Sippl, Charles J., *Microcomputer Dictionary*. Howard W. Sams & Co., Inc., 1981.

Spencer, Donald D., *Fun with Microcomputers & Basic (Painless Programming for Kids and Adults)*. Reston Publishing Co., 1981.

Stern, Nancy B., *Flowcharting, A Tool for Understanding Computer Logic*. John Wiley & Sons, 1975.

Waite, Mitchell, and Pardes, Michael, *Basic Programming Primer*. Howard W. Sams & Co., Inc., 1979.

Waite, Mitchell, *Computer Graphics Primer*. Howard W. Sams & Co., Inc., 1979.

Williams, Robert, and Taylor, Bruce, *The Power of Visicalc*. Prentice-Hall, 1982.

Additional Listings

Spectrum Books, 1983 Catalog, Prentice-Hall.

Personal Guide to Personal Computers, Peter Lundstrom, 1982. Available at authorized Apple Computer dealers.

Understanding BASIC, by Richard Peddicord. Alfred Publishing, 1981.

Understanding FORTRAN, by Herbert R. Ludwig. Alfred Publishing, 1981.

Understanding COBOL, by Richard Peddicord. Alfred Publishing, 1981.

Understanding PASCAL, by George Ledin, Jr. Alfred Publishing, 1981.

Understanding ARTIFICIAL INTELLIGENCE, by George Ledin, Jr. Alfred Publishing, 1981.

Magazines

There are about 100 magazines that specialize in computers. Here are some of the better-known ones:

Byte
Commodore
Compute
Computers and Electronics
Computer Graphics World
Computerworld
Creative Computing
Datamation
Infosystems
InfoWorld
Interface Age
Nibble
PC: The Independent Guide to IBM Personal Computers
Personal Computing
Popular Computing
Power Play

8

YOUR WHEELS

CONTENTS

Part I: Cars—New and Used

Part II: Other Vehicles

Part I: Cars—New and Used

SHOULD YOU BUY A CAR?

Introduction

If you are one of about 18 million teens who will reach the age of eighteen by 1988, you will be old enough to buy a car, wherever in the country you may live.

But should you? Buying a car is just about the biggest investment you can make at this age, and the expenses go far beyond just the price of the car. Look at depreciation—the fact that your car will be worth less the instant you drive it out of the showroom and will be worth less and less as time goes by. Look also at the cost of gas and oil; maintenance and repairs; taxes; parking, garaging, and tolls; liability and collision insurance (especially if you are a single male).

Car prices will continue to go up, too, in line with the costs of their production—natural resources, labor, tools, government regulation, marketing, advertising.

In Five Years, Your Car May Get 80 MPG

If your big, old status-symbol car is lucky to get 15 miles per gallon (mpg) with a tail wind, how would you react to a new model from a top auto maker on sale to you within a few years that would get 70 to 80 mpg? A car that would shift itself constantly and automatically turn its engine on and off, if only for seconds, to save fuel?

Far out? Not at all. The automakers always have been able to produce "economy cars." The 1902 Cadillac achieved 25 to 30 mpg, *Car & Driver* magazine recalled recently. And the 1936 Economy Run was won by a Willys that got more than 33 mpg.

In just the past five years, "downsizing," weight-dropping and lean-burning have almost doubled fuel efficiency, despite the negative fuel factor of antipollution devices. And the automakers are confident they can redouble your fuel savings in another half-decade.

So should you postpone buying? Not necessarily. For you can be certain that this next leap forward in fuel economy will be almost as costly as the last five-year advance. Fuel economy is expensive, and the industry expects to create the new mpg numbers with electronically controlled, souped-up, hot-rod engines coupled with smarter, more versatile transmissions. Souped-up hot rods, even small, are costly.

To enjoy 75-mpg efficiency in a family-size car, you probably will be driving a miniature version of the same turbocharged diesel engines installed today in many eighteen-wheel trucks, with what amounts to an extension of the truckers' nine-to-ten speed transmissions (a device called a "constantly variable shift"). What's more, a computer may be turning your engine off and on automatically during stop-and-go traffic.

Of course, diesels have been on the market for decades. Turbochargers and variable transmissions are hardly new either, but they will get electronic controls to make them more durable and efficient. Turbochargers boost the engine's output by raising its air pressure.

Diesels already run under higher pressure than gas engines, a basic reason even uncharged diesels get better mileage. Still, since standard diesels must be heavier to take the pressure, they cost more. Turbocharging them will add to fuel efficiency—and to costs.

When fuel was cheap, engines could be inexpensive and inefficient. Turbocharged diesels with ten-speed gearboxes paid off only on the biggest eighteen-wheelers. Now the automakers think fuel prices will remain high enough to bring the cost/benefit tradeoff level down to minicars and minimileages.

Should you keep your paid-off gas guzzler and absorb the costs? Trade to a slightly used unit with better performance? Buy a new model with even better fuel efficiency and smaller repair outlays?

Or should you try to wait for the streamlined diesel dreams of later in the 1980s? You can pay now, or pay later. But one point is sure: the 70-to-80-mpg car may be cheaper to run but it won't be cheaper to buy.

HOW TO BUY A NEW CAR

Introduction

You've taken everything into account and you still have decided to buy. Now: new or used? Expense will help you make that choice.

The average price of a new model today is around $10,000, even though new cars are getting better in quality and design. A small or medium-sized car will cost less than a luxury model. However, when it comes to small cars, it's a dealer's market, with small gas-savers—which get 30 to 40 mpg—selling, despite the fact that they seat only four people in most cases, and that even with new kinds of safety features, they still come out way behind big cars in an accident.

In some ways, midsize cars are the best and most versatile—with most getting 30 mpg on the highway. A small car with an automatic transmission doesn't get a lot more.

The cost of running any car is up, but the cost of running a new compact has jumped sharply. For a while, these costs could be decreased a little by the use of a diesel engine and fuel, but diesel fuel prices have gone up to meet, in some cases, the price of gasoline, and diesel fuel can be difficult to find.

A subcompact could be a way to save on the costs of running a car. A subcompact may become even more attractive to you when you consider that the average price of a new compact car in the early 1980s was in the $7,500 to $8,000 range, typically equipped.

The Environmental Protection Agency (EPA) puts out a gas mileage guide you can get from any local car dealer. It categorizes cars by size, model, passenger capacity, engine size and type, fuel-delivery system, and mileage estimates. If you can't find a copy, write the EPA, Washington, DC 20460; get the guide! It may help you decide what you want in your car.

There are other publications you can use to help you make these decisions. Consumer's Guide puts out an entire auto series which rates specific models and comes out at different times of the year. All should be available at your local library. *Consumer Reports* publishes an annual car issue each April, and magazines such as *Car & Driver, Road and Track, Motor Trend,* and *Automotive News* usually rate a few models in their monthly issues.

Comparison Shopping

Once you've done your essential homework, you'll be able to make some of the important choices about what you want in a car. Here are guides regarding what to do before you visit any dealer.

1. Set a maximum price you want to/can pay, and stick to it. Take into account the running costs of the car, and try to estimate what the monthly payments on the car will be over a period of, say, three or four years. Depending on how you finance the car, this will vary. (You'll find more information about financing your car later in this chapter.)

2. Ask yourself why you're getting the car, where you'll usually be going in it, and how much room you'll need. That will help you choose a make, size, body type, engine, and transmission.

3. If you have more than one car in mind, compare prices, taxes, preparation costs, extras and options, the warranty and the gas mileage. You'll probably have to visit a dealer to get some of this information, but that's fine. Visit several dealers to educate yourself before making your final choice.

4. Once you've test-driven each model, compare the ability of each to pass on the road and how well it brakes; the amount of interior space it gives you; the smoothness of the ride; the repair record of that make and model; its handling and looks; the availability of service for it; and the reputation of the dealer, about which you can learn by asking friends who've bought from that dealer or by checking him* out with the local Better Business Bureau.

5. Ask yourself how long you think you'll keep the car. This could determine the best kind of car for you. Buy later in the year if you think you'll keep it more than a few years. If you plan to keep it only a few years, buy a used model.

6. Try to buy a car the dealer has in stock. Delivery can take eight weeks, and the dealer wants to unload cars he has in stock since he's paying interest on them from when *he* bought them.

7. Decide about options beforehand so a glib salesperson can't talk you into expensive extras you don't really want.

8. If you are interested in a high-powered sports car (which can cost more to insure), don't believe the 0-60 stats about them. Test procedures influence the results, and a manufacturer will simply choose the one which gives his car the best result. The same is true

---

*The male gender is used for convenience and simplicity. It refers to either a male or female.

of the often-heard "drag coefficient," which tells how easily the car overcomes aerodynamic drag. Cars with low drag coefficients are said to use fuel more economically.

Computerized estimating services can also help you choose. For a fee, these services will run a printout of the car and its option costs for the dealer, so you'll know what the dealer paid for it. Some even arrange for you to buy it at that price and pick it up at a dealer near you.

Choosing a Dealer

Choose a dealer close to home. It will be more convenient for repairs, and the dealer won't be able to avoid you (which some may try to do).

Choose a dealer who is a member of NADA, the National Automobile Dealers Association. Also make sure he is franchised by an auto manufacturer. You can always complain to the company if your dealer is uncooperative.

Ask your friends and neighbors about local dealers. You also might consult the teacher of an automotive work course at your school. Ask if the dealer gives good prices; if he is reliable when it comes to service; if he honors his warranty; what his hours are. He's no good to you if you can't manage to see him.

Read the warranties of the different dealers, and ask an informed person you trust to explain them to you. Warranties are usually for twelve months, but the mileage requirements can vary. (More about warranties later in this chapter.) Ask the dealer for the manual and warranty for any cars you're considering. Take them home and read them. Ask about anything you don't understand. Be wary of confusing or unclear terms. You can't feel secure in your purchase if you don't know exactly what you're paying for.

Negotiating with the Dealer

Depending on where you live, you may start out with a few strikes against you in this phase of car buying. As a rule, you'll get a better deal if you live in the suburbs or in a rural area than in a big city. Any dealer must make a profit, but the costs of running a dealership are higher in a big city. Once you are in a position to bargain with the dealer, however, here are tips to help you:

• Don't let yourself be rushed or intimidated, especially by a commission-hungry salesman.

• The sticker price is negotiable, but the amount depends on the popularity of the model.

• Ask the salesman for the manufacturer's invoice. This will tell you how much he paid for the car.

• You may have a car that you are thinking of trading in toward the purchase of your new one. Don't tell the salesman whether you've decided to trade in with him. Stick to the price for the new car you want. As a rule, you can get more for your car by selling it yourself, even though this is more trouble. (More information about selling or trading in your old car later in this chapter.)

• If you do decide to trade in with your new car salesman, don't have much faith in his statement "I'm giving you more than the book says (for your car)." There are many used car price books.

• Don't be trapped into taking your loan or insurance from the dealer. You'll almost surely get more favorable rates from your bank and insurance company (which, at this point, you must have).

• Do get this information from your dealer: the price of the car, how much the monthly payments will be, and how large a down payment he will require.

• When you decide to buy, get a written agreement containing *all* the verbal promises the salesman may have made to you. Make sure it has been approved by the sales manager. Read it; cross out any and all blank spaces. Be certain you understand every word in the agreement, and don't sign until you do. Keep in mind that items such as preparation costs and undercoating are included in the retail price of most cars. (More about that in a moment.)

• Establish exactly when the car will be delivered and what you can do about this delivery if the date is missed.

All of this won't happen the first time you visit the dealer, even though he might like it that way. The first time out, visit several dealers and get brochures on all the cars in which you are interested. If the model is in the showroom, take a few minutes to familiarize yourself with it so that when you are reading about it later you'll be able to remember how it looked and felt.

The second time back, you may be ready to test-drive. Despite what a salesperson may say, a serious test drive cannot be accomplished by going around the block for fifteen minutes with the dealer. His insurance policy may dictate that he go with you, but insist on driving the car for as long as it takes you to decide how you'll feel driving it every day. Agree to buy only after you've made your choice at home first. The salesman might try to get your signature right after you've made your test drive, when the feel of all that new plush is fresh in your mind, but *don't*.

When you do test-drive, use roads you usually use and drive the way you usually drive. Here are points to check:

• The controls—are they easy to see and use, or will you have to fumble to turn on the air-conditioner?

• Does the car give you good visibility, or is the design such that your view in your rearview mirror is blocked?

• Does the car steer easily? Will you want power steering, if that is what your test car has?

• Is there a good ventilation system? This is especially important if you don't plan to buy air-conditioning.

• Does the car run quietly enough so you can carry on a conversation at a normal level?

• Does the car accelerate smoothly and easily? Does it have enough power to go up a hill?

• Take note of the car's braking ability. Can you stop short if you have to? Decide if you want power brakes, if that is what the car has. Brakes can be *too* sensitive.

• What about the way the car handles going over bumps? Decide if you want front-wheel drive, which means that the engine's power will be applied to the front wheels instead of the back. (Four-wheel drive means the power is applied to all four wheels.)

If you like the car, get the price—including tax, license, and registration. Then *go home* and make your decision.

In general, if the dealer can come within $100 of your calculated price, it's a good buy. If you buy your car at a sale time, you may get an even better deal, not because the prices are really any cheaper, but because the salesman is under more pressure from the manufacturer to sell. This pressure may cause him to go to extraordinary lengths to sell you a car, including:

- *The Demo Ride.* The salesman may push you to test-drive, but not because he wants you to make a more informed decision. He thinks your good sense will be smothered under the aura of a new car.
- *The Turnover.* If the salesman sees that he's not getting anywhere with you, he may turn you over to the sales manager, who may then hand you over to the general manager, in an attempt to wear you down. Insist on dealing with one person.
- *The Deposit.* The salesman may try to get a deposit from you during your talks, thinking that you will be less likely to walk away without buying once you have given him your money. Don't make a deposit until your offer has been approved by the management.
- *The Raise.* The salesman says he'll sell to you at your price, goes off to see the sales manager, and comes back to tell you that his boss won't okay the deal unless you agree to pay more. *Don't.*

Buying Options

The ten options people (that definitely includes teenagers) buy most frequently are: automatic transmission, power steering, air-conditioning, power brakes, AM/FM stereo radio, tinted glass, tilt wheel, cruise control (keeps the car going at a steady pace during long trips), remote control mirrors, and styled wheels or wheel covers.

But don't buy these options just because everyone else gets them. Ask what each will do for you. Some add weight to the car and cause lower gas mileage; others take power from the engine and battery, which can also lower your gas mileage; mechanically intricate items can cost you substantially extra money for repairs.

Options can raise the price of your car by as much as 50 percent. Dealers get a big markup on them, and they'll go all out to try to sell options to you, especially if you're an inexperienced buyer. Be especially careful about adding too much to your car. Other people may not be impressed by your power sun visors.

Also, some manufacturers offer only option packages—such as power steering, but only with power windows, automatic speed control, and an AM/FM stereo radio. Some options are available only if you buy the top-of-the-line car.

Tips to help you play the option game:

• *Undercoating* is applied to all cars made by Ford, Chrysler, or General Motors. GM does not even offer additional rust protection as an option, so if you buy a GM car, you should never see a charge for undercoating on the sticker or the invoice. Ford will provide additional undercoating for a minor cost. Chrysler will too, but how much it will cost is between you and the dealer. The whole practice of undercoating is under investigation by consumer affairs departments and organizations due to reports of dealers charging as much as $800 for what they call "rust-proofing." Rust-proofing is a bigger job than undercoating, involving the injection of chemicals inside the body of the car to prevent rust. Ford charges $150 for this, so beware of the dealer who tries to sell it to you for five times that much.

• *A big engine* costs more, uses more gas, and costs more to maintain. Six cylinders are sufficient for most cars; four are usually enough for a small car. The *area* of the cylinder is more important than the *number* of them.

• *Automatic transmissions* cost more to fix, add several hundred dollars to the price of your car at the start, and use more gas. But you'll have to learn to drive a stick shift if you don't want this option. If you plan to trade in or resell your car, get an automatic. It'll add to the value of your car.

• *Air-conditioning* will be valuable at resale time if you live in a warm climate. It can also cause your car to overheat on a hot day in stop-and-go traffic.

• *Power steering and brakes* are good if you have a big car. They'll allow you to steer and stop more easily, and they make parallel parking easier.

• *Remote control outside mirrors*. You should get these, on both sides.

• *AM radio*. If it's not standard, don't buy it. For the same money, you can buy your own AM/FM elsewhere.

• *A CB radio* is useful in the exurbs, but can be hard to use in the city, since so many people are using the channels. If you live in a rural or semirural area, buy a cheap set and use it only for emergencies. Get a magnetic roof mount for the antenna.

• *Rear defoggers and wipers* are especially good for hatchbacks.

• *A vinyl roof* may look nice, but it's useless.

• *Power windows* are a waste of money. They use electricity and can break.

• *Computerized gas gauges, digital clocks, etc.* are still pretty expensive when weighed against what they actually do.

HOW TO BUY A USED CAR

Introduction

Even if you have traditionally been a new car buyer, consider buying a secondhand car. Used cars are still the most economical, despite the upward push in prices. Most people who buy a car for personal use buy a used car (three out of four), and each year 50 percent more used cars are sold than new. The reason is that the best way to save money on a car is either to drive a new one until it becomes "very" used, or to buy a well-maintained used one in the first place. Since fewer new cars have been sold in recent years, late-model cars are hard to find—a force working against you. Owners are keeping cars longer, reducing the availability of older used cars as well.

The operating costs of used cars can be 10 to 55 percent less than that of their new counterparts. But the primary reason a used car remains a bargain is that car depreciation is "front loaded"—bigger in the early years, lower later on. The first 30,000 miles of driving cost you about two-thirds more than your second 30,000; this second, in turn, costs about 20 percent more than your third 30,000 miles. And though maintenance costs increase as mileage rises, they don't go up as fast as expenses go down. To save the most, buy a well-maintained one- to three-year-old car and keep it three years or longer. It should still have a number of good years left in it, and most of its depreciation is behind it (that is, it has lost most of the value it will lose). The longer you keep the car, the lower your costs per year and per mile.

But if the *new* car marketplace has been called the last bastion of horse-trading, just use your imagination to find a name for the *used* car marketplace. You've all seen comedy skits about the slick used car salesman who swindles an unsuspecting soul out of his last dollar for a heap that won't take him to the end of the street. This chapter should help you steer clear of such trouble.

Used cars are subject to a higher markup as a rule—22 to 50 percent, compared to 12 to 15 percent for new cars. And when you buy a used car, naturally you're opening yourself up to risks that don't go with a new car. The car may have been in an accident, or its odometer may (illegally) have been turned back so it won't show the true amount of mileage the car has traveled. It may be a lemon someone doesn't want to or couldn't fix. You might (unwittingly) end up buying a former taxi or police car which has traveled 50,000 or 100,000 miles a year, 12 to 18 hours a day, and has been through a lot of rough travel (think of your favorite police chase scene in the movies). The odds are 1 in 6 that you will get such a car if you shop for one- to two-year-old cars. The chances are 2 in 5 that a one-year-old used car has been in an accident, and for a two-year-old car the odds are 3 out of 5. Understandably, if a car has been in an accident, the police department or taxi company will probably trade it in. A huge number—750,000—of seriously damaged one- to three-year-old cars go to used car lots each year, which is one good reason to avoid the "used-car only" salesman.

If you're thinking of buying a real oldie—pre-1975—keep in mind a new disadvantage: it's becoming harder and harder to find the high octane, premium gas these cars need. They can't use unleaded gas, and oil companies are not making much high octane leaded fuel anymore. If you're good with cars, you can tinker with the engine so the car will run well on regular gas, but more likely you'll have to use some kind of octane booster. The boosters, however, are very flammable and toxic. You also can use water or a water/alcohol mixture to reduce "knocking."

Buying a Used Car from a Dealer: What to Watch Out For

One surprising fact about used cars is this: the newer they are, the more likely they are to have a lot of miles on them. And when doing any used car shopping, or any car shopping for that matter, bring a friend to give you a second opinion. Two heads *are* better than one in this case.

Despite a 1978 federal law which calls for a $50,000 fine and one-year jail sentence for anyone convicted of turning back a car's odometer, "odometer rollback is still out there, sorry to say," according to the New York State Department of Motor Vehicles, which reports an increase in rollback by used car dealers. Certainly it is possible for a private individual to turn back an odometer, but it doesn't happen as often since people skilled in this craft charge a lot of money for their service. The illegal practice of odometer rollback is on a nationwide increase. So, watch out.

The law also requires every seller to sign an odometer mileage statement, asserting that the odometer shows the true mileage, or giving the reason it doesn't. A good way to estimate the car's mileage is to assume 20,000 miles per year during the first four years of a car's use. Take a careful look at the driver's seat—if the odometer says 10,000 miles but the seat looks as though it's been through a war, be suspicious. Examine the accelerator, brake pedal, and tires, too. They're good indicators of how much a car has been driven.

Other swindles to be on guard against when buying a used car:

• *Doping.* You are told that the used car you want has been totally reconditioned. But once you get it home, it develops a wide variety of problems just temporarily covered up by the owner or dealer.

• *Bushing.* After you have made a deposit, the dealer raises the price of the car. If you make a deposit, insist that the dealer sign a statement saying that the car will be delivered at a certain time, at the agreed price.

• *Packing.* The dealer adds extra fees to the purchase price. Don't sign until you're satisfied that all charges are legitimate.

• *Bait and Switch.* You go to a car lot to find a car you saw advertised at a certain price, but when you get there—no car. The ad was designed to "bait" you to the lot with the purpose of then "switching" you to a more expensive model.

• *Highball.* A dealer offers you a great price for the car you're trading in to keep you from going elsewhere. You agree, but when it comes time to make the deal, he lowers the offer on the pretext that your car really isn't as good as he first thought.

• *Lowball.* The other side of the coin: a dealer offers you a great price for the car you want, but then raises it when you actually come back to buy.

General Rules for Used Car Shopping

The used car market is a jungle, but there are ways to hack through the bush. While there are numerous used car price guides, most banks use the National Automobile Dealers Association's guide to determine what the car you are buying is worth, and, therefore, how much of its price the bank will help you finance. There are also other publications which will tell you about different models in different years, and what the models sell for. The *Used Car Rating and Price Guide, 1971–81* from Consumer's Guide gives a recall history for each model, and explains any other problems with it that have been reported, such as rust.

To get additional recall information, use the National Highway Traffic Safety Administration's recall hot line (800-424-9393). The NHTSA will give you general recall information for vehicles dating from 1962 to the present, if the recall was related to the safety of the car.

Other general tips to help you through the jungle:

- Stay away from cars for which it might be difficult to get parts. If you buy from a dealer, make sure that he is well stocked. For very old cars or imports, it may be especially hard to find parts.
- Decide what you want, how much you're willing to pay for it, and stick to your decisions.
- An older, low-mileage car might be better than a newer, abused one, especially if you plan to keep the car more than one or two years. A three-year-old car with 30,000 miles on it may be a better buy than a two-year-old one with 60,000 miles on it.
- Take a friend with you for that valuable second opinion.
- Stay away from big gas-guzzlers. They may have a snob appeal among your peers, but this is temporary. And each time a new line of fuel-efficient cars is introduced, the basic value of these oldies drops.
- Most used car sales are final.
- Don't buy a car that is more than four years old if you plan to keep it as long or longer yourself.
- Taxes and insurance will be lower on an old car because almost surely it was bought for a lower price than a new automobile.
- Never buy a car at night. Wait until you can see it in the daylight.

• Shop at clean, reputable lots displaying a wide range of cars. Stick with ones that offer a warranty or a trial period.

• Expect major repairs to be necessary at any time if you buy a car with more than 50,000 miles on it.

Buying from an Owner

Most used cars are sold by private individuals, and there are advantages to buying from a private owner. You'll probably be able to get a good car for less money, and if that person is the original owner, you'll know you're not getting an ex-taxi or –police car. The owner can give you a wealth of information about the condition of the car and its maintenance history.

However, you won't get any kind of guarantee that the car will pass inspection. It's also hard to know what the car is worth. Price guides are based on averages and on other cars, not the one you're considering. Use them as guidelines: they will tell you the difference between the car's wholesale and retail price, so you can bargain without suggesting that the owner take a loss on the car. Know the wholesale value of the car, and don't pay more than 10 percent above that price when you're buying from a private individual.

When dealing with an individual, you usually won't be presented with a contract to sign when you buy the car. But the two of you should write up some kind of contract stating that you are the new owner of said car, that it was agreed to be sold as is (or any other details about the sale), and the specified price. If you have made any kind of repair agreement with the owner, keep records of all repairs so there's no doubt about who's responsible for them.

Try to convince the owner to agree to some kind of money-back guarantee, even if it's only for a week or two.

And perhaps most important, have the owner show you documentation that will verify he/she is indeed the owner of the car. If you buy a hot car, you'll end up *out* the car and your money, and *in* a whole lot of trouble.

An owner usually will not hold his/her car for you without a deposit. Fall and winter are usually the best times to buy from individuals—the sellers may be hoping to use the money from their sales to buy new cars, and may want to shop for them at this time of year. It's a good time for bargaining.

A final note: Many friendships have gone under due to the sale of a used car. Keep your friends. Look elsewhere for your car.

Choosing a Used Car Dealer

When choosing a used car dealer, use the same criteria you'd use to find a new car dealer, and stay away from those who sell only used cars—they're the ones to whom taxi companies and police departments wholesale cars that are too badly damaged to sell retail. Even if the car you're thinking of buying from a used-car-only dealer isn't one of the above, the chances are the dealer didn't sell the car to its previous owner and so can't tell you anything about its history. In addition, he won't have as complete a repair facility as a dealer who sells both new and used cars, since he doesn't have to fix any new cars that are under warranty. And there's much more of a chance that he has had the odometers on his cars turned back than there is that a private individual has done so. Check with your local Better Business Bureau to see if there have been any complaints about the firm.

Understanding Car Talk

When you decide to shop for a used car, one of the first places you may look is your newspaper. But instead of ads written in English, you may find that they look as if they were done in speed-writing.

Here's a translation of auto shorthand:

a/c: air-conditioning
at: automatic transmission
cb: citizens band radio
conv: convertible
cpe: coupe
cyl: cylinders (4, 6, 8)
dlr: dealer
dr: doors (2, 4)
hdtp: hardtop
lo mi: low mileage
pb: power brakes
pd: power disc brakes

ps: power steering
p seats: power seats
pw: power windows
rad ti: radial tires
sed: sedan
spd contrl: speed control
tape: tape player
std tr: standard transmission
vnyl: vinyl top
wrnty: warranty
wgn: station wagon

Once you've translated the shorthand, decide if the ad seems realistic and truthful to you. Good places to look for ads are *Motor Trend*, *Car and Driver*, and *Road and Track* magazines.

Other Shopping Hints

Shop the new car dealers in your area to see if they have any new trade-in cars for sale. These cars will have a warranty the dealer will honor in his service shop.

Tend to smaller, lower-priced cars with few options. That way you'll get fewer gimmicks you don't want.

The value of a car depends on its condition (obviously) and on the area of the country in which you're buying. Used car guides, such as the NADA guide, take this into account. (If you live on the West Coast, look at *Kelley's Auto Market Report*, available at banks or libraries, for the average value of a model in a given year.) Check the pamphlet *How to Buy a Used Car*, published by Consumer Reports, for prices and other information. The yearly published new car issue from Consumer Reports gives a list of used cars to avoid. And *Car/Puter's Auto Facts—Used Car Prices* is available from Davis Publications (380 Lexington Avenue, New York, NY 10003).

Avoid shopping in late spring/summer, when demand for vacation transportation is at a peak and it's a dealer's market.

Whatever car you are considering seriously, spend the $25 or $50 it may cost to have a mechanic check it out. If he/she tells you not to buy the car, your money has been very well "wasted."

Comparison shop for deals on insurance and financing. Shop for these first: it may not be possible for a car to be held for you while you make the rounds for your money.

Dealing with the Dealer

After you've done your homework, you'll be ready to visit a dealer. Trading with a horse trader can be tricky, but it's not impossible.

First, don't come in and announce. "I have about two thousand dollars to spend. What do you have for that price?" Let him show his hand first.

When you talk about a purchase price, make sure that it includes any repairs you know you will have to make on the car.

If he agrees to a price, but then says "I'm losing money on this deal," or "I'm breaking even," don't believe him. No one works to lose money or break even. Would you?

Try to get a thirty-day guarantee on all or all major repairs, or at least a guarantee that the car will pass inspection. Usually it will be a 50-50 deal for the first thirty days, but in that case, watch out that your dealer doesn't double the repair charges so you end up footing the whole bill.

Learn about the car first: don't rely on the dealer's sales talk. He'll tell you just about anything.

Ask the dealer for the names of customers who bought from him more than six months ago, and get in touch with them to see how they've made out with their cars.

Even if the car you are considering has an inspection sticker, the car may not necessarily be in good condition. Inspection procedures in most states don't require that the mechanic look at the engine or transmission, and if the dealer has a friend who is a mechanic, he may have been able to get a sticker with no inspection at all.

If the dealer won't sign the statement required by law saying the odometer is accurate (the statement is available from the State Department of Motor Vehicles and branch offices), don't buy the car—regardless of the reason he gives. For tips on how to figure a car's mileage on your own, reread the pages earlier in this chapter.

Take notes as you talk to the dealer; inspect the car; and test-drive it.

How to Inspect the Outside of a Used Car

When you've settled on a year, make, and model of a car you want, and have chosen that one special car from perhaps hundreds, you can learn a lot about it without even moving it an inch.

• Look at the car's body. Ripples in the metal, uneven paint, different colors of paint, rust, a gritty surface, or loose bumpers may mean the car has been in an accident.

• Open and close the doors, windows, hood, and trunk. Do they move easily and fit right?

• Kicking the tires may be a cliche, but tires can reveal a great deal about a car's history. Do you see any bald spots? The wheels may need balancing. Is one front tire more worn than the other? This may mean poor alignment of the front wheels or front end wear.

• Is there gummy soot in the tail pipe? The engine may be burning oil, and you may have to make expensive repairs later on.

• Inspect the seats and carpet. Look for rust on the floor. Make sure the front seat locks in place and adjusts easily if more than one person will be driving it. Check the seat belts and shoulder harnesses if there are any. Do they adjust easily and lock securely?

• Inspect the gas and brake pedals—do they look worn? Right here is a good indication of the car's age.

• Start the engine, or try to. If it sounds rough or doesn't start right away, it may have a bad battery or electrical system.

• While the engine is running, have your friend look for smoke from the exhaust. If it's blue, it may mean bad valves or rings. If it's black, you may have carburetor problems.

• Accelerate (in neutral) and see how the engine responds. If it makes a clunking noise or rumbles when you press the pedal or let up on it, the engine may have bad rods or main bearings—and that means trouble.

• Listen for a whining sound if the car you're in has an automatic transmission. If you hear it, get out and look underneath to see if the transmission fluid is leaking. Look on the underside of the engine, transmission, and rear axle.

• Take note of how far you have to turn the wheel before the car starts turning. The amount of "play," as it's called, should not be more than two inches. If the wheel is stiff, or if you hear a clunking noise when you turn, the car may have front-end problems.

• When you press the brake, the pedal should stop firmly, as if it's hitting the floor. It shouldn't be spongy. If you can, have one of the front and rear wheels taken off so you can check the brake linings. Are there any signs of fluid leakage on either the inside of the wheels or the master cylinder?

• Turn on the windshield wipers, all the lights, the turn signals, the climate controls, and the radio.

• Test the car's suspension system. Try to make the car bounce by pushing down hard on each corner of it. If it keeps bouncing after you let go, the car may have worn shock absorbers. Hold the top of each front tire and try to rock it. If it seems loose or makes a noise, the bearings or joints may need work.

• Check the fan belts and hoses.

The Road Test

Now that you've given the car a thorough external inspection, you're ready to move it. A good dealer should insist that you test-drive the car—if he won't let you give a car a road test, don't buy it.

As when you're buying a new car, the road test should not be four right turns back to the dealer's lot. Go on many different kinds of roads, particularly the kinds on which you usually drive. Take a friend with you and leave the dealer at the shop, if you can. If the dealer's insurance agency requires that he go with you, ask him please to sit in the backseat.

Wherever you go, be sure to:

• Stop and start several times, so you can see how the car accelerates and brakes. It should gain speed without hesitating, and when you brake you shouldn't feel a pulling to one side.

• Ask your companion to look out the back window for smoke as you slow down. If there is any smoke, especially if it's blue, the car may have bad rings. (This is the same test you did while stationary, but it's wise to do it when the car is actually in motion as well.)

• Make turns when you are going both fast and slow. If the car sways or if the wheel seems stiff, the front end may need to be checked and the front shock absorbers replaced.

• Take some bumps. Does the car seem to be falling apart around you?

• Drive in a straight line through a puddle and have your friend look at the tracks. He/she should see only two sets of tracks, not four. If there are four, the wheels are not properly aligned.

• You might even want to have the car you're thinking of examined and driven again by someone else. It's a good way to make sure you weren't the victim of a staged car performance. I know it seems a long, drawn-out process, but if there's one time you definitely should *not* go shopping for a car, it's when you have "car fever."

Have all verbal promises written down, just as if you were buying a new car. Be sure the person who authorizes the guarantees has the power to do so. And don't sign any agreement unless it's all filled out, with lines through any blank spaces. The contract must be specific about the provisions of your guarantee.

Buying a Rental Car

Should you decide to buy a used rental car from a rental agency, the probabilities are your car will be no more than twelve months old with somewhere between 17,000 and 23,000 miles on it. You'll get a complete service history and documentation, and the company's reputation will stand behind your car. You won't get any car that has been in more than a minor accident—those that have been in major ones will be sold elsewhere.

Most rental cars have to pass a 55-point physical to stay on the road. A top car-renting firm offers a 12-month, 12,000-mile warranty including parts and labor. Rental companies sell more cars than either private individuals or dealers, so they can afford to sell from $200 to $500 below the book price of a car.

The rental companies will give you eight hours to test drive the car and bring it to your mechanic. You can be sure that it has been maintained well.

Try Leasing

That great American fall tradition—the introduction of new car models—is being wiped out by the brutal reality that new cars cost what houses did thirty years ago.

If you qualify—unlikely, unless your parents will stand with you—another alternative to buying a new, used, or rental car is to lease-buy a new car from a leasing company and enter into a straightforward "open-end" lease. If your credit is good (imperative), you'll pay only the equivalent of two months as down payment—perhaps $400 to $600. Then you will pay the equivalent of regular monthly installment purchase payments for three or four years, as you would on a car bought on the installment plan. But at the end of a three-year period, you still won't own the car.

A terrible deal? Not as bad as you might think. You've paid only $400 to $600 "down" (up front), and you have the right to buy "your" leased car from the leasing company at a price specified when you signed the lease. Since you're driving the car and you can baby it, you have a used car bargain. Assuming interest rates have fallen, you can borrow to buy your own "used" car over another two or even three years. In effect, you will have engineered a low down payment and four- to six-year loan for a new car.

Beware the pitfalls, though. Read the fine print carefully. It's your car, and for the lowest payments you probably must license, insure, and maintain it, just as though you really owned the car. Shop around for the lowest payments. Resale values on cars with identical sticker prices may be hundreds of dollars apart.

Don't Forget Government Surplus

The U.S. Government will sell you a car that might be practically new. Test cars used by the Department of Transportation may have racked up all of twenty-five miles.

The cars are sold at auction, with "spot" or sealed bids. But once you buy a car, it's yours. Period. There are no warranties, and the cars are in a variety of conditions. Here are some examples: A 1976 four-door sedan with 43,000 miles on it sold in the early 1980s for $1,400, and one with 36,000 miles on it sold for $1,600.

You have a few days to pay for the car, and you must make your own arrangements for hauling it away. You can't test drive the car, but you can start the engine and look it over just like any other car.

For information write to the Customs Service in Washington, DC, about its cars, or to the Defense Department Disposal Service (Bidders Control Office, P.O. Box 1370, Battle Creek, MI 49016), about Defense Department property.

In the Washington, DC, area, the General Services Administration holds a vehicle auction on the second Wednesday of every month at 11 A.M. It takes place at the Surplus Sales Center, Washington Navy Yard, Second and M Streets, S.E., Building 197. You're allowed to inspect the vehicles two days before the sale is scheduled.

WARRANTIES FOR NEW AND USED CARS

Shop for your warranty just as you shop for everything else associated with your car. At least for the first year of ownership, the warranty can mean the difference between you paying for repairs and maintenance and the manufacturer or dealer paying for these expenses.

Car repair is inherently expensive, since it is done on an individual basis, while your car is mass-produced when it is built. If your car suffers 25 percent damage, fixing it might cost as much as you paid for it new.

Most warranties last for twelve months, but the mileage allowances may vary. The conventional warranty is for 12 months or 12,000 miles, whichever comes first. In the early 1980s, the state of the American auto industry caused a "warranty war" among major auto makers, with some offering a 5-year/50,000-mile warranty on maintenance and certain major repairs. Other manufacturers are warranting the engine and giving free maintenance for 2 years or 24,000 miles, whichever comes first. Extended service contracts are becoming increasingly popular, but before you buy one, keep in mind how much it costs and how well equipped the dealer seems to be for repairs. The longer you keep the car, the greater the chance that you will be in an accident which may require costly repairs. You can save on needed repairs by buying an extended warranty or service contract from your manufacturer— but these have "deductibles" (fixed portions of the cost of any repair which you agree to pay), and you must buy the warranty when you buy the car.

Your warranty should cover: the transmission, front and rear suspension, air-conditioning, brakes, electrical system, radiator, and turbocharger. You should be able to tell exactly what your warranty covers—beware of anything that is written so you can't understand it.

The mileage stipulation on a warranty is important, for as the car passes certain "milestones" you can expect specific repairs to be necessary.

After 12,000 miles, you might have to attend to the brakes, alternator, cylinders, hoses, shock absorbers, muffler and exhaust system, batteries, electrical system, pumps (water, oil, and fuel), and various minor repairs.

Beyond 50,000 miles, you can expect some major repairs, perhaps to the transmission, valves, or engine.

Warranties for used cars can be outright phonies, so beware. Question other people who have bought used cars from your dealer about whether the dealer honors his warranties.

The warranty should be included in the price of the car, and your best bet is to take over the car's original warranty. The car you are thinking of buying would have to be less than a year old for you to do this, but if you are buying a demonstrator, a salesperson's car, or a relatively new one you should be able to arrange this. Get the warranty in writing; don't take anyone's word that your car is covered. And any kind of warranty you get from a used car dealer should run for at least thirty to sixty days or it really isn't worth much.

Keep this valuable document in a safe place, and follow its instructions, such as taking it for monthly checkups, to keep it in effect.

TAKING DELIVERY OF YOUR CAR

Finally, the big day arrives when you become a car owner, perhaps for the first time. But before you get caught up in all the excitement, grabbing the keys and waving good-bye to the person who delivered your car, make sure you've received what you paid for.

- Check the exterior and interior. Do all the side panels and moldings match up?
- Operate all the options, such as power windows.
- Get your copy of the invoice and make sure it matches the car.
- Take the car for a short test drive. If you find any problems, have the dealer fix them before you sign for delivery.

And by all means, if you find trouble in the first few weeks you have the car, go back to the dealer and have him repair it while the car is still under warranty.

MAINTENANCE

Costs of Driving

The American Automobile Association (AAA) has calculated that in the early part of this decade it cost $6.56 per day to own a compact car, whether it moves or not. This is a national average.

You may think that once you've bought your car, any more expenditures will be incidental. The AAA, however, estimates that in the early 1980s the national average cost of driving a compact car 15,000 miles a year was $3,654 per year, or 24.4 cents per mile.

There are two types of costs of driving: *running costs,* which include gas, oil, maintenance and repairs; and *fixed costs,* such as insurance, licensing, depreciation, registration, taxes, and finance charges. Depreciation is the basic difference between what you paid for your car and what you'll sell it for.

The AAA broke the costs down as follows:

Running Costs

Gas and oil	$1011/year
Maintenance	$150/year
Tires	$94.50/year
Total	$1,255.50/year

Fixed Costs

Insurance	$449/year
License, registration, tax	$54/year
Depreciation	$1,356/year
Finance charges	$539/year
Total	$2,398/year

The AAA has changed its "typical" car from a midsize to a compact to reflect what most people drive.

Costs of Maintenance

Maintenance costs are the costs of running your car—amounts you'll pay for gas, oil, lubrication, spark plugs, batteries, tune-ups, and a multitude of other things. On average, maintenance and repair charges account for 25 percent of the cost of a recent-model car, and 40 percent of the cost of a ten-year-old car.

In 1980, Americans spent $521 maintaining and repairing each of their cars, for a total of $63 billion on maintenance and repair alone.

But maintenance has gone up the least of all elements of car costs. In fact, in 1950, maintenance accounted for 28 percent of a car's costs over a ten-year period, on average. In 1980, it accounted for 20 percent.

These charts show the costs of maintaining a medium-priced, midsize and compact car over ten years. The figures are for 1980.

Year	Compact Cost Per Mile (cents)	Percent of Total Cost of Running Car
1	1.69	4.19
3	2.20	5.50
5	2.43	6.94
10	3.04	11.28

Year	Intermediate Cost Per Mile (cents)	Percent of Total Cost of Running Car
1	2.30	4.52
3	2.99	6.22
5	3.31	7.49
10	4.14	12.12

As the charts emphasize, maintenance costs, even when averaged over the years of a car's life, rise as the car ages. They also account for a greater percentage of the total cost of running the car. But since the car's value drops less sharply as the years go by, you still will save money by holding on to your car.

Study the last column of the charts. Independent of rising prices due to inflation, it tells you what portion of your car costs should be spent on maintenance at various stages of your car's life.

Exceeding 55 MPH Costs Billions

If you drive within the legal 55-mph speed limit on the open road today, you're a rarity. The 55-mph limit is federal law, but on highways speeds of 65 mph to 70 mph are so much the norm that if you drive at 55, you feel you're making a fool of yourself.

The 55-mph speed limit was enacted in 1975 as a result of the oil embargo in 1973–74 with the combined goals of conserving energy, cutting imports, and yet still allowing highway travel to continue at a reasonable pace. Those goals are as valid as ever, but an unexpected "bonus" has been the saving of up to 4,000 lives a year on the highways. Highways designed for safety are safe only if you, a motorist, make them so. The faster you drive, the less time you have to react and make decisions. And in a collision, the chances that you will die are *doubled* with each ten miles of speed over 55 mph. The savings in fuel and in lives will be deeply eroded if the 55-mph limit is weakened or abandoned by the states.

The case for the 55-mph speed limit has been proved beyond doubt. At lower speeds, you reduce the risks of death and injury, conserve gasoline, and are in better control of your vehicle.

We're buying smaller cars in mounting numbers because they are energy efficient, but we lose our savings on fuel when we speed. At 55 mph, fuel efficiency is 10 to 30 percent superior to efficiency at 56 to 75 mph. And the costs (as well as the dangers) of speeding are zooming.

Deaths from motor vehicle accidents exceed 53,300 a year. Every eleven minutes of each day of the year there is a death as a result of an automobile crash in the United States, and every nine seconds there is an injury, ranging from moderate to tragically severe. Disabling injuries from motor vehicle accidents total 2 million annually. Each one of the more than 146 million of us who drive cars can now expect to be involved in an automobile crash once every ten years. Costs—including losses in wages, medical expenses, administrative and claim settlement expenses, costs of insurance, and costs of property damage—will top $40 *billion* each year. That's far in excess of the budgets of many countries. It's all so wasteful, and so contrary to our best interests!

The drain on this nation's economy and health has reached staggering proportions. The price tag of these crashes has soared to $20.1 billion a year, up from $14.4 billion as recently as 1975. Among health problems, the costs of car crash injuries are second only to cancer, outranking even the cost of coronary heart disease, and the waste (as well as loss of productivity) resulting from car crashes cannot even be calculated.

Save on Maintenance from the Beginning

The costs of maintenance and driving are obviously very high. What can you do to save on them? From the start, when you buy your car, there are ways to save money.

- Buy a smaller engine—a four or six cylinder model rather than an eight cylinder one.
- Choose fewer options. The fewer you buy, the fewer you'll have to maintain and repair.
- Try to do most of your driving in moderate weather. In the summer, you'll have to use expensive air-conditioning, and in the winter you'll need antifreeze and snow tires.
- Take advantage of the better rust-proofing methods now available.
- Buy radial tires, which wear longer. Also get electronic ignition and disc brakes.
- Keep a repair log and note the mileage at which each repair was made.

In addition to yearly maintenance, do a checkup every spring, when chances are you'll start to do most of your driving. Check:

- The ignition system and air filter.
- The oil. Change it to multigrade or summer weight.
- The radiator. Drain and clean it.
- The battery. Check the fluid levels and charge; take the rust off the terminals.
- The exhaust system. Look for leaks in it.
- The tires. Change snow tires to regular tires. Look at your shock absorbers and front alignment.
- Any accumulated moisture from the winter. Have your car lubricated to guard against any rust caused by moisture.
- All belts and hoses.

Maintenance Musts

Oil

Without motor oil, the engine of your car would grind itself to pieces. Its parts might start to fly through the hood of your car while you were driving.

Check the oil whenever you stop for gas. This is the single most important step in car maintenance. Replace the oil whenever necessary with the grade of oil your owner's manual recommends, and also replace the oil filter as often as your manual says to.

Battery

The battery, which provides the power to your car's electrical system, should be inspected regularly according to the instructions in your manual. Even if you have a "maintenance-free" battery, you still must check the cable connections. A while ago, the connectors on my car blew out while I was in a service station. Lucky for me: five minutes later I would have been on the New England Thruway.

Radiator

Check your radiator, especially after highway driving. Rinse away any dirt with a garden hose.

Check your coolant monthly, in the manner your owner's manual states. Measure its level relative to the bottom of the filler neck. Add the type of coolant your manual suggests.

Lights

To make sure all of your car's lights are in working order, have a friend stand by while you activate headlights, high beams, turn signals, taillights, and hazard lights.

Hoses, Belts, and Filters

Check the hoses to your radiator, air-conditioner, and heater every six months for leaks, cracks, and to make sure they're still firm.

Change your air filter according to the manual. If you drive in an unusually dusty place, the air filter should be changed every 3,000 miles. Also check drive belts and water hoses to make sure they're not cracked or leaking.

Fluids

Check your brake fluid, and clean the filler cap before you remove it. The level should be ¼" or less from the top of the reservoir.

Transmission fluid is essential to an automatic transmission and should be checked regularly. (See the information on automatic transmissions later in this section.)

Power steering fluid should be checked whenever you check your oil. Your owner's manual will help you find the pump on your particular car. It has a dipstick, just as the oil does, and it should read between the "add" and "full" marks. Add power steering fluid according to the instructions in your manual.

Keep a constant supply of windshield washer fluid in the reservoir for this purpose. In winter, make sure it has sufficient antifreeze.

Shock Absorbers

Bounce the car over each wheel to see how the shock absorbers are working. The car should not bounce more than once after you've let go.

Tire Pressure

Buy an air-pressure gauge and check the pressure in your tires regularly. Don't rely on simply eyeballing them, since looks can't tell you everything. Correct tire pressure is vital for the safe handling of your car as well as for the long life of your tires. (See the information on tires later in this chapter.)

General Motors calls the owner's manual "the most unread book in the world," but I've referred to it above in just about every maintenance procedure. For your sake and the sake of your car, pretend it's a best seller. Read it.

Body and Interior

To maintain your car free of rust, keep it clean and dry and wax it. Wash it underneath, and get rust-proofing to supplement the undercoating it comes with. Rust-proofing is injected inside the car's body, so it helps stop rust from the inside—before you ever see it. You can fix holes caused by rust before they spread with a kit from a store that sells car parts. Follow the directions on the package: basically it involves sanding the area and patching it with fiberglass.

You can fix a dent yourself, but it can mean a lot of work. Get a reference book from the library to help you through the process.

For scratches, use the small canister of touch-up paint that comes with your car, but always use a brush smaller than the scratch. If your vinyl roof rips, immediately patch it with waterproof tape in case it rains. By doing so, water won't get under the vinyl and cause it to come away from the metal roof of the car. There are kits to repair vinyl tops that won't produce perfect results but will greatly improve the damage.

To fix holes in the carpet of your car, first cut out the damaged area and use it as a stencil to cut a piece of the same shape from under the seat.

Glue the edges and insert the new piece. Then set a weight on it, and when it dries, use a nail to rake across the piece so it will blend in with the rest of the carpet.

How to Stop Little Problems Before They Become Big Ones

Your car can't come running over to you to tell you it has an ache or pain, that something's wrong—but it has its methods of telling you about its problems. You just have to know how to listen.

Make it a habit to glance under your car to see if it has left anything on your driveway. Some stains don't mean anything; some mean a lot:

- If you see clear water stains, don't worry about them. They're probably just condensation from your air conditioner.
- Clear brown or green stains near the front of the car may be coolant leaking from the radiator hoses or the radiator itself.

- Dark brown, gray, or black oil may indicate a leak in the oil system. Take your car in for repairs.
- Red oil at the rear of the car may be transmission fluid. If it's at the front on the driver's side, your power steering fluid may be leaking. Go to your mechanic.

Your car also sends smoke signals. If you see white smoke coming out of the exhaust when it's cold out, it may be just condensed water. But if this happens when it's warm, you may have an engine problem.

Bluish black smoke usually means big trouble. You may have worn piston rings, valve guides, or valve stem seals; get professional help. If you see black or gray smoke, have the carburetor checked—it's probably not mixing air and fuel correctly.

Apart from stains and smoke, if you find that your engine is roaring loudly, you may have trouble in the exhaust system. In the pages on big repairs later in this chapter, I'll tell you more ways to spot signs of trouble in your car before they demand costly work.

Some Handy Hints on Giving Your Car Home Care

You're in a dwindling minority if you still leave all maintenance work on your car to the repair shop. An all-time high of 78 percent of us do at least some car maintenance.

You're in a steadily rising majority if you do your own tune-ups and install your own spark plugs. Nearly 37 percent of all tune-ups are now done by backyard do-it-yourselfers, and nearly half of America's car owners install their own spark plugs.

As for women, we're becoming so involved in our own auto home repairs that the shine has worn off the news.

The top jobs done by do-it-yourselfers include installation and changing of antifreeze, oil, air filters, spark plugs, windshield wiper blades, batteries, headlights, oil additives, V-belts, and mufflers.

For $10 to $15, you can get a preview of work your car needs at shops offering electronic diagnosis. The diagnostic center will tell you what's wrong and what needs to be done to fix it. The stores may also rent repair bays and tools as well. Even after renting the equipment, you may save as much as 75 percent on some of the jobs. If you repair the car yourself, you'll save money—and don't forget the old adage that if you want something done right, do it yourself.

But if you're considering doing some of your own repair work, you will need to start with some basics as ready reference. You'll need a record of the make and model of your car, the year it was manufactured, spark plug designations, number of cylinders, number of carburetor barrels, figures for cubic displacement. Also you'll want to have in your file the crankcase oil capacity and, if you have air-conditioning, the type of the equipment.

You'll find most, if not all, this information in your owner's manual. The manual also frequently lists the recommended brands and types of parts for replacement.

Parts

It's relatively easy to pick parts on sight. Catalogues are generally available in stores which give you the specified numbered part to meet your car's requirements.

When selecting parts, buy only the well-known brand names or the private label brands of the recognized chain retailers in whom you have confidence. This is particularly important in the selection of such items as points sets, spark plugs, generators/regulators, gasoline, oil and air filters, filler caps, distributor caps, and condensers.

Be skeptical of so-called "gypsy" parts, which are knock-offs or copies of brand name items. They are cheaper but frequently lacking in quality. You can encounter manufacturer warranty problems on your car, too, with the installation of gypsy products—in addition to buying an inferior item that won't stand up as a brand item would. Read the container with care, since some producers even style their cartons and packages to imitate the genuine parts and confuse you into buying the inferior item on impulse.

Check whether parts are supplied by the Original Equipment Manufacturers (OEMs), which consist of the parts-supplier divisions of the auto producers, independent companies which manufacture for the automakers, and manufacturers which specialize in the production of quality replacements. All of these producers follow stringent manufacturing standards required by the auto producers.

You can also buy shelf products from the remanufacturer who rebuilds such items as starters and water pumps—even engines. New

OEM and replacement equipment are more expensive than rebuilt parts.

Try Your Favorite Junkman

What can you, a relatively unsophisticated car owner, do except gasp in horror at official investigations disclosing that a stunning 53 cents of every $1 we spend on car repairs is wasted—and the fraud is nationwide?

Answer: Shop the automobile junkyards for spare parts.

Start copying the body shops and service garages, which regularly patronize yards where wrecked, vandalized, and otherwise abandoned cars are dismantled in usually successful searches for replacements to install in your car at inflated prices.

You can—and you will—save big money by visiting auto graveyards and learning as much as you can about doing it yourself.

Dismantling cars has become a vast and sophisticated business for the "auto parts recyclers," as many of them like to be called with their newly achieved status.

The head of one suburban New York firm known as "the Onassis of auto parts recyclers," for instance, catalogues, cleans, tests, and stores every recoverable part of a car. In seconds, thousands of parts are traceable with the aid of an IBM computer.

You could save up to 50 percent on your repairs by shopping the auto junkyards—and that translates into beating the crooks in the auto repair field by using their own weapons and your own know-how.

But you must have guidelines:

• Wherever possible, use a licensed yard. Police departments stress that you should obtain a receipt for your purchase that assures you bought a legitimate item.

• Get the advice of an experienced mechanic about what is wrong with your car or what part needs replacement. Don't be your own diagnostician! Eliminate the danger that you'll get an incorrect or inadequate part.

• Don't buy a road-tested electrical part. It can be cheaper, but the fact that the yard found it to be functioning when it was removed as salvage does not necessarily mean it will perform satisfactorily for you. If you can, get a bench-tested electrical part.

Perhaps the yard will test it for you. Get a guarantee, if you can, covering a specific period of time.

• On any purchase of an engine and transmission, don't fail to supply the size and model number of your car.

• Don't buy an engine or transmission that has gone over 70,000 to 75,000 miles. Ask if the yard has kept a record of the accumulated mileage on these items.

• Bring in the old part for comparison and verification that the part you are seeking will interchange with it. If you can find the part number, this also will help ensure that you are getting the correct item.

• If you are not planning to replace the part yourself and will need the services of a mechanic, get an estimate of the mechanic's costs for time and labor before you start your parts search.

You can save substantially if you shop the auto recyclers for parts and if you are alert to the traps in the yards. Before you make a single move in this direction—and it's a new and challenging one—get as much information as you can to make sure that you are shopping wisely.

Avoid Big Repairs

Maintaining Your Automatic Transmission

Your transmission is the mechanism which sends the power from your engine to the wheels. An automatic transmission is a set of gears which shifts automatically depending upon how much power you need. It operates under the pressure of transmission fluid which lubricates and cools it.

Fluid is the blood of your automatic transmission—be sure you always have enough. There's a dipstick in the engine compartment at the rear of the engine with which you can check it. Drive for about fifteen minutes so the car is warmed up. Stop the car, put it in "park," take the dipstick, wipe it off, and insert it as far as possible. Wait a few seconds, remove it, and repeat the procedure a few times. If the line is at the "add" mark or below it, see how much (in pints) you need and consult your manual for the correct kind of fluid. Pour it slowly into the tube with a funnel, then replace the dipstick.

Keep the engine's cooling system in good repair—overheating can cause transmission trouble. Remember that other engine problems can cause transmission trouble, too. A good mechanic should always check your ignition timing and the vacuum hoses which link the engine to the transmission.

Have an engine tune-up once a year, and change the fluid in your transmission at least every 24,000 miles. It should always be pink or red. If it's dark brown, burnt-smelling, foamy, or milky, your transmission may be slipping. This is one of the most common transmission problems. When you shift, the transition will be drawn out, and the engine may race for a second as it slips.

If you see fluid marks on your driveway, have trouble shifting, or experience racing between shifts, you could have trouble. These symptoms don't necessarily mean you need an overhaul—you simply might be low on fluid.

Don't be afraid to take your car in for transmission repairs. Rough or rapid shifting can be fixed easily. If you have trouble passing another car when you accelerate quickly, you may just need an adjustment to the pedal linkage. You can help your transmission last: accelerate gradually; don't force it to work so hard.

(For further information on transmission repairs, read the transmission material later in this section.)

Tune-Ups

When do you need a tune-up?

- When your gas mileage drops 15 percent or more.
- If your engine idles fast even when it's warmed up.
- If your engine stalls, loses power, idles rough, knocks, or pings.
- If your car becomes hard to start or misfires.
- If you see black exhaust coming out of your car.
- If your engine runs rough, hesitates, or runs on after you turn it off.

Watch for changes in how your car runs, and see if these changes happen only under certain conditions. If your car has any of the above problems, it doesn't necessarily mean major repairs are needed. The idle speed or ignition timing can be adjusted easily.

Even if your car doesn't exhibit any symptoms, give it a periodic tune-up—every 12 months or 12,000 miles for a car that uses leaded gas, and every 2 years or 24,000 miles for a car that uses unleaded gas.

Check these items: cylinder compression; ignition, carburetion, and pollution systems; idle speed; ignition timing; points; plugs; condenser and distributor cap and rotor; as well as the battery, choke, and vacuum hoses.

Look at the points, plugs, condenser. Anything else that can't be cleaned or adjusted should be replaced. A thorough tune-up includes adjustment of the idle speed, ignition timing, and choke, and a road test of the car.

The price: near the beginning of the decade, $45 to $65 for a V-8 engine.

There is a great range in the prices of tune-ups because they can include or exclude so many things. If you have a 1973 or 1974 car, its gas mileage probably won't be very good no matter how well it's tuned, although a tune-up should make your car peppier.

You can do a tune-up yourself if you're good at mechanics and can follow directions. You'll need tools, some car parts, and a repair manual for your car. There should be a decal in your engine compartment with the manufacturer's specifications for your engine.

If you have a fuel-injected rather than a carbureted car, have the ignition tuned by a specialist. In these cars especially, watch the fuel filter and replace it on schedule since fuel-injected engines are more sensitive to dirt than carbureted engines.

How to Shop for a Mechanic

Key Guide: Don't wait until your car is in bits and pieces on the highway before finding a mechanic—then you'll have to take the first one you find, regardless of how much he costs. Shop around when you have plenty of time and there's nothing wrong with your car.

Ask your parents, friends, and neighbors who's reliable in your area. Going to a local station is sound because if you buy your gas there, the station owner will know you. But be sure your gas station is more than just a gas pump and can handle big repairs.

Stick to licensed repair shops. You have choices about where to go for car repair: there's your dealer; an independent mechanic; or a specialty shop for problems with mufflers and transmissions. If you're knowledgeable about cars, you might be able to rent a repair bay and do your own work.

If you like the work your dealer has done, go there first—especially if your car isn't too far out of warranty. You've already bought something from him, so he should try to cooperate with you in the hope that you'll buy your next car from him. He should have all the parts your car needs, and he's familiar with the car. The problem you're having may be common in your model, and the dealer and manufacturer may have a policy to fix it even beyond the warranty period.

If you decide to try an independent mechanic, make sure that the shop is conveniently located, and that it has all the parts and tools needed to fix your car. Wherever you go, you may be required to make appointments well in advance.

Specialty shops can save you money. They have a lot of expertise, as well as all the parts you might need for your car.

But how do you know if you've selected a competent repair shop?

- It will want you to return for any future repairs you may need.
- The mechanic will try to accommodate you in scheduling.
- He/she will explain what is being done to your car and what is wrong with it in terms you can understand.
- The mechanic will take whatever time is necessary to find out what repairs are essential—or if nothing's really wrong, will tell you.
- Go to a shop where you can see the mechanic personally and talk to him. In some shops, you may only be allowed to see the person who writes repair orders. He/she may even be a sales representative and will want to give you an overdose of repairs. The mechanic will feel personally involved with the job if he/she has talked to you about it.
- Take a course in auto mechanics at your school or at a local college. This doesn't mean you have to do the work yourself, but if you know what it takes to make a car run, you'll be able to recognize a good job.

Most mechanics are honest people trying to do a good job. Car repair may be the nation's number one product complaint, but most of those complaints don't involve direct rip-offs. The complainers contend that unnecessary work was done, or that a part should or shouldn't have been replaced. If you get a second opinion before you have any work done, you'll be able to avoid these problems.

Another option is full-service chains. These are really car "department stores," and one advantage of having repairs done by a chain store is that if you find yourself in another part of the country when your repair comes undone, you can go into any affiliated shop and have your car fixed at no cost. These shops also have arbitration systems which you can use if you're unhappy with a repair job.

The AAA runs an Authorized Repair Service which both members and nonmembers can use. Garages sign up to become part of the service, and they agree to provide to AAA members accurate written estimates, old parts that were replaced, ninety-day warranties for repairs, and arbitration by the AAA of problems between members and shops. There are 1,700 such shops across the country. If these garages offer service in a certain area of repair, they must have a mechanic certified in that area. You can get a list of these garages from your local AAA club. (Even if you are an AAA member, you still must pay for repairs.)

Check with your Chamber of Commerce or local consumer protection agency on who has a good reputation. And the National Institute for Automotive Service Excellence (NIASE) certifies mechanics with tests on the various systems of a car. Mechanics pay for, study for, and take the tests on their own time. They have to be recertified every five years and wear a shoulder patch displaying the areas in which they are certified. Shops that employ these mechanics have signs saying so. The NIASE publishes a list of certified mechanics: for a copy, write to the Institute (1825 K Street, N.W., Washington, DC 20006).

How to Deal with a Mechanic

When you've decided *where* to go—what kind of repair facility you want—and perhaps have even chosen *who* you want to work on your car, make sure you're getting *what* you want.

Always get a detailed estimate of the cost of the proposed repairs. Have the mechanic estimate the amount of time he'll spend on each job so you can have an idea what to expect for labor charges. Afterward, ask for any parts that were replaced as proof the work was done. (The repair shop should offer to do this.)

Go to a shop which guarantees its work. Some guarantee it for 4,000 miles or 90 days, whichever comes first. Some of the specialty shops have guarantees that apply nationwide: if you have work done in one shop and are dissatisfied with it, you can go to any other shop and have the problem rectified.

If the price you are being asked to pay for a part seems high to you, ask to see the mechanic's parts price list. (But don't ignore the cost of labor.) If the shop won't show you the price list, that's a bad sign—go elsewhere.

When you do find a good place, stick with it. Most shops give familiar faces the best treatment.

Avoid Monday or Friday appointments when you call to set one up. These are the busiest days at most repair shops.

If you are having a tune-up, know beforehand exactly what you are getting. There are as many different kinds of tune-ups as there are mechanics.

When you visit any mechanic, describe in detail what the problem is, but don't try to tell the mechanic his business. You may hurt more than you'll help.

If you must drop your car off without waiting to see the mechanic, leave a note on the windshield explaining what you want done, and what the symptoms of trouble were. Put your name and phone number on the note, and add that you want to be called first if any additional repairs are deemed necessary.

If you've gone to a big repair shop and see only the person who writes orders, make a list of the repairs you want, date it, and sign it. Then the shop can't pad your repair order with items you didn't want, and you won't have to pay for them. If you want diagnostic work done, you'll have to pay for it.

There are extra steps you can take to help your mechanic waste less of your money and his time.

• When you notice something wrong with your car, note when it happens. Has the car warmed up yet? Is it hot out? Is the problem worse when you accelerate? If you can't remember, write that down, too.

• Liken sounds your car makes to something familiar, such as someone banging on a tin can.

• Test-drive your car after repairs are made, and don't pay until you're satisfied.

If you choose a lower-priced job after visiting several garages, know the risks. Will it mean you'll be back in another month for added repairs? It will be worth the time, money, and hassle to you if you have it done correctly the first time. Don't try the Band-Aid approach too often.

If you're concerned about getting an honest estimate of what repairs will cost from the mechanic who's doing the work, try getting another opinion from a diagnostic center (mentioned earlier in this chapter). The diagnosticians won't be fixing your car, so they should have no reason to try to sell you more repairs than you need.

Mark your car's parts. Not only will this help protect you in case of theft, but also you will be able to see if the parts have been replaced.

Before you ever have to take your car in to be fixed, call your local Better Business Bureau for information about state laws which apply to car repair and the consumer as well as the rights and responsibilities of both you and your mechanic under the law. This knowledge may help head off trouble.

How to Save on Big Repairs

Transmission Work

If you think you have transmission trouble, your mechanic can probably tell what the problem is by road testing your car. But before you agree to have your car taken apart, ask the cost.

As a rule, watch out for shops that have a flat rate for transmission repair, or a very low rate (less than 2 percent of what you paid for the car).

If the mechanic tells you that your transmission needs only an "adjustment," don't believe him. Most new automatic transmissions can't be adjusted at all, and old ones can be adjusted only slightly.

In general, the more accurately you can describe what's wrong, the less open you'll leave yourself to transmission repair difficulties. Specifics such as "It races between shifting," "It shifts late or misses a gear," "I hear a clunking noise when it slows or goes into a lower gear," or "It doesn't shift out of first gear" will help your mechanic evaluate the problem. A good repair shop will ask you for this information. The mechanic also should ask you the year and make of the car and how long you've had the problem. He should check the fluid and the motor mounts. Perhaps he'll first put the car on a lift to inspect it.

Once you've described what's wrong, make sure what you say is written down. Take a look at it. If you can't read it, most likely the mechanic who works on your car won't be able to read it either.

Go along on a preliminary road test to be sure the mechanic is finding the same problems you are. Don't allow the transmission to be removed from your car and opened up until the problems you cite have been written down and the car has been road tested. (If the transmission does need to be taken apart, don't fall for the "metal shavings" gimmick. These shavings will accumulate in the transmission case as a result of normal use. Don't let a repair shop use them to "prove" to you that you need an overhaul of your automatic transmission.)

Get an itemized, written estimate of what the job will cost, and a written promise that the final price won't exceed the estimate by more than 10 percent. Avoid "five o'clock surprise"—when you go to the repair shop at the end of the day and discover that your job will cost you six times what you were told it would. The estimate should include removal and inspection as well as repair, and reassembly and replacement in original condition if you decide you don't want the job done, or you want to get a second opinion.

Ask about the warranty: find out what is and isn't covered by it. Beware of places that offer warranties on their work only at extra cost. A good shop will give you its best work regardless of the cost of the job. Don't be taken in by claims of "deluxe" or "super deluxe" jobs.

If any of your family, friends, or neighbors have had transmission work done, ask where they've gone for it. And make sure that the mechanic you select is certified in transmission repair by the National Institute for Automotive Service Excellence (even though this is no guarantee of good work). Check out the shop you're considering with the Better Business Bureau as well.

Valve Jobs

This repair can cost you as much as 4 percent of what you paid for your car. Symptoms of valve trouble include decreased gas mileage and an engine which runs poorly or lacks power. Your mechanic must do a compression test to find out if valves are the cause of your car trouble.

Engine Overhaul

This could cost you one-fifth of what you paid for the car. You might consider buying a rebuilt engine instead. They're just like new ones, especially if they've been rebuilt in an engine factory. Installing a rebuilt engine costs the same as having yours overhauled, but it's much faster. Be sure that the engine you get is actually rebuilt and not just used. When you're dealing in motors, watch out for places that:

• Say they'll replace your motor for a certain set rate, which seems low. They may add extra charges later, charge you more if your motor is unusable, or leave certain parts out of your car that you need to make it run.

• Offer credit. *They* won't give you credit; you'll have to pay cash and get a loan from a bank.

• Advertise one-day service. It's highly improbable.

• Give a mileage guarantee for their work, but don't give you a time limit on it.

Accidents

If you've been involved in a bad accident and have an expensive repair ahead of you, your insurance company probably will pay to have a good job done on your car. Don't head for the nearest bargain-basement repair shop.

When Repairs Go Wrong

You can avoid many problems by getting a second opinion before you turn your car over to anyone for repair. But when you have a complaint about the way your car's been treated, what should you do?

·1. Talk to the person in charge of the shop, someone not in the service area. State the facts, be calm, and don't be apologetic. And be armed with all the papers you collected during the repair.

2. Find out if the shop has an arrangement with an arbitration service such as that run by the Better Business Bureaus or the Automotive Consumer Action Panel. (The BBB's program does not have the force of law. Repair people must cooperate.)

3. When you call or write to any consumer protection office, give your name, address, phone number, the name of the garage and where it is, the make and model of the car, and how much the problem has cost you. Keep the originals of all letters sent to you; send out copies only of all correspondence, bills, etc.!

4. Ford, Chrysler, and General Motors have arbitration services to deal with repair problems. Details are in your owner's manual.

5. Keep in mind and be warned that many protective car repair laws assume that you've received a written estimate and signed the repair order.

6. If available, there's the Small Claims Court.

7. Above all, don't pay until you're satisfied with the work. Once the repair shop has your money, you're over the barrel.

CAR CRASHES

How to Cut the Horrifying Total and Costs of Car Crashes

At the end of every weekend along a stretch of one of this nation's most magnificent, wide, and costly superhighways, in northern Westchester County, it is becoming a rarity *not* to see a car or two rolled over into the fairly deep ditch that separates the north and south lanes. Along a stretch of a narrow old highway divided by a typical guardrail, it also is a rarity not to see a newly crushed rail signifying a weekend accident in which at least one car has crashed into the barrier, killing or injuring an unknown number of people.

At the beginning of this chapter, you read about the astounding costs of car accidents and resulting injuries in the United States today. The drain will swell; the price tag will increase. The chances that you and your car will be involved will grow.

As this decade progresses, at least 50 percent of all cars purchased in the United States will be classified as small cars. At the same time, manufacturers will be making trucks larger so they can carry bigger payloads to save fuel. Just ponder how this changing vehicle mix increases your hazards.

With more and more small cars—meaning more and more cars that admittedly give the occupants less protection in crashes—on our highways, the 55 mph speed limit's gains will be overwhelmed by the upsurge in deaths and injuries. Small cars, large cars, trucks, vans, and vehicles of all sizes will be crowding our highways and roads. What, then, can be done?

It may make you wince to read this, but the facts are that little hope of success lies in crackdowns on drunk drivers or in safety-belt protection campaigns. None of the costly attempts to change driver behavior on drunk-driving or on safety devices has worked here or abroad.

More than half of all fatal crashes today involve a drunk driver, so this is a vital area for exploration. A bright note in recent findings is that programs combining understandable drunk-driving penalties with widespread, highly visible enforcement might reduce crash deaths somewhat—but such programs would necessitate such possibly unpopular activities as police roadblocks and staking out drinking spots along highways, in addition to incurring huge continuing costs.

Another startling finding is that high school driver education, coupled with early licensing for youngsters completing such courses, is contributing to thousands of avoidable teenage deaths each year. In areas where driver ed has been dropped, teenage deaths in crashes have plunged.

Reinstatement of the motorcycle helmet use laws that have been repealed by dozens of states in recent years (via lobbying by motorcycle groups) would save thousands of lives. In states that repealed the laws, deaths of cyclists have jumped 30 percent.

In small cars themselves, demand for crash-protection features is necessary and indisputable. The carmakers (here or abroad) will respond to it.

And then there are our roads. The states must intensify supervision of hazardous and improperly installed guardrails and not let up on their drives to eliminate the hazards. Roll-over crashes must be reduced by modifying the depth of ditches and embankments on highways, new or old.

The problems are obvious, the solutions diversified and costly. But how do you like the odds that you'll be in a crash in a few years?

Buckle Up

Since the day you first switched on a TV set or opened a magazine, you've been bombarded with public service announcements to wear your seat belt, and with news stories of the terrible consequences of failure to do so.

You know all the excuses: you're lazy, in a hurry, or careless—"just this once it won't matter." You can't believe seriously that you, or anyone you know, will die or be maimed as a result of leaving the belt unfastened. You're bored by the whole subject.

You must be: only one in five of you wears a seat belt regularly!

But automotive accidents are the number one killer of teenagers in this country. The staggering numbers:

• More than 8,800 teens died in car accidents *each year* early in the decade. Teens fifteen through nineteen alone represented over 17 percent of all deaths caused by car accidents. Of those, one-third were drivers, one-third were passengers in cars driven by other teens, and the rest were outside the car—bicyclists, pedestrians, innocent bystanders. Many thousands more were injured, and many were disfigured and maimed for life.

• Of the 14,300,000 drivers under twenty early in the decade, 10,000 were involved in fatal accidents, and about 5 million accidents of all degrees of severity, according to the National Safety Council.

How do you value a life?

Are you yawning now? Picture almost 9,000 people—imagine the packed stadium at your school, or the population of your town or campus—snuffed out. Think of the total waste of life, the lost potential, the hideous cost to family and friends.

Hospital emergency room staffs see victims your age practically every day and a common refrain is, "If kids could only see what they do to themselves." Visit the emergency room when an accident victim is wheeled in. You just might be shocked out of your complacency.

These figures should also remind you of the stupid risks you take while driving by speeding, drinking, and getting high. You imperil yourself, your passengers, and anyone unfortunate enough to be driving or walking nearby. It's not too smart, either, to ride along with someone whose driving scares you, or who you know is drunk or out of control.

There's no special protection for you because you're cool, popular, athletic, pretty, or smart.

So buckle up. Tell your passengers you won't start the car until they do, too. If you don't like the way your friends drive, let them know. When someone's loaded, take away the keys or, at least, refuse to go along. You can *always* find another way home. And don't let anyone insult you or make you feel foolish. Instead, challenge the insulter to tell you what's so funny or weird about protecting your own life.

Am I trying to frighten you? You bet I am! The slaughter of young people on our roads and highways is a national tragedy that impoverishes us all.

Isn't it better to be a little frightened and cautious—and alive?

Buckling your seat belt is the single most effective way to save your life—or reduce injuries—if you are in an auto accident.

Automatic seat belts are cheap to install, but they are easier to "defeat" as well. These devices are available on German imports, and German officials found a high degree of owner removal. Would you follow the same pattern on a U.S. car system?

The most effective safety devices are the manual hip-and-shoulder harnesses already installed on all new cars. The problem is to get you to use them—to buckle up—because teenagers particularly are lazy, forgetful, obstinate.

A real answer could be a different type of law that the insurance industry should have been backing all along: fines for *not* buckling up, and an automatic legal presumption of "contributory negligence" for anyone in an accident who wasn't buckled up. If you were hurt, your award would be reduced if you had not fastened your seat belt; if you hurt someone else, his award would be increased. Now that's incentive.

TIRES

Your tires are what separate you from the road—an important factor in determining the experience you'll have with your car. A tire can cost you $100 a year or more, especially if you live in a snowy climate where you'll need topflight snow tires and may have to replace them more often.

Don't assume that the tires your car comes with when you buy it (new or used) are best for you and the way you drive.

Types of Tires

There are three kinds of tires.

- *Bias* are the least expensive. They give the smoothest ride, but they wear out faster. In this model, the cords wrap around the tire at an angle. Average life: 15,000 to 20,000 miles.
- *Belted* tires cost more, but they wear longer. They give a "harder" ride than a bias tire, since they have a belt of fiberglas under the tread. Average life: 25,000 miles.
- *Radial ply* tires are the finest quality tire made today. Their plies run across the treads, like chains. If you have steel-belted radials, they have a steel belt under the tread. These tires wear long, handle well, and can increase your gas mileage by 3 to 5 percent. Average life: 40,000 miles, so they may be the least expensive over time.

In general, tires can be tubeless or tube-type, but just about all tires made today are tubeless.

Retreads

Consider retreads, and save half the cost of a new tire. If the tire has been retreaded well, it will last as long as a new one.

- Retreads account for one of every five replacement tires sold in the United States for passenger cars, while 98 percent of the world's leading airlines are using quality retreads, and trucks and government vehicles also are major retread users.

• It takes 2½ fewer gallons of crude oil to retread a tire than to manufacture a new one—an obvious oil-saving factor.
• Retreads also have a true cost/performance edge. A good retread will deliver the same mileage as an equivalent new tire, making its cost per mile much lower.

You should get the same warranty for a retread as you'd get for a new tire, since "retreaded" means that new tread has been put on the casing, which is the most expensive part of the tire. If you buy retreads, go to a dealer who gets his tires from a shop that inspects tires before retreading them.

Or, have your own tires retreaded. An advantage is that you know what condition your tires are in. Have it done at a shop which retreads tires for taxis or government fleet cars, such as police cars. But don't retread your tires more than once, or if they've been damaged. And the tires must have at least ¹⁄₁₆″ of tread *left* in order to be retreaded. For more details, write to the Tire Retread Information Bureau and ask for its packet of basic data (TRIB, P.O. Box 374, Pebble Beach, CA 93953).

Snow Tires

How much snow do you get where you live, and is it cleared right away? If you live in a rural area where snow arrives in October and doesn't seem to disappear until May, you'll probably want to get a very open, heavy tread. But this type of tire won't be good for driving on dry roads.

A similar rule applies to studded tires: great for ice and snow, but not for dry roads. Studs work best on radial ply tires, and only on new tires that have holes for them. Don't replace your studs once they wear down. Studs are illegal in some states, and prohibited in others except during the snow season, from October to April.

How to Buy Tires

You know the familiar number one rule: find a good dealer. Your tire dealer should be honest about what kind of tire is right for you as well as about what it costs. And by all means he should honor his warranty.

Just as when you were choosing a car dealer, ask your friends where they bought their tires, what they thought of the product they got, and the service they received. Compare prices and look for sales, *but beware:* some sales are phony. Compare warranties (more about tire warranties in a moment). Do they include mounting and balancing the tires, plus the sales tax? How many miles or months do the warranties cover? Are the tires guaranteed for life against road hazards? Some warranties include partial payment for a new tire.

Here are tips on tire buying:

• Don't buy tires when you're in a hurry, and don't wait until a crisis before you look for tires or a spare. Always keep a good spare, so you're not at the mercy of a rip-off artist when you're on the road.

• Question the sales pitches dealers give you. Be especially wary of "Buy three, get one free" deals. If you were a tire salesman, would you give anyone a free tire? And a half-off deal on two tires means half off the price of the second tire only.

• Make sure the dealer registers your name and address and the identification numbers of the tires you buy so that he can get in touch with you in case of a recall. This is a federal law.

• Don't be impressed by tires which are called "first line" or "premium." These labels aren't formal classifications based on any standard; they're just dealer talk. Tires are rated according to traction, tread wear, and high-speed performance.

• On the side wall of all tires you will find the following information: the size of the tires, the maximum pressure to which it can be inflated, the brand name, the manufacturer's code number, what the cord is made of, and the number of plies or the word "radial."

• Don't agree in advance to have the dealer put on the tires for you. First find out how much it will cost, and if it's more than a few dollars, go elsewhere.

• When you're buying, take into account the kinds of roads you'll be driving, whether or not you'll be carrying heavy loads, and the way you drive.

You must decide on the size tire you want, the number of plies, and the kind of cord material—don't buy more tire than you need. Radials are good for long mileage, but they may not be necessary if you do most of your driving around your campus or hometown. Most tires have polyester cords, with fiberglass used for the belts. Steel is also used for belts, in radial tires, and sometimes in belted bias tires.

Never buy a smaller size tire than the size your car came with; always use the same kind of tire on all four wheels. If you get one new tire for the rear, pair it with the one that has the most tread. Never mix tires on the same axle, and never mix radial tires with any other type of tire. Whatever type you do get, try not to exceed 55 miles per hour for the first 50 miles of the tire's use—allow it to break in.

Before you put any new tires on your car, check certain parts of your car that are directly related to how well tires will perform. Make sure the front end is aligned correctly. If it isn't, the tires will wear unevenly, creating bald spots. Be sure that your brakes are working properly, that the wheel bearings are in good condition, and that the wheels are balanced.

With new tires, buy new valves as well, since the old ones may be damaged. Tires should then be mounted, and balanced on the wheels. There are two methods of balancing:

- *Static.* The tire is balanced with the wheel not in motion. This costs $1.50 to $2 per tire.
- *Dynamic.* Here the wheel is in motion, as it is when you drive. This is slightly more expensive ($4 per tire), but a better way to balance your tires.

Tire Grading

Tires are graded by number to give you an idea of how long the tread should last. A tire with a grade of 60 should last about 18,000 miles; one with a grade of 100, 30,000 miles; with a grade of 150, 45,000 miles; and with a grade of 200, 60,000 miles. External factors also will affect the mileage you get.

The traction of the tire is graded A, B, or C, according to its ability to stop on a wet road. "A" is above average, "B" is average, and "C" is below average. Here again, though, external factors can affect a tire's ability to stop when wet.

Tires are graded, too, for how well they perform at high speeds. The grades are A, B, and C, but only racing tires are given a grade of A. Never buy a tire that says "only for racing" or "not for highways'' on it. That tire can't legally be sold for use on public roads.

Tire Warranties

Tire warranties are among the most lenient of all product warranties. Most protect you against road hazards even if the damage done to the tire was entirely your fault, but they usually don't cover punctures, irregular wear, or driving with a flat tire.

Always get your warranty in writing. It will be based on the list price of your tire, so if you've bought the tire on sale, discount the warranty by the same amount. Most replacement policies work this way: if your tire fails with 80 percent of the tread left on it, you get 80 percent toward the price of a replacement tire.

Tire Care

Take care of your tires and you may not have to use your warranty. Using a small air pressure gauge, check the pressure once a week. Do this before you drive, when the tires are cool. In general, the pressure should never exceed thirty-two pounds per square inch for a 4-ply ''B'' tire, or forty pounds for an 8-ply ''D'' tire. When the tire pressure is right, you'll have better traction, steering, and braking.

In summer, you may find that pressure has increased by as much as six pounds. Don't release it. You can tell if the tire is under- or overinflated by where the wear is. If it's on the outer edges, you haven't enough pressure, if it's in the center, you have too much.

Rotate your tires every 5,000 miles, and when you do, check your wheel balance, front-end alignment, and suspension. Radial tires should be kept on the same side of the car—simply move the front to the rear and vice versa. But if you have other types of tires on the front and rear axles, rotate them on the same axle. To work your snow tires into the rotation, move your spare tire to the left front wheel, and the left rear tire to the right front wheel. Store the front tire you replaced with the spare and replace the snow tires with the front tires in the spring.

Eventually your tires will become ''bald,'' and must be replaced. Do this *before* there is only $\frac{1}{16}$" of tread left on any tire. If you continue to drive with that borderline tread, you will be fifty times more likely to get a flat than you would with a new tire. The tire is worn when bars start to appear across the face of it, or when you can put a penny upside down in the tread and still see the top of Lincoln's head. Some states have laws requiring you to replace bald tires.

Store tires flat, in a cool, dry place away from the sun. If you store them on the rim, reduce the pressure inside to ten pounds, then reinflate when you put the tires back on the car.

GASOLINE

How to Choose

Leaded or unleaded, regular, super regular, or premium—the choice of gasolines available today is enough to confuse a long-time driver and certainly you, a teenager and new driver. The kind of gasoline you use will be crucial to your car's performance, though, so it pays off to be informed when you go to the pumps.

The type of car you have will help you decide which gasoline to use. If your American car was built after 1975, it will require unleaded. In fact, it is illegal to use leaded gas in such cars. However, as your post-1975 car gets older, it may develop a need for more octane, as deposits from its oil and gas build up. This fact has led oil companies to create "super unleaded." And since there are fewer and fewer pre-1975 big cars on the road, many of the companies have reduced their production of premium leaded gas. So if you've decided to buy a big oldie, you may have trouble finding gas for it. You can switch to an unleaded gas of at least a 92 octane rating (that's the number that appears on the little yellow sticker in the lower right-hand corner of all gas pumps).

A higher octane won't give your car more miles per gallon or more power, necessarily, so try to stay away from premium unleaded unless your car "knocks" or "runs on." "Knocking" happens when the fuel doesn't burn evenly through each cylinder. It burns and then explodes, making the "knocking" noise you hear. If it happens only occasionally and not too severely, it won't damage your car, but if this noise is heavy and sustained, it will cause engine damage.

When your car seems to keep running after you've turned off the engine, it means that the fuel and air mixture is still entering the chamber, and even though there's no spark there to ignite it, it ignites because of the high temperature in the chamber.

Using the wrong gas also can cause stalling and hesitation.

How to Increase Your Gas Mileage

The best fuel economy ever achieved is 376.59 miles per gallon. That car coasted part of the way, however, and the fastest it ever went was 12 miles per hour. It had no windows, springs, or generator. And if I could show you a picture of it you would turn away in disgust.

But you can increase your miles per gallon by up to 30 percent. First, check what mileage you're getting now. Fill your tank and drive until it's empty. Note your odometer reading when you start and finish. Repeat this procedure. Then divide the number of gallons your tank holds into the number of miles you drove the second time. If it seems you're not getting much mileage for your money, follow these rules:

1. Drive smoothly, at steady speed. Don't stop and start suddenly, or speed.

2. For your best mileage, drive between 45 and 50 miles per hour.

3. Keep your tires inflated two to three pounds above the lowest recommended pressure listed in your owner's manual.

4. Keep your gas tank full in the winter so water vapor won't condense in the tank, and your fuel line won't freeze. Gas antifreeze in the winter will prevent this.

5. Don't waste gas in the winter with long warm-ups. Instead, start slowly and increase your speed as the engine warms up.

6. If you're stuck in traffic and if you think you'll be longer than a minute, turn your engine off. You'll use more gas idling than it will take to restart your car.

7. Don't believe ads telling you about substances you can pour into your tank to make gas last longer.

8. If you're handy with cars, get yourself a good shop manual so you can keep your car tuned. Even if you're not handy, keep

your car tuned. This alone can improve gas mileage by as much as 10 percent.

9. Buy a vacuum gauge to tell you when you're accelerating more than needed.

10. Don't have extra fuel tanks put in your trunk—they're extremely dangerous if you're hit from behind. If you decide to get a fuel tank despite this warning, you could be subject to a $10,000 fine if the tank allows more than a certain amount of gas to evaporate.

11. Don't risk a similar fine if your dealer is found to be tinkering with the emission control device on your car in an attempt to increase your gas mileage. Doing this will not greatly affect your gas mileage since these devices are really part of the engine, not just attachments to it.

12. Keep your spark plugs, points, and PCV valves in good condition.

13. Don't waste money with a dirty air filter. This can cost you a mile for every gallon you use at 50 miles per hour. Check your owner's manual to see how often you should replace your filter.

14. Have a mechanic check the spark plugs to make sure the plugs are not misfiring and shooting new gas out the exhaust.

15. Also check that your front wheels are properly aligned. Your car will use extra gas trying to correct its course if they're not, and tires also will wear out more quickly, at a cost of 0.3 miles per gallon.

16. Make sure your brakes are properly adjusted. If not, they may drag on your wheels and cause your car to work harder and use more gas to overcome them.

17. Consider baggage if you go on a long trip. Luggage will weigh down your car and decrease gas mileage.

18. If you buy a manual transmission and operate it correctly, you can increase gas mileage by 15 percent. (This statistic was calculated for a car that would get 25 miles per gallon with an automatic transmission.)

19. Buy steel-belted radial tires: you can get 5 percent more gas mileage.

20. Combine local trips so you do most of your driving when your car is warmed up. A cold car gets only half the gas mileage of a warm one.

21. Keep in mind that when you travel, the brand and grade of

gas you may use may be different in various parts of the country. They're blended differently in accordance with the climate.

22. If you have a manual transmission, shift into high gear as soon as possible. High gear is where you'll get the best gas mileage.

23. Think with care about the fact that a big car with luxury options (air conditioning, power steering, a V-8 engine, automatic transmission) will cost you an estimated $223 more to drive over 10,000 miles than a car without these options.

24. Use a multigrade motor oil such as 10W-40 instead of 30-weight. Change your oil as often as suggested in your owner's manual.

25. Replace the clutch on your manual transmission when it begins to slip.

26. Recognize that diesel fuel will give you more miles per gallon than gasoline. So even though it costs about the same per gallon as gasoline, it will be more economical in the long run.

How to Operate a Self-Service Gasoline Pump

If you pump your gas yourself, you'll pay several cents less for it per gallon in most cases than if you have it pumped for you. What follows is Study Course Gas Pumping 101:

- Stop smoking before you start to pump gas.
- Then take the cap off your gas tank.
- Take the nozzle from the pump, turn the handle to "on." This should change all the numbers on the tank to zero.
- Put the nozzle in the gas tank, and squeeze it about halfway.
- When it clicks off, take it out, turn the lever on the gas pump to "off," and hang up the nozzle.
- Reminder: put the cap back on your gas tank.

Diesel Engines

Even though diesel fuel can be hard to find, it can provide you with some savings on your fuel bill. An informed estimate is that on average, diesel fuel gives 25 percent better mileage than gasoline.

Cars with diesel engines are said to have higher trade-in values than their counterparts with gasoline engines.

A diesel engine doesn't need a tune-up because there are no spark plugs. Nor is there a carburetor or distributor. But the oil and filter should be changed every 5,000 miles and the crankcase ventilation every 15,000 miles.

These cars drive the same way other cars do, but they must be started differently. When you turn the key, a light will go on telling you to "wait," usually for a few seconds. (You are waiting for the engine's chambers to heat to a sufficient degree so that when the fuel is sent into them it will ignite without a spark.) Then you press the accelerator and start the engine.

Gasohol and Alcohol

Gasohol, which is made up of nine parts of gasoline to one part alcohol, is disappearing from use. It began to cost more to produce than gasoline, since it is made from corn—when the price of corn went up, the price of gasohol did, too. At one point, it cost about 10 cents a gallon more than gas, and its popularity faded with the worldwide oil glut early in the decade when prices of gasoline began to fall.

Alcohol, however, can be used to raise the octane level of gasoline. Be warned though: both alcohol and gasohol can corrode aluminum and some kinds of fuel hoses.

EMERGENCIES

How to Prevent Accidents

No matter what the statistics predict, in reality your odds of being in an accident depend on how and how much you drive. It's expensive each time you're in an accident: in addition to the cost of fixing your car, your insurance premium will be raised because the insurance company figures you become a greater risk.

The best advice I can offer you about accidents is how to avoid them.

• If you will be drinking and driving, have no more than one drink an hour, and wait one hour after the last drink before you drive.

- Depression, anger, fatigue, and cars don't mix. Driving under these conditions often leads to *fatal* accidents. Don't go driving to relax. Take a walk.

- When driving at night, don't go so fast that your car can't stop within the range of its headlights.

- Good driving doesn't mean just controlling the car. What's going on in your head is most important. Sense what's happening around the car and try to determine dangerous situations—you can't react until you know what's happening. You've all seen public service announcements telling you to "watch out for the other guy." Do it! This is called "defensive driving." Keep space around your car so you can move out of trouble.

- Speed limits are designed for ideal conditions, not heavy traffic, snow, or nighttime driving. But on highways, be careful not to go *too slowly*. Stay with the flow.

- When you're poised at an intersection waiting to make a left turn, don't sit with your wheels turned in the direction of the oncoming traffic. If you're hit from behind, you'll be pushed right into it.

- While you're on the ramp entering a highway, look ahead and to the sides. Plan your move. Don't make a sudden stop. When you exit, start toward your goal at the beginning of the ramp rather than cutting over at the last minute.

- As a rule for following a car, allow two seconds between you and the car in front of yours. Choose an object at the side of the road to judge the time. When he passes it, you should pass it no sooner than two seconds later. Don't tailgate. If someone is tailing you, slow down and let him pass. If he's really in a hurry, he will. If someone cuts you off, back away from him. Don't get angry and tailgate, or change lanes constantly.

- Keep using your rear- and sideview mirrors. Look once every few seconds.

- Even if you have the right-of-way, don't assume the other driver will yield. Slow down, blow your horn, or do both at the same time. If you're going through an intersection, look left, right, then left again before you proceed.

- To avoid being hit from the rear, tap your brakes once or twice before you stop to light your brake lights and warn the driver behind you that you'll be stopping.

- Curves—right-hand ones, especially—are dangerous. They're

usually blind because of trees and the like. You have to slow down, or you could be forced into the next lane of traffic.

• Changing lanes is one of the leading causes of highway accidents. If someone wants to change lanes, make room. Try to stay out of other cars' blind spots. Pull even, or stay clearly behind. Use your signals when you want to change.

• When you're taking a long trip, take a break every 100 to 150 miles to keep from getting "white-line fever."

• The worst kind of collision, without doubt, is head on. Your chances of surviving are not good. If you see a car coming at you over the center line of a road, try to go right, even if it means hitting something else. Blow your horn and brake hard. The slower you're going, the less impact there will be when you meet the other car. I know it sounds easier than it is, but the key is not to panic when you're confronted by any emergency.

Malfunction on the part of your car can lead to major accidents. But if you know what to do, you might be able to avoid them.

• If one of your front tires blows out, your car will pull to the side of the blowout. The steering wheel will vibrate also, but hang on. Stay off the brake and gas, slow down, and pull off. If one of your rear tires blows, the back of your car will pull to one side. Behave in the same way as you would if a front tire blew.

• If you skid, don't brake, even though that will be tempting. Take your foot off the gas, and turn your wheels into the skid to help straighten out the car. If you then skid the other way, steer that way.

• Should your hood fly up in front of you while you're driving, try to stop smoothly and pull over. Peek through the opening created when the hood is up (between the lower edge of the hood and the car) or look out the window. You might try lifting the hood of your car sometime when it's safe and seeing what kind of view you get from each of the two vantage points.

There are steps you can take from the day you order or buy your car to make sure it's safe. When you shop for cars, take note of the different safety features they come with. Ask the dealer to list the safety aspects of each car you look at. Federal law requires him to do this. Ask if the car you're interested in has ever been recalled for a safety problem.

All cars come with seat belts. Use them.

Once the car is in your driveway rather than the dealer's shop, do your part to make sure your car is safe. If you get a recall notice, follow its instructions. Abide by inspection laws. Don't allow your car to be "stickered" without a thorough inspection.

What to Do if You're in an Accident

The first move you must make at the scene of an accident is to see if anyone has been hurt. If you can't assist the injured person yourself, send for help. Route other cars around the scene. Call the police, no matter whose fault the accident appears to be. A police officer is accustomed to observing these situations. Exchange license and registration numbers with the other driver. Get his/her name and address, as well as the phone number and the name of the insurance agent. Note the make, model, and year of the other car. Get the names of any witnesses, or at least their license plate numbers. And finally, note the name, badge, and station numbers of the police officer who arrives at the scene.

Check the physical circumstances surrounding the accident. Where were the cars when the accident happened? How fast were they going?

Don't tell the other party what kind of insurance you have (though you may give out the name of your agent), and even if you feel the accident was your fault, don't admit it right then and there and say your insurance will cover everything.

There may be circumstances surrounding the incident that haven't come to light yet. Don't sign anything saying you haven't been injured. Pass on any correspondence you receive from the other party to your insurance agent; don't try to answer any questions on your own.

Always keep these two items in your glove compartment: (1) the insurance identification card your agent will give you; and (2) a copy of the accident report form you need to fill out for your insurance company or for the police. Get copies in advance.

Call your insurance agent whenever you are in an accident, even if the other person claims responsibility. That person could change his/her mind later. Don't refrain from calling because you feel your accident wasn't serious enough to warrant raising your premium. More damage or an injury may show up later and you may lose your policy or not receive full benefits for not letting the agent know soon enough.

It's always a good idea to follow up the first phone call you make to your insurance company about any accident with a registered letter containing all the relevant information—the policy number, agent's name, circumstances surrounding the accident, and any other vital facts.

How to Prevent Breakdowns

Good car maintenance is the best way to prevent breakdowns. There are certain parts of a car, though, that are most commonly at the root of breakdowns.

• *Your tires.* Look for signs of wear, and replace worn tires. Always have a spare with you, and the tools to change a flat. If you fix a flat with a tire inflator and sealant, this is only a temporary solution. Check tire pressure often.

• *Worn belts* are a common cause of breakdowns. The belts shouldn't give more than half an inch when you press them, and if they're frayed or cracked, replace them.

• *Your battery* should have enough fluid. The cables should be on tight, and not corroded.

• *Overheating* reveals a cooling system problem. Radiator hoses should be free of leaks and cracks, and not swollen. Have your mechanic check the coolant regularly.

• *Brake failure* is one of the most serious breakdowns you can have. Your brake pedal shouldn't go more than halfway to the floor. After you've pushed it once to test it, push it again—and count to ten. If it keeps going down, you could have a master cylinder problem. (If you have power brakes, you must turn on your car to test them.)

You can get a good idea of how ready your car is to be driven as soon as you turn the key and your dashboard panel lights up. The lights should all go out, most importantly the oil-pressure light. If it doesn't, don't drive. You could destroy your engine.

What to Do if Your Car Breaks Down

When your car breaks down, get off the road immediately, if you can. If you don't, you may compound one disaster with another by leaving yourself open to an accident with another car or risking being hit yourself while you try to work on your car.

Raise the hood and turn on the flashers or "hazard lights." Tie a white cloth to the antenna or door handle. If you must stop in the middle of the road, place flares (which you should have with you) 10 feet in back of the car and 300 feet back as well. Place another one 100 feet in front. Don't put flares anywhere near spilled gas.

Don't leave your car and start walking unless you know where you're going. Lock your doors and stay inside while you wait for help. The fact that your hood is raised, your lights are on, and the white cloth is tied to the door or antenna will alert people to your situation. If someone comes over saying he wants to offer help, roll down your window just a little—enough to ask him to call for help. Don't get out of the car or let him in. Many roadside muggings occur this way.

Always keep the following items with you so you can help yourself as much as possible when your car breaks down: a fire extinguisher, jack, spare tire, flares, flashlight, fuses (know where the fuse panel in the car is), lug wrench, jumper cables, siphon jump, duct tape, wire, a paper clip, tire inflator, plastic water bag, screwdriver, and adjustable pliers.

Common Car Troubles

If you turn the key in the ignition and nothing happens, turn your headlights on. If they go on and don't dim when you try to start the car, jiggle the lever in park or neutral while you turn the key. If they *do* go dim, you may have a loose battery connection or corroded terminals. Turn off the ignition. Try loosening the bolts that hold your cables to your battery and prying the clamps apart. Lift the cables off and use a knife to clean the surfaces that connect. Put the cables back, the grounded one last. These should be on so firmly that you can't turn them. If your car still won't start, the battery is either dead or disconnected, and you need a jump. Always be careful working with a battery; it contains acid which can explode.

What if your engine turns over but won't start? You have a problem involving either the air, spark, or gas—possibly all three. The engine might be flooded. If you see gas on the engine, get help. If you don't, floor the pedal and turn the key for ten seconds. If it still doesn't start, tap the carburetor lightly near the gas line, and try again. To check the spark, pull out a spark plug wire, open a paper clip, and push it into the "boot." Hold the "boot" with a rag so that the clip is about one-eighth of an inch from any bolt on the engine. Have someone crank the engine, and watch for a spark.

To see if you're getting gas, take off the top of the air cleaner to see if the choke valve is open. Open the choke and look inside while someone pumps the gas. If you don't see gas, get help.

Suppose you are caught in a traffic jam on a hot day, and suddenly you see the "hot" light on your dashboard come on. Smoke comes out from under the hood. Your car is overheating. Pull off the road, turn the engine off, and wait. If you can't pull off just yet, turn off the air-conditioner, radio, etc., shift into neutral, and accelerate lightly. (This will also help prevent overheating in the first place.)

When you do pull over, don't take off the radiator cap—you'll be scalded with boiling water. Look for a leak in one of your radiator hoses. If you find one, wait until the car cools and tape the hose. Loosen the radiator cap one notch when it cools, and proceed to the nearest service station. Check the coolant level, and add water if necessary. If your fan belt is broken, but the radiator is full and the cap is on tight, you can drive until the light comes on, then stop and let it cool. In this way, you can limp along until you get to a service station.

If the alternator light comes on while you're driving, don't stop and turn off the engine; you might not be able to start it again. Keep driving if you can, until you get to a service station. But watch your temperature and oil lights. If your brake light is on, you have either your front or rear brakes left, and that's enough to stop you. But head for a mechanic!

How to Jump Start a Car

1. Put the cars together, but not touching. Get out your jumper cables. Turn off everything in both cars.

2. For this procedure, the batteries must be of the same voltage—most are 12 V. They must have grounded negative posts.

3. Take a red clamp and put it on the positive terminal of the dead battery. Put the other on the positive terminal of the good battery.

4. Put one black clamp on the negative post of the good battery and the other on any metal bracket connected to the engine block of the other car. You can attach it to the engine block itself, but not near the carburetor or battery. Keep the cable away from fans and belts.

5. Start both cars. If the one with the dead battery doesn't start right away, let the other one run and try it again. Once you do start the stalled car, keep it running, and remove the clamps in reverse order.

How to Change a Tire

Get far off the road so you have room to work. If you can't pull over, keep driving with your flashers, even if you ruin a tire or a wheel— it's better than getting hit yourself. At least a few thousand people are killed each year while working on their cars on the road.

Study your owner's manual for any specific instructions about changing *your* car's tires.

Put the car in park, on level hard ground. If it's a manual, put it in gear. Put on the emergency brake. Place some wood or a rock in front of the opposite corner wheel so the car won't roll.

Use a screwdriver or the tapered end of a lug wrench to get the wheel cover off.

Do one turn on each lug nut.

Take out the spare. Jack up the car according to the manual (two or three inches, usually).

Take off the lug nuts, and put them in the wheel cover so you don't lose them. Pull off the flat tire.

Put on the spare, and tighten the nuts by hand. Be careful not to knock the car off the jack. Lower the car until the tire just touches the ground, and tighten the nuts with the wrench.

Don't tighten the nuts in circle sequence; they could loosen as you drive. Do one, and then the opposite corner. Lower the car.

Don't put the wheel cover back. This will remind you to fix the flat as soon as you can.

How to Handle Serious Emergencies

• *Dropped drive shaft.* One of the most serious emergencies you can have in your car is a dropped drive shaft. This shaft runs under the car from the transmission to the rear-end differential and gives the rear wheels power to make the car go. The universal joints hold it in place. If your drive shaft gives way, slow down and pull over so it doesn't dig into the road.

You can prevent this from happening by having your universal joints checked and lubricated regularly. Listen for noises under the car and be on guard if it vibrates.

• *Stuck accelerator.* What if your accelerator pedal sticks? If you're on an open road, tap it to see if it springs back. (What is actually sticking is the throttle, which is what you push with the accelerator pedal.) Try to pull it up with your toe. Don't reach down with your hand. If this doesn't work, turn the ignition to the "off" position, not "lock." Apply your brakes—don't pump them—and pull over.

• *Brake failure.* If you lose your brakes, pump them to see if they come back. If they don't, shift into a lower gear and gradually apply the emergency brake. If you're driving through water and the brakes get wet, you may lose them for a few minutes. Go slowly and press them while you're driving to dry them out.

Watch Out for Tricks on the Road

There are crooks who make their living standing along highways pointing to motorists' cars as if something is wrong with the cars, motioning the motorist over to the side of the road, and telling them to go to the nearest service station (with which they are in cahoots).

As a teenager, be warned *now:* dishonest mechanics specialize in swindling you, a motorist far from home. Your car should be in its best condition before you take it on a trip; if you leave yourself in a position where you may have to patronize mechanics with whom you have no previous relationship, you may open yourself up to such tricks as the following:

• A mechanic may "pour" your oil from an empty can, or not push the dipstick all the way in when he's checking the oil level, or may try to sell you new oil and a filter by showing you a dirty dipstick. All oil looks "dirty" once it's been in the engine.

• "Honking"—in which a mechanic slashes your tires while you're not looking. Or if the tires have been taken off, they won't be put back on until you buy new ones.

• A mechanic may wobble your wheels to try to sell you new ball joints. All wheels wobble somewhat when they're raised in the air on a hydraulic lift.

• A garage attendant may drain the acid out of your battery, then "prove" to you that it's dead with a hydrometer check.

• Or may bend your wiper blades, then say you need new ones.

• Or may boil your battery by putting baking soda or Alka-Seltzer in it, or put soapy water on it to make it seem damaged.

• Or may spray your engine with chemicals to make it smoke.

• Or may slash your fan belt.

• Or may switch your ignition wires so you can't start your car. (This will also hurt the engine.)

• Or may bend the wires on the alternator to make the red warning light glow.

• The mechanic may squirt oil on your engine to make it appear your fuel or oil pump is leaking.

• The gas attendant may give you fuel from one pump but charge you the higher price from another pump.

• Any person in the garage may try to steal or misuse your credit card. The shop may use it to imprint blank bills which they will fill in later. They also may add to or otherwise alter your slip after you've gone. So before you sign, cross out any blank spaces on the slip and keep a copy of it so you'll have a record of what you signed for.

Keep your doors locked at all times. Best tip of all: be aware of everything that is being done to your car. Have an oil check repeated if you're suspicious about it.

If you're going on a really long trip (say, across the country and back) get new tires before you start (unless yours are practically new) and take along a good spare. And if you'll be taking along a camper, get two good spares for it.

Choose garages which belong to the Independent Garage Owners of America. They work together, and if one does work unsatisfactorily, another member garage will fix it.

You won't be able to make any repairs without money or credit. Leave yourself $200 for emergencies and take your travel and other appropriate credit cards with you.

Consider joining an auto club. (See the section on auto clubs later in this chapter.) The clubs usually have some kind of rescue mechanism you can use if your car breaks down away from home.

When you have any repairs done on the road, don't do any more than you must to get your car going. Have more expensive, preventive measures done at home. Suspect any mechanic who finds a problem you haven't noticed while driving and recommends that you have an expensive repair done to *avoid* "big trouble."

How to Drive in Bad Weather

Whether your problem is fog, rain, snow, or ice, there are ways to help avoid accidents caused by bad weather.

First, decrease your speed. Speed limits are set for ideal conditions. Don't follow cars as closely as you otherwise might, since you may not be able to stop as suddenly. Roads are most slippery at 32 degrees Fahrenheit when there may be water on top of ice.

Clear your windows completely. You may see people on the road who've cleared only the space on the front windshield on the driver's side. They think they can see, but they're cutting off three-quarters of their field of vision.

A car that has been tuned well will start more easily in the cold than one that hasn't. Turn everything off before you try to start the car. Crank it for only thirty seconds, then let it rest for one or two minutes. Don't do long warm-ups—start slowly and speed up as your car warms up. Idling clogs your engine with sludge.

Fog

If you must drive in fog at night, use your low beams—they will create less glare. You also can buy fog lights, which you install below your headlights. Go slowly, use your wipers and defroster, and be alert. If you must pull over, turn off your head- and taillights. In the fog, a person behind may see only your lights ahead of him/her, think you are still on the road, and try to follow.

Rain

Slow down, especially on curves. Don't make any sudden moves. Go slowly through deep water so your brakes don't get wet. Whatever bad weather you're in, keep your head- and taillights clean or they won't illuminate as well. If you're going fast on a wet road, you may find yourself ''hydroplaning''—riding on a layer of water rather than the road. If you're losing control of the car, take your foot off the gas, don't brake, and just let yourself slow down. Your wheels will start to cut through the layer of water and will make contact with the road again.

Snow

In addition to snow tires, tire chains aid driving in snow and ice. They allow you to stop in about half the distance you otherwise would on snow. If you do get stuck in snow, don't immediately start spinning your wheels. Get out and look at the situation. Throwing some sand behind the wheels may do the trick for you. (Always have some sand with you in the winter.) If you must maneuver out of snow, don't turn your wheels—you have the most power when they are straight. Start slowly, and don't let your wheels spin. Rock back and forth to gain traction.

Should you find yourself in the worst of all possible situations, snowbound in an isolated area at night, stay in your car. Run the engine and heat ten minutes per hour, so you'll keep warm but not use all your gas. Keep your window open a bit for air while you do it. Clear the snow from behind your tail pipe so the exhaust doesn't back up into the car. Tie a scarf to the antenna, and light a flare.

Keep a snow emergency kit with you: a shovel and sand, flares, matches, candles, a scraper and brush, tire chains, booster cables, a jack, flashlight, deicer, and additional antifreeze.

How to Prepare Your Car for Bad Weather

Driving in very bad weather is never pleasant, but there are ways to decrease the amount of wear and tear the weather puts on your car.

Get antifreeze early and keep good snow tires. Have new wiper blades and enough washer fluid. Check your heater to be sure it is operating after a summer layoff; check the defroster, too.

Test your brakes. Do they apply evenly on both sides? If they don't and you're on ice, they could send you skidding.

Buy new ignition points if you don't have an electronic ignition. In fact, have your car tuned altogether.

If you live in a very cold place, use lightweight or multiviscosity oils to take the strain off your battery.

Weather-strip your car, and fix any holes in the floor or roof.

AUTO THEFT

How to Prevent It

More than 1.1 million cars are stolen each year in the United States, and car theft has been rising steadily since 1977. But the most amazing fact is that in 1976, when a million cars were stolen, 80 percent were unlocked and 40 percent *had the keys in the ignition!*

People made it easy for thieves to steal their cars. In fact, most were stolen by amateurs.

There is no known device that will make it impossible for a professional thief to steal your car: if he wants it, he'll get it. The precautions you can take are designed to make it hard for a thief to steal *your* car so he'll look elsewhere.

- Keep doors locked and windows rolled up tight.
- Replace the door lock buttons your car came with. Use tapered ones that a thief can't "hook" and pull up.
- Don't leave attractive possessions or new purchases in a visible place in your car.
- Keep your car in a garage, or, if you must park outside, park in a lighted place.
- Don't hide extra keys under the mats or in other "secret" locations in your car. They're no secret to a thief.
- Don't get out of your car and leave it running with the keys in the ignition for even a second. If you've had a breakdown, turn off the car, lock it, and take your keys.
- Park your car in the driveway with the front end to the street, so your neighbors can see if anyone's tinkering with it.
- Get different locks for your doors, ignition, and trunk.

• Put an antitheft device warning decal on your car. Even if you have no device, it may prompt the thief to try another car.

• Buy a hood lock.

• Don't keep the title to your car or its registration in the glove compartment unless state law requires you to do so. You'll just be making it easier for a thief to sell your car.

• When you park your car in an open lot, don't tell the attendant how long you'll be away. Leave only your ignition key with him. (Incidentally, some lots now have rules which allow you to leave only your ignition key with them.)

If your car is stolen, you can protect its parts by having marked them in advance with your initials, or better yet, your driver's license number and state. Ask your local police department if any group in your area is sponsoring an antitheft program and has an engraving tool that you can rent and use to mark your car. Even a spot of nail polish on your car's major parts may help you identify them. You also can identify the car by dropping a business card down the slot between the door and window.

There are more complex gadgets you can buy to help keep your car safe from thieves. Most cost between $10 and $100. Let an expert install them, or, when you buy your car, ask if there are any antitheft devices you can buy as options.

The devices range from switches that prevent your car from being started, to sirens that go off if your car is shaken or if the doors are opened, to mechanisms which prevent fuel from running to your carburetor after the car has gone more than a few hundred feet. There are armored collars which circle the steering column and cover the ignition switch; and crook locks, which lock the steering wheel to the brake pedal.

The ignition-kill device costs between $12 and $15. It has a button which you must push to deactivate the "kill" so you can start the car. The trick is where in the interior to put the button so the thief can't find it, but you can—and be able to start the car without being a contortionist.

The motion detector costs about $10. When your parked car is shaken or even bumped, a siren or horn will go off. A siren kit, which costs about $100, is the most expensive and sophisticated gadget. It goes off when the ignition is turned after a preset delay.

There's also a special way to remove the ignition key if you don't want it to go off.

There are inconveniences to each of these devices. Your alarm may go off if you haven't locked the car door correctly the first time and go back to open it and relock it. Your siren may start to scream while you're unloading packages if you take longer than the delay time to do it. You either have to keep the ignition on, or leave the key in the "accessory" or middle position. Maybe it's more trouble than it's worth to you to have such a device.

Theft Insurance

Theft insurance should be included in your comprehensive auto insurance. When you shop for this insurance (more about this later), look for:

Is there a theft deductible?

Does the insurance cover items stolen from or with your car?

Does it provide for a rental car for you to use if your car is stolen?

What to Do if Your Car Is Stolen

You'll be understandably distraught if your car is stolen, but nevertheless you'll have to provide some important information to the police, your insurance company, and perhaps the National Automobile Theft Bureau. Here's a copy of a form you should fill out now and carry in your wallet so that you'll have all the answers ready.

Vehicle Information:

Make _____ Year _____

Model _____ Body Style _____

Vehicle Identification Number _____ Color _____

Type and Size of Engine _____ Type of Transmission _____

Ignition Key Number _____ Trunk Compartment Key No. _____

Repair work, dents, secret marks or anything else which would help
identify your car _____

License Information:

License No. and State _____ Year License Expires _____

City Registration Number _____

Additional Information:

Insurance Co. _____ Policy Number _____

Agent _____

Bank or Finance Co. Holding Title _____

Account Number _____

Purchased From _____

Address _____ Date _____

Optional equipment or other items usually kept with auto (give serial
numbers) _____

Once your car is stolen, you must have this information for
the authorities to help them find it:

Date of Theft _____ Place of Theft _____

Time of Theft _____ Odometer Reading _____

Personal Items in Car When Stolen _____

Law Enforcement Agency Contacted _____

Date _____ Complaint Number _____

Officer Investigating Theft _____

Insurance Company Contacted (Date) _____ Claim Number _____

Claims Representative _____

Auto Recovered At _____ Date _____

By (law enforcement agency) _____

Condition of Car (list damage) _____

FINANCING YOUR CAR

The "cheapest" way to pay for your car will be with cash. But, as a teenager, you almost certainly will not have several thousand dollars sitting around unused waiting to be spent on a car. Assuming that you don't, you'll have to borrow the money.

As a rule, the first places you shop for a car loan are a bank or credit union, if you or your parents have access to either. Dealers, auto finance companies, and small loan companies are usually the most expensive sources of credit. A credit union may lend you the most, whether you are buying a new or used car. It will be more expensive to borrow for a used car from a bank, especially if the car is five or more years old.

The trends in car loans are toward longer repayment periods—as long as five years at some bigger banks. There is also a move to decrease payments to 20 percent or less.

When you compare financing terms, be sure you are comparing the same down payment and repayment period. Here is a checklist for you to use to make comparisons:

	Lender No. 1	Lender No. 2	Lender No. 3
Price of the car, including taxes, options, other expenses.			
Minus down payment.			
Minus trade-in allowance for your old car.			
Amount to be financed.			
Amount of monthly payments.			
Number of monthly payments.			
Total amount of monthly payments.			
Total dollar cost of auto loan.			

Try to make the biggest down payment you can and repay the loan in the shortest period of time. This is the way you save on finance charges. Obviously, the less you pay for your car, the less you'll have to borrow. You'll also pay less for insurance. Consider shopping for a trade-in value that will cover your down payment. If it will cut the cost of your loan, put up collateral. (Collateral is any money or other items of value you have with which you guarantee loan repayment.)

If you've never used credit before, you may need a cosigner for your loan (say, your parents).

All of the terms of your loan must be spelled out in writing, no matter who the lender is. (This is required by the Truth in Lending Law.) Understand all the terms before you sign. If you want to prepay, will the lender refund future finance charges? Is there a penalty for late payments? Will you receive a warning before repossession, should your situation deteriorate to that? If your dealer offers you "easy payment terms," what exactly does that mean?

Shop separately for your loan and insurance, and shop for them first. The terms you may have to accept for financing may not be satisfactory to you, and you may decide to wait awhile before buying a car.

A final note: if either you or your parents have a whole life insurance policy, you may be able to borrow against it to raise cash for your car at a lower rate than anywhere else.

INSURING YOUR CAR

You start out with one big strike against you when you shop for car insurance just because you're in your teens. Individuals under twenty-six—especially those who are single, male, nonwhite, and live in major cities—have the highest accident rate and therefore must pay the highest premiums, perhaps in excess of $1,000 per year. This may be four times as much as other drivers pay.

Types of Car Insurance

You'll have several kinds of car insurance.

• *Collision insurance* will pay for damages to your car in case of collision with another car or object. It will have a deductible—an amount set by you which you agree to pay yourself whenever you have a claim.

• *Liability insurance* will pay for claims against you if you hurt other people or their property.

• *Medical payments coverage* pays for your medical bills if you are hurt while riding in your car.

• *Comprehensive coverage* protects you if your car is stolen, catches fire, or is hit by any of a wide variety of other perils. You also can have *"uninsured motorist" insurance*, which covers you or anyone else riding in your car if any of you is killed or injured by an uninsured motorist. Your liability insurance is designed to pay other people who claim to have been injured by you. Similarly, their coverage pays you, unless they don't have any. This is the purpose of uninsured motorist insurance.

Most states require that you have a certain set amount of liability insurance. The states that don't will ask you to prove you can pay a certain amount in case of a claim against you.

If your car is more than three years old, or worth less than $1,000, drop your collision insurance. You cannot collect more than the value of your car in a claim, and it might cost more than your car is worth to fix it. Most lenders will insist you carry collision insurance until your car is paid off.

Don't buy duplicate coverage. If your health insurance covers your medical bills for injuries to you while in your car, don't buy medical payments insurance.

Your state may require you by law to have the minimum amount of *"no-fault" insurance.* Under this type of policy, your company pays you, regardless of whose fault the accident was. If there are "no-fault" laws in your state, you may be able to save on liability insurance.

How else can you, a teenager, save on insurance, since it is so expensive for people in your age bracket?

Saving on Car Insurance

• To reduce your premium from the start, buy a less expensive car.

• Take as high a deductible as you can afford. A good rule of thumb may be one week's pay. The typical deduction is $100, but if you raise to a $200 or $250 deductible, you save 10 percent on your premium. Raise it to $500, and you save 35 percent. Raise it to $1,000, and save 50 percent. If you raise a $50 deductible on your comprehensive coverage to $100, you'll save 20 percent.

• There are other discounts which you should check. If you take a state-approved driver education course, you may be eligible for a 5 to 10 percent cut. If you take a defensive driving course offered by the National Safety Council and pass it, you also may save 10 percent. If you're sixteen or over and have a B average or better in school, or if you go to school 100 miles or more from home and must drive there and back, you may be eligible for a rate cut. All drivers are eligible for "good driver" rates. If your car is actually a second family car and you use it less than a specific percentage of the time, you can save. And you can save on comprehensive coverage if you have an antitheft device on your car. There are discounts if you drive less than a certain number of miles per year, or if you don't smoke or drink. You can also save by having your car insured in your family's name with yourself as the principal driver rather than in your name with you as the sole driver. Shop around for insurance and ask questions! Rates *vary!*

Other tips:

• Get a "plain talk" policy rather than one written in "legalese." Does your policy pay for towing charges or a rental car while yours is out of service?

• Once you have insurance, inform your company of any change in your age or marital status which may affect your rate.

• Don't file claims just above the level of your deductible—you'll spoil your "good driver" record.

• Buy comprehensive insurance that covers only fire and theft, not every possible act of God, and you can cut your premium by more than half.

• Pay your premium yearly and save finance charges.

• Though it will actually increase the cost of your insurance, you may want to raise your liability premium $10, $20, or $30 in order to boost the limit of your coverage substantially. If you can afford it, it's well worth it. Juries often make huge awards to a victim's family in a fatal accident.

Dealing with Your Insurance Company

What are your rights under the law in dealing with your insurance company?

• If your company says you aren't covered for a claim, it must show you the provision which prohibits coverage.

• It must acknowledge receipt of your claim within ten work days. It must answer any communications within seven, and investigate your claim within fifteen work days.

• If your car is totaled, you can get a replacement car or cash (the cost of buying a comparable car in your area).

• Your company must pay you within ten work days after you receive agreement from it.

What if your insurance is canceled? Call your agent. He must give you an explanation. Correct any misinformation in your file—the cancellation may be a mistake. If your insurance has been canceled because you have been determined to be too great a risk, shop around at other companies. If none is willing to serve you, go into the "assigned risk" pool. Companies in this plan usually must keep you for a few years, and then, if you maintain a good record, you should be able to get regular insurance. Understandably, "assigned risk" carries a high premium.

AUTO CLUBS

Are auto clubs worthwhile for you? Will the membership fees (usually in the range of $30 per year) be money wisely spent? For answers ask yourself these questions:

Do you go to pieces over even a slight on-the-road breakdown? Are you totally unfamiliar with your car and its workings? Do you often go into unfamiliar territory with your car? If the answer to any or all of these questions is yes, then join an auto club.

About 30 million people in the United States belonged to these clubs at the start of the 1980s. Different clubs offer different services. Among them are: emergency road service, auto insurance, trip planning, bail and bond, and legal defense reimbursement.

There are national clubs and regional clubs. Some clubs which call themselves national are more active in some parts of the country than others. If you do most of your driving in one area, you might want to join a club that specializes there.

Shop for rates and discounts. Read their literature, and ask friends about clubs to which they may belong. Specific questions to ask are: Is the club full-service? Is it nationwide or regional? Does it serve you directly, or just pay you back for your trouble? Is it basically just trying to sell you insurance? Are there conditions you must fulfill to receive benefits while you're on a trip?

If you're interested in a national club, call its local office to make sure it offers all the services that are advertised nationally. And don't become lazy about shopping just because you've joined an auto club. Make the rounds when you're looking for insurance. Your club may try to sell it to you, but it probably will be cheaper on the outside.

(See Chapter 12, *Take a Vacation*, for further travel and auto club information.)

GARAGING AND PARKING

It may startle you to learn that your car will spend 95 percent of its life parked. If you use it to commute in a major urban area, your yearly parking costs may run between $500 and $1,500, and your daily costs between $2.50 and $10. These prices appear headed only one way—up—as the 1980s progress and the demand for land increases.

If you're a student, you're among the lucky few if there is free parking at your school. As of the late 1970s, 75 percent of this country's universities and colleges charged students for parking, saying it took away from their classroom space.

But there are ways to save on keeping your car parked and garaged:

• Carpool—and try to arrange with the garage for different people to use the space every day, week, etc.

• Use a garage not located directly in town. You might save as much as 20 percent. You might also consider a garage even farther away, from which you would take a subway or bus into the city.

Even with the added expense of public transportation, you might still save on parking.

• Check if your garage will allow you to park a compact car at a cheaper rate, since your car will be able to slip into a tiny space other cars can't use.

• Investigate the garage's monthly rates. Even if you don't park every day, the cheaper monthly charge may still allow you to save money.

RENTING A CAR

Your age may be trouble if you want to rent a car, since you must be eighteen or over even to consider it. Among the major companies, Hertz and National will rent to you if you're at least eighteen. Hertz, however, requires that you have *your own* major credit card, not one in your parents' name. National may rent to you even without such a card, but its policies differ from city to city, so you must call the office near you to find out if you're eligible.

Some smaller companies will rent to women eighteen years of age. Call the ones in your area to find out what their policies are.

If you can rent, consider it if you won't be driving on a constant basis; if you don't want to take out a loan for a car; if you simply can't scrape up the money for that big an expenditure at this time; or if you want to get rid of an old car that you are now paying to garage and insure and rent a car only when you need one.

Rules of the Road for Renting a Car

Rental rates are determined by the type and size of the car, how long you keep it, and how many miles you drive it. Some companies include a certain number of "free miles"; others have discount plans. Some charge flat rates, while others charge per day and per mile. Lower rates are usually available on weekends. Some agencies are more flexible about exactly when you must return the car. Smaller firms may give you cheaper rates, but you may be getting a two- or three-year-old car, in contrast to Hertz, which rotates its cars every nine months. There's nothing wrong with driving a car that's a few years old if you get what you're paying for.

Larger firms will allow you to pick up your car at one location and drop it off at another.

It's easy to comparison-shop for a rental car. Most of the companies have toll-free numbers.

When you rent a car, check it to see that it has no unstated defects, that its mileage is indeed what it has been claimed to be on the form you'll be given, and that there is a full tank of gas. If you aren't paying by credit card, you may have to leave a hefty deposit (a few hundred dollars).

Understand how you will be charged for gas. There is a move in the industry toward "dry" rates, in which you pay for gas and aren't reimbursed. If the company is to charge you for gas, the charge will be based on the mileage you traveled. Start with a full tank. If you return it with more gas than it had when you picked it up, insist on a credit. (There is one company, however, that does not do this.)

You must be insured while driving a rented car. You must have collision insurance (to cover the costs of repairing the car), liability insurance (to cover the costs of injury or property damage to others), and medical payments insurance (to cover your medical bills).

You can take care of collision insurance through a "full collision damage waiver," which means that you pay (depending on the firm) up to $6.50 per day to absolve yourself of any responsibility for collision damage. If you turn down this waiver, you'll be held responsible for, say, the first $500 worth of damage to the car. If you're not renting for a long period of time, pay the waiver. Some companies will ask for a deposit of a few hundred dollars if you refuse the waiver. One company holds you responsible for the first $250 worth of damages even if you take the waiver.

The nationwide agencies provide adequate liability coverage, but smaller ones may not. Ask the company for the limits of its coverage.

The third type of insurance, for your medical payments, will be offered to you by the firm for a fee.

Questions to Ask

If you live in a major urban area or are visiting a popular vacation center and need a rental car, you may have as many as 100 different

rent-a-car companies from which to choose. How can you, a teen-ager, possibly tell the difference between them?

You may be in for a nasty surprise when you rent your next "bargain." Get the answers to the following questions particularly:

Is there collision damage waiver insurance, and is it optional?

The collision damage waiver (CDW) is one of the most confusing areas of rent-a-car policy. It is not insurance. Accepting CDW usually means that you, the renter, will not be held liable for the cost of repairing accidental damage to the car while it is in your possession. Declining CDW means that you, the renter, may be held liable for the costs of repairs from the first $500 of damages to the full cost of the car.

Policies on CDW vary widely. For instance, at several companies CDW was mandatory at up to $6.50 per day over the advertised daily rates in the early 1980s. At one company, even after accepting CDW, renters were still liable for the first $250 of damages. Some companies require a cash or credit card deposit if you, the renter, refuse CDW.

Do all companies have twenty-four-hour emergency road service?

No. If you are driving any distance from the original renting location, the availability of twenty-four-hour road service is a major point.

Some companies will rent to you only if you plan on driving within a 200-mile radius from the renting location. If you break down after hours, you may have to wait until the next day—not very comforting at 3 A.M.

Do you pay for gasoline you don't use?

Most companies charge you at a standard rate for the gas used: you receive a full tank at check-out and are charged for gas based on the mileage at check-in. Should you return the car with more gas than when you rented it, you will get a credit for the difference. At one company, however, any gas left on return becomes the property of the rental company, to be resold to the next renter.

How do you know if you are eligible to rent a car?

Check eligibility requirements if you are under twenty-five. Companies have different eligibility requirements, depending on how you intend to pay—in cash or with a credit card.

Do all companies offer courtesy phone service?

No. Some rent-a-car companies have no phone service at the airport. You must arrange for a pickup at the time you make your reservation or once you arrive at your destination. If your plane is late, you may find that some "bargain" operators close at 5 P.M.

Do all companies have courtesy buses?

No. Some drop off cars at hotels or other designated locations; some have only in-city locations. You may have to take a cab to pick up your car, with all the extra costs that involves.

How often do courtesy buses run?

Smaller companies often can afford only one bus. If you miss it, you must wait for the bus to complete the airport circuit before you will be picked up.

Aren't all reservations computerized?

Most rent-a-car companies do not have computerized systems, must write out contracts by hand, and must get credit authorization by phone. These procedures can add significantly to check-out time.

SELLING OR TRADING IN YOUR CAR

There are many reasons you may want to sell your car or trade it in toward the purchase of a new one, but when maintenance costs become a regular expense, you certainly will start to think about it.

If you sell your car yourself, you'll probably get more for it. But a trade-in will be faster, and can be arranged right when you buy your new car. It may take you several months to sell your car yourself. Trade-in values can vary from dealer to dealer, but the price difference between the trade-in value and the price of your new car is what's really important.

Selling the Car Yourself

Selling the car yourself will save you the 10 percent or more a dealer tacks on as his profit. (Some dealers get as much as a 22 percent markup.) There are responsibilities that go with selling a car yourself, though. Find out about title laws in your area, and any other laws pertinent to auto sales. In some states, if you trade in your car, you pay a lower sales tax on your new car.

You must give the person to whom you sell a statement verifying that the odometer is correct. You can get this form from any car dealer or the motor vehicle department in your state.

Selling your own car involves deciding how much it is worth and then advertising that you have something to sell. To advertise you can simply tell everyone you know that you're selling your car, put notices on bulletin boards at school or at work, paste a sign on your car (with your phone number) saying For Sale, or put an ad in the paper (this last will cost money). To save space, use the "car shorthand" discussed earlier in this chapter.

Newspaper ads will not only help you sell your car but will also aid you in determining how much to charge for it. Look at prices others are asking for your model and year. Use the NADA (National Automobile Dealers Association) guide to car prices, available at most banks and libraries, or the Kelley *BlueBook*.

If you want to figure the price yourself, here is the method:

1. Find the list price. Subtract 10 to 15 percent, and add local sales tax.

2. Subtract the amount by which your car has depreciated. In the first year, it will have lost 30 to 32 percent of its value; in the second year, 24 to 26 percent; in the third, 18 to 20 percent; in the fourth, 7 to 8 percent; from the fifth through seventh years, 3 to 5 percent each year; and from the eighth through tenth years, 1 to 2 percent each year.

3. Take inflation into account. Get the Consumer Price Index for the year you bought the car and the year in which you are selling it. Divide the new index by the old, and multiply the wholesale price by your answer.

4. Add 10 to 12 percent for your profit.

Keep your car's condition in mind. How much will the new owner have to spend on it if you've run it down? On the other hand, if you've spent a lot of money on your car to improve it, add to its value. You also can add to the value of your car by washing, polishing, and waxing it, touching up any scratches with paint, cleaning the inside, vacuuming the carpet, emptying the storage areas, and perhaps even cleaning the engine. These are all ways to make a would-be buyer feel better about paying a certain price for your car. Also check the fluids, tires, and light bulbs in case the prospective buyer wants to take the car for a test drive. (Before you let him or her drive it, be sure he or she has a license and that you have insurance for other people who drive your car.)

Don't invest in major repairs or a whole new paint job. A newly painted car may make people think you're trying to hide something. Be honest about the car, but be firm about the price. Don't begin by telling people the price is "flexible"!

If a buyer indicates interest in your car but must get a loan for it, ask for 5 to 10 percent of the price in cash or a teller's check in order to hold it. (See "Cashier's Check" in Chapter 3.)

Should you decide to trade in your car to a dealer, he will classify it according to how easy it will be for him to sell. He may use an appraisal form, noting what he will have to do to the car to sell it.

When to Trade In Your Car

The odds have shifted greatly in favor of keeping your car as long as you can! Your car should last fifteen to twenty years if you care for it properly. And it should hold up for 100,000 to 150,000 miles if your driving habits don't abuse it.

In the past, traditional wisdom held that a car should last 10 years or 100,000 miles, whichever came first. Traditional wisdom also held that the age and mileage limits probably would roughly coincide—that you average about 10,000 miles a year for each year of the decade that you drive the jalopy.

But several recent developments are undercutting this wisdom—and the bottom line is producing startling new results.

Beyond all other factors is the Anti-Rollback Odometer law, which has produced indisputable evidence that many of your parents' generation who sold cars (dealers, wholesalers, auctioneers, even individuals) were routinely turning back the mileage on car odometers.

Thus, when a car was sold, the 50,000, 60,000, or 70,000 miles its odometer had recorded would be rolled back to read 20,000, 30,000, or 40,000 miles. So when the old buggy literally started to fall apart in its ninth, tenth, eleventh, or twelfth year, with 90,000 or 100,000 miles on its clock, a logical conclusion was that the odometer was accurate and that, therefore, most cars would last "only" 100,000 miles.

But big trucks routinely rolled as many as 100,000 miles a year. Admittedly, these trucks usually got top maintenance and tender loving care, since they cost $50,000 to $60,000 each to buy new. They would undergo major engine overhauls every 150,000 miles or so—and they were made of heavier gauge steel, while their components also were of sturdier, more heavy-duty stuff than those cars.

But 500,000 or 600,000, sometimes 750,000 miles—six, seven, eight, nine years of useful truck life? This had to force a reappraisal. While cars were smaller, lighter, and usually less well-maintained, they obviously were going farther than most people had previously imagined.

Detroit has made progress in building its cars. Components last longer and do not have to be repaired or serviced as often. As a result, maintenance costs, while rising in absolute terms, actually are declining as a percentage of total outlays.

Auto analysts are looking more carefully at "scrappage" or "junker" totals. The traditional concept that any car registered in one year but not reregistered in the next was scrapped or junked has been giving a false impression. What about those 300,000 cars per year stolen and never recovered? They have not just disappeared; most of the cars have been shipped to other countries and continents (South America, South Africa) for resale.

These stolen and reshipped cars have then been driven tens of thousands of miles more.

And finally, newer cars are being driven greater distances each year than older ones—15,000-plus miles against an assumed national mileage average for all cars of 10,000 miles per year. A new "first" car may be driven more and farther than "normal." Then as the auto is replaced and becomes a "second" car, its annual mileage increase may slow. Or if it is sold, the second owner may drive it less than the original buyer did. "Fleet" cars—and the majority of new cars do go into government or business "fleets," into smaller business car pools, or into other nonpersonal service—are traded relatively more often than cars bought for personal use. (The comparison is 5.2 years for cars bought new for personal use against 2.25 to 2.50 years for fleet cars.)

In brief, the figures we have been trusting have been misleading, incomplete, or plain wrong.

To make my basic points unmistakably clear:

1. New developments in the entire sphere of personal car ownership—the Anti-Rollback Odometer law; the vast improvements in Detroit's building of new cars to last longer and to require repairs and service less often; the rising recognition that official figures on junking and scrappage of cars have been misleading us—underline the money-saving message that you, a young owner, can keep your personal car much longer than you've been led to believe.

2. To trade in a car every two or three years is emerging as a ridiculously shameful waste of money which millions of young Americans cannot afford. In some cases, trading in your personal car after it has been driven 50,000 to 55,000 miles may be a wise decision—but in most cases, it is not.

The traditional trade-in yardsticks are obsolete. Don't trade in too soon!

Part II: Other Vehicles

BICYCLES

Selecting a Bicycle

For most of you, bicycles will be the first vehicles you own. The best kind for you to buy will depend on what you want to use it for and also on how good a cyclist you are. Don't buy "too much bike" for your level of ability.

Types of Bicycles

One of the major characteristics which distinguishes types of bikes is their number of speeds. If you're planning to ride short distances on level ground and want a durable bike, get a one-speed. It will be heavy (fifty to sixty pounds) and hard to pedal up hills, but in flat areas this will be best for you. Single-speeds work well for beginners.

Three-speeds, which weigh between thirty-five and forty pounds, are good if you'll be cycling in an inner city or going up small hills. They're for you if you've outgrown a one-speed but can't yet handle a ten-speed. Five-speed bikes are good for touring or taking short trips. If you want or need to go long distances with little effort, get a ten- or twelve-speed bike—these are the most popular, versatile bikes. One of these will provide you with exercise and fun, is good for touring or racing, and is easy to dismantle and take along on a trip. Don't go to a fifteen-speed unless you'll be taking very long trips on fairly steep hills. Five- to fifteen-speed bikes weigh less than thirty pounds.

Prices are in these ranges: a single speed, with either a traditional or racing style frame, from $50 to $200; three-speeds run between $75 and $300; ten-speeds start at about $100 (although this variety would be found in a department store rather than a bicycle shop) and can cost $1,000; and fifteen-speeds start at $300 to $400 and run up to $1,000 and over.

Prices vary because there are different ways to make a bike. Less expensive bikes are made of steel welded to form a tube. The metal, however, could be weakened by such welding. Cheaper bikes are also not reinforced where the tubes join each other and other parts of the bike.

Features to Look For

The best frame to buy is "double-butted"—the tubing is thicker at the ends, where the most stress occurs. Look for lugs on the frame—these are sleeves of metal which act as braces where one tube of the frame meets another.

If you want to use your bike for racing, look for an aluminum rather than a steel alloy frame. Rims (for the tires) should be made of aluminum alloy. Steel is heavier, and is used on lesser quality and children's bikes.

The "hubs" at the center of each wheel should be made of one-piece machined aluminum—avoid stamped metal hubs. If the bike you're interested in has "quick-release" hubs, it will be easier to change a flat tire.

Wheels should have thirty-six spokes in the rear, and thirty-two or more in the front. Smaller-sized bikes (twenty-four inches) will probably have twenty-eight in both front and rear. All spokes should be thicker at the ends than in the middle.

The crank and chainwheel, which make up your pedaling mechanism, also should be made of aluminum alloy.

When you shop for brakes, you'll find that side-pull brakes will be the least expensive, but they may not grip evenly. Buy center-pull brakes, or high quality side-pull ones made from an aluminum alloy.

Tires come in two types: tubular "sew-ups"—so called because the casing is sewn up all the way around the tire—and the tube-type tires. Novices and intermediate riders should buy the tubular types because they are less likely to get flat (and they are easier to fix when they do). "Sew-ups" are more prone to get flat, but are lighter and can be changed in a matter of seconds. Racers understandably prefer sew-ups.

Curved handlebars, often called "racing" handlebars, may look uncomfortable, but the position into which they put your body makes you less resistant to the wind and will ease your pedaling. The lower portion of the bars, where you hold them, should be 10 degrees less than horizontal. No handlebar, racing or otherwise, should be wider than your shoulders. If a bike you like doesn't have racing handlebars, or any other part you want, buy this part separately and have it put on your bike.

You will find the people best skilled to change parts on your bike or assemble it in the first place in a bike shop. Just about all bikes require some assembly when you buy them. You'll also need to be fitted for your bike, and a bike shop is the best place for that. You can find your size by subtracting nine to ten inches from your inseam, but your bike may still need adjustment. Test ride it to make sure it "fits." As you ride it, note if there are any sharp edges or parts sticking out on the bike that could hurt you.

When you choose your bike, decide whether you want hand brakes (caliper) or foot brakes (coaster). Most models, other than single speeds, come with hand brakes; be sure your hands are strong enough to squeeze them tightly. Hand brakes work by causing two pieces of rubber to squeeze each tire and stop it. Keep in mind that, since brakes get wet in the rain, they may not stop quickly. And test the brakes in the store.

What frame size and style do you want? If you want a "boy's" bike, whether or not you are a boy, straddle it. You should be able to stand with both feet on the ground and clear the bar by about an inch. This style is more popular because it is stronger, and since it is more rigid, it handles better. But if you don't want a "boy's" bike, you don't have to get a "girl's" bike. There is another frame made called the *mixte,* which has a horizontal bar higher than a "girl's" bike but lower than a "boy's."

You can get two kinds of seats, *tourist* or *racing.* The tourist seat is more padded; the racing seat is firmer and more pointed. Some cyclists feel it is less comfortable, but others say that when it is broken in it is as comfortable as a tourist seat. Don't mix the style of your seat and handlebars—if you have one racing style, have both racing style. Both styles can be adjusted for comfort.

Accessories

You don't need a catalogue of accessories for your bike, but you should have:

- A chain or cable with a key lock to tie the bike to a pole to prevent theft.
- A bell or horn, especially if you ride in the city. If you do ride in the city a lot, you should have a gas-powered horn as loud as a car's.
- Bags and carrier baskets, depending on your needs.
- Reflectors on the front and rear fenders and the pedals. Also have the separate flashlight-type lights which strap onto your arm or leg and move with you.
- A mirror—but don't rely on it. Always turn your head to see who's behind you.
- Two tire pumps—a frame-mounted one to take with you and a foot-weighted one at home.
- A bicycle repair kit, which you can buy or make yourself. It should include basic tools, a tube or tire patch kit, and a can of pressurized lubricant.
- A helmet, which you should wear, especially when you ride in heavy auto traffic.
- Chain guards to keep clothes from getting caught in the bike.

Maintenance

Once you have acquired your bike and everything else you want to go with it, keep everything in good working order. The main points: tighten, lubricate, and clean. Listen for noises that might mean problems with your brakes, gears, or tire pressure. The correct pressure should be stated on the side of the tire. Do your lights work? Are all your reflectors in the right place? Tighten all nuts and bolts. Check your gear-chain tension once a month. Grease your bearings, and whenever you use oil or spray lubrication on your bicycle, don't get it on the tires—it damages rubber.

Twice a month, wipe your bike with a damp cloth. Use kerosene to remove tar. Wax the frame and any chrome on the bike. Sit on the seat. Does it tip forward or back? Tighten it so it's level. Are there any bent or broken teeth on the chainwheel? You may have to take the bike to the dealer so a new one can be installed. Spokes should be tight, rims unbent.

If your foot brakes aren't working correctly, your dealer should look at them. But if you have hand brakes, make sure the cables aren't worn or frayed. Oil the levers, and measure the brake shoes to see if they are evenly spaced from the rim ($\frac{1}{8}$″ to $\frac{1}{16}$″).

Insurance

You can buy bike insurance, but before you do, check whether your bike is covered under your parents' homeowner's insurance. In any case, register your bike with the police—you will have a better chance of getting it back if it's stolen.

Rules of the Road

You can be a good or bad bike rider, just as you can be a good or bad auto driver. To ride well, your bike has to work properly. Brakes should stop you within 15 feet at 15 miles per hour. If you have foot brakes, you shouldn't have to backpedal more than 60 degrees before your brakes go on.

Here are other rules of the road:

- Stay to the right, or in a bike lane.
- Don't ride with someone on your bike.
- Use hand signals when making turns, and obey all other traffic rules, signs, etc.
- Obey all local bike laws as well.

- Ride single file if you are with a group.
- Watch for gratings in the road, sewers, or subways.
- Be wary of car doors swinging open, and cars pulling out from the side of the road.
- Don't carry so many packages that you can't see where you're going or control your bike.
- Be especially careful when making left turns. A good method is to cross the street first on your bike, then proceed in the new direction.

MOPEDS

The moped derives its "mo" from motor, and its "ped" from pedal. Having both, it's really a motorized bicycle.

These vehicles, which get from 95 to 100 miles to the gallon and usually cost from $400 to $600, are becoming more and more popular. Anyone who can ride a bike can ride a moped—it has no gears or clutch, just a few simple controls. It requires some pedaling, but it is by no means strenuous. In fact, some manufacturers are now making "mopeds" without pedals.

A moped has a single-cylinder engine which provides 2½ to 3 horsepower. By law, the top speed it can achieve is 30 miles per hour—or else it is a limited-use motorcycle. This is the most efficient motorized passenger vehicle. It is not suited for all roads, though, and if used where it shouldn't be, such as on highways, it can be dangerous. Mopeds are great for short-distance commuting, especially if you live in a small- or medium-sized town. You can take the vehicle with you on trips in your car or camper. It doesn't require much maintenance, and is great at getting through traffic.

As far as regulations go, all mopeds must be registered, and you must have a driver's license to operate them. Most states don't have a special road test for moped drivers to take as they do for motorcyclists. Some states do require that you have special insurance; others make you prove you can pay a certain amount in damages in case of an accident. Check with your state's motor vehicle department for specific regulations. Moped insurance runs about $150 per year. Don't just assume you can buy one and ride it.

The most expensive mopeds, which cost about $1,000, can be

hard to get parts for. Ask about availability of parts for whatever model you consider.

Regardless of your state's regulations, wear a helmet whenever you ride your moped. You can get hurt just as badly from a fall while going 30 miles per hour as you can while going faster.

MOTORCYCLES

Motorcycles are dangerous—particularly for *you*, a teenager. The danger of your being involved in a fatal accident is *four times greater* than it would be if you were riding in a car. And the chances of your being injured in an accident are *ten times greater* than they would be if you were involved in a car accident. Most of these accidents happen to people under thirty.

This is the reason insurance for motorcyclists is so expensive. However, you can save with a motorcycle driver-training course. You probably will need to take this course anyway because most states will require you to pass a separate road test for motorcycles, even if you already have a driver's license.

If you do decide that a motorcycle appeals to you, don't buy "too much cycle" for your abilities. Find a dealer who will not try to sell you a Hell's Angels–type machine.

Types of Motorcycles

Motorcycles, or "bikes," fall into two basic categories:

1. Dirt bikes are made for riding on trails. You can recognize them by their front fender, which is mounted far from the wheel.
2. Road bikes have a close-mounted front fender made of metal.

But what size should you get? And what do they cost?
That depends on what you will be using your bike for.

Selecting Your Bike

To start with the smallest styles, *minibikes* are lightweight, scaled-down motorcycles. They are ridden mostly by youngsters, since they have a low, short frame and 12" to 18" wheels. They have an engine size of 100 cc (cubic centimeters) or less. Minibikes are good for learning to ride a motorcycle, or just for fun, but they're not intended for traffic or any street use, or for two riders. They range in price from $400 to $800.

After *mopeds*, (described in the preceding section) come *motor-bikes*. These run between $500 and $800, are ridden on or off trails, have a 50-cc to 80-cc engine, get 80 to 90 miles to the gallon, and run on 8 to 12 horsepower. Anything bigger is a *motorcycle*.

If you want to ride around town on your cycle, stay in the 70-cc to 125-cc range. Bikes this size cost between $600 and $1,000. If you want to ride on highways, you must move up to a machine with a 250-cc engine. Once you become more experienced, you may find that such a bike will be more comfortable to ride than a smaller one. These sizes (70 cc to 250 cc) will be cheaper than the bigger bikes to run and insure, as well as to buy.

As you become a more skilled rider, you may want to use your bike to commute to and from school or work. To do this, you will need a bike with a 250-cc to 400-cc engine that will cost an average of $1,700. It will have about 40 horsepower and get about 60 miles to the gallon.

The upper echelon of motorcycles, used for long-distance touring, ranges from 500 cc to 1300 cc. The largest motorcycles have 120 horsepower, more than some small cars. In this group, mileage figures run from 40 to 90 miles per gallon, and prices from $1,000 to $6,000.

Cycles are available with automatic transmissions, but most have a five-speed clutch. There is no reverse gear; simply walk your bike backwards. Some models have electronic ignition.

Regardless of power or style, a motorcycle fits you if you can plant both feet on the ground while you are seated. Beginners, however, should have a bike with at least sixteen-inch wheels, and one that weighs no more than 200 to 300 pounds.

Accessories and Cycle Safety

Most cycles don't come with windshields, but for $45 to $90, shields are a good investment. So is a tire inflator you can carry with you to patch small holes in your tires. A ''fairing''—a piece which fills in the area below the handlebars, providing you with protection in the front of your cycle—is a good safety feature, even though it may cost about $250.

A helmet for motorcycle riding, which can cost $65 to $125, is essential. Look for one that has passed the "Snell Impact Test." This means it will provide a certain standard of protection for your head should you hit it in a fall. And leather jackets aren't just for motorcycle glamour—they are good protection if you fall. And don't ride in shorts or sandals. Wear sturdy boots and gloves, and carry rainwear with you. When riding at night, wear brightly colored clothes, and place reflective tape on yourself and your bike.

Buying Your Bike

There isn't really much room for bargaining when it comes to motorcycles; they're generally sold at list price. Most come with a 6-month/6,000-mile warranty.

You can buy a used motorcycle, either from a private individual or a dealer. You can save money, just as you can buying a used car, but be cautious. Have a mechanic look over any bike you are considering. Since motorcycles are accident-prone, any new paint or mismatched paint could be covering repairs.

These machines can be financed just as cars can, but dealer financing can be expensive. Pay cash for your cycle if possible, or try to get a loan against your savings account from a bank. A motorcycle loan from a bank can be as expensive as one from a dealer.

Insurance

When you're on a motorcycle, you're going as fast as a car but are less stable and can't be seen as easily. That explains why insurance rates are so high. Your rates will depend on where you live, your age, and your driving record. If you are single, male, and under thirty, you may pay as much as 150 percent of the basic car-insurance rate. Shop around. Some companies specialize in motorcycle insurance. You'll save if your bike is less than 200 cc and if it weighs 300 pounds or less.

Know specifically what your policy covers. Liability insurance may cover only you, the owner/driver, and it may not be effective if you've been speeding or racing. It also may not cover medical payments for injuries to you.

Maintenance

Your motorcycle will be safer and you'll be less likely to have to collect on your insurance if you've maintained it. Just like a car, your motorcycle should be tuned up once a year. If your dealer has a good service department, you can tune up your bike there. Before you ride, check tire pressure, chain tension, and fluid levels. Every bike comes with an owner's manual, which will tell you how to check the control cables and oil level, as well as how to clean the exhaust system and ignition points. It will also tell you how to adjust the brakes, spark plugs, handlebars, and front shock absorbers.

To see whether the spokes are tight, spin the wheels while holding a metal object against them. Listen for a ring, which means one is loose. If only a few are loose, tighten them yourself, but if most are, have a pro look at your wheel. When you wash your cycle, be careful not to get water in the engine; you could damage it.

RECREATIONAL VEHICLES

Selecting an RV

''Recreational Vehicles'' (RVs) is industry talk. You call them campers and trailers. Since RVs range from a converted van costing $10,000 to a $35,000 motor home, it is especially important when selecting an RV that you know what you will use it for. How far will you go? How much will you use it? How many people will be with you? Where will you camp? And perhaps most important of all, how much money do you want to spend?

If, when you camp, you like to stay in one place but go off on short side trips, get a vehicle you will tow rather than drive so you'll have your car to use separately. If you think camping isn't camping unless it's done in a tent or tentlike place, then a folding camping trailer is for you.

Talk to dealers and people you know who have RVs. Rent a vehicle to test-drive and compare before buying. When you buy an RV, look for the seal of the Recreational Vehicle Industry Association. This means the RV has met certain national standards.

Types of RVs

What are the different kinds of RVs available, and how much do they cost? From a van to a motor home, there are three basic categories:

1. *Folding campers* have collapsible sidewalls made of canvas, plastic, or fiberglass which are mounted on wheels and towed behind you. Cost: $2,000 to $3,500.
2. *A truck camper*, which fits onto the bed of a pickup truck and is portable. Cost: $2,000 to $6,000.
3. *Travel trailers*, which you tow with a car or truck and which don't have to be hooked up to water and gas lines at a campsite. Cost: $4,000 to $15,000.

These prices depend on length and the kinds of facilities with which the RVs are equipped. (One note about truck campers: as of the early 1980s, forty-eight states did not classify them as vehicles but as personal property, which means they can't be titled, licensed, or registered. Industry experts say vehicle classification could lead to lower-cost financing and insurance for them.)

Financing and Insurance

RVs must be financed and insured in the same way as other vehicles. Financing is available from your dealer, bank, other financial institution, or credit union, usually for a period of seven or eight years with a 20 to 25 percent down payment. To insure your RV, go to a firm that specializes in such insurance. If you go to the same firm from which you bought your auto insurance, claims against your RV may jeopardize your car insurance. Ask your insurance agent about this possibility. Wherever you go for coverage, your policy should be broad enough to cover you while you are on vacation—if necessary, to pay for emergency lodging, towing, food that you may need, etc. Buy a comprehensive policy to cover the theft of any of your possessions from your trailer or camper.

Maintenance

Maintaining your RV can be as complicated or simple as your vehicle is. If you have plumbing and appliances, check the electrical, water, and sewer systems frequently, and especially before you travel. If your RV is motorized, check its fluids and brakes and follow all the maintenance procedures you would for an auto. If the vehicle is towable, you must maintain the towing apparatus. Each vehicle comes with an owner's manual; your dealer can also give you more details on how to care for each make and model. An important warning: drain the water from your RV in the winter so it won't freeze in the pipes and rupture them.

Fuel Economy

Poor fuel economy has always been a monkey on the back of RVs. They have become more economical in recent years, but there are steps *you* can take to save gas and money:

- Pack your things inside instead of strapping them to the outside of the vehicle. You'll cut down your wind resistance.
- Plan your trip. Wandering around wastes gas.
- Don't weigh down your RV. For every 100 pounds you add, subtract 1 percent in fuel economy.
- Plan to avoid rush hours in cities you pass through.
- For each 5 mph you exeed 50 mph, you'll get one mile less to the gallon.
- Eliminate jackrabbit starts.
- Check your vehicle's motor timing, ignition system, battery, tires, wheel alignment, oil, and air filter before you travel.
- If your RV has appliances, turn them off when not in use.
- Use your electrical hookup or batteries rather than the generator.

Rules of the Road

Practice driving your RV before you take it on a trip. Whatever type you have, it will handle very differently from a car, and if you're towing something, you'll have to get used to that, too.

Your owner's manual will tell you how much weight your vehicle is capable of towing. Then, to equip your car or truck for towing, you may need a heavy-duty clutch, differential, or transmission, different shock absorbers, a large radiator or fan blade. Get a weight distribution hitch with which to tow more than you'll ever pull. Have an expert install it.

Whether you're towing a trailer or driving a motorized unit, obey these safety rules: Slow down. Signal well before turns. Remember that winds may blow your trailer from side to side. And you must back a trailer very slowly. Place your right hand at the bottom of the wheel, and move it in the direction you want the trailer to go.

SMALL TRUCKS AND PICKUPS

You've at least seen some of the new breed of "minitrucks" on the roads these days. As the name implies, they're smaller and therefore less expensive than the traditional "4-by-4" pickup. (The term "4 by 4" refers to four-wheel drive.) A full-size pickup can run between $8,000 and $14,000 with options. You can buy a smaller truck for $6,000 to $8,000.

These trucks will give you more miles to the gallon than a "4 by 4," that is, 27 miles per gallon versus about 10 or 12. Minitrucks can tow trailers or small boats, and they can hold campers on top of them. Basically, they carry anything a full-size truck can, just not as much of it—a maximum of 1,000 pounds. Some have four-wheel drive.

The smaller trucks are gaining in popularity because they are easier to handle in cities and suburbs. They're good on narrow roads, handy at small public campsites, and great for short camping trips. So, before you buy, ask yourself what you want to use your truck for.

As far as comfort in driving goes, just about any option you can buy for a car is available for a truck—electric windows, bucket seats, power steering, tilt steering wheels, etc.

DUNE BUGGIES

Most people call any vehicle that moves on sand a dune buggy, but a "dune buggy" is just one type of dune buggy.

Both dune buggies and three-wheelers, as the other type of vehicle is called, can be used anyplace with sand where vehicles are allowed. They have wide, low-pressure tires to enable them to navigate dunes, and are used mainly for recreation.

A three-wheeler can be bought for under $1,500, and can be used in sand or silty soil. Many beach areas rent them, so try one out if you're thinking of buying. Most are not meant for the street, although they do attain speeds of 35 to 75 miles per hour.

A dune buggy runs on similar principles, but is more expensive. It is excellent on sand, but not as good in rocky places, because it has four wheels, which may make it more difficult to maneuver.

Dune buggies are not toy vehicles! Accidents involving them can kill people. Use common sense and courtesy when driving them.

SNOWMOBILES

I can't show you a picture of the first snowmobile, but it was a far cry from the sleek-looking cabs on skis that you see today. Now snowmobiles come with just about every option you can think of— bucket seats, AM/FM stereo—and some even go in reverse. They have speedometers, disc brakes, and nice, high windshields. On some models, if you want, you can get handlebars with built-in handwarmers. (Snowmobiles don't have steering wheels.)

A snowmobile operates with an engine which provides power to the skilike "tracks" on which it moves. The average price of a new snowmobile in the early 1980s was $1,800, but the price will depend on how strong an engine you get. You can buy a used snowmobile for as little as $100, depending on its condition.

Today's models have better shock absorption than in days past. They're also wider and have more padding in their seats to make it easier to go over bumps. They have bigger gas tanks for longer trips, but they cost a lot in fuel. A full tank may only last for a day's riding. You must insure your machines and some states require you to license them.

It's not advisable to drive a snowmobile more than a half hour without a helmet because of the noise it generates. New models are much quieter today, but still wear a helmet when riding one for safety reasons.

Snowmobile trails are opening up across the country. A 3,000-

mile national scenic trail from Vermont to North Dakota is in the works.

VANS

A van can be decorated to look like your living room, or can be a one-seater with a whole lot of empty space. But regardless of their use, these vehicles are increasing in popularity. Two million trucks (vans and pickups) are being sold a year, and there are now 36 million of them on the road.

Vans which can carry twelve to fifteen passengers sold for $10,000 to $16,000 in the early 1980s, the price depending on how customized the machine is.

What you have in your van will determine gasoline mileage, but you probably will get in the neighborhood of eight miles to the gallon. Your fuel economy will depend also on the size of the van.

Vans are sturdier than cars, depreciate less in their early years, and last longer. Borrow or rent one for a week and see how you like driving it.

Van Pooling

The van pooling craze isn't crazy; it saves money.

One of the fastest growing trends in transportation in the United States is "van pooling." By getting into a "van pool," you as a person going to school or work will:

- Cut your commuting costs by more than 25 percent.
- Reduce your travel time more than 35 percent.

And since your co-riders also use van transportation, your group is helping to ease pollution, cut traffic congestion, relieve the parking pinch, and conserve gasoline.

Stop kidding around about car pooling and van pooling! Share your driving with other commuters to school or work and you'll save truly eye-popping amounts.

IF YOU'RE CHARTERING A BUS

How do you go about chartering a bus for any purpose—at a reasonable price and without fear of being either dreadfully disappointed or even gypped?

What are the rules to guide you when, in many trips involving fifteen or more of you, you must charter a bus to take the place of an individual car?

The bus is not a form of second-class transportation. Convenience, flexibility, low cost—these have been the prime factors behind the popularity of the bus. In countless instances, people can't operate a car or can't afford one—which could easily include you, because of your youth, location, or income level. And even those who haven't had any special reason to take a bus have often preferred to "leave the driving" to them.

Here are vital hints for you:

What are guidelines for prices?

Prices are generally quoted in one of two ways, depending on the trip's distance. For local work of up to fifty miles in one direction, the price is quoted on a per-hour basis.

For trips of more than fifty miles in one direction, prices are usually quoted on a per-mile basis, the exact amount depending on the type of bus required. In addition, there is usually an hourly charge if the trip goes over a specified number of hours, because the driver must be paid, no matter whether the bus is moving or standing still.

What are hidden cost pitfalls to look out for?

Does the quoted price include tolls, parking charges, permits? Is the cost of the driver's lodging and/or food included if yours is an overnight trip? Check each of these items in advance.

Order the bus to report as late as possible to reduce unproductive waiting time for the inevitable last-minute arrivals. Use box lunches and save money on roadside food purchases.

Also, for your own comfort, make sure the bus you charter has sufficient baggage capacity for your luggage—particularly ski gear. Make sure the seating capacity of the bus itself is adequate.

What is a "short" trip for a bus?

Up to 500 miles is an accepted rule of thumb. Cost aside, a plane might be more comfortable and convenient for a longer trip. But, the flexibility of the bus can't be approached by the trains or planes.

What guides do you have for young bus travelers?

Wear loose-fitting clothing. Have a sweater handy. Travel light.

What about valuables and breakables?

Carry them with you. Most companies will insure items up to $50 in value, free of charge, with added coverage available.

Any tips for making the time pass?

Take a guide book or map and figure out where you are—landmarks, history, products, etc. A camera buff will enjoy the perspective from a ride high off the road. Read, sleep, use a transistor radio or tape-record with a personal ear-plug.

How do you find the right company for a charter?

A good source is a local college which uses dozens of charters for its athletic teams and knows the reliable firms.

9

PETS

CONTENTS

CAN YOU PASS THIS "TEST"
FOR OWNING A PET?

I saw it begin a few miles down the road from our exurb home, where a family had a litter of mixed breeds for sale. Two young teenagers in a passing car begged their parents to stop and take a puppy. I agree there's nothing more adorable than a puppy. So the parents stopped and . . .

Thus starts the abandonment of 25 million pets in this year alone—dogs and cats doomed to die either in dog pounds or on our streets as a result of accident, disease, or starvation.

Do you know what you are doing when you accept a pet? More large dogs recently have been abandoned on the streets than at any time in the past quarter-century—because the owners couldn't bear the feeding and caring for a large animal. Answer these questions before you take on the burden.

• *Can you accept the fact that it won't be a baby forever?* Sure, an adorable little kitten will fit into your pocket, a cuddly puppy will snuggle into your lap. But both will become gawky adolescents capable of knocking over breakable objects and creating havoc with your family's household routine. Animal shelters are full of pets that were rejected when they grew past babyhood.

• *Are you prepared to give a pet lifetime care?* Fully grown, a dog or cat is still totally dependent on you for all its needs. You must provide it with food and water, change its litter box or walk it regularly, watch over its health, keep it clean, and take it to the vet if it becomes ill. You must discipline it and still give it attention and affection so it stays the loving pet you wanted.

• *Are you ready to have it spayed or altered?* You must assume the responsibility and cost of having your animal spayed or altered.

• *Have you the time to feed and care for it properly?* Cats usually give themselves enough exercise, but dogs must be taken for walks and runs regularly. Feeding for either has to be regular and dependable. Grooming is of utmost importance to long-haired breeds, and not for looks alone—matted and tangled hair creates excellent hiding places for fleas and causes skin disorders. Some pets require other kinds of care which can be quite extensive. To parents who read this, leaving the chores to teenagers to give them a sense of responsibility is unwise and unfair both to your offspring and the animal.

• *Can you give your pet daily attention and companionship?* A pet is a living creature with a constant need for affection and reassurance, and needs daily human contact.

• *Can you afford the financial responsibility of ownership?* In addition to food, there are shots, checkups and vaccinations, veterinarian fees, licenses, and medicines. Unexpected costs may include damage to a neighbor's property, legal fees, torn clothing, and destruction of furniture and carpets.

• *Has your entire family discussed the subject?* Adding an animal requires adequate research and preparation. Impetuous, unplanned pet ownership can lead to misery for everyone.

Note: Never give a puppy or kitten as a gift unless you ask the prospective owner first whether the pet is really wanted.

Write or phone Friends of Animals (11 West 60th Street, New York, NY 10023), about its subsidized low-cost spaying program that costs about one-third of what you would pay a private vet. Phone: (800) 631-2212, except in New Jersey where is is (201) 922-0060 and in New York City (212) 247-8077. And if you've answered ''no'' to one of the questions above, give up the idea of getting a pet.

P.S.: All the above applies to all pets, to a greater or lesser degree: fish, horses, lizards, rabbits, and so on.

IF YOU PASS THE PET "TEST," HERE ARE GUIDES ON BUYING

Here are significant guidelines to consider before you make any purchase of a pet. In this case, the guidelines are for puppies.

• Carefully check the temperament and health of the puppy. All puppies should be outgoing. Don't buy a timid pup. Dogs that hide when you attempt to touch them or jump away when you approach are more than likely to turn out to be disappointments.

• Figure out what you will have to spend not only for the pet, but also for trips to the veterinarian and possible hospitalization of the pet. (These are not puny sums! I know.)

- Learn as much as you can about the type of animal before you buy. Read pet magazines. An important source of information is a visit to pet shows at which the breed you think you favor is being shown. These dogs are usually the best of the breed.
- If you're planning to buy a purebred, discuss the advantages and disadvantages of the different breeds. You will see the greatest variety at the pet shows and can talk with the owners and trainers who know most about the breeds.
- Discuss with a veterinarian the breed of the animal you want to buy, the type of home you have, your family's habits, your free time.
- If possible, buy from a breeder. Seldom are breeders in the business just for money. Their primary interest is in improving the breed, as opposed to strictly financial gain. When you finally settle on the breed you want, tell the breeder what you can afford to spend and how your family lives. Then the breeder can be of great assistance in helping you reach the best decision.
- While most sellers of pets are honest, there are major risks. You must beware of the sale of sick animals, untrustworthy guarantees associated with a sale, delay or inability to secure registration papers, unsatisfactory work performed in dog-grooming schools, and unsatisfactory training by dog obedience schools.

Also be wary of inadequate vaccinations given to pets; misrepresentation in sales (such as mixed breeds advertised as purebreds), and pet adoption services that don't spell out fees in adoption.

A special committee under the sponsorship of the Better Business Bureau of Metropolitan New York, Inc., has drawn up a list of "Pet Guidelines" that lists the seller's responsibilities, standards of advertising, and minimum guarantees for a dog or cat. Among other points, it notes that the new pet owner should be given information about the care of the animal at the time of purchase. This list is free; write the BBB (257 Park Avenue South, New York, NY 10010).

Also inquire for guidelines at your local ASPCA or write to them at 441 East 92nd Street, New York, NY 10028.

10

BE SMART AND SAVE

CONTENTS

HOW TO WIN THE BATTLE OF THE PENNIES

Prices will continue to rise. There are ways you can cope and not just hand over your money without a whimper.

- Check the prices of every product and service you buy. Never just take an item and pay whatever is on the tape. You well may be paying a lot more than you thought, or more than the cost of a competing product with a less highly advertised brand name.
- Compare prices of similar items. Some products cost literally dozens of times more than less highly promoted brands.
- Check out all sales and bargains to make sure the "bargain" is not just an everyday price labeled a discount. This applies especially to seasonal items that have just passed their peak.
- Clip all cents-off coupons. Whether you want to be bothered or not, you're involuntarily paying for these programs when you buy at regular prices. Use the coupons and save what is offered.
- Watch out for the cost of credit. Under the Truth in Lending Law, it is your right to be told the annual percentage rate and amount of the finance charge on credit. Must you buy on borrowed money?
- Look for automatic changes in contracts that add to your costs without your being notified or asked. Banks have been known to send you a notice without asking you to sign, just announcing that certain service charges have been hiked or even created from scratch. Sellers of oil and other items have been known to put a low-keyed note on their bills, again without your signature, that they will charge an annual 18 percent finance fee on bills unpaid within thirty days.
- Beware of trick clauses in big contracts. Read that fine print!
- Think about what you are buying. Most of us eat too much, and too much of the wrong things. Why create health problems and add to your medical bills?
- Don't try to keep up with your peers. It isn't sophisticated to show that you can throw money around wildly.
- Question your assumptions on long-term spending habits. If you take the time to write down your expenses, you well may find items that could be cut back or even dropped with no ill effects.

• Use advertising creatively to learn about new products or services that can save you money. Don't be manipulated by ads that may rate "A" as entertainment, but "F" as a basis for buying.

• And always remember: If it sounds too good to be true, it is. The warning, "Sign now, or it will be too late," should flash a big yellow (or outright red) light.

SHOP FOR GIFTS BY MAIL— DO IT RIGHT AND SAVE

A full 25 percent of our population is now shopping by catalogues and thereby eliminating the annoyances of waiting in lines, depending on indifferent-to-insolent store employees for service, and worrying about deliveries or carrying gifts home.

Why not you, too, a modern teenager? Why not avoid the swindlers who seek to gyp *you*, more than any other age-group, by street sales at holiday season of phony perfumes, watches, umbrellas? Why don't you join the "easy shoppers" now? Save on time, avoid poor service? Why not learn the rules for shopping by mail— which will become more and more routine as you become more and more an adult?

While I hadn't been noticing particularly, direct mail merchandising soared to a $60-billion-a-year business and is slated to balloon to a $600-billion-a-year industry by the end of the 1980s. And while in Chapter 11 you will be alerted to be on the watch for the con artists who use the mails, there are many more rules which will make shopping through the mails a joy and success, rather than a bitter letdown.

A first warning is: start your Christmas shopping at least a month ahead of your desired delivery date.

Take full advantage of the toll-free numbers provided by many companies to get your order in the works. And if you're cutting time close (which you well may try to do), you may find it's worth paying a little extra for your gifts to be shipped special delivery or by air express.

Make sure the mail-order house with which you are dealing gives you a "satisfaction guaranteed" provision in its ad or catalogue. If you have any questions about whether the company is reliable, or if its name is unfamiliar, check it through your local Better Business

Bureau or the Direct Marketing Association in New York. If you're still not satisfied, check your local consumer affairs office or the Federal Trade Commission.

Most big companies guarantee satisfaction, or "your money back." Another reassurance for you, a wary shopper, is a notice that the medium which runs the ad is backing up the mail order house with its own guarantees.

Always double-check the way you've filled out the order form to make sure that you have supplied all the necessary information and that it's readable. If you send in a sloppy form, the wrong merchandise easily may be sent or it may be delayed in reaching you.

Never pay by cash. Make a copy of the order and the mode of your payment (money order, personal check, credit card). Keep a record of all the pertinent information, as well as the catalogue or ad on which your order is based. The only way a mail-order house can stay in business is by being responsive to its customers and responsible in its methods and merchandise. Follow the rules and you'll find the orders easy to fill out and the deliveries satisfactory.

But back to my first warning: be fully aware of the time factor! Most mail-order houses specify that merchandise will be shipped within thirty days of receipt of the order. Read the catalogue with care to find out whether the delivery of the item or items you are ordering is guaranteed in sixty days or more. If, for any reason, shipment is delayed, you should be notified and given the option to cancel—with your money refunded within seven days of receipt of your cancellation notice.

Whether you have the merchandise sent to you or have it sent as a gift to a relative or a friend, it should be examined on receipt. If it is damaged, if something is missing, or if it is not what was ordered, notify the mail-order house immediately. If the company provides special return-mail forms for this possibility, use the forms, and return the articles by United Parcel Service, insured parcel post, or any other shipping means that will give you a receipt for your records.

Of course, before you make any decision to buy from an ad or catalogue, make sure all the information you need about the product is listed (depending on what it is): dimensions, weight, color, choices, packing, price, extras, shipping instructions, etc. And don't be caught with a gift you bought from a picture, which you discover late Christmas eve must be assembled from a bunch of sticks!

TRY THRIFT WITH YOUR GIFT

Of course, you'll buy Christmas/Chanukah gifts, and birthday and other gifts from time to time through the year.

Empty as your wallet may be right now, you'll respond to the spirit of the holiday season with cash or credit. How, then, do you spread the highest amount of cheer for the least money?

• Know your recipients. If you know their hobbies and interests, you can buy remaindered books on those subjects. If you know their favorite causes, make a donation in their names and send a card stating that it's been made; the charity will send an acknowledgment to them. The donation could be to a local hospital, the public library, each recipient's church, the women's movement, whatever. They all need money.

• If you cannot afford an expensive gift, work out a "theme gift" with several small parts. For instance, you could give the tennis buff some accessories such as headband, sunglasses, tennis balls, etc. Wrap each gift separately, then tie them together with a big bow.

• You can make people happy by giving them an I.O.U. for services, enclosed in a colorful envelope. You could promise to babysit for an evening of your recipient's choice, fix an electrical appliance, cook a gourmet meal, bake a cake.

• Personally baked goods are always welcome and cost very little. The same is true for homemade candies or a frozen gourmet dish, such as a frozen capon pie.

• Give some seldom used possession, such as an heirloom silver cup. This would go to a favorite relative, and the holiday season is a good time to give it (no money involved).

• Save by shopping for special and evocative items at flea markets and thrift shops. All you need to do is clean the items and wrap them in attractive gift paper.

• Shop at factory outlet shops in your area for bargain purchases. When you buy at any factory outlet or discount store, shop early in the morning before the holiday crowds arrive.

• A welcome gift might be cuttings from a treasured household plant. Start on this gift as soon as you can.

• Practical gifts always will be welcomed. Socks, dish towels, wine vinegar, travel umbrellas, or extra alarm clocks impressively wrapped are more thoughtful than impractical luxuries.

• Newspaper and magazine subscriptions are a relatively inexpensive gift that most people appreciate. Be sure to send your own card stating that you have ordered the gift subscription. Don't count on the publication's circulation department letting your recipient know during the holiday season.

• For last-minute cash for small gifts, cash in your penny collections. Most banks will now pay far more than $1 for every $1 in pennies brought in. They must be in paper rolls, of course.

WITH AN ENCYCLOPEDIA, LOOK SMART

Every year more than 1 million American families buy encyclopedias—still largely from sales representatives who come to their homes, despite a growing trend toward purchases in bookstores, shopping centers, theme parks, and other over-the-counter outlets. The books range from single-volume reference works, priced from $10 to $100, to multivolume sets costing as much as $1,000 or even more if they have leather bindings.

At the latter extreme, the purchase of an encyclopedia is likely to involve one of the largest single outlays your family will make after a home or a car. Yet this purchase—often a once-in-a-lifetime occasion—is not easy.

There are two main types of encyclopedias:

• A specialized encyclopedia that concentrates on a specific subject area, such as art, sports, science, music. In the field of music, for instance, your choices range from the one-volume *Harvard Dictionary of Music* (cost around $25) to the twenty-volume *Grove's Dictionary of Music and Musicians* ($2,000). What you buy will depend on how much you want to know and, of course, on how much you want to spend.

• General-interest encyclopedias are designed to provide the answers to questions in your business or personal life and to help you in your schoolwork. Here, too, the price range is extremely wide—

from less than $100 for a single-volume work or a limited multivolume set all the way up to the major multivolume sets that you or your parents usually buy on the installment plan, paying $25 to $50 a month.

Encyclopedias geared for children from the third or fourth grades through junior high school include *Britannica Junior* and the *New Book of Knowledge*. The age or school level of intended readers is a key factor.

Falling in the "young adult" category, but also suited for the entire family, are *World Book* and *Compton's*.

Adult references suitable for college students are *Encyclopedia Britannica, Encyclopedia Americana, Collier's,* and *Academic American*.

With the present "knowledge explosion"—knowledge doubling every ten years or so—it is now more important than ever before for people to have some access to knowledge they can readily retrieve and understand.

Factors to consider in choosing your encyclopedia (most major multivolume sets are generally not sold in stores) include:

• *Authority*. Nearly all reputable encyclopedias identify their editors, advisers, consultants, and contributors, together with their credentials, usually in the first volume, and all but the shortest articles are signed. Spot-check names in fields in which you may be an expert.

• *Accuracy*. Study articles on several subjects you know something about—a favorite sport or hobby or your profession—to see whether the information is factually correct, as well as sufficiently comprehensive.

• *Objectivity*. Check on controversial subjects—birth control, homosexuality, nuclear energy—to see that the presentation is well balanced and without any apparent bias.

• *Up-to-dateness*. Check the latest copyright date on the back of the encyclopedia's title pages. Do not confuse with printing dates, which may or may not indicate any significant revisions. Some encyclopedia publishers issue supplementary annual yearbooks, available at a small extra charge.

• *Also consider:* clarity of writing style; quality and reproduction of illustrations, photographs, maps, charts, and other graphics; and ease with which you can find facts through index and cross-references. Be sure the sales representative shows proper identification; be wary of any salesperson who pretends to be conducting a survey.

Even after you've signed a contract, you can still change your mind. A Federal Trade Commission rule covering in-home sales mandates a three-day "cooling off" period during which buyers of goods costing $25 or more may cancel their contracts. Be sure you get two copies of a "Notice of Cancellation" form. This is vital protection for you!

HOW TO USE A BARGAIN: A DESK DICTIONARY

If you are entering college or senior year in high school and you are asked to describe the DNA molecule, diagram a jet engine, or give the formula for a benzene ring, where would you look for the answers?

If you must find the answers to such questions as how far Mercury is from the earth, what the ten winning hands in a poker game are, or which language is spoken by more than any other on earth (would you believe Mandarin Chinese, by 585 million?), how would you tackle the assignment?

Or what is an azimuthal equidistant projection? An X-disease? Archimedes' screw? Rebus? Truth table?

You'll find the answers to the above and thousands of other similarly provocative questions in a familiar book that millions of you have at home, school, or office: the desk dictionary.

Today's dictionaries are rapidly becoming a passion of mine, for they are far from mere collections of words and definitions. (I actually have caught myself reading a dictionary as I would a top mystery story, even though I picked it up initially just to check a definition or spelling.) The ones I own cover a vast array of subjects, including medicine, chemistry, anatomy, geography, biology, and many more. If you, too, are looking for answers, consult your inexpensive desk dictionary before you sink money into one more textbook.

As a student struggling with expenses, you may be pleasantly surprised to find a dictionary—at an average cost of $10.95—a one-step reference book to backstop your studies.

In a good desk dictionary, for instance, you can get descriptions of the human heart, linear perspective, the diesel engine, all 104 chemical elements, including atomic weights and numbers, the runic alphabet, world money tables, longitude and latitude, human vertebrae, on and on.

Leafing through the book, you would find the complete metric system, a diagram of the human brain, dimensions of a basketball court, a complete list of radio frequencies, parts of an incandescent lamp, signs of the zodiac, the Braille alphabet, the months of the Muslim calendar.

It's been a long time since dictionaries contained only A-to-Z entries. While the A-to-Z vocabulary listing is the heart of any dictionary, within that listing—and also in the front and back—there is a wealth of information that you, as students, will find useful. The dictionary is now designed with students in mind.

As just one illustration, my edition of *Webster's New Collegiate* (the largest-selling desk dictionary in the world), contains, among other things, a separate list of some 2,600 biographical names. It includes 12,000 geographical names, 500 foreign words and phrases, a list of 2,600 American colleges and universities, a full page devoted to the alphabet tables of the Hebrew, Arabic, Greek, Russian, and Sanskrit languages.

Other desk dictionaries which I own have similar listings. The dictionary in front of me now, for example, describes and diagrams a hyperbola, defines PNR, RDF, AAUN, a toggle joint, mortise and tenon, a worm gear, illustrates a cross section of the inside of a pomegranate, and also shows what an amoeba looks like, as well as what a human cell appears to be.

A desk dictionary can be loosely defined as a hardcover book containing some 155,000 entries. Its average length is roughly 1,500 pages. There are many excellent desk dictionaries on the market now. Ask your librarian, teacher, parent, or bookstore owner which one suits your needs the best.

Item: In the mountains of northwestern Bohemia is a small town known in the early sixteenth century by its German name, Sankt Joachimsthal. When a silver mine was opened nearby to mint coins, the coins were known as joachimstaler, later shortened in German to taler, then known in the Dutch form of ''daler,'' then borrowed into English and into Spanish as "dollar." It was Thomas Jefferson who proposed that the dollar be the monetary unit of the United States, and so the Continental Congress resolved on July 6, 1785.

Source: The dictionary.

NEW RITE OF SUMMER: THE GARAGE SALE

Summertime, U.S.A. The air is filled with smoke from countless backyard barbecues, the whine of newly repaired power mowers, and cries of "Isn't that darling? And it's only $1!" at garage sales near and far. Less well-known a mere generation ago, except for occasional backyard bartering sessions of a few accumulated collectibles gathering dust and rust in attics and basements, garage sales are now big business.

Beginning with spring training and lasting to the final games of the college football season, garage sales have multiplied. The first sale usually takes place after the youngest child has flown the nest, and may well include bric-a-brac that has soared in value. This new rite cuts across all economic lines, from the tract homes of California to the affluent suburbs of New York. It truly has become a uniquely American phenomenon, circa 1980s.

Garage sales are becoming more sophisticated. Ads are run in local, regional, and even nearby big-city newspapers. Utility poles are plastered with copies of the announcement, which is written by the most proficient copywriter known to the family. Attendance can create traffic jams in normally quiet neighborhoods.

By summer's end, millions of Americans will have initiated or participated in a garage sale. For many, it will provide hundreds of dollars of needed vacation funds or expense money for family essentials.

If you shop at garage sales, concentrate on tools, yard and garden equipment (which can be restored to top condition easily), housewares, and furniture.

You may uncover an occasional antique, but don't count on it. The organized search for valuable antiques has become so intense that most homeowners already know the value of those they possess.

But, do look for inexpensive records. And you'll discover big values in old book collections if you look hard (older editions of famous encyclopedias or dictionaries, for example).

Clothing can also be a terrific buy.

For all of you who are buyers, here are some suggestions:

• Arrive early to get a parking place as well as first pick at the complete selection.

• Be prepared to negotiate. Have a good idea of what you want and, if the quality is good, be ready to make an offer—or, if you think the price is fair, to buy. If the item requires a major cash outlay, make your offer, advise the seller you will call back in a few hours, and leave your phone number in case someone else enters a bid in your absence.

• Have cash in your pocket for your purchases, and be ready to haul away whatever you buy.

• If you can, make a day of it. Check community papers and cover several sales in a morning or afternoon. And realize from the start that there are no returns and no refunds.

Are you planning to hold a garage sale or help your folks arrange one? Here are your guides:

• Select your date well in advance, skipping holidays and dates of big weekend events that might be televised (the World Series, opening games of the National Football League).

• Investigate all local regulations governing sales, parking, etc. If, for example, local zoning restricts parking in your area, include this fact and suggest alternatives in your local ads.

• Price sale items realistically. Visit other garage sales and get yardsticks on pricing. Ticket your items low enough to get rid of them within a few days. Cut your prices on the second day, maybe by as much as 50 percent.

• Arrange items by category; mark them clearly. Check whether sales taxes apply and figure out how to record them. Separate the good stuff from the "white elephant" merchandise.

• Consider serving coffee to enhance a feeling of goodwill. Encourage your shoppers not only by accurate directions to your sale but also by your pleasant attitude. In short, use grace and common sense.

EVEN YOUR ODDS: SWEEPSTAKES AND CONTESTS

To all of us television viewers and newspaper readers, it often appears that companies compete strenuously to offer the most lavish contests awarding millions of dollars in cash and prizes. Every Sunday supplement carries details of a new contest; magazine ads regularly feature sweepstakes; and radio and television programs are punctuated by ads announcing the latest, most rewarding contest yet.

Playing these games and contests can be a lucrative hobby. Cash, cars and gasoline, travel, homes, electronic entertainment equipment, and lesser prizes entice millions of us each year into filling out contest blanks. Sooner or later, just about everyone is lured by the promise of big winnings.

Some devotees of contests have won (and win) as many as fifty prizes a year. More than $100 million in cash and prizes are awarded via approximately 500 national events annually.

Because of the huge number of contestants and wide variety of entries, the odds are heavily against your winning. But multiple entries are usually allowed, and there is clear evidence that a well-planned strategy can strengthen your chances of coming out a winner.

To assist you, for instance, there are now at least a dozen contest newsletters—all of which give you valuable guidelines.

Here are suggestions to help you plot your next campaign:

• Remember that a *contest* may require some element of aptitude, such as providing a correct answer or composing a limerick. A *sweepstakes* requires only that you submit an entry form (luck over skill.)

• Follow the rules to the letter. If the instructions tell you to print, don't write in longhand. If a card size is specified, use it. Don't send a 4-by-5 index card if the rule specifies a 3-by-5-inch entry.

• Pick entries requiring skills over luck, assuming you have at least some skill. You may do better if you can write a jingle in a contest where there are fewer entrants. Research the product you are targeting. Learn as much as you can about its features. Read the instructions carefully for helpful clues.

• Enter on a regular basis. Be alert to new sweepstakes and contests. In addition to watching TV and reading newspapers, observe grocery shelves and supermarket and store windows. Submit multiple entries.

• Keep an expense record. If you plan to make this a regular habit, you can deduct such expenses as stationery and postage from your federal income tax when you win.

• Thank the sponsors if you are a winner. With enough appreciative responses, they may devise a similar contest—at which you have become skilled.

• Each state has laws regarding sweepstakes. If you have questions about your state's laws, write to the attorney general.

11

TEENAGERS ON GUARD!

The Rackets That Can (and Do) Swindle You

CONTENTS

MUGGERS, PICKPOCKETS, AND
PURSE-SNATCHERS

Ten Ways to Thwart a Mugger

I've been mugged and had my purse yanked from my arm at one of New York City's fanciest corners: Park Avenue and 51st Street. One result is that I have tried to learn and obey the rules to reduce the chances that I again will be a victim.

Below are ten valuable rules to protect you in what the chairman of Burns International Security Services, Inc., calls "the age of the mugger, the criminal who turns a street robbery into a vicious act of violence."

1. *Where you walk.* Always walk near the curb to avoid passing close to dark doorways. Don't take shortcuts—day or night— through alleys, backyards, empty buildings, or parking lots—a habit you, a teenager, adopt almost naturally. If you are in a dangerous neighborhood or fear you're being followed, walk down the center of the street if possible.

Familiarize yourself with the areas you walk through frequently and note which stores, restaurants, or gas stations are open late at night. Run to the nearest one if a mugger approaches. Walk on well-lighted, well-traveled streets, even if it makes your journey longer. Don't stray from the crowd in any public place and don't—as a young girl, particularly—window-shop at night.

2. *Walking technique.* Walk briskly, appear confident, act as though you know exactly where you're going. Don't walk slowly or appear distracted, or with your head stuck in a newspaper or book.

Watch the people who approach you, and avoid being confronted. Move out onto the street if necessary, or step into a store. When you walk at night take a companion or, even better, travel in a group. Be particularly careful on a Friday—payday for many workers and muggers, too.

3. *Keep alert.* Make sure you're not being followed when you get off a bus or subway. Be very careful after leaving a bank or store where you've just showed money in your purse or wallet or just cashed a check. Don't be lured to unsafe places by strange sounds;

hurry away and alert the police. Always carry enough change for carfare and an emergency phone call.

4. *Caution on subways.* Wait for your train near the change booth or turnstile, not way down the platform. Never enter an empty subway car by yourself. Try to sit near a conductor or transit policeman.

Avoid subway cars full of overly boisterous teenagers near your own age. Note the location of the emergency cord. Never fall asleep on a subway!

5. *Danger in elevators.* Be patient, wait for your car. Stairways are notorious hangouts for muggers. If you suspect someone in the car when the door opens, walk away. Don't enter an elevator with someone who doesn't get off when the car reaches the main floor. When you do get on an elevator, stand by the control panel and if attacked, hit the alarm and as many buttons as you can so the door will open at the nearest floor.

6. *Safety behind the wheel.* In congested areas, drive with your doors locked and your windows raised so no one can reach in. If someone tries to break in at a red light, drive through the light and sound your horn. Always look inside your car, especially in the back seat, before getting in.

7. *An armed attacker.* If you're confronted with a weapon, don't provoke an attack. If only your money is at stake, experts urge you to give it up. Keep calm; the mugger may be easily excited if he is drunk or drugged. If possible, observe your attacker so you can describe him later to police. A description of his shoes can be especially helpful since criminals rarely change them after committing a crime.

8. *When to resist.* If you are attacked, don't fight back unless you're convinced you have to fight for your life, a decision you must make instinctively. What you decide will depend on your personality, sex, physical condition (you already have your age in your favor), the size of your opponent, whether he is or is not armed. Don't turn a robbery into a fight for life.

9. *If you must fight.* If a mugger attacks despite your cooperation, your best defense, if possible, is to break away and run for safety. But if you must fight, go all the way.

Do anything to hurt the mugger. Attack him where he is most vulnerable—the groin, eyes, throat. Bite, scratch, kick, and scream. There are no rules of etiquette in a street fight for your life.

10. *Weapons.* Law enforcement officers advise you not to rely on

lethal weapons—guns and knives—to defend yourself. They're too easily taken away and used against you.

Other "weapons," however, may help. A police-type whistle or compressed air siren is good to have. A hat pin, ballpoint pen, key ring in the fist, nail file, or umbrella also can hurt, shock, or scare away a potential mugger—and perhaps save your life.

Coping with Pickpockets and Purse-Snatchers

Have you ever experienced the heart-tugging feeling of reaching for your wallet or purse only to discover that it's gone? If so, you are among the millions of Americans who each year are victimized by pickpockets and purse-snatchers.

To avoid becoming a pickpocket's prey, you first must know how each type operates. One type of sneak thief deftly slips your wallet from your clothing; another specializes in taking wallets from women's purses; a third simply snatches a woman's handbag and then runs away with it.

Here are fifteen basic precautions and safeguards for you:

1. If you are a man and can do so, carry your wallet in the front pocket of your pants, or your inside jacket or shirt pocket rather than your back hip pocket. (Pickpockets don't like to face their victims.) If you must carry your wallet in your back pocket, at least have the pocket buttoned. You also might place a pocket comb in the wallet sideways so the ends stick out on both sides. With the comb teeth pointed upward, it's virtually impossible for a thief to remove it.

2. If you must carry an unusually large amount of cash, consider buying a money belt with a zippered pocket on the inside. (For a vacation trip, as an example.)

3. Always be on guard if a stranger approaches you for any reason: to ask for a light, directions, the correct time, etc. Most pickpockets work in teams. The first man or woman stops and distracts you while the other bumps against you and lifts your wallet. Watch out, too, for the type of pickpocket who spills your coffee or drink and swipes your wallet while brushing you off and apologizing for his clumsiness.

4. When you take out your wallet in a store, bank, or other pub-

lic place, never let strangers see your cash or a string of credit cards. Carry your credit cards in a separate case, so they're not exposed every time you open your wallet.

5. If you see a sign in any public place that says "Beware of Pickpockets," do not reach to check your most valuable possession. You'll only locate it for any pickpocket who's watching.

6. If you're being followed by a person you suspect is after your wallet or purse and there's no policeman or friendly crowd around, drop your valuables in a mailbox to protect them.

7. When you enter or leave a theater, sporting event, transportation terminal, etc., secure all your valuables. Button up your clothing and clutch your purse tightly. A congested area is the pickpocket's best-loved environment.

8. In a supermarket, always keep your purse on your arm and never (as so many women do) put your purse in a shopping cart or open shopping bag. These actions merely invite the pursesnatcher.

9. If your purse *is* stolen in a store, demand that the store personnel help you find it. A thief will often remove the cash and discard the bag inside the store.

10. Carry your clutch-type purse upside down and open. If someone grabs it, the contents will then spill on the ground.

11. Hang your high-risk shoulder bag from your shoulder and keep your hand and arm on the outside of the bag. Outside pockets are particularly vulnerable. Generally, it is not wise to carry a shoulder bag with the strap across your body. You could be seriously injured if a determined purse snatcher grabs the bag and runs with it.

12. In a snack bar, movie, etc., always hold your purse in your lap. If you place your purse on the seat beside you, a thief behind you may tip the seat so the purse falls to the floor. The thief then will pick it up and courteously return it to you—minus the wallet.

13. Take special care when riding subway trains. Many women lose their purses when a thief reaches out the window of a departing car and snatches the purse of a woman on the platform. Thieves leaving a subway car will also grab the purses of women sitting near the doors.

14. To minimize your loss should a thief be successful, never carry more money than you need and carry only the credit cards

you expect to use that day. Some people carry their money in several different places.

15. If your purse is stolen, notify the police immediately and contact the issuers of all your credit cards and licenses to protect against charges to you for unauthorized use of your credit cards. Don't be fooled by calls to your home advising you that your cards have been found and are being mailed to you; this just gives thieves more time to use the cards. Keep at home a complete list of your credit card and license numbers and the addresses and phone numbers of whom to contact.

CON MEN—HOW TO BEAT THEIR "BARGAINS"

Probably the biggest unreported crime in the United States is the so-called confidence game. It also is among the most difficult kind of crime to control because you, the victim, usually become an unwitting accomplice and you, the victim, often are eagerly seeking "bargains."

Although the variations of the confidence game are limited only by the con man's imagination—and he belongs to a notoriously inventive breed—the favorite scam involves the selling of "bargain" merchandise.

A stranger approaches you and offers to sell you a brand-new color TV set for $50. When you ask where it came from, the man just winks—a lure in itself.

You pay him the $50 and he tells you to meet him at a local warehouse. You wait for him, but he never shows up.

What recourse do you have now? If you go to the police with a tale of being robbed by a man who offered to sell you a new color TV at one-tenth its retail value, you're in for some embarrassing questions. Most victims do nothing.

Or you see on a street corner a person offering watches, or jewelry, or perfume, or umbrellas (particularly on a day when the rain is coming down in torrents), or snowshoes, or boots (on another day when an unexpected blizzard dumps a foot of snow)—at bargain prices. You stop.

It's a few weeks before Christmas and you're broke (as usual). You look at a watch, a perfect gift for your mother or girlfriend and it is a bargain at the price being quoted. The confidence man's spiel is intriguing. You buy, wrap the watch as a gift, give it proudly—and find that within a few hours or days at most, your gift is discarded as worthless.

The same goes for the jewelry, which turns out to be junk—although at least it's attractive junk. It's no bargain at the price you paid.

As for the perfume, it does have a scent similar to the fragrance of a famous name and it is in a bottle that looks the same to an uneducated eye such as yours. But that's about where the similarities end.

The umbrella turns inside out and becomes useless before you even get home. The snowshoes and boots tear, leak, even fall off.

If your reaction to all this is "I would never be so foolish," don't be so sure. The key elements in the confidence game are gullibility and honesty—and the crucial requirement for its success is winning the victim's confidence.

How can you protect yourself from confidence men? Above all others, follow these rules: if a stranger offers you something valuable at a ridiculously low price, be suspicious. If the person requests money in advance, insist on notifying the police. The con man usually will disappear fast.

GETTING NOTHING FOR SOMETHING

Beware the Sting of a Free Loan Offer

If you were offered an interest-free loan of $1,500 for three months—ninety days during which you easily could invest the money at whatever return you can get today, and that rate is far, far above zero!—would you grab it?

A veteran consumer finance firm headquartered in Des Moines, Iowa, dangled this financial goodie off-and-on before new customers for months. The company operated in approximately thirty-five states, was a respectable and savvy company, and it attracted thousands with ads promising: "Interest-free loan! Special get-acquainted holiday offer lets you borrow up to $1,500 without interest for three months."

A free loan is tempting at any time. With the cost of borrowing at high levels at the time, it was close to irresistible.

How, then, can consumer finance companies such as the one described above extend loans, even for so short a span as ninety days, interest-free? Here's the tale behind such consumer finance ad campaigns:

• The company's "interest-free" loan is available only to new and "qualified" customers. The company retains the right to determine who is and who is not "qualified." Its goal is the customer who in the past has rarely even thought of visiting a finance company, much less actually used one.

• The short-term loan is truly "free" only to the borrower who can repay it in full within the allotted three months. In general, you would be in the group who cannot raise this much cash in so short a time. Thus the terms of the offer, which seem so appealing across-the-board at first glance, in themselves help to limit the loans to the category of borrower who usually doesn't need loans in the first place.

• If a customer fails to repay the interest-free loan within the ninety-day period, the finance company levies finance charges on the full amount of the loan from day one. In fact, the loan program is so structured that all participants sign regular installment loan contracts when they accept the "interest-free" money. In effect, they are paying a finance charge each month along with a portion of the principal. At the end of the ninety days, when they repay the full amount of their loans, the finance charges are refunded.

An estimated 15 to 20 percent of the 15,000 customers who obtained interest-free loans during a recent Thanksgiving–Christmas–New Year's holiday season did not repay the full amounts of the loans within the three months. These borrowers then became regular finance company customers, paying the highest rates legally permitted on their loans.

The rates which finance companies charge vary, depending on the state in which they conduct business. Because they customarily cater to higher-risk borrowers than do banks, credit unions, and other financial institutions—which is their stated function in the money markets—finance companies usually charge much higher rates than these other lenders. They also frequently impose higher finance charges on the individual seeking a small loan (which could be you) than on the borrower obtaining a big sum of money.

There is no disputing the value of the consumer finance company's funds to the higher-risk, small borrower—which is the reason the companies have flourished for so long a period and have grown to occupy so significant a place among our lending institutions. But there are few, if any, free lunches in real life—especially from consumer finance companies in business to make profits from their operations.

The very offer of a loan at zero interest should arouse your skepticism. The source of such generous loans should raise your cynicism to a high notch. Investigate every line of small print and read between the lines as well before you *even consider* accepting.

Advance-Fee Credit Card Companies

Establishing a credit rating takes time, an employment history, and good money management. But "companies" do exist to help you bypass these potential obstacles when you want to get a credit card such as MasterCard or Visa.

There are advance-fee credit card promotions that advertise on TV or radio, in classified ads or through direct mail, to tempt you with promises of easy credit, regardless of your income and previous credit experience. Catch: the company that collects your money to get the card does not issue the card itself.

A typical promotion will require that you pay in advance to learn more about the offering, join the plan, and obtain each credit card. For your money, which can total as much as $150, you may receive information about credit, credit card laws and regulations, and credit-granting institutions. Or perhaps the ad claims that you may be entitled to one or two cards for your money.

These promotions can be frauds.

• Frequently, the ad or literature does not disclose all fees, including the annual amount charged by the credit-granting institution for each card. The offering often fails to mention that you must establish an account at the institution (such as a savings or commercial bank) to obtain a Visa or MasterCard. These are known as secured credit cards. Failure to disclose these fees is a serious omission and signals the need to investigate thoroughly before you send in a dime.

Before you send your check or money order, be sure you understand all the fees involved. Do you know exactly what you will receive in exchange for your initial investment?

• Many of these offerings may mislead you because they convey the impression that anyone paying the initial fee is likely to obtain a card.

• Many neglect to state clearly that you will most likely have to pass some kind of credit check by the credit-granting institution.

• Some companies are simply selling information about how to obtain a credit card. The information may be merely a booklet which describes credit, summarizes state and federal laws and regulations, and lists credit-granting institutions.

• Check with a local bank to see whether the bank cooperates with any of these companies, or if they've even heard of the one which has caught your attention.

• Ask the bank, too, whether it will grant credit to a teenager, such as you, with no credit history, according to the conditions described in the promo.

• As with any advance-fee company, proceed with caution before you give them any money. Double-check that there is a money-back guarantee.

Self-Help Books and Gizmos

Mail-order books, exercise gadgets, creams, and potions—all promising ecstasy through self-improvement—continue to clog the post office. Capitalizing on the average person's anxiety and the young man's or woman's disappointment with appearance, health, romantic success, and other vital concerns, these books and ''treatments'' feed expectations they can't possibly fulfill.

Do you see yourself in these fantasies?

• You can't seem to lose that last ten pounds, or you want to distribute them someplace else—like your chest or biceps.
• Maybe you're shy and uncomfortable around strangers. You despair of ever having a date.
• Or you're ready and willing to marry a millionaire, if only you knew where and how to meet one.

Then one day, you flip through a magazine or catch an ad on late-night television that promises quick, painless success. The ads say something like:

"Melt away fat in hours! No diet, no exercise! Eat, drink, and be merry, and still lose!"

"I lost 25 pounds in two weeks and transformed my life!"

"I changed from a mousy, unexciting girl to a sensuous, passionate woman in just 10 days! Now I can share my secret with you closet femmes fatales!"

"Tired of those laughs in the locker room? I was, too, until I learned these easy tricks and added inches to my chest and arms. Guess who's laughing now?"

"Ladies! Add 5 to 10 inches to your bosom in two weeks! Beautiful, shapely curves at long last! Wear bikinis with pride! Brand-new, scientific, and permanent treatment!"

Sound familiar, don't they? Yet these are hypothetical ads, dreamed up after checking out the back pages of some national magazines. Each item claims the latest, or most advanced, or most secret, or most successful treatment *ever*.

When you finish one of these ads, you will be asked to send from $5 to $15 (plus postage and sales tax) for your opportunity to read or try the product. But what you actually get is a story of the author's experience plus opinion, or a useless and flimsy elastic strip, or a smelly cream.

Yet you thought you were buying a self-help guide, right?

The ad didn't specify that you would be reading someone's personal experience and opinions.

Go back and look at the fine print. You will rarely see an ad state in boldface type "author's experience," or "in the opinion of the writer." The ad you see or hear may simply imply success going far beyond the contents of the book or manual. Wouldn't it be wonderful if those claims were universally true? The free descriptive booklets promoted in some of these ads won't enlighten you further. They simply tease you into opening your wallet with additional stories and extravagant claims.

Now that you know the ads promise more than they deliver, how do you protect yourself when you're still interested in the subjects—your body and your love life?

• Study the whole ad, not just the headline and pictures. The fine print might contradict, or at least qualify, the claims in the headlines. And who are those people in the pictures, anyway?

• Remember that the author's experience and the testimonials from satisfied readers (usually identified as "G.Z., Iowa," or something like that) nearly always reflect the most successful results. They are not typical of the average experience.

• Realize that any book offering a "cure" or "permanent treatment" for a disease that has baffled science is a joke that trades cruelly on public fears, pain, and wishes. When research scientists find a cure for arthritis, or even the common cold, it will be front-page news.

• Leave medical problems to medical experts. Details of the suffering and treatment of one person usually don't apply to someone else.

• Beware of inflated claims to deflate your body. Unfortunately for many of us, and despite the claims of the "quickie" diet books, the best way to lose weight and keep it off remains a balanced diet, fewer calories, and exercise under professional supervision.

• Promoters know that dissatisfied customers rarely bother to ask for their money back. If you're one of them, don't be too lazy, or too timid, to complain. Just be prepared to wait for that check and to have to ask for it, again and again.

• As the cliche goes, if a claim sounds too good to be true, it is!

Get-Rich-Quick Books and Schemes

Ad campaigns for miracle cures and dramatic weight-loss plans shrink in comparison to those for get-rich-quick books and schemes.

"Obtain riches beyond your wildest dreams!" they proclaim. "Stay in debt and make huge profits!" "Erase your debts like magic." "Invest just $10 a month and earn $125,000!"

Do you feel a tug on your wallet when you read these feverish (and often conflicting) headlines? Everyone wants more money. We all—including you, a teenager—dream of outwitting the banks, the government, and our current pile of bills. That powerful incentive lurks behind the popular self-help come-on.

While the above "ads" are fakes, the real ones don't differ very much. Authors can write whatever they want—a precious freedom guaranteed by the Constitution. As long as ads for these books accurately reflect the contents, there is little basis for challenging the advertising when each statement in the ad is factually accurate. The problem is that, lumped together, all the testimonials, headlines, and illustrations con you into thinking that you, too, can get rich this way.

The spectacular success of all varieties of mail-order self-help books has induced subsidiaries of some nationally known companies to cash in on this trend and market what might gently be called "questionable" books. Backed by money and experience, these companies hire writers and produce and publicize books that pander to your daydreams, manipulate your fears and frustrations, and seduce you with extravagant claims.

If your fantasies threaten to overtake your common sense and skepticism when you're confronted with these silly claims, remember:

• Anyone in his/her right mind with a scheme to make zillions will not sell it to you, a total stranger, for $5.95 plus tax and postage.

• Basically, there is no quick and easy—not to mention foolproof—way to make money. You will have to earn it by work and smart investment.

• Beware of claims of preposterous returns for minimal, if frequent, investment ("only $15 a week yields $125,000," etc.).

• Stop short when you read a claim such as: "No experience or financial wizardry needed." Spend your money on a lottery ticket instead. Your odds are better.

• Don't be lulled by an author's claim of outwitting the banks and authorities or, for that matter, of disclosing a great secret. For instance, someone who trumpets, "Let me be the first to teach you debt is profitable," is preaching nothing new. The economies of the Western world have in recent decades been built on a vast foundation of public and private debt. So, even though each statement in the debt ad may be accurate on its own, together they mislead you.

• Only one person gets rich from these books, newsletters, and assorted schemes. The author/promoter should produce a testimonial that reads: "I grossed a fortune in just six months. I wrote a get-rich-quick manual, slapped a $10 price tag on it, advertised in national magazines, and sold it to 100,000 gullible people. Now, for my sequel. . . .''

Phony Sales

''Digital clock radio, manufacturer's suggested list price $99.95, our sale price $65.95!''

''One week only! Brand new cameras, our price only $79.95 —$150 value!''

''Gold chains $49.95! Must sacrifice! Value to $99.95!''

These particular ads are phonies, but they represent accurately the widespread deceptive advertising practices in print and on the airwaves: ads for nonexistent savings based on false comparative prices.

If you're asking why the print and broadcast media don't police ads to eliminate these insidious deceptions, the answer is simple: they lack the money, time, knowledge, and inclination to monitor and double-check each and every ad. Essentially, you must rely on yourself to bring the same tools—common sense, alertness, skepticism—to ads that you bring to any store, flea market, garage sale, or other shopping situation.

Look at those hypothetical ads again, starting with the sale on digital clocks. The claim ''based on the manufacturer's suggested list price'' is among the most frequently misused by retailers attempting to claim savings on many categories of merchandise. Often—not always, but often enough—the saving is nonexistent because neither the advertiser nor the competition sells the merchandise at ''list price.''

Or consider the ad for a camera in which the store offers a 50 percent saving during a week-long sale. The claim, ''Our price $79.95 —$150 value!'' grabs your attention. The word ''value'' should mean the price at which the identical camera is being offered, at the same time, by other competitors in the same trade area. If you check around and find competitors offering the same camera at the same price, where is the saving?

And those lovely gold chains aren't described fully, are they? The original price was not mentioned, nor is there a description of lengths, weights, and types of links. Deliberately vague ads mean you should be even more cautious than usual: some of the merchandise may not be on sale *at all*.

"Freebies"

A long-standing deception swirls around the word "free," as in "free gift with minimum purchase," "free parking," and the like.

The word "free" means unconditionally given—no strings attached! When a business promotes a gift with the qualification that you have to buy something to be eligible, the details should be clear to you, the reader or viewer. Be sure that the regular prices stay the same, that there is no reduction in the quality and quantity of the merchandise, and that the "free offer" is temporary. If the offer drags on endlessly, the alleged "freebie" is not. You did not get something for nothing.

A common variant: stores that have continuous sales on identical items and don't identify themselves as discount outlets.

• Be suspicious of any company that matches this description—you not only don't save money, you might even pay extra.

• Check the validity of an ad campaign by collecting the store's print ads for several weeks. If the "sale" lasts indefinitely or if the merchandise costs the same after the "sale" ends, look elsewhere.

• Beware of stores that have "going out of business" signs plastered on their windows month after month. These stores renew their leases and restock their shelves while their owners skip to the bank—with your money. But, first they gyp you. You may even bargain with the clerk to "reduce" the price and still wind up paying more than a discount or department store would charge.

• Be especially wary of this kind of store when you are traveling. These swindlers concentrate on customers (teenagers especially) who don't know the city or town and have no sense of prices away from home. And when you are on vacation, relaxed, and prepared to indulge yourself, it's easy for them to separate you from your money.

WHEN GETTING AHEAD CAN
PUT YOU BEHIND

Scholarship Matching Services

With college costs climbing relentlessly to record highs, and sources of financial aid declining to new lows in recent years, you, a teenager eager for a college career, can despair of affording higher education. Having heard of companies that offer—for a fee—a computer search for scholarships and financial assistance, you wonder whether they really do match students with sources of money. How do they work?

In general, they feed information you provide—a detailed profile of your economic, academic, and financial qualifications—to a computer data base. As a farfetched example, if you are a blond, brown-eyed aspiring astronaut, someone somewhere may have left a scholarship for a person who fits that description. Since it's so obscure, only the computer knows about it, and that's the lure of these services. There are so many sources of financial aid it's hard to research them all. After you receive your list of sources (usually between ten and twenty) you apply for each scholarship yourself. The service provides names and addresses only.

You can expect to pay up to $70 for these services. Is it worth it? Figure out the answer for yourself:

- The service provides customers with information about funding sources for which the deadline has passed.
- Or the consumer is ineligible (not being blond, brown-eyed, etc.)
- One of the sources, for which you paid, is the financial aid office of the school you plan to attend, or another, equally well-known source.
- The promotional material implies that only sources of funds for which no repayment is required will be called up from the computer.
- They sell information you could get from your school guidance counselor, the library, or financial aid office of your college.

If you plan to use one of these scholarship funding companies, investigate its claims thoroughly. Contact your local Better Business Bureau and ask about the reputation and success rate of the company you want to use. Many are reputable and supply valuable information to their customers. Don't be ripped off by the fringe of swindlers that blotches the reputation of the entire field.

Talent Promoters and Assorted Star-Makers

So you want to be a star. You're in your teens, you've been told since you were a baby how pretty/beautiful/handsome you are, you believe what you've been told—and you're ready to start.

Hundreds of firms offer their services to teenagers just like you who yearn to work as professional actors and actresses. Most of them—talent marketing companies, casting services, talent agencies—are reputable and perform the services they advertise, but some, trading on your hopes and fantasies, lure you with flattering promises, take your money—and run. How can you, the newcomer, recognize these con artists?

Imagine a company that places ads in shoppers' weeklies and small local papers, on late-night television, and on radio, promoting this deal: pay $700 and they will put your photograph in a book they send to agents and producers who seek new faces and talent.

Agents and producers, in fact, never look at these promotions, if they make it past the secretary.

Next, the newcomer (you?) goes to the company's office and willingly writes out a check or pays the cash amount asked. You are then instructed to have lots of photographs taken at a special photographer's studio. You will pay for this, too, of course.

Never be conned: you should be able to choose your own photographer, and you do not need hundreds, or even dozens, of photographs when you are starting out.

Weeks—or months—later, you ask the company why you haven't heard a word from anybody. Why haven't you been offered a job?

Later still, when you have small children of your own, and you are extravagantly proud of their looks and accomplishments, don't be a sucker for a smooth-talking ''agent'' who approaches you in a shopping mall and says that, for only $500, he can arrange to place your child on a TV show or in an ad.

The real talent on display here belongs to these marketing companies, which swindle you out of money for no services at all: pure loss to you, pure profit for them.

Some variations on this theme:

• A company sends you a letter urging that you mail in your screenplay, outline or concept, plus $100 to have your offering transformed into a synopsis to be sent to movie studios. Since you just happen to have a great idea for a movie, you jump.

Save your money. Studios and producers will never read anything not submitted by an agent.

• You write song lyrics but don't know how to compose music. You hear of a company that, for a mere $400 per tune, not only develops a song but will record it on an album with eleven other such songs, and send you one copy. In addition, the company promises royalties from the record, which will be sent to dj's and radio stations, if it sells more than 25,000 copies.

The company needs at least ten or so patsies to put out one record, and you can be certain nothing will be done to promote it. Unless you and the other patsies have extremely large families, you will never see a dime and will have done nothing to advance your career.

• Your passion is invention, and you think you've come up with a classic. You see an ad about a company that takes worthy inventions and markets them, after the inventor puts up some seed money—say, $5,000.

What the company's ad neglects to tell you is that it can't do patent research, so your gizmo may already be patented and developed elsewhere. The company also fails to tell you that it doesn't actually manufacture, distribute, or otherwise develop your grand invention.

The key to each of these schemes is advertising. Can you think of any reason why a talent agent, music promoter, or screenwriter's agent needs a lot of your money to market your talent or creation? In general, only the phonies advertise, especially in throwaways and non-trade papers, to separate eager fame-and-fortune seekers from their money.

Success in creative endeavors requires talent, hard work—and some luck. The phonies live off people who can't or won't wait, or who refuse to assess their abilities realistically.

Guidelines to protect you, the teenager:

• Be suspicious of any ad that requires your money to develop your special talent or interest; or any ad that promises success and fame in exchange for your check.

• Don't rush. Before signing any deal, check with all reliable sources, starting with the Better Business Bureau or your local Consumer Protection Agency. An honest promoter will not force you to sign a contract immediately.

• Don't be afraid to ask questions about how the advertiser will use all that money. How successful is it? Can you verify its report? Can you speak with someone similar to yourself?

• Do some research—go to the library, talk to people in the business.

• Don't pay any advance fee that is more than you can afford to lose. Some businesses may charge a registration fee, but it should be a reasonable amount.

• Don't be fooled by flattery. These businesses want to make money; you don't have to make it easy for them.

• Comparison shop, just as you would for a car or stereo system. The Yellow Pages and trade publications can steer you to similar companies, and you may find a better deal.

• Find out from a state or local consumer agency whether this kind of business is licensed or otherwise regulated. Get a copy of any guidelines.

• Don't sign anything, especially a check, until you're absolutely certain you understand what you will get for your money and you're assured of a money-back guarantee.

Model Agencies

• A teenager in Nogales, Arizona, answered a "help wanted" ad placed by a New York modeling agency in the local paper. After mailing off her picture and a registration fee, she cherished the hope they would send for her, at her expense, and launch her on a modeling career.

• After months of waiting, a seventeen-year old girl in Brooklyn finally received seventy-two color slides from her modeling manager with instructions to enlarge thirty of them to 8-by-10 inch glossies. And then, suddenly, the "manager" disappeared, along with the several hundred dollars the girl had sunk into "developing" her career.

• A young woman of similar age in Atlanta phoned the local Better Business Bureau after reading an announcement in the newspaper that a representative from a New York modeling agency was interviewing candidates in a hotel suite downtown. Did the agency exist? Was the agent on a genuine scouting trip? A few phone calls to New York determined that yes, the ad, the agency, and the offer were genuine.

Every year, hundreds of aspiring models fall victim to ads in the "help wanted" section of the paper that read something like this:

Model M/F, immediate openings for fashion types/real people/commercial. F (5′2″–5′11″) & M (5′6″–6′2″). Also children.

What this "bafflegab" means is that any person who yearns for a career as a model should watch out. Where is the mention of an actual job? Exactly what are the openings for? Study the height requirements. How many young women do you know who are shorter than 5′2″ or taller than 5′11″? Likewise, do you see many men shorter than 5′6″ or taller than 6′2″ (forget about the Los Angeles Lakers!)? Doesn't that height range suggest the majority of people? Finally, and most curious of all, where does the ad mention anything about appearance, weight, or photogenic quality?

The would-be successors to Brooke Shields who respond to these ads can expect to pay—and keep on paying—for the following:

• On arrival, you'll hand over a $10 to $20 registration or consultation fee. If you're quite short, they'll say, "That's okay, you make a fine character type."

• A portfolio. "That costs $400, but we'll split it with you because you've got a future!"

• You need to take some classes: $25 for makeup, $25 for hairstyle, $25 for walking and, you guessed it, $25 for body language.

- And, of course, you need a composite—a card that shows you in three or four poses and which you leave at job interviews called "go-sees."

Now. . . . It's weeks after your first visit to the agency, you're almost broke, and you haven't worked at all. What sort of job is this?

"We never guaranteed you work," the agency says, and it's true.

Some preliminary legwork on your part will save you the hassles and heartbreaks of this kind of experience.

- Recognize the telltale signs of a scam: advance registration fee; nonspecific ads in the "help wanted" column; and pressure. Pressure to leave a cash deposit and pressure to sign on the dotted line.
- Additional clues: the promoter schedules appointments for after work hours and away from an office, avoids answering your specific questions, expects an immediate deposit for your photographs, and requires the balance before you even see them.
- Avoid an utterly negative experience by checking out the firm's performance record with local consumer protection agencies or the Better Business Bureau—before you make another move.
- Be realistic. Modeling, as a business, is incredibly hard to break into. Be honest with yourself and determine whether you meet the stringent physical and photogenic requirements. If not, try to console yourself that most people don't. But if you are one of the fortunate few who might, write to the New York Better Business Bureau and request the BBB's subject report on modeling.

Private Employment Agencies: What to Look For

As a teenager, the odds are high you will go to an employment agency as a primary source of jobs early in your career. And thousands of employment agencies place ads in newspapers from coast to coast to which millions of jobseekers turn each week. Most agencies attempt to match job-hunters with jobs they really want; satisfied clients and companies mean repeat business, essential to an agency's success. Some agencies even specialize in particular career fields.

Almost all states require that employment agencies be licensed;

many limit the fees agencies can charge and otherwise regulate their practices. In some states, agencies charge clients a percentage of a year's salary, calculated on base (not take-home) earnings. The amount is usually between 5 and 10 percent. Agencies also may charge the company for finding you, the perfect candidate.

At few times in your life will you be under such stress as during a prolonged job search. You can't afford to lose time, money, and hope to a sleazy, disreputable outfit. When you deal with an agency, these tips will help you select those that deliver:

• Be certain the agency is, in fact, what it says. Does the word "agency" appear prominently in the ad? Don't confuse employment agencies with job counselors, who charge an advance fee for their work but don't actually place clients. Beware, too, of the advance fee schemes that spell trouble, as in "Guidance while you hunt for jobs. $25, inclusive."

• Determine who pays the fee and under what terms. If you pay, make sure you understand the schedule of payments spelled out in the contract. Until you accept a job, employment agencies do not charge for their services. Some might request a deposit or registration fee that they refund if you do not accept, or are not offered, a job.

• If the ad says "fee paid," check that your new employer, not you, will pay the fee. When an agency claims "never a fee to the applicant," the employer picks up all the charges.

• Many states allow the agency to collect a portion of the fee from you if you accept a "fee-paid job" but quit within a specified number of months. Get the details in writing. Find out, too, what the policy is should the job fall short of your expectations within a few days. If the job goes sour and the policy is to refund your money, find out about the time limit on your eligibility.

• Watch out for "job bait." Most ads and most agencies are legitimate, but you will occasionally encounter ads that lure you to an agency office. For example, the "assistant to the president, minimal skills, great benefits, $350 per week," that somehow turns into a file clerk position at $200 is suspicious. In short, verify that the agency's advertised job really is available.

You can protect yourself from agencies that advertise deceptively:

• Monitor the ads for several days or weekends. When the same ad appears day in and day out, the job probably doesn't exist and it's "bait" to reel you in.

• Ask questions. Request as much information over the phone as you can, but realize that the agency will not divulge the name of the company in the ad.

• Keep the ad you answer and match it up with the agency's when you get there. Write out all your questions before you go so if you get rattled you won't overlook any details.

• Watch out for "cute" ads that amuse you but fail to describe the job duties, skills, or experience required, and stress great benefits.

• Don't let an agency employee mislead you into confusing the type of business with the job description. A real estate firm may need a switchboard operator, but the agency's ad should not read "broker seeks assistant to work with clients."

• Never return to an agency that advertises nonexistent jobs or refers you to a firm that doesn't need new employees.

• If your state requires a license for employment agencies, be certain to deal with licensed agencies only.

• If you have questions or doubts about an agency, check with your local Better Business Bureau and with the National Association of Personnel Consultants (NAPC), the industry's self-policing organization (1432 Duke St., Alexandria, VA 22314). More than 2,000 firms nationwide belong to the NAPC, and each member subscribes to a strict code of ethics. The NAPC will send you, upon request, a directory of member firms that includes an analysis of industry practices.

Magazine Sales—Target: Teenagers

The ad leaps out from the Help Wanted column: "Gals/Guys, excitement, travel, and money! Must be 18. No experience necessary." A phone number follows.

Before you grab the receiver, think: you have no idea what this is about. Details such as a job description—*if* it's a job—are absent, as is an explanation of why you must be eighteen.

You probably won't know until you interview that these ads are generally placed by magazine-subscription services. The companies generally recruit young, unattached people to go door-to-door selling subscriptions to all sorts of magazines. Applicants must be eighteen in accordance with interstate travel laws.

Here's how these work:

The ad, placed in a local paper as a crew swings through town, invites applicants to call, or visit room 1 at Motel XYZ. You go and learn that the job is selling subscriptions. If it's summertime, chances are you will travel through northern-tier states and in winter, crews travel south.

Crews numbering from five to a dozen people pile into vans and drive from city to city, with the crew manager assigning work quotas to each member. You can expect to stay in hotels and motels and to work through small cities and towns very quickly.

Many of these companies are legitimate, and buyers actually receive their magazines. However, Better Business Bureaus, Travelers' Aid Societies, the Departments of Public Safety, and hotels that have been left with unpaid bills know the fakes very well. In fact, many big-city newspapers won't carry these ads unless they are assured that return transportation is guaranteed if the worker is fired or becomes disenchanted.

Before you even consider applying for one of these jobs, ask the following questions and refuse to be satisfied with half-baked answers:

• Will you receive a salary or commission for your work? How is the commission calculated?

• Exactly who pays for transportation, lodging, and food? That hefty commission or salary will melt away if those expenses are deducted from your paycheck. And, speaking of deductions, are Social Security contributions and income taxes deducted, or do you go home with a tax liability?

• What are the plans for travel? Who drives the cars or vans? What insurance coverage is carried in what name and amounts?

• Where will you stay? How many to a room? Where will you eat?

• And, most vital of all, are you guaranteed your return home?

Don't be taken in by an ad that promises travel to a city you've wanted to visit all your life. Under this sales scheme, this privilege will require you to work long hours at door-to-door sales while traveling and living in close proximity with complete strangers.

Overseas Employment Deals

No matter how savvy a job-hunter you become, you might find yourself tantalized by ads in the "help wanted" columns that read like this:

"Overseas employment opportunities! Gals/guys, no experience. Summer and full-time!"

"Alaska! Land of opportunity and jobs! Full-time, part-time jobs, big money!"

You're intrigued. You write for details and receive a form letter explaining that, for $25 or $50 or even $200 you will be provided with all the information. Perhaps, though, the sum is smaller—the first time—to defray "mailing and handling costs."

Guess what you get in exchange for money you can't afford to lose when you're out of work and looking, hard, for a job? You will receive a list of jobs culled from local newspapers and hence out of date, or a list of all the hotels in Austria, or a directory of American companies doing business overseas. In short, nothing you couldn't have discovered if you spent some time in the library or with your guidance counselor.

Advance-pay schemes wear many disguises. Learn now the telltale signs and avoid disappointment and anger at watching your money disappear. *Be cautious about paying money to anyone in advance* for information or applications about jobs. You will almost certainly regret it.

HEALTH CLUBS

The fitness craze is here to stay, in tandem with an explosion in the health-club industry. Everywhere you turn, health clubs that offer nautilus machines, saunas, whirlpools, indoor tracks, and a brace of classes spring up practically overnight. For an annual membership fee, you can join, jog, jounce, and jolt yourself into shape.

Most health clubs deliver on the promises specified in the contract you sign. But be alert to the following:

• Failure to honor the cancellation clause in the contract.
• Crowded, unsanitary conditions.
• Nonavailability of advertised facilities—heated swimming pool, steambath, whatever.
• Inability to transfer membership from one unit of the club to another unit in another city or state.
• Preopening membership sales that never result in a club. Promoters rent space and advertise preopening specials. Excited at the prospect of a new, fully equipped health club in your town, you rush to sign on the dotted line, although the "opening" is still months away.

Don't do it! If you're intrigued by an ad like this, do your homework: ask about the promoters' history, find out if they've requested building permits, check your city ordinances. Some cities have statutes against payment until the facility opens. Ask if you can sign up for the same fee when the facility opens.

Many health clubs rely on a membership that signs up and never visits the premises. To ensure that you get your money's worth from your health club:

1. Visit the club at the time of day or week you expect to use the facilities. If you will only be able to go after work, early in the evening, visit the club then. If people are knee-deep at the nautilus or lined up outside the sauna, you will be tipped off that you can't expect to use the equipment when you want to.

2. Ask and get the facts about how many members the club has and how many they service regularly.

3. Inquire about the cancellation clause in your contract, and read the contract thoroughly before you sign.

4. Expect—but don't give in to—high-pressure sales pitches. When you visit a club, you will be urged to join before you leave. Resist this tactic. You owe the salesperson nothing—no matter how much time or how much fun you had together. Allow yourself plenty of time to go home and think about what you've seen and decide whether it meets *your* requirements.

5. Most important of all, investigate the club's financing. Typically, you will sign up and agree to make monthly payments, but you don't have to accept the health club's financing plan! Chances

are, these costs will be comparatively high, but you are entitled to shop for credit elsewhere, such as a bank or credit union.

DATING AND ROOMMATE-MATCHING SERVICES

Item: You're new in town and need a roommate and apartment fast.

Item: It's been a while since you met someone so attractive you just had to ask for a date.

Smart businesspeople have capitalized on these two situations—and their infinite variations—to start up two big businesses: date-finding and roommate-matching services. Similar problems may arise in each business, so if you decide to use either—or both—here's what to look for:

• Many dating services wind up with rosters overloaded with members of one sex or the other. Ask how many men and women are registered in each age bracket.

• Beware of addresses that are post office boxes only. Also, be suspicious when you can never get the company on the phone but must leave a message with a service or answering machine.

• If the company advertises "computerized service," ask where the computer is located.

• Be realistic. Just because you know in excruciating detail your requirements for the perfect date or roommate, don't expect to find him/her on a computer printout. Spare yourself disappointment and don't be too specific in your descriptions. Of course, be honest: if you can't live with pets or wouldn't dream of kissing someone who smokes cigarettes, say so.

• Ask about refund policies in case you don't get the promised number of referrals. Many roommate services state in their promotional literature that fees are nonrefundable.

YOUR COMPLAINTS

How to Use the Mail Fraud Law

The heaviest artillery you, an American teenager, have in the federal consumer protection arsenal is the mail fraud statute—adopted way back in the nineteenth century—which prevents swindlers from using the mails to carry out schemes to gyp the American consumer of all ages, including teens, often the most believing and therefore the most vulnerable.

The scope of this law covers any scheme to cheat you if the mails are used in any way to promote the gyp. There is virtually no important activity which does not use the mails in some way and, thus, there are no deliberate frauds of any significance which this law cannot reach.

What's more, penalties for violating the mail fraud statute include up to five years in jail and a $1,000 fine for each piece of mail sent, or received, as part of the scheme.

Of course, this does not mean that an unintentional mistake or a debatable statement in an advertisement or sales pitch constitutes deliberate fraud. Such mistakes, or statements, would not violate the statute. The issue here is fraud, not stupid error. This is a warning, designed to alert you on how to use this vital law to help protect yourself.

The mail fraud section is enforced by the U.S. Postal Inspection Service, one of the oldest and most effective law-enforcement agencies. This is an elite corps responsible for protecting the mails from theft, burglary, embezzlement, and use in aid of fraud.

Among frauds investigated by the postal inspectors have been confidence schemes, pyramid franchising, sales referral schemes, and massive consumer gyps involving large numbers of consumers.

Under the mail fraud statute, U.S. attorneys from coast to coast bring prosecutions. Some of the attorneys have established consumer fraud units to use the statute systematically. Follow these simple rules on using the law:

• If you are suspicious about a transaction (say, to buy a car or a TV or stereo equipment by mail), be sure to keep the originals or copies of all papers you send or receive, including postmarked envelopes. Do this automatically, even if you have no reason to feel suspicious. Your envelopes in particular may supply the jurisdiction of the postal authorities.

• If you feel that a serious fraud may be involved, notify the postal inspectors, in care of your local post office. If they agree that a violation is involved, after investigation, they can send the matter to the U.S. attorney.

- If you have evidence that a widespread fraudulent scheme may be involved, you may wish to contact the U.S. attorney's office directly as well.
- Frequently, complaints to the postal inspectors result in refunds to victims. But keep in mind that the mail fraud section does not enable the government to rule on individual complaints or require individual refunds. Nor can you, as a complainant, insist on being kept informed about the progress of any investigation. That must remain confidential unless and until formal charges are brought.

Despite its simplicity and its tough sanctions for violations, the mail fraud section does have serious weaknesses. What priority is given to improving the mail fraud law to add to your protection rests on how much you realize the power of the weapon in your hands—if you will only use it. Wake up while you are a young consumer, and have time to fight and beat the crooks before they beat you!

Step-by-Step to Satisfaction

Back in the early 1970s your parents automatically rushed to a copy center and ran off forty sets of complaints to send to everyone from Ralph Nader to their local Federal Trade Commission office whenever a product didn't work, on the premise that this was the most effective way to frighten the maker into fixing the thing. That may have made sense in that long-passed consumer heyday, but it sure doesn't in the new atmosphere of the 1980s.

The wisest advice for this era is to start with a low-key polite request to the company itself. Assume the maker is honest and not a crook. Do it in writing, so there's a piece of paper to be passed on to the proper people. If your paper lands in the wastepaper basket, go to stage two: Write directly to the president of the company. Explain that you are a good customer and describe the facts in detail, including what was said to you about the item, what went wrong, what you did to solve the problem, your lack of satisfaction.

In each of these polite but firm letters to the company, send photocopies of papers you have, such as advertising, the guarantee (if any), canceled checks, etc. Do not send originals because you probably won't get them back.

If none of this works, escalate your activities. Tell the president politely that unless something is done, you will be compelled to complain to all proper authorities. Send out no copies of this letter, since by so doing you will already have done whatever you can and your letter won't serve as a warning at all.

Next try voluntary groups. The local Better Business Bureau (BBB) may be able to help you, or the Chamber of Commerce.

The BBB may be able to offer you a chance to arbitrate your dispute before an impartial private party on an informal basis, if the firm agrees. If not, you can still contact various government agencies.

There may be a specific agency dealing with the industry involved, such as a state insurance department, motor vehicle bureau that registers auto repair shops, education department monitoring vocational schools, etc.

If you are not sure, go to a general consumer protection law enforcement agency such as the state attorney general's office or local consumer protection agency. If the company involved has a license of any kind, the licensing agency may give you help or advice.

The Federal Trade Commission in Washington or its nearest regional office may assist you, though federal involvement is thinning out. If the mails were used in what you believe was a full-fledged fraud, contact your local postal inspector. Copies of envelopes you received from the firm will establish mailings under the law.

If you still have not been helped, you may want to consider a lawsuit via your local small claims court, where you don't need a lawyer. Or you can hire a lawyer—on a contingency (the lawyer is paid out of the proceeds if you win). Legal Aid and other community legal services are not getting the funds they need to help much.

Or you simply can refuse to pay. The "holder in due course" rule says a financing agency connected with the seller is subject to the same defenses as the seller (if the product was no good). You could be sued, though, and could lose and be subjected to enforcement procedures such as garnishment of wages. If you are given a bad credit rating for nonpayment, you can demand your side of the story be included in your credit file.

From your first low-key protest to this is a long, long way. If you do it right from the start, you'll be out from under well before.

STOLEN GOODS: A BIG BUSINESS
AND GROWING

Dealing in stolen goods is a big and ever-growing multibillion dollar business. Your odds of innocently buying stolen property are increasing, and your chances of getting caught, whether innocent or not, are rising as well.

States, counties, and cities have begun to pass strict laws forcing merchants who buy and sell used items to keep meticulous records of who sold them what, and to whom, in turn, they sold it. These laws should help catch both the "fences" and the reputable dealers who are lax in their bookkeeping.

Courts, too, are getting stricter in meting out punishment or damages in cases of thefts, even those that occurred years ago.

You wouldn't knowingly buy or sell stolen goods. But right now you could have some purloined object in your home.

Do you have clothes or other items that a family member got "cheap" from "someone at work" or school? A record or tape bought for less than half the list price at a "discount" store? A scarf, watch, bracelet, or other trinket bought from a sidewalk vendor at an absurdly low price? An "almost new" television set from a moonlighting appliance "repairman"? Everything from silverware to old books, purchased from a stranger who rented a motel room for a weekend and advertised he would buy or sell family heirlooms and antiques?

Even if you suspected all was not as advertised, you got a receipt for your money and a bill of sale, if the price was large enough. You convinced yourself that "it's legally mine."

But, despite your receipt, you could be way out on a limb if what you bought is hot merchandise. "Your" property could be confiscated, with no compensation to you.

One spectacular example: in the summer of 1981, a federal judge ruled that two paintings by the fifteenth century artist Albrecht Durer that had been stolen from a German museum in 1945 by an Allied soldier and, according to the court, sold later to an American lawyer, had to be returned. The lawyer bought the two paintings for $50 in 1956; today, their estimated value is at least $10 million. Furthermore, without even requiring a trial, the U.S. judge ordered the paintings returned to the East German government.

Thefts involve more than simple warehouse robberies or the traditional highway hijacking of routine goods from delivery trucks. With auction houses now operating worldwide, organized crime is into almost every type of "hard goods" from gems to tape recordings, from tapestries to religious relics.

Thefts are from libraries, museums, banks, universities, private collections—even churches. The government of Peru has waged a worldwide campaign to halt thefts of artwork, gold, silver, paintings, and pottery swiped from Peruvian churches and worth an estimated $500 million.

A rash of thefts of religious books and articles from New York–area churches and synagogues over the past few years has prompted clerics to imprint invisible markings on rare items to aid identification of stolen objects.

So, whether the items are rare artifacts, coins, books, and jewels, or whether they are everyday appliances, records, clothes, or furniture, they have one thing in common: the buyer winds up the loser, no matter how innocent the purchase may have been.

The goods are confiscated. You, the buyer, wind up without the goods, without the money you paid, and, with luck, only the reputation that you were stupid.

12

TAKE A VACATION

Don't Let a Vacation "Take" You!

CONTENTS

RULE NUMBER ONE: PLAN EARLY!

If you're planning to travel, you have at your fingertips an enormous amount of material to help you arrange a great trip. Invest some time and energy before you go and you will be rewarded with a memorable tour. Write to local chambers of commerce or state tourist information bureaus and they will shower you with pamphlets, maps, and guides. Consulates and government travel offices distribute a limitless supply of promotional material. Student travel organizations can direct you to fare discounts, cheap accommodations, and special deals designed exclusively for students and young people. Call a nearby college or the state university for advice and referrals.

As you rev up for a vacation, rule number one is: *plan early* to ensure that you enjoy your trip and stay within your budget.

Organizations

Consider writing to, and possibly joining, the following organizations as you plot out your trip.

American Automobile Association (AAA)

If you intend to drive, join the American Automobile Association. Among the benefits: free trip-planning services as well as emergency road assistance. Membership entitles you to discounts on car rentals and you can purchase traveler's checks free of service charge. You renew your membership yearly: first-timers pay a one-time application fee. The AAA can also assist you with details about international car registration and international drivers' licenses. Check your phone book for the local AAA affiliate, or write to the American Automobile Association (8111 Gatehouse Road, Falls Church, VA 22047).

American Youth Hostels (AYH)

Membership in AYH not only entitles you to sign up for its trips but, even more important, allows you to stay in an international network of inexpensive hostels geared to young, active travelers. Annual membership fees are low; in the early 1980s rates were $7 for those under eighteen and $14 for single members over eighteen. You receive a list of domestic hostels with your membership. For an application and further details, write to AYH (1332 "Eye" Street, N.W., Washington, DC 20005, or call (202)-783-6161 or from March through October, toll-free: 1-800-424-9426). (More on hosteling is included later in this chapter.)

Canadian Universities Travel Service (CUTS)

Are you heading north to the Maritime Provinces, or dreaming about a ride on the Trans-Canadian Railroad? Write to CUTS to learn about student rates, tours, and special programs for Canadian citizens. (The address: 44 George St., Toronto, Ontario, Canada M5S 2E4; also branches in Halifax, Nova Scotia; Ottawa, Ontario; Saskatoon, Saskatchewan; Edmonton, Alberta; Vancouver, British Columbia; Montreal, Quebec.)

The Council on International Educational Exchange (CIEE)

The Council on International Educational Exchange is the source for your international student I.D. card as well as invaluable information about budget air fares and accommodations, both here and abroad. Write for the Council's annual *Student Work/Study/Travel Catalog*, and request any supplemental updates. CIEE also publishes directories of budget lodgings both in the United States and abroad. (Its address in New York is 205 East 42nd Street, New York, NY 10017, and in San Francisco, 312 Sutter Street, San Francisco, CA 94108.) Also, check your phone book for campus and local affiliate offices.

Travel Guides

Wherever you decide to go, consult a couple of travel guides and books. Aside from firing your imagination, they will yield all sorts of terrific advice and, in some cases, valuable coupons. Many books are geared for student and budget travelers; most are updated yearly. Among them:

U.S.A. and Canada

The Best Free Attractions, John Whitman. Meadowbrook Press (18318 Minnetonka Boulevard, Deephaven, MN 55391), 1981. Regional editions for East, South, Midwest, and West.

Budget Travel in Canada, Jan Myers/Canadian Universities Travel Service. St. Martin's Press, 1981.

Fodor's Budget Travel in America. Fodor's Modern Budget Series (2 Park Avenue, New York, NY 10016), updated yearly.

Hosteling USA: Official AYH Handbook, Michael Frome. East Woods Press (Charlotte, NC), 1981. Available from American Youth Hostels.

Let's Go: U.S.A., Harvard Student Agencies. St. Martin's Press, revised annually.

National Directory of Budget Hotels, Raymond Carlson. Pilot Books (347 Fifth Avenue, New York, NY 10016), revised annually.

The Rites of Spring: A Student's Guide to Spring Break in Florida, Bruce Jacobsen and Rollin Riggs. Arbor House, 1982.

Road Notes: A Student's Guide to North America's Adventures and Delights. Datsun Student Travel Guide/Rand McNally and Company, 1980.

Roadfood, Jane and Michael Stern. Random House, 1981.

Where to Stay USA from $3 to $25, Marjorie A. Cohen. CIEE/Frommer Books, revised annually.

Abroad

Fodor's Budget Travel: Europe. Fodor's Modern Guides (2 Park Avenue, New York, NY 10016), revised annually. Others in the *Fodor's Budget* series: Britain, Caribbean, France, Germany, Italy, Japan, Mexico, and Spain.

Frommer's Europe on $20 a Day, Arthur Frommer. Simon & Schuster, revised yearly.

International Youth Hostel Handbook, Number 1: Europe and the Mediterranean. International Youth Hostel Federation, available from American Youth Hostels (1332 "Eye" Street, N.W., Washington, DC 20005), revised annually.

International Youth Hostel Handbook, Number 2: Asia, Australia, and the Americas. International Youth Hostel Federation, available from American Youth Hostels (1332 "Eye" Street, N.W., Washington, DC 20005), revised annually.

Let's Go: Europe, Harvard Student Agencies. St. Martin's Press, revised yearly. Others in the *Let's Go* series: Britain and Ireland; France; Italy; and Greece, Israel, and Egypt.

Traveler's Survival Kit, Roger Brown. Oxford, England: Vacation-Work, 4th edition, 1982. Distributed in United States by Writer's Digest Books (9933 Alliance Road, Cincinnati, OH 45242).

Whole World Handbook: A Student Guide to Work, Study and Travel Abroad. CIEE (205 East 42nd Street, New York, NY 10017), updated yearly.

Additional Listing

Free Stuff for Travelers, Bruce Lansky. Meadowbrook Press (18318 Minnetonka Boulevard, Deephaven, MN 55391), 1981.

DRUGS

Avoid! Beware! Stay away from! Forget! Don't use illicit drugs while traveling. It's that simple. You can be fined, or even arrested, in the United States if you are caught with any amount of a "controlled substance," and even though state laws and local attitudes vary, don't try to outsmart anyone. You could wind up looking far more than stupid.

Getting busted at home is a petty annoyance compared with what can happen overseas. If you're abroad and want to sample the homegrown, forget it—your friendly dealer might also be a police informer. Believe the unpleasant and scary stories that abound of Americans imprisoned for possession or trafficking in illegal drugs. Depending on the country, if you are arrested, you might not be jailed but you will almost certainly be deported and perhaps told to stay away for life. And if you are imprisoned, don't depend on United States consular officials to help set you free. They can only provide a list of attorneys, visit you in jail, and notify your family.

You will be subject to the laws of the country in which you're caught, as well as entitled to your rights under them, and those laws and rights are often very different from the ones at home. (Not to mention local hygiene and sanitary facilities.) Never try to smuggle drugs across international borders, and don't let *anyone* persuade you that it's safe. Expect that you and your belongings will be searched—thoroughly—at border crossings, and never underestimate the fact that customs agents know places to look that will astound you.

OVERSEAS TRAVEL: THE BASICS

Passports

When you travel abroad, the first item you need is a passport. Since processing an application takes from two to four weeks, allow ample time, especially during peak summer months. Should you need to leave within forty-eight hours, the Passport Agency provides rush service, but you must show proof of your departure date.

Apply for a passport at any one of the U.S. Department of State Passport Agencies, local post offices, or see a clerk of any Federal, state, or probate court (check the phone book). If you are applying for your first passport, or if you are over eighteen and your most recent one has expired, go in person to any of the above places. Otherwise, you can apply by mail. For a complete application, you need proof of U.S. citizenship (birth certificate, previous passport, or naturalization papers), identification that furnishes a picture or physical description (driver's license, for example), and two recent 2" by 2" photographs. Passports cost $15 in the early 1980s, and renewals cost $10. Your local passport agency or post office can answer any other questions, or write to the Office of Passport Services (Department of State, Washington, DC 20524) for its free pamphlet, *Your Trip Abroad.*

Your passport is the single most valuable item you carry with you. U.S. passports are coveted on overseas black markets, so guard yours at all times. If you lose it, immediately notify the local police and the U.S. consulate. The consulate will issue you a new five-year passport, which in the early 1980s cost $14.

Visas

A visa, or written permission provided by a government to enter its boundaries, is a requirement in many countries around the world. Each country makes its own rules: for some, you must apply in advance of your trip and submit your passport plus additional photographs. Others issue you a visa upon arrival. Before you leave the United States, check the requirements of the countries you plan to visit by contacting the nearest consulate or embassy, or request from the Office of Passport Services its free pamphlet *Visa Requirements of Foreign Governments.* If your plans include an extended stay as a student or worker, you may need a special visa, so ask about that, too. If you travel with an organized tour, be sure that the operators provide you with instructions or applications for any visas you need.

Customs

Coming home, after you reclaim your baggage and before you're reunited with your family or friends, you will be stopped at the customs gate. Expect the customs agent to examine everything you acquired while abroad, and hold on to all your receipts for this purpose. To save yourself frustration and aggravating delays, acquaint yourself with the basics.

• You are allowed to bring back with you $300 of duty-free goods, which are items obtained for your personal or household use and those marked as presents. The next $600 is taxed at a flat 10 percent rate. If you visit American territories (Samoa, Guam, and the United States Virgin Islands) your duty-free allowance rises to $600; a 5 percent charge is added to the next $600 of goods. Any total above the $600 extension, no matter where bought, will be taxed at the prevailing rate which, for some categories, is high.

• You can bring home one quart of liquor (or one gallon if bought in American territories) when you're twenty-one or older, one carton of cigarettes, and 100 cigars. You cannot bring in Cuban cigars unless you're returning from Cuba.

• You can mail back to the United States an unlimited number of gifts valued at $25 or less. Packages must be marked "unsolicited gift," and you can send one gift per recipient per day. Don't break up sets, such as a salt grinder in one box and a pepper mill in a second: packages are subject to mail inspection.

• Request that local sales taxes be listed separately on invoices so that taxes are not considered part of the item's price, thus raising the amount of duty you owe or eating into your exemption.

• If a value added tax (VAT) is charged in countries where you buy anything, ask the shopkeeper for a receipt showing the sum of the VAT so you can present the receipt to the U.S. customs inspector. The inspector will validate it for you; then you can return the receipt (keep a copy!) and ask for a money order totaling the specified amount.

• Get receipts for everything you buy, no matter how small the item or its cost. Customs officials have detailed and current knowledge of the value of most goods brought into the United States.

• Use the Generalized System of Preferences (GSP), a surprisingly unfamiliar benefit to overseas travelers. It enables you to bring home items normally subject to duty completely duty-free if the items were bought in a country covered by the law. The GSP was designed to help developing countries improve their export trade; it covers more than 100 countries and an astounding variety of goods. Products and countries covered are added and deleted according to current economic conditions, so before you leave, call the nearest customs office and ask if the countries you plan to visit are included and whether items you expect to purchase are covered, too. Also request the Custom Service's free booklet, *GSP and the Traveler*.

• Before you leave the United States, register with Customs any foreign-made items you are taking with you (such as Japanese cameras or French bikes). If you neglect this step, customs officials might assume you purchased them abroad and charge duty.

• Don't try to cheat. There isn't a hiding place customs inspectors don't know.

• Ask for a copy of current pamphlets from the U.S. Customs Offices (P. O. Box 7118, Washington, DC 20044), including *U.S. Customs Pocket Hints, A Gift . . . Are You Sure?, U.S. Customs Trademark Information, Importing a Car*, and *GSP and the Traveler*.

International Student I.D. Card (ISIC)

Next to your passport, the most useful document to have overseas is an International Student Identity Card (ISIC). In fact, it's essential if you plan to use student flights and other student fares once abroad. With it, you get reduced or free admission to many theaters, museums, cultural, and historic sites, as well as discounts at some restaurants and lodgings. An extra benefit: the ISIC provides you automatically with medical insurance up to $1,000 for the life of the card.

Only if you are a full-time high school or college student are you eligible for this valuable item. Apply for your card through the

Council on International Educational Exchange (CIEE) (205 East 42nd Street, New York, NY 10017), or check your phone book for a branch office near you. Collect the following information to submit with your application:

• Proof of full-time student status: a transcript of grades for the immediately preceding semester, or a letter on school stationery signed and sealed by the registrar or dean, or a copy of your current I.D. card. High school students should send either a report card or a letter from the principal or guidance counselor on school stationery.
• A vending machine-sized photo (1½″ by 2″) with your name printed on the back.
• A certified check or money order for the application fee.

CIEE provides so many services to young travelers—and not all restricted to students—be sure to write for its catalog, which includes an application form for the ISIC.

HOW TO CARRY MONEY

Figuring out what to do with your travel money—even when you have it—can stump you. Take the time now to organize your finances and your wallet.

• Experienced travelers avoid carrying large sums of cash and *never* leave their wallets and valuables unattended. Heed their example: buy a money belt and tuck your spare bills inside.
• Never pack your wallet, traveler's checks, and plane tickets in your luggage. Suitcases and backpacks have a distressing tendency to go astray; that's bad enough, but will be calamitous if you're stranded, too.
• Unpack and check your wallet before you leave home. Remove library cards, department store charge cards, and museum membership cards—anything that you won't be needing but would have to report if lost. These just add to clutter and won't help you where you're going. Hold on to your school I.D. and driver's license, of course.
• Domestic travelers: don't assume that you can use personal checks nationwide. Most U.S. banks will not cash out-of-state checks, and some stores and businesses will be reluctant to honor your personal check for your purchase.

• When heading overseas, purchase a small amount of currency for your first stop before you leave. Balance the possibly high service charge and less than ideal rate of exchange against the reassurance of having local currency when you arrive—it's worth it. Note that most airports and ports of entry have banks on the premises that keep unusual hours suited to tourists.

• Incidentally, many countries expect you to prove that you have money to support yourself while within their borders. You also may be asked to show your return plane ticket.

Traveler's Checks

You probably will carry your funds in traveler's checks. Most banks sell them, frequently with a commission added on of 1 percent of the total you buy, but if you shop around you can purchase checks commission-free. All companies promise prompt refunds of lost or stolen checks and it has become such a competitive business that they offer additional services that make it worthwhile for you to investigate carefully.

American Express

Many banks and all American Express offices sell these checks at a commission of 1 percent. Members of the AAA can buy American Express checks without a service charge from most AAA affilates. You also can purchase money orders and checks in the same currencies as the traveler's checks: French francs, German marks, Canadian dollars, Swiss francs, British pounds, and Japanese yen. If you have an American Express Card, you can purchase checks abroad with your personal bank check (you can't charge them to your account). Emergency services for when your checks are lost or stolen include a temporary I.D., a phone call at no charge, notification to your credit and charge card companies, and cash for a personal check up to $200.

Barclay's Bank Ltd.

Barclay's sells its checks either in U.S. dollars or pounds sterling; either way, they are commission-free. Consult your phone book for a Barclay's office near you or write to its main headquarters in New York and ask for an office list (100 Water Street, New York, NY 10005).

Deak-Perera

This financial company, based in New York and with branches in other American cities, sells several kinds of traveler's checks at no service charge. The basket of currencies includes: U.S. dollars, Swiss francs, French francs, German marks, Hong Kong dollars, Italian lira, Australian dollars, and Japanese yen. (New York headquarters: 29 Broadway, New York, NY 10006.)

Thomas Cook

You can buy Thomas Cook traveler's checks at any Thomas Cook office, commission-free; if you purchase them at a bank, there will be a 1 percent service charge. Also, expect to pay a commission on foreign currency checks: British pounds, French francs, Australian dollars, Canadian dollars, Hong Kong dollars, and Japanese yen.

Before you buy checks, consider your itinerary, particularly if you're going abroad. If you plan to stay in one country for a while, you might want to buy traveler's checks in that currency. Then you won't have to fret about the daily rate of exchange or wonder whether a shop or restaurant is helping itself to a hefty service charge.

Conversely, if you plan to skip from country to country, you might want to buy traveler's checks in dollars—and small denominations (tens and twenties)—so you won't be stuck with a lot of cash to convert into a third currency or back into dollars. (You lose money twice that way, since the banks charge on each transaction.)

When you do cash checks, ask at the banks if the banks charge for each check or for the transaction itself and plan accordingly.

Credit Cards

Bring a major credit card along if you have one. Of course, the bills find their way home too, so keep your credit line in mind as you budget your trip.

Some advantages and some pointers:

• You can use a card to rent bicycles and cars without paying a large cash deposit. If you're under twenty-one, you might not be able to rent a car without a credit card.

• MasterCard and Visa allow their cardholders to obtain a cash advance at any institution which issues the cards. American Express will let you cash a personal check for up to $1,000 in the local currency.

• Another plus for American Express cardholders: you can receive mail sent to any one of the American Express offices or agents abroad. This is the toughest card to acquire, but if your parents or older brother or sister has one and is willing to sign a guarantee form, American Express will issue a card in your name for an annual fee of $35.

• Credit cards are often useless at budget restaurants and lodgings, which accept cash or traveler's checks only.

• You may have to spend a minimum amount before you can use the cards at all.

• Despite their worldwide popularity, you can't use credit cards everywhere, and you may be asked to pay a surcharge for the "privilege" of using a card at all. Check receipts carefully before you sign, and ask to have unexplained charges spelled out.

• Keep in mind that charges incurred abroad will be converted from the foreign currency into American dollars. Save your receipts, and when your bill arrives, check the conversion rate and scrutinize your charges.

GETTING THERE

Air

With federal deregulation of airfares, it has become impossible to predict either domestic or international airfares with any accuracy. Competition for passengers is fierce; skirmishes among airlines can save you money. Checking fares is a nuisance, but the savings well may stagger you.

Follow these guidelines:

• Look for advertisements about airfares on TV, in local newspapers, and in Sunday travel sections. Airlines often promote special deals that are available for a limited time only. But read the small print on restrictions and deadlines!

• Check out your airlines as never before, and take the time to study which airline will give you the best bargain and biggest discount to the spot you've chosen. Many airlines are offering special package tours that include airfare and hotel room and even discounts at selected casinos, restaurants, and car-rental agencies.

• As a rule, it's cheaper to travel during the week than on weekends, and cheaper still to travel at night.

• Since deregulation, several small, no-frills airlines have cropped up. These airlines offer cheaper seats than their big rivals while providing fewer amenities, such as movies and meals. Check whether they are flying your way.

• Find a reputable travel agent to help unravel the tangled skein of fares. It costs nothing to use travel agents; they receive their commissions from the airlines. But since commissions on budget flights are necessarily smaller, you may have to shop around until you find an agent who wants to help you save money. (For more information on travel agents, see "Using a Travel Agent," later in this chapter.)

• Contact the nearest student travel service, even if you're not enrolled in school. Chances are, this service will be most knowledgeable about airfares, charters, and current bargains.

Domestic Flights

Domestic flights come in many varieties, and major airlines routinely list several rates for the same flight. Ask the airline you call if they offer excursion fares, supersavers, and night supersavers (or whatever name the airline uses for a special fare). Call more than one airline; compare fares among carriers.

Here is a short course on different budget fares as of the early 1980s:

• *Excursion fares* usually work best for short trips. Often no advance purchase is required, but the time of day you can fly may be restricted.

• *Supersaver* tickets can save you a lot of money, particularly for long distances. You must purchase a round-trip ticket at least one week in advance and remain at your destination for a specified amount of time. If you plan to buy a supersaver, try to buy far in advance of your trip, especially if you plan to fly during peak seasons or holidays; advance purchase protects you from sudden fare increases.

• *Charters* are not a common form of air travel within the U.S. Since the stipulations on available domestic charters vary from airline to airline, you probably will need a travel agent to assist you in finding a flight. Restrictions on domestic charters are usually quite stiff: you must purchase your ticket well in advance, leave and return on the scheduled dates, and, if you are forced to cancel, you can lose a substantial amount of the cost unless you have cancellation insurance. Try to find another way to get wherever you're going.

International Fares

International airfares vary as much as their domestic counterparts. Small upstart airlines help keep the pot stirred by offering fares that undercut larger carriers, and you can choose from many more charters for overseas travel.

As rate structures stood in the early 1980s, four categories of airfares prevailed: (1) charters and student fares, (2) stand-by, (3) no-frills airlines, and (4) SUPER-APEX and APEX fares. This order corresponds roughly to the fares' ascending costs.

• *Charters and student fares.* Charters can be the least expensive flights. On most charter flights you can book right up to the time of departure (if there's room), fly either one way or round trip, and arrive at one city and leave from another. Charter deals change from year to year, so a travel agent or student travel service can give you the best current advice. Another excellent source of information on charter flights is the Council on International Educational Exchange. CIEE publishes regular updates to their *Student Work/ Study/Travel Catalog* (which you should acquire, anyway), listing fares and instructions for booking flights. CIEE itself offers charters to Europe from New York and the West Coast; its publications provide the details. Don't despair if you're not a student; you may be eligible for some of the flights anyway.

• *Standby* can be a rewarding, if risky, way to fly. If you do plan to try standby, do so off-season when competition for scarce seats lessens. Otherwise, brace yourself for frustrating and upsetting delays, missed connections, and wasted time. Particularly in July and August, standby can be a nightmare. You can purchase standby tickets in advance but you have no reservation on any flight. Only on the day of departure will the airline know the availability of seats, although the line might indicate to you the chances for a seat on any given day. Each airline has its own system, mysterious though it may be, of assigning standby seats. Ask about the airline's policy. Ask, too, whether it keeps a list of standby passengers and, if so, ascertain your number on the list. Equip yourself with books, magazines, and an ample supply of food and drink; you might not leave when you expect to.

• *No-frills.* Some of the newer airlines fall in the category of "no-frills." Many offer standby, excursion, and other fares; ask, too, about additional student discounts. Travel agents and student travel services will steer you to the good deals.

• *APEX and SUPER APEX* fares usually are the cheapest of the regular budget fares offered by the airlines. APEX stands for Advance Purchase Excursion Fares. Regulations stipulate that you book and pay for your tickets at least several weeks in advance; that you reserve your return flight within a specified period of time; and that you pay heavy penalties if you cancel or change a reservation. Here again, a travel agent can best guide you through the maze of fares and regulations.

Train

Travel by train can be an efficient and scenic way to speed you toward your destination, but in the United States it is not cheap. Amtrak, the country's major passenger line, has slashed service and raised fares. Moreover, Amtrak offers no student fares or reductions (although it sells the USA Railpass to foreign visitors). But there are ways to beat, or at least minimize, the high cost of train travel at home.

• Ask about excursion fares. These are reduced round-trip fares that come with restrictions on when you can use them.

• Amtrak occasionally offers special deals that include unlimited travel for a specified number of days. Ask your travel agent or Amtrak representative.

• Check for local competition. In the northeast, for example, Conrail often has lower fares than Amtrak for the same destination. The schedule is not as flexible, but do you really care?

• Don't buy food on the train. Bring your own snacks and beverages and avoid the dining car and snack bar. You'll eat better for less.

Train travel overseas is a different story. In Europe, you can plan to take as many trains as you want. The reason: the Eurailpass and BritRail pass. These tickets grant you, a foreigner, unlimited mileage within their respective areas: the Eurailpass is valid in sixteen countries; the BritRail pass is limited to the United Kingdom. Check with the Council on International Educational Exchange, American Youth Hostels, or a student travel service to find out current youth rates for these tickets. These sources also can bring you up to date on train fares in Canada and elsewhere, as can current editions of guidebooks such as those in the *Let's Go* series.

If you plan to travel extensively by train, you might enjoy reading the adventures of some great travel writers. Paul Theroux has written two delightful books about "training" in exotic places: *The Great Railway Bazaar*, about the Middle East and Asia, and *The Old Patagonian Express*, about train journeys through the Americas. And in *The Big Red Train Ride*, Eric Newby describes his adventures on the Trans-Siberian Railroad.

Car

If you plan to travel extensively—or exclusively—by car, bring along friends or relatives to help cut expenses. Otherwise you will find driving a very costly way to get around.

Before you leave home, join the American Automobile Association (mentioned earlier in this chapter) or another automotive club, and take advantage of membership benefits. The AAA, for example, can provide you with details about international auto registration and international drivers' licenses, along with domestic services.

Check your car insurance and make sure it covers you in all the states you plan to visit. If you plan to drive your car in Canada, ask your insurance company for a Canada Non-Resident Inter-Province Motor Vehicle Liability Insurance card. This slip of paper is required to provide your insurance coverage to provincial officials in case you have an accident. South of the border, Mexican auto insurance laws are stringent, and United States insurance usually is not valid for more than forty-eight hours after you enter the country. You probably will need a more expensive Mexican policy for longer trips.

Whatever you do, *look into your coverage before you leave home,* so that a fender-bender (or worse) doesn't wreck your trip.

A little care can help save you money on the road. Keep your car in good shape, with the tires inflated at the proper pressure. Check the oil and water regularly, and, unless absolutely necessary, keep the air-conditioner turned off. You can help stretch a gallon of gas with these measures, and gas will be one of your primary concerns as you plan a road trip. (For more on saving fuel, see Chapter 8, *Your Wheels.*) Although it is merely guessing to predict the cost or availability of gas far in advance, watch news reports and check with your local gas station to get a sense of price trends and supply.

Bicycling

Bicycling is exploding in popularity as a way to travel as well as to sight-see once you've reached your destination. When you decide to cycle, you discover quickly a network of thousands of miles of bike trails across this country, and in Canada and Europe, too.

As a cyclist, your first resource is Bikecentennial, a nonprofit organization that provides its members with a terrific variety of services:

- The bimonthly *BikeReport*, which is geared for touring cyclists.
- *The Cyclist's Yellow Pages*, an exhaustive resource guide that lists overseas publications, U.S. cycling organizations, state-by-state lists of bicycle resources, and is updated yearly.
- Informative pamphlets on how to get in shape for a bicycle trip, how to transport your bicycle, and others in a series.
- A bookstore that carries over 200 titles about bicycling, camp-

ing, and other related activities at home and abroad. Catalogs are sent out regularly; nonmembers can request a copy, too, but members can purchase books at discounts of up to 50 percent.

• Maps, route information, and other useful guides to help you plan a successful trip.

Request membership details from Bikecentennial (P.O. Box 8308, Missoula, MT 59807).

American Youth Hostels offers cycling tours and publishes useful guidebooks for cyclists, including its *North American Bike Atlas*. One noteworthy feature of many American hostels: they are located along established bicycle paths.

Long-distance bicycle trips demand careful planning and quality equipment. You need to own or rent a good ten-speed bike and know how to repair it. Practice riding near home with your camping gear loaded on the bike to get accustomed to balancing the extra weight. Practice routine repairs, too.

You can also bring your bicycle along with you and unpack it when you reach your destination. Airlines, buses, and trains allow you to transport it, but each method—in fact, each company—has its own restrictions. Call the carriers you plan to use and find out *exactly* what those restrictions are, and pack accordingly. Whether you fly or ride, you will have to dismantle and box your bicycle. A bike shop can sell you an inexpensive, sturdy box that meets your needs or, in some cases, you can purchase a box at the station or airport. Don't forget to ask the carrier about insurance!

Overseas travelers are subject to extra guidelines; you can also expect extra charges. Ask the carrier, and check out U.S. customs rules, too.

Most guidebooks now contain sections for cyclists in response to the growing popularity of this mode of travel. If your plans include the United States, take a look at *Cyclist's Guide to Overnight Stops* by Seymour Levine (Ballantine Books, 1982). The guide is divided into three regional editions—eastern, western, and central; hence, three volumes that include capsule descriptions of each lodging and the prices and forms of payment accepted.

CAMPING

Renting Camping Equipment

The wilderness beckons you to explore; to fish, climb, camp, canoe, raft—escape! But you anticipate such high costs that your fantasy sinks into the sunset. Well, dream on. By renting virtually every item you need for wilderness travel—from a sixteen-foot trailer that sleeps six and includes stove and water supply, to tents, camp stoves, lanterns, and sleeping bags for less elaborate expeditions— you can slash the costs of your trip. And if you pool the costs among friends, your expense shrinks further. Purchases of camping gear can equal or easily surpass your income for the next year or so. Since you may not yet know whether you plan to camp on a regular basis, why spend huge sums on something you might use twice a year?

Other advantages to renting: you may not be liable for damages to equipment unless there is evidence of abuse; some rental outlets offer a damage waiver, for a fee; you can rent the most up-to-date gear.

When you rent equipment, you sign a contract. State laws vary on the minimum age required; you can find out by phoning the attorney general's office or the department of state. Don't give up if you're still too young—perhaps an older brother or sister or friend will join you and will sign the essential papers.

Start your expedition with the Yellow Pages. Look under listings for "Rental Services, Stores and Yards," or under specific headings such as "Camping Equipment." Shop around by phone for the best prices and policies.

Other tips to check out before you sign on the dotted line:

- Ask about liability for damage to any item and liability waivers.
- Be sure you understand the proper use of each piece of equipment, no matter how obvious it seems. Ask, too, how to correct typical problems—and which ones to anticipate.
- Be clear on deposit and payment procedures. Can you pay with personal checks and credit cards?
- Know exactly when the gear must be returned to avoid additional charges. If the store tacks on a late fee, ask how long a "grace period" you have and how they calculate late charges.

Renting can help you make those "wild" dreams come true. Just be sure to do your homework first.

Planning Your Camping Trip

During the summer, some of the most crowded tourist spots you can find are campgrounds—proof of the immense growth in popularity of camping. If you have a car or bicycle, camping is a wonderful way to see the country; if you travel by bus or train, camping requires more planning but is still feasible and enjoyable.

As you organize your camping trip, consult one of the many national directories of campgrounds. There are now more than 20,000 campgrounds in the United States and Canada; the trick is to find one with the facilities and location you want. Some resources:

• *Rand McNally Campground and Trailer Park Guide.* Updated yearly, this guide is divided into eastern and western editions. A third volume includes the United States, Canada, and Mexico.

• *Rand McNally Backpacking and Outdoor Guide.* Also updated yearly, this volume is a how-to- and where-to-enjoy guide; maps included.

• *Camping in the National Park System; Guide and Map to the National Parks;* and *Lesser Known Areas of the National Park System.* These are all publications of the U.S. Government. Order them from the Superintendent of Documents (Government Printing Office, Washington, DC 20402). Write first for a current price list.

Essentially there are two types of campgrounds: public and private. Campgrounds administered by the federal or state governments are public and typically located in state and national parks, wilderness, and other designated areas. Prices are low to moderate (under $10 a night in early 1980s), but reductions in staff and funds may result in higher fees in the next few years.

Private campgrounds, run by individuals or companies, augment the public system. Perhaps the best known is the nationwide chain Kampgrounds of American (KOA). You can get a directory of KOA campgrounds for a small fee by writing to KOA (P.O. Box 30558, Billings, MT 59114), and you can make reservations via a toll-free number: 1-800-548-7063.

Camping requires equipment. If this is your first camping trip, *rent* what you need. Buy as little as possible until you decide whether you enjoy the realities of camping and you discover what style suits you best. This is particularly true since you shouldn't scrimp on camping gear. You will need at bare minimum a good sleeping bag, tent, cooking kit, and possibly a cookstove.

Ask for advice, write away for catalogues from camping supply outlets, and visit reputable camping outfitters. It will take time to sort through all the options, not to mention the serious outlay of cash to equip yourself properly.

A final note, campers: national park campsites are wildly popular and fill up early. Have on hand a list of alternatives to fall back on in case your first choices are everyone else's first choices, too.

WHERE (AND WHAT) TO EAT

When you travel on your own (as opposed to traveling with an organized tour) you will have to provide yourself with food at least a few times a day. You can cut down on food costs and enjoy yourself at the same time by adhering to a few simple guidelines:

• Avoid junk food. Aside from its dubious nutritional value, junk food gobbles up your loose change.

• Eat breakfast. Breakfast can be the least expensive and most sustaining meal of the day. Check to see whether it's included with your overnight accommodations, and fill up.

• Plan to picnic. You can buy the groceries you need at any market in the world and take advantage of local delicacies, such as produce and cheese. Then, find a convenient spot and feast!

• Include in your travel kit a good pocketknife, can and bottle opener, plastic "silverware," and sturdy plastic plate and mug.

• Patronize fast-food restaurants judiciously. Although you can save money at these places (not always as much as you might think) and you can count on the quality and taste, you'll miss part of the fun of travel. Seek out new experiences for your taste buds, too.

• Guidebooks can direct you to inexpensive, interesting restaurants. Consult the list at the beginning of this chapter, and see what others you can find at the local library or bookstore.

• Look for college newspapers when you hit a new town. They usually carry advertising for inexpensive restaurants near campus. Similarly, "alternative" newspapers are a good bet for ads and leads on cheap meals.

HEALTH HINTS FOR THE ROAD

Even with all the hours you spend arranging, rearranging, and dreaming about your trip, you might overlook one crucial area: your health. You can demolish the most fabulous vacation by failure to follow through on these basic suggestions:

• Obtain a copy of the current edition of *Health Information for International Travel,* available from the Superintendent of Documents (Government Printing Office, Washington, DC 20402). You'll find sound advice for handicapped travelers, as well as details on vaccinations, food and water treatment, and other essentials. The book is updated yearly, as is the price.

• Read the sections on health, what to do if you get sick, and innoculations in the free pamphlet, *Your Trip Abroad.* Write to the Bureau of Consular Affairs (Department of State, Washington, DC 20520).

• Call your city or county health department and ask about necessary vaccinations. The department receives updated information from the federal Center for Disease Control (CDC) in Atlanta and can also advise you where to go locally for shots. In a pinch, call the Quarantine Office at the CDC, tell them which countries you plan to visit, and ask what shots you need (telephone: (404)-329-2572).

• Have a dental check-up before you leave.

• Carry a small first aid kit: aspirin or aspirin substitute, motion-sickness pills, antacid, antihistamines, and a remedy for—you guessed it—"tourista," such as Kaopectate. Equally important, include bandages, antiseptic cream, sun block or sunscreen, and insect repellent. If you are bound for exotic places, ask your local health department or doctor for advice about additional precautions, such as quinine for malaria.

• Don't pack prescription medicines in your luggage—carry them with you. First, luggage often goes astray; second, it's subject to abuse and temperature extremes that can alter some medicines.

Make certain you have an adequate amount; include a copy of your regular prescriptions written according to the drug's generic name. Foreign manufacturers may have a different brand name for the same drug, but generic names work everywhere.

• Leave medicines in their original, labeled bottles and vials.

• Tote along a spare pair of prescription eyeglasses or contact lenses.

• If you have diabetes, carry insulin and needles in your carry-on baggage. Luggage compartments, especially in airplanes, are often very cold, and insulin can freeze. Insulin, syringes, and you belong together. And don't forget to bring food along for when you en-counter typical—and uncontrollable—snafus.

• Join Medic Alert if you have chronic conditions or allergies. As a member, you wear a bracelet or necklace engraved with your medical problem, file number in the Medic Alert system, and the toll-free number of the twenty-four-hour answering service. In an emergency, this medallion can save your life. (Medic Alert Foundation, P.O. Box 1009, Turlock, CA 95381, or toll-free: 1-800-344-3226.) (For more on Medic Alert, see Chapter 14, *Your Health*.)

• Obtain a list of Western-trained, English-speaking doctors in 450 cities around the world from the International Association of Medical Assistance to Travelers (IAMAT). The doctors agree to a fixed fee schedule: one price for office visits and a second, higher fee for hotel visits. The booklet is sent to you free, although IAMAT encourages donations. (IAMAT, 736 Center Street, Lewiston, NY 14092; telephone: (716)-754-4883.)

• Intermedic also will send you its list of English-speaking doc-tors in more than 200 cities worldwide. Participating doctors agree to provide services—either in offices, or hotel visits, or hospitals—for preset fees. Single membership cost $6 yearly in the early 1980s; family membership cost $10. (Intermedic, 777 Third Avenue, New York, NY 10017, telephone: (212)-486-8974.)

• Write for a catalogue from the World Health Organization (WHO). Some of its publications can help you chart your medical needs when you plan foreign trips. (WHO Publication Center, 49 Sheridan Avenue, Albany, NY 12210.)

• Finally, if you get sick within a year after you return home, tell your doctor where you were! Some bugs invade your body but take months to introduce themselves, and this information can help the doctor diagnose your ailment promptly—and correctly.

WHERE TO STAY

As a young traveler, the kinds of accommodations open to you are varied, ranging from budget motels and hotels to college dormitories to campsites. Finding reasonably priced lodgings won't be difficult, but it will require initiative and planning on your part, and you must be prepared to do without certain amenities (such as color TV and swimming pools).

Some Options

In the United States and Canada, seek out budget motel chains. Many of these operate regionally, so you will do well to consult one of the hotel directories mentioned at the beginning of this chapter. Budget hotels and motels fill up quickly, especially during peak seasons. Make your reservations early and confirm them before you leave home.

A second option for domestic travelers in the summer is college and university dormitories. The easiest way to find out which schools rent rooms is to consult a guide such as the CIEE's *Where to Stay USA*. The accommodations may be Spartan, but college campuses can be great places to spend part of your vacation. Students can guide you to popular hangouts and suggest sightseeing tips and campus activities, such as concerts and galleries, for you to investigate. Usually, too, there are plenty of inexpensive restaurants and other attractions located nearby.

A third choice, if you are city-bound, are Young Men's Christian Associations (YMCAs) and Young Women's Christian Associations (YWCAs). Not all Ys offer overnight lodgings, but many do and often at prices comparable to those of budget motels. Their urban locations make them especially desirable places to stay, so write well in advance to guarantee yourself a room. To obtain a list of YMCAs nationwide, write to the Vanderbilt YMCA (224 East 47th Street, New York, NY 10017; telephone: (212)-755-2410). Most YMCAs accommodate women and families, but ask first. Write to this address for a list of overseas YMCAs, too.

Similarly, YWCAs offer inexpensive rooms with shared bathroom facilities. Most YWCAs will only house women, and non-Y members pay a small surcharge in addition to the regular rate. Write to the Data Center, YWCA (135 West 50th Street, New York, NY 10020; telephone: (212)-621-5115) for a list of the 123 YWCAs nationwide that have overnight lodgings; you will then have to write to each YWCA to make your reservations. If you plan to be in town a while, ask about reduced weekly rates.

Youth hostels, mentioned earlier in this chapter, provide a fourth budget alternative, and there are many from which to choose. Hostels are low-priced dormitory-style accommodations; a prerequisite for using the worldwide network is membership in American Youth Hostels. In fact, you can stay at some hostels without a membership card (with a surcharge tacked on), but if you plan to use hostels extensively, join. Be aware that hostels run according to strict rules: most are closed between 10:00 A.M. and 4:00 P.M., enforce evening curfews, and prohibit drinking and smoking. Moreover, many hostels in the United States are inaccessible by public transportation. Hostels can be a terrific place to stay—but you must do your research in advance. (More about hosteling and hostel trips in a moment.)

Finally, as a teenage domestic traveler, you should know of the Travelers Aid Society. Staff workers may be able to help you find a place to stay in an emergency—look for their offices at bus and train terminals and airports. But careful planning should eliminate any need to contact them for shelter.

If you travel abroad, you have some of the same options described above—plus. Consult guidebooks and, most important, plan far ahead. You will have lots of competition wanting to stay at inexpensive pensions, bed-and-breakfasts, and hostels, especially in peak seasons.

Tip: European train stations often have a special booth staffed to help travelers find hotel rooms. Still, it's always best to be prepared.

The following guidelines will help you pare hotel bills wherever you travel:

• If you can, make a reservation by a toll-free reservation system. Save the expense of a phone call.

• Ask for room rates by category. Even budget accommodations vary in price at the same establishment.

- Don't use room service. It's never inexpensive.
- Likewise, don't use hotel telephones. Find a pay phone and avoid steep surcharges.
- If you are driving, ask whether you will have to pay an additional parking fee.
- Observe check-out times. If you want to stay an hour or two beyond the scheduled check-out time, ask the manager if you may do so without extra charge.
- Find out whether your lodgings are on a public transportation route. Find out, too, how to get there from the train station, bus depot, or airport. If you have to rely on taxis to get around, you haven't found much of a bargain.
- Double up. Single rooms invariably cost more.
- Don't be shy—ask about student rates. Failing that, ask about business rates, off-season specials, and other discounts.

Hosteling

As mentioned earlier, membership in American Youth Hostels (AYH) opens to you a worldwide network of youth hostels—inexpensive, dormitory-style accommodations that provide beds, baths, and simple meals or kitchen facilities. In the early 1980s, there were 266 hostels distributed unevenly across the United States and more than 5,000 in 50 countries. At home, prices range from $2.50 to $7.50 a night; overseas, prices can be even lower, depending on the country.

AYH membership entitles you to sign up for travel programs, which typically include hiking, bicycling, and other outdoor activities, both in the United States and abroad. In one year at the start of the decade, for example, AYH offered a sixteen-day bicycle tour of the People's Republic of China and a three-week safari in Kenya. Domestic costs that year started at $345 for two-week cycling trips and escalated to $840 for six weeks on the road. Overseas trips generally are more expensive and, like the ones at home, are more costly for short tours. Trip prices include all group expenses: lodging, food, transportation for the duration of the trip, accident and health insurance, and other costs. List prices *do not* include transportation to the trip's assembly point (this means you pay extra for air or train fares), personal spending money, required equipment, travel documents, and membership dues. In other words, AYH trips are not necessarily inexpensive, but you can find affordable trips from the broad selection AYH offers.

AYH tours are divided among several age groups so you are assured of being with people your own age, along with an experienced and older guide. To join an AYH trip, you must be at least fourteen years old; all hostelers must be in good physical and emotional health, as certified by a doctor.

Membership costs vary according to category: if you're under eighteen, you'll pay about half the fee of a single, older individual. For current details on membership and tours, write to American Youth Hostels (1332 "Eye" Street, N.W., Washington, DC 20005, or call (202)-783-6161 or from March through October, toll-free: 1-800-424-9426).

HANDICAPPED TRAVELERS

If you are disabled in any way, you must obey in full the number one rule: plan ahead! Investigate all the options available to you. Then, as businesses adopt a more humane attitude about the problems handicapped people encounter while traveling, you'll find it increasingly easy to get around, see the sights, and find a place to stay.

Some tips to get you started:

• Rehabilitation International U.S.A. publishes the indispensable *International Directory of Access Guides*, and will mail you a single copy free of charge. Updated annually, the guide consists of hundreds of entries for access guides for cities, towns, parks, and transportation systems worldwide. (Rehabilitation International U.S.A., 20 West 40th Street, New York, NY 10018.)

• Virtually every travel guidebook now includes a section of tips for handicapped travelers. Study them.

• The U.S. government has publications that can help you plan your trips. Write to the Consumer Information Center (Department G, Pueblo, CO 81009) for an updated catalogue of pamphlets. Perennial titles include: *Access Travel*, which describes facilities and services at 472 airport terminals around the world, and *Golden*

Eagle/Golden Age/Golden Access Passports, which itemizes savings and reduced fares for handicapped travelers at our national parks.

• Look at a copy of *Health Information for International Travel*, another U.S. government special, available from the Superintendent of Documents (Government Printing Office, Washington, DC 20402).

• Also, see *A Travel Guide for the Disabled: Western Europe* by Mary Meister Walzer (Van Nostrand Reinhold, 1982).

USING A TRAVEL AGENT

A good travel agent helps you plan—and achieve—the trip you dream about. A savvy agent will save you substantial amounts of money, get you the maximum possible in convenience and special programs, find the best ''bargain'' deals in off-season travel, and offer advice on the little details that make a trip memorable, such as getting into the visitor's gallery at the House of Commons or finding your way around the San Diego Zoo. Under a Federal Government deregulation ruling in late 1982, the airlines were given unprecedented flexibility in selling tickets through just about any medium they wanted, but travel agents were not as severely downgraded as anticipated. Nothing really has changed so far; consumers have not benefited from the easier access to plane tickets; the travel agents are fighting back hard. So, how do you find this wonderful resource?

First, realize that travel agents receive their pay in the form of commissions from suppliers (airlines, hotels, resorts, car-rental agencies, etc.). Thus, with the exception of long-distance phone calls, wires, and cables, travel agents ''work'' for you for free.

Today, there are approximately 20,000 travel agencies in the United States. Look in the Yellow Pages of your phone book to get an idea of the number in your vicinity. Which agent is right for you?

• To avoid confusion, start by asking a trusted relative, classmate, or friend if they have used a travel agent they liked. You can then balance their recommendations against your preferences in personal service.

• Another excellent clue: find out how long the agent has been in business. Agents prosper from repeat business, which comes from satisfied clients—so the longer the agent's experience, the better for you. An estimated two-thirds to three-quarters of a travel agent's business comes from repeat customers.

• Look for professional accreditations. A travel agent has an official appointment from at least one transportation conference to issue tickets and to represent the group in arranging and selling tours and trips. These include such groups as the Air Traffic Conference (ATC) and the International Air Transport Association (IATA). Agencies which meet the financial and business requirements of these powerful organizations receive door stickers attesting to the approval of the organizations.

• The largest travel trade association in the United States is the American Society of Travel Agents, Inc. (ASTA), which requires members to have at least three years experience plus appointment by a minimum of two major transportation conferences. You can identify the ASTA insignia of members in the Yellow Pages.

The questions you ask a travel agent before you make your final arrangements are vital. Among ASTA's suggestions:

• What are the types of hotel accommodations available? Do they include meals? Is there a service charge?
• What do sightseeing tours include? Are the trips full-day or half-day? Are admission charges included?
• What are the cancellation privileges?
• How far in advance should reservations be made for charter flights? What happens to your trip if the flight is canceled?
• What do you need in terms of passport, visas, vaccinations, innoculations?
• What kind of clothing do you need for your destination? What are the average temperatures and climate conditions?
• How close to the hotel is the beach? (Or tennis courts? Or golf course? Or other facilities? Be skeptical here!)
• What is the name of the tour operator? When do you receive the itinerary? How many people will be in the group?

With these questions to start you off, you can carry on and ask other questions of basic concern to you. You will learn quickly how valuable the right agents (or how useless the wrong ones) can be.

TOURS

You may decide that an organized tour will provide you with the most enjoyable and affordable trip. If so, you will have hundreds of tours from which to select, both at home and abroad. The variety of trips designed for teenagers is astounding: among your choices are camping trips, deluxe bus tours, theme trips (great cathedrals of Europe, for example), and educational and study programs. You should have no trouble finding a tour that fits both your interests and budget if you choose this option.

Before you decide on a specific tour, though, be warned: there has been no evaluation compiled of the youth tour business, although a few tour groups have been accredited by the American Camping Association. It's up to you to investigate your chosen tour thoroughly.

To find an interesting selection of tours, look in the Sunday travel section of your local newspaper and glance in the back of the Sunday *New York Times Magazine* (you'll find it at your library).

A guidance counselor at school, friends, or a student travel service can also offer worthwhile suggestions. Write away for brochures and then read them carefully. Make a list of questions to ask the tour operator—things you must know to decide whether this trip is for you.

Keep in mind these suggestions when you decide on a tour:

• Ask the tour operator for referrals of previous clients. If he/she will not or cannot provide you with alumni references, forget it! They're not being straight with you.

• When you do speak with tour veterans, ask about the group's leadership, since the leaders will be important people in your life for the duration of the trip. Ask if the tour was well organized, fun, and lived up to its promises. Finally, ask the veterans whether they recommend the trip to you. If yes, why? If not, why not?

• Speak with the tour operators and ask how they recruit group leaders, whether the operators and leaders receive any special training, and what is the ratio of members to leaders. Request a description of qualifications and referrals of previous leaders.

• Find out whether the tour operator screens applicants. Is everyone accepted who applies? Are potential group members interviewed? Are you being interviewed? Answers to these questions truly reveal how the tour groups are put together.

• Be certain that you understand exactly what expenses are covered by your payment and what the refund policy is should you be forced to withdraw or should the tour be canceled. Look for any hidden costs that might confront you with unwelcome surprises. Ask, too, about tips and gratuities. Determine how much spending money you will need and how much free time to expect. Don't overlook any factors that might add to (or diminish) your enjoyment of the trip.

A good tour operator should be happy to give you all this information. Don't be afraid to ask questions—it's your money and your trip.

Several well-known national organizations sponsor rigorous and unusual tours. You already know about the American Youth Hostels. Others include:

• *The Sierra Club,* which sponsors hundreds of trips around the country. You can choose among canoeing, hiking, and riding programs—you'll have no trouble finding a trip to match your energy level. Write to the Sierra Club (530 Bush Street, San Francisco, CA 94108) for details. Local chapters of the Sierra Club also sponsor outings; check your phone book.

• *The Wilderness Society* emphasizes travel to undeveloped areas of the country. Learn about ecology and natural history while hiking or horseback-riding through breathtaking scenery. For information, contact the Wilderness Society (Western Regional Office, 4260 Evans Avenue, Denver, CO 80222), or the national headquarters, (1901 Pennsylvania Avenue, N.W., Washington, DC 20006).

• *Outward Bound* has rigorous programs which challenge your sense of adventure and encourage you to test and expand your limits. Financial aid is available for most programs, and forms will be sent to you on request after you apply to an Outward Bound School. Requests are evaluated both on need and a first-come-first-served basis; nearly 30 percent of Outward Bound students take advantage of the financial aid program. Find out more by writing to Outward Bound (National Office, 384 Field Point Road, Greenwich, CT 06830), or phone toll-free: 1-800-243-8520 (except Connecticut, where the number is (203) 661-0797).

• *The Experiment in International Living* promotes international understanding through travel abroad, language study, and homestays, in which participants live as part of a family in another country. The EIL, or Experiment as it is often called, is a private, nonprofit organization that offers summer and academic semester programs for high school and college students. Most, but not all, are built around the homestay experience, which gives young Americans the chance to see another country from the inside.

Additionally, visitors from more than thirty countries take part in EIL programs in the United States.

For more details, write to the Experiment in International Living (Brattleboro, VT 05301). Tel.: 802-257-7751.

SUMMER CAMP

Summer camp. The words evoke images of white-washed cabins, piney woods, long days spent sailing, swimming, playing tennis, horseback riding; and evenings spent listening to the snap and hiss of campfire flames. You meet and live with interesting people of your age group, develop new skills, and polish old ones—chiefly outdoors. You can indulge a passion for sports—soccer, basketball, tennis; the arts—theater, music, dance; educational programs—languages, computers; weight reduction; and many, many others. If you have a particular health problem (diabetes or limited mobility, for example) don't write off the idea of summer camps; there are special facilities for campers with similar problems. Hundreds of camps await your choice: your biggest problem will be selecting the right one.

How to Choose a Camp

When choosing a camp, your chief considerations are location, program, and, of course, cost. Since you'll find camps in every state, one approach is to select a geographic region and explore its possibilities. Other hints:

• Camps often are operated by religious and civic organizations. These affiliations can determine a camp's program and participants.

• At the very start, decide the kinds of activities you like and the skills you want to learn to help you define the type of camp you want to attend.

• Sort through the staggering variety of choices with a copy of the American Camping Association's *Parents' Guide to Accredited Camps*, which is updated annually. You can buy it from regional offices of the ACA or write to the American Camping Association (Bradford Woods, Martinsville, IN 46151).

To be accredited by the ACA, camps must be inspected every three years and pass certain standards of administration, program, personnel, and campsite. The guide doesn't rate camps; instead, it provides a state-by-state list, including fees, facilities, name and address of the director, number of campers, and age brackets. One index includes detailed charts that let you locate a specific program in a particular state; a second index lists camps that appeal to anyone with particular health or educational needs.

• Another useful resource is the Sunday *New York Times Magazine*, which carries camp advertising. Look for it at your local library. And check your local newspaper regularly!

• Don't overlook your high school guidance counselor, and ask religious groups and civic organizations for recommendations.

• Flip through the Yellow Pages under "Camps."

• Those of you interested in camps in the Northeast should request a copy of *A Guide for Selecting a Private Camp*, from the Association of Independent Camps (157 West 57th Street, New York, NY 10019).

• Start investigating camps in the fall, even though it seems that summer is light-years away. Good camps fill their enrollments early. After you find camps with stimulating programs and affordable costs for you, write for their brochures and applications. Then you and your parents will want to meet with the director. You can't make a smart decision based on glossy pictures and testimonials.

Since camp can be expensive, don't hesitate to talk about money. Find out exactly what the camp's fees include, and let the following checklist help you:

• Is there an application fee?
• Does the total payment include transportation to and from camp?

- Are insurance and health coverage included?
- Is there a separate laundry fee? Can you make alternative arrangements?
- Are excursions and day-trips covered?
- Are extra fees added for such activities as horseback riding and computer time?
- How much spending money will you need?
- Do you need special equipment or clothing?

Most camps include in their tuition the services used by all campers: lodging, food, athletic facilities, infirmary, laundry, and so on. But still, you deflect unwelcome surprises by asking, first.

You can find ways to beat the high cost of summer camp, too:

- Investigate nonprofit camps, some of which adjust their fees to your ability to pay. The ACA *Guide* lists camps for the "economically disadvantaged." Ignore how terrible that sounds; the list comprises hundreds of camps.
- If your parents are paying, tell them they might be eligible for a tax deduction under the day-care provisions in the tax law. Don't be embarrassed by the sound of "day care." It might make all the difference whether or not you can afford to go to camp.

If you attend weight-loss camp, have your folks look into possible tax deductions for medical expenses.

Incidental costs can creep up on you. Good examples include visiting day and transportation of your belongings:

- Find out whether your parents will have to stay overnight for visiting day. Are there good hotels or motels nearby, and what are their rates?
- If you have to send your belongings to camp, look into United Parcel Service and third-class mail for bulky objects, such as your duffel bag.

Some of you are in classes for "gifted children." Did you know that you can attend camps for gifted children, too? Start your search at the state department of education, and you will almost surely find state-sponsored and other agency-sponsored projects that offer rewarding programs. Most states have within the state department of education a bureau for gifted and talented children, and you'll also find state art councils a help, particularly if the councils sponsor programs. Look for ads in specialized publications covering dance, arts, or music. Ask high school and private teachers (and perhaps your classmates and friends) for advice.

If you have a camp in mind, you and your parents should visit it as soon as you can. Ask for a list of past instructors and talk with them to get a feel for the facility and program.

In addition to checking the food, housing, and arts facilities, study the list of sponsors—then get ready for some detective work. For example, a state department of education tells you that the educational system endorses the camp. If a camp is completely sponsored by the state government, ask probing questions about the funding. If state and local arts and humanities councils are involved, you are dealing with people who are deeply sensitive to art and who make their influence felt in running the camp.

Travel and tourism department participation in sponsorship frequently means the camp will offer a series of public concerts, dance programs, or art exhibits by campers. If the camp is getting funds from national organizations such as the National Endowment for the Arts or the American Federation of Musicians, consider that a ''plus.''

From your parents' standpoint, funding from private foundations keeps costs down. And from the camp's viewpoint, well-known private sponsors make it easier to attract other contributors.

Most camps are improving admission and scholarship policies. Admission is no longer a matter of talent alone, but has been broadened to include highly motivated teens with potential talents. Does this sound like you? And scholarships often are available to those who truly need them.

Using a Camp Referral Service

If you become thoroughly confused after investigating a number of camps that offer a feast of programs, you might want to use a camp referral service. Some of these advertise in the ACA *Guide*, and you can find others in the Yellow Pages. A good service will match you—your interests, your preferences—to a camp, and receive a commission from the camp itself. But, before you entrust your summer to an agency, check it out, too.

A good agency visits the camps where it places clients so it can represent the camps accurately. The agent is not content to mail you a fistful of brochures, but will interview you and your parents and then recommend a camp tailored to your requirements and budget. In the fall, the agent should follow up with a detailed questionnaire or phone call to ask about your experiences. Also ask the agent about other placement services. Can you get information about tours, summer school, and private school, as examples? And, of course, check with the Better Business Bureau if you have any doubts.

Summer comes but once a year. Don't let a fast-talking agent or camp director convince you to spend your precious time—not to mention money—on a camp that suits neither your interests nor your budget.

TRAVEL ODDS AND ENDS

It's all in the planning. Be alert to the endless possibilities. Equip yourself properly. Free your precious vacation time for fun, relaxation, and learning, instead of hassles and chores. Herewith a grab bag of travel hints:

• Check bulletin boards, student newspapers, and magazines for timely information on offbeat, rewarding trips and programs.

• Stock up on essentials before you leave. Sure, you can buy film, batteries, tape cassettes, and tampons abroad—often at three or four times the amount you expect to pay at home.

• If you're traveling to a resort with your family, ask about special programs for teenagers. These might include day-trips, introductions to local teens, and sports events.

• Does the idea of herding sheep in Australia or sampling other occupations around the world appeal to you? Order a copy of *Working Holidays*, from the Canadian Bureau for International Information (141 Laurier Avenue West, Suite 809, Ottawa, Ontario, Canada K1P 5J3). The book includes addresses of organizations that can place you in jobs around the world, as well as travel information and practical advice.

• Earthwatch provides teams of volunteers to scientists to assist with a variety of research. Most projects are timed for summer vacations, and volunteer shifts last two to three weeks. For information on field research projects, costs, and scholarships, write to Earthwatch (Box 127, 10 Juniper Road, Belmont, MA 02178).

• Many prep schools and colleges offer special programs for high school students. Usually you can receive academic credit, and many are designed to give you a taste of a college freshman's experience. For programs near you, check with your guidance counselor; also contact local prep schools, the state university, or simply write to the admissions office of a school about which you know and ask whether it has such programs, or can suggest some to you.

• Consider a temporary membership in Assist Card Corporation of America. If you encounter problems such as canceled flights, lost travel documents, illness, or other emergencies, membership entitles you to call on local Assist Card representatives. Its function is to remedy the problem, be it legal, financial, personal, or medical in origin. You can buy memberships for as few as five days (in the early 1980s, that cost $25). For details, write to Assist Card Corporation of America, Inc. (745 Fifth Avenue, New York, NY 10022), or call, toll-free: 1-800-221-4564 (except New York, where it's (212)-752-2788).

13

LEISURE IN YOUR LIFE

CONTENTS

Stretches of free time invite you to try new activities, catch up on postponed chores, read, play games, and just relax. It's your time, to spend as you choose.

Except . . . most hours spent away from school and work are devoted to essential tasks: sleeping, doing homework, eating, practicing, helping out around the house. Surely, though, you find some spare moments for activities that give you special pleasure.

Leisure time provides your chance to refresh yourself and use the energy pent up in classrooms and carpools. True recreation helps you meet the challenges you face every day by allowing you to concentrate on activities (or nonactivities) that make you happy, and respond to needs that don't get fulfilled in study hall. And you have fun in the process.

Each of you enjoys many ways of relaxing and "recreating." Some ways are highly structured, such as games; others essentially are free form, including everyone's favorite: hanging out.

Obviously, leisure time covers hobbies and sports, time-honored ways of recreation that can require cash outlays, lessons, and special supplies. In short, recreation can cost you money. So to enjoy this precious time to its fullest, plan ahead. Which pastime can you afford now? Which might you save up for?

To choose hobbies and sports that you enjoy, think about activities that intrigue you now. The most popular hobby in the world will bore you if it doesn't excite your imagination. Consider, too, how much free time is actually yours—whether it occurs in blocks or little fragments, and how you can put either to use. Not least, factor in the costs of your choices. Some of the best things in life may be free; others may cost very little once you make the initial purchases (hiking, jogging); and some can be quite costly (scuba diving, parachuting).

We are a nation of hobbyists and sports enthusiasts. Every year, we spend tens of billions of dollars on recreational activities, yet so much of this is wasted because we buy unselectively. Quality equipment—for whatever purpose—is expensive. If you tire of its purpose quickly, you've wasted your money.

When you plan and budget your allowance, recreation will account for a hefty percentage. Before you take up a new pastime, do your budget homework for the activity itself. How much do lessons cost? Will you need them? Does it require special tools and materials? How about clothing and equipment? Can you rent any of these items before you begin? Or borrow from a friend, so you can take your time to decide how much you like the activity?

You can divide your recreation expenses into predictable categories and decide how much you want to spend, or actually have available, for each one. Here are sample categories to help you plan the costs of your leisure time:

- Hobbies: special equipment, materials, books, instruction
- Sports: equipment, clothing, travel, tickets, lessons
- Special events: concerts, dances, etc.
- Daily recreation: movies, records, and tapes

You may develop additional categories to help you protect your budget. The sums you allot for recreation will change as your interests develop, you discover new activities, and you have more to spend.

This is the most flexible line in your budget—expenses sensitive to your fluctuating allowance, babysitting schedule, after-school job, full-time employment. Awareness of the costs of your favorite activities will help you derive even more pleasure from them, for by planning ahead, you free time to relax and enjoy them.

VOLUNTEERING: MORE THAN STUFFING ENVELOPES

When you hear the phrase "volunteer work," do images form in your mind of gnomes bent over cartons of envelopes, licking labels, and gluing on stamps? Or do you envision eager, cheerful people thrusting unwelcome flyers on reluctant passersby? Volunteer work encompasses these tasks, and they can be vital to the success of a project—and fun besides. But volunteer work involves other jobs as well, so if you think it is limited to tedious, meaningless chores that no one wants to do, you are shutting yourself out of a valuable, challenging way to use some of your free time.

Millions of us volunteer some of our spare time to serve thousands of institutions and causes. In fact, according to a national survey conducted early in the decade, 47 percent of Americans aged fourteen and above contribute their time to help others in such organizations as schools, hospitals, churches, and social service and cultural agencies; and an additional 5 percent assist their friends in informal ways, such as donating a pie to a church bake sale or driving a disabled neighbor to the supermarket or a doctor's appointment.

A really impressive statistic: 53 percent of teens aged fourteen through seventeen spend some of their leisure time in volunteer work.

If you'd like to be among them, you'll find you are welcome among volunteers in many nonprofit enterprises, from theater groups and cultural and educational organizations to health, social service, and religious agencies.

Volunteerism is a central value in many national youth groups, the Girl Scouts, the YMCA, 4-H Clubs, and the Boy Scouts among them. Religious youth groups and civic organizations sponsor volunteer activities for their members. Local branches of any of these can fill you in on details and will be delighted by your interest.

Many of you can test out career interests while you learn new tasks and meet intriguing new people. If you're interested in the health professions, a hospital or nursing home is a natural target. Future veterinarians will profit from working at an animal shelter, rescue league, or local office of the ASPCA. Museums, historical societies, and theatrical groups—cultural outfits that operate on shoestring budgets—often need volunteers to help with special assignments, as well as to serve as receptionists, guides, sales help, and telephone operators.

Does politics enthrall you? No better civics lesson exists than to volunteer in a political campaign. You can count on work at least every two years and, depending where you live, local elections may occur between Congressional and national races.

Are you passionately involved in a cause? Volunteer your time: whatever side of an issue you take, a group exists to publicize it and needs help in raising funds, publicity, and countless other chores.

The point is that whatever your interests, talents, age, and skills, you can find a volunteer job that will be fun and satisfying to you and to the agency. Volunteer work can clarify career choices or simply provide an outlet for your enthusiasm, energy, and concern that remain untapped at school or work.

The bonuses of volunteering are huge. You feel involved in an important activity. You see the contribution you make. You meet people with similar interests and values. You develop interests and abilities that, completely unknown to you, lie hidden inside you.

To find out more about volunteering, write to "Volunteers," P.O. Box 4179, Boulder, CO 80306.

HOBBIES

Getting Started

Do you like to tinker with Lionel trains, collect beer cans, play chess, weave belts, braid rugs? These and hundreds of other pastimes that provide hours of pleasure and amusement fall under the heading of hobbies. A hobby can be sophisticated or simple, sedentary or active, but all hobbies have in common enjoyment and planned use of spare time.

A satisfying hobby is a surefire hedge against loneliness and boredom, and can even become a source of income (see Chapter 1, *Where Does Your Money Come From?*).

You doubtless have sampled many as you've grown up; discarded some and perhaps postponed trying new ones until you're older or have more money. Whatever your hobbies are now, look for ways to derive even more fun (and maybe profit) from them:

• Check out classes offered through YMCAs, YWCAs, park and recreation programs, community colleges, high schools. Low-cost instruction can introduce you to new activities without requiring a big investment in materials and tools. Among common offerings: making jewelry, working with stained glass, ceramics, woodworking, refinishing furniture, painting.

• Find out about crafts clubs in your area. At these you'll learn about new techniques, tools, and developments; meet people, swap information, and exchange ideas. You also can help develop outlets to sell your finished products through craft fairs and flea markets organized by the clubs, as you improve your skills. Another outlet: local crafts councils.

• Read up on your favorite crafts. The crafts section of your library and bookstore will introduce you to all levels of proficiency and suggest new crafts to try. An encyclopedic reference, *Reader's Digest Crafts and Hobbies* (Reader's Digest Association, Inc., 1979), provides a step-by-step guide to creative skills such as bookbinding, macrame, candlemaking, collage, leatherworking, and winemaking. All the basics of the crafts revival are in this reference.

• Perhaps your interests lie in collecting things—shells, dolls, stamps, coins, comic books. An association exists for every collectible, as well as books and magazines that list current prices and availability of different goods. Learn which ones are authoritative for your specialty so you can stay up-to-date with changes in the market. Join groups that stress your interest. Find out what dealers have the best reputations. Building a good collection takes time as well as money. Maintaining it requires your attention and devotion.

If finding current data about your collection is a problem, you can plug that information gap with Collectrix, a pocket-sized reference guide that is published three times yearly. It notes all forthcoming books about antiques and collectibles, and lists new editions of standard price guides, remaindered copies, and out-of-print volumes. While not recommending specific titles, it does let you know what's available, and when.

To find out about subscriptions, write to Collectrix (146 Front Street, Hempstead, NY 11550).

Organizations and Associations

Look through the *Encyclopedia of Associations* (Gale Press, current edition) which should be in the reference room at your library. One whole section lists associations for every imaginable hobby, craft, collectible, game, and sport. Some of these are specifically for teenagers and will provide you with current information and ideas for your specialty. Here's a suggestive sample:

National Model Railroad 　Association Box 2186 Indianapolis, IN 46206	Teen Association of Model 　Railroading 1028 Whaley Road, Route 3 New Carlisle, OH 45344

(The Teen Association is for thirteen to twenty-year-olds interested in model railroading, contests, building, and operations.)

American Numismatic Association
  (coins)
Box 2366
Colorado Springs, CO 80901

American Philatelic Society
  (stamps)
Box 800
State College, PA 16801

(There are nine pages of listings in the *Encyclopedia* for organizations appealing to stamp collectors!)

National Woodcarver's Association
7424 Miami Avenue
Cincinnati, OH 45243

Handweavers Guild of America
The Exchange
Farmington, CT 06032

Embroiderers Guild of America
6 East 45th Street, Room 1501
New York, NY 10017

World Pen Pals
1690 Como Avenue
St. Paul, MN 55108

(World Pen Pals is a clearinghouse for 40,000 teenagers to exchange letters and match up with pen pals.)

United States Chess Federation
186 Route 9-W
New Windsor, NY 12550

American Radio Relay League
225 Main Street
Newington, CT 06111

Beer Can Collectors of America
7500 Devonshire
St. Louis, MO 63119

Many of these associations publish directories and magazines to keep you informed about special classes, programs, new developments, techniques, and other useful information so you can fully enjoy your chosen hobby.

Focus on Photography

Photographs freeze memorable events in our own lives and those of leaders and heroes; remind us of travels; can be works of art and subjects of study. Photography continues to zoom in popularity as a hobby (in fact, it's a national passion). We spend billions annually on cameras, film, developing costs, supplies, courses, exhibitions,

publications. Cameras accompany us to sporting events, family reunions, and destinations near and far. Authentic shutterbugs
never go anywhere without a camera (or cameras!).

Photography appeals to millions of us, but many never bother to
learn how to enjoy the fullest use of cameras and accompanying
gear—films, lenses, filters, flashes. To become a really good photographer takes time and practice, although the basics can be mas-
tered by anyone with a simple camera and a few rolls of film.
More complex skills require more complicated equipment and
study.

Most of you probably have cameras right now that were given to
you as birthday presents or bought with your savings. You know
that cameras can cost from $25 to thousands of dollars, depending
on their features and manufacturers. Professional equipment and
attachments can be costly indeed. You are aware, too, that even a
simple camera can provide sharp pictures and easy handling. Still,
it's very easy to become confused about what you need.

Since photography, more than many hobbies, requires that you
spend money to enjoy it, it's vital that you do your homework before you buy. Hundreds of books and magazines are devoted to the
subject; read a few and be conversant with apertures and f-stops
before you shop. Experienced photographers love to talk about
their equipment, so speak up and ask for advice. Explain your current skills and aspirations. If you want to learn how to develop pictures, arrange to visit a friend's darkroom or ask at a local camera
shop where you can observe the process before you spend hundreds of dollars to equip one. Investigate photography classes at
local community centers, shops, and community colleges. Photography is so incredibly popular that low-cost classes often compete
with each other for students in the same town—to your advantage.

Many organizations sponsor activities around photography for
teenagers. Among them: Scouting groups, 4-H clubs, YMCAs and
YWCAs, and civic groups. Your phone book and a few calls will
lead you right to them.

As you immerse yourself in photography, develop a relationship
with a reputable camera shop. As you upgrade equipment, ask
about trade-ins and resale value, since used camera equipment is a
popular choice with many photographers. Read the instructions
carefully for each new piece of gear so you'll know how it works
and what results to expect.

Photographs may be magic, but the techniques and tools used to create them are very real. Be sure you understand such basics as loading and advancing the film, using the flash, setting shutter speeds and lens openings, and changing batteries. Learn what kinds of film work best in different situations, light settings, and speeds.

Photography is a lifelong hobby that provides hours of pleasure, creative expression, and lasting results. Once you're hooked, you'll stay with it forever. The following publications will help you get started, or continue on your way:

The Amateur Photographer's Handbook, Aaron Sussman. Thomas Y. Crowell, 1973.

The Basic Darkroom Book, Tom Grimm. New American Library, 1978.

Beginner's Guide to the Single Lens Reflex Camera, Nikon Educational Services, 1978.

The Darkroom Handbook, Michael Langford. Alfred A. Knopf, 1981.

The Joy of Photography and *More Joy of Photography,* Editors of Eastman Kodak. Addison-Wesley, 1979 and 1981.

The Photographer's Handbook, John Hedgecoe. Alfred A. Knopf, 1977.

Successful Photography, Andreas Feininger. Prentice-Hall, 1975.

Kodak Publications—obtainable at local photography shops or write for information to Eastman Kodak, Dept. 841GS, Rochester, NY, 14650.

Time-Life series on photography.

The 4-H Club has produced a number of manuals to help you enjoy photography more and learn how to mount slides, produce a slide show, and other offshoots. For a list, write to "Educational Aids," National 4-H Council, 7100 Connecticut Avenue, Chevy Chase, MD 20815.

THE SPORTING LIFE

The cost of sports instruction and equipment can outpace your budget if you don't plan for it. Every year, parents attending the World Figure Skating Championships reveal that their children's lessons, equipment, and travel expenses total thousands of dollars annually. The costs represent a major portion of the family budget.

Keeping Costs Down

Life at the top of even amateur sports depends on a huge financial commitment, and merely beginning a sport can be expensive. But you can minimize start-up expenses in a number of ways, still learn the game, and have a good time.

• Economize wherever you can. No one ever played superior tennis because he/she was wearing the latest designer sportswear. The clothes may look swell, but they get sweaty and crumpled just like any others. A pair of shorts and T-shirt will be perfect. Similarly, do you really need a fancy warm-up suit for jogging? Or can you wear your sweatshirt and sweatpants from high school gym classes? Of course, in sports that require specialized clothing for safety and comfort, buy what you need for proper protection.

• Before you invest in state-of-the-art equipment, decide whether you truly enjoy the sport and expect to continue it. Should you purchase equipment, buy what you need to assist your development—give yourself room to grow. You don't need professional caliber equipment if you're just starting out or have middling abilities. Test your commitment to the sport: will you really play more often with top-of-the-line gear, or will it gather dust in your closet, along with other relics of past enthusiasms?

• When you rent gear, make certain you understand the agreement's terms and have looked for hidden fees and penalties. Check that the equipment is in good condition when you receive it, and return it in the same condition. For some kinds of sporting goods, stores will deduct rental costs if and when you decide to buy.

• Take a block of lessons before you buy the clothes and equipment. Inquire about classes at community facilities: high school, community college, Red Cross, YMCA or YWCA, junior colleges, and universities. For most sports, you don't have to drop a fortune at an expensive health club to learn the basic skills and rules of the game.

• Local park and recreation councils sponsor classes and leagues for a number of sports—tennis, golf, and soccer among them. Low-cost instruction and organized games are designed to appeal to amateur players of varying abilities.

• Ask coaches and physical education instructors for advice about lessons and equipment. They have current working knowledge of the local sporting scene: who are the good instructors, where to get the best deals on equipment, and so on.

• The tennis racket, jogging shoes, or catcher's mitt beloved by your friends may not be the best choices for you. Elaborate advertising campaigns may persuade you that only with *this* product can you play the sport—a claim that is rarely true. Buy what suits you and your abilities, not what works for your friends or looks smashing in a magazine.

• Don't neglect to buy or rent safety equipment. All the lessons in the world will be useless if you fail to wear and use recommended gear and procedures. Sports injuries are soaring and many of them have debilitating and lifelong consequences. That means: wear helmets, goggles, gloves, mouth guards—whatever is required for the sports you participate in.

• The best opportunities to buy sports equipment and clothing are during pre- and postseason clearance sales. For instance, spring is a fine time to buy football helmets; sales on ski equipment sprout in March; swimwear buys are best right after the Fourth of July during midsummer clearances. Shop around and protect yourself by dealing with reputable sporting goods stores.

• Finally, resist temptation to replace fairly new gear with the latest, most feverishly promoted products. Will they really improve your game, speed, endurance, strength? Or do you simply have to work out more often and try harder? Equipment, after all, doesn't provide the muscle power. You do.

In the following pages, a few of the most popular sports will be highlighted. We can't possibly cover all the athletic options you have today—from hang gliding to gymnastics to basketball—but you'll find that often the rules for starting out are the same. With proper equipment, a little instruction, and some like-minded companions, a sporting interest can bring you both good fun and good health.

Jogging/Running

In the 1970s, everyone was off and running—and the boom continues. New marathons, half-marathons, minimarathons, and assorted other road races multiply; clothing and shoe manufacturers design new products for both serious runners and those who want to look the part; we snap up books and magazines that cater to this sport.

Running is big business in addition to great exercise. All the paraphernalia surrounding jogging can obscure a simple truth: all you really need to run is a good pair of shoes and socks. That's it. The elegant warm-up suits, windbreakers, designer shorts, and T-shirts may look great, but they improve neither your speed nor endurance. Only you can do that, by means of daily or regular runs, training, and discipline. (Make an exception, though, if you're a girl who wears a C-cup or larger bra—you might want to try a sports bra that provides lots of support and relieves the discomfort and jouncing caused by running and other sports.)

For those of you who are seriously eager to learn about diet, warm-up exercises, physiology, conditioning, and all the other subjects that fascinate runners, turn to the books and magazines at your library and bookstore. Among them: *The Complete Book of Running*, James Fixx (Random House, 1977), *The Runner's Handbook*, Bob Glover and Jack Shepherd (Penguin Books, 1977), and *Runners World* and *The Runner*, each published monthly.

Whether you're a newcomer to the sport or a daily jogger, you must have good running shoes. Once you've bought a pair, expenses plummet to nothing, or next to nothing, until the shoes need repair or replacement.

Shoes can cost from $25 to more than $100 for a pair, but they're worth the money for the protection they give your arches, feet, and legs. Simple sneakers aren't adequate to the stresses of regular and prolonged jogging. And the investment in a good pair of running shoes will keep you on the track or roadway even when your muscles cry out for a break!

The main clues to finding good running shoes are comfort and fit. Give yourself lots of time at the store—and buy at a sporting goods or runners' supply shop where experienced runners can fit you and explain different models. Bring along the socks you expect to wear while jogging—an obvious point, perhaps, but often overlooked. Avoid ordering shoes by mail since you can't try them on and fit to your larger foot, the way you can in a store, until you hit on a model you like. Most running shoes are now made of lightweight nylon and/or leather and are carefully designed to support your foot, ankle, and arch. Quality shoes are easy to find.

Virtually all running shoes are constructed with a half inch to an inch of cushioning to protect feet and shins from the shock of slamming down on pavement. Heels are built up higher than toes to prevent strain on the Achilles tendon and enclose a "cup" to support the runner's own heel. Any runners with orthopedic problems should see a podiatrist and get special inserts fitted to their shoes. If you have any inserts, tote them along when you buy shoes.

The same rules apply to fitting running shoes as street shoes and boots: half an inch between your big toe and the inside of the front of the shoe. No pinching, no wobbling. You definitely want to be able to wiggle your toes. If you run for fun, not competition, consider studying the shoe ratings included as features in magazines such as *Runners World* (every October). Expert runners caution you not to rely completely on these surveys—not every highly rated shoe will fit you or work for you.

When you bring your new shoes home, allow yourself time to break them in. A ten-mile run in a new pair is not wise. You can easily wind up with blisters and, after hobbling back to the store, accuse the salesperson of selling you crummy goods.

Before you toss out your old shoes, try patching or resoling them. Typically, runners first wear down the outer soles on their shoes; these can be repaired easily if caught in time. Early detection is important to you anyway, since run-down heels place additional stress on feet and legs and can precipitate injuries. You will find a selection of products made of rubber or rubberlike substances which you apply to soles and let ''cure'' or dry for up to several days. These products work equally well on tennis sneakers and other sports shoes.

Do not be carried away by the mystique of running shoes. Whether you run five miles or five blocks daily, you need good shoes and can find them at a price you can afford. The colors, the stripes—is that how you want to spend your money? It's not the shoes that make you run a sub-three-hour marathon, is it?

Golf

Golf's pleasures and challenges, plus the success achieved by Nathaniel Crosby, Nancy Lopez, and other young players, lure more of you onto the courses each year. The National Golf Foundation estimates that 1.8 million Americans under eighteen play golf regularly and that many more of you play occasionally. But many people—surely some of you—who are interested in the sport shy away because they assume they can't afford it. While it's true that golfing equipment can run into thousands of dollars at the upper levels of the game, you can outfit yourself with a few clubs for less than $100 and, more important, you can rent equipment until you're ready to buy.

Beginning golfers, however, need instruction. If you fit that classification, seek out classes in your community. Try such facilities as the YMCA, Park and Recreation Departments, municipal golf courses, and high school and college physical education departments. Group lessons are inexpensive and will acquaint you with the game's basics; private instruction can cost from $10 to $100 an hour, depending in part on the pro's reputation. As your skills improve, you may decide to invest in some private lessons, but by then you will be better equipped to evaluate your needs and your teacher.

Look for instructors who have been certified by the Professional Golfers Association (PGA) or Ladies Professional Golfers Association (LPGA), particularly when you choose private lessons. The teaching divisions of these organizations certify their professionals and require periodic reexamination, so you'll have instructors who know the most current techniques and training methods.

To play golf, you will need some clubs, shoes, and other equipment. If you plan to buy clubs, go to the pro shop at a golf course, a golf specialty store, or a reputable sporting goods store. To enjoy the sport fully, you need clubs that fit your height and grip, are not too heavy, and won't bend or snap.

To help you choose, you need the counsel of a knowledgeable player or pro. "Multipurpose" clubs, such as some sold at big discount stores, frequently are a waste of money. Another tip: regular players are constantly buying new sets of clubs to replace their current ones. Look for ads in the classified section of your newspaper and check in at the local pro shop. These clubs are perfectly all right; players just keep searching for the ideal set that will help them realize the dream of coming in under par every round.

Similarly, when you buy golf shoes, keep in mind the fitting pointers you employ whenever you buy footgear. If they're not comfortable, try another pair. You walk a great deal on the golf course and if your toes are pinched, how can you get around?

Golf, more than many other sports, requires expensive equipment, so look into renting what you need for the first few times you play. In the long run it's much more economical to rent than buy cheap, shoddy putters and irons that break apart. Renting gives you a chance to decide gradually whether you like the game; pro shops and golf specialty stores are happy to satisfy new customers by renting quality goods. Read the rental agreement carefully, as you would read any other contract.

Scuba Diving

When you see on TV a Jacques Cousteau or National Geographic special about marine life, do you yearn to explore the mysteries revealed by the cameras? About 2.6 million Americans live out this dream as they wriggle into wet suits, strap on air tanks, and dive into oceans and lakes, near and far. In fact, divers spend about $500 million a year on scuba equipment and travel. ("Scuba" is an acronym for Self-Contained Underwater Breathing Apparatus.)

Alluring as it might sound, you can't just drive to the nearest beach, buckle on a tank, and dive in. Divers must be certified by an agency such as the National Association of Underwater Instructors before they can rent equipment and refill air tanks, both here and in the Caribbean. To be certified, you must take a course of lessons that lasts from twenty to twenty-five hours and includes lectures, pool work, and open-water diving. Courses cost from $150 to $250; not all include equipment rentals in the fees. Know before you sign up what gear you are expected to buy or rent during your lessons.

Once you are certified, the waters of the world open up to you. Scuba diving is popular in the Mediterranean, Caribbean, Australia, and other exotic destinations; serious divers plan vacations around their favorite sport. The equipment used for this dramatic pastime can give your budget a jolt: early in the decade, the cost of a full set of gear—including wet suit, fins, mask, snorkel, watch, tanks, inflatable vest, lights, regulators with gauges, and the rest—totaled more than $1,000 and could easily amount to $2,000. Rental costs often may be applied to future purchases, so always ask about this provision.

Approximately 200,000 people take the plunge each year. To learn more about the sport (and perhaps to join them) look for copies of *Skin Diver* magazine, or check the Yellow Pages under "scuba diving."

Skiing

Skiing is winter's royal sport and the sums we spend on it are princely indeed—almost a billion dollars a year on equipment and clothes alone. Clever skiers schuss their way to money-saving values on their purchases and lift tickets by doing their homework on how and where to cut costs.

Since skiers thrive outdoors in bitterly cold temperatures, warm clothes are essential. The most fashionable—and often most expensive—garments don't always stand up to wind, wet, and cold, no matter how great they look. When you shop for skiwear, look for the following:

• The fabric is the most important component of any skiwear, providing you with softness, warmth, durability, and flexibility. Outer fabrics should be waterproof, water repellant, and tear-resistant. Check wind resistance by trying to blow through the parka—if you can blow through the fabric, so can the wind.

• Look for a collar that can be turned up to protect you from the wind and sudden temperature drops, plus a storm collar and cuffs to hug your neck and wrists and keep out snow and wind.

• Examine the seams. Thread should be made of high-tensile polyester, and seam allowances should be overlocked to prevent raveling. Top stitching reinforces seams.

• A parka should have a placket either over or under the zipper to provide extra protection from the wind. Make sure that the zipper tape is strong and that the zipper itself is stitched properly to the garment. A large pull lets you zip up even while wearing your mittens.

• Ski bibs should be water repellant and have snow cuffs around the ankles. Most well-made bibs are made from a nylon shell with a lining to break the wind and to trap body heat.

• Buy a wool hat and ski mittens. Body heat is lost quickly through extremities, and if your body isn't warm, there's little heat left for your feet and hands. Covering your head avoids excessive heat loss and forces warmth down to your hands and feet. Wool not only insulates from the cold, but its natural fibers even work when wet. Mittens are superior to gloves because they allow each finger to transfer warmth to the next.

To save money on skiwear (in fact, any winter sports clothing), buy off season. You can save from 30 to 50 percent on list prices by buying ski clothing in March and April instead of December. Having done your homework in ski magazines and on the slopes, look for classically styled, durable, and functional skiwear. Leave the trendy styles to others; otherwise your purchase will look dated before you can really enjoy it—next season. Be sure you're buying this year's merchandise. Be on guard against a wide variety of items that have been placed on sale to lure you to clean off the merchant's shelves.

You'll find other savings on the path to chair lifts and T-bars. As young skiers, you can take advantage of a number of discounts and budget trips.

• Students at many resorts frequently receive discounts on lift tickets. Bring along your student I.D. or proof of age.

• Many resorts offer discounts to guests who purchase multiple-day lift tickets. Usually, the minimum is two or three days.

• Some resorts offer half-day lift tickets—a real boon to those of you who like to ski and to sleep late, too, after sampling *après*-ski activities.

• Package rates at many ski areas include a full-day lift ticket, ski rentals, and a group lesson.

• Group rates are offered at most ski resorts. Requirements range from ten to twenty-five people per group.

• Rent before you buy equipment unless you already are an avid and frequent skier. If you ski only a few times each year, you'll never enjoy the maximum use of your expensive gear. Renting also lets you test what kind of skis and boots are best for you. (You can rent other winter sporting goods, too: cross-country skis, snowshoes, skates, and sleds.)

• For ski vacations, check out youth-group sponsored trips. Churches, synagogues, community groups, the YMCA, American Youth Hostels, and colleges sponsor many of these every year. You travel and ski with a group of fellow enthusiasts, often accompanied by a chaperone (so your parents won't worry), and at lower prices than a comparable group of adults would pay. Your accommodations, naturally, will be less luxurious, but you'll be so busy skiing and thawing out by the fire that you'll never notice.

• Student travel agencies have up-to-the-minute information about where the good skiing deals can be found and what package tours are best for you and your budget.

• Ski off-season whenever possible and benefit from reduced hotel and lift rates.

Swimming and Boating

Water sports entice millions of Americans to beaches, pools, and lakes every year. From surfers in Hawaii to sailors off the Maine coast, practically everyone enjoys some activity that puts them in, or on, the water.

The backbone of most water sports is swimming. While you can row on a quiet pond or kayak down a river without knowing the difference between the crawl and the breaststroke, common sense should tell you how dangerous it will be if you capsize and can't make it to shore. Few activities surpass swimming for strengthening, toning muscles, and building endurance, besides being such great fun.

Swimming is probably the most widely taught sport. To find out where to learn how to swim inexpensively and safely, phone a local chapter of the American Red Cross, a YMCA, a local high school or college, or the Parks and Recreation Department. About 75 percent of the 3,000 Red Cross chapters offer swimming instruction; the others can steer you in the right direction.

You need a well-trained, conscientious instructor. Seek out teachers who have been certified by a nationally recognized organization, such as the YMCA and Red Cross. These instructors have completed rigorous training programs that stress water safety and effective teaching methods.

The Red Cross offers five basic swimming courses, from beginners to advanced (all include diving, too), and several water safety ones. As a prerequisite for the most difficult—the advanced lifesaving course—you must be at least fifteen. If you want to take the Water Safety Instructors' course, you must wait until you are eighteen. While pools and beaches don't always require the WSI certificate, it can help you find a job as a lifeguard. Swimmers at any level of ability—even inveterate waders—can sign up for a basic water safety course that teaches the essentials in a few short lessons.

Community Red Cross- and YMCA-sponsored classes are inexpensive. Usually, you can expect to pay a pool or locker room fee and not much more.

Similarly, if you want to learn boating skills, you can find low-cost instruction through the same channels plus the Coast Guard Auxiliary and the U.S. Power Squadron. If you choose to take lessons from a commercial boat dealer, *ask* about his/her certification.

Any boating course should stress hands-on training: you get in the boat and make it move. The Red Cross, for example, offers courses in sailing, rowing, canoeing, kayaking, and outboard motors. Each takes a prescribed length of time. Acquire a copy of *Safe Boating: A Parent's Guide* or *Small Craft Safety Demonstrations* if you plan to include boating in your way of life. Its guidelines are invaluable.

The costs of boating courses will vary widely. Commercial classes are most expensive, so phone around for the ones best suited to your budget. Red Cross boating classes rely on volunteer instructors; your costs should be limited to fees, required books, and overhead. If you become interested in teaching boating skills, the Red Cross trains instructors and instructors' aides. All boaters are taught the revised 1980 Inland Navigational Rules.

Boating safety need not be expensive and it's absolutely essential. Before you go out on the water, make certain that the craft carries whatever equipment is required by federal and state law. Ask the dealer or rental agent for a list of suggested additional gear, and, of course, have with you a life jacket or preserver that *fits*.

No matter how sophisticated your aquatic activities, learn about water safety and how to swim. It could be your life you're saving.

Tennis Everyone?

Whether you dream of succeeding John McEnroe or Martina Navratilova (in a few years, of course) as the best player in the world, or you are content to play tennis now and then, chances are you own a tennis racquet. An astonishing number of us do—almost one in every four. Surveys indicate that about 5 or 6 million teenagers are hard-core tennis freaks, playing twice weekly at least, and another

8 million of you are "moderate" players, that is, on the courts a few times each month. Close observers of the game list many reasons for the continued popularity of tennis with teenagers: among them, the increase in college and high school teams or leagues, and the availability of tennis scholarships to good players in an era of increasingly expensive college tuition. And there's the lure of seeing kids your own age play competitively, turn pro, and then earn prize money that catapults them into the financial company of rock stars.

If you've been thinking about dusting off your racquet or buying a new one and starting lessons, here are some pointers:

• You need a tennis racquet to play the game, but how do you choose one? In a typical case, you acquire your first racquet as a family member's hand-me-down or a present bestowed for some special occasion. The problem is, it doesn't "fit" you. When choosing a racquet, key considerations are weight, size of grip, balance, material, and, not least, price. You basically want a racquet that "feels" right and is comfortable to hold and swing. If you're not sure what that means, do your homework before you even go to the sporting goods store. Specialty magazines, such as *World Tennis*, run regular features about racquets that discuss their composition and the advantages or drawbacks of different models. Consider these your required reading. Learn enough basic information so you can ask good questions and begin to evaluate the racquets you try. Talk to tennis coaches at school and ask what they recommend for players at your level. Since manufacturers are competing fiercely now for a share of the market, you can benefit by learning about different product lines and which companies make racquets for your stage of development and size of budget. Any tennis instructor will have recommendations for you as well.

Racquets can cost from $40 to $50 to three times that much. Try to choose wisely and well. Don't rush into a purchase; tennis racquets are often sold at discount or on sale. Allow time for comparison shopping.

• To enjoy the game fully, you must know the fundamentals; this means instruction. You can choose to take private lessons at $20 to $25 an hour or so with a teaching pro at private tennis centers or country clubs. As an alternative, group lessons will cost you much less (an average of $4 to $8 an hour), and you will be learning with other players at your level, so you can measure your skills against your peers and decide how serious you are about mastering the game.

To locate classes, contact municipal sports clubs, high schools and community colleges, and other local sports facilities. Perhaps your high school coach or phys ed instructor offers classes or knows someone who does. Or, write to the United States Tennis Association (51 East 42nd Street, New York, NY 10017) and request a list of member clubs located near you where you can get involved with the sport.

• The qualities to seek in a tennis teaching pro are those of any worthwhile sports instructor: a good coach, enthusiastic about the game, knowledgeable about techniques and training methods, and patient! Look for a person who has played tennis competitively, perhaps at the college or professional level.

About 6,000 pros teach tennis, and approximately half belong to the United States Professional Tennis Association. About 2,000 instructors have joined the Professional Tennis Registry and have attended a program and been certified in teaching tennis. Ask prospective instructors whether they belong to either organization. But, most important, find a teacher with whom you feel comfortable who can guide you through the levels of the game.

14

YOUR HEALTH

Everything You Want
(or Need) to Know

CONTENTS

HEALTH EXAMS

When and Why

Except for sex, what is as baffling, entertaining, funny, weird, disturbing, and exciting as your own body? As its owner, you're responsible for its maintenance and performance, but chances are you understand better how a car or the space shuttle works. And even though you spend hours worrying and wondering about your body's astonishing development and growth, you're still not entirely sure what's going on. Sometimes you think you're going crazy and that you'll never grow up, or get periods regularly, or rid your complexion of acne, or grow a beard. Your list of complaints is long and detailed.

Perhaps, too, you wonder how often you should see a doctor and why, especially if there's nothing wrong with you and, in fact, you feel great—mostly. Physicians who specialize in caring for adolescents recommend that you see them often—every year or two—particularly early in your teens, and these are the reasons why:

• You grow and develop so fast. Regular checkups monitor these processes and detect any problems early—or reassure you that there are none.

• While you're so busy with these changes, you occasionally get confused or frightened. Doctors can help allay your fears and explain just what, exactly, is happening to you, what else to expect, and even when to expect it.

• Acne, menstrual cramps, "growing pains," and other problems really can interfere with your life. But you don't have to endure them or wait until you "outgrow" them. Talk to your doctor and ask for help.

• Many conditions that blossom in adulthood can be detected in adolescence before they cause medical problems. (Hypertension—high blood pressure—is a good example.) The idea is to identify these potential health hazards early and intervene so as to change the long-term outlook, or deflect future problems completely.

• Some of you pick up habits that lead straight to trouble: smoking, overeating, excessive drinking, drug abuse. You can benefit from a doctor's advice and counseling, even when you're sure you already know everything you need to.

• Doctors will also check for infectious diseases, such as mononucleosis, rubella, hepatitis, sexually transmitted diseases, and others to which you might be exposed.

• Most of the health problems you develop in your teens are products of rapid growth and development. As illustration, orthopedic problems, such as scoliosis (curvature of the spine), endocrine disorders, and gynecologic ailments (excessive menstruation, lack of menstruation) can all be diagnosed by regular checkups and corrected.

The Exam

Your individual requirements will differ, but basically a health exam screens out problems to treat and issues for you and your doctor to discuss. Here are the essentials:

1. *A thorough discussion*—before, during, and after the exam—when you and the doctor talk about your concerns, the exam's results, and other medical topics.

2. *A series of checks:* heart and lungs; blood pressure; height and weight; skin; genital development; orthopedic development; thyroid. Also, expect the doctor to examine you for scoliosis, a condition that affects teenage girls more than any other group.

3. *Lab work*, including tests for tuberculosis (in high-risk areas); a hematocrit, or blood chemistry to check for iron deficiency; a urinalysis; and any other tests indicated by your medical history.

4. *Some counseling.* It's hard to keep track of everything you need to know about nutrition, exercise, rest, and stress. Doctors who work with young people want to talk about these, and also sexual concerns, pregnancy, venereal disease, drug abuse, smoking and alcohol. That's quite a list! Most doctors aren't interested in preaching to you, but they want very much to help you keep informed. A major part of your health care consists of this important dialogue with a physician you can trust and in whom you can confide.

5. *Referral.* If your health screen uncovers any disorders, your doctor might recommend that you see a specialist.

6. You will also be counseled about *self-examination* (and if not, ask!). Most of you have heard this term and probably assume it applies only to women, who are instructed to examine their breasts every month. But men are now encouraged to learn self-examination of their testicles. The reason: cancer of the testicles is the third most common malignancy found in men twenty to thirty-four years old. Most testicular cancers develop ''silently''—with few or no symptoms, and no pain. And, as with all diseases, early diagnosis enhances the outlook for successful treatment. The actual technique is easy, but you should be instructed by a doctor or other health professional. Self-examination is recommended every six months or so, following a bath or shower.

The Cost

How much should all this cost? Health exams aren't inexpensive, and while costs vary across the country, an average exam runs between $80 and $100. Check first with your doctor, especially about lab work, since tests can add greatly to the expense. Many of you will be covered under your parents' health insurance policies or family memberships in Health Maintenance Organizations.

If you're worried about the expense, though, call the adolescent (or pediatrics) unit of a local hospital and ask for advice; check the phone book for community health services; or call local hot lines and explain your problem. You'll be able to get the care you need.

Then get the most from your checkup. Listen to and act on the doctor's suggestions. It's hard to believe, but habits and patterns you adopt *now* affect—even determine—your health in years to come. You play a vital role in keeping yourself well, and the choices you make ultimately are yours alone.

The Famous Doctor-Patient Relationship

You expect your doctor to treat you as a special, grown-up person. Have you stopped to think that your doctor deserves the same appreciation from you? You develop half the doctor-patient relationship; observing commonsense suggestions will make your visits easier and more successful for both of you.

When you call to make an appointment, tell the receptionist how old you are and identify the reason you want to see the doctor. Some physicians have special office or clinic hours for teens. This is a good clue that the doctor sees a lot of people your age.

Ask in advance about confidentiality. If you expect to pay for the appointment, ask about fees and payment schedules on the phone. You will be respected for such an adult, responsible approach.

Most doctors will tell you that they respect your privacy, but that if they feel it's necessary to your health and well-being to discuss something with your parents, they will first talk about it with you and then decide when and how to approach them. Some issues are too important *not* to involve your parents.

Some other pointers:

• Be on time for the appointment itself. Sounds simple? Yet it's easy to leave too late to get to your appointment on time, or to forget about it completely. And, if you must cancel, phone at least a day in advance. Other patients are waiting to see the doctor, too.

• Take a shower or bath first. Doctors, like everyone else, appreciate cleanliness.

• Wear uncomplicated clothes. Since you're probably going to undress, at least partially, save time and aggravation by choosing simple clothes.

• Bring your health records from home. Your parents probably have records of your immunizations and childhood diseases. Find out all you can about your family's medical history, your past illnesses, and your physical development (height and weight charts are a great asset if you have them). This information helps a new physician evaluate your current development and place it in context.

• Girls, include your menstrual history calendar, plus the date and duration of your last period. Doctors learn a great deal from this simple record, and it's a terrific habit to cultivate and continue.

• Jot down your questions, requests, and concerns *before* the appointment. Some issues might be hard to talk about, and you'll become nervous and distracted. Concentrate, instead, on how relieved you'll feel later if you bring up what's on your mind now.

Doctors comment that patients expect them to read their minds. Since they can't do that, it's up to you to tell them your concerns. Try very hard to mention tough issues early enough so that you have time to discuss them. The doctor's job is to treat the whole you—to help you, not to judge and not to snitch. What you say won't shock them.

Ask whatever questions occur to you during the examination. Far from thinking you're dumb, a doctor will welcome your interest. If you don't understand an explanation, suggestion, or direction, say so! Doctors sometimes get carried away with medical jargon and forget that the rest of us don't speak "medicalese." There's no procedure or problem that can't be explained in plain English.

Occasionally, health-care professionals can be as shy with teenagers as you can be with them. The reasons: they want to treat you with respect but aren't sure how; observe your privacy, but find out all they need to know; give you information, but not overwhelm you with facts. If, though, you see a doctor a few times and can't break the ice, it's perfectly okay—in fact, advisable—to look for another one.

Doctors ask a lot of questions about medical subjects—symptoms, sexual activity, medical history, and so forth—and about nonmedical ones, too. Answer them truthfully. Your doctor isn't going to scold you or "tell on" you, and information that you provide is central to diagnosing any problem correctly. Also, many factors affect your overall health, such as how well you sleep and eat; how much exercise you get; whether you feel a lot of tension at home; how well you're doing at school; whether you have an active social life; whether you use drugs or a birth control device—the list goes on and on. So, even if it seems your doctor is prying, keep in mind that he/she is *trying* —to help you.

MEDICAL FACILITIES: YOUR CHOICES

When you find the right doctor and medical facility, you're on your way to developing a durable relationship with a person you can count on in many situations—for help in a crisis; when you simply want sound advice or reassurance; or when you need treatment and medication. Choosing the right doctor and environment can take time and effort, but you'll be rewarded by knowing that when you take good care of your health, you're taking good care of your future.

Sources of information about health care include your high school infirmary and guidance counselor, who should have current information about medical problems, local clinics, and doctors who specialize in treating people your age. People who work with teens usually have special training, as well as an ability to relate well with your age group and really listen to what you have to say. You will find exceptions, of course, but you should be able to link up with caring and helpful doctors, nurses, physician's assistants, and staffers by seeking out facilities that specialize in health care for you and your peers.

You can choose from a number of medical resources. Here's a rundown on some of those available to you:

Private Physicians

You may decide that it's time to see a doctor other than the pediatrician you've known all your life. If you select a private physician, you'll realize quickly that drawbacks accompany the advantages. They are, chiefly, expense and the issue of trust.

Private doctors simply cost more. Before your first appointment, explore the costs and ask what procedures and lab tests to expect. Ask also about the obligatory fees for routine office care. These questions are entirely legitimate and help promote openness between you and your doctor.

Your second problem is that it can take time to find someone you trust. Often it's simply a matter of chemistry between you and the doctor. To get started, ask first for recommendations from friends and classmates, your current doctor and school nurse, your guidance counselor, and from other health care professionals you know. Also, call the local medical society, or write to the Society for Adolescent Medicine (P.O. Box 3462 Granada Hills, CA 91344) for a list of doctors who live near you and belong to the Society. Members can be internists, pediatricians, or other specialists, but all have additional training in and sensitivity to the needs of teenagers.

One further issue to clarify with your new doctor is how he/she approaches counseling. You may meet someone who can't offer you unbiased advice about birth control, for example, or keep your conversations confidential. This should be rare. But since you're naturally concerned with these areas, raise them immediately on the phone or in person.

College Health Services

Campus health services have traditionally been a source of jokes about alleged incompetence, medieval medical practices, and antiquated attitudes. These services, though, can offer good routine medical care and, in emergencies, prompt referrals to hospitals and local practitioners. If you're in college, chances are your school will provide most of your health care for a number of years, and it's a good bet you'll visit the clinic sooner or later—so learn early what's available and how to use it.

College health plans are generally financed by a fee charged to each student on an annual, semester, or quarterly basis. In a sense, these plans are structured like Health Maintenance Organizations (HMOs)—you've already paid for medical care whether you need it or not. (More about HMOs in a moment.) The school, meanwhile, has an incentive to keep you healthy—and that means broad preventive and educational services. Typically, you are entitled to unlimited use of the medical facilities and a specified number of counseling sessions per year, but each school has services tailored to its population. Often, too, you'll find an on-site pharmacy that provides prescription medicines at cost. If you are referred to a local specialist, you pay that doctor on a fee-for-service basis.

College medical records are confidential. Don't hesitate to ask for birth control, counseling, testing for sexually transmitted diseases, and any other ailment that bothers you. If your health suffers, your school work and social life are bound to follow.

Free Clinics

Free clinics, by their very nature, vary from community to community. Some are established, vital contributors to health care on the local scene (such as The Door, in Greenwich Village, New York City), and offer a full range of medical and counseling services. Medical care really is free at these centers, although your contributions will be welcomed; consequently, the financial base is not always secure. One feature of free clinics worth noting is that reception areas are always jammed with other patients. Be fore-warned and bring along a book or magazine—you may have a long wait before you see a doctor or physician's assistant. Since medical personnel at these clinics often donate their services, they are committed and caring people who want to help you get thorough, competent medical care. To find out about free clinics near you, check the White Pages of the phone book, or call a local hospital.

Adolescent Clinics

About 120 clinics that specialize in comprehensive care for teenagers are scattered across the United States and Canada. Their staffs—consisting of doctors, nurses, and health care-professionals with extensive training and interest in teenagers' health problems and special requirements—concentrate on total health care. As a rule, these are hospital-based clinics that offer low-fee services, with rates often based on the patient's ability to pay. Adolescent clinics stress well-care and patient education, and provide a broad array of counseling services (family, individual, crisis, etc.). These clinics—in fact, most facilities that deliver health care to teens—are open after school and in the evenings to make it easy for you to use them. And it's not uncommon to find video games and other distractions to help you pass the time while you wait. Most adolescent clinics will match you with a primary care physician who becomes "your doctor" for all subsequent treatment.

To find out whether there's an adolescent clinic near you, check the phone book, or call a local hospital and specify that you're interested in adolescent clinics. You can also write to the Society for Adolescent Medicine (P.O. Box 3462 Granada Hills, CA 91344) and ask for its list of clinics, which is complete and up-to-date. As a rule, you'll find clinics located in medium-sized and large cities, but there are exceptions.

Youth Clinics

Youth clinics are linked to county or state medical services and are useful resources for birth control, treatment for sexually transmitted diseases, counseling, and other routine medical needs. You'll find them listed in the White Pages of your phone book.

The ABCs of HMOs

For most of you, your parents take care of finding doctors, paying the bills, and completing insurance forms. But the day will come when these become your responsibilities, so, in anticipation, consider getting acquainted with a health-care delivery system that remains unfamiliar to many but is growing in popularity: Health Maintenance Organizations.

An HMO is a system that provides comprehensive inpatient and outpatient health services in exchange for a fixed, prepaid fee. When you belong to an HMO, you are provided with umbrella coverage that includes everything from routine examinations to dermatology, crisis counseling, abortions, pediatrics, eye examinations and even, in some HMOs, dental care. Participation offers some relief from the ravages of the drastic price spiral in health-care costs while guaranteeing you the array of health services you need.

Most people who belong to HMOs join as part of a group at their workplace, union, or trade association, and choose the HMO instead of a group insurance policy. More than 50,000 businesses offer their employees this option, ranging from such corporate Goliaths as IBM, Xerox, and AT&T, to small companies employing twenty-five to thirty workers. Employers contribute the same sum to the HMO premium as they do to an insurance policy; if the HMO costs more, you, the employee, pay the difference, though sometimes the HMO actually costs less. You also can join an HMO when a local organization holds an open enrollment period (usually once a year) during which anyone who applies must be accepted.

HMOs can be a good choice for comprehensive health care for young people. All the health-care professionals are gathered under one roof and you don't have to shop around for different practitioners. When the time comes for you to line up your health-care services—particularly after you finish school, move to a new town, or get a job and receive fringe benefits—you will want to learn more about HMOs. Good sources include:

Communications and Information
  Department
Group Health Association of
   America, Inc.
624 Ninth St. N.W., Suite 700
Washington, DC 20001

Office of HMOs
Department of Health and Human
   Services
12420 Parklawn Drive
Parklawn Building, 3rd Floor
Rockville, MD 20857

Meanwhile, those of you who currently belong to an HMO with your parents will benefit from finding out what special services and educational programs your HMO has designed for teenagers.

HEALTH INSURANCE: THE BASICS

''Why'', you ask yourself, ''do I need to know anything about health insurance? I'm young, I'm healthy, and my parents (or school or job) take care of all that. I'll find out what I need to know when I get older.''

With health-care costs gobbling up a huge percentage of our incomes, insurance is worth some study. Think how often you hear about a catastrophic illness or accident that devastates a family's finances when it lacks this coverage.

Approximately eight out of every ten Americans under sixty-five are covered by health insurance—under either individual policies or group plans offered by employers, unions, and professional associations. Without health insurance, many millions of people would be crushed financially by even routine medical costs. This does not mean insurance is inexpensive, however.

Insurance operates on a simple principle: people pool their money and share the risk of unforeseen medical hazards—illness, accident, surgery, hospitalization, and the like. In general, health insurance covers expenses for those events over which no one has control. Think of it as a reverse gamble: winners pay losers—that is, individuals who don't get sick or otherwise use their benefits help pay the expenses of people who do by means of their insurance payments.

Teenagers generally experience few illnesses and medical problems that require lengthy hospital stays or expensive care. But you are in the group at highest risk for car accidents—and in an accident's aftermath, you might need hospitalization, surgery, and other lifesaving medical treatment. In that event, and without insurance, you or your family would pay medical bills for years.

Most of you are covered under your parents' insurance policies, which they acquire through work or directly from an insurance company. As a rule, you are protected until your nineteenth birthday or up to age twenty-two or twenty-three, depending on the policy, if you remain a full-time student. *College students:* Check your parents' policies before you purchase the school's policy (not its health-care plan, which is a separate program). Often, the school's policy duplicates your parents' coverage so you, or they, pay twice. A rule of thumb for insurance is to pay the least amount for the maximum coverage to suit your situation.

You can't plan for every medical problem that will arise, and no policy pays all your medical bills all of the time. But, when the time comes, do shop for health insurance. Don't be satisfied that one policy is enough or that all coverage is the same. Insurance companies compete with each other to offer the best packages; you will benefit if you take the time to compare them.

Learn all about your insurance benefits at school or work. Once you have your own coverage, review it periodically and look for gaps and ways to plug these holes with supplemental policies.

When you have questions about health insurance, you can get information from the following sources:

- The consumer information departments of the various insurance companies.
- Your company's benefits counselor, or a trade union or association officer.
- Your state health insurance department.
- Your insurance agent.
- Health Insurance Association of America (1850 K St., N.W., Washington, DC 20006).

THE SKIN YOU LIVE IN (AND CRY OVER)

Your skin functions as a protective envelope for your body. It maintains body temperature and moves wastes—important work for an organ weighing about twenty-five pounds. Most of the time, you are preoccupied with the skin on your face and its uncanny ability to misbehave at the worst possible times. In fact, you probably ignore the skin on the rest of your body, assuming (wrongly) that it requires scant attention. You subject it to days of intense sunbathing, for example, or infrequent baths.

Skin tends to take good care of itself if it's kept clean and treated gently. That, dermatologists counsel, means daily washings with mild soap, controlled and reasonable amounts of sun, and prompt attention to any problems that develop, such as changes in moles, development of eczema or rashes, and other common—and treatable—problems.

Surviving Acne

Facts

• Americans spend about $100 million each year in over-the-counter acne remedies. That sum does not include cosmetics designed to hide telltale bumps and spots.

• We spend another $18 to $24 million on prescription sales of topical medicines—ointments, creams, and such. The amount spent on antibiotics (such as tetracycline) for acne relief is unknown.

• Acne accounts for 14 percent of all patient visits to doctors for skin care, and 27.5 percent of visits to dermatologists.

• Teenagers account for almost 6 million visits to office-based dermatologists every year; the majority seek relief from this common scourge.

• Outpatient and physician fees top $190 million annually.

A study prepared for the American Academy of Dermatology reveals the details at which these huge sums hint:

• Clinically significant acne—that is, acne requiring medical attention—affects 20 to 25 percent of all persons between fifteen and twenty-five years old.

• Acne tends to be more severe among boys. Nearly 50 percent of the boys examined had moderate to severe acne; about 34 percent, or one-third, of the girls fell into this category.

• Slightly more than 86 percent of all seventeen-year-olds have some degree of facial acne. In fact, age seventeen seems to be the peak year of acne among teens.

• The tendency toward acne increases to a depressing degree during the teens.

• Finally, survey data indicate that more than 68 percent of all teens have some facial acne. That means some blackheads, pimples, or bumps, but not necessarily acne severe enough to require medical treatment.

True/False

You've been blitzed with numbers and facts. Now, take a moment to look at this true/false quiz—then on to the good news:

- Acne is caused by dirty skin.
- Chocolate, greasy foods, and soft drinks induce acne.
- Sexual activity promotes pimples, blackheads, and all the rest.
- Sexual abstinence promotes pimples, blackheads, and all the rest.
- Vitamin deficiencies lead to acne.

Did you guess "false" to each question? Each is a popular myth that has been exploded by medical research. You don't have to gobble a candy bar and wash it down with soda to celebrate, but acne doesn't condemn you to life without the occasional French fry or corn chip, either.

What It Is

Acne, in fact, is a normal, predictable part of teenage life. As you know, it consists of blackheads, whiteheads, pimples, and boillike lesions on face, neck, shoulders, and chest. These areas of skin secrete the most oil, or *sebum,* and are most prone to the sequence of events that culminates as zits.

During puberty, increasingly high levels of hormones in the body cause oil glands in the skin to enlarge. The skin of acne-prone people reacts to these hormones, and a complex series of changes is set off that leads to those characteristic eruptions. Stress, incidentally, can aggravate acne, but by itself does not cause it. Hormonal changes during a woman's menstrual cycle also affect acne, and many teens know their periods are due with the arrival of a new crop of pimples.

Even though every article you will ever read about acne tells you to wash frequently, acne *is not* caused by dirt. Blackheads, for example, are not impacted bits of grime but, rather, oxidized material trapped inside a pore of your skin.

While acne is not exactly a life-threatening disease, it can make you painfully self-conscious and miserable. Knowing that just about everyone else suffers with it is slight consolation, especially before a big date or key job interview.

Treatment

Treatment of acne is like one of those good-news/bad-news jokes:

The bad news is that there is no cure for acne, although it usually clears up after several years.

The good news is that it can be controlled in most cases. You needn't be stoic, grit your teeth, and endure its course. And just because your parents say you'll outgrow it later doesn't mean you shouldn't seek treatment now.

So, ignore the myth that acne will go away if you just leave it alone. Acne can progress and get worse, particularly in severe cases. The end result can be unsightly scars and a very unhappy person. If your acne doesn't respond to your best self-help efforts—a careful cleaning regimen, over-the-counter preparations used according to directions, and careful diet—you can benefit from seeing your family doctor or a dermatologist.

Since individual cases differ in severity and kind, the treatment a doctor gives you may not be what is prescribed to your friends. Here's a quick rundown on current remedies:

• Tetracycline, which is an antibiotic, has been judged an effective treatment for acne. Be sure that you understand its side effects if it's prescribed for you, though. In some patients the medicine causes mild nausea; others become ultrasensitive to sun and burn quite easily. Women who take tetracycline are prone to vaginal yeast infections since the medicine apparently upsets the natural pH balance.

• A successful new treatment is vitamin-A acid (also known as RETIN-A). This must be prescribed for you by a physician and used strictly according to directions—and only on your face. RETIN-A is applied to the skin and, in the short run, seems to make acne much worse. But if you follow through on the treatment (of course you will!) the outer layers of your skin will peel and finally, a new layer of soft, clear skin will emerge. Even though the new skin may be free of blemishes, however, treatment with RETIN-A does not remove older acne scars.

• Birth control pills are rarely used as a treatment for acne these days. The levels of estrogen (female sex hormones) now included in most versions of the Pill have been judged too low to be effective or to justify the risks entailed in using them in acne treatment (remember, all medications have risks and side effects). Occasionally a doctor might suggest a high-dosage estrogen pill; if this happens to you, ask the doctor for an alternative remedy and check first with a gynecologist.

Your doctor will almost surely issue a set of treatment instructions. Expect specific suggestions about diet. He/she may also prescribe medicines that reduce oiliness and produce mild peeling. Additional preparations may include tinted medicines that match your natural skin tones and help dry the skin. Expect, too, to be warned not to squeeze, pick, scratch, pop, and otherwise torment your acne. When done improperly, these actions can lead to more inflammation—and permanent scars.

But whatever treatment your doctor prescribes, it will be up to you to follow the routine and use the medicines faithfully. You, after all, will be in charge of your daily skin-care regimen, and all the prescriptions in the world will be useless if they stay bottled up.

As a rule, acne soaps and treatments will dry your skin. Contrary to all those commercials on television, dry skin does not cause wrinkles and you won't turn into a prune on your twenty-fifth birthday if you use these preparations. Sun dries your skin—so limit your exposure to sun, and use sunscreens if you plan to keep your skin youthful and supple. (More about suntanning in a moment.)

Doctors recommend the following skin-care routine for most teens. It won't cure, or even prevent, acne, but it will keep your skin healthy and clean. It won't shrink your pores, either. Their size, like the color of your eyes or the texture of your skin, is determined by heredity.

Here goes:

Treat your skin gently. Wash all of it daily with a mild soap, and wash your face twice, at least, to remove excess oil, bacteria, and grime. Keep your hair off your forehead and face, and keep your hands down! Resist cupping your chin in your palm or resting your cheek against the heel of your hand.

Shampoo regularly, too. Acne-prone teens frequently have dandruff, another annoying condition that can't be cured but can be managed. (Acne and dandruff are related problems with similar causes.) Healthy hair can easily withstand gentle, frequent washing—and many of you doubtless shampoo every day. Beware of blow-dryers, though; excessive heat can dry out your hair.

When you choose cosmetics, buy water-based foundations and powders, and stay away from heavy oils and creams which will clog your pores and dull your skin. Now that all makeups list their ingredients on packages and bottles, you can check for the presence of oil and shun those that list oily substances prominently.

Dermatologists: Expensive Luxury?

A visit to a nearby dermatologist to help control your acne can, in the long run, be less expensive than buying every over-the-counter preparation in the drugstore. If you're really troubled by your acne, you can benefit from a consultation. Depending on the severity of your problem, the region of the country in which you live, and the number of visits, you can pay from $25 to $75 for treatment. Whether office visits are included in your or your parents' insurance policy depends on the plan. Dermatology consultations are featured in many HMO plans; if a dermatologist is not on staff, one is on call for referral of patients.

Treatment for acne scars (which includes *dermabrasions*, a process in which the skin is planed smooth—covered later in this chapter) usually cannot be undertaken until acne is well controlled (by your late teens or early twenties), but is now often covered by insurance because it is considered a reconstructive, or therapeutic, rather than a cosmetic treatment. Again, particulars vary, according to individual insurance policies. Check with your carrier or your parents' carrier before you go ahead with a costly treatment program.

If you live near a medical school, contact the department of dermatology and inquire about local skin clinics. Many schools and affiliated hospitals hold regular clinics that are staffed by residents who can give you expert care at reduced fees. You might not see the same doctor every visit, but you can lop off as much as a third of your medical bill in this way. And major medical insurance often will cover a portion of the clinic fee, too.

Sunbaking Dos and Don'ts

That glorious tan you get every summer from baking in the sun without any protection can leave your skin looking tough and leathery by the time you're forty. That already sounds old, but what's worse is that you'll look as though you're fifty-five.

Overexposure to the sun's rays results in loss of skin elasticity, which translates into wrinkles, folds, and sagging skin—and you'll be spending fortunes at the cosmetic counter and plastic surgeon trying to remedy the carelessness of your youth.

Once your skin loses its elasticity, little can be done to restore it. Moreover, most of the 300,000 cases of skin cancer treated in the United States each year are linked closely to overexposure to the sun. Skin cancer kills more than 5,000 people annually but, if treated in time, most skin cancers are curable.

Remember how her Mammy nagged Scarlett O'Hara and her sisters to stay out of the sun and remain pale, proper southern belles? Our society, instead, values tawny, burnished skin, and, as soon as the weather turns warm, millions head for the nearest patch of sun. If you're among them, you probably baste yourself with baby or mineral oil and roast. After you recover from a sensationally painful sunburn, you'll have a nice base tan, but you've needlessly strained your skin and depleted some of its vitality. Skin is elastic when we're young but it loses that elasticity as part of the aging process (sorry, it's inevitable). You hasten that process by thoughtlessly overstraining it.

Don't get annoyed and stop reading here. No one is telling you to avoid the sun or forbidding you from ever getting a suntan. What you should do is work on that tan gradually:

- Avoid the sun's burning rays between 10:00 A.M. and 2:00 P.M., if you can. (Of course, you don't want to do this—you know these are peak tanning hours, so you'll be out there.)
- Turn your reflector over. Better yet, don't buy one. Spend the money on a hat, instead.
- Since you'll almost certainly ignore this good advice, at least purchase a good sunscreen. The most effective one on the market today is 5 percent PABA (para-amino-benzoic acid) in 55 percent alcohol base. PABA penetrates the inner layers of your skin and blocks out virtually all the burning rays for six to eight hours. The good news is that PABA allows tanning rays to bronze you gradually. That boring word, moderation, is the key to successful tanning.
- Use of a potion containing baby oil or mineral oil and iodine provides no protection at all. All these preparations do is keep the skin lubricated—not a bad idea, but totally useless as a tanning agent.
- Black skin can burn, too, though not as easily as light skin.

If you doubt that sun ages your skin, take a mirror and look at your bottom. Chances are it has rarely been exposed to the sun. And it's unwrinkled and smooth, right? As in the cliché, "Soft as the skin on a baby's bottom?" Now look at your face. Even in your teens, little lines have begun to appear. Some of these result from your skin's exposure to the elements—chiefly, sun.

But the good news is that a gradually acquired tan can actually help protect your skin. *Melanin,* the pigment that determines skin color, can shield you from burning rays. The problem: melanin takes weeks to be produced. You don't speed up the process by baking for hours. What you speed up is the likelihood of a painful burn and prematurely aging skin. Even when you can't see it, the cells know.

Resources

For more information on skin and hair care, you can request information from the American Academy of Dermatology (AAD) (820 Davis St., Evanston, IL 60201). The AAD prepares patient information booklets on such topics as acne, black-skin care, and sunbathing. Enclose a business-size self-addressed stamped envelope with your letter.

Check a copy of *The AMA Book of Skin and Hair Care,* edited by Linda Allen Schoen (Avon Books, 1978) in a bookstore or library. As you would expect from doctors, the information is sensible, reliable, and cautious. And as you know very well, your favorite magazines run many articles each year about skin and hair care. Often, though, the articles simply repeat the commonsense advice you read the month before, in another article and another magazine. There just is no magic cure-all to skin and hair problems. The cures lie in moderation, medical care when necessary, and patience. Proper care will ease the trials of skin problems for most of you.

Keep Alert

Be a wise consumer. Learn to read labels and approach claims with skepticism. Some acne remedies, for example, contain oil in their solutions or creams. If you use a cosmetic or other topical product and get a skin reaction, stop using it immediately and try another instead. Often, you may have an allergy to perfume or dyes. Learn what remedies, soaps, and products work for you, and always use any product in moderation.

And any time you notice changes in your skin—enlargement of a mole, change in skin color, patches or scales—seek medical advice. Occasionally, these symptoms may point to a serious underlying medical problem; at the very least, they can be annoying or uncomfortable.

EAR-PIERCING

In your grandmother's day, only women had their ears pierced—and only one hole per ear. Fashions have changed, and you probably know guys who've pierced an ear or two, and girls who've had several holes pierced in one lobe. If you haven't had yours pierced yet, you must have wondered about it—whether it hurts and is safe, and what happens if you don't wear earrings for a while.

Ear piercing is a safe, painless procedure when done under antiseptic conditions and with proper equipment.

What this means is: *don't* let your friends pierce your ears for you (and don't do it yourself!). The complications from pierced ears that doctors see most frequently stem from the do-it-yourselfers who simply didn't take adequate care either with the actual piercing or the follow-up routines.

The best way to have your ears pierced is by your doctor. Most pediatricians and internists will perform this routine procedure, and it isn't expensive. (If your doctor doesn't pierce ears, ask for suggestions about someone who does.) Usually doctors pierce ears in one of two ways: by inserting a surgical stainless steel needle and then quickly poking a 14 karat gold stud into the new hole, or by using a device similar to a staple gun that ''shoots'' the earring into your lobe. The doctor may apply a local anesthetic or pinch your ear lobes to numb them temporarily, but either way the procedure is quick and bloodless.

Many jewelry and department stores have ear-piercing clinics on site that offer special rates if you purchase a pair of earrings. Prices can be as low as $5.00 for this service. But be careful! Many people have their ears pierced at these shops without incident or infection, but first double-check to see what technique is used, how neat the place appears, whether the operator's hands are clean (don't laugh!), and what antiseptic precautions are employed. Assure yourself that the earrings are really 14 karat gold or surgical stainless steel.

Infected ears are no fun and can lead to more serious (and expensive) health problems. Avoid infections with these follow-up routines:

• Swab your ears with alcohol at least two or three times daily while they heal.
• Twist the earrings around to keep crusts from forming and to establish the holes.
• Let your ears heal! You'll grow tired of the gold studs and eager to play with new earrings, but hold off. If your doctor tells you to wait a month before changing earrings, that means four weeks—not two and a half or three.
• For the first six months or so after your ears are pierced, dip earrings into alcohol before you insert them.
• Make sure the scars are fully formed—at least six months— before you wear metals other than 14 karat gold, surgical stainless steel, or sterling silver. You might be allergic to other alloys, and that can lead to itchiness, pain, and even infection.
• If you have any of the following problems, consult your doctor before piercing your ears: you bleed easily and heavily; you know you're allergic to some metals; you have a tendency to form keloids (raised fibrous scar tissue); you get infections frequently. These problems don't mean that you can't have your ears pierced, but they do indicate that you should ask a doctor's advice.

Once your ears are pierced, your biggest expense will be earrings. After all, your goal is to build an earring wardrobe for different outfits, occasions, and moods. It's worth the effort, and small cash outlay, to have your ears pierced properly, painlessly, and healthfully.

TATTOOS

The next time you go to a beach or resort, check out the number of people with tattoos. Chances are you'll be amazed—and those are just the ones you can see! A lot more tattoos lie hidden under swimming trunks and bikini tops.

Tattoos are one of the few subjects in American life for which you can't get statistics. But men and women, young and old, celebrities and just plain folks get tattoos on every imaginable part of the body and for all sorts of reasons. Many of you will at least think about getting one, so you should know what to expect.

Tattooing is an ancient practice, known worldwide, that seems to regain popularity every decade or so. Today, tattoos are applied by puncturing the skin with a needle dipped in pigments, transferring the dye underneath the skin's surface. While it's not a pain-free process, it shouldn't hurt too much. Small tattoos cost as little as $25; full-body tattoos, applied over months, can cost thousands of dollars.

Even in our sanitary age, there are still risks associated with tattoos. Some people have a sensitivity to red and yellow dyes used in tattoos that can cause swelling, scarring, and itching, particularly when exposed to sun.

The possibility of infection, although rare, still exists. Most tattoo parlors undergo regular inspections, and tattoo artists sterilize their equipment and clean your skin. Whatever you do, don't get tattooed while in the Far East.

Each state has its own policies regarding tattoo parlors. In some states, it is still illegal; others have licensing requirements.

Consider your tattoo a permanent fixture. It won't wash or scrub off, and removal is expensive, painful, and not always successful. Among the removal methods used:

• *Excision*. The tattoo is removed surgically—cut out—and the area is stitched up. Eventually, a scar forms.

• *Dermabrasion*. This is the same treatment that is used for planing the skin to smooth out acne scars. In these cases, dermabrasion planes away the tattoo. But since pigments are "locked" into deep layers of the skin, dermabrasion doesn't always remove the color, and can leave scars, too. (More about dermabrasion is included later in this chapter.)

• *Other removal techniques* include lasers, salt, and acid. Any treatment to remove a tattoo should be handled by a doctor. See a plastic surgeon or dermatologist and have the tattoo evaluated properly. No responsible person will try to remove a body tattoo.

And the cost will depend on the size and depth of the tattoo, as well as the prevailing rates in your area.

VISION

Who's Who and What's What in Eyecare

If you can't remember when you last had your vision examined, it's probably time for a check-up—and this is especially true if you're about to go away to school. But who do you see when you go to an "eye doctor"? There are two eye-care specialists who examine your eyes and test your vision.

Ophthalmologist

An ophthalmologist is a medical doctor who specializes in total care of the eyes. He/she is trained and qualified to treat all eye and visual-system problems as well as general diseases of the body. Treatments include prescribed eyeglasses or contact lenses, medications, surgery, or other medical therapies as needed. The intensive training ophthalmologists receive concludes with three or four years of residency following college, medical school, and internship.

Optometrist

A doctor of optometry examines, diagnoses, and prescribes scientific treatment for eye and vision conditions. When examining eyes and related structures, optometrists determine the presence of vision problems, diseases, and other abnormalities, and utilize drugs for diagnostic purposes when required (and where permitted by state law). Optometrists can detect systemic and eye diseases and will refer patients to the proper health professionals. They also treat their patients by prescribing and adapting lenses, contacts, or other optical aids, and by using visual therapy and training to preserve or restore visual skills. Their special training calls for six or seven years of college and professional-level education.

Optician

Opticians are in a different category. They dispense prescription eyewear, but are not permitted to examine your eyes or prescribe treatment. They do, however, ensure that your prescription eyewear meets high standards, is ground accurately, fits properly, and stays in good repair.

The Eye Exam

You probably can think of many things you'd prefer to spend money on than eye care, especially if you think you see perfectly well and are unaware of any vision problems. But 52 percent of the American public wears corrective lenses, and we spend approximately $7.5 billion annually on eye examinations and corrective eye wear. Approximately 95 percent of all vision deficiencies can be corrected wholly or in part, experts believe. Moreover, when you have a thorough eye exam, the ophthalmologist or optometrist looks for signs of general diseases, too; often, an eye exam is the first clue to a serious problem such as diabetes, glaucoma, multiple sclerosis, kidney diseases, and many others. All from looking deep into your eyes!

This checklist helps you prepare for your next eye exam and tells you what to expect.

- A thorough eye examination that can last up to an hour and will include a lot of questions and tests—which vary from patient to patient.
- A review by your doctor of your medical history, including questions about your vision and that of your family.
- An examination of the interior and exterior of your eyes for signs of eye disease and general health problems.
- Tests of your ability to see clearly and sharply at near and far distances.
- Tests for nearsightedness, farsightedness, astigmatism (a problem in focusing light rays), and other conditions.
- Checks of your eye coordination and the muscles around your eyes to make sure your eyes work as a team.
- Tests of your ability to change focus from near to far distances, and vice versa.
- Tests of your judgment of colors and peripheral (side) vision.

• If indicated by your medical history, tests for glaucoma, a disease that, if untreated, causes blindness.

When all the tests and questions are completed, your doctor studies the data and decides how best to treat any newly disclosed problem.

The chief vision condition affecting you, as a teenager, is near-sightedness—the ability to see clearly what is up close, but the inability to see at a distance. (Farsightedness is the opposite.) In fact, nearsightedness, or *myopia*, increases from a total of about 3 percent of five- to nine-year-olds to more than 17 percent of all teens, so it makes good sense to have your vision checked regularly. Your vision affects your school performance, and you know how important that is to your future goals.

When you see your eye doctor, don't neglect to mention your special activities and needs. If you play sports, for example, ask about protective eye gear.

Costs

More and more of you have your vision-care and eye-wear costs covered, at least in part, by your parents' employer or union health-care plans. But no matter who is paying for eye care, ask in advance about basic fees and services.

• Find out how much a basic examination costs and what tests are included. Sometimes a lower fee can mean an incomplete exam. Your test results might lead to additional tests not covered by the basic fee.

• Don't confuse an office, or consultation, fee—which is a minimal charge for time, in most cases—with the basic examination fee.

• Remember that the basic charge won't include the cost of medicines or eye wear.

• Doctors may add a separate service charge to cover time spent in designing, fitting, and verifying prescription glasses. Protect yourself and ask in advance!

Eyeglasses and Contact Lenses

When your vision exam indicates you need eyeglasses—and it will for about 22 percent of all teenagers—your ophthalmologist or optometrist will write a prescription that contains the necessary information to have lenses ground to correct your vision problem. The two of you will determine whether eyeglasses or contact lenses will best meet your needs. Your vision condition may limit the choices open to you. For example, you may have certain physical characteristics that rule out contact lenses—your eyes simply won't tolerate them, or they won't improve your vision. Your doctor will (or should) explain clearly the advantages and disadvantages of each kind of corrective lens to help you make an educated decision.

Eyeglasses

When you decide on glasses, discuss the following with your doctor:

• *Lens size.* You may want oversize lenses for your new glasses, but not every prescription can be ground into the big lenses without distorting peripheral vision.

• *Lens material.* If your glasses are too heavy to wear comfortably, ask about plastic lenses which are lighter than glass. The optical quality of plastic lenses equals that of glass, and both meet federal standards for impact resistance. But plastic scratches more easily and requires more care in handling and cleaning. You can have an antiscratch coating applied, at extra cost. Plastic lenses are good choices if you must wear thick prescription lenses, if you want oversized frames, or if you play and exercise vigorously. If, however, you want light-sensitive lenses (which turn dark in bright light) or sun lenses that screen out infrared rays, you will need glass. (More about sunglasses in a moment.)

• *Tinted lenses.* Tinted lenses are available in practically all shades of the rainbow. Deep tints affect your color perception to some extent, so talk over your preference with the doctor. Plastic lenses tint uniformly—the color is not lighter in the thinner portions and darker in the thicker, which can be a problem in tinted glass. However, you can avoid unevenly tinted glass lenses by getting ones that are color-coated on the surface rather than tinted throughout. In that case, though, you will want a protective coating applied in case the tinted layer scratches or wears off.

• *Frames.* You can spend hours selecting the perfect pair of frames from the dizzying display in front of you. Choosing the right pair involves more than staring in a mirror with a new model perched on your nose, though. Look for a frame that is well made, the right size, and fits comfortably, in addition to suiting your face, wardrobe, and budget. Be sure to have the frames adjusted to your head and face, not only to eliminate discomfort but to avoid any distortion of your vision.

Good eyewear is not inexpensive, but you exercise more control over the cost of your glasses than you may think. All the elements you factor into your decision—lens material, type of frames—add to the cost of new glasses. Keep the following in mind as you make your choice:

• Large lenses are more expensive than smaller ones.
• Plastic lenses generally cost a bit more than glass; extra coatings will add even more to the price.
• Tinted lenses cost more than clear ones.
• Special sun-sensitive lenses are more expensive than standard sunglasses.
• You pay dearly for the little insignia on designer frames. You will be able to find almost identical styles with a little hunting. Also, save by comparison shopping for the same model frames—note the manufacturer's name, model name, and model number of the frames you like; then check around.
• Don't be talked into spending more than you want or can afford by pushy salespeople. Since the frame determines the size of the lens blank, and the lens size, in turn, plays a part in the placement of the prescription within the lens, you might not be able to cancel an order once it gets sent to the optical lab.
• Ready-to-wear glasses waste your money. Mass-produced eyeglasses are nothing more than magnifying lenses mounted in frames.

A few eyeglass dos and don'ts to help you get the best glasses and save you money in the long run:

• Don't have your completed glasses mailed to you. The frames must be readjusted to your head to ensure that you look through the optical center of the lenses. Otherwise the glasses almost surely won't work properly and can distort your vision.

• Always verify your prescription with the doctor after you pick up your new glasses. When you order your glasses through the prescribing doctor, he/she should verify them automatically. This step guarantees that the prescription was filled accurately by the optical lab and contains no imperfections.

• Never buy manufacturer's seconds, even when you are told they meet your prescription. Microscopic flaws have altered the prescription, or why else would they be seconds?

• Advertising has stimulated consumer interest in shopping for eyeglasses, yet one recent authoritative study found that consumers could not comparison shop for eyeglasses by ads alone. Many variables determine the price of a pair of glasses, so the buyer has to visit shops and compare glasses offered at similar prices. Ads simply can't tell the whole story for a product as individual as your prescription eyewear.

• Many doctors provide glasses at lab cost, adding a fee for this service. Ask your doctor about this: the total might be the same, or even less, than you'd pay in an optical shop.

Contact Lenses

More and more Americans are choosing contact lenses for their prescription eyewear. About 13.9 million wore contacts in the early 1980s, or about 4 percent of the 52 percent of the total population wearing corrective lenses. New lens materials and improved fitting techniques make it possible for mounting numbers of people to wear contact lenses comfortably and safely.

As the decade began, contact-lens research focused on new extended-wear lenses; in 1981, the Food and Drug Administration approved two extended-wear soft lenses to correct nearsightedness. Even so, these new lenses are a subject of controversy among eye-care specialists. What is *not* controversial is that the overall future for contact lenses is bright indeed.

"Typical" contact lens wearers are young women (one third of all wearers are women between seventeen and twenty-four); but the number of young men who choose contacts increases yearly. Today, about 42 percent of teenage girls who wear prescription lenses choose contacts.

Since few people notice contact lenses, they appeal to most wearers for cosmetic reasons. If you want contacts instead of glasses because you think you'll look better, don't feel a bit embarrassed. Why shouldn't you look your best? Moreover, one study of teenage girls indicated that wearing contacts encouraged longer daily wear of needed prescription lenses. If you feel you look good, you won't mind wearing corrective lenses.

If you suspect you need corrective lenses you will, of course, have your eyes examined thoroughly by a qualified specialist. Since additional tests will determine whether your eyes can adapt to contacts, your optometrist or ophthalmologist will:

• Look for signs of eye disease and other abnormalities on the exterior of your eyes and lids, as well as the interior.
• Measure the curves and diameter of the cornea (the transparent covering over the black and colored parts of your eyes), the diameter of the pupil when it is fully dilated, and the distance between the eyelids, for each eye.
• Check the quantity and quality of your tear flow.
• Observe how often you blink.
• Depending on the results of these and other tests, add more tests to the exam.
• Talk to you about your motivation to wear lenses. Specific handling and wearing instructions are provided for every kind of contact lens, and your doctor wants to make certain you are willing to take good care of your eyes and lenses.

Contacts cannot be made directly from your eyeglass prescription. When you choose contact lenses, find an eye-care specialist who is experienced in fitting and servicing lenses. He/she will guide you through the process of getting—and getting used to—your new lenses.

Expect an adaptation period, no matter what kind of lenses you get. Your eyes must become accustomed to the friction, the different way of getting vital oxygen, and a change in tear flow. Your specialist will start you on an adaptation schedule designed for you after it's determined that your lenses fit properly and that you know how to apply, remove, and care for them. You will be supervised for the first month or so, and the doctor will check on the fit. Soon, your vision will be tested while you wear the new lenses.

Every contact-lens wearer must return periodically for checkups. The length of time between office visits depends on the kind of lenses you wear. Just in case your eyes don't adapt well, ask your doctor about returning unusable lenses, too.

All contact lenses are made of plastic and—with very few exceptions—fit over the cornea. They are shaped to correct the anatomical distortions that cause vision problems. Of the many types in use, the following are prescribed for most problems:

- *Standard hard lenses.* The first contact lenses available, these are still chosen by more wearers than any other. They correct most types of vision problems, including high degrees of astigmatism; have the longest life span; and are available in tints (and bifocals). However, they require a long adaptation period and must be worn consistently: if you don't wear them for several days, you must readjust to them. You can wear them for a maximum of fourteen to eighteen hours daily. As a rule, these are the least expensive lenses, and you can choose from a wide variety of tints that will, at little extra cost, enhance your natural eye color.
- *Gas permeable lenses.* More expensive than hard lenses, these are also more comfortable at first and require a shorter adaptation period. As a rule, though, they don't come in tints.
- *Soft lenses.* Made of water-absorbent plastic, these lenses fit flush against the cornea and require very little adjustment time. They are difficult to dislodge, even during active sports, and you can wear them infrequently. Routine care of soft lenses is complicated, though, and you must adhere to a daily regimen of cleaning as specified by the manufacturer. Failure to do so can lead to eye infections and clouding of the lenses. Soft lenses need replacement every year or so and, initially, are the costliest choice. A tint can be added in a customizing process that will add to the expense of the lenses, as well as to the length of time to obtain them. Once applied, though, the tint is durable and unaffected by the cleaning process.
- *Extended-wear soft lenses.* Professional opinion about extended-wear lenses is divided; you should know, however, that these are not appropriate for all vision problems. They can be worn continuously for periods of two weeks and, in special circumstances, even longer. They are quite costly and require more frequent replacement than other types.

Once you decide to get a pair of lenses, you probably will start to notice all the ads that offer great deals on the price. Check out these supposed ''bargains'' thoroughly. Today, contacts still cost more than glasses, even though prices for contacts keep falling. Many of these offers don't add up.

Before you order contacts from a shop you locate through advertising, get satisfactory answers to these questions:

• Does the price include a thorough examination by a licensed optometrist or ophthalmologist? (Remember that opticians can't examine eyes and that licensing is required for all eye-care specialists.)
• Are you given specific, detailed instructions about applying, removing, and caring for lenses? Is an adaptation period designed for you?
• Are any additional charges tacked on after your lenses are fitted? What are they?
• Are the lenses tested on your eyes before you accept them? What is the shop's policy on returns if you can't adapt successfully to lens wear?

The total cost of contact lenses may shock you. Yet, when broken down into its components, the price should start to make sense. Of the initial cost of hard lenses, only about 15 to 20 percent is applied to the lenses and supplies themselves; for soft gas permeable and silicon lenses, the percentage rises to between 30 and 35 percent. The remaining sum covers office visits, vision examinations, a specified number of follow-up office visits for patient aftercare, and professional fees.

When you have to replace lost or damaged lenses, the cost depends on how much time and which services you require of the specialist. Ask about insurance to cover these losses. Also ask which kinds of lenses require frequent replacement and which are prone to tearing and breakage.

Contact Lenses and Makeup

Most cosmetics have an oily base that can coat contact lenses, fog your vision, and irritate your eyes. You don't have to avoid makeup—in fact, you probably got contacts in the first place to enhance your appearance, and want to boost the effect with cosmetics. Fine. A few tips to help with successful application and wear:

- Avoid using any hand cream, skin cream, or face lotion before touching your lenses. Ditto for cream soaps.
- Apply your lenses *before* putting on your eye and face makeup.
- Avoid lash-extender and other oily or flaky kinds of mascara. Your best bet is a waterproof type.
- Similarly, try a form of eyeshadow that is not powdered, to avoid particles drifting onto the surface of your eyes.
- Apply foundation and blush carefully. Particles from powdered blush can blow into your eyes, too.
- Use hair spray *before* you apply your lenses.
- Keep nail polish remover away from your eyes—the fumes will irritate them.
- First remove your lenses; then remove makeup.
- For other suggestions about makeup and its application and removal, ask your eye-care specialist.

Nonprescription Sunglasses

Whenever you buy a pair of nonprescription sunglasses, whether for fashion or protection against glare, you participate in a business that takes in $830 million each year. Americans purchase about 86 million pairs of sunglasses annually, and many of you undoubtedly waste your money on poor-quality items. Knowing what to look for when buying sunglasses will save you money and, even more important, protect your precious eyesight.

Decide before you go to the store what kind of glasses you want. If you choose "fun glasses"—those with lightly tinted lenses—don't rely on them for protection from the sun. They look great but, since the lenses don't filter out powerful infrared and ultraviolet rays, you can seriously damage your eyes.

"Sunglasses" should screen out 75 to 90 percent of sunlight, according to the American Optometric Association. All nonprescription lenses must meet FDA impact-resistance standards. You can find optically correct lenses made of plastic or glass, so you can decide which you prefer.

You can select among a variety of lens types and coatings:

- *Basic sunglass lenses* are evenly tinted in a solid color, most often gray or green. Gray permits truest color vision; dark green absorbs the most infrared radiation, but only in glass. Some people believe that brown lenses improve contrast on hazy days. Experts caution, however, that dark or medium blue tones can interfere with some wearers' ability to distinguish colors—definitely a safety hazard while driving. You can choose among practically any tint—the selection is as wide as the rainbow.

• *Photochromic, or light-sensitive, lenses,* respond automatically to the amount of available light by darkening in sunlight and lightening as the sun lessens. Currently, all photochromic lenses are made of glass and are available in strengths that screen out up to 85 percent of available sunlight. Investigate your choice carefully. Several types are on the market, and some have a narrower range—less sensitivity to light—and don't alter as much. All photochromic lenses need a breaking-in period before they adapt easily to different amounts of light.

• *Polarizing lenses* appeal to those of you bothered by excessive glare reflected from water and highways. These lenses contain a filter that absorbs glare and lets useful light reach your eyes. You'll find them in both plastic and glass.

• *Coatings.* Among the popular coatings you can choose from, mirrored lenses are definitely the most dramatic—you can look out but no one can see in. Not only do they look cool, by the way, but they really are cooler to wear because they protect against infrared rays. One problem: they require a hard protective coating since they scratch easily.

• *Gradient lenses* vary in intensity of tint. Some are quite dark at the top and light at the bottom, others are dark at both the top and bottom with a pale midsection. You can find them in all colors and coatings, including mirrored styles.

As dazzled as you are by your choices, you can be even more so by the price. But you can find glasses to fit your budget. Just bear these hints in mind:

• Plastic lenses, as a rule, are more costly than glass.
• Photochromic and polarizing lenses are generally more expensive than standard ones.
• The more coatings (antiscratch, mirror, and so forth), the higher the price.

• Designer frames are designed to remove cash from your wallet. A little hunting will bag a pair of (almost) identical frames.

During your sunglass-buying expedition, follow these guidelines to help you buy better glasses:

• Detect cheap, nonoptical glasses with an easy test: hold them up at arm's length and look through them. Focus on a straight edge in the distance, and move the glasses back and forth, up and down. Does the straight line—a doorframe, for example—curve, jiggle, zigzag, or distort in any way? If so, find another pair.
• Check lenses for overall evenness of tint.
• Examine gradient lenses carefully. The tones should blend smoothly and the lenses should match.
• Look in the mirror. You shouldn't be able to see your eyes clearly if you're wearing high-quality sunglasses.
• Test for fit. Toss your head back and forth, shake it, lean forward. Determine that the glasses fit comfortably and stay put. They should fit snugly—but painlessly—on the bridge of your nose and around your ears.
• Don't overlook the quality of the frames. You want your glasses to withstand months of use—and abuse—on your head, in their case, on the car seat, and wherever else you stash them. Look for sturdy, well-constructed frames. Check the hinges to make sure the screws are securely fastened.

Vision and Athletics

Teenagers lead active lives, and millions of you regularly jog, tumble, and swim yourselves into shape. That's a great boost for health, appearance, and personality, but be especially careful to protect your eyes while exercising and growing strong and beautiful.

Each year, about 160,000 children between five and seventeen years old suffer eye injuries, mostly while horsing around or playing sports. Yet if kids were taught eye-safety rules, provided with safety equipment, and taught how to use the equipment, 90 percent of these injuries could be prevented.

While all athletes need eye protection, certain sports present higher risks than others—particularly racquet sports, in which 3,200 Americans annually suffer eye injuries. These injuries are no joke, and some lead to blindness.

Professional athletes are serious about their vision. Their livelihoods depend on their exceptional skills and visual acuity:

• Sugar Ray Leonard canceled a title defense in 1982 to undergo surgery for a detached retina. He later retired from boxing.
• Kareem Abdul Jabbar, center for the Los Angeles Lakers, took to wearing goggles after suffering two eye injuries.
• While a college senior, Arthur Ashe discovered he couldn't read road signs from a distance as well as his teammates, so he had his vision examined.
• Back in 1967, Tony Conigliaro of the Boston Red Sox was beaned by a pitch. He suffered a severe head injury that impaired his sight and helped shorten his major league career.

Sports that present hazards to your eyes and vision include, in addition to the racquet sports (tennis, squash, paddle tennis, racquetball), handball, ice hockey, badminton, golf, archery, baseball, basketball, fencing, boxing, karate, fly-fishing, and any sport played with a projectile—something that hurtles through the air.

Prevent eye injuries by wearing protective equipment, whether or not you wear glasses. And urge your friends to do the same.

You can choose from a wide variety of protective gear for just about every sport:

• Sturdy eyeglass frames with industrial strength impact-resistant lenses are great for wearing while biking, playing golf, and archery.
• Sports frames with special features—such as padded bridges, headband attachments, deep-grooved eye wires—and formed to your face suit active sports such as basketball, baseball/softball, and racquet games.
• Goggles, designed primarily for protection and adaptable to prescription or nonprescription lenses, can be worn for racquet

sports, volleyball, basketball, swimming, water-skiing, snow-ski-ing, scuba diving, and skydiving.

• Eye/face guards can be designed to wear over your prescription glasses while you are playing such high-risk sports as hockey and any game with a racquet.

• Leave your helmet on! A smack on the head can harm your vision, too.

Note: Contact lenses are no substitute for protective eyewear when playing sports.

Even after you're equipped with the right gear, learn about the potential hazards in your sport. Tennis players, for example, are at greatest risk from the ball. Your own vision skills help prevent injuries; so does controlling your temper and telling your partner to do the same. Several players have suffered serious eye injuries from being hit by a ball slammed in anger or frustration.

Basketball players are most subject to eye injuries when beneath the basket where arms, elbows, and hands flail about as players grab for rebounds.

Any time you suffer a serious blow to your eyes, seek help at once. Damage to your eyes may not be apparent to you, the victim, so prompt attention is vitally important.

Finally, you can learn about your vision from your skill and enjoyment of sports. Problems you encounter while playing may be related to vision and not to clumsiness, laziness, or a "bad attitude," despite what the coach says. Among the clues:

• Playing worse, rather than better, even after arduous practice.
• Frequently blowing easy plays.
• Squinting.
• Poor eye-hand-foot-body coordination—essential to all sports.
• Consistent problems in hitting, catching, throwing, or passing a ball.

Even Olympic athletes can improve their competitive performance by honing visual skills. If they can, you can.

You play a central role in protecting your eyesight. Protective eye gear may look funny to you, but at least you'll be able to see what you look like.

DENTAL CARE

The Basics

By now there isn't one of you who doesn't know the ABCs of dental care. As veterans of countless hygiene classes and even more between-meal treats, you know the rules: brush and floss your teeth regularly, cut down on foods containing sugar, use fluorides daily, and visit the dentist at least twice a year for a thorough cleaning and examination.

But you ignore, postpone, or otherwise disdain good dental habits because they just don't seem very important, and the threat of dread diseases, rotting gums, and false teeth seems irrelevant to you, still in your teens, whose favorite meal is snack and whose toothbrush is always someplace else.

Did you know that, other than the common cold, tooth decay remains the most prevalent disease in the United States today? Unlike a cold, though, you can prevent cavities by following a simple regimen. Saving your teeth is largely up to you, and trust me, it's worth it.

Decay strikes most often during the teen years. If you get a lot of cavities, you are not brushing, flossing, using disclosing tablets, and performing the other rituals that can protect your teeth.

In your mouth's development, your second molars erupt by the time you're thirteen. The third molars, commonly called wisdom teeth, erupt when you're seventeen or older—but human jaws have grown shorter throughout the centuries, and most of us don't have enough room in our mouths for four more teeth. Wisdom teeth often develop at awkward angles or become impacted behind the second molars. Your dentist monitors the development of these teeth because they can cause so much trouble and pain. If they develop normally, they are usually left alone, but if X-rays and other evidence prove they are impacted or are pushing other teeth out of line, out they go in a surgical extraction, usually in your late teens or early twenties.

Preventive Care

Dentists stress preventive care, and with good reason. It works. For example, if you are among the 110 million Americans who live in communities that have fluoridated water supplies, you help inhibit the growth of cavities every day. Studies have shown that 20 percent of you, today's teenagers—who have been drinking fluoridated water since birth—are cavity-free. The remaining 80 percent suffer nearly 70 percent less decay than those of you who do not have fluoridated water. The American Dental Association predicts that, over a lifetime, people who consume fluoridated water can have 65 percent fewer cavities and 90 percent fewer tooth extractions.

Fluoride toothpastes, mouthwashes and gels can further boost your resistance to tooth decay. Fluoridated water and mouth rinses do not, by themselves, relieve you from the duties of brushing, flossing, and caring for your teeth properly.

Another weapon in the prevention arsenal: sealants. Ask your dentist about this inexpensive treatment. The dentist coats the biting surfaces of your teeth with a special clear plastic that prevents the growth of cavities by keeping the surface clear of plaque. (Plaque is a sticky, thin, colorless layer of bacteria constantly forming in your mouth. Bacteria in plaque combine with sugar in the foods you eat, creating acids that attack tooth enamel, starting the chain of decay.) Usually, sealants are painted on twice yearly.

In addition, get hold of some disclosing tablets. When you chew on one, a harmless and temporary vegetable dye stains the plaque you left behind after brushing your teeth. You will learn which areas of your mouth need extra attention when you brush and floss.

Don't let fear keep you from visiting the dentist. About half of all Americans don't see a dentist regularly, and of that group, 10 percent say they avoid checkups because they are afraid. What they don't know—but you do now—is that various technical advances have reduced the pain of dental care. And, too, dentists use a wide range of techniques to help you relax, including video games in the waiting room, headphones and piped in music, relaxation exercises, biofeedback, and hypnosis. Ask your dentist if he/she uses any of these methods, and find out what you can do to help yourself unwind.

Excellent brushing and flossing habits are vital in preventing periodontal disease, the number one cause of tooth loss in adults. This disorder affects gum tissue and supporting bone structure which deteriorate slowly and, if left untreated, cause teeth to loosen and eventually fall out. In most cases, periodontal disease is painless in its early stages, so as a teen you may not realize you have it. A virulent form of periodontal disease, called periodontosis, has been found to affect permanent teeth in teenagers. It seems to appear more often in girls and progresses at a rate three to four times that of adult periodontal disease. In other words, you can't postpone good dental habits on the theory that gum disease happens only to adults.

Don't restrict preventive care to brushing and flossing and smart eating habits. When you play active sports, wear a mouth guard! Ask your coach or dentist what kind of protective gear you need for your sport. It's worth the small investment to save your teeth from chips, breaks, or worse.

Appearance

No matter now conscientiously you brush, floss, and obey the commandments of preventive dentistry, you can't always do much to conceal imperfections or remove stains. But your dentist practices esthetic dentistry for these problems, and can make your teeth prettier more quickly and less expensively than you might think with a technique called *bonding*.

Bonding repairs teeth that are chipped or cracked at an average cost of one-third to one-half the cost of a conventional crown, and can eliminate the need for caps altogether. The dentist etches the tooth with acid to permit the plastic material to stick to the enamel, and then molds layers of this plastic into the gap or paints it on the surface to repair the problem. After the stuff is applied, the restoration is ''cured'' by means of a chemical process that frequently uses ultraviolet light. Teeth that have been repaired by bonding may need reapplications after a few years, but the process still is less expensive than capping. It's also painless.

Dental Specialists

Since you want to be a smart dental consumer, here's what other dental specialists do to help preserve your teeth—and your smile.

Pedodontists

Pedodontists, or pediatric dentists, treat children and young adults. They supplement their dental training with two to five years of postgraduate study in psychology and child development. They understand thoroughly the special problems you might encounter.

Endodontists

Endodontists treat diseases of the dental pulp. They are the specialists who perform root canals, a procedure that preserves a tooth that, if left untreated, would eventually have to be pulled. Diseases of dental pulp are most commonly caused by a break in your tooth or a deeply penetrating cavity that you ignore too long.

Periodontists

Periodontists diagnose and treat diseases of gums and supporting tissues. Treatment restores healthy gums and preserves teeth. Treatment, by the way, usually consists of surgery for advanced cases. It's definitely something you want to avoid, which is possible by employing good dental habits!

Prosthodontists

Prosthodontists specialize in treatment for those who have lost some or all of their teeth and require dentures. Chances are you will never need to see one, especially if you maintain those terrific habits of dental care!

Orthodontists

Orthodontists specialize in diagnosing, treating, and preventing faulty positioning of teeth and surrounding structures—and that includes giving you braces. More about these later!

You and Your Dentist

During the time you live with your parents, you probably visit the dentist they chose and you know, and you are comfortable with his/her treatment. But the day will come—perhaps it already has—when you must choose a dentist of your own. You'll certainly have a lot of dentists from which to choose: the American Dental Association (ADA) listed over 136,000 dentists in active practice in 1982. About 90 percent of that figure worked in private practice.

As in any medical relationship, you want to find a dentist with whom you can have a personal, long-lasting relationship. You want your dentist to take time to talk with you, understand your fears, and treat your problems with skill and sympathy. Here are ways to make it easier for you to find one you like and can work with successfully:

• Contact the local dental society for names of dentists in your area. If you live near a university dental school, ask its staff about local practitioners, and inquire, too, about the school's dental clinic.

• Nearby hospitals with an accredited dental service are good sources of referrals. So are your family physician and local pharmacist.

• Ask friends, co-workers, and neighbors to recommend dentists they trust. Of course, don't accept their recommendations on blind faith—not everyone's standards are the same. Investigate a little further.

• Check the latest ADA directory, which lists current members. You can find it at your local library. The roster will provide you with names only, however.

• Ask about fees, even over the phone. Ask, too, what to expect during your first visit.

• Learn from that first visit. Your selection process continues once you are in the dentist's chair. Does the dentist take your dental and medical histories, including the name and phone number of your physician? Does he/she ask about any allergies, or whether you have medical problems such as diabetes or hemophilia? Does he/she take a full series of dental X-rays before starting treatment? Does the dentist teach you how to avoid and prevent cavities and other dental problems?

• What procedures exist if you have an emergency—and no appointment? What about emergency referral services?

• Check for signs of good dental practice. Are you draped with a lead apron during dental X-rays? Is the office clean and neat? Does the equipment appear modern and well maintained? Are you advised on good dental care to follow between visits?

• Find a dentist who has an office near your home, school, or workplace so you can avoid lengthy trips. Select one who doesn't keep you cooling your heels in the outer office regularly, and one who sends reminder notices when you need a checkup.

• If your dentist is disorganized, find another and request that your dental records be sent along.

Also on your dental checklist:

• If you carry dental insurance, check in advance which services are covered by the policy. Bring essential documents with you to the office.

• Always question the need to extract a tooth—even those accursed wisdom teeth. Extractions might be inexpensive remedies now, but they can cost you a fortune later in dental appliances, false teeth, and other dental services.

• Don't be seduced by bargains in dental care. There aren't any. Initially high expenditures—amounts that seem pretty scary—can easily turn out to be less expensive when averaged over your lifetime because you'll be spared later dental catastrophes. Preventive dentistry makes good sense economically. Your teeth were meant to last a lifetime. They will, if you take proper care of them now.

Dental Insurance

While increases in dental costs remain below the rise of the Consumer Price Index, good dental care is not cheap. In addition, only about 50 percent of the population sees a dentist regularly.

Against this background, dental insurance makes good sense: about 75 million Americans currently have that protection, and the ADA predicts that by 1985 almost 100 million of us will be covered.

Virtually all dental-insurance plans are sold to groups: companies, unions, associations, school groups. Perhaps your parents are covered by a dental plan that takes care of your expenses. If you are about to look for a full-time job, be sure to ask whether a dental plan is part of your fringe benefits.

Dental insurance differs in principle from medical insurance. Basic dental coverage takes care of recurrent, predictable events such as cleanings, examinations, and cavities. Think of dental insurance as a way to prevent small problems from mushrooming, rather than as a financial safeguard against catastrophe (a principle of medical insurance coverage).

Dental plans vary widely, but most cover a broad range of basic services. These generally include: examinations, X-rays, teeth-cleanings, fillings, crowns, fluoride treatments, root canal treatments, extractions, some other types of oral surgery, and treatment of gum diseases. Some policies also include orthodontic insurance. As a rule, policies do not cover hospitalization costs involved in dental treatment and treatments provided for cosmetic reasons only.

Getting Wired: Braces

Have you ever laughed at the tall stories about braces—the one about the kid who receives radio signals on his wires and can tune in to the Rolling Stones during geometry class? How about that couple, each wearing bands and wires, who got locked together during an impassioned good-night kiss? They're great stories—and completely false.

By now, though, you know some facts about orthodontics, even if you are not a veteran of braces, retainers, rubber bands, and countless hours after school at the doctor's office. As mentioned earlier, orthodontics is that branch of dentistry that diagnoses, treats, and prevents faulty positioning of teeth and surrounding structures. Did you know that the orthodontist's goals also extend to improving the health and function of the patient's mouth? Severe untreated orthodontic problems can lead, eventually, to tooth decay, diseased gums, loss of teeth, and other unpleasant effects. The cost of treating these unnecessary problems later on can far outstrip the cost of prompt orthodontic care, to say nothing of the unnecessary pain involved.

Less dramatic problems can affect your health and emotional well-being. Orthodontic problems affect, to some extent, an estimated 89 percent of Americans aged twelve to seventeen. Of that 89 percent, 29 percent are classified as severe cases—meaning that treatment is either very desirable or necessary.

Of the 4 million Americans in orthodontic treatment, 80 percent are under twenty-one. Treatment, or at least preliminary evaluation, can start as young as age seven or earlier. Your dentist or orthodontist may have practiced "interceptive" techniques on you—recognizing that problems were developing in your mouth, he/she headed them off by a variety of means. For many patients, this kind of attention reduces the need for full-scale treatment later.

The remaining 20 percent of orthodontic patients are adults—men and women over twenty-one who voluntarily undergo orthodontic treatment. Most choose orthodontic treatment to make their smiles prettier, or their dentist recommends orthodontics before other required dental work can be started. Or, troubled by symptoms such as a clicking jaw or even facial pain, a person seeks orthodontic advice. Whatever the reasons, lots of famous people have waited until they were grown up to undergo this treatment: Linda Gray of "Dallas," Barbara Walters, Dick Smothers, Phyllis Diller, Michael Jackson, and Diana Ross, to name a few. If you think that someday you will want orthodontic treatment, don't assume you'll be too old.

Many companies and unions include orthodontic insurance in their dental policies, and increasing numbers of employees receive this valuable benefit. Ask your parents about their policies, and keep it in mind when you look for a full-time job. You may want it for yourself, since a dental/orthodontic policy will pay up to $1,500 per person in lifetime benefits.

Choosing an Orthodontist

Choose an orthodontist with great care, for this is a person you must trust and with whom you will spend a lot of time. Some general dentists may be able to handle your problem if it requires limited treatment, but if a specialist is called for, ask your dentist to recommend one or two orthodontists. Orthodontists are specialists who have completed two academic years of continuous advanced studies after dental school. Currently, over 9,000 orthodontists work in the United States and Canada.

Ask friends for referrals. Quiz them about why they like a particular orthodontist.

If you live near a dental school, ask a member of the department of orthodontics for advice. Ask, too, about orthodontic clinics run through the dental school program.

Consult with two orthodontists and weigh their suggestions.

However, don't expect a complete evaluation and diagnosis for the price of a consultation. Once you decide on treatment, the orthodontist takes diagnostic records that include X-rays, photographs, and plaster models. After the orthodontist studies these data, he/she tells you what the prescribed course of treatment is for you.

It's your mouth, so ask a lot of questions and understand the answers. For example, find out in detail about your problem, the proposed treatment, what will happen if you don't correct it, and whether another method of treatment might work.

Inquire about fees and payment schedules. Fees vary widely, depending on the severity of your problem, length of treatment, type of appliance to be used, and other procedures. Orthodontics is not cheap! But the results last your lifetime and the cost, averaged over the length of treatment, might not be so terrifying.

Your orthodontist decides whether to use fixed or removable appliances. In general, fixed appliances—bands and wires—give the control needed for long-term treatment; removable appliances tend to be limited to short-term work.

Control your impatience when you are reminded again to brush your teeth. Successful orthodontic treatment—which is what you want, after all the time you've spent and aggravation you've endured—depends to a huge extent on you. Humor your orthodontist and follow his/her instructions to the letter. Your regular visits will prove whether you're obeying orders or not—and if not, you simply prolong the treatment. Don't forget to wear that retainer after the bands are removed!

Department Store Dentistry

How does the idea sound of visiting the dentist while between stops at sportswear and shoes in your local department store? A new development in delivery of dental-care services permits you to do just that.

The first clinic to be placed in a retail store was in California back in 1977. Since then the numbers have mushroomed and, in 1982, encompassed seventeen department store and five drugstore chains for a total of ninety-one retail store dental facilities in seventeen states and the District of Columbia.

Department store dentistry appeals to patients because it's so convenient. In general, these facilities keep the same hours as their host, including some evenings and weekends. That can be a real boon to busy patients. They promise speedier care and, often, lower fees.

Here's how they work: a separate administrative group leases space from the store and then subleases it to the dental group providing the actual services. Bulk purchases of equipment and supplies and shared overhead costs help keep expenses down; profits are calculated, at least in part, on the number of patients treated each day minus expenses. Questions to ask, should you decide to sample this kind of care, include:

• What services are included in the advertised fee? What costs are involved in different routine treatments such as fillings and the always-popular scaling and prophylaxis (cleaning)? Unadvertised costs can jack up your expenses to equal those for a private dentist.

• Does the facility emphasize preventive care? How about continuous long-term care?

• Will you see the same dentist and technician regularly? Can you establish a relationship with staff members? And, too, what's the rate of staff turnover?

• How do they handle dental emergencies?

If you're unsure of the answers, call your local consumer protection agency, Better Business Bureau, or dental society for advice.

HEARING

Hearing Loss

Statistics on hearing loss in the United States tell a startling story. More than 16.2 million Americans suffer from some degree of hearing loss, and more than 11.5 million suffer from uncorrected hearing loss. Approximately 5 million are under eighteen.

Looked at another way, this means that one out of every thirteen people suffers some hearing impairment.

Did you know that loss of hearing is the most widespread malady in the United States today, affecting more people than heart disease, cancer, and a host of other ailments—combined?

You probably don't pay a lot of attention to your hearing, and take for granted that you can play your records as loudly as you please, don headphones and turn up the volume, and otherwise abuse your hearing. Not only are you wrong, you may damage your hearing now and not realize it for years to come.

Hearing loss among young Americans is increasing dramatically, and a disturbing increase of noise in our society suggests that this trend will continue, since noise is the most common cause of hearing loss. What kinds of noise affect you? Chief villains include loud rock music (loud music of any kind, actually), motorcycles, traffic, use of power tools, and sports racing.

If you fail to wear hearing protection when using tools, riding dirt bikes, or racing cars, you harm your hearing.

Prolonged exposure to loud rock music can cause inner ear damage that may result in permanent hearing loss. Key words to remember are "prolonged" and "loud": the combination of intensity of sound with length of time you're exposed to it is crucial. The higher the decibel level, the less amount of time it takes to hurt your hearing. For example, the average intensity of music at a disco is 110 decibels. At that rate, half an hour's exposure can cause hearing loss. One expert has said that listening to rock music at over 108 decibels for more than five minutes a day will, over several years, result in hearing loss.

Noise affects the ability to hear at very high frequencies, so a loss can remain undetected for years. These high frequencies don't affect normal conversation.

The effect is cumulative; it adds up over time. Your tendency to turn up the volume to hear better merely increases the problem—an audio "Catch 22."

Does all this grim information decree that you turn off the records and tapes and deprive yourself of good music? Not at all; just give yourself and your ears a break. Observe some simple guidelines:

• Stereo equipment is not harmful; people misuse it. Turn the volume down!
• Use headphones less frequently and at lower volumes. Headphones can be dangerous because the noise has less distance to travel and has nothing to absorb and cushion the sounds. Keep this in mind, too, when wearing portable headphones.

• Don't sit next to the speakers at home, at a concert, movie, or disco.

• Don't be embarrassed to wear earplugs—the soft, malleable kind. In fact, no one need notice them. The plugs reduce sound, but don't block it completely.

• Give yourself a breather. Remember that combined volume and duration of exposure damage your hearing, so take breaks by turning the sound off, or way down, going outside, or taking a break from whatever the source is.

• Boycott excessively loud amplification, and complain. Shopkeepers, restaurant managers, and club owners get the hint quickly when customers stay away or gripe audibly. It might not seem too cool, but think how you'd feel if you couldn't hear yourself complain.

• Think, too, about the many rock performers who have suffered great hearing losses but won't go public with the news. They fear this revelation will repel fans in droves.

The only relief for a noise-induced hearing loss is amplification of remaining hearing—that is, a hearing aid. Surgery can sometimes correct hearing loss caused by other agents, such as heredity, illness, and head injuries. (Don't remove those helmets during sports or when riding motorcycles!) Surgery does not work for all of these, however.

Basically, hearing loss falls into two categories: *conductive* and *sensorineural*.

Conductive loss, which can be caused by wax blocking the ear canal or infection of the middle-ear tissues, often responds well to medical or surgical attention.

Sensorineural, or nerve loss, is traced to the inner ear and is caused by damage to nerve fibers, hair cells, or both. Since this type of loss responds poorly, if at all, to medicine or surgery, the only remedy is a hearing aid.

Nearly everyone, whatever the category of hearing loss, can benefit from medical or surgical treatment or amplification. You just need to ask for help, and promptly. Your family doctor can answer your questions, or you can direct them to Hearing HelpLine, a toll-free service sponsored by the Better Hearing Institute. Operators will send information and list sources of help in your area. Call during business hours, eastern standard time: 1-800-424-8576.

What to Do if You Can't Hear

If you think you're losing your hearing, don't wait around for it to improve. Your family doctor or clinic will direct you to an ear specialist, called an *otologist* or *otolaryngologist*, who will test your hearing, diagnose the problem, and help you with medical or surgical treatment.

If the otologist determines that you need a hearing aid, you will be referred to a clinical *audiologist*, who is trained to measure hearing and to help rehabilitate and counsel patients, or to a hearing aid specialist. Hearing aids neither cure hearing loss nor prevent additional loss, but they do enhance your remaining hearing.

When you purchase a hearing aid, read and understand the instructional brochure and the terms of your contract. Study the warranty.

Your further questions on hearing aids can be answered by the National Hearing Aid Society (NHAS), and operators will send you a resource packet on request. (NHAS, 20361 Middlebelt Rd., Livonia, MI 48152; toll-free telephone: 1-800-521-5247.) Services are free.

THERAPY: WHAT, WHY, AND WHEN

Your Body Tells You

"It's just a phase. You'll get over it."

"These are the best years of your life. Someday you'll look back and wish you could do it all again."

"Everybody has problems. What makes you think you're so special? Don't be such a baby!"

"You have to be crazy to go see a shrink."

If you're unhappy and confused, comments like these can make you want to scream—they reflect the apparent insensitivity of parents, teachers, even friends. But *you know* you hurt inside. You're just not sure what to do.

How do you know when it's time to seek outside help?

You give yourself clues all the time. Pay attention to what you are trying to tell yourself.

Your body lets you know when something is wrong, with typical problems such as: you can't sleep; you can't seem to wake up; you're always exhausted; you lose your appetite for no real reason;

your weight drops off; you can't seem to fill up; you gain rapidly; you suffer blinding headaches; your stomach hurts.

If you never feel well, first have a checkup to determine whether there is an organic problem causing your distress. Often, common illnesses such as hepatitis, mononucleosis, and even the flu can make victims feel depressed, lethargic, and cranky. But if you get a clean bill of health and the symptoms persist, ask your doctor for advice and counsel about a therapist.

Watch for dramatic (violent) changes in your behavior: loss of interest in school, sports, your car, any or all of your regular activities and favorite places and people; plummeting grades; poor concentration; easy boredom; crippling and engulfing waves of panic.

Note any frightening actions and self-destructive behavior. Do you drink too much? Drive too fast? Eat constantly? Starve yourself? Or, perhaps, do you isolate yourself and withdraw from everyone who cares about you? That makes sense if you think that no one knows or understands the first thing about you.

Any or all of these signs indicate that it's time to talk to someone and perhaps receive professional help. When problems disrupt your ability to function normally and cause relationships to suffer, professional assistance can help you pull things together and to focus on issues that make life so difficult.

It may happen that parents, a teacher, doctor, or friend suggests to you that you see a therapist. If so, don't dismiss the idea. The suggestion doesn't mean that you're crazy! Sometimes a crisis may arise that you can't resolve on your own—a separation or divorce of your parents, the death of a close relative or friend.

Today, an estimated 34 million Americans get professional counseling and psychotherapy. There is no reason to feel that you're a freak, or weird, or totally nuts to have problems that you can't untangle alone. In fact, when you're unhappy, the urge to see a therapist can reveal how much you want to feel better and take care of yourself. If you had a virus or broken bone, you'd see a doctor and have it treated, wouldn't you?

Finding a therapist is a real challenge, especially when you feel unhinged to begin with and uncertain about every aspect of your life. You may have no idea where and how to begin or whether you or your parents can afford this special help.

Anything this important might take a little time to resolve; start now to learn where, and who, the resources are.

The Mental Health Professionals

First, familiarize yourself with the mental health professionals. There are more than 90,000 of them, and most divide into the following groups.

Psychiatrists

Psychiatrists are medical doctors who specialize in mental disorders and who have completed a three-year residency (advanced training) in psychiatry. A board-certified psychiatrist has passed the written and oral examinations of the American Board of Psychiatry and Neurology and has practiced for at least two years. Only psychiatrists can prescribe drugs and medical therapies.

Psychologists

Psychologists are specialists who have a master's or doctorate in the study of human behavior. Their interest lies in understanding, preventing, and treating emotional and mental disorders. Each state has established its own licensing requirements, but usually experience is expected to supplement classroom training.

Social Workers and Psychiatric Social Workers

Social workers and psychiatric social workers have master's degrees or Ph.D.s in social work and have completed programs designed to train them in such techniques as therapy and consultation. Most are accredited by the National Association of Social Workers.

Psychiatric Nurses

Psychiatric nurses are clinical specialists who are registered professional nurses with advanced training and degrees in mental health. They conduct individual, family, and group therapy, according to their training, and work in a variety of agencies and private practice.

Psychoanalysts

Psychoanalysis is a treatment technique, not a profession. Most psychoanalysts are psychiatrists, although, in increasing numbers, training institutes accept clinical psychologists, social workers, even lay people. Men and women who become psychoanalysts are already fully trained and practicing mental health professionals when they begin their new training.

Psychotherapists

Psychotherapists are any mental health professionals who treat patients. Just about anyone can call himself or herself a psychotherapist and operate a private practice, since the term is so broad; therefore, it's essential that you protect yourself by learning all you can about a potential therapist. Ask whoever refers you about the individual's type of training and professional qualifications.

Finding a Therapist

When investigating a therapist's qualifications, feel free to contact local professional associations, or check national directories of the American Psychiatric Association, the American Psychological Association, and the National Association of Social Workers (these should be at your library or county medical society). When you talk to the therapist, assure yourself of his or her training, experience, and professional associations. Don't be overwhelmed by a wall plastered with diplomas and certificates. Vague answers will signify that this "therapist" has something to hide.

During your initial phone calls with prospective therapists, include questions about their areas of expertise, availability for appointments, and fees.

If you proceed and arrange a consultation, consider it a mutual interview and ask as many questions as you want. This is *your* therapy, and your choice of therapist is central to its success. No one has yet devised a formula for choosing the ideal person; it's very much up to you.

Therapy doesn't have to be expensive. Many patients with limited financial resources see therapists regularly either in private practice or through community mental health centers. Basic costs for private practitioners are based on their training, location, and reputation, among other factors. Psychiatrists traditionally are the most expensive, with fees soaring to $100 an hour and more in some instances. Psychologists charge between $25 and $75 an hour, and psychiatric social workers receive between $20 and $40 an hour. But these are approximate figures only and shouldn't deter you from seeking help: most therapists are willing to reduce their fees based on your ability to pay. And don't ignore your health insurance (or that of your parents) as a way to help reduce your out-of-pocket expenses. Also, local community mental health centers offer less expensive therapy, and although these clinics don't always have glowing reputations, millions of people receive excellent and successful treatment this way. Wherever you go for therapy, mention financial considerations early in your discussions and be up front about your ability to pay.

But after all this introduction, how *do* you find a therapist?

• Speak with your family doctor. Here's someone who has known you for a long time, knows the local scene, and can link you with a good therapist who is skilled in dealing with teenagers. If you're worried about confidentiality, say so! Most doctors and therapists will honor your wishes, and if for some reason they cannot, they will tell you why.

• Haul out the phone books. Look in the Yellow Pages under "social service agencies," "family and children's agencies," "mental health facilities," and professional titles. When you make your calls, explain as clearly as you can your problems and the sort of help you want. Check the fee for an initial consultation.

• Search for any friends in therapy. Ask them about their treatment and therapists. Of course, the process is intensely personal, and different people's reactions to the same therapist vary tremendously. Still, discussing it with your friends can suggest to you how to proceed and with whom.

• Explore such community resources as the YMCA, YWCA, women's centers, and community mental health centers. If you live near a medical school or therapeutic training institute, speak to a staff member about special services for teenagers.

• Check with the denominational helping agencies—such as Catholic Charities and Jewish Welfare Board—that match people with social services. Call on them, no matter what your religious background.

• Ask for counsel from rabbis, priests, and ministers who often advise members of their congregations; they also can refer you to agencies and individual therapists. The American Association of Pastoral Counselors (3 West 29th Street, New York, NY 10001) will help you find a minister, rabbi, or priest with accredited counseling skills. Not all clergy are qualified—or interested—in counseling.

• Use the community hot lines—terrific sources of current information and referrals. They can provide you with short-term emotional release, since calls to them are confidential and anonymous. You can say whatever you want.

• Contact the outpatient mental health department of local hospitals, especially teaching hospitals (those affiliated with a medical school). Professionals still in supervised training, or those just starting private practice, often charge less and are more willing to adjust their fees.

• If you're living on campus, you can go to your school's health center for counseling. For more comprehensive treatment, the staff can advise you about professionals in the community and tell you which ones offer sliding-scale fees.

• Finally, the Family Service Association of America (FSA) assists individuals and families with every imaginable kind of problem. Its scope is so broad, in fact, that you should request information about them whenever crisis threatens, whatever its nature. For a list of FSA accredited member agencies near you, write to the main office (44 East 23rd Street, New York, NY 10010). Services, in general, are low in cost or payable on a sliding scale.

Reaching out to any of these people and services will not be easy when you feel so terrible—getting up in the morning may be all the activity you can handle. But try, as hard as you can. You can leave all the confusion and unhappiness behind.

Read More about It

A number of books specifically for young people deal with common emotional problems and include suggestions for overcoming them.

Look at *Why You Feel Down and What You Can Do About It: A Psycho-therapist Tells Everything You Wanted to Know about Teenage Depression*, by Irma Myers and Arthur Myers (Charles Scribner's Sons, 1982). Also check out *Help: A Guide to Counseling and Therapy without Hassle*, by Jane Marks (Julian Messner, 1976). Chapters in *The Family Handbook of Adolescence, The Healthy Adolescent, The Teenage Body Book*, and *Don't Worry, You're Normal* (see pages 632–33) offer insights that you can use while you decide how to handle your problems. *A Parent's Guide to Child Therapy*, by Richard Bush (Delacorte Press, 1980) explains different modes of treatment, kinds of therapists, and problems children and teenagers encounter.

GYNECOLOGY

When to See the Gynecologist

- Your mother suggests that it's time for you to see "her doctor."
- You're about to leave home for college.
- You experience cramps, swelling, and general grouchiness before and during your period.
- You worry that your body isn't developing. You're fifteen, you don't menstruate, and your breasts remain flat.
- You're at least eighteen years old.
- You need advice about birth control, since you're sexually active.

Any of these and similar occasions or complaints lead you to an obstetrician-gynecologist or "woman's doctor," a physician who, specializing in medical care for women, concentrates on reproductive and sexual organs and functions. *Obstetrics* focuses on care of women through pregnancy, labor, delivery, and immediately after childbirth; *gynecology* covers all other areas of health care involving the reproductive organs.

According to the standards of the American College of Obstetricians and Gynecologists, you should undergo your first gynecological exam by the time you're eighteen or when you first become sexually active. (For information on birth control, see Chapter 17,

Times of Trouble and Feeling Bad.) Gynecological care is vital once you're sexually active since you need advice about contraception and the risks of unwanted pregnancy, and with sexual activity your risk of contracting infections in your reproductive system increases sharply. Experts counsel that you should have a full pelvic examination yearly (your doctor may want to see you every six months). The exam includes a Pap smear (a screening test for cervical cancer) and checks for vaginal infections and sexually transmitted diseases. (For more on sexually transmitted diseases, see Chapter 17, *Times of Trouble.*) In addition, you should call the gynecologist if you notice any unusual symptoms or changes involving your reproductive system. If you're fifteen or older and you have never—or only rarely—menstruated, consult a gynecologist or other doctor.

Choosing a Gynecologist

During her lifetime a woman well may see an obstetrician-gynecologist more than any other doctor. Many women consider an ob-gyn their primary care, or regular, doctor. Common sense tells why: yearly checkups and Pap smears alone dictate many visits. You can understand easily why you want a doctor you like, trust, and can talk with openly—someone who will respect your confidence.

You have available a number of good sources of referrals:

• Your family doctor (internist or pediatrician) or another health-care specialist can recommend an ob-gyn for you.
• The local medical society has a list of practitioners in your vicinity.
• A nearby medical school will have a department of obstetrics and gynecology; you can ask a staff member for advice by phone.
• Virtually every hospital has a maternity ward. Ask to speak to a physician or nurse at a hospital near you.
• Your friends, as always, can recommend doctors they like. But, since standards always differ, find out what they like and dislike about their gynecologist, and why.
• If there's a special teacher at your school whom you respect and trust, ask her!
• The American College of Obstetricians and Gynecologists (ACOG) will send you a list of members in your area (more than 90

percent of ob-gyns are fellows of the college). Send a stamped self-addressed envelope with your letter and, if you live in a relatively unpopulated area, mention the nearest metropolitan region. (Resource Center, American College of Obstetricians and Gynecologists, 600 Maryland Ave., S.W., Washington, DC 20024.)

• The Resource Center also will send you single copies of ACOG's patient information booklets. Send your request for a list of titles, along with a self-addressed stamped envelope (SASE), to the address above. Sample titles: *The Gynecologic Examination, Menstruation—Normal and Abnormal*, and *Ob-Gyn: The Woman's Physician*. Enclose a SASE each time you write for a booklet.

What to Expect Once You're There

When you first get to a new doctor's office, you might feel nervous and shy. Minimize those feelings by asking important questions over the phone:

• Find out about fees and extra charges for lab tests, including a Pap smear and tests for sexually transmitted diseases and herpes.
• Ask whether the doctor has staff privileges at a local hospital. Which one?
• Is the doctor a partner in a group practice? If so, can you expect to see the doctor of your choice regularly? If not, what provisions are made for emergency care?
• What is the doctor's payment policy? Should you bring your wallet or checkbook, or will you be sent a bill?

Once you actually arrive at the appointment, the doctor will have questions for you. The first stage of the exam will include inquiries about your health and your family's medical history. Be ready to talk about any illnesses, allergies, medications, and your menstrual and reproductive history.

The second step is a thorough physical that includes measurement of your height, weight, and blood pressure, and an examination of your abdomen and internal and external pelvis. The doctor will feel your breasts and teach you how to examine them each month. At this point, the doctor will take a Pap smear—a swab of cells from your vaginal walls and cervix.

Lab work, the third part of your exam, consists of any tests such as urinalysis, Pap smear, and others indicated by your medical history and current problems. Some lab work can be performed in the doctor's office, but many procedures are sent to commercial medical labs for analysis (which takes more time and can be expensive).

Routine care is covered in many medical-insurance policies. An annual exam and Pap smear are considered preventive care, which may not be covered.

Your Menstrual History: Key to Your Reproductive Health

Your menstrual cycle is an intricate, continuous process that involves ovulation, hormonal ebb and flow, changes in the uterine lining, and finally, sloughing of that lining by means of the menstrual flow. As you know, menstruation involves your whole body and is controlled by your brain and pituitary gland. Your cycle may already be well established while your friends never know when to expect their periods, or the reverse may apply. But no matter where you are in your development, an excellent habit to establish *now* is a record of your menstrual periods.

On a calendar (you can find special calendars for this purpose) jot down the first day of your most recent period. Check off each day you have menstrual flow. When your next period begins, repeat this process. At the *menarche,* or when you first start menstruating, your periods may vacillate wildly because your system is still working out its own timing, but eventually you will establish a fairly predictable schedule. For example, if your most recent period began on October 1 and your next starts on October 31, you have a thirty-day cycle. When you chart your periods over time, you will recognize when disturbances or problems arise that require special attention, and you will understand better your body's rhythms.

Tampons and You

In your lifetime, you can expect to menstruate the approximate equivalent of six years. That's a significant amount of time, and one reason why it's vitally important to understand menstruation, to "demythologize" this fact of life, and to learn to live comfortably with your body and its rhythms.

Menstruation is an economic fact of life, too. American women spent almost $640 million on sanitary napkins (which includes ''mini'' and ''maxi'' pads) in 1981, and another $400 million on tampons.

Yet, menstruation still may be one of the most misunderstood and controversial subjects around.

• About 42 percent of all women think it's unwise for young women to use tampons before they experience sexual intercourse. A recent survey found about 30 percent of teenage girls agreed with this statement. Among men, 48.5 percent of 14- to 17-year-olds, and 32.2 percent of 18- to 21-year-olds thought so, too.

• A startling 31 percent of 14- to 17-year-old girls did not know what menstruation was (in this era!) when they experienced their first period.

• Another shocking 26 percent of the population believe women cannot function as well as usual while menstruating.

• And 8 percent—which works out to 14 million people—believe that women should make an effort to stay away from other people during their periods!

But here's good news: today, ten times as many teenagers (fourteen to seventeen years old) learn about menstruation in school as in a former era did people over fifty-five (33 percent versus 0.3 percent). American men and women today support teaching about menstruation in school (91 percent).

Misunderstandings still prevail about tampons and sanitary protection, however. Did you know that commercial sanitary napkins were first sold after World War I, and that tampons weren't even on the market until 1936? Your grandmothers had very different supplies when they first started menstruating.

Let's torpedo some of the myths now:

Myth: Tampon use in some way causes you to lose your virginity.
Fact: Virginity has nothing to do with successful use (or failure to use) tampons. A tampon is inserted into the vagina through an opening in the hymen that allows menstrual flow to exit. Only a statistically small percentage of young women is unable to use tampons. If you are among them, see a doctor.

Myth: A tampon can get lost inside your body.
Fact: Impossible. Muscles around the entrance to your vagina grip the tampon in place. You may be tense however. Relax, breathe deeply, and you will "relocate" the tampon.

Now is the time to establish good hygiene habits:

• Bathe or shower regularly during your menstrual cycle.
• Don't wear a tampon between periods to absorb normal vaginal secretions. Doctors will tell you that the vagina cleans itself, and a regular, clear discharge is normal and healthy.
• You don't need "deodorant" sanitary products. In fact, many women are allergic to the perfumes used in scented pads and tampons, and these women wind up in the doctor's office.
• Use the proper absorbency tampon for your needs, which will vary during your flow. Using a more absorbent tampon than you really need can soak up the natural fluids that lubricate your vaginal walls and that help maintain the normal pH balance.
• Read the instructions in your box of tampons carefully.
• Change tampons as needed, but at least every six hours and definitely before you go to bed and when you get up in the morning.
• Learn to use menstrual pads and tampons correctly. Abuse can lead to discomfort and even infections that can be costly and unpleasant to cure.

Many doctors recommend that young women learn to use tampons and get to know their own anatomy. It can be a bit difficult at first, but you'll soon get the idea.

Read All about You

Books on women's health care are a mini-industry within the publishing business. Among the many titles in your bookstore or library:

Bell, Ruth, *Changing Bodies, Changing Lives: A Book for Teens on Sex and Relationships*. Random House, 1980.
Cooke, Cynthia W., M.D., and Dworkin, Susan, *The Ms. Guide to a Woman's Health*. Berkley Books, 1979.
The Diagram Group, *Woman's Body: An Owner's Manual*, revised edition. Simon & Schuster, 1981.

Holt, Linda Hughey, M.D., and Weber, Melva, *The American Medical Association Book of WomanCare*. Random House, 1981.

Madaras, Lynda, and Patterson, Jane, M.D., *WomanCare: A Gynecological Guide to Your Body*. Avon, 1981.

Stewart, Felicia, M.D., Guest, Felicia, Stewart, Gary, M.D., and Thatcher, Robert, M.D., *My Body, My Health: The Concerned Woman's Book of Gynecology*. Bantam Books, 1981.

BOYS: THE DOCTOR AND YOU

Boys, when you visit the doctor, expect a thorough examination of your genitals. Your penis will be checked for any growths, such as warts, and other abnormalities. If you weren't circumcised, the doctor wants to make sure that your foreskin retracts smoothly. Too, he/she will look for tumors as well as hernias (abnormal protrusions of an organ inside the body) by examining your testicles. The doctor will sometimes feel your prostate, a gland lying next to the bladder, for any irregularities. In addition to screening out any problems, your doctor is looking to see that your body is developing properly by monitoring changes in your genitals—an increase in the size of your penis and testicles and the growth of pubic hair, for example. And, as mentioned earlier, you should be counseled about self-examination, which can be of vital importance in early detection of cancer of the testicles.

Many of you worry about your height. Actually, the range of what is "normal" for teenage boys is surprisingly wide, but if your height concerns you, don't hesitate to talk it over with your doctor. It's too important an issue to fret over silently. And don't be shy of discussing other questions about your body's development.

While your growth spurt can take place at any time during your teens, and lasts a few years at least, it will be preceded by some changes and growth of your testicles. Your physician will be on the lookout for these changes and can explain them to you.

PLASTIC SURGERY

When you hear the phrase "plastic surgery," do you imagine glamorous celebrities having their noses straightened, their faces lifted, their tummies tucked? Do you envision people older—much older—than yourself? Then it will be news to you that, while those are all standard procedures, plastic surgery is limited neither to those few operations nor celebrity (read rich) patients. And patients fit into all age categories, too.

In fact, a survey conducted among members of the American Society of Plastic and Reconstructive Surgeons early in the decade revealed that 11 percent of all patients are under sixteen, and another 14 percent are between sixteen and twenty-five.

Not all plastic surgery is esthetic—that is, performed to improve your appearance—although that's an important part of what plastic surgeons do. Many of their operations are designed to correct congenital problems such as cleft lips and palates and to repair scars caused by accidents, burns, and other misfortunes. An estimated 60 percent of teenage patients have reconstructive-repair work.

Plastic surgery doesn't always require a hospital stay. Often, surgery can be performed on an outpatient basis, with doctors having fully equipped operating and recovery rooms in their office suites. Use of these facilities can slash your medical bills! Nationwide, the savings average 30 to 40 percent. Basically, the surgeon's fee will be the same wherever the operation takes place, but once in a hospital, you have to add on the operating room, recovery room, overnight stay, anesthesiologist, and other incidental costs. For elective, nonreconstructive surgery few, if any, of these expenses will be covered by health insurance.

Having surgery performed in the doctor's office is important to you in another way. Since you already know the doctor and have visited the office before, you'll often be more comfortable and relaxed when you return for the procedure. Those surroundings may be less intimidating than a strange, big, impersonal hospital.

Many operations can be performed on an outpatient basis, and the criterion is not so much the operation but the patient's general health status and need for postoperative care. In other words, if you're strong and healthy, and can get good postsurgical care from a parent, there's often no reason to go to the hospital.

Common Procedures

A brief guide to the most common cosmetic procedures performed on teens follows.

Rhinoplasty

Probably the most common operation among teens, rhinoplasty is nose surgery that improves the shape and size of the nose by removing excess cartilage and tissue and rearranging and reshaping what remains. Almost always, the work is done inside the nose, leaving no scars. Generally, surgeons wait until their patients are fourteen or so to let the nose assume its adult shape and character. Rhinoplasties can easily be performed on an outpatient basis. Postoperative care involves minimizing the swelling and discomfort that follow. It's vitally important to obey—to the letter—the set of instructions given by the doctor. Patients can usually return to school or work within ten days to two weeks of surgery, or even earlier. Fees, early in the decade, ranged from $1,200 to $1,800.

Otoplasty

You might know this operation as "pinning back" the ears. Otoplasty consists of reshaping the ears' external cartilage, occasionally removing some cartilage, and placing the ears in proper alignment with the face and head. Since ears reach their full growth before age five, otoplasties can be performed on children as well as teens and adults. (By the way, otoplasties do not correct—or cause—hearing problems.) The operation can be performed either in a hospital or outpatient clinic, depending on the patient's requirements. During postoperative care, a wraparound bandage is worn as a turban for a week or so, and most patients return to school or work within a week or ten days of surgery. Costs ranged from $800 to $1,200 for the operation early in the decade.

Dermabrasion

By planing down the skin's surface, dermabrasion reduces the scars and pits caused by severe acne, chicken pox, and injuries. During the treatment, the area of skin is frozen and a rapidly rotating brush or abrasive tool is moved across the site, removing upper layers of skin. Since the procedure leads to swelling and crusting, dermabrasion patients generally remain at home for a week or more following surgery, but the procedure itself can be performed at an outpatient clinic. After the dermabrasion, patients are warned to stay out of the sun for some time. Skin will be very sensitive and susceptible to sunburn and irritation. Recent patients also are cautioned about medications, since splotchy, oddly pigmented skin can result (no birth control pills, for example). Also, dark-skinned people may not be good candidates for dermabrasion, since their skin pigment can alter after the skin is planed. Doctors generally recommend that their patients be at least in their late teens before undertaking dermabrasion, and also wait until acne is in a quiescent stage. Of course, details vary with individual cases. Early in the decade, dermabrasions ranged from $500 to $1,000. Depending on the policy, many insurance companies consider dermabrasion a therapeutic treatment and reimburse at least a portion of the cost.

Breast Reductions

Surgeons perform more than 32,000 breast reductions annually, many of them on young women. This operation is reserved for women whose breasts are so large they cause physical problems, including pain and spinal and postural difficulties. Doctors wait until their patients are fully developed before they perform this surgery, which is a major operation that requires hospitalization. Surgical costs alone run from $2,000 to $2,500, on average. Doctors rarely perform breast augmentations—enlargements—on women under twenty, or before a woman reaches full maturity.

Other Procedures

• One treatment for acne scars now in early stages of use is collagen injections. Only doctors who take a special training course offered by the manufacturer are allowed to use this method, which consists of injecting highly refined collagen into depressed scars. Sometimes, follow-up injections are needed to elevate the scar to the level of the surrounding skin. So far, this treatment has been quite successful, but it's still unclear whether repeated injections will be needed in the future to maintain the results. Patients are first tested for allergies, and some people prove to be poor candidates because they have a history of allergic reactions. Your doctor will take a complete medical history before proceeding with this treatment.

• An earring may be ripped from a pierced ear and tear the lobe. Plastic surgeons can repair the earlobe in a simple, straightforward procedure either immediately or months after the wound heals. And your ear can be repierced safely, away from the scar.

Choosing a Plastic Surgeon

Approximately 4,000 doctors practice plastic surgery—including, in addition to board-certified plastic surgeons, dermatologists, otolaryngologists (ear, nose, and throat specialists) and ophthalmologists trained in plastic and reconstructive surgery. The number of doctors practicing plastic surgery is soaring. Rising, too, is the number who, with no special training, perform cosmetic and therapeutic operations. You, the would-be patient, must be as vigilant as you can when you select a plastic surgeon, to spare yourself the grief, pain, and expense of being treated by a phony. They are out there, ready to prey on overeager and gullible teens. Pay close attention to these hints on finding—and evaluating—a reliable plastic surgeon.

• Consult with your doctor for the names of plastic surgeons. The reputation of those who do good work gets around a medical community quickly (as does the reputation of deadbeats!). If your doctor is unable to recommend anyone, call the local medical society or a nearby medical school, name the operation you want, and ask for referrals of local plastic surgeons.

• Contact the American Society of Plastic and Reconstructive Surgeons (ASPRS), which has a patient referral service. At no fee, you will receive the names of three ASPRS members in your region who are experienced in the type of surgery you want. (ASPRS, Suite 1900, 233 North Michigan Ave., Chicago, IL 60610.)

• During your consultation, ask the doctor where (and in what specialty) he/she did a hospital residency training. Find out at which hospitals the doctor has staff privileges, and don't hesitate to call the hospital and double-check.

• Carefully examine his or her qualifications. Board-certified plastic surgeons have passed extensive examinations given by the American Board of Plastic Surgery. Members of the American Academy of Facial Plastic and Reconstructive Surgery (AAFPRS) should be board-certified or board-eligible in their specialty, which is usually otolaryngology. You can check by writing to AAFPRS (1101 Connecticut Ave., N.W., Suite 700, Washington, DC 20036). Request its pamphlet, *How to Select a Cosmetic Facial Surgeon*.

• Make certain *your* doctor actually will perform the operation and supervise your postoperative care.

• Ask whether there are other methods to treat your problem or improve your appearance.

• Reach prior agreement with the surgeon about all fees.

• Be sure the surgeon takes the time to explain the procedure thoroughly, explain its risks and limitations, discuss what kind of anesthesia will be used, and tell you what to expect as you recuperate. The doctor should document your case with photographs and, in general, willingly answer all your questions. Shy away from any surgeon who hesitates to answer you satisfactorily, or who gives evasive answers and suggests that you're too suspicious. That attitude tells you one thing: look for another doctor.

• No ethical physician will guarantee beautiful or perfect results. What you want, and have every right to expect, is a sober assessment of the range of results likely in your case.

• When you talk with a plastic surgeon about the kind of cosmetic surgery you want, he/she (most plastic surgeons are men, still) will be interested in learning about you—why you want the surgery and what you expect for results. Do you anticipate an improvement in your appearance, or a completely new you? Some teens really do think that having a prettier nose will transform their lives and miraculously make them successful. Of course, having the surgery and knowing you look better *will* make you feel terrific—and those are great reasons for doing it. And it's important that you want the surgery for yourself—not to please someone else.

• Sometimes, the doctor will ask a prospective patient to come back in a year or so and talk again about the operation. Why? Because, in the doctor's best professional judgment, that patient doesn't yet understand everything that's involved and has unrealistic fantasies. Or maybe the patient's parents seem much more eager for the surgery than the patient does. A good way to judge whether you've found the doctor who's right for you is to check out whether he/she takes time to explain possibilities and to speak with you—without your parents.

• You'll also be asked about your medical history. Some people aren't good candidates for plastic surgery for medical reasons such as uncontrolled diabetes, anemia, or a tendency to bleed. Says one plastic surgeon: "I look to see that a teenage patient is mature and sensible, and I give him or her sufficient time to make a decision. The patient has to want the surgery for himself."

All these precautions are necessary to protect you. A minority of patients is treated by incompetent, inexperienced surgeons who have no business wielding a scalpel and who don't screen patients carefully. You can contribute to your own problems by overeagerness and inflated expectations. Because you can't take "no" for an answer, you shop around until you find a doctor who will accept you for surgery. Don't be insulted if a doctor suggests you wait a year or two before an operation. It may be hard for you to accept in the short run, but that decision is really for your benefit. Your body, or your soul, may not yet be ready, and you'll have to live with the results.

MEDICATIONS

Your Guide to Nonprescription Pain Relievers

Item: Every year, Americans swallow approximately 20 billion aspirin or aspirin-containing tablets. That figure does not include aspirin substitutes, such as Tylenol.

Item: Aspirin manufacturers produced 81,000 pounds of aspirin *per day* in 1981. That equaled 2½ grains of aspirin—or about half a standard aspirin pill—for every person, daily.

Item: We spend more than $1.3 billion annually on all categories of over-the-counter pain remedies—headache pills, effervescent tablets, arthritis formulas, remedies for menstrual cramps. That total is expected to rise as we continue to cut back on visits to the doctor's office and increase our trips to the pharmacy.

Each of us has a favorite brand that we swear by to relieve our various aches and pains. Despite the thousands of products on the market, though, there are actually only two generic nonprescription pain relievers available: acetylsalicylic acid (aspirin) and acetaminophen (most commonly known by the brand name Tylenol). Medical research has demonstrated that both drugs relieve pain and reduce fever, and are safe and effective when used properly.

Read (or listen) between the lines next time you're assaulted by advertising for the latest and best pain-killer in the entire galaxy. Advertisers love to use the expressions "most often recommended by doctors," or "used by doctors," when the mysterious ingredient is usually aspirin or an aspirin substitute. The higher prices you can expect to pay for these brands simply cover the manufacturers' feverishly inflated advertising.

Aspirin has been the traditional choice for relief of minor ailments for generations, but, in recent years, acetaminophen has been in an upsurge because it does not have aspirin's possibly adverse side effects.

Which pain reliever for *you*? Keep these points in mind:

• Know what you're taking. If you have stomach disorders or ulcers, any medication containing aspirin should be avoided, for aspirin can cause local irritation of the stomach lining. If you have an iron deficiency anemia (common among the elderly), choose acetaminophen since it does not cause gastrointestinal irritation or blood loss.

• If you are an aspirin-sensitive individual, carry a Medic Alert card to notify any physician unfamiliar with your condition. (More about Medic Alert in a moment.)

• If you have arthritis, learn which of two major types you have: osteoarthritis (most common) or rheumatoid. Either aspirin or acetaminophen can effectively relieve the pain and stiffness resulting from osteoarthritis, but only aspirin can treat the inflammation involved in rheumatoid arthritis.

• If you're preparing for surgery, ask your physician what pain-killer to choose. Acetaminophen is generally recommended because use of aspirin a week or two before any surgery—including tooth extraction—can increase bleeding at the time of the operation.

• Don't mix medicines. Always avoid taking more than one medication at a time without a doctor's advice.

• When your physician prescribes a medication, be sure to ask about its possible interaction with your pain reliever, if you are taking one, and any other medication you may be using. Alcohol is a drug, too—so it is not advisable to drink if you are taking any medicine.

• Always follow label directions. Do not take any medicine for a prolonged period without the guidance of your doctor. Strictly avoid larger doses than recommended. Overdoses of any drug can cause serious side effects.

• If you accidentally overdose, call the local poison control center, emergency room, or your physician at once. And always keep in mind: there is no substitute for your physician's advice. Call your physician any time pain persists or is of an unusual type or severity. Pain signals you that something is wrong.

There is no doubt that we are moving toward a new era in which we will save countless tens of millions of dollars a year in our purchases of drugs—prescription and nonprescription—by buying under their generic (rather than their well-advertised brand) names.

There is also no doubt that when we do buy medicines this way, we will be compelled to be more knowledgeable about what we're buying for what purposes, how to use the drugs, and in what amounts. The debate over the side effects of aspirin has been going on for years—and the cons as well as the pros have been widely publicized. This sort of public education is clearly beneficial—and should be a model to be copied in other areas.

Using Medicines Properly: Rx for Consumers

Read labels carefully and begin educating yourself about the medications you take. Learn to recognize common names such as acetaminophen. Analyze all advertising for both prescription and OTC (over-the-counter) drugs as carefully and intelligently as you can. Get expert help—pharmacists are trained to interpret the chemical mysteries of these remedies.

Try a single-ingredient, nonprescription item for nonemergency problems and check whether it works before you turn to combination pills and potions.

Find a pharmacist you can trust and talk with frankly. Pharmacists cannot prescribe medicine, but they can guide you to useful economical remedies if you ask them.

Learn about the medicines you take. Ask the doctor and druggist what to expect from a medication and how you will know when it's working. Find out if it will interact with something else you take regularly, such as medication for allergies.

Inquire how you should ingest the medicine—on an empty stomach, for example, or following a meal. How often? Are there foods you should not eat while on this medication? Are you supposed to take it only until you feel better, or until you finish a prescribed supply? Illnesses often recur because we stop taking a drug as soon as we feel healthy, even though the problem has not been cured. That means another (expensive) trip to the doctor and a second round of the prescription.

Squeeze every gram of effectiveness from your medicines. Store them properly so they don't weaken or change chemically. Keep them in their original containers so you can always identify them. If you have "leftover" prescriptions—ointments, pills, potions—toss them out. They will simply clutter your medicine cabinet, lose their efficacy, and quickly become useless.

Never let friends "borrow" your prescriptions! Their medical histories and problems are very different from yours, and even when symptoms sound familiar to you, it's no favor to them to lend your medicines.

Don't be swayed by advertising and testimonials into buying a medication you don't need. The fact is, every medication has side effects and none should be used to excess. For example, abuse of laxatives—a common problem among teens—can promote dependency on them and cause damage to the intestines. What side effects will occur and for whom depends on the contents of the medicine and your particular body chemistry. Each of us is an individual, and each of us reacts to varying substances in our individual ways.

Taking medications that you don't need is often a harmful move. It is never a helpful one.

Medic Alert

If you live with chronic—and hidden—medical problems such as diabetes, epilepsy, and allergy to penicillin, you know well the special precautions you must take when you receive medical treatment. But suppose you are in a car accident or contract some disease while far from home: you can't explain your medical history, or you're too frightened and forget. That's a prescription for trouble. It's unpleasant to imagine such events, but you don't have to fantasize for long. Ensure your own safety and health by joining Medic Alert.

Members of this life-saving (and nonprofit) service wear a bracelet or necklace stamped with a red caduceus—the internationally recognized symbol for medicine—and the words "Medic Alert." On the flip side are engraved your medical problem, file number in the Medic Alert system, and a toll-free phone number of the emergency answering service, which can be called any time of the day or night.

When you complete a Medic Alert application, you will be asked for all relevant medical details: blood type, allergies, current medications, date of birth, any medical problems, doctor's name, and relatives to contact. In an emergency, the police or hospital staff can call Medic Alert, read the operator your file number, and retrieve this crucial information.

Emergency medical identification saves lives. Over 1.2 million people worldwide know this and belong to Medic Alert. The cost is minuscule, particularly when weighed against the benefits. Depending on the type of metal you choose, and whether you want a bracelet or necklace, prices start below $20.

Members most often request medallions for diabetes, epilepsy, heart conditions, contact lenses, allergy to penicillin, and allergy to codeine. But people also ask for identification of their blood type, home address, and even allergy to insect bites. Medic Alert will engrave whatever you wish.

You can request an application and information by writing to Medic Alert Foundation (P.O. Box 1009, Turlock, CA 95381), or call toll-free: 1-800-344-3226. (For other tips on health safety during international travel, see Chapter 12, *Take a Vacation*.)

BOOKS: LEARNING MORE ABOUT YOU AND YOUR BODY

Your library and bookstore should have on their shelves a number of books about teenagers and all aspects of health. Among the recent books, and those recommended by health professionals, are:

Lauton, Barry, M.D., and Freese, Arthur S., *The Healthy Adolescent: A Parents' Manual*. Charles Scribner's Sons, 1981. Don't be put off by the word "parents" in the title—this book is useful and comprehensive. Hardcover.

Johnson, G. Timothy, M.D., and Goldfinger, Stephen E., M.D., *The Harvard Medical School Health Letter Book*. Harvard University Press, 1981, hardcover; Warner Books, 1982, paperback. Explanations of common medical problems, written for interested lay readers.

McCoy, Kathy, and Wibbelsman, Charles, M.D., *The Teenage Body Book*. Simon & Schuster, Wallaby Books, 1978. A question-and-answer format enables the authors to examine all facets of a health problem and health concerns in a friendly, informal manner. Paperback.

McCoy, Kathy, *The Teenage Survival Guide: Coping with Problems in Everyday Life*. Simon & Schuster, Wallaby Books, 1981. Questions and answers; continues health discussions and branches into topics of familiar—and frequent—concern. Paperback.

Schowalter, John E., M.D., and Anyan, Walter R., M.D., *The Family Handbook of Adolescence*. Alfred A. Knopf, 1979. Written for both parents and teenagers to consult on every aspect of health and development.

Simon, Nissa, *Don't Worry, You're Normal: A Teenager's Guide to Self-Health*. Thomas Y. Crowell, 1982. Explores all aspects of medical care and health. Paperback.

These last two books are for your parents. Present them on that inevitable day when they drive you around the bend once too often, when it seems that they don't understand anything, and certainly don't remember what it's like to be young:

Ephron, Delia, *Teenage Romance: Or How to Die of Embarrassment*. Viking Press, 1981. With drawings by Edward Koren.

Rinzler, Carol Eisen, *Your Adolescent: An Owner's Manual*. Atheneum, 1981. With drawings by Devera Ehrenberg.

Laughter, it is said, is the best medicine. You might want to read them, too.

INFORMATION: TOLL-FREE HELP LINES

Information about numerous health topics is a phone call away. Call these toll-free numbers when you have questions and want assistance quickly:

- *National Health Information Clearinghouse*
  (Sponsored by Department of Health and Human Services)
  Operators will refer you to sources of information for every imaginable health-related issue:

703-522-2590 (Washington, DC; Alaska, Hawaii, Virginia)
1-800-336-4797 (everywhere else)
Hours: 8:30 A.M. to 5 P.M., Monday through Friday

- *Cancer Information Service*
(National Cancer Institute, National Institutes of Health, Department of Health and Human Services)
Operators provide information about cancer treatment and on-going research; fill requests for pamphlets and other literature on cancer; and refer you to local centers for help and treatment.
202-636-5700 (Washington, DC)
1-800-492-6600 (Maryland)
1-800-638-6694 (everywhere else)
Hours: 9 A.M. to 5 P.M., Monday through Friday

- *Hill-Burton Hospitals; Low-Income Assistance*
(Department of Health and Human Services)
Receives inquiries about Hill-Burton hospitals, which are required by law to provide free or reduced charges to those who qualify because of their low income.
1-800-492-0359 (Maryland)
Hours: 9 A.M. to 5 P.M., Monday through Friday

- *Second Surgical Opinion Hotline*
(Department of Health and Human Services)
Operators will refer you to a nearby specialist for a second opinion after your doctor recommends surgery. This well-established practice helps you make an informed decision about surgery. You can also request a copy of *Thinking of Having Surgery*, a free and very useful leaflet.
1-800-492-6603 (Maryland)
1-800-638-6833 (everywhere else)
Hours: 9 A.M. to 5 P.M., Monday through Friday

15

LOOKING GOOD
And How to Do It

CONTENTS

READY-TO-WEAR: YOU AND YOUR CLOTHES

Introduction

"I don't have a thing to wear!"

How many times have you muttered or thought those words as you stood before a closet crammed with clothes? It's rare that you really don't have a thing to wear; more likely, you can't find anything in the chaos of your drawers and shelves that is either clean or in good repair.

Just a little organization can prevent at least some of your cries of distress. You build a successful wardrobe by planning around a core of basics tailored to your activities, and by acquiring clothes that suit your style and budget while discarding those that don't. The best wardrobes—for men and women—contain pieces that mix and match to create many different looks.

Here's how to plan a campaign for your wardrobe. This strategy will work for you at any age and in any season:

Start with what you have now. Since you probably have forgotten what you own, inventory your clothes and, in the process, try on every single item. Make a pile of those that no longer fit, are worn or outdated, or that you never wear.

Sort through the pile of discards and reach a decision about each piece immediately. Ask yourself: will a new accessory transform this dull old thing? If not, toss it back into the heap. Later, give unwanted (but still useful) clothes to charity, rummage sales, or sell them to a used-clothing store.

Next, itemize your remaining clothes according to categories: school clothes, play and sportswear, dress, outerwear, and so forth.

Look for the gaps. Which pants and skirts need new shirts and sweaters? Which clothes can be spruced up with new belts, scarves, ties, other accents? While you're at it, weed out anything that needs repairs and fix it, *now*.

As you plan your wardrobe, keep in mind your personal style. What clothes make you most comfortable—classic, preppy, trendy, a mix of styles? In what activities do you participate, and what clothes best suit those activities? Make notes to keep your ideas fresh.

Before you buy anything new, do your fashion homework. Look through magazines and newspapers, wander through fashion departments of local stores, check out window displays, and look at passersby. Find out what is making fashion news this season. Observe how outfits are put together and what shapes, colors, and styles are dominant. Figure out ways to adapt the clothes you already have to the new looks. Often, an alteration or new accessory will be enough to revise dramatically something that seems hopelessly outdated and boring. Perhaps, too, not all the new styles work for you—even fashion models can't wear everything—but you might be able to modify some of the key elements and create a look for yourself. This tactic will stretch your clothing dollars, too.

Now, are you ready to go shopping? Not quite!

Tailor Your Budget: You and Your Parents

A traditional source of argument between parents and children is clothes—everything about them. Discussion about clothes disrupts many households, but with effort and thought you can help keep the home front on a more tranquil level.

Most of you buy your own clothes with money your parents give you, with your earnings, or a combination of both. Periodically, sit down with your parents and, together, discuss your clothing needs and agree on what is included in a clothing allowance. For example, you may believe that accessories are covered; this assumption might come as a total surprise to your folks. Allocate money for big-ticket items such as coats and boots and think ahead to next season and even next year. Be flexible and ready to compromise by setting up lists of priority and dream items. Quality clothes are expensive: what purchases are most important and necessary to you? Avoid overloading your wardrobe with clothes of limited use when you are on a tight budget.

New School—New Wardrobe?

Back in the early and mid-1970s, students reflexively bought a new pair of jeans each September and considered themselves outfitted for any social or academic engagement. Times have changed, and with them, high school and college attire.

A classic opportunity to revamp a wardrobe is when you go away to school. Generations of students arrive for their first year away from home with trunkloads of clothes that immediately get shoved from sight or traded away. Among the reasons: your parents' outmoded ideas of what is essential to campus style, and your own uncritical acceptance of what the magazines prescribe for fashionable students. Either of these approaches can lead to disaster—wasted money and useless clothes.

Going away to school is a terrific and scary adventure. You want to look your best when you meet the people you will live with during the next four years; you'll want and need new clothes. But before you drop a fortune, assess your present wardrobe and buy only what you need, right now, to survive for the first few weeks. Hold off on a complete overhaul until you've been at school long enough to get an idea of what your schedule and activities will include. A closetful of dance dresses and ballet slippers is useless if you suddenly take up camping. Preppy tweed jackets and corduroy trousers will make you gag if the weather is always hot and humid.

Also, before you go, don't fail to discuss your clothes budget with your parents. I repeat: decide together whether clothing will come from your allowance or from an additional sum. Add in dry cleaning, laundry, and repair expenses. These can mount up.

Men have an easier time of planning a campus wardrobe, unfair as that may seem. Plan your clothes around the basics—good trousers, sports jackets, and sweaters to augment your jeans, T-shirts, and sports clothes.

Once you establish your clothing allowance and your lists of necessities and preferred purchases, you're almost ready to go. Except. . . . Where should you buy *your* clothes and accessories.

A Detour through the Stores

You probably shop regularly at local stores and know what kind of merchandise to expect there. But are you familiar with the differences among different kinds of stores?

Department Stores

Big department stores offer a range of quality and prices for many kinds of merchandise. They provide customer services such as private dressing rooms, experienced sales staff, store credit, and alterations. Department stores run well-advertised sales at regular intervals throughout the year; learn which ones mark down the type of clothes you need. Columbus Day and Veterans Day (October and November), for example, are great times to shop for winter coats and jackets.

Specialty Stores

If you've ever shopped in a boutique, you know what specialty stores are like. These offer a limited array of goods tailored to the tastes of a particular kind of customer. Some sell only sportswear, or underwear and lingerie, or menswear. The variety of specialty shops is dizzying, especially in larger cities. You'll find that clothes in these shops sell at middle and higher prices, but sale prices are usually competitive with and sometimes better than those in department stores.

Factory Outlets

Factory outlets usually sell merchandise manufactured by one company and its subsidiaries; the racks hold perfect clothes, irregulars, and seconds, so you must examine each piece carefully before you buy. Visit conventional department and specialty stores first; check out the styles, prices, and fabrics. This background will help you shop more successfully.

Independently owned factory outlets sell several brands at off prices. It's typical at any outlet for you to share dressing rooms, pay in cash, and receive little assistance or fitting advice from salespeople.

Discount Stores

Here you'll find clothes at the lower end of the price spectrum. Quality is variable, but you can find good clothes and enviable bargains if you sort through the merchandise. *Army-navy surplus stores* are time-honored sources of low-priced, sturdy, and versatile clothes for both men and women.

High-Fashion Discount Outlets

These stores offer tremendous bargains on brand-name clothing, but you must be well briefed on the latest fashions to weed out what's a bargain and what's not. Discount outlets are usually located in or near large cities. Wise shoppers visit these places regularly, since the best new merchandise stays on the racks a few days, at most.

Catalogue Sales

Often these are operated as divisions of large department stores. The range of goods mimics that in the store; prices are competitive. Their advantage: you can shop at home and at any time, since you place your order by phone or mail. The big disadvantages: you can't try things on; returning unsatisfactory clothes is a chore; delivery and handling charges add to your cost.

Used-Clothing Stores

Clothing exchanges run by charities and schools, rummage sales, thrift shops, and flea markets are great sources of fashion finds at rock bottom prices. The hitch: know what you are buying. Check every piece thoroughly, no matter how inexpensive, and decide whether the asking price matches its condition.

SHOPPING AT LAST

Tips to Help You Shop Wisely

Shopping can be tremendous fun or a nerve-racking ordeal. Since it's probably one of your favorite activities, you already have some strategies for making it an entertaining pastime. Here are more tips to help you shop wisely:

• Buy quality merchandise for the basics that you will wear many seasons: coats, boots, raingear.

• Don't be snowed by designer labels. Depending on where you make your purchase, you might receive a fake. Unscrupulous manufacturers rake in millions by counterfeiting designer-label jeans, for instance; before you buy designer jeans at a discount house or flea market, check them out at a department store. Examine the construction and hardware. Tug on the fabric and seams. Be warned: when you buy fakes, the real designer will not replace or repair poorly manufactured jeans.

• Fads are fun but by definition also short-lived. Limit the most trendy items to accessories and frills that accent, not replace, your wardrobe.

• When you're attracted to a sale item, judge it the same way you do other clothes: Will it complement your wardrobe? Is it well made? Will you actually wear it? How often? A bargain that stays in your closet is a waste of money.

• Think about the maintenance costs on clothes you want. Can the item be washed? Or must it be dry-cleaned? Will dry cleaning break your budget? Study the hangtags and labels so you'll know how to give your clothes proper care *before* you buy.

Invest in clothes that fit well and flatter your face and figure. In the long run, these are the real bargains, because you wear them often and enjoy years of use. Consider these tips as you try on clothes:

• Check that seams, hems, buttonholes, zippers, and pleats are finished off neatly. Examine plaids, stripes, and large prints—they should match at seam lines.

• Lapels on coats and jackets should lie flat and be layered with interfacing to hold their shape. Armholes should fall comfortably from your natural arm line and not bind. Shoulders should extend the width of your own. And the garment should fit comfortably over the clothes with which you plan to wear it.

• Buy according to fit, not size. Manufacturers each have patterns designed to their own specifications, and the size that fits you in one label may be impossibly tight in another. That doesn't mean you've gained weight since yesterday; contemporary clothes sizes are simply unpredictable.

• Are you on a diet? Don't buy clothes expecting to diet into them in a week or two. Buy what you can wear now. Clothes can be altered and taken in a size or two, but it's very difficult to have them let out.

• If a garment doesn't feel right when you try it on, no matter how it looks on the hanger, it won't look good on you. That's why trying on clothes is so important. Look at yourself in a three-way mirror; bend, sit, and stretch. Be honest with yourself and resolutely return uncomfortable clothes to the rack. Keep looking—you'll find something else to wear, especially as you acquire shopping skills and the confidence that goes with them.

Underneath It All

If your clothes budget is stretched pretty thin and you're still looking for ways to economize, peel down a layer and save on underwear and nightclothes. Will you really sleep better in a lacy nightgown or elegant pajamas, or will a flannel nightshirt or T-shirt work just as well? Designer-label underwear may strike you as exotic and glamorous—a lot of people think so, since designers are making new fortunes this way—but why not stick to tried-and-true budget brands that fit as well, last as long, and cost half as much? Seriously, who is going to read the *labels* on your underthings—and why?

Manufacturers resolutely refuse to make long-wearing panty hose. Beat their efforts to make you spend your entire allowance on their products by saving pairs with one ruined leg. Snip off the useless side and wear two panties with one leg each. The waistbands will be marginally more bulky, but in many of your clothes it won't matter and no one will know.

Look for sales on bras, slips, camisoles, and bathrobes. Many of these items with your favorite labels are priced at deep discounts, particularly during such bonanzas as after-Christmas sales and during Washington's Birthday and Labor Day sales. And don't overlook underwear counters at discount houses, army-navy, and dime stores as places to stock up on socks, underpants, and T-shirts.

KEEP IT CLEAN

Whether you love to shop and buy stylish new things, or hate the chore and buy clothes under duress, you'll extend their wear and pleasure to you if you take good care of them. This means more than tossing clothes in the washing machine from time to time or sending them off to the dry cleaners. Attending to details prolongs the wearability and value of your clothes and keeps them looking snappy and fashionable. Incorporate the following suggestions into your clothes-care routines; in the long run, you'll save money on cleaning, washing, repairs, and replacement.

• Inspect new clothes for loose threads, wobbly buttons, faulty zippers and snaps, and fraying seams—before you leave the store, if you can. If you find a flaw serious enough to shorten the garment's life-span, exchange the garment or get a refund. Otherwise, resew the buttons, snip the loose threads. Check your clothes regularly as you wear them and make repairs as needed; fix hems on skirts and pants before they start to drag; patch your jeans while the holes are still small.

• Save hangtags and care instructions along with your sales receipts in a box set aside for this purpose. If you've followed care instructions to the letter, according to the tags, and your clothes nonetheless become damaged, return the clothes to the store. Honest merchants will refund your money or exchange the item and send the original back to the manufacturer. If the idea of complaining intimidates you, bring along a friend. If the store refuses to honor your complaint, call the Better Business Bureau or local consumer protection agency and let them know.

• Dress, and undress, carefully. Fully unbutton, unzip, and unfasten the item you're about to put on or take off so as not to stress seams, necklines, cuffs, and waistbands. Avoid rips and snags by removing sharp-edged jewelry and watches. Wait until your deodorant dries, and hold the makeup until after you've dressed.

• Look before you lean and sit. Be alert for fresh paint, chewing gum, greasy crumbs, soot, oil, and other substances that can attach themselves to your clothes.

• Before you pack your pockets, check that pens have their caps snapped on tight and don't leak, that candies are wrapped, that makeup and perfume bottles are closed. Don't load up with heavy change, wads of keys, and big bulky items that can rip seams and cause pockets to sag out of shape.

• Leave good clothes in the closet when you tackle messy jobs such as moving furniture, weeding, waxing the car, painting. Wear an apron, old shirt, or smock when you wash dishes and cook.

• Be ready for foul weather with a raincoat or storm coat, boots, and umbrella.

It's important to store your clothes properly to help preserve their looks and wear:

• Hang clothes on wood or plastic hangers instead of tossing them over a chair or on the floor. (Wire hangers can rust and stain clothes; besides, they're the wrong shape.)

• Fold—don't hang—knitted items such as sweaters, scarves, jerseys, and T-shirts.

• Leave space between each hanger. Let each item breathe and hang properly: see that collar buttons are fastened; cuffs, shoulders, and sleeves hang straight; collars and lapels lie smoothly. Otherwise, clothes will mat or wrinkle and look messy when you start to put them on.

• Cover your infrequently worn things in garment bags to keep them dust-free.

• Let wet and damp clothes dry out thoroughly before you put them in your closets.

• Clean and mend your clothes before you store them for a season. Dirt and grease will set into the fabric and become even more difficult to remove as months go by. In particular, wash or dry-clean woolens to get rid of moth eggs and remove stains and food that attract insects. An extra benefit: when the weather changes again, your clothes will be ready and waiting.

Extend the life and appearance of your clothes by proper cleaning. When you buy a new piece, *read those hangtags and labels!* Will it be easy to care for, or will you have to spend a lot of money and time to keep it wearable? If you're buying fabric, ask the salesperson for a care label for the bolt of material. Federal Trade Commission rules state that yard goods manufacturers must provide care information on each bolt of cloth and must supply merchants with labels.

Before you wash clothes, empty all pockets; turn cuffs down; shake out crumbs, dust, and grit; sew on loose buttons. Sort through and separate your clothes into piles that require the same amount of wash time, action from the machine, and water temperature.

Generally speaking, if an item is to be dry-cleaned, the sooner it's brought in, the better the chances the stains can be removed. Find a dry cleaner who does the work on the premises.

Learn about fabrics and fabric care by keeping up-to-date through news and magazine articles. New materials and techniques for caring for them come on the market with dazzling speed.

SEW YOUR OWN

Many of you, encouraged by sewing lessons in home-ec and crafts classes, will decide to buy a sewing machine. If you intend to make many of your clothes, a sewing machine will pay for itself quickly and will reward you with distinctive, handmade originals. You will find that the choice of patterns, fabrics, buttons, and trim is limitless; you can spend hours deciding what to make and which materials to use.

Choosing a Sewing Machine

But first, you need a machine. You can find them for as little as $200; prices escalate rapidly according to the company and the kinds of features on each model. Investigate and compare brands to find one tailored to your skills and your budget.

Even before you start to shop, ask yourself: What will I use the machine for? Approximately how often? Decide your current level and the kinds of skills you want to learn. You want to choose a machine that can accommodate your current abilities as well as let you expand them. It's silly to spend hundreds of extra dollars for features that sound great but that you never really intend to use, such as decorative cams or computer memories. Besides, you always can trade up—that is, exchange your machine for a more sophisticated one.

Discuss your purchase with a more experienced sewer: a friend or home economics teacher. Don't be shy about asking for advice—especially when you're about to spend such a large sum of money. You want to enjoy your purchase, not rue the day you made it.

Bring along scraps of fabric of varied weights and textures—cottons, corduroy, wool, knits—when you go to look at machines. Use each scrap to test each model; try different stitches and gauges to round out your knowledge of each machine's performance.

As you test each one, keep your comfort and machine's use uppermost in your mind:

• The machine should be at a comfortable height and allow adequate leg room.

• The foot pedal should operate smoothly and not slide around on the floor. Chances are, the store will be carpeted, so pick up the pedal and see if it's ribbed or rubberized on the bottom.

• Check that the needle threads easily, the bobbin rewinds simply, the machine runs and adjusts smoothly and quietly, and the thread tension balances easily.

• Test the buttonhole maker, if possible. Look at any attachments and understand how each one works and fits on the machine.

• Make sure the machine is easy to clean and maintain.

• If the machine is portable, lift it to make sure you can actually carry it yourself.

• If it is a console, measure it to be certain that it fits the space you have and that the cabinet's construction is sturdy.

Don't let a salesperson talk you into features you don't want. Before you make your selection, double-check the following:

• *The warranty.* Does it cover parts and labor? How long do repairs take and where are they made? For what length of time is the warranty good?

• *The price.* What does the dealer include? Are you entitled to any instructions or lessons? How about sewing books and manuals?

National brands go on sale, just like any other appliance. Machines made by well-known companies are often easier to maintain and have repaired, so, if you prefer, time your purchase to a sale, thereby saving money and gaining assurance of good service.

IF THE SHOE FITS . . .

Nothing ruins the effect (on both you and onlookers!) of a great outfit faster than a pair of ill-fitting shoes. When you have to plaster your heels with bandages, hobble around, and grimace every time you take a step, you cancel the positive impression made by your appearance from the ankles up.

A shoe wardrobe to fit your clothes and different occasions in your life represents a considerable investment. Although shoe prices have risen less than the general rate of inflation in recent years, they still cost plenty.

22 Guidelines

To stretch your shoe dollars, pay heed to these guidelines for shopping and caring for footgear. Your wallet—and your feet—will feel the difference.

1. There is no mystery to buying shoes that look good and fit properly: shoes should fit when you try them on. Don't rely on breaking them in and having them stretch to fit correctly. Would you buy clothes that don't fit right (other than jeans, which are usually bought too tight), bring them home, and attempt to "break them in"? Don't do it with shoes, either (though boots may require some breaking in).

2. In general, most people's right foot is larger than their left; determine which of yours is larger and fit shoes to that one.

3. Feet swell during the day: *avoid* buying shoes first thing in the morning.

4. Wear the type of socks or panty hose you expect to wear with the shoes. Their thickness will affect the way shoes fit.

5. When you try shoes on, stand with your weight distributed evenly and check the length and width of the shoes. Do you have room to wriggle your toes? Is there about half an inch between the end of your big toe and the shoe? Does your little toe lie flat, or can you see it bulge against the side of the shoe? Is the arch long

enough, and does it support your foot comfortably? Does the shoe fit snugly and painlessly? And, if you're trying on sandals or shoes with open toes or heels, does your foot stay inside, or do heels or toes dangle over the edges?

6. Walk around and take as much time as you need. Are the shoes flexible? Can you walk comfortably? Do the shoes pinch, or do they flap because they're too big?

7. Look in the mirror. Do the shoes flatter you? Will they look good with your clothes?

8. When you buy jogging shoes or sneakers, apply the same guidelines; also see to it that they are not too tight over the instep, and that the quarter (padded section that rises above the heel) fits snugly. Otherwise they will chafe and cause blisters.

9. Never buy shoes according to size without trying them on.

10. Look for good materials and quality construction when you buy shoes. Seams inside unlined shoes should lie flat and the innersole should be smooth; lined shoes should have porous, fungus-resistant innersoles and no buckles or bumps in the lining. Counters (the stiff piece of material around the heel of the shoe) should be firm but not rigid, seams should be stitched evenly, and hardware attached securely. Check to see that the heels don't wobble. To find out what shoes are made of, look inside. The Federal Trade Commission requires that shoes with man-made components be labeled to indicate where those materials are used. Although all-leather shoes do not require labeling, manufacturers do so as a selling point.

Boots require additional fitting pointers:

11. Never buy boots that fit tightly around the calves and interfere with circulation.

12. Be aware that some boots are more difficult than others to break in. Your heels will slip at first in Western-style boots, for example, until they mold to your feet. Break them in slowly or you can wind up with painful blisters.

13. If you have a high instep, knee-high boots without zippers or laces will be difficult to pull on and take off.

14. Feel inside the boots to make sure the stitching and seams are smooth and that zippers are placketed to prevent rubbing against your ankles and legs. The counter should be firm; watch

out if you feel sharp edges through the lining because they will wear through and dig into your heels. Good boots have a steel shank to support your arch.

The average person's feet stop growing around age eighteen. That doesn't mean your feet can't stop growing when you're younger—or older. Don't be surprised to discover that even in your late teens, shoes you bought last year are now too short.

Once you get your new shoes home, preserve their looks and life-span with simple good care:

15. Alternate pairs of shoes daily. If you wear the same ones day in and day out, you'll wear them out quickly. Shoes need to rest and dry out (all feet perspire).

16. Clean leather shoes with mild soapsuds or a leather cleaner, let them dry, and then polish them. Remove all stains—mud, grass, grease—as soon as possible. And if shoes get wet, stuff them with newspaper and leave them to dry thoroughly. However, don't park them on top of the radiator, since heat will cause leather to crack. Remove salt, water marks, and chemical stains with saddle soap, then rub the shoes and apply a thin film of mineral oil.

17. Insert shoe trees overnight to help restore shoes to their original shape.

18. Clean suede shoes and boots by using a bristle brush to remove dirt. Rub a gum eraser over stains and embedded grime. Because suede requires special care and is easily damaged by salt and water, it is a poor choice for winter and foul weather footgear.

19. Use a damp cloth to take care of patent leather shoes. To maintain patent's flexibility, apply a leather preservative and, to restore the shine, a special cleaner designed for patent leather.

20. Clean vinyl and other synthetics with detergent or soap and water. Remove tar from synthetics with a cloth dampened with lighter fluid.

21. Handle fabric and straw shoes gently. Clean them with special cleaners designed for these materials, or use a mild detergent dissolved in water. Don't toss them in the washing machine unless the manufacturer recommends it.

22. And keep shoes in good repair. Reheel them promptly as soon as they start to run down. In addition to looking sloppy, worn-down heels strain your feet and accelerate wear and tear on

the shoes themselves. Leather shoes and boots usually can be resoled—an expensive procedure, but often less than the cost of a new pair.

HOW TO BEAT THE HIGH COST OF BEAUTY

Buying Tips

How old were you when you first played with your mother's lipstick and mascara or your father's shaving cream and after-shave? The urge to groom and beautify ourselves is an ancient one— archaeologists have excavated beauty kits from long-lost civilizations around the world—and most of us apply cosmetics and toiletries daily to make ourselves more attractive and stylish.

If, like most of your peers, you love and study cosmetics, you could teach your parents a thing or two about current trends, brands, and colors. But do you know how to buy cosmetics and toiletries wisely, how to use and store them, and even when to throw them away?

Most of you monitor at least one fashion magazine, and you certainly watch what your friends wear (and how they wear it). Typically, you spend some (even all) of your allowance on a new product you see in an ad or your friend's purse. Before too long, you have a drawer cluttered with tubes, jars, compacts, brushes, and assorted junk that you rarely, if ever, use. Cut down on the jumble, and the expense, with a few quick steps:

• Organize. Sort through and throw away items you never use. Know what you have and where the gaps are before you dash off to buy a new eye shadow, blusher, or shaving cream. When the cosmetics companies promote a line of colors for a new season, you may discover a nearly identical shade in your own collection, since the "new" colors at the center of lavish ad campaigns are often old ones in different packages.

• Save good brushes from old, discarded cosmetics (not mascara or eye shadow, though). Rinse them in warm, soapy water and let them air dry.

• Look for the best prices on the brands you buy. If you purchase all your toiletries and cosmetics at drugstores, you probably miss bargains at the supermarket or discount store down the block or at the mall.

• Buy products that you know you will use, and save the splurges for something really intriguing. If you rarely wear nail polish, bypass the pretty bottles and gorgeous colors.

• Don't buy cosmetics in container sizes larger than you can use. But do buy economy sizes of toiletries you use often. Usually, the bigger the bottle or tube, the lower the price per ounce.

• Take advantage of trial and sample sizes that manufacturers sell to introduce new products. Frequently, these are real—if temporary—bargains.

• Stock up on staples. If you pass a store with a special on your favorite products, buy several—but not a ''lifetime'' supply. The products are not meant to last forever. Restrict your stockpiling to items that have a long shelf life: soaps, shampoos, conditioners, shaving creams, razor blades, talcum powder, and the like.

• Learn to read labels. The Food and Drug Administration requires that cosmetics companies list the ingredients in each product on its package. The major ingredient is listed first, with others following in descending order of importance. Your scrutiny may reveal that the ingredients in expensive preparations you favor and those in cheaper brands are almost identical. You will be paying for the company's name, fancy packaging, and advertising blitz.

Saving Tips

How many times have you walked into a store with a specific shopping list and walked out with a bag full of extras? Cosmetics and toiletries are often impulse purchases, and teenagers in particular turn themselves loose when in the vicinity of a cosmetics counter. If you can't restrain yourself from buying the newest brands and products, at least set a budget figure and don't overspend. In addition:

• Look for sales. Cosmetics and toilet articles frequently go on sale after Christmas and during the summer.

• Be aware that many department store cosmetics clerks work on commission. They will try to sell you an entire product or treatment line. You do not have to buy everything just because you're told how fabulous you will look. But, by all means, ask for the adviser's help and recommendations.

• Be on guard against the favorite lure of a gift (or purchase) with purchase. Brand-name companies offer special sizes of cosmetics they want you to try attractively packaged in a tote bag, ceramic pot, or other imaginative container. The catch: you have to spend $8 or $10 or even more before you can buy, or receive, the special promotion. If you are planning to buy cosmetics anyway, you can get some great bargains, but just as easily you can be induced to spend money you hadn't budgeted. These promotions are usually advertised in local newspapers and last a week or two.

Using Cosmetics Safely

Rely on your good judgment whenever you buy and use anything on your face and body. Common sense tells you not to buy a product that smells bad or has been opened.

If you think you have an allergy to a product, stop using it. Many people suffer adverse reactions to a variety of preparations: deodorants and antiperspirants, mascaras, hair coloring and permanents, depilatories (chemical hair removers), even face creams. Protect yourself by first reading through instructions on any new item. This is a critical step when you buy hair coloring, perms, and depilatories. Follow the step-by-step instructions for patch tests to the letter; don't continue the treatment if you develop a rash or your skin is broken.

Recognize what "hypoallergenic" means. The FDA requires that any cosmetic manufacturer who uses the term "hypoallergenic" run a battery of tests to prove that the cosmetics really cause fewer allergic reactions than other, similar products. Hypoallergenic cosmetics are not medicated, however—unless they are designed for a specific purpose, such as acne, and state this on the package. By the way, you could react against ingredients in hypoallergenic products, too, and the products can be contaminated with use just like any other cosmetic.

Safe use of cosmetics prevents discomfort and waste and lets them work for you. Most cosmetics contain preservatives that inhibit the growth of bacteria which can cause infections and reactions. Makeup is relatively uncontaminated and pure when you buy it; careless use and handling encourages the growth of bacteria. Heed these warnings:

- Admire your friend's makeup and toiletries, but don't use them. And *don't lend* your own.
- Shun department store testers and demonstrations. You can pick up someone else's germs—such as the herpes virus that causes cold sores—or donate your own. Never use lipsticks, mascaras, and eye shadows that aren't new and aren't yours.
- Don't use makeup if you have open cuts or irritated skin.
- Use fresh water—not saliva—to moisten brushes for eyeliner, shadows, cake mascara, and brow coloring.
- Use mascara wands carefully. Keep them from touching the surface of your eyes or your lids. Bacteria from your skin can then grow on the wand and eventually lead to sties, inflamed lids, and even severe infections.
- Throw away contaminated products, or those that have been cluttering your shelves for a long time. As a general rule, keep cosmetics for no longer than two or three years—it's even recommended that you toss them out after a year. The preservatives in mascara start to lose their effectiveness within six months, so no matter how infrequently you use mascara, throw it away. That means the brush, too—no refillables for you.
- Don't mix the leftovers from old bottles of makeup or other preparations. One may contaminate the other.

Cosmetics manufacturers appeal to our vanity with their promise of beauty and success from a bottle, brush and jar. They succeed in prying loose billions of dollars from American consumers every year. Frequent shopping sprees eat up allowances and budgets until you learn what products work best for you, which you enjoy, how to take care of them, and where to buy.

DOLLARS AND SCENTS: PERFUMES AND AFTER-SHAVES

One vital word on perfume and after-shave: *moderation*. Use fragrances sparingly—the objective is to entice those nearby, not knock them over. Your perfume or after-shave should not arrive in a room before you do. Since most people's sense of smell is weakest in the morning, beware of dousing yourself in a shower of scent.

A light touch with the stopper or spray will save you money; your supply will last longer. Any perfume can turn rancid once it's been opened, if it's stored in direct sunlight or is subjected to extremes of heat and cold. Colognes, toilet water, and after-shave, all of which contain more alcohol, keep for a much longer time.

When you select a fragrance, don't choose one just because it smells provocative on your friends. Your skin chemistry determines how you will react to the combination of oils, alcohol, and other ingredients in a particular perfume, and your skin chemistry is unlike anyone else's—even that of a brother or sister. As you test fragrances, try only two or three at one time or else your nose will get hopelessly confused. Let each one dry and absorb into your skin; then see how long the scent lasts and how it changes as you wear it for a few hours. These simple precautions will help you buy the fragrances you—and those around you—will enjoy.

BAUBLES, BANGLES, AND BEADS

When your mothers were teenagers, practically every girl owned a charm bracelet and the trick was to acquire as many dangling charms as there were links on the bracelet. Meanwhile, your fathers accumulated pairs of cuff links and tie tacks with every birthday and graduation. Fashions in jewelry, like everything else, change; most of you now favor rings, earrings, pendants and chains when you buy—and ask for—jewelry.

American teenagers spend almost $290 million yearly for jewelry, including school rings and pins, watches, and costume and fine jewelry. Jewelry is an accessory that adds sparkle, fun and whimsy, or elegance and sophistication to your appearance. As a complement or counterpoint to your clothes, jewelry makes a statement about your style and personality.

Costume and Fine Jewelry

Basically, jewelry falls into two broad categories: costume and fine. Fine jewelry is made of precious metals, such as gold, platinum, and silver, and can be ornamented with gemstones, pearls, and enamels. Costume jewelry is an enormous catchall category that includes pieces made of wood, ceramic, shell, glass, even silver and semiprecious stones.

Buying Costume Jewelry

Costume jewelry is not always inexpensive—workmanship and design weigh heavily in the price, with some pieces costing as much as fine jewelry. Inexpensive costume jewelry won't dent your allowance much, but when you make your purchases, be alert for rough edges and clasps that can snag clothes and scratch skin, dyes that rub off and stain, cheap fastenings, and earring backs that wobble and fall off after one or two wearings. While costume jewelry is not expected to last a lifetime, you want to wear it out gradually—not the day you buy it! To get your money's worth from costlier costume jewelry, look for the details on design and craftsmanship. Check that stones are set securely, that enamels don't flake, and that fasteners are secure.

A money-saving tip: if you enjoy crafts, study fashion magazines to see what costume jewelry designs you can adapt with materials purchased in art supply and craft stores. Make contemporary designs at a fraction of the cost; as a bonus, your originals will make distinctive gifts.

Buying Fine Jewelry

Most of your fine jewelry comes to you as gifts for birthdays, holidays, and graduations. If you buy fine, expensive jewelry, here are the basic facts:

• Usually, fine jewelry is made of gold. Look for the stamp that signifies the gold content: for example, 18K or 22K. *Karat* designates a degree of gold purity; don't confuse it with *carat*, which states the weight of a gemstone. Pure or solid gold is 24 karats. Most contemporary jewelry is 14 karats—14 parts gold mixed with 10 parts of another metal. Certain metals, when mixed with gold, change the color of gold—for example, gold alloyed with copper assumes a reddish tinge.

• Gold-filled, or gold overlay, must by law contain at least a layer of 10 karat gold permanently bonded by heat and pressure to a supporting metal. The gold must weigh $\frac{1}{20}$ of the total metal content. *Gold-filled* jewelry is stamped with "GF." *Gold electroplate* is a film of gold at least 7 millionths of an inch thick, and *vermeil* is gold at least 150 millionths of an inch thick bonded to sterling silver. Sterling, in turn, must be $92\frac{1}{2}$ percent silver. Knowing these technical definitions will help you buy wisely.

• Pearls have their own vocabulary. *Oriental pearls* are made exclusively by the oyster, and are rare and expensive. *Cultured pearls*, formed when a mother-of-pearl bead is inserted into the oyster's shell and then coated with natural secretions, are very popular and fashionable. *Simulated pearls* aren't pearls at all: they're beads coated to look like the real thing.

• When you decide to buy diamond and colored-stone jewelry, find a reputable jewelry shop where you can be helped by a knowledgeable salesperson. Fine jewelry is a *costly* investment. Since few—if any—of you are jewelry experts, you will have to rely on a salesperson's honesty and reputation.

Look for these qualities in fine jewelry:

• The stones should be *set* into or on the metal—never glued. Pearls and stone beads should be strung with knots between each one (this prevents them from flying about in case the string breaks).

• Look for safety catches on gold chains and bracelets. Rings should fit exactly. Findings (ear wires, posts, pin backs) should be soldered or attached securely.

Ask the salesperson to write out the details of your purchase on the sales receipt. This information serves two purposes: you need it for insurance records, and it's useful if you decide to trade in the piece at a later date. Many jewelry stores allow you to trade in jewelry and apply the value to other pieces. Protect yourself by getting this service guaranteed in writing on the sales receipt, next to the description.

Heed these "don'ts" for buying jewelry:

• Don't buy from street peddlers. They won't be around when your shiny ring turns green or your new watch stops running. Moreover, the brand names and copyrighted designs they hawk are usually counterfeits—and worthless. Many peddlers practice a classic scam: they sell a watch with its insides plucked out.

• Don't respond to mail-order teases that advertise diamonds, rubies, other gems, and gold chains at minuscule prices. Your cash outlay might be small, but so is the item—tiny, in fact. Pendants typically are not much thicker than tinfoil, chains are fragile and break easily, and the "gemstones" are about the size of a pinhead.

• Don't be pressured into buying something that you don't want. Reputable salespeople will not twist your arm to buy costly diamonds and solid-gold watches. If you feel that you're being pushed around, leave the store.

Care and Maintenance

"A diamond is forever," the saying goes. Fine jewelry, when cared for properly, will indeed last a lifetime, at least. Follow these basic suggestions and keep yours beautiful for years to come:

• Store jewelry in a box, and keep each item in its own compartment to prevent tangles, scratches, and misplaced treasures.

• Don't wear fine jewelry to the beach or swimming pool.

• Clean silver jewelry with a soft cloth and good silver polish. In a pinch, toothpaste or cigarette ashes remove tarnish.

• Rinse fine jewelry with a mild soapy solution and dry it with a soft, lint-free towel to remove body oils, perspiration, and make-up.

• While pearls become more lustrous with wear, keep them free of cosmetics and grime. Wipe them frequently with a damp cloth, and have necklaces restrung periodically. Store your pearls in a separate box or compartment of your jewelry box.

• Clean costume jewelry with a mild soap and dry it thoroughly with a soft cloth.

• Don't immerse costume jewelry made of beads, feathers, dyed shells, papier-mâché, or other materials that can run or fade. Dust them off and wipe with a damp cloth.

Watches

From Mickey Mouse watches to expensive, diamond-encrusted heirlooms, the variety of watches is dazzling, and never more so than in December, when most watches are purchased. The impulse to track time is as old as humanity. Space-age technology has designed ever more accurate ways to do so.

When you choose a watch (or request one as a present), a number of factors determine the price. The style, case, band, and special features account for a big percentage; the same basic watch movement may be used in many models made by one company. The most expensive watches, made of gold and platinum and sometimes studded with gems or accented with other precious metals, can cost as much as a house. Among the least expensive, L.C.D. (Liquid Crystal Display) watches that feature digital faces and even microcalculators tell time with remarkable accuracy.

Whatever kind of watch you buy, bear in mind the purpose for which you will use it. A delicate dress watch may not stand up to the demands of your daily activities—school, work, sports—while a sports watch may not complement the clothes you wear to discos and parties.

Handle your new watch carefully and follow these common-sense guidelines to prolong its usefulness and appearance:

• Before you set and wind it, read the instruction booklet. Some models, especially those equipped with day, date, and alarms, can be confusing to start up.

• Read the guarantee to know what is covered and for how long. Store it along with the sales receipt in a safe place.

• Don't try to fix a watch yourself—except for replacing a battery, assuming the manufacturer provides instructions.

• Have your watch cleaned and serviced every two years or so. If maintenance costs outstrip the watch's value, buy a new one.

• Don't squirt perfume or other sprays on your watch. The liquid can seep inside and gum up the works; it also corrodes the band.

• Just because a watch is water resistant (most new ones are), don't wear it swimming or in the shower. (Ignore this advice if you own a diver's watch.)

• Avoid exposing your watch to shocks and direct hits. Even though most watches are shock resistant, why risk it?

• Don't risk overwinding. An automatic watch will keep itself wound for thirty-six hours or so, even when you're not wearing it.

Wind hand-wound models once a day; as soon as you sense resistance in the spring, stop to avoid overdoing it.

• Replace leather or fabric watchbands as soon as they start to wear out. The strap might break when you're not paying attention, and you'll lose your watch.

16

YOUR DIET

Budgeting, Buying, and Balancing It

CONTENTS

THE FAMILY SHOPPING

More and More of You Are Doing It

No longer is the supermarket the social gathering place for homemakers. Now, *you* are as likely to meet your friends there as your mother is to meet hers. That's another result of women pouring into the job market: chores traditionally done by the woman of the house now have to be split up among all the family members. Seven out of ten of you are elected (or elect) to do the family shopping.

Advertisers know it. That's why supermarket items are advertised in teen magazines and on the TV programs you watch. If they can coax you into thinking that "Soft Z Silk" gets your clothes cuddly soft, you'll buy "Soft Z Silk" when you see "detergent" on the shopping list.

With over 10,000 food products on the shelves, shopping for the family gives you an excellent opportunity to test your hawk-eye consumer skills.

Before You Leave the House

Make a Shopping List—Or Take the One Made Up for You

• There is nothing more frustrating after you have gone shopping than to come home and find that you have forgotten the milk. What a waste of time (and gas, if you have to drive) to go back for one item. Follow your list.

• Don't buy items not on your list. Wait a week. See whether you really want or need the items you didn't buy.

Take All the Coupons You Need

Checkers across the country are picking up the refrain, "Do you have any coupons?" Coupons have become a way of American life. *Use them!*

• Cut them out. Wednesday's newspapers usually have a good supply. So do women's magazines.

• Collect them. Have others clip and save them for you. Participate in the clipping exchanges found in most public libraries. (You bring in the coupons you won't use, and take those on file which you will.)

• Shop the stores which will double the face amount on your coupons. If all else is equal with the stores, it's a good deal.

• Don't try to slip by a coupon for an item you're not buying. The store will embarrass you by refusing to honor it.

• Before you consider using a coupon, check to see if there's an expiration date on it. Some have them; some don't.

• If you don't need or like a product, don't buy it, coupon or not. The best way to use coupons is on a product you like and already use regularly—or on a new product which sounds interesting and with which you'd like to experiment.

Don't Shop Hungry

When you shop on an empty stomach, you are sure to boost your impulse buying. Surveys reveal that those who shop with their stomachs grumbling spend up to 17 percent more than those who shop after having eaten.

Take Along a Hand Calculator

If you don't have a calculator already, buy one. It will allow you to keep track of your expenditures as you go through the store, and will save you from that moment of shock when the cashier totals up your groceries at $56.28 and you (with $50 in your pocket) scramble to figure out what to put back. That's the kind of experience everyone needs—but just once!

Shopping the Labels

Decoding the labels is necessary in order to know what you are getting and how much you are spending for it.

Unit Pricing

On the edge of the shelf, under the article you are considering, is a label. Here is what it means:

To use this information to your advantage, keep these tips in mind:

1. The items you intend to buy have to be listed on the shelf (and in the proper place, so you don't go scrounging around).

2. You must know some conversion rates. For example, 2 pints = 1 quart; 16 fluid ounces = 1 pint; 1 pound = 16 ounces; 1 pound = 454 grams.

3. You must know what and how much you need. Sure, the five-pound package of American cheese gives you a better unit price per pound than the twelve-ounce package. But if you are the only one who likes American cheese (and then only once in a while), and you buy the five-pound package, you will wind up throwing out cheese and money.

4. Unit pricing refers to cost, not quality. The fact that something is inexpensive (or expensive, for that matter) doesn't mean it tastes bad or good.

List of Ingredients

Ingredients must be listed in descending order of proportion. (This is true for all food products—name brands or generic.) Chicken noodle soup, for example, which lists ingredients as:

Chicken stock, enriched egg noodles, chicken, water, salt, carrots, corn starch, monosodium glutamate, unbleached palm oil, chicken fat, dehydrated onions . . .

contains more noodles than chicken, more salt than carrots, and more monosodium glutamate than dehydrated onions.

Nutritional Information per Serving

While food manufacturers are not required to list nutrients on the label unless they advertise something about the nutritiousness of the product, many do anyway as a service to the consumer.

Most of us, for example, have had the experience of staring at a cereal box while eating breakfast and seeing the words "Nutritional Information Per Serving." The listing of vitamins, minerals, fats, carbohydrates, protein, plus the calorie count is at least interesting. And you can make it helpful in planning your daily intake of food.

RDA means "Recommended Daily Allowance," which is the amount of a vitamin or other nutrient the average adult should have each day. Teen RDAs may differ from adult RDAs.

Dating Foods

In most states, foods which are perishable or semiperishable are marked with a date. This indicates the date the product should be taken off the shelves—either by you from your own shelf, or by the store if it has not been bought.

For food in the dairy section, the date is usually fairly close to when you are shopping. If you're doing your shopping on July 1, the milk gallon may be stamped July 4. If you don't think you or your family will drink a full gallon by July 4, buy a half-gallon or a quart. In the case of milk, the "pull" date is often the "sour" date. Some dairy case items—cold cuts, ice cream, fresh dough products—allow for some storage time in your refrigerator.

For shelved products, the pull date is often months and sometimes a year from the day you are shopping.

Dating tips:

• If you see a product which is outdated in the regular display section, tell the store personnel. It should be removed promptly.

• Outdated bread and cakes are often set aside in a special display position and offered at greatly reduced prices. These can be good buys. While not *fresh* fresh, they are still tasty and safe for consumption.

• If you do discover that you have bought an out-of-date item that was not marked on special sale as such, take it back and get a refund.

Grading and Stamping Food

USDA. You hear about it. You see it stamped on food products. It is nothing mysterious. It means that the United States Department of Agriculture (USDA) has measured the quality of the product for taste, texture, and appearance—not nutritional content.

In the case of meat, anything sold in interstate trade must be inspected and passed by the USDA and so stamped. To you, the seal means the meat is from healthy animals and that the processing and packing plants and their employees have passed certain standards of health, sanitation, and safety.

In addition, most meats we buy are graded by the USDA—but grading is not required by law. The shield tells you the grade. These are the ones you'll see most often:

USDA PRIME	Most expensive. Not many stores sell it. Tender, juicy, flavorful.
USDA CHOICE	Sold commonly in most stores. Quite tender, juicy, flavorful. The grade most frequently bought.
USDA GOOD	Sold commonly in most stores. Fairly tender. Generally less fatty than "choice." Less expensive, too.

Other food products—such as eggs, butter, canned and frozen fruits, and vegetables—also have USDA grades. The grading systems vary for each item, but you can be fairly certain that if you see a Grade A, you're buying a good product.

Don't be concerned if there is no grade at all on a label. Grading is voluntary, and is paid for by the packer or processor who requests it. But even those who request it are not required to use it on their labels.

Computer Stripes

As we enter the computer age, we're taking our groceries with us. Those bars with numbers below them that you see on most packaged goods are product equivalents of our Social Security numbers. Each product has its own set of bars and numbers—its own Universal Product Code (UPC). (See p. 665 for an example.)

At computerized checkout counters, the clerk runs the UPC over or under a scanner and the price is automatically recorded and printed. The UPC eliminates the need for individual pricing of all items in the store.

How to Spot a Bargain or a Bummer—16 Tips

1. *Pick up a flyer in the front of the store.* Pull your cart out of the mainstream of traffic and pause for a moment to see what is on sale. Always take along some extra money so you can spend it on a real bargain. If staples (foods that are basic to your family's diet, such as ketchup, flour, peanut butter, jam, tomato sauce, tea bags, coffee) are on sale and can be stored safely for a long time, it is a good idea to stock up on them while there's a good offer.

Especially important: *shop the meat specials*, since the cost of meat makes up such a large percentage of the amount of money spent on food. *You can save as much as one-third on your family's meat bills* (even more, if you're shopping for yourself) simply by stocking up on meat that's sale-priced for the week rather than buying it at regular prices. Adapt your week's menus to suit the sale.

Carefully examine the packaging of the advertised meat specials and make sure you're getting the advertised sale price. If the supermarket has no packages left at the special price, get a rain check—a Federal Trade Commission rule requires that advertised specials be adequately stocked at or below the advertised special prices.

2. *Experiment with "No-Frills" foods.* In your local supermarket, you may see whole shelves of canned and packaged foods which carry simple black-and-white labels and price tags up to 40 percent lower than what you usually pay. These are the "No-Frills" foods.

They all list their contents and are equal in nutrition to well-known brands, but are less pleasing in packaging or size or content. Because they are not advertised or elaborately packaged, they're less expensive.

It's worth a try. Buy a couple of No-Frill items each time you go to the market. See if you (and your family) like the product as much as the well-known brand you use now. If so, switch. If not, forget it.

3. *Buy what's in season.* April may be cherry-blossom time, but it isn't time for cherries. Even if you manage to find cherries in the

market, you'll wind up choking on price, if not pits. Buy what's in season, and therefore in abundance. Summer fruits and vegetables, for example, cost 50 percent less in season than in winter. But don't buy the first of a crop; prices will go down and taste will go up as the supply increases.

4. *Be careful when you buy meat.* It's the most expensive item on your shopping list. Try to steer yourself and your family away from eating beef. It hits three high Cs—calories, cholesterol, and cost.

When you do buy meat, keep in mind that the weight labels can be confusing. A weight of 2.5 means 2½ pounds—two pounds, eight ounces—not two pounds, five ounces.

You can figure two to three cooked servings from each pound of roast beef, pork, lamb, veal, whole ham, trimmed fish, and certain types of steaks and chops. Figure fewer servings per pound when meat is loaded with fat, bone, or gristle (T-bone steak, for example).

5. *Pluck a tender chicken by noting its color.* The bird should be a creamy color—neither too yellow nor too white.

Figure about one pound per person for a whole chicken.

Chicken, one of the most popular and least costly of all main-dish foods, is worth more—hence more expensive—in parts than whole. So unless you or your family only eats legs, for example, your best bet is to buy the whole chicken. Cut-up chicken is a few cents more per pound, but can be worth the difference to a busy family.

6. *Don't squawk at a large turkey.*The bigger the bird, the more meat it will have in proportion to bone, so you get better dollar value. A turkey weighing less than twelve pounds is one-half waste.

Other tips:

- A self-basting bird costs more per pound than its plain sibling.
- The law says turkey loaf may contain as little as 35 percent turkey.
- If you or your family does not like the wings, legs, or giblets, check into buying just a turkey breast. It costs more per pound than the whole bird, but in the long run it may be less expensive for you.
- Turkey leftovers make great snacks and second meals. Cookbooks and magazine and newspaper recipes can help you create wonders with the leftovers. (I even know people who bake turkeys just for the leftovers!)

7. *Buying fresh fish* is dependent on your sight, touch, and smell. It's tricky because there is no mandatory federal inspection in this area—just a voluntary program which covers only 30 percent of the fish products processed in the United States.

The inspected products will carry the seal "U.S. Department of Commerce, Packed under Federal Inspection." But since most fish is *not* inspected, you must depend on your senses for what's good.

If you're buying fresh seafood, be sure the lobsters, crabs, clams, or oysters are alive when you purchase them. Note that shrimp is sold by color and count size. Smaller shrimp cost less.

8. *Avoid fishy cans.* Make certain the flesh of the canned fish is firm and uniform in color. If the flesh next to the can is darker, return it to the store. If the fish is packed in oil, the oil should be clear.

Know the difference between "white meat" and "light meat" tuna. Only albacore is white meat. Tuna that is "light meat" comes from the yellowfin, skipjack, and bluefin varieties.

9. *Fruit drinks are not fruit juices.* Check the cans. Last time I looked, some of the fruit drinks had as little as 10 percent fruit juice—not your number one source of Vitamin C.

10. *Beware of frosty frozen foods and damaged cans.* Buy neither. If a frozen food package is damaged, don't buy it. Don't buy packages stacked above the freezing line in the store freezer; these could be in the process of thawing, or indeed actually thawed. In some instances they have thawed and are being refrozen.

In no circumstances should you buy a leaking, bulging, or severely dented or damaged can. This could mean the product has spoiled. If you uncover such a can in your pantry, toss it out.

But suppose such a can slips by you in the store and on the pantry shelf, and you open it expecting to eat its contents. If you detect a foul odor when you open the container, do not use the food. *Don't even taste it.* Botulism, a possibly fatal food poisoning, can occur in improperly canned foods.

11. *Crack the egg color mystery.* Brown or white? The color makes no difference; it is determined by the breed of hen that does the laying. What's inside is the same for both.

12. *About the size of eggs.* Eggs come small, medium, large, extra large, and jumbo. Although larger sizes cost more by the dozen than smaller ones, the rule of thumb is that you get more for your money (by weight) if you buy the larger size, assuming its cost is no more than 10 cents above the size below it.

13. *Soda: by the can? No, buy the bottle.* A two-liter bottle will cost considerably less than its equivalent five or six cans. The cans generally hold twelve ounces, but suppose you don't want that much at one time. Once you open the can, your time is limited before it loses its carbonation—which is fine only if you like flat soda. (Always remember to screw the bottle top back on tightly, or bottled soda, too, will lose its fizz.)

Some states have bottle laws. Return your empty bottle for the deposit, and the soda costs you even less.

The one time cans make sense is when you want a soda away from home. Then cans are handy.

14. *Buy goodies so that they're "time-released."* Don't buy all the good stuff so that it has to be eaten within twenty-four hours or it will spoil. It would leave holes in your pocketbook and your stomach if you opened the refrigerator five days after you went shopping to find the raspberries moldy, the cake stale, the yogurt sour, and the sliced ham dried up.

15. *Help pack the bags.* That way you will be able to keep all the frozen and refrigerated foods together, making unpacking a simpler chore.

16. *Watch the cash register when checking out.* This is not so easy; you're usually busy unloading the cart while the cashier is ringing up items. If you can't watch everything, at least look up when something on sale or particularly unusual is being recorded. Cashiers are human; they make inadvertent mistakes like the rest of us.

The Shopping Cart Experiment

One of my teenage friends agreed to grocery shop with me for some of the items she usually buys. She, we decided, would play the eagle-eyed consumer. I would play the casual consumer.

I got the name brands, and disregarded specials, coupons, and generic foods. She hunted, compared, and used coupons—but she didn't buy second-rate products or any brand she didn't like, even though it might be on sale.

We went shopping for the same items in the same store. Here is the partial list of our results:

Item	She	I	Difference
2 yogurts	$ 0.68	$ 1.18	$ 0.50
1 6½-ounce can tuna	0.79	1.11	0.32
1 quart mayonnaise	1.21	1.69	0.48
1 pound coffee	2.09	2.35	0.26
1 1-pound package spaghetti	0.34	0.45	0.11
1 2-liter bottle of soda	0.79	1.19	0.40
1 29-ounce can sliced peaches	0.75	0.99	0.24
1 8-ounce bag of potato chips	0.99	1.19	0.20
1 1-pint 8-ounce jar vegetable oil	0.89	2.39	1.50
1 1-pound 3-ounce package chocolate cookies	1.10	1.49	0.39
1 12-ounce jar chunky peanut butter	1.09	1.29	0.20
1 1-pound package corn oil margarine	0.59	1.09	0.50
1 frozen pizza (small, approx. 1-pound size)	1.59	1.95	0.36
	$12.90	$18.36	$5.46

Savings
About 30 percent

The prices in the market may vary depending on the year and where you live, but there always will be a dramatic difference between the expenditures of a careful consumer and a casual one—even on a run-out-for-a-few-things shopping list, such as this one.

Hurry Home and Protect Your Investment

• Don't stop at a friend's house en route home and risk food spoilage.

• Once you're home, unpack the frozen foods first, then move to the refrigerated products.

• Meats go on the coldest shelf, loosely wrapped. Fruits and vegetables belong in the vegetable crisper unwrapped or in plastic bags with air holes.

• Don't leave items in brown bags. They become surprise packages: you forget what's in them and when you do get around to looking . . . *surprise*. Moldy, unrecognizable globs.

• Shelf items are last to be put away.

• *Note:* some shelf food must be refrigerated after it is opened.

Mayonnaise and spaghetti sauce, *yes;* peanut butter, vegetable oil, *no.* Check the labels.

NUTRITION: WHAT'S GOOD AND WHAT'S GOOD FOR YOU

True or False?

How much do you know about what goes into your body?

1. Four pancakes with syrup and a glass of milk is enough to fuel your body for about an hour of walking.
2. Athletes need twice the protein intake of nonathletes to function properly.
3. Yogurt is yogurt, whether it is in a container or frozen.
4. Having a tuna sandwich on pita bread with milk and a tangerine would shock nutritionists if this is your breakfast meal.
5. Honey is the only healthful sweetener on the market.
6. If one all-purpose vitamin pill is good for you, two should be twice as good.
7. Oysters, raw eggs, and rare meat increase your sexual potency.
8. To lose *one* pound, you must eat 3,500 fewer calories than your body needs.

The Answers

1. False. Assuming a calorie count of 665 for the pancake breakfast, you would have to walk for about an hour and a half to use up all the calories you consumed. Biking for an hour would do it, though, and if you swam or ran for an hour you would lose weight on that breakfast.

2. False. This is a myth which has no scientific support. What athletes need more of is calories and carbohydrates.

3. False. While all yogurt is nutritious, most frozen yogurt is loaded with sugar and additives and ranks on a par with ice cream when it comes to calories.

4. False. Nutritionists are not easily shocked—they would say

great to this tuna sandwich breakfast because the meal contains fish, bread, dairy, and fruit products and is well balanced.

5. False. Honey is no different from sugar. It has about the same number of calories; it is not any better for your teeth; it's no better for your system; and it's often more expensive. Neither is good for you.

6. False. If you eat well-balanced meals (more about this in a moment), nutritionists are not in agreement that vitamin pills should be taken at all. But if you have a less-than-perfect diet and do choose to take vitamin pills, be aware that those vitamins which are fat-soluble—A, D, and E—are stored in your body and can be harmful, even toxic, if they are not utilized.

7. False. These protein foods, as well as others, are important to your general well-being. But as for increasing potency, sorry. They just don't have any special magic.

8. We finally come upon something that is *true*—and 3,500 is a lot of calories! One painless way to take off weight is to determine how many calories your body needs to maintain its present weight and then simply eat 100 fewer calories a day. Give up one cookie a day and over a year's time you'll have dropped *ten pounds*.

How did you do? If you got seven or eight right, congratulations—you're a top banana.

Five to seven right and you're a fair pear—read on.

Four or less and you're a nutritional crab apple. You'd better bone up on what's good for you, if you want to stay healthy.

Healthy Doesn't Equal Wealthy

Don't try to save money by sacrificing good nutrition. Fortunately, you won't have to.

The key to good nutrition is good balance. You must choose what you eat with care from among the five basic food groups. Sometimes it's difficult because of the fast-paced life you lead.

What You Need in the 5 Basic Groups

• *Meat, poultry, fish, and beans group.* You need at least two servings (three ounces each) of cooked beef, lamb, veal, pork, fish, or organ meats daily. Substitutions for one meat serving can be two to three eggs; ¾ cup nuts, dry beans, peas, soybeans, or lentils; ¼ cup peanut butter; ½ cup cottage cheese.

What's in it for you? Protein, phosphorus, vitamins B_6 and B_{12}, and other vitamins and minerals.

• *Milk group.* Teens need more of this group than adults of the same height and weight. You need four 8-ounce servings daily. As you enter your twenties, cut down the number of servings to two.

The group includes milk in any form. Serving substitutions include 1 cup of yogurt; 1½ cups of ice cream; 2 ounces of process cheese food (American cheese); 1⅓ cups of cottage cheese.

What's in it for you? Calcium, riboflavin, protein, and vitamins A, B_6, B_{12}, and D (when the product is fortified with this vitamin).

• *Fruit and vegetable group.* You need at least four medium servings a day, and at least one of them should be something high in Vitamin C (such as an orange, a grapefruit, melon, strawberries, or a tomato). Every other day you should have a deep yellow vegetable (such as squash or sweet potato), or dark green fruit (such as honeydew) or vegetable (such as asparagus, broccoli, collards, spinach) to provide you with vitamin A. Potatoes, by the way, are part of the fruit and vegetable group.

What's in it for you? A good source of most vitamins and minerals.

• *Bread and cereal group.* You need at least four servings a day from this group. Count as one serving a slice of bread; 1 ounce dry cereal; ½ cup cooked cereal, pasta, or rice. Some whole grain bread or product should be included daily.

Very active people, as most of you are, need more than four servings daily. If you are a teen athlete, you have hit the jackpot in this group.

What's in it for you? B vitamins, iron, some protein, and other nutrients.

• *Fats, sweets, alcohol group.* No serving sizes are suggested because other than calories, this group provides little of nutritional value. Nutritionists believe that you will ingest enough fats and sugars if you eat a balanced diet from the other food groups.

Wouldn't you know it? This group includes such items as pastries, butter and margarine, mayonnaise, salad dressings, and sweets of all kinds.

What's in it for you? Nothing much except pounds.

- *Don't forget fluids—four to eight cups a day. Water is the elixir of life.*

What's Right for You?

Following is a chart developed by the National Academy of Sciences which outlines the recommended daily allowances of the nutrients which will keep you healthy.

Balancing Tricks

How do you go about slotting everything you need for a healthy diet into your hectic schedule when you're too late for breakfast? When you hate breakfast? When you're grabbing a snack for lunch? Or eating dinner before or after everyone else?

- *Make breakfast fit your schedule and desires.* Pancake batter can be made the night before and refrigerated until morning. You can grab some juice as you leave the house and stagger your breakfast throughout the morning. Or whip up a blender shake with nonfat dry milk (you can't tell the difference between it and its cartoned equivalent, except that the dry milk is much less expensive), an egg, and your choice of other good ingredients: honey, wheat germ, fruits. You can also heat up last night's macaroni and cheese; or make breakfast pizzas on English muffins; or create your own hot cereal by adding warm milk to graham crackers.
- *Plan ahead.* Cut up vegetables and hard-boiled eggs and make sandwiches in advance. But don't put the mayo, mustard, or ketchup on the sandwich until the last moment—they tend to soggify the bread.
  Plan leftovers to be used as another meal, either in the same form (cold chicken), slightly altered (sliced chicken sandwich), or disguised (chicken divan).
- *Make sandwiches wonderful by imaginative combinations.* Doesn't ham and swiss cheese with sliced tomato and lettuce on rye do a nice job hitting all four food groups? What about a tuna and celery on whole wheat pita bread with lettuce and a glass of milk? There are hundreds of combinations you can invent.
- Don't make anything. Just grab the right things. It may not fit your idea of a ''meat and potato, sit down with the family'' dinner

**Food and Nutrition Board, National Academy of Sciences—
National Research Council Recommended Daily
Dietary Allowances, Revised 1980**
*Designed for the maintenance of good nutrition of practically
all healthy people in the U.S.A.*

	MALES			FEMALES		
Age (years)	11–14	15–18	19–22	11–14	15–18	19–22
Weight (kg)	45	66	70	46	55	55
(lb)	99	145	154	101	120	120
Height (cm)	157	176	177	157	163	163
(in)	62	69	70	62	64	64
Protein (g)	45	56	56	46	46	44
Fat-Soluble Vitamins						
Vitamin A (μg RE)	1000	1000	1000	800	800	800
Vitamin D (μg)	10	10	7.5	10	10	7.5
Vitamin E (mg α-TE)	8	10	10	8	8	8
Water Soluble Vitamins						
Vitamin C (mg)	50	60	60	50	60	60
Thiamin (mg)	1.4	1.4	1.5	1.1	1.1	1.1
Riboflavin (mg)	1.6	1.7	1.7	1.3	1.3	1.3
Niacin (mg NE)	18	18	19	15	14	14
Vitamin B-6 (mg)	1.8	2.0	2.2	1.8	2.0	2.0
Folacin (μg)	400	400	400	400	400	400
Vitamin B-12 (μg)	3.0	3.0	3.0	3.0	3.0	3.0
Minerals						
Calcium (mg)	1200	1200	800	1200	1200	800
Phosphorus (mg)	1200	1200	800	1200	1200	800
Magnesium (mg)	350	400	350	300	300	300
Iron (mg)	18	18	10	18	18	18
Zinc (mg)	15	15	15	15	15	15
Iodine (μg)	150	150	150	150	150	150

(and it isn't), but when all else fails, peanut butter and banana slices on crackers with a container of yogurt and a handful of raisins is a well-balanced, though strange, dinner. Just don't make a habit of this kind of "on the fly" eating.

• Slow down. Enjoy the warmth of sharing a leisurely meal with people you care about.

Natural Foods

They're Expensive. Are They Really Healthy?

As of 1982 there was no officially adopted definition of "natural foods." Unofficially, though, the Federal Trade Commission describes these as foods free of artificial and synthetic ingredients and minimally processed.

But there are "natural foods" on the shelves which contain food coloring, monosulfate, thickening agents, white flour, partially hydrogenated oil, tannic acid, and other quasi-"natural" substances. All that "natural" products seem to have in common is that the word "natural" on their labels perks up sales.

Have you uncritically allowed yourself to believe that "natural food" means healthy food, and have you been willing to pay the extra money that these foods cost for a shot at instant good health? Have you believed (erroneously) that health-food candies such as carob-coated treats sold in health food stores are good for you? Do you realize that "health bars" contain just as much sugar, fat, and salt as regular candy bars?

Natural foods are peaches, sunflower seeds, eggs, lamb chops, and the like. If you buy food that is fresh, you will be getting the most natural, the healthiest, and the most reasonably priced food available.

Choosing Bottled Waters Is a Matter of Taste

Q: What's "nouveau," American "chic," in drinking in homes and restaurants across the land?

A: Bottled water, that's what—a European habit which goes back to the time of Julius Caesar, known to Michelangelo, and immortalized in the story of Ponce de Leon and his search for the fabled fountain of youth.

While our nation is known the world over for having the best tap water available anywhere, sales of bottled waters have tripled in the last decade. And whatever the reason—style or dieting or fear of contamination—one of every 200 Americans now drinks bottled water, with the perpendicular climb showing no sign of slowing.

But if you are part of this switch, do you know what you are really drinking? Do you know how to buy? The odds are you don't.

A first key fact is that it's just about impossible for one bottled water to be described as "better" than another. The differences depend entirely on individual tastes. Don't be fooled by fancy names or bottles. Drink what tastes good to you.

No matter what the conflicting claims, all bottled waters must meet certain bacteriological, chemical, and physical standards, and must be bottled under strict regulations covering cleanliness of processing, containers, shipping, and storage. And all must be labeled under Food and Drug Administration rules.

Many of the terms used to describe a water's source are confusing:

• Bottled waters described as "artesian" (water pumped from a well), "natural spring," or "mineral water" (spring waters), come from natural springs or wells. They are bottled, minerals intact, directly from the source, unfiltered and unprocessed.

• Bottled waters described as "purified," "artificial," "formulated," "drinking water," or "springlike" also come to just about the same thing. The terms mean the water has been scientifically treated to remove such impurities as chlorine and sulphates. Minerals are frequently added. Although the levels may differ, the contents of purified bottled waters are generally the same as artesian, natural spring, or mineral waters.

• As for purification treatments, the different methods include distillation, deionization, electrolysis, and filtration. Most purified bottled waters are filtered.

• You also may be easily befuddled by the mineral (or salt) content. It's misleading, though, to limit the term "mineral water" to natural spring waters, because all bottled waters, except distilled, have minerals.

If you're choosing between carbonated or noncarbonated (still water), it's your taste which must dictate your purchases. "Naturally carbonated" (or "naturally sparkling") means that carbon dioxide gases captured at the source are added to the water during bottling. Artificially carbonated water has carbon dioxide added.

On price: roughly 75 percent of bottled waters on the market are purified and tend to cost a little less than the imported varieties. But don't forget: One bottled water can't be called better than another. It's all a matter of personal taste, so experiment on your own and reach an intelligent decision.

CALORIE COUNTING

Calorie Counters Beware

"Why can't I look like Jennifer?"
"Why can Peter drink two milk shakes with his three cheeseburgers and two large orders of fries and never gain a pound?"
"Why when I diet do I lose weight in my face, the only part of me that's thin to begin with?"

We're all different. Jennifer's built differently from you; Peter's more active than you are; people lose and gain weight differently.

But if you really do want—or need—to lose weight and keep it off, you must cut the number of calories you take in while still maintaining a balanced diet.

For a diet (either to lose *or* gain weight) to be successful, it has to:

- Conform to your personal food likes and habits.
- Provide you with all the nutrients your body needs, and in the correct balance.
- Allow you to snack and eat in public places.

If it doesn't do all that, you'll quit it in no time because it will interfere with your health, disposition, and social life.

Stay away from fad diets. They're trouble! (See Chapter 17, *Times of Trouble.*)

The USDA Diet

The U.S. Department of Agriculture provides these guidelines for those trying to control weight. (For those who want to gain, just reverse them.)

1. Cut down on high-fat foods, such as margarine, butter, highly marbled or fatty meats, and fried foods. Salad dressings, cream sauces, gravies, and many whipped dessert toppings are also high in fat.

2. Cut down on sweet foods, such as pies, cakes, and candies; also soft drinks and other sugar-sweetened beverages and punches.

3. Cut down on, or eliminate, alcoholic drinks.

4. Cut down on *portion sizes*. (A bunch of grapes is fine; a bowl of grapes is fattening.)

5. Eat low-fat and skim-milk products, such as ice milk and skim-milk cheeses. These provide fewer calories and are nutritional substitutes for their whole-milk counterparts.

6. Choose cooking methods which help cut calories. Cook foods with little or no added fat and avoid deep-fat fried foods. Trim off visible fat and either broil or roast meat and poultry on a rack. If braised or stewed, drain the meat to remove the fat. Broil or bake fish. Steam, bake, or boil vegetables. For an occasional treat, stir-fry vegetables in a small amount of vegetable oil.

7. If you're counting calories, be sure to count the nibbles (even the gum) and drinks enjoyed during social events and throughout the day.

Paying More for Less

Your eagerness to pay extra for the built-in maid service that comes with convenience foods has been for years a widely acknowledged factor in your swelling food budgets. But not so well recognized—or even admitted—has been your growing willingness to pay substantial additional amounts for "packaged" willpower. Anxious about overweight, you are spending hundreds of millions a year on special diet products, featuring fewer calories but also providing smaller portions and less food value.

"Paying more for less" is just another signal of your spreading

nutritional illiteracy and susceptibility to inviting ads and supermarket displays—or both. Whatever the explanations, the result is
costly to you and me.

There's a diet counterpart these days for just about every food
you can think of—fruits, vegetables, jellies, salad dressing, TV din-
ners, sour cream, cookies, eggs, etc. Yet, you can easily convert
many of these items into diet specials yourself at far less cost.

To illustrate: a package of low-cal, fruit-flavored gelatin makes
four servings of ten calories each. But you can claim a saving of at
least 300 percent merely by buying unflavored gelatin and flavoring
it yourself with leftover coffee, fruit juice, diet soda, or whatever.

Then there are many foods which are both naturally low in calories and in price and which should form the basics of your diet.

Consider low-fat milk products. While fluid skim milk usually
costs a few cents per quart less than whole milk, the real savings in
money and calories is nonfat dry milk. It cuts calories in half, reduces cholesterol intake, and is usually priced at roughly half what
you pay for fluid skim or whole milk.

Or consider the simple apple. If bought fresh by the pound,
these cost half as much as the price for the equivalent in foil-
wrapped dried slices.

Low-income consumers have been the usual target for most nutritional information. But the unspoken assumption that only these
consumers are malnourished and in need of education is unrealistic! Obesity is as much a symptom of malnutrition as starvation.
Middle- and upper-income families need to be educated about a
balanced diet as much as anyone.

Meanwhile, you can get sensible, if not inspiring, nutritional aids
from the USDA. *Food and Your Weight*, Home & Garden Bulletin
(#001-000-03735-8, cost: $4.50), and *Calories & Weight: Pocket Guide*,
(#001-000-04164-9, cost: $3.75) are both available from the Superin-
tendent of Documents (U.S. Printing Office, Washington, DC
20402). Be sure to compare the calories in regular foods with those
in their diet counterparts. (Read their labels).

EATING OUT

"Meet you for lunch in the cafeteria."
"Want to go out for a pizza before the movie?"

Sound familiar?

That's because we all do it. Eating out has become a way of life for two main reasons:

- We have to. We're at work or school and can't go home.
- We want to. We're using eating out to socialize.

Since about a third of every dollar spent on food goes to eating out, here are ways to get the best value from brown bags to doggie bags.

Brown Bagging

First of all, you don't have to use drab brown bags. Ever think of toting food in a basket, a colorful tote bag, a small hat box?

3 Good Reasons

1. With the possible exception of government-subsidized school cafeteria lunches, brown bagging provides you with the least expensive way of eating out.

2. Packing your own lunch means getting what you like to eat. Your decision is limited only by your tastes, imagination, and what's in the house when you're ready to do your packing.

3. There's a certain reverse snob appeal in brown bagging. Brown baggers have the shrimp salad in pita bread, fresh fruit, cheese and crackers, cold chicken, and homemade brownies that even the greasy hamburger devotees envy once in a while.

Make It Fun, but Make It Easy

Brown bagging gives you a chance to experiment. If you usually have strawberry yogurt, add a little culture to your life and try a different flavor, such as piña colada. Add banana or bacon to your peanut butter sandwich. Mix apple bits into your tuna salad. Look for intriguing recipes in newspapers and magazines.

If you like soups or hot drinks not available where you brown-bag it, buy a wide-mouthed vacuum bottle (thermos) to accommodate your tastes.

Caution: the general rule for safe eating is that foods that are meant to be hot should be hot; foods meant to be cold should be cold. Most foods keep without spoiling at room temperature for the three to four hours between when you pack your lunch (or take it out of the refrigerator, having packed it the night before) and the time you eat it. Be careful, though, with perishable items such as mayonnaise. The big no-no is serving unrefrigerated foods made with mayonnaise, especially in the summer.

Vending Machines—for the Quickest Meal of All

Since you don't expect a three-course gourmet meal to drop down when you pop in the coins, you cannot be too disappointed with the simple standard fare that vending machines provide. Although you pay slightly more for the convenience, who can squabble about the speed with which the food is served?

Vending machine dealers must comply with local board of health standards. Certain foods—such as candy, cake, and potato chips—must be dated for freshness. The frequency of servicing is dependent upon the amount of traffic at the machine. It can range from daily to once a week.

What happens if the machine eats your money without providing you the foods to fill your stomach? A time-honored remedy—kicking it—can lead to broken toes and/or broken machines. Instead, tell the proprietor of the establishment what happened. Vending machine companies generally provide proprietors with a kitty from which to give refunds. Even if that is not the practice at your locale, *you are still entitled to a refund.*

But don't keep feeding a broken machine. One quarter lost must be refunded. Twenty dollars' worth of quarters is another matter.

Cafeterias

Prices at school cafeterias are almost always lower than those of private establishments. Cafeterias also offer well-balanced meals, and food services are expanding the traditional sliced turkey, gravy, peas and carrots, and mashed potatoes lunch. In the New York State University system, for example, dieticians ask students for "recipes from home" so that they can be served in the cafeteria to spruce up the standard fare and to make students feel more comfortable at school.

Cafeteria pluses: low prices; someone else does the preparation and cleanup; wide selections, ranging from institutional-type food to ethnic dishes.

Minuses: you can get caught up buying more than you'll eat, or choosing a poorly balanced meal; the food can be boring.

Picnics and Parties

Tips on How to Keep the Costs Down

Picnics (the brown-bag lunch with pizzazz) and parties don't have to be expensive to be fun. Here are a few ways to help you combat costs.

• Prepare a budget and stick to it. Figure out how much you can spend for food, drinks, decorations, etc. If you see you are exceeding your budget, reassess the situation. Can you cut down on the number of people you're asking? (This automatically reduces the overall costs.) Do you need such elaborate decorations? Must you serve crab meat dip? Will onion soup dip do instead?

• There are lots of ways people can share in party preparations. Some can bring their favorite records; others can bring the drinks; others can shop for the "dry" goods, such as napkins, paper cups, potato chips; still others can help you prepare the food. Sharing, in addition to saving time and money, also gives a terrific psychological boost to a party. Everyone feels the event is partly his/hers and will make every effort to ensure its success.

• Let everyone assemble his/her own sandwich, sundae, omelette, whatever. If you put all the cold cuts on a platter, people will have more fun assembling their own sandwiches than they would if you did it for them. Besides, when the party's over, there may be a pound of roast beef left, but it will be in a pile of neat slices to be used another day and not in someone's half-eaten sandwich. The whole "assemble it yourself" concept cuts down on waste and increases your time to have fun at your own party.

• Buy the largest available bottles of soda. You can always save what you don't drink.

Beer, Wine, and Hard Liquor

If you are of drinking age, here's what you should know about beer, wine, and hard liquor—in addition to the serious trouble these substances can cause (see Chapter 17, *Times of Trouble*).

A quarter-keg of beer contains about 120 eight-ounce glasses. If you are having a big party (over thirty people of drinking age who prefer beer), this is a better bet than individual bottles or cans—even if you wind up with extra beer in the keg.

Wine can be bought at all prices. The choice can be intimidating—racks line the liquor store's walls and aisles, stuffed with imported and domestic wines. This is where your local, reliable liquor store will be most helpful. Don't be embarrassed to ask for assistance. People three times your age are as confused as you are.

Buying guides that will be helpful no matter what your taste in wines:

• Decide how much wine you need before you shop. The rule of thumb is a half bottle of wine or twelve ounces per person for dinner for a two- or three-course meal.

• Don't overlook large bottles. A magnum of wine is 51.2 ounces, and American jug wines are very economical.

• Wine makes a super punch when combined with fruit juices—and it goes a long way.

Less expensive brands of hard liquor are often indistinguishable in taste from the more expensive brand names. (Often the house brands are made by the nation's top distillers.) Use them—especially when you're combining liquor with mixers or fruit juices.

Look for liquor sales. Although liquor prices often are controlled in any given area by state laws and other factors, sales do occur and bargains can be found. The best time to find liquor sales is after a big holiday.

Figure on 12 to 15 drinks per a fifth of liquor; 18 to 20 per liter; and 40 to 45 per 1¾-liter bottle.

Fast Food

Can you beat this combination: something that tastes good, is affordable, great for your social life, and nutritious to boot? Hats off to the fast food establishments! Fast food is not necessarily synonymous with junk food—you just have to choose the right combinations.

Your social life and your tastes in food are subjects I'll avoid. But affordability and nutrition are topics I will tackle. Here's how to get the *most* and the *best* for your fast-food dollar.

• Don't assume that just because a place serves fast food, it's the least expensive place to eat. Long gone are the days when a company advertised that you could get a whole meal for under a dollar. Like other food establishments, fast-food chains have also raised their prices to meet their escalating costs.

• Order a meal which is nutritionally sound. Experts suggest these sample menus:

Tacos with grated cheese and shredded lettuce & tomatoes
Lemonade

Chicken with cole slaw and mashed potatoes
Milk

Pizza with a tossed salad
Lemonade

• If you're anxious about calories, skip the toppings on the pizza, the special sauces on the hamburgers, the dark meat of the chicken, the megacalorie dressings on the salads, and the shakes.

• Instead of the extra soda or shake, ask for water or head for the water fountain. Not only is water good for you, it's free.

• Order the minimum and test whether the theory "your eyes are bigger than your stomach" holds. The beauty of fast food is that you can always go back and get more—fast.

• Fast food doesn't mean fast eating.

Dining Out Is Different from Eating Out

You are leaving a fancy restaurant. You carefully planned this big night out, but now you feel like choking—not from food; from frustration.

You know you've been taken. The meal cost twice the amount you expected. You almost fainted when you looked at the menu initially. On your tight budget, you were lucky to have walked away with 50¢ in your pocket.

What went wrong?

• The entrée prices seemed within your price range, but everything else on the menu also had a price next to it.

Moral: next time, dine out where the dinner is *prix fixe* (price fixed). *À la carte* (a separate price for each item) is fine if you have lots of money or a small appetite.

• Your date ordered escargots and almost gagged when the waiter brought out snails.

Moral: don't order anything you don't understand. Ask the waiter, who will be happy to translate. Dining out on a limited budget is not the time to experiment. If there is something you have never had and someone else at the table orders it, it is perfectly okay to ask for a taste, but don't shoot your whole dinner on *filetto alla tartara* (steak tartar—raw chopped sirloin, seasoned) unless you have had it before and know you like it.

• You ordered the crab meat special, described so enticingly by the waiter, and were shocked to find it cost $3 more than the most expensive entrée on the menu.

Moral: ask the prices of the specials if you think you might order one; then you can judge whether or not it's within your budget. If more people would do this, perhaps waiters would start reciting the accompanying prices as well as the accompanying spices.

• You went to a restaurant in the middle of the city which you had heard was frequented by celebrities. You didn't see one.

Moral: it's an expensive gamble to go to a midtown restaurant where overhead and rent may be 30 to 50 percent higher than a neighborhood restaurant, just to see a celebrity. The restaurant's higher operating costs are passed on to you. Anyway, celebrities are smart. They don't want people gawking at them while they're eating, so they eat at *your* neighborhood restaurants.

• You ordered the cheapest bottle of wine (which still seemed steep to you) and you felt like a fool when the wine steward put the cork down in front of you and stood there waiting for you to do something.

Moral: do your fancy drinking at home before dinner—the typical markup on wine in restaurants is around 100 percent. If you do have wine with dinner, the wine steward will expect you to sniff the cork to approve the bouquet, and to sip the wine to okay the taste before he pours wine for others at the table.

• You each ordered an appetizer, entrée, salad, and dessert, and you both were so full you could hardly get up from the table.

Moral: order one appetizer, one salad, and one dessert. Ask for two forks for each of these courses. It is perfectly acceptable. In some good restaurants, the waiters will even suggest it.

If you do over-order, ask for a "doggie bag" so at least you'll be able to savor the food the next day.

• You thought your date would offer to leave the tip—at the very least!

Moral: discuss who is paying for what in advance, so nobody is caught short. While it used to be a male's responsibility to pick up the tab, this is no longer true. If both people are in the same financial position, it makes good sense to split the bill. The young woman should offer to pay half, and the young man should consider the offer without wounded pride. The person who has done the asking out can decide about the split-bill arrangement—and should not feel guilty about accepting.

When a group is eating together, the easiest thing is to split the check evenly, unless one diner gorged himself with caviar and truffles and another on a diet had one scrambled egg. If that happens, see who ate what and tally accordingly. (Best to decide in advance.)

• You felt you had to give individual tips to the headwaiter (he got you a table near the fountain), the doorman (he parked your car), the hatcheck girl (she hung up your coat), the rest room attendant (he handed you a face towel)—as well as your own waiter.

Moral: avoid restaurants where you must give individual tips to a large staff.

• You felt a little uneasy about the waiter's tip. You didn't know if you should figure the tip on the cost of the dinner alone or with tax and liquor added onto it—and the whole process required more math than you could do in your head.

Moral: the average tip is 15 percent of your food and drink bill (exclusive of tax). If the service was poor, you are correct to leave less. If good, you can leave more—closer to 20 percent.

The easiest way to figure the tip is to take 10 percent of the bill, then halve that amount to get 5 percent. Add the 10 percent and 5 percent together, and that's your 15 percent.

Food and Drink Bill	$48.20
10%	4.82
½ of 10%	2.41
	$ 7.23 = tip

But leave $7.25. It is tacky to leave pennies; instead, round the tip off to the nearest nickel, dime, or quarter.

If you can't figure the tip in your head, ask the waiter for a pen and figure it out on a tissue.

A toast to your next meal out! May it be a thoroughly digestible experience.

GRABBING A SNACK

It was awesome. Six members of a soccer team came into a pizza parlor at five in the afternoon and polished off four large pizzas "with everything" (anchovies, sausages, meatballs, pepperoni, peppers, onions, extra cheese) and a dozen sodas, and then dispersed to their respective homes for dinner.

You are lucky. You have the ability to digest almost anything at any hour of the day or night.

Since snacking fulfills so many needs beyond the physical—social, psychological, emotional—nobody would ever suggest that you do away with it. There are, though, ways to make snacking more nourishing and less costly.

The High Cost of Snacking

You work hard for your money, according to a 1981 report by the National Center for Educational Statistics in a report, "Youth Employment during High School." The report says the amount of time that the average teenager spends working is more than he or she spends at any other activity—except for going to school. And that includes teens from high-income as well as low-income families.

Assume for a moment you make $4 an hour at your part-time job. How long would you have to work for the following snacks at a local eatery?

Two slices of pizza (90 cents each) and a 50-cent soda?

A $1.80 quarter-pound cheeseburger and a 90-cent shake?

A $1 hot dog and an 80-cent lemonade?

A $2.50 meatball wedge (submarine, grinder, hoagie) and a 50-cent can of fruit juice?

A $1 ice cream cone?

The answers (rounded off) are 35 minutes for the pizza snack; 41 minutes for the cheeseburger snack; 27 minutes for the hot dog snack; 45 minutes for the wedge and juice; and 15 minutes for the cone.

If you're working to put money away toward a goal—your post-high school education, a car of your own, a microcomputer, or simply to pay for the gas you use in the family car—snacking costs can take more than a nibble out of your paycheck.

Fill Your Stomach—Don't Empty Your Pockets

• With all deference to our soccer friends, *don't stop for a snack on your way home to dinner.* If you do stop, at least limit your intake. Chances are there is enough food to fill you up awaiting you at home. If you don't eat it (because you're full from snacking) and it has to be thrown out, that's an additional waste of money.

• *Bring snacks from home.* Buying food—including snacks—at the supermarket is considerably less expensive than buying something "out." By bringing your own snack to a movie, for example, you will save money—in addition to being able to bring what you like, instead of choosing from a limited selection at the candy stand in the lobby.

• *Choose affordable snacks.* Everyone is going for ice cream and you want to go too, but you know that most of the money in your pocket is for this weekend. Life is full of choices. If the weekend is important to you, but you still want to be with your friends who are going for ice cream, maybe you can join them and settle for a single-dip cone.

• One of the best ways to avoid snacking out is to *have interesting snack ingredients at home.* One family I know has created a snack shelf in the pantry; one in the refrigerator; and another in the freezer. And each is clearly marked "Stuff for snacking: eat at your own risk." I'm told that the complaint "There's nothing to eat in the house!" is rarely heard.

By providing a variety of nutritionally sound snacks, this family was making a conscientious effort to save money by making snacking *at home* attractive. While I was there I observed a variety of snacking patterns among the four teenagers who lived at home.

One wanted peanut butter and crackers and milk, and that was that. Another wrapped meat and cheese slices around pretzel sticks before downing a homemade thick shake. Another took out a slice of frozen meat loaf and warmed it in the microwave oven, adding a few raw string beans. The fourth grabbed a dish of fruit and put a scoop of cottage cheese in the middle. They told me that sometimes they liked to be creative snackers and other times they just wanted to be able to grab something they liked. The snack shelves served either mood.

17

TIMES OF TROUBLE AND FEELING BAD

What You Can Do about It

CONTENTS

SELF-HELP FOR COMMON
CHRONIC AILMENTS

Arthritis

Arthritis, a chronic disease that afflicts more than 31 million Americans, is the nation's leading crippler. Although not really common among teens, it is not limited to the middle-aged or elderly people you see in television pain-reliever commercials. In fact, 250,000 people under eighteen have arthritis. The term, which literally means inflammation of a joint, refers to at least 100 different conditions, each with its own symptoms, patterns, and modes of treatment.

If you, your family members, or friends are diagnosed as having arthritis, you will naturally want more information. Your best resource is the Arthritis Foundation, based in Atlanta and with 150 offices around the country. When you write, you will be sent pamphlets and referrals to local treatment centers and self-help groups. If there is not a branch located near you, mail your letter directly to the Arthritis Foundation (1314 Spring St., N.W., Atlanta, GA 30309).

Of particular importance for young arthritis patients is a membership organization founded early in the decade as an offshoot of the Arthritis Foundation. The American Juvenile Arthritis Organization (AJAO) sponsors a number of activities for young patients and their families. Members receive a newsletter and participate in regularly scheduled meetings of local self-help groups that can include, among other agenda items, guest speakers such as vocational counselors, doctors, and psychologists. The purpose of these groups is to demonstrate to young patients that they're not alone and that there are ways to cope and prosper. The national AJAO underscores that point with references to helpful publications for arthritis patients as well as for others with handicaps and chronic diseases.

Learn about the legitimate, helpful treatments and resources available to you if you have arthritis. Don't turn to quack devices and miracle cures. Those who do throw away a staggering $950 million each year.

Allergies

American pupils lose about 130 million school days every year because of asthma, and another 37 million school days from hay fever. Asthma alone causes an estimated two-thirds of all school days lost to illness.

Allergies can be a real trial, causing sniffing, red-rimmed, itchy eyes, hives, and a number of irritating, uncomfortable, and unattractive symptoms. But, worse, allergies can—in some instances—be life-threatening. Often they are life-altering—you may have to eliminate certain foods from your diet (strawberries, to choose a common example), change jobs, or even move to a new region. If you know you are allergic to certain substances, such as penicillin, wear a Medic Alert bracelet (see Chapter 14, *Your Health*), or other indicator of this allergy so you won't inadvertently receive the wrong treatment in an emergency.

A good resource for questions about allergies is the Asthma and Allergy Foundation of America (9604 Wisconsin Ave., Suite 100, Bethesda, MD 20814). You can get answers to a host of questions—what to do about possible allergic reactions to chemicals in your environment; facts about possible interaction of medicine you take regularly with drugs and alcohol; and pamphlets, lists of resources, and information about clinics and programs that specialize in treating allergy patients. Sooner or later, just about everyone experiences an allergic reaction to something, so it's important to know that allergies can be managed and controlled.

Other resources: The National Institute of Allergy and Infectious Diseases (Information Office, Bethesda, MD 20014)—part of the National Institutes of Health; and the National Jewish Hospital and Research Center/National Asthma Center (3800 East Colfax, Denver, CO 80206).

Diabetes

If you live with diabetes, you are not alone. The National Diabetes Data Group estimates that one in every twenty Americans is affected by this disease. About 6 million Americans know they have diabetes (2.6 percent of the population), and another 6 million are estimated to have it but do not yet know it. Diabetes affects one in every 1,000 people under age 17, experts say.

Basically, two types of the disease exist: juvenile diabetes, or insulin-dependent (Type 1), and adult-onset, or non–insulin dependent (Type II). In each form, diabetics are unable to produce enough insulin—the substance that regulates the body's amount of glucose, the product of sugars and starches in the food we eat. As carbohydrates break down into glucose in the digestive system, the glucose builds up, and cannot be used properly. It remains in the bloodstream and does not reach the body's cells, where it's needed to produce energy. Wasted glucose builds up in the bloodstream and spills out in the urine. (Testing urine for glucose is the easiest way to test for diabetes.) Meanwhile, of course, the body is deprived of vital energy.

Most people with juvenile diabetes are diagnosed in childhood or teen years. Even though it's a chronic disease, millions of people lead productive and vigorous lives—Mary Tyler Moore, Catfish Hunter, and Ron Santo among them. Prompt detection and strict control of diabetes are essential. It's a tough illness to live with, as you know if you or a family member is diabetic, but it is not the calamity it was only fifty or sixty years ago.

A simple series of tests will determine whether you have diabetes. If so, you can begin a program to control the disease. If you experience one or more of the following symptoms regularly, visit your doctor or clinic:

- Frequent and copious urination.
- Unusual thirst.
- Extreme and frequent hunger accompanied by weight loss.
- Fatigue, drowsiness, exhaustion.
- Annoying and persistent itching of the skin and genitals.
- Development of skin disorders and infections.
- Sudden changes in vision; blurring and other visual difficulties.

Help is close by for those of you with diabetes or a diabetic family member or friend. Contact your local branch of the Juvenile Diabetes Foundation International (JDFI) or write to the main office (23 East 26th St., New York, NY 10010; call toll-free 1-800-223-1138) and ask about the AIDD program. JDFI developed

AIDD (Association of Insulin Dependent Diabetics) as a self-help program for teenagers and young adults specifically. Activities include regular meetings where members talk about their management routines, invite guest speakers, discuss common problems and successes, and support each other in an open, friendly atmosphere; one-on-one counseling for newly diagnosed diabetics and their families; a library of materials; fund-raising; and public education. The program, begun in 1979, is expanding rapidly and new chapters are forming around the country. If there's no branch near you, the JDFI welcomes your energy and ideas about starting one.

The JDFI will send you pamphlets that are targeted to different readerships, including parents and teachers, that explain different aspects of the disease. You might want to acquire some and educate your elders.

Epilepsy

Epilepsy, a mysterious, disturbing disease to many people, affects an estimated 1 percent of the population—more than 2 million people—and 100,000 new cases develop annually. The condition is a chronic disorder of the central nervous system which is characterized by uncontrolled, temporary malfunctions in the brain's electrical systems. These discharges cause seizures of varying intensity and type.

Epilepsy is not a symptom of mental illness, retardation, contagious disease, or cancer. Usually it develops in childhood or adolescence, although accidents, injuries, and illness can cause it to develop, too. At present, epilepsy cannot be cured, but about half of those with this disorder can control their seizures with regular medication, and most others can attain at least partial control.

If you have epilepsy or are close to someone who does, you can get assistance and information from the Epilepsy Foundation of America (4351 Garden City Drive, Landover, MD 20785). Request booklets that explain the disorder, its causes and treatment; and ask for referrals to clinics and comprehensive programs that provide diagnosis, treatment, medication, counseling, and services such as vocational rehabilitation and disability counseling. You can also get answers and advice regarding problems with applying for jobs, use of alcohol and other drugs, participating in sports, and other daily activities. Local chapters sponsor self-help groups and special programs for teenagers. People who want to start their own self-help groups can receive advice and encouragement from either a local affiliate or the national office.

Most states allow people with epilepsy to get drivers' licenses, but usually you must submit written proof from your doctor that you have been free of seizures for a prescribed period of time. Check with your state department of motor vehicles.

Headaches

Severe headaches are no joke; in fact, they are a major cause of lost days at school or work. If you suffer headaches that don't respond to standard aspirin therapy, ask your doctor to check for other ailments—headaches often are a symptom of disease and emotional stress. If you suffer migraines and have questions about new treatments, dietary advice, and current information, write to the National Migraine Foundation (5252 North Western Ave., Chicago, IL 60625). It provides practical, useful information and suggestions, and a list of treatment centers for people who suffer debilitating migraines. When you write, you will receive a sample of the newsletter, a brochure of pertinent facts about headaches, and a list of in-state doctors and treatment centers.

Scoliosis

Scoliosis—curvature of the spine—strikes teenagers, especially teenage girls, more than any other group in the population. (See pages 563–65, Health Exam: When and Why.) If you are diagnosed as having scoliosis, you and your family will find this booklet extremely helpful: "Scoliosis: A Handbook for Patients." It explains the different forms of the problem and modes of treatment. To get a copy, send $1 to the Scoliosis Research Society (444 North Michigan Ave., Chicago, IL 60611). The organization itself comprises doctors and research scientists who specialize in studying the causes of and seeking cures for this ailment.

Living with scoliosis and the lengthy treatment required for most cases can be very hard on you, your family, and friends. The Scoliosis Association, a national self-help group, sponsors a number of local chapters throughout the country. To find out more about its activities and to learn whether there is a chapter near you, write to the Association (1 Penn Plaza, New York, NY 10119). Enclose a self-addressed stamped envelope (business sized) with your letter.

FEELING BAD

Suicide

Each year, April and May bring a sharp increase in the number of suicides. Psychologists conjecture that suicidal people, seeking release from their tormenting inner pain—made even more intolerable in contrast to spring's brilliance—submit to their self-destructive urge.

Teenagers figure prominently among the victims of this tragedy, which is on the increase in our society. The facts of teenage suicide are grim indeed.

- More than five young Americans, aged ten through nineteen, kill themselves each day.
- Suicide is the second cause of death among teens, after car accidents, and roughly equal to homicide. Since many accidents are actually disguised suicides, and since many suicides are reported as accidents, the actual figure probably is higher. Moreover, these numbers do not include ''slow'' suicide—self-destructive behavior, such as drug and alcohol abuse.
- The suicide rate for young people has more than tripled in the last ten years. It is four times higher now than in 1955.
- Three times as many teenage girls attempt suicide as boys; three times as many boys succeed.
- Many suicides occur from miscalculation or mistake: overestimating the number of pills to make oneself sick, for example.

If You Feel Suicidal

Only you know how unhappy you really feel. But no one has to live in such pain and isolation. Help is all around, perhaps in unlikely places, but it is there. Friends or a trusted adult, such as a teacher or member of the clergy, care enough to listen to your problems and suggest ways of coping. If you can't talk to your parents, call on a trusted relative or family friend. In addition, many communities have suicide hot lines. Operators at community hot lines will listen sympathetically and propose courses of action for you to take.

The National Runaway Switchboard and Runaway Hot Line (formerly called Operation Peace of Mind) have national toll-free hot lines as well as listings of agencies in your region that can help lead you out of a bad situation. Callers to any hot line remain anonymous but the operator will have to know where you're calling from to route you to an appropriate local agency. (See the end of this chapter for the toll-free numbers.)

Call the Samaritans, an international suicide prevention organization with several branches in the United States, including Boston, Providence, Chicago, Keene (New Hampshire), and Cape Cod. Volunteers befriend and listen without offering judgments, quick solutions, or unwanted advice. People from all over the country phone the Samaritans; the Samaritans do not have a national toll-free hot line, but their regional hot lines are listed in the White Pages of your telephone book.

It's hard to ask for help, sometimes. You may feel that you can't express the hopelessness and hurt you feel. You may want to try special or professional help to sort through the confusion, but feel too unsure or unsafe to ask. But help *is* there—reach out for it.

If Someone You Know Talks About Suicide

The idea of suicide is so scary and ominous to you that you don't want to think about it or hear about it. But when someone you know talks about suicide, you must listen as calmly as you can and be a supportive, caring friend. The fact that this person has reached out to you lets you know that you are trusted and that your friend wants to be taken seriously. Experts say that teenagers, especially, are not really convinced that they want to die, so you, a friend, must seize the moment to prove that someone—you—cares. If you find yourself dealing with a potentially suicidal person, or someone you suspect is a threat to himself or herself, here are some guidelines:

• Take the threats seriously. When someone says, "You'll be better off without me . . . I think I'll kill myself," don't offer encouragement, even if you think that it's all a joke. And should someone give you a treasured possession accompanied by a comment such as, ''I won't need this where I'm going,'' take that as a clue and ask questions.

• Look for hints in the person's behavior, attitude, and language. The worst, most persistent myth about suicide is that people who talk about killing themselves never actually do it. The tragic fact is that almost everyone who commits suicide—or tries to—has given previous warning. Eight out of ten completed suicides actually told someone in advance that they were considering it.

• Don't be afraid to ask, ''Do you feel so terrible that you sometimes think about killing yourself?'' You won't be giving a suicidal person morbid ideas or encouragement! Studies show that most of us fleetingly consider suicide at some point (usually not too seriously), and the idea is not a new one. In fact, you may help lift an agonizing burden by initiating an open, free discussion of your friend's feelings.

• If your friend answers ''Yes,'' follow through. Get details—when, where, how. Find out whether your friend has made an attempt before. Weigh the answers, and if the situation seems urgent, get immediate help. Do not leave your friend alone. Stay until help arrives or the immediate crisis passes.

• Most suicidal people want not irrevocable death but an escape from the terrible pain they feel. However, even after your friend unburdens some of the pent-up feelings and the tension drops, the ordeal isn't over, and neither is the conflict. Don't be satisfied if your friend says, ''I'm okay now, you can go home,'' or ''Why don't you hang up, you must be tired.'' As soon as you can, contact the police, the emergency room of a nearby hospital, a community hot line, your parents, or another adult you trust. You cannot resolve this crisis by yourself, and should not try to—but you can be a lifesaving friend.

Phobias

A Gallup Youth Survey conducted early in the decade indicated that nine out of ten teenagers endure at least one completely irrational fear or phobia. Fears of snakes and hypodermic needles top the list of the most common phobias, followed by fears of falling, rodents, heights, bugs, darkness, and flying. Notice that all of these fearful situations share one quality: in most cases, each can be avoided—a cause for sighs of relief all across the country. In general, fears of a single object or situation rarely interrupt or restructure daily activities. However, other phobias are not so harmless. Some people experience phobias about driving on freeways, riding in elevators, and being in enclosed spaces. One type—agoraphobia—cripples the lives of its victims even more, robbing them of peace of mind and self-esteem.

The term *agoraphobia* comes from the Greek for "marketplace" (in fact, the ancient *agora*—market—is a popular tourist spot in downtown Athens). It means, literally, fear of the marketplace; others define it as fear of open places, or fear of fear—a fear that resides within. However it is explained, it can devastate the lives of its victims and their families, and it is estimated that this problem afflicts from six to ten people per thousand in varying degrees of intensity. People with severe cases of agoraphobia are unable to leave their homes, even for work, school, social events, or doctors' appointments. Some even retreat to one or two rooms in their homes. To avoid any situation that provokes a panic attack, agoraphobics forfeit the activities that most of us take for granted. Telltale signs of agoraphobia include:

- Severe anxiety
- Depression
- Frequent episodes of panic
- Fear of going out alone
- The accumulation of many fears: for example, fears of driving, department stores, escalators

In general, agoraphobia begins with constant anxiety and escalates to encompass these other symptoms—not necessarily all of them, by the way. If you believe you fit this pattern, the sooner you get help, the easier it will be to overcome this problem. Many research scientists are now exploring agoraphobia and possible causes and treatments.

Help is available. The Agoraphobia and Anxiety Center at Temple University keeps on file a list of treatment centers and programs for phobias, especially agoraphobia, around the country. Requests for information will be answered more quickly if you include a self-addressed stamped envelope. It helps, too, to explain your problem and name the nearest city. The center also offers a comprehensive treatment program of its own. (Agoraphobia and Anxiety Center, 3975 Conshohocken Ave., Temple University, Philadelphia, PA 19131.) Fees in different programs usually depend on the type and duration of treatment; most are covered by health insurance.

Social fears, another class of problems, conspire to keep many teenagers at home or isolated from friends. Typically, these include fear of parties, or of the opposite sex, or of school. How can you tell when to get help for any of these fears? Only you know whether they prevent you from going places, fulfilling obligations, and enjoying yourself. You don't have to live with this discomfort—look into the resources for counseling in your community and get help quickly; the sooner you respond to these problems, the easier it will be to conquer them and get back to feeling good.

A number of programs work by behavior modification—helping people overcome their fears by increasing their exposure to those things which frighten them, together with counseling and supervision. For example, many people have been able to overcome their fear of flying with special programs that ultimately get them up in a plane. Among them: Fearful Flyers Seminar (Captain T. W. Cummings, 2021 Country Club Prado, Coral Gables, FL 33134) and Fly Without Fear (310 Madison Avenue, New York, NY 10017). Local travel agents can help you locate other programs that help people master this common fear.

TROUBLE AND FOOD

Eating Disorders: Anorexia Nervosa and Bulimia

Francesca Louise Dietrich—Kessa—lives in a nice apartment on New York's Upper West Side with her parents (her older brother and sister live elsewhere), excels in school, and works very hard at her dance classes. An offhand comment by Madame, her instructor, that she should firm up a bit and lose a pound or two instigates a diet that, very soon, consumes Kessa's life. As she deprives herself of sustenance, she becomes obsessed with food and develops a bizarre set of rituals for eating and maintaining order that claims all her time and leaves no energy for school, social, or family life. Her formerly excellent grades slip, but she retreats into her own world and doesn't care. The doctors who treat her don't know what to do, and neither do her parents. Eventually, her pediatrician teams her with a clinical psychologist and they join battle against her disease. At 5'4", she weighs 98 pounds when she stops eating; by the time she's hospitalized, she weighs 63½ pounds and is almost dead from starvation.

Kessa's story, a frightening case study of a teenager suffering from anorexia nervosa, is told in the novel *The Best Little Girl in the World*, by Steven Levenkron (Contemporary Books, 1978), a clinical psychologist at Montefiore Hospital in the Bronx.

Kessa is lucky. Hard work, good treatment, and her own will eventually pull her through. It used to be that up to 20 percent of anorectics died from the irreversible effects of long-term starvation. New therapies have now decreased that rate to 1 percent or less.

Those afflicted with anorexia need immediate medical and psychiatric care. This is *not* a disease that responds to self-help books and well-meaning friends. Most victims are young women, ranging from twelve to twenty-eight; the highest concentration of anorectics occurs in the sixteen- to eighteen-year-old bracket. Health experts estimate that currently fewer than 10 percent of anorectics are men.

A related and equally self-destructive and frightening syndrome afflicts even more young women—as many as one in five college students, and an estimated half of all anorectics. See if you recognize anyone you know in the following remarks. They were spoken by a young woman on a national talk show in response to the question: "How did it happen to a nice girl like you?"

"I am a very nice person, I'm a perfect person. I don't get angry. You look at my desk at work, you come to my apartment and you look at the way I am, I am very controlled. My relationships are controlled. I was a perfect little girl. I never stamped my foot. I never got ugly and I never dealt with anything that I was feeling and even now the only area of my life that is out of control is when I am eating that (Sara Lee) cake and I can put my life back in control by going in the bathroom, throwing everything up, washing my hands, and walking out thinking, 'phew.' "*

This "perfect person" is describing bulimia—a disorder in which the victim binges by consuming thousands of calories and then

Donahue quotes Copyright © 1981 by Multimedia Program Productions, Inc.

purges her system by inducing vomiting or diarrhea. In fact, bulimia is considered the gorging-purging phase of anorexia nervosa.

These two are life-threatening illnesses that require prompt medical attention. Unlike a cold or flu, they do not vanish if they do not receive care, and the consequences can be devastating on both the victims and their families. The longer the behavior lasts, the more difficult it becomes to correct. Severely malnourished patients must, in some instances, be hospitalized before they can begin the psychotherapy and other treatments necessary to restore their health.

No matter how severe their symptoms, anorectics and bulimics can be incredibly convincing that nothing whatever is wrong, and clever in hiding their behavior from people close to them. An anorectic might sit down to a meal, carve up her portions of food into tiny pieces, dawdle, drink some water, and leave, saying she isn't hungry today. Or she may cook elaborate meals for her family and not eat a morsel. Here's how one bulimic described her behavior: "I worked very closely with two roommates very intimately for a period of two to three years. They did not know until I disclosed this to them this summer. We had one bathroom. I was renowned for my long showers. The water ran forever. Nobody has to know."*

Not all victims display each of the following symptoms, but study them. It will be incredibly difficult to ask for help for a friend—or yourself—but you must.

- Abnormal weight loss
- Refusal to eat, or eating only tiny portions of food
- Denial of hunger
- Distorted body image (belief that one is obese when, in fact, victim is painfully thin)
- Intense fear of becoming fat
- Preoccupation with food
- Infrequent or complete absence of menstruation
- Excessive physical activity
- Vomiting
- Binge eating
- Abuse of laxatives, diuretics, and diet pills

*Donahue quotes Copyright © 1981 by Multimedia Program Productions, Inc.

- Severe weight loss—25 percent or more
- Constant cold—low body temperature

Why do these strange, frightening afflictions strike young women so often? No one really knows, but study of these problems continues. Meanwhile, help is available for anorectics, bulimics, and their families. If you or someone you know fits these patterns, write to the following organizations for advice:

American Anorexia Nervosa Association, Inc. (AANA)
133 Cedar Lane
Teaneck, NJ 07666
(201) 836-1000
(Weekdays 10:00 A.M. to 2:00 P.M. E.S.T.)

The AANA puts people in touch with treatment centers, self-help support groups for families, and other community facilities around the country. It can also provide background information, advice on counseling, and a speakers' bureau. Members receive a newsletter, too.

Anorexia Nervosa and Associated Disorders, Inc. (ANAD)
Box 271
Highland Park, IL 60035
(312) 831-3438

ANAD provides counseling and information to anorectics, families, and health professionals. Its free services include a referral list of therapists, hospitals and clinics; a directory of self-help groups; and a list of suggested reading material.

Overweight and Obesity

Name three school friends who are not concerned with their weight.

Give up? That's a tough question simply because most of us worry about our weight and appearance, and this holds true for teenagers with a vengeance. It's hard enough to deal with bodies that change so unpredictably and fast; excess weight simply compounds the problems and anxieties that so many people feel.

In advertising, in department stores, and in movies, we are exhorted to be lean and fit. Yet most of us don't measure up to the ideals, and people who are overweight often feel—and are encouraged by some to feel—like social misfits.

Obesity is a major health problem in our society, and one of the nastier features of long-standing obesity is that it is a factor in the development of other health problems, such as some circulatory and heart problems and arthritis. The longer a person remains obese, the greater the risk of developing ailments related to obesity.

Learn to distinguish between "overweight" and "obese." Although we tend to use them interchangeably, they have different meanings.

Overweight refers to a condition when one weighs more than is average for one's height. This amount can be as low as a few pounds. Athletes, for instance, often weigh more than might be expected for their heights, but who would consider them overweight? For them, excess weight comes from muscle mass, not fat. Highly developed muscles weigh more.

But *obesity* means overweight totaling at least 20 percent more than expected on the basis of height. Obese people carry around too much fat, an amount that can be measured using a device called a skin-fold caliper.

Obesity is a confusing subject, even among medical professionals. The causes remain murky—generally they are pinpointed as a combination of genetic, metabolic, cultural, and environmental factors—but each person's makeup is unique and no one explanation satisfies everyone. No confusion exists about the process, though. Obesity results from either an excessive intake of calories, or a failure to use up those consumed. Curiously, a fat person doesn't necessarily ingest more calories than a thin one; studies have shown that obese, inactive teenage girls actually eat fewer calories than their thin classmates.

The solution—as you know from seeing countless magazine articles, books, and television commercials—is diet and exercise. But the bedrock of that solution is knowledge of good nutrition and good eating habits. (See Chapter 16, *Your Diet.*)

The hard truth is that there is no easy, painless way to lose weight—yet millions of us jam the bookstores and pharmacies, grabbing the latest diet book or aid that promises magical results with minimal efforts. Some of these fads endanger health. You, as teens, are particularly vulnerable because your bodies need certain nutrients to enable you to grow and develop. The diet plan your mother uses is not necessarily the right one for you.

Dieting is tough work—sometimes too tough to undertake alone. Fortunately, if you don't want to do it alone you don't have to. A number of nationally known diet groups sponsor programs and regular meetings, including some for teenagers, and you probably can find at least one group nearby. Among the well-known groups are Weight Watchers, Diet Workshop, and Overeaters Anonymous. The first two programs work according to diet plans; the third is a self-help and support group.

At Weight Watchers, new members receive a personal-program diet plan and instructions for living with it. The versions include diet plans for men, women, and young people, and the program accommodates preferences such as vegetarianism. Once a week you are weighed—in private—and your weight is monitored by the instructor. The program encourages steady, controlled weight loss and, following attainment of your desired weight, you learn to stay slim on the Maintenance Plan. You pay to attend the weekly weigh-ins and lectures, which are key elements in the program. If you want more information about Weight Watchers, information about their summer camps, or a copy of *Be the Best*, a booklet written for young people that includes a diet plan, write to Weight Watchers International (attention Teen Department, 800 Community Drive, Manhasset, NY, 11030).

You hate groups? Or you can't bear the idea of discussing your weight in a roomful of strangers? You can diet on your own—millions of people do, with varying degrees of success. How well you do is up to you. You can plan a diet with your doctor or other health professional. Both can help you with choices of foods as well as strategies for sticking to your program. Whatever route you take, your success is ultimately up to you.

TROUBLE AND SEX

Birth Control

The subject of birth control can arouse so much passion that the purpose of the many devices, creams, and pills becomes obscured. It's really very simple, though: use of birth control lets you plan when—and when not—to have children. These devices, creams, and pills are not instruments of torture designed to drain the spontaneity and pleasure from a relationship or diminish your feelings. Besides, how much fun can you have when you both worry about unwanted pregnancy?

Deciding which method of contraception to use is an intensely personal act, but to make the best choice for you and your companion, learn the facts, consider your priorities (expense, convenience, readiness to handle unwanted pregnancy), and discuss your feelings and requirements with a doctor, counselor, or other health specialist. Base your choice on what you are most comfortable with—you need to be confident of using your method automatically and correctly, every time.

Complete, current, and reliable sources of information will make your deliberations easier. Sources which can supply you with what you need to know:

Your doctor, a local clinic or health department, an adolescent medical unit at a nearby hospital, a family service agency, the community hot line, the local Planned Parenthood chapter, your campus health center. These are primary resources and often dispensaries of birth control information and devices.

In the library and bookstore, look for current materials on this subject, such as *Congratulations! You're Not Pregnant: An Illustrated Guide to Birth Control*, by Peter Mayle and Arthur Robins (Macmillan, 1981).

Nonhelpful and error-prone sources include graffitti, second- or third-hand testimony ("I heard that Susie said that Mary used . . ."), and rumor ("There was this article, I don't know who saw it, about a fail-safe . . ."). Don't try any hearsay suggestion until you first check it out with a *reliable* source.

Only one method of birth control is one hundred percent effective: abstention. Even sterilization can be unsuccessful—and no doctor performs vasectomies or tubal ligations on teenagers, anyway. Many children have been born to couples who swore they were infertile.

A few more cautions: no method is completely convenient and fun to use. But the health risks associated with pregnancy, particularly for teenagers, are much greater and more common than those associated with any form of contraception. Moreover, the drastic consequences of unwanted pregnancy far outweigh the inconveience of using birth control.

Types of Birth Control

Assume, for safety's sake, that no time of the month is risk-free. Even before you become sexually active, think about what method of birth control might be right for you. Contraceptives can be classified in a number of ways:

Those which the man uses or participates in: condoms, withdrawal, sterilization, rhythm.

Those which the woman uses or participates in: the Pill, IUD (intrauterine device), diaphragm, vaginal suppository, spermicides, rhythm, sterilization.

Available over-the-counter: condoms, vaginal suppository, chemical spermicides.

Those which require a doctor's examination and prescription: diaphragm, IUD, Pill.

Effectiveness

The free, traditional methods such as withdrawal, postcoital douche (never!), and luck don't work. They are safe and cheap enough, but are accompanied by a high probability that in nine months you'll be sending out birth announcements.

More effective are condoms and spermicidal agents, particularly when used together. Inexpensive and easily purchased, they are popular and convenient. Be absolutely certain to follow instructions to the letter.

Rhythm, the method sanctioned by the Roman Catholic Church, is based on meticulous recordkeeping and requires planning and motivation. Even when employed in the best circumstances, rhythm has a high rate of failure, since it is not possible to predict every variable in a woman's menstrual cycle. Instruction from a knowledgeable health professional is essential: don't assume you know which days are "safe" and which are not. By the way, women *can* and *do* get pregnant during their menstrual periods.

The diaphragm, surging in popularity, is safe and quite effective when properly used and fitted. It must be used with a special spermicide (not the kind you use alone). The actual diaphragm should be replaced every two years—or sooner, if you gain or lose more than ten pounds, have a baby, or if it tears or cracks. The tube of spermicide can be replaced as often as needed and can be purchased in any drug store without a prescription.

The two most effective methods of birth control are the IUD and the Pill. Before you choose either, find out about the pros and cons—you may decide that neither is appropriate for you, at least right now. Each carries certain medical risks, aside from accidental pregnancy. Many doctors will not fit a woman with an IUD before she has had a child. Before you can get the Pill, a doctor will want your complete medical history and will perform a pelvic exam.

Whatever your choice, *don't* economize on birth control. Trying to save money on birth control is a false move when weighed against the enormous costs of pregnancy, delivery, and child-rearing. Terminating a pregnancy is costly, too, both emotionally and financially, and, while an alternative, is *not* a method of birth control.

And be warned: no device will work if it is left in its container!

Pregnancy

About 10 percent of all teenage girls will get pregnant this year. The United States has the highest incidence of teenage motherhood of any Western nation—53 per thousand, as compared with 32 per thousand in England, for instance. Of these, 25 percent of young mothers receive no prenatal care; their first contact with the medical establishment occurs in the delivery room.

If you are among the pregnant 10 percent, you are faced with some tough decisions. For some of you, pregnancy spells disaster, and presents the biggest crisis of your life. Others of you will plan joyfully for motherhood and welcome your condition.

Whether your pregnancy is planned or not, go into action the moment you have reason to think you're pregnant. Don't drag your feet. The classic symptom is a missed menstrual period. However, women often miss periods: stress (such as worrying that your period is late), illness, travel, poor nutrition, and irregular schedules can throw off your body's timing. Other telltale signs of pregnancy include constant fatigue, frequent urination, tender and swollen breasts, vaginal discharge, and morning sickness. Actually, "morning" sickness can occur at any time, but it usually strikes early in the day. (Fortunately, it tends to disappear after the first three months.)

If you are sexually active and your period is two weeks late, have a test and confirm—or refute—your suspicions. To find out where to get this test, call a local hot line, women's center, chapter of Planned Parenthood, Public Health Clinic, or community hospital. Check ads in local and college papers for free or inexpensive testing. In a pinch, you can buy a home pregnancy test for about $10, but they are not totally reliable. If any pregnancy test is negative but your period doesn't materialize within the next week or ten days, have another one. At this point—especially if the test comes out positive—a doctor should examine you and look for changes in the color of your cervix (it becomes "bluish") and feel for changes in your uterus.

Early confirmation of pregnancy is vital. You can't hide it for very long, and you have important decisions to make.

Wanted Pregnancy

If you plan to bear the baby, your life will now include regular appointments with an obstetrician. A number of precautions will become routine: avoiding alcohol, tobacco, and other drugs—even aspirin, unless you have your doctor's permission.

Your body's nutritional needs alter drastically. You will modify your diet under a doctor's supervision to suit new and changing requirements for the duration of your pregnancy.

If you have chronic medical problems, such as diabetes, you need special medical care. In this case, the Juvenile Diabetes Foundation International (mentioned earlier in this chapter) can send you vital facts about pregnancy and diabetes. For more complete information about genetic counseling and screening programs throughout the country, write to the National Genetics Foundation (555 West 57th St., New York, NY 10019).

Very young mothers are at high medical risk—in some cases, their bodies are too immature to withstand the stresses of pregnancy and labor. Young mothers commonly experience high blood pressure and toxemia, a bacterial blood infection. If you're a very young mother, you *must* see an obstetrician regularly to avoid—or at least detect—problems such as these.

Unwanted Pregnancy

If yours is a problem, unwanted pregnancy, wishing it away will not work. The sooner you accept this fact, the sooner you can deal with your condition and decide on a course of action.

Your first hurdle may be telling the father and your family. Since this can be the most terrifying aspect of the situation for many girls, you may decide now to seek help. The resources you used when you had your pregnancy test can advise you or direct you to counseling services. Use them: usually they are offered free or at low cost. Once there, you'll find it pretty hard to shock these counselors, most of whom are women. They will help you explore your options clearly and plan your strategies. For example, if telling your parents scares you, a counselor might suggest that you confide in a trusted relative or friend and together go to your parents.

The point is: you must do something! That something, however, should *never* include self-induced abortion. No matter how grim the situation seems to you, you have choices and there are people to help you. A self-induced abortion can make you sterile or kill you. You'll almost certainly wind up in the hospital and compound whatever problems you had hoped to solve.

You have four choices in a problem pregnancy: to bear the child and keep it; to marry the father and rear the baby; to give the baby up for adoption; and to have an abortion. Each alternative is painful to think about and raises a wide range of issues: emotional, religious, financial. And each course of action calls on you to examine your life's goals, assess what you can realistically do now, and probe your feelings honestly and bravely. Each route has costs— both long-range and temporary.

Many of you will need help. Social service, family service, and denominational (Catholic, Protestant, Jewish) welfare agencies can offer counseling, advice on adoption procedures, and arrangements for adoption if that is your choice. Also you can turn to community hot lines, family service agencies, the United Way, Public Health clinics, and the clergy. All are listed in the phone book.

Financial aid for pregnant teens varies from state to state, county to county and, in this era, year to year. Contact your state or county welfare agency if you need information on local eligibility requirements and instructions for application procedures.

Abortion to terminate an unwanted pregnancy is a difficult decision to make. As this is written, abortion is legal everywhere, but regulations affecting its availability, eligibility for public funding, and other issues change often and make long-term predictions impossible. To get up-to-date, accurate information about abortion in your state, call the National Abortion Federation's toll-free hot line. You also can ask questions about the medical and psychological aspects of abortion, need for parental consent, and for a copy of a consumer's guide for choosing a high-quality abortion facility. The hot line is open Monday through Friday, 10 A.M. through 6 P.M., E.S.T. Number: 1-800-223-0618; in New York City: (212) 688-8516.

Planned Parenthood, with its 188 local affiliates and chapters, provides services ranging from counseling and pregnancy testing through abortion and prenatal care. All Planned Parenthood clinics welcome teenagers and some even provide special hours for appointments. Planned Parenthood's services won't empty your wallet, either. Call your local branch or, for a list of centers, write to the Planned Parenthood Federation of America, Inc. (810 Seventh Ave., New York, NY 10019).

Reading

When you discover that you're pregnant, you will profit from reading up on the subject as you sort through the feelings raised by this enormous event. Good places to start:

- *The Teenage Body Book,* by Kathy McCoy and Charles Wibbelsman, M.D. (Simon & Schuster, Wallaby Books, 1978). Includes a thoughtful, balanced, and sympathetic chapter about pregnancy.
- The Consumer Information Center offers a number of booklets dealing with different aspects of pregnancy, prenatal care, and infant and child care. (Consumer Information Center, Department G, Pueblo, CO 81009.)
- Helpful pamphlets about pregnancy and your body's new requirements are available from the American College of Obstetricians and Gynecologists (Resource Center, ACOG, 600 Maryland Ave., S.W., Washington, DC 20024). Enclose a self-addressed stamped envelope. Single copies of each pamphlet are free.
- *Pregnancy, Birth and Family Planning*, by Alan F. Guttmacher, M.D. (New American Library, 1973). Covers all subjects from conception (and contraception) through delivery.
- *Preparing for Parenthood*, by Lee Salk, Ph.D. (Bantam Books, 1980). Explores different aspects of parenthood and the issues to consider.
- Books about exercise and nutrition during pregnancy cram the bookshelves in libraries and stores. Talk to your obstetrician and ask for advice about which ones to read.

Other Sources

There are also other sources to help you:

- *Practical Parenting*, a bimonthly newsletter, helps parents cope with children at all stages of development. You can obtain a list of more than sixty newsletters as well as magazines for parents by writing to Practical Parenting (Department PPL, 18326B Minnetonka Blvd., Deephaven, MN 55391).
- Purdue University's Child Development Department has developed a set of newsletters which track a child's development every month until he/she is six years old. Send your child's birthdate (or expected birthdate) along with your inquiry to Growing Child (22 North Second Street, P.O. Box 620, Lafayette, IN 47902).

Sexually Transmitted Diseases

STDs. The term sounds like the acronym for a component of your home computer or a late-model car. But, in fact, STDs stands for Sexually Transmitted Diseases—sometimes called venereal diseases after Venus, the Roman goddess of love.

Why the name change? Among the reasons: most people think of only two diseases when they hear the term VD, yet researchers have identified more than twenty STDs. In addition, the new term is more descriptive, less judgmental, and signifies a move away from associating STDs with sexual promiscuity and moral laxity. Along with the new term comes an emphasis on how STDs relate to other medical problems such as infertility, birth defects, and cancer. For instance, a mother with an *active* case of genital herpes can transmit the disease to her new baby as it passes through the birth canal. Therefore, women with active herpes need extra medical care.

STDs are not a shameful and embarrassing secret. They are common ailments that demand prompt attention the moment you suspect, or are told, that you have one. Immediate attention guarantees that you don't pass the disease on to someone else, who may, in turn, donate it to a third person (STDs are often called the gift that keeps on giving). And, of course, you want your disease attended to in order to avoid jeopardizing your health or that of any children you may someday have.

There are *no* effective home remedies against any STD. A physical exam and lab tests are essential for a proper diagnosis, and exact diagnosis is critical because each STD requires specific treatment.

Symptoms

Especially in women, some STDs do not produce any symptoms. An astonishing four out of five women with gonorrhea have no symptoms at all. Consequently, health professionals recommend that sexually active people be tested for syphilis and gonorrhea at least once a year.

Nevertheless, here are a number of common warning signals. If you experience even one of the following symptoms, check it out with a doctor.

In men:

• *Discharge.* A discharge or drip that is white, clear, watery, or thick can develop with gonorrhea and other STDs, particularly nonspecific urethritis.

In women:

• *Discharge.* Most women routinely have some normal vaginal discharge, but if you develop one that changes in color or consistency, that is irritating or causes itching, have it checked out.
• *Lower abdominal pain.* Lower abdominal pain may be a symptom of gonorrhea or pelvic inflammatory disease. Sometimes it is accompanied by fever. Whatever its cause, it must be diagnosed and treated properly.

In both men and women:

• *A burning sensation and frequent urination.* Pain and frequent urination are signs of many diseases. In all cases, diagnosis is required to identify and eliminate the problem.
• *Sores. Painless* sores anywhere on the genitals may be signs of syphilis or chancroid. *Painful* small sores on and around the genitals are symptoms of herpes.
• *Lumps and bumps.* Vaginal warts are bumpy, cauliflowerlike

growths around the genitals. Usually they are painless, but they are contagious, so treatment is mandatory. A rash can indicate the second stage of syphilis.

• *Itching.* Crabs and scabies are the little devils that cause intense itching in any infested area of the body. They are spread by close physical contact and cluster around the genitals. In women, itching can also be caused by vaginal infections that are not transmitted sexually, such as yeast infections.

No completely effective way to prevent STDs now exists, but ways to protect yourself and your partner are available, and you should use them.

Condoms help reduce transmission of STDs for both men and women. They should be worn for the duration of sexual activity.

Some health professionals recommend that you urinate and wash your genitals after sexual contact, since there is evidence suggesting that these measures can help prevent STDs. But they also caution that this is not a fail-safe routine; you should not rely on it.

When you're feeling amorous, any precaution may seem depressingly unromantic. But the consequences of failing to pay attention are considerably worse.

• Be alert for any symptoms. If you are suspicious, see a doctor or go to a public health clinic. Look in the Yellow Pages under "venereal disease" or "sexually transmitted disease."

• Follow the prescribed treatment diligently. That includes no sex from the time you suspect a problem until completion of the medication and the doctor's okay.

• Notify your partner(s) at once. Others deserve to know so that their cases can be cleared up, too.

• One bout with an STD does not make you immune from others, and you can contract the same disease more than once.

• Reminder: if you notice something that troubles you, ask!

Herpes

A current cause for concern nationwide is the spectacular increase in cases of genital herpes. Herpes viruses are quite common: there is Herpes simplex (responsible most commonly for cold sores), Herpes Type 2 (Herpes simplex virus 2, or HSV-2, the cause of genital herpes), and Herpes Zoster (the cause of chicken pox, the third most commonly transmitted disease in the country—gonorrhea is number one).

Genital herpes typically causes lesions in the pubic zone; blisters may occur within a few days to a week after infection, which requires intimate physical contact. A tingling or burning sensation in the affected area usually occurs, and fever and headaches may develop. The little red blisters often break open and become painful open sores; generally, though, they heal on their own. The bad news about genital herpes is that it recurs and that there is no known cure at present. The first episode lasts, on average, three weeks; subsequent attacks may last five days or so.

Once you are infected by herpes, the virus lingers in your nervous system for life. In 1982, only one proven treatment for genital herpes was on the market. Called acyclovir, it is a creamy topical medicine that retails for about $20 a tube; applied during the initial bout, the medicine speeds healing and relieves the symptoms. But it is not a cure.

Beware of the rip-off artists who have moved in to prey on the discomfort, hopes, and unhappiness of people with herpes. Researchers are busily searching for, testing, and pursuing possible remedies to cure and alleviate the disease.

For additional information about herpes, write to the Herpes Resource Center (HRC, Box 100, Palo Alto, CA 94302). Enclose a self-addressed stamped envelope (business size) with your request. The HRC sponsors local chapters that arrange regular meetings at which members talk about their problems, frustrations, and successes in living with herpes.

Information

Local community hot lines are an excellent source of information about different STDs and local arrangements for treatment. Also:

- The National VD Hotline
  1-800-227-8922 (except Alaska and Hawaii; the line cannot receive calls from these states)
  Weekdays 8:00 A.M. to 8:00 P.M.; Saturdays and
  Sundays 10:00 A.M. to 5:00 P.M.; all Pacific Time

The National VD Hotline is sponsored by the American Social Health Association. Operators have a complete list of public clinics, compiled on a state-by-state basis, and can refer callers to a clinic in their vicinity. You can also request written information about STDs, including herpes.
  Write to:

• The American Medical Association
  P.O. Box 821
  Monroe, WI 53566

• Planned Parenthood Federation of America, Inc.
  810 Seventh Avenue
  New York, NY 10019

  Ask for its publication *9 Common Sexually Transmitted Diseases.*

• American College of Obstetricians and Gynecologists
  Resource Center
  600 Maryland Avenue, S.W., Suite 300
  Washington, DC 20024

  Enclose a self-addressed stamped envelope, and request a copy of *Important Facts about Venereal Diseases.*

  Treatment of STDs is confidential. The American Academy of Pediatrics suggests to its members that all examinations and treatment be considered a private matter between patient and doctor. Public venereal disease clinics provide free, confidential care and are located nationwide. In any state, your parents do not need to know about or consent to your treatment, even if you are still a minor. All cases of gonorrhea and syphilis must be reported to the federal Center for Disease Control, but all they get is a report of a case and your gender; the CDC receives no personal data.

THE BIG THREE: SMOKING,
DRINKING, DRUGS

Introduction

The desire to alter a state of consciousness is as old as humanity. Anthropologists note that virtually every society developed a distilled or fermented beverage, and many groups developed religious beliefs that revolved around the ritual use of drugs.

Drugs have been—and continue to be—used for all sorts of reasons: as medication, to get high, to calm down, from boredom, from a desire to experiment. We use certain drugs routinely, with scarcely a second thought: aspirin and caffeine are good examples. Other drugs cause much more of a stir: alcohol, marijuana, amphetamines, cocaine, PCP, all the rest—''up'' and ''down.''

Alcohol and tobacco are two of the most abused drugs around. A drug is any chemical substance that produces behavioral, emotional, physical, or mental changes in the user. You can argue that drug use is sanctioned by society—think of all the ads for coffee, aspirin, cigarettes, and alcoholic beverages. Ironically, the cost to society of drug abuse—especially when you factor in tobacco and alcohol—is so huge it defies belief.

When does use of a substance, whatever its nature, become a habit and dangerous to your body and mind? Will using these substances create problems for you? When and what kind? What, exactly, is substance abuse?

Smoking

You don't want to read another sermon against smoking, right? You know that it's bad for your health, pollutes the air, befouls your hair and clothes, and burns up your spare cash. There is not a single redeeming feature about smoking, but if you're a smoker you don't want to be reminded of that truth. Anyway, you plan to quit someday.

Since you've already read this far, here are more facts:

• Smoking causes wrinkles. Dermatologists report that women who smoke are prone to develop little wrinkles sooner than nonsmokers—the act of smoking speeds the facial skin's aging process.

• Smoking decreases your sense of taste and smell, and leaves you with foul breath (hence, more money spent on breath mints and mouthwash!).

• A smoker's risk of dying in a fire or smoking-related accident is much higher than the risk for nonsmokers. Smoking-related accidents can occur when, for example, a driver gropes for a lighter or dropped cigarette and removes his/her hands from the steering wheel of a car. And everyone has read horror stories of families incinerated in a blaze caused by a cigarette butt that smoldered in a pillow and then burst into flames after everyone went to bed.

• Babies born to teenagers who smoke tend to weigh less than those of nonsmokers, and the incidence of miscarriage among teenage smokers is almost twice as great as for teenage non-smokers.

• Medical evidence indisputably links cigarette smoking to major health problems: cancer of the lungs, lips, tongue, mouth, pancreas, esophagus, bladder; increased risk of heart attack and stroke; and emphysema, a devastating lung disorder. Most smokers start while still in their teens. Chances are, if you reach age twenty without smoking, you won't take up the habit later.

• How much does a pack cost you each day? Multiply that by 365. Or do you smoke two packs? What else could you do with that money? A stereo might be nice. . . .

• There is more—much more. All of the bad effects of smoking don't show up for years. But reread this list and you'll see some that affect you right now, every day.

Now the sermon: smoking causes nothing but trouble. It is the nation's number one health problem and is the leading cause of preventable deaths. The amount of money spent on smoking and its consequences is almost incalculable: the cost of cigarettes; amount spent on treating the sick; time and money lost in productivity; cost in human lives. Research scientists are trying desperately to devise a cure for cancer; for many of you, the ''cure'' is up to you.

When Mark Twain said that quitting was easy—that's why he had done it so often—he could have spoken for millions of Americans. When you decide to quit, you will have a number of options to make it easier. You can go cold turkey or use gradual withdrawal; you can go it alone or you can get help. Many techniques and programs have been devised to help smokers become exsmokers. To get information about them, turn to:

American Cancer Society (or local affiliate)
777 Third Avenue
New York, NY 10017

American Lung Association (or local affiliate)
1740 Broadway
New York, NY 10019

American Heart Association (or
local affiliate)
7320 Greenville Avenue
Dallas, TX 75231

5 Day Plan to Stop Smoking
Seventh Day Adventist Church
Narcotics Education Division
6840 Eastern Ave., N.W.
Washington, DC 20012

Office on Smoking and Health
U.S. Department of Health and
Human Services
200 Independence Ave., S.W.
Washington, DC 20201

National Interagency Council on
Smoking and Health
7320 Greenville Ave.
Dallas, TX 75231

About 15 percent of all teenagers smoke; that percentage has declined over the years. Do you think that 15 percent is still too many?

Drinking

Basically, drinking is fun. Why else would so many people do it? Over 100 million Americans drink at least occasionally—only about one in three adults doesn't drink at all. An estimated 70 percent of all teenagers drink at least sometimes, which makes alcohol the main drug used by young people.

Since you probably will include alcohol in your lifestyle, you owe it to yourself, to your health, and to your future to learn all you can about how to use, enjoy, and handle it. The problem now is that many of your peers don't do this.

The National Institute of Alcohol Abuse and Alcoholism estimates that *1 of every 20 teenagers has a serious drinking problem.* Of that group, *1 in 10 will become an alcoholic,* just as 11 million Americans are now. Currently, 3½ million teenagers are problem drinkers, and alcohol is a factor in the leading cause of death and injury among young people: motor vehicle accidents.

Here are the basic facts about alcohol, which, although you might already know them, tend to evaporate from memory:

• Alcohol is a drug. It alters moods, causes changes in behavior and in the body, and can be habit-forming.

• People assume that alcohol is a stimulant because they become less inhibited, livelier, and more amusing after a few drinks. Although alcohol does first go to work on the part of the brain that controls inhibitions, it is nonetheless a *depressant*—it acts on your central nervous system and gradually slows down all your body's functions and reflexes.

• Alcohol interferes with sexual feelings and performance. Those of you who have read *Macbeth* remember the character in Act II, Scene 3 who says "It provokes the desire, but takes away the performance." Impotence, even when temporary and alcohol-induced, can be a painful, unhappy experience.

Most of you will drink. The trick is to learn to drink properly so that you can enjoy it in moderation and control its use, rather than have it control you.

• Don't drink faster than your body can burn up alcohol. That works out to one drink every two hours for the average-size person.

• Eat something before or while you're drinking. Food in your stomach will slow the alcohol's passage into the bloodstream and into your brain.

• S-i-p, don't gulp.

• If you're in a crummy mood, hold the sauce. Anger, depression and tension are aggravated by alcohol and can be made *much* worse. Have you heard the term "crying jag"? It describes the times when someone who, already unhappy when he/she starts to drink, becomes morose and weepy and can't stop crying. If you're angry, you might become obnoxious and rude to people you really care about.

• Combining alcohol and other drugs is a major mistake. Two or more drugs can multiply each other's effects and make you feel terrible—or worse. At the least, you may become sleepy or dizzy, get a headache, throw up, or pass out. In addition to increasing your risks of accidents, serious injuries, and death, you also can create serious medical problems for yourself.

• Physical activities and alcohol are another bad mix. Seventy percent of fatal falls, 69 percent of drownings, and 40 percent of work accidents stem from alcohol.

• Time sobers you up, not coffee by the quart or cold showers. Alcohol needs time to leave your system.

• Do you really need another reminder about drinking and driving?

Health professionals consider alcohol a major problem for young people now. They point out that alcoholism—abuse of this drug—

differs for young people and tends to be sudden and severe. Older people develop chronic problems—that is, long-term patterns of behavior and abuse.

But substance abuse of any kind requires help, and alcoholism is a treatable disease. How do you know if you, or someone you care about, needs help? Clues: problem drinkers are those whose drinking causes trouble in major areas of their lives—school, relationships, jobs, health, and the law. Basically, if you're unhappy and your relationships have started to suffer because of your drinking, you have a problem that needs attention right away. Don't wait until a crisis or accident compels you to get help.

• The National Institute on Alcohol Abuse and Alcoholism (NIAA) maintains a state-by-state listing of most public and private treatment facilities. The NIAA collects and disseminates current information on all aspects of alcohol, drinking, and alcoholism, and they can answer almost any question. (National Clearinghouse for Alcohol Information, P.O. Box 2345, Rockville, MD 20852.)

• The National Council on Alcoholism, Inc., maintains a list of nonprofit organizations in more than 100 cities that refer clients to doctors and to public and private agencies that provide treatment for alcoholism. Some organizations on the list provide counseling and treatment services in addition to referrals. (National Council on Alcoholism, Inc., 733 Third Avenue, New York, NY 10017.)

• For a list of agencies concerned with alcoholism and supported by the state governments, write to Alcohol and Drug Problems Association of North America (1101 15th St., N.W., Suite 204, Washington, DC 20005).

• Local Alcoholics Anonymous (AA) chapters, Al-Anon family groups, and some Alateen groups are listed in most telephone books. Or, write to Alcoholics Anonymous (P.O. Box 459, Grand Central Station, New York, NY 10017). You will be sent information on local facilities and other informative material.

Many local AA groups have special meetings for young people. AA's goal is to help alcoholics sober up, stay sober, and work out better patterns of living. Alateen, also part of the AA movement, is specifically for teenaged children of alcoholics; the purpose of the groups is to help those whose parents' drinking creates problems in the teenagers' own lives.

Similarly, Al-Anon is based on the AA model and is designed to help non-alcoholics in a family—or friends and business associates of an alcoholic—deal with the emotional problems triggered by an alcoholic's behavior.

• The Family Services Association of America will send a list of member agencies on request. Most offer counseling for alcohol-related problems. (Family Services Association of America, 44 West 23rd Street, New York, NY 10010.)

Learn about alcohol and respect its effects! Alcohol causes very big problems for teenagers, and you fool yourself if you think you and your friends are immune. We *all* wish we were immune from the unhappy results of excessive and problem drinking, but statistics and stories tell us otherwise.

If you think you or someone you know has a problem and you don't want to work through the mail, talk to someone in your community whom you trust—a friend, relative, doctor, or member of the clergy.

Drugs

The Statistics

The United States is a society that spends at least $120 *billion* a year on drug abuse and its consequences. Ours is a nation in which up to 40 million people use marijuana, 15 million use cocaine, and in which there are about 500,000 heroin addicts. Since 1972 our use of cocaine has risen faster than our use of marijuana, according to the Narcotics Intelligence Estimate. Over the past five years, reports the National Institute of Drug Abuse (NIDA), cocaine-related admissions to drug-abuse clinics have soared 300 percent.

Although considered nonaddictive and an "entertainment" drug by many of its users, cocaine has ruined careers, destroyed families and businesses, and taken the lives of people whose names are household words. Yet, the typical user is a person a teenager considers close to a "role model": affluent, in his twenties or thirties, and apt to be a professional man, an athlete, or an entertainer.

Every estimate must, if anything, err on the low side. Yet this is a risk Dr. William Pollin, director of the National Institute of Drug Abuse, insists on taking. Just as you cannot measure the cost to society of drug abuse in terms of damaged or lost lives and expectations, neither can you measure it in terms of dollars. The very nature of the subject—ranging from the shameful to the illicit to the criminal—tends to prevent the accumulation of "hard" data.

Behind the staggering total of $120 billion a year wasted on drug abuse costs lie a number of estimates. The National Narcotics Intelligence Consumer Committee—a federal interagency group that lists NIDA among its members and is chaired by the Justice Department's Drug Enforcement Agency—offers the following estimates of the range of street values of drugs for 1980 in billions of dollars:

Heroin	$ 7.9 to $ 9.5
Cocaine	26.8 to 32.2
Marijuana	18.3 to 26.8
Hashish	1.5 — 1.5
Other drugs	14.0 to 20.0
Total	*$68.5 to $90.0 billion*

Until a short time ago, some experts would have favored the low side of these estimates, especially in cocaine, but recent drug arrests have shaken their thinking. On one day in the spring of 1982, a cocaine bust in Miami turned up drugs worth about $1 billion on the street. The very next day in the Bahamas, agents seized cocaine worth $130 million on the street.

A study commissioned by the NIDA (statistics follow) included the cost of drug abuse to society in certain categories, but did not count the street value of drugs. Nor did it count an estimate for property stolen to support the heroin habit—over $6 billion. And largely ignored as well were the costs to society of drugs other than heroin, since heroin provided the hard data. In some cases, the figures go back to 1975.

- *Crime-related costs:* $11.2 billion, including careers in crime, those parts of the police, court and penal systems involved, other factors.
- *Losses in productivity:* $4.2 billion, resulting from unemployability and absenteeism, but largely confined to males eighteen to twenty-four who were heroin addicts.
- *Treatment in health facilities:* $1 billion plus.

Compared with our other social problems, drug abuse is a massive evil.

Are we making progress or are we still losing ground?

While heroin is a hidden problem for the middle class because of the stigma attached to its use, there are signs of a trend reversal in the last three years.

For instance, on the positive side, the most recent NIDA study of high school seniors shows that the daily use of marijuana, which peaked at 10.7 percent in 1978, dropped to 7 percent in 1981. The annual use of cocaine, which had doubled from 1976 to 1979, stabilized early in the decade. The annual use of PCP ("angel dust") dropped more than 50 percent from 1979 to 1981, or from 7 percent to 3.2 percent.

On the negative side, though, the use of amphetamines and over-the-counter diet and pep pills has increased sharply. There's still a long way to go.

An overwhelming two-thirds of the high school class of 1981 admitted to some drug use, the NIDA reports—a conservative yet still tragically high figure, higher than that of any other developed country in the Western world.

What's more, accounting in part for the trend reversals are certain social changes over which we have little control. Nationally, drug abuse peaked in the late 1970s along with the percentage of the population made up of adolescents and young adults, and then drug abuse began to decline. Coincidentally, so did record sales. Inflation and cuts in spending money added their impact.

There were changes in perception, too, however. Marijuana is no longer considered "no big deal," as it was in the late 1960s. Among high school seniors, 30 to 55 percent now see regular use of marijuana as damaging.

There is also an increasingly negative attitude toward drugs and dramatic declines in their usage at the college level, some surveys show.

The discovery that the brain manufactures its own morphine—endorphin—may lead us to understand that the heroin addict's brain may not produce a sufficient amount of endorphin. That's a concept we couldn't have considered ten years ago, let alone have tested. "Antagonists," to block the effects of drugs and remove the craving for them, are in the making, including one for marijuana.

But, new and more powerful psychedelic drugs are in the future. In a decade or two, their usage will double—with unforeseen results. Do not forget! LSD, PCP, and the amphetamines were virtually unknown only twenty to thirty years ago.

Look-Alike Drugs

Peruvian flake. Ultracaine. Florida Snow. Toot. Little bottles with big prices, filled with crystalline powder and on sale at your local head shop or by mail order. Sold as novelty items and "incense," the sales pitch runs that the powders look, taste, and feel like the real thing. And the real thing, as you have guessed, is cocaine. The vials warn that inhalation may cause excitement, stimulation, and even toxic effects—but, for users, that is the whole point.

As for uppers and downers—speed and Quaaludes—they're hard to get, and expensive. So, to fill a "gap," a number of look-alike pills are manufactured and sold. All are appealing because they are legal and easily available. But look-alike amphetamines and sedatives, while legal, are *not safe*, and constitute a serious drug-abuse problem. These drugs are a combination of over-the-counter ingredients found in many commercial diet pills and decongestants. Since they do not contain controlled substances—or mislabel their ingredients—they are hard for authorities to curb.

These drugs are usually a combination of caffeine and antiallergic agents such as ephedrine sulphate and phenylpropanolamine. The latter two are commonly used as appetite suppressants and nasal decongestants. The fake downers contain one or more antihistamines, the ingredients found in sleep preparations and cold tablets. Since antihistamines tend to make users feel drowsy, use of fake cocaine can make people feel mellow and relaxed.

But here's the kicker: these drugs can be tremendously dangerous. A number of deaths have been linked to their use. And when taken in combination with alcohol, they can have unpredictable and terrifying results.

Want to know more? Here's what else to dislike about them:

• People who don't normally abuse drugs are introduced to look-alikes and told they're legal and safe. In turn, these fakes give the impression that real, controlled substances are neither as potent nor as dangerous as they really are.

• Physicians and poison centers are deceived by the fakes. When this happens, treatment of emergency patients can suffer.

• There's no product control. The Food and Drug Administration has analyzed samples and discovered mixtures of varying proportions of ingredients under the same labels. You don't know what you're buying when quality control doesn't exist.

• Here's what they do. The cocaine substitutes can collapse blood vessels, depress heart muscle strength, and cause low blood pressure. Phenylpropanolamine constricts blood vessels, increases heart rate, raises blood pressure, and causes collapse in massive enough doses. Since you have no idea what a massive dose might be in any given batch, you place yourself at the mercy of the unknown.

• You may buy the fakes and think you have the real stuff. To get high, though, you have to increase a dose (dangerous in itself). When you finally acquire real speed, or real downers, you overdose because you take too much.

Just because look-alikes appear harmless doesn't mean they are harmless.

Information and Resources

Drug abuse becomes a way of life that is difficult—even impossible—to leave. When you recognize that you or a friend needs help to control a drug problem, or if you just want information about something you don't understand, dozens of organizations and agencies will send you information, suggestions, and referrals.

If you have a drug-related problem and need help, write to Narcotics Anonymous (P.O. Box 622, Sun Valley, CA 91352), or Addicts Anonymous (Box 2000, Lexington, KY 40507).

The most current information about the prevention and treatment of drug abuse is yours for the asking from the government. Write to National Clearinghouse for Drug Abuse Information (Room 10a-56, 5600 Fishers Lane, Rockville, MD 20857). Important booklets include *Let's Talk about Drug Abuse*, which explains popular drugs and their effects clearly and briefly.

Your state has an agency that is responsible for drug-abuse prevention and treatment programs. Check the phone book.

Another national source is the National Association on Drug Abuse Problems, Inc. (355 Lexington Avenue, New York, NY 10017).

The National Institute on Drug Abuse developed the Pyramid Project to provide assistance, instruction, and support for the development of drug-abuse prevention efforts around the country.

For information about Pyramid and for referral to programs in your area, write to The Pyramid Project (Pacific Institute for Research and Evaluation, 3746 Mt. Diablo Blvd., Suite 200, Lafayette, CA 94549; or call toll-free: 1-800-227-0438).

TROUBLE AT HOME

Family crises aren't restricted to a few families in distant towns. All too often, they occur here and now, and maybe to you. How do you recognize them and what can you do? How do you cope with conflict, confusion, and unhappiness that never seems to go away?

Different kinds of problems happen within families. Some reside in the parents and make life difficult for everyone else: child abuse, alcoholism, drug abuse, illness. Others involve stresses between mothers and fathers: quarrels, separation, divorce. And a death in the family can devastate everyone: the wounds take a long time to heal.

If and when problems such as these happen at home, you do have resources and ways to cope.

Child Abuse

Society doesn't legislate the quality of relationships within a family, but it does set certain legal and moral standards that a child's parents or custodians are expected to fulfill. You have the legal right in every state to protection from physical harm and severe emotional impairment. Also, you have the right to adequate food, clothing, shelter, medical care, and access to education.

Child abuse means purposeful injury to a child, usually by a parent or other family member. Every state has laws on what constitutes child abuse which spell out what acts are to be reported to authorities.

For general purposes, categories of child abuse include major physical injury, minor physical injury, sexual maltreatment (including incest, exploitation, rape, and molestation), deprivation of necessities, emotional maltreatment, and abandonment.

Since 1976, there has been a 91 percent increase in the number of reported cases of child abuse! Teachers, doctors, individuals—those who suspect child abuse and those who are its victims—are speaking up and reporting these crimes.

Still, child abuse is not always easy to recognize, and it is even harder to report, especially when it happens to you. It is a terrible ordeal for anyone to endure, and one that is not the victim's fault.

If you are a victim of child abuse, or know someone who is (all forms occur to teenagers, unfortunately), reach out for help: turn to local community service agencies, hot lines, clergy. Call a women's crisis center, the police, or a trusted adult—a teacher, perhaps. Rape and sexual abuse victims can contact the rape crisis center. Every state has Children's Protection Service agencies, specially equipped to handle these problems. Many states and localities also operate child-abuse hot lines. Find out if there's one near you.

Parental Problems

Alcohol, Drug Abuse

Parents often have problems that entangle everyone in the family. Alcoholism and drug abuse frequently destroy or weaken families—no one is unaffected. Living with an alcoholic or drug abuser is painful; recognizing that you can't solve the problem or make the person quit this behavior is even more difficult. Help yourself, even though you can't help your parent or sibling. For help dealing with an alcoholic family member, look in the phone book under Alcoholics Anonymous (discussed earlier in this chapter) and contact Alateen, which helps teenagers learn to cope with alcoholic family members, and Al-Anon, a self-help program for family members of alcoholics. In these settings, you can share your feelings with others who know exactly what you are living through.

Divorce and Separation

Divorce and separation are problems that involve the whole family, your future, and your financial and emotional security. It's hard to watch parents separate, no matter what your age, and like most people in this situation, you will experience many conflicting feelings. You may decide that you need counseling, or want to talk with someone outside your family. Now that you know where resources can be found in your community, use them. Another way to learn about dealing with divorce is to read about how others handle it. Look for:

Gardner, Richard A., M.D., *The Boys and Girls Book about Divorce* (Bantam Books, 1971).

Mayle, Peter, and Robins, Arthur, *Divorce Can Happen to the Nicest People* (Macmillan, 1980).

Richards, Arlene, and Willis, Irene, *How to Get It Together when Your Parents Are Coming Apart* (Bantam Books, 1976).

Rofes, Eric, ed., *The Kids Book of Divorce* (Random House, 1981, hardcover, and Vintage Books, 1982, paperback.) Written by a class of eighth graders in Cambridge, Mass., this book explores, in their words, feelings, problems, and all the common themes of divorce and its effects on a family.

Salk, Lee, *What Every Child Would Like Parents to Know about Divorce* (Warner Books, 1979).

Other books with useful suggestions and comforting advice for times when you and your family are in crises include:

McCoy, Kathleen, *The Teenage Survival Guide: Coping with Problems in Everyday Life* (Simon & Schuster, 1981).

Schowalter, John E., M.D., and Anyan, Walter R., M.D., *The Family Handbook of Adolescence* (Alfred A. Knopf, hardcover 1980, paperback 1981).

Books don't contain all the answers, but they can offer reliable, valuable guidance.

TROUBLE ON THE STREETS

Rape

Rape. Few words evoke the terror and anger of those four letters. Teenage women are among the most likely victims of rape and sexual assault; studies indicate that about half of all rape victims are between the ages of ten and twenty. More frightening still, rape is a violent crime that is on the increase in our society.

These are the straight facts about this vicious act—a misunderstood crime for which the victim still too often pays.

• Rape is a violent crime that no woman invites. Women do not provoke rape by the way they dress, act, or talk—a truth borne out by police statistics and government studies.

• Men rape to dominate, humiliate, and control women. Rape is not a crime of passion, and its goal is not sex or pleasure.

• Rapists use violence, threats, and weapons: women who "comply" do so to avoid death or serious injuries.

• Rape is not always committed by strangers. In fact, more than half of all rapes are committed by friends, relatives, or acquaintances of the victims. This is particularly true when children are raped.

• The FBI estimates that 1 in 10 women will be raped, and that 1 in 4 will be sexually assaulted before they reach age sixteen. Any woman, regardless of her age, race, or occupation, can be a victim. Rape knows no geographic bounds—in fact, half of all reported rapes occur in the victim's home.

• Men and boys are raped, too, by other men, but the chief targets are female.

You owe it to yourself to learn the skills and information required to protect yourself. The key element is your attitude. Research indicates that attackers—muggers, rapists—select victims whom they perceive as helpless and vulnerable. A calm, confident attitude can deter crime (*any* crime) in many cases.

To learn about self-protection, call a local crime prevention board, police department, or women's center. If your school offers a self-defense course, take it; if not, call a local community college and ask if it teaches self-defense techniques. Here are additional tips, suggested by the New York City Advisory Task Force on Rape:

1. Examine your daily routines to figure out where and when your vulnerable moments occur, and modify your habits, if possible, to eliminate these moments. For example, do you park your car in a lonely parking lot? Find another lot, or park in another space (and *always* keep your doors locked). Always be alert, and don't be afraid to change your plans if you sense danger or feel uncomfortable. Better to be late or rude—and safe.

2. If you are attacked, try not to panic. As best you can, assess the situation, breathe deeply, and think about options. If possible, observe your attacker so you can describe him clearly later. Do whatever you must to ensure your safety—that is the most important thing of all. You must remember that whoever attacks you is a severely disturbed person.

3. A woman who has been raped requires immediate medical

and legal help. If this happens to you or a friend, call a rape crisis center (listed in the phone book, or ask the operator) and call the police. Even before a rape victim bathes and changes her clothes, she must see a doctor, since police need physical evidence that can be obtained only from her body and clothing. Her medical needs will include:

- A pelvic exam to check for internal injuries.
- Medical treatment for any internal or external injuries.
- Tests to collect evidence for the courts.
- Information about any medication or recommended treatment.
- A VD test within six weeks of the attack; any follow-up care.
- A pregnancy test within six weeks of the attack; follow-up information about abortion or other alternatives.

4. The victim may very well need counseling, in addition. A rape hot line or agency within the hospital is the best place to recommend the appropriate kind of therapy and the correct people to see. Counseling can be a lifesaver during the difficult times when a woman recovers from the attack, reports the crime and, if possible, prosecutes the rapist. Each step is a difficult, emotionally draining procedure.

Anyone who is raped needs time, support, and care to recover from this ordeal. All rape victims deserve support and credit for having survived.

Shoplifting

Did a promising trend begin to emerge early in the decade? According to figures compiled in a survey by the National Coalition against Shoplifting, the number of teenagers who admitted to shoplifting began to decline while the number of those caught and punished actually rose.

Shoplifting costs $26 *billion* nationwide. That sum *includes* the 6.9 percent of retail store sales, loss of merchandise, the cost of prevention (security guards and devices), and prosecution. But that same figure *excludes* time off for employees to testify in court against shoplifters, the total cost to the criminal justice system, and sales tax revenues lost to cities and states. Thus, the total cost is actually much higher. It costs all of us an additional 2 to 9 percent of the price of our purchases to cover these staggering shoplifting losses: merchants estimate how much they lose and pass the charges on to us.

Shoplifting is hardly the harmless, amusing prank so many teens believe it is!

The reason shoplifters offer for their actions lack both originality and remorse:

- The stores already make enough money—look at the prices they charge.
- They won't miss this item—whatever it is.
- It's a dare—for the fun of it. "I'll see what I can get away with."
- It's a way to impress friends and show off. Or to make new ones, to be accepted.

Very few teenagers who shoplift actually need the item they steal. Of course, there's a big difference between needing something to survive and "needing" the latest Fleetwood Mac album because everyone else owns it and you don't.

If you shoplift—occasionally or often, it doesn't matter—take heed: your chances of getting caught *and* punished continue to increase as stores and law-enforcement officials develop new strategies against shoplifting and shoplifters. They have decided not to tolerate such high losses anymore; retailers are taking vigorous action against shoplifters caught on their premises. In addition to being lectured and scolded by store personnel, more shoplifters are detained until their parents can be notified. Many stores now expect a parent to come down and pick up his or her child before the shoplifter will be released. And although fewer shoplifting cases actually seem to go to trial (because stores are handling the problem on their premises) the percentage of those found guilty and fined is rising, too.

The conclusion: merchants, security guards, police—all are taking shoplifting very seriously these days. You should, too.

Fascinating footnote: surveys repeatedly indicate that teenagers think society as a whole is too lenient with shoplifters. Respondents are often quoted as saying they think police and the courts should punish shoplifters more severely for their actions. That now seems to be happening, and with telling results.

Vandalism

How would you feel if you walked into your bedroom and saw obscenities painted all over one wall, your TV antenna twisted like a pretzel, and your records scratched up in a spokelike pattern?

Or if you opened your locker to find your down ski jacket slashed and feathers covering the pages of your ripped notebooks?

You might be threatened, angry, furious, or depressed—or all of these—because you were the victim of a vandal.

When someone defaces or destroys part of your environment without your consent—that's vandalism.

The above are examples of vandalism which affect you personally.

Public vandalism affects us all. A jammed public phone can be a serious problem when you have an important call to make. A turned-around street sign can cause you to lose your way. A defaced building is an eyesore to the entire community.

Vandalism among teens crosses all socioeconomic groups and has been increasing at an alarming rate—although it is not only an adolescent activity. Adults are vandals as well.

Between $250 million and $500 million is spent annually to repair the damage done to public and private facilities by vandals. In time that money comes out of our pockets—either in the form of higher taxes or higher rates and prices charged by the companies whose property has been damaged.

The Reasons

Psychologists and sociologists have offered myriad reasons for the destructive behavior.

- Anger
- Boredom
- Discontent
- Lack of meaningful work
- Influence of TV violence

- Physical designs of our environment which provide opportunity for vandals
- The breakdown of authority figures (parents, teachers, law-enforcement officials are not as threatening today as they have been in the past)
- The lax enforcement of punishment

How to Fight Back

Society's acceptance of this antisocial behavior has been one of the major reasons vandalism has flourished. Recently, though, as vandalism personally affects more and more people, an awareness has developed that this behavior should be tolerated no longer.

Teens who have been personally vandalized by schoolmates are becoming intolerant of this acting out and are mobilizing. On the rise are human-relations clubs (which foster respect for others), victims' clubs, youth advocate programs, and student governing boards which are trying all sorts of creative programs to curb vandalism.

You are the best people to deal with vandalism as it affects your age group. You understand that horseplay is part of the fun of your teen years. You also know that destruction is another story entirely. Studies show that once you think behavior is destructive, you are tough on the offender.

Student governing boards have found one of the most effective ways of dealing with vandals is to have the victim confront the offender and negotiate how the destruction can be repaired. (Not the offender's parents. The *offender*.)

This does two things.

It takes the anonymity out of the act. (The vandal didn't merely break into a locker, slash a ski jacket, and rip some notebooks; he broke into *Nicole's* locker, slashed *her* ski jacket, and ripped *her* notebooks.) And it teaches the vandal how much work and money is involved in repairing the damage he created. (Trying to get spray-painted obscenities off the face of a building can be an endless, exhausting job—not worth the ten minutes of "fun" the vandal had putting them on.)

Peer pressure: you know how much influence it can have on your life—both positively and negatively. Join the groups that are trying to use it to reduce the vandalism which plagues our communities.

Know Your Rights

If you've ever watched a police show on TV (in other words, all of you!), you have an idea of what happens when a person is arrested. The thought that this could ever happen to you might seem laughable, but people are arrested for many crimes—among them, drunk driving, vandalism, drug-abuse violations, larceny, and theft. In 1980, for example, of 1,385,000 arrests of people under 18, a full 68,444 were for drug-abuse violations. And in the decade 1970–80, the arrest rate for driving while intoxicated rose a spectacular 473 percent. If you or any friends engage in any criminal behavior, the chances of your getting caught have risen, and experts expect that trend to continue.

If you are arrested, you will be read your "Miranda" rights, which inform you of your right to remain silent, to make one telephone call, and to have a lawyer. That's precisely what you should do. Don't fool around with the police, offer excuses, or say anything at all. Use your phone call to contact your parents or someone who can get a lawyer right away if your situation requires one. It is not farfetched to suggest that, along with the names of doctors, dentists, and others to call in an emergency, you or your parents should have the name of a good criminal lawyer. If, however, you have little money, you are entitled to free legal representation by an attorney from the Legal Aid Society or the Public Defender's Office. The procedures that follow arrests are complicated and technical, and require expert help to guide you through them.

Generally speaking, every state determines the age at which its citizens are considered adults for legal purposes—the so-called age of majority. States set minimum ages for such activities as drinking, obtaining a driver's license, making a contract, serving on a jury, and attending school. In most states, then, you can be considered an adult for some purposes but not for others.

The subject of legal rights and young people is fascinating and one with which you should not remain unfamiliar. To learn more, a good place to start is *The Rights of Young People: The Basic ACLU Guide to a Young Person's Rights*, by Alan Sussman (Avon Books,

1977). The book, in a question and answer format, is short on jargon and technical language, and long on clear, concise explanations of subjects as diverse as adoption, medical care, and procedures in criminal actions. (For students' rights, see the following section.)

If you think your rights have been violated, or if you are in legal trouble and don't know what to do, contact your local Public Defender's Office, or Legal Aid Society, or local branches of the American Civil Liberties Union.

Organizations concerned on a national level with legal issues involving young people—and which can help answer basic questions and suggest appropriate agencies to turn to—include:

American Civil Liberties Union
Juvenile Rights Project
132 West 43rd St.
New York, NY 10036

National Juvenile Law Center
St. Louis University
3642 Lindell Boulevard
St. Louis, MO 63108

Youth Law Center
693 Mission St.
San Francisco, CA 94105

TROUBLE AND SCHOOL

With all the influences and activities competing for your attention, you may feel at times that school takes up too much of your time. In fact, school might seem like a total waste.

While some of you doubtless enjoy school, or at least some aspects of this daily ritual, it's the rare person who never considers just dropping out—quitting, hiking across country, getting a job. For most of you, these fantasies remain just that, but others—confused, bored, or maybe even lazy—call it quits too soon. Here are issues, and alternatives, to consider:

Truancy

Skipping school, constant tardiness, and other disrespectful behavior ultimately bounce back to you. Your teachers aren't wounded that you don't show up, your classmates learn to live with your erratic appearances, and life goes on. But what happens to *you*?

When will you finish school, and in what shape? In fact, *will* you finish school?

Dropping Out

Dropping out of school with neither job skills nor plans for continuing your education is almost always a mistake. Unless you have exceptional, recognized talent, you foreclose most options for your future. The majority of jobs, even those employing only basic skills, require a high school diploma to go with them. Employers want to see that piece of paper because it signifies that a person is serious, literate, can complete a task, and has met certain standards. Experts concur that high school dropouts can expect lower lifetime earnings than peers who complete high school. Most job and apprenticeship training programs require a high school diploma. And the National Education Association stresses that job market survival skills in the coming decade will include literacy, decision-making ability, and the ability to function in ambiguous situations. You may not see an immediate tie-in with your English lit class, but knowledge and experience add up, and you owe it to your future to equip yourself as best you can.

Before you drop out, look for alternatives. Talk to a school guidance counselor or teacher. Surely you can find at least one person to trust and talk to. Many school districts combine work-study programs that let you earn your diploma with credits for both classes and work experience. Night classes, which free your days for work and allow you to study at your own speed, are another possibility. Find out whether your community sponsors any alternative schools and explore that option, too.

Stick it out. You will, eventually, appreciate the effort and the lift it gives your self-esteem and financial goals.

If you're bored because school seems a little simpleminded and your courses are too easy, contact local community colleges and ask whether you can augment your program with classes outside the school. Enlist a guidance counselor or teacher if you aren't certain how to enrich your school life. Don't allow yourself to feel mired and bored: it can be all too easy to let your schoolwork slide if overconfidence edges into cockiness. You could wind up in big trouble and sabotage your goals, all at once.

Cheating

A national survey early in the decade revealed that 66 percent of all teenagers admitted to cheating on exams—and 15 percent confessed that they had been caught. Most admitted that it is morally wrong, and blamed the pressures to excel and succeed for their cheating.

Next time you consider cheating, think about what you expect to gain, and locate your sense of self-responsibility. Simply put, cheating is a bad habit, and the consequences, if you're caught, will at best be painful and embarrassing. At worst, your academic record will be tainted—a ''little'' fact that can haunt you as you plan for your education and career.

Students' Legal Rights

It may come as a surprise to learn that students have legal rights, particularly since favorite terms to describe high school include ''prison'' and ''jail'' and ''torture.'' School administrators have great authority in your lives, but, essentially, they are limited to issues concerning education. They are entitled to respect and obedience, and you are entitled to your rights.

One way to learn about them, whether you are in high school or college, is to read *The Rights of Students: The Basic ACLU Guide to a Student's Rights*, by Alan H. Levine and Eve Cary (Avon Books, 1977). Check your library and bookstore for additional references.

TROUBLE AND MONEY

Debt

''He that goes a borrowing goes a sorrowing,'' Benjamin Franklin wrote in *Poor Richard's Almanac*. Overlook the sexism of his language and that observation holds true, all too often, today.

As a group, teenagers rarely dig themselves into the kind of financial rut that parents do—you don't have the opportunity, really—but you can accumulate big debts. Moreover, as soon as many of you find your first jobs, go off to college, get credit cards, and start buying goods on ''time''—change your financial lives— you'll wind up in the hole, too.

Why? Because you've never learned to handle money, credit, and debt properly. You have spent most of your life learning how to earn a living and very little on how to budget, spend, borrow, and save.

If you find yourselves in financial difficulties, the reason is that you don't understand the disciplines of living within your income and on a budget. The problem becomes abruptly acute the day you move into your own apartments or houses or dormitories. And typically you're in a hurry to move out, set up your own home, buy a car and other essentials, or pal around with your friends at school. The book you are now reading may represent your *first* training at home or school on how to budget and how to plan for financial needs—fixed expenses, savings, and luxuries.

Consider the following typical situations:

You move into an apartment with a high school friend at the time you start your first job. You decide to buy a car—you've wanted one all your life. But can you afford car payments right now? Have you looked at your expenses and measured them against your income? Do you, in short, have a budget? Look at your finances:

• What are your fixed expenses every month? These must include rent, utilities, perhaps insurance payments. Your first obligation is to pay these bills on time. Include *savings* as a fixed expense or you'll never, never, discipline yourself into saving!

• How much is left? For food, medical care, trips to the dentist, clothes, transportation?

• How much do you spend on entertainment and recreation? How much do you have for gifts you must buy? Contributions?

• Do you still have enough money in your pocket at every pay period? Or do you have to borrow from someone, or juggle your expenses? Hold off on a utility bill, or let a store payment slide?

Be honest. If you can't handle your current expenses comfortably, if you must nickel-and-dime it a week before your paycheck is due, how will you meet monthly installments on a car loan? It's a huge disappointment, and frustrating—but you can't afford car payments right now.

Take this process one step further. You already include in your fixed monthly costs your regular car and insurance payments. You'd like to buy a videocassette recorder. Repeat the process. Ask yourself: Can I afford another set of payments? Maybe you want a vacation this year. Will you have to choose? Choose now, before you tie up any more of your present and anticipated income.

You go to college, away from home for the first time. Your parents send an allowance every month, and you have a checking account. Although you'd like more money, you admit you're in pretty good shape, except that you always seem to be low—or broke—by the twentieth or twenty-fifth of every month, a week before the next lifesaving check comes through. Meanwhile, the clothing store near campus offers easy credit to students, so you get a charge card. You also apply for and receive a charge account at the school bookstore. You are not permitted to charge over a certain dollar amount at either store, but it doesn't take long until you charge to the maximum. Problem: where's the money to pay those bills going to come from? And—whoops—you forgot that you owe on that mail-order record club, too.

You must make choices. Local charge cards can lure you into trouble: a bill follows every purchase by no more than a month. A good rule of thumb for many college students is that if you can't afford to pay for an item, in cash and right now, you can't afford it. Period. If you're among the lucky minority who manage your finances well and have money at the end of your allowance period, apply for local charge cards. But if you already have trouble meeting expenses on your allowance, your alternatives are (1) to ask your parents to raise your allowance, and document your case for more money (this tactic may not work—they may not have the money, or may feel you already live well enough, or may have other reasons for declining your request), or (2) to look for a part-time job, or type term papers, or come up with another way to earn cash.

Another possibility is trim your budget to what's really important to you. Meanwhile, *pay those bills.* Try your best to make the full payments, on time, even though it means skipping dinner out with the crowd or missing a weekend at another campus. These pleasures are only temporary, but imperiling your credit rating is a long-term threat. If you find you can't make the full payments on time, talk with the store managers, decide what you can afford to pay each month, and work it out together. Often they will be happy to agree to your proposals, provided you're honest with them.

And, when your bills are finally paid off, don't charge up a storm again!

Credit Counseling: What and When

Debt doesn't just happen. Careless, reckless spending and failure to plan ahead lead to trouble. But at any point, you can intervene and reassert control over runaway spending habits. You can see a credit counselor and work out a strategy to prevent current debts from overwhelming you or perpetuating bad habits. It's no crime to seek help: in fact, it is a lot more comfortable than ignoring your mail because you know your bills are in those envelopes waiting for you.

Key times to organize your finances occur often: whenever your status changes and with it, your income, expenses, and goals. For example, when you move away from home, go to college, get your first job, or acquire a new roommate, stop to examine your new financial obligations, or you could easily find yourself in trouble.

Heed these warnings that you're about to slide dangerously into debt:

- You use your long-sought credit card to get cash advances to tide you over and pay for routine expenses.
- More and more of your income is spent on paying off debts.
- You have to decline invitations and social events because your choice is between dinner and your department store bill.
- You borrow often from friends and family—and you're none too swift about repayment.

A nonprofit credit-counseling agency will help you overhaul your current spending. You will be encouraged and advised to work out a repayment schedule where you make full payments to your creditors. This means you will have less—or even no—discretionary income for the time being. Your income is a finite resource; you can't mint dollars to pay for movies, or dinner, or a weekend camping trip. If your woes are really severe, you may have to reduce your payments; credit counselors advise that, whenever possible, you avoid that step. Any time you reduce the sum you pay off each month, you risk weakening your credit rating, and that will haunt you when you want to borrow money for a new car, or look for an apartment, or apply for a new round of credit cards.

Credit counseling can be found under "consumer credit counseling" in your Yellow Pages. You also can find these services through the Family Service Association and such local organizations as church groups, the YMCA, and YWCA.

For names and addresses of agencies near you, write to the National Foundation for Consumer Credit (8701 Georgia Avenue, Suite 601, Silver Spring, MD 20910), or the Family Service Association (44 East 23rd St., New York, NY 10010).

Expect to work out a financial plan that will avoid calamities and help you build a sound, secure financial future. Just the process of filling out an application form—explaining your income, routine obligations, and economic goals—may help you to work out a satisfactory plan.

Pay Your Bills—or Pay the Piper

If you are a young adult in debt and are falling slightly behind in your payments, the laws and enforcement agencies have been giving you more and more protection in recent years against abuses by some creditors and debt collectors. But the reality remains: you, the consumer, in general must pay whatever you agreed to pay for whatever you buy. The consequences if you don't can be mighty unpleasant to you in many instances.

• Usually, the creditor will try first to reach you to convince you to pay. This pressure is entirely proper.

• If such dunning fails, you may be sued. This means you will lose automatically by default unless you file an answer in court saying why you think you don't have to pay. If you do contest the debt, you will have to appear in court, at least for any trial—meaning you must take time off from work or school or whatever. And unless your reason for not paying is good, you will lose.

• If you lose a lawsuit, the creditor has the legal right to take assets of yours to pay the amount due (sometimes with legal expenses added). This usually includes at least such assets as bank accounts, but not such possessions as household furnishings, except when the money owed was used to buy them.

• The creditor can in most states also serve a paper on your employer ordering him/her to deduct 10 percent of your wages (unless you are in the lower income brackets, in which case complicated limitations apply). This means annoying paperwork for your boss as well as deductions from your paycheck until all owed money has been repaid.

• Long before these events, the creditor normally will notify a credit bureau that you are delinquent. This information then may be provided to other creditors from whom you wish to obtain credit.

• The bad mark on your credit rating is not necessarily erased just because you eventually pay the bill. On the contrary, the fact that you did not pay initially on your own will remain on file for a long time. And if you go bankrupt to get out from under your debts, you will lose valuable assets you have. Your credit rating will show this for seven years.

• Frequently, a "security interest" exists in property you bought with the money borrowed. In such cases, that property can be repossessed to help pay your bills. If, after the property is sold, the creditor still has not collected the full amount, you can be sued for the balance (a "deficiency"). You could wind up losing a car you purchased, plus whatever you paid for the car, and still owe more money, even though the car has been repossessed. To collect the deficiency, the creditor may obtain a garnishment on your wages.

• A creditor may put a lien on your house, too, if you happen to own one and if it isn't exempt under the laws of your state. This prevents your selling the house unless the creditor is paid, and may permit the creditor to sell your house to pay the debt and give you whatever is left.

• If you owe money to a bank, and have deposits or other assets in an account there, the bank can "set off" what it owes you and what you owe it simply by taking your deposit to satisfy the claim—without even going to court. You are the one who may have to go to court if you claim the institution is wrong.

• If you are sued and defend, you may have to get a lawyer to guide you through the complicated legal procedures—unless you have the time and knowledge to handle it on your own. Unless you can qualify for free legal services under some special program, you may owe a legal bill as well.

Sound rough? It is! But it is also rough on those who do pay their bills, because if some debtors can get goods and services without paying, the cost of their defaults is included in the prices we pay for everything we buy.

Illegitimate collection tactics by collection agencies, such as late-night phone calls and spreading "deadbeat" rumors about you, are prohibited under the Federal Fair Debt Collection Practices Act and by many state laws and Federal Trade Commission decisions.

There can be a number of reasons that you do not pay a bill: you may indeed not owe the money claimed. The transaction may never have happened. An error in billing may have occurred. The goods were defective and the warranty, if any, was breached, entitling you to return the goods or deduct something. You have defenses against the seller in any of these instances, and you have rights under the FTC "holder in due course" rule. But before refusing to pay, consult an attorney, or a consumer protection agency, or a knowledgeable person you trust who can give you sound advice. Don't fight blindfolded!

SWITCHBOARDS AND HOT LINES— A SUMMARY

With America's highly developed telecommunications network, you can dial a joke or a horoscope, get an up-to-the-minute weather report, learn the latest sports scores, report emergencies, and talk endlessly with family and friends around the globe. In Chapter 14, *Your Health*, you learned about some health-oriented hot lines. Just as important, life-preserving help is never more than a phone call away. No matter how troubling the problems you encounter, how low your spirits plummet, or how bleak your future seems, someone at the other end of the receiver wants to guide you to the assistance you need.

You probably are already familiar with hot lines in your area. Hundreds of communities around the country sponsor them. They dispense advice and referrals, and lend a sympathetic ear to callers of all ages, backgrounds, and woes. You can find these hot lines listed in the White Pages of your phone book, or you can ask directory assistance. Consider them a primary resource for information: operators can help you cope with the spectrum of human cares. Many towns and cities have hot lines expressly for people who are considering suicide—trained and understanding counselors befriend and guide callers through a crisis and, if requested, recommend sources of help and treatment.

The following nationwide toll-free hot lines serve hundreds of thousands of callers each year:

Runaways

National Runaway Switchboard
1-800-621-4000
1-800-972-6004 (Illinois)
929-5150 (Chicago)

The Switchboard, based in Chicago, operates twenty-four hours a day, year round, and serves the entire continental United States and some islands in the Caribbean. It helps callers in a number of ways. It delivers runaways' messages to parents, and can arrange three-way calls among parents, the runaway, and a trained switchboard operator. In addition, its volunteers have available listings of more than 7,000 resources and agencies that provide services to young people at low (or no) cost. Most callers to the switchboard are teenagers; the average age is sixteen. All callers remain anonymous, though if you request referrals to an agency, the operator will need to know where you're calling from. The operator will help identify your problem, discuss your options, and link you with an agency in the community where you are located. Established in 1974, the hot line now handles more than 200,000 calls each year.

Runaway Hot Line (previously called Operation Peace of Mind)
1-800-231-6946
1-800-392-3352 (Texas, except Houston)
524-3821 (Houston)

This hot line, operating out of Houston, is funded by the Texas Governor's Office of Volunteer Services. Like the National Runaway Switchboard, it reunites runaways with their parents via the phone and provides referrals of legal aid, shelter, medical assistance, and food, from a national data base. Operators try to match your problems and financial situation with appropriate social service agencies, many of which limit their services to people eighteen and under. The hot line operates around the clock—and around the year.

Abortion

National Abortion Federation
1-800-223-0618
688-8516 (New York City)
Weekdays 10:00 A.M. to 6:00 P.M., E.S.T.

Sexually Transmitted Diseases

The National VD Hotline
1-800-227-8922 (except Alaska and Hawaii)
Weekdays 8:00 A.M. to 8:00 P.M.; Saturdays and Sundays
10:00 A.M. to 5:00 P.M.; Pacific Time

18

MOVING OUT, MOVING ON

CONTENTS

Graduation is a memory. Your thoughts now focus on starting a home of your own. Chances are, your first move away from your parents' house will be to an apartment or shared house, if not to a college dormitory. Few, if any, of you can currently afford to purchase your own condominium, co-op, house, or mobile home.

No matter what arrangements you make, moving out on your own is a momentous step—at once exhilarating and scary. To minimize the hassles and make your move a happy and successful one, here are some things you should know.

How to Select Housing

Each of us has a wish list of features to incorporate into our dream house or apartment. Identify which ones appear on your list as you study real estate ads and visit different apartments and houses. Decide what features are essential for you and which ones are frills:

- *Location.* Close to work or school, public transportation, and shopping centers.
- *Buildings and grounds.* Well-maintained building; locked entrances; clean and brightly lit public areas (halls, laundry room, vestibules, stairs); adequate fire escapes and fire exits.
- *Living space.* Sufficient storage room; good ventilation; well-placed windows; weatherproofed windows and screens; shades or venetian blinds; good plumbing and modern fixtures; well-built doors and cabinets; sturdy locks; adequate electrical outlets; sound floors; well-proportioned rooms; and fringes—dishwasher, central air conditioning, wall-to-wall carpeting.
- *Services.* Laundry room on premises; live-in superintendent; parking space or garage; trash disposal; tight security; locked mailboxes.

The perfect apartment incorporates all of these qualities into its design and operation, and at a laughably low rent. But since you live in the real world, you will have to make compromises on at least some of these; however, never rent an apartment in which you feel unsafe, no matter how minuscule the rent. If you think the building is a firetrap, or the neighborhood seems dangerous, stay away. Your peace of mind (and that of your parents) is worth a few more dollars a month for a better location—not to mention your life!

Another factor you must consider is size. If you plan to live alone, chances are you don't need more than a studio (efficiency) or one-bedroom apartment. Naturally, extra space is always welcome—to create a study or workroom, or to house guests. If you have roommates, try to arrange matters so each of you has your own bedroom, along with the shared common spaces.

The key to your choice is rent. The old rule held that one month's rent should not exceed one week's take-home pay. That guideline has gone the way of gas at 29 cents a gallon and nickel ice-cream cones. (They really did exist, and not so long ago, either!) Consider this an ideal figure, though. If you can't meet it, shrug philosophically. You have lots of company. Do try to limit your rent to a week's gross pay; certainly not much more than that.

Before you rent, establish your budget, either alone or with your roommate. Set a comfortable ceiling for your rent—that means, allow yourself so much and no more for rent. Be honest. Rent is one expense you can't defer until you have extra funds. If you cannot afford an apartment of your own right now, consider a share, or add another roommate. Or wait just a little longer.

Finding an Apartment

Whether you live in a big city or cozy suburb, finding an apartment takes time, energy, and initiative. The following rundown describes tried and true methods, plus a few surprises:

• *Newspaper ads.* A typical ad might read something like this: "6 rms, rv vu." In fact, this shorthand also was the name of a Broadway play, but it typifies the language found in newspaper real estate listings. In case you didn't guess, it translates into "six rooms, river view."

The specialized vocabulary of real estate ads takes some time to learn, but, once decoded, is actually quite descriptive. In time, you'll learn that what ads leave out can be as significant as what they stress, and certain words indicate special problems. "Charming'' often can be a euphemism for run-down, for example. ''Needs work'' is a dead giveaway that the place is a shambles.

In any event, when you start looking for an apartment or house, spend time reading through the ads and get a feel for what is on the market, what the range of rents is these days, and where to find places you can afford. If you don't understand an ad, call the newspaper's advertising department and request help. Experienced apartment hunters know that the best time to check ads is Sunday; better yet, buy the real estate section on Saturday and start phoning. Make appointments to see as many apartments as you can arrange and don't be deterred by a busy phone signal. A lot of other people read the ads, too.

• *Real estate agents.* If you want a shortcut to finding an apartment, consult real estate agents who specialize in locating rentals for a price. Typically, you pay them one or two months' rent (or a fixed percentage of one year's rent) if you rent one of their listings. Expect to follow up on their leads every day—some agencies deal with so many customers that you can get lost. Don't be afraid to push or nag. They don't make any money from you until you sign a lease.

• *Rental services/apartment finders.* Before you rush to sign up with a rental service, find out what, exactly, you're buying. You usually pay a fee to see the service's ''exclusive'' list of apartments. The catch: frequently, the listings are culled from the newspaper and, in fact, are identical to the ones you've already read.

• *Apartment management.* Either the superintendent or the building's owner can help you rent an apartment. Contact these people in buildings you've already scouted and know you like. Generally, management companies are found in cities; they take care of renting vacant units. To find the managing company's name, look for a sign on or near the door or in the vestibule.

• *The grapevine.* A time-tested method of finding shelter is to tell absolutely everyone that you're looking for an apartment. Ask around and don't be shy about it. It works.

• *Local sources.* Check bulletin boards at the supermarket, library, community center, student union; read through campus newspapers; stroll through neighborhoods, look for signs, befriend doormen and superintendents.

• *Be inventive.* A medical student in New York slipped inserts offering a finder's fee for getting him an apartment into copies of a best-selling mystery at a local bookshop. Bold tactics can pay off.

Once you actually find an apartment that you want to rent, take your time whenever possible. Check the plumbing, consult your wish list, bring along a friend, and ask for advice. Try to contact someone who lives in the building and ask about building services, such as heat and hot water. Quiz tenants, too, about the presence of vermin, such as cockroaches and ants, if you're at all suspicious. Satisfy yourself that whatever problems appear to you are manageable and that you can live comfortably in your new home. Try not to sign a lease under pressure. In a tight housing market, you may lack the luxury of time but, whenever possible, give yourself a day or two to decide.

Taking Possession

Once you sign the lease, you won't be able to wait for the day when you can move in, hang up your clothes, plug in the stereo, and settle down. Before you do:

• Call the phone company and find out what monthly service options are available. Ask about and compare service charges for all models. Choose the options that fit your budget and phone habits, and expect to pay a deposit (refundable when you terminate your service) before you receive your new number and the company hooks your phone into the system.

• If utilities (gas and electricity) are not included in your rent, phone the local company. The company will need your name, address, apartment number, and the exact date you plan to move in so it can turn on the juice. You may have to pay a deposit first, or it will be tacked onto your first monthly bill.

• Most landlords carry insurance that covers all their rental property. That insurance does not cover your personal belongings, however, so as soon as you can, investigate and buy a renter's policy to insure your belongings against fire, flood, theft, vandalism, and other natural and man-made disasters. You may choose a policy that includes personal liability protection and medical payments to others. Compare insurance policies before you buy. Costs vary according to a number of factors, including your location, duration of the policy, the amount of protection you want, and what you want covered. Riders for jewelry and silverware can be prohibitively expensive.

Home Is where the Lease Is

As a renter, direct your most critical questions to your landlord. When you find a place you want to rent, don't get so excited that your judgment goes AWOL and you forget to ask basic, essential questions. Guidelines:

• When you put down the application fee, ask if it commits you to take the dwelling if you are accepted. If you reject the unit, will any charges be deducted from your application payment? What happens to the fee if the prospective landlord fails to provide you with a satisfactory dwelling? How long will it take after the application for the landlord to advise you of an acceptance?

• When you tour the dwelling, make a list of all damages and needed repairs. Ask the landlord if he/she will repair them before you sign a rental agreement. Have the landlord make a list of damages. Keep a copy of that list, and get a completion date for repair of damages.

• If the landlord refuses to repair the problems, ask him/her to sign an acknowledgment that you have pointed them out. Have the landlord attach a copy of the reported damages to your lease.

• If you still plan to rent, despite the damages, keep a copy of the report for your records to protect you against claims when you move out. Find out what repairs are your responsibility as a tenant. Have this spelled out in your rental agreement.

• Obtain in writing the address and phone number where the owner or landlord can be contacted, so you can locate either one in an emergency.

• Be sure you understand all terms of your lease. Ask questions about the "legalese." If need be, ask a parent or friend for assistance. Don't rely on oral promises; everything must be in writing.

• If the landlord has set up rules and regulations to preserve his property or to safeguard tenants, learn what the rules are before you sign.

• Be clear on all deposits required. There may be a cleaning deposit, which allows the landlord to clean or paint after you move; a damage deposit, which must be returned when you leave the premises unless you caused excess physical damage; a security deposit sometimes used interchangeably with a damage deposit. *Read* your lease to discover if there are any reservations or conditions affecting refund of these deposits.

• Find out whether the landlord, or the city, has a policy for subleasing. Never sublet your apartment unless you know it's legal; similarly, don't rent a sublet if you have any suspicions that you could be evicted by the landlord.

When you sign a lease, you sign a legal document. A lease spells out the amount of rent charged for the unit; what services are included for the rent; the duration of the lease; when the rent falls due; the responsibilities of both landlord and tenant. You are protected from sudden rent increases unless the lease allows increases in certain circumstances, such as a rise in fuel bills. Heed the list of dos and don'ts contained in the lease (no pets, for example). Many leases include riders—that is, extra clauses not contained within the body of the lease. Study each one thoroughly before you initial or sign it.

Your signature on the dotted line commits you to major responsibilities. These include: keeping the apartment clean and neat; disposing of your garbage; safe use of heating, plumbing, and electricity; prompt payment of rent; and careful maintenance of the landlord's property. In return, the landlord contracts to keep the building in good condition; maintain all common areas; provide for garbage removal; supply all services required by local law (heat, hot water); and maintain appliances and services.

The landlord-tenant relationship can become complicated, especially in a dispute. In general, state and local laws cover most facets of this relationship, and the federal government stays out of this area with a few critical exceptions. Be aware: no landlord or real estate agent can deny you housing on the basis of your sex, race, religion, or national origin. If you have reason to believe that you have been discriminated against, do not hesitate to call your local civil rights commission, division of the American Civil Liberties Union, and local housing authority. In addition, contact the Director, Fair Housing and Equal Opportunity (Department of Housing and Urban Development, Washington, DC 20410: telephone: 1-800-

424-8590; or 202-755-7252 in Washington). HUD officials are on guard against the following types of housing discrimination:

- *Steering:* being directed to buy or rent in a particular neighborhood or building.
- *Redlining:* being denied a mortgage for a home in a location boycotted by lending institutions.
- *Discriminatory sales:* being rejected as the buyer of a home for other than financial reasons.

As a would-be tenant, learn what your rights and obligations include. Contact tenants' groups in your community and find out whether a tenants' association exists in your new building. And, as always, turn to books for guidance:

Ardman, Harvey, and Ardman, Perry, *The Complete Apartment Guide* (Collier Books, 1982).

Blumberg, Richard E., and Grow, James R., *The Basic ACLU's Guide to a Tenant's Rights* (Avon Books, 1978).

Division of Communications, American Bar Association, *Landlords and Tenants: Your Guide to the Law* (ABA Press, 1982). Order from the Publications Department, American Bar Association, 1155 East 60th Street, Chicago, IL 60637.

Wise Rental Practices (U.S. Department of Housing and Urban Development). Free. Order from Consumer Information Center, Dept. G, Pueblo, CO 81009.

Landlords' Tenant Blacklist: What Can Be Done

An overwhelming majority of tenants are not aware that a special organization has been created to provide landlords with information on whether you have been a troublemaker while a tenant elsewhere. The organization's purpose: to help landlords avoid tenants who make too many complaints, call in the press, bring lawsuits, or just become pests.

If the service becomes widely available and accepted, an almost inevitable result will be that if you get into a fight with your landlord, you might have difficulty getting another lease.

If you find that the toilet doesn't flush and the landlord says it's your fault, it might seem wiser to keep quiet and pay to have it fixed yourself. Otherwise, you could find yourself on an official

"Troublesome Tenant Table" ("TTT" is not a real name, but the substance of this report is real).

On the surface at least, the TTT seems completely legal. It's in the same category as a credit bureau keeping tabs on your record of paying your bills. And the use of blacklists has a long history.

In the nineteenth century, lists of factory workers who joined unions or were troublemakers were compiled. Members of the information exchange could refuse to hire those named on the lists. Some groups of employers used "Yellow Dog" contracts, under which workers promised never to join a union. If a worker joined one, he could be fired and blacklisted.

Now labor laws ban such practices. But there are no laws to prohibit the new tenant blacklist. TTT could be considered a consumer-credit-reporting program, if the landlords extend credit and do not require advance payment of rent.

Even if permissible under existing law, TTT could well be questioned legally because of our increasing recognition of threats to our privacy. And tenants injured by TTT could bring libel suits against the former landlord and TTT agencies if any statement in the reports could be proved to be false and malicious. The courts could award punitive damages.

But let's be realistic. Most tenants don't have the money to finance a major lawsuit. Lawyers might hesitate to take on a case of this type, since their fees would be based on a most speculative recovery. A legislative ban on TTT could run into a constitutional barrier, not because of the issue of impairment of freedom of contract, but because of First Amendment protection of freedom of expression. To prohibit exchange of truthful information presumably would raise at least an issue of violation of the First Amendment.

Assuming you still believe TTT requires some supervision, there still are other options. A TTT agency could be required to supply tenants with full copies of all information furnished to TTT by any landlord, with the name of the person furnishing the information, the date, and any proof.

A TTT agency could also be required to supply the tenant with the name and address of anyone requesting or receiving data on the tenant. The requirements could become onerous enough to discourage TTT services. And if interstate activity were involved, even the Federal Trade Commission might become involved to bar supplying of information to an out-of-state landlord.

TTT is a service that can be good or bad, helpful or harmful, depending on how it is used. In an era of scarcity of space to rent in which to work or live, TTT is a phenomenon that virtually created itself. Now it's up to you to view it and use it wisely.

YOU AND YOUR ROOMMATE

Your roommate uses your last smidgeon of basil and you planned to make your special tomato casserole tonight.

You leave the cap unscrewed from the toothpaste tube, to your roommate's eternal annoyance.

He/she often forgets to switch off the electric coffee machine.

You never wash your dishes.

Habits and disagreements such as these can break up a marriage. They can be equally disruptive among roommates, even if you have been friends since grade school. If you expect to avoid these crises and enjoy a harmonious relationship:

• Decide whose name will appear on the lease, who will receive the utility bills each month, and under whose name the phone will be listed. If you all want to be included in the phone book, identify yourselves by initials only for protection from crank callers.

• Devise a cleaning schedule and assign tasks on a regular or rotating basis.

• Agree, before you move in, how to divide grocery bills and cooking chores. Don't neglect to include condiments (ketchup, for example), spices, dishwashing supplies—every item that both (or all) of you will use.

• Do not—repeat, do not—assume that tasks will be accomplished and problems vanish without your active participation.

• Make sure boundaries and private property rights are respected. Don't borrow anything unless you're 100 percent sure it's all right. Replace what you break.

• Talk now about ownership of jointly purchased items so that if and when you go separate ways, you can take along what belongs to you. And put it in writing, to avoid acrimony.

• Discuss your feelings about guests—the frequency of their visits and length of stay. Work out a policy, but expect to be flexible.

• Plan regular conferences to air any differences and resolve lingering resentments and new problems.

• It should go without saying, but respect your roommate's privacy.

APARTMENT BASICS

Equipment

Setting up your own home costs money, and your first few months on your own will be especially expensive. Practically every day you'll discover a critical need for some item you can't postpone buying—such as a plunger or oven cleaner. Following is a list of the basics; amend it to your special requirements and taste.

Kitchen Equipment

• Dishes and flatware for four; also assorted bowls, platter, butter dish, salt and pepper shakers, coffee mugs.

• Glasses: four each for tall drinks, juice, and wine.

• Pots and pans: two frying pans (large and small), two sauce pans (one large, one small), and covers; kettle, teapot, coffeepot; casserole dish; muffin tins; cookie pan; pie plate; 8-by-8-inch baking pan.

• Utensils: can opener, bottle opener, corkscrew, measuring spoons and cups, knives, mixing bowls, colander, strainer, knife sharpener, cutting board, pancake turner, spatula, ladle, kitchen towels, apron, potholders.

Kitchen Appliances

• Toaster or toaster oven; hand mixer; popcorn machine.

Bed and Bath

• Two sets of sheets and pillowcases for each bed; two blankets or one blanket and comforter for each bed; bedspreads; pillows.

• Two sets of bath towels, hand towels, and washcloths; shower curtain; bath mat.

Essentials

Broom; dustpan; sponges; wastebasket; iron, ironing board; laundry bag or hamper.

Cleaning Supplies

Dishwashing liquid; ammonia; cleanser or scouring powder; window cleaner; pail; rubber gloves; steel wool; floor wax; furniture polish; bathroom-tile cleaner; rags or paper towels; laundry supplies: detergent, bleach, fabric softener, presoak, spray starch.

Keeping Costs Down

If a move is in your future, start to plan now and purchase what you can to break up these big expenses. Study newspaper ads and advertising supplements. Be alert for good buys on bedding, towels, housewares, and other household goods. Stores often hold "white sales" on sheets and towels in January and again in late summer. Time your purchases and save. Don't be too proud to use an old set of dishes and flatware from your family to help you get started while you figure out what, precisely, you need, and decide on your taste and style.

Thrift shops, garage sales, and flea markets can yield treasures to furnish your kitchen and other rooms of your new home.

Renting Furniture

You are furnishing your very first home away from home. You're uncertain about your taste. Perhaps you can't afford the high prices of new furniture. Or maybe you don't want to pay movers to transport your bedroom suite across country. Or you lack eligibility for credit. Whatever your situation, you might consider renting furniture. Should you decide to do this, your home will join 500,000 others in the United States that are now partially or totally furnished with rental furniture. The Furniture Rental Association, based in Columbus, Ohio, estimates that at least 500 rental showrooms, where you can find the pieces you want, operate around the country.

Selecting and renting furniture are similar to buying, up to a point: you decide what pieces you need, where you will place them, allocate a budget, compare prices and styles at different showrooms. But instead of signing a credit or sales slip, you sign a rental agreement.

In general, the longer your rental agreement, the lower your monthly payments. Charges for rental furniture vary according to your region of the country, the kind and number of pieces you rent, and the duration of the rental agreement. Also, consider two other costs before you rent: pick up and delivery charges, and deposits. Typically, you will be expected to pay one month's rental charge as a deposit. It will be refunded when the furniture is returned and found to be in satisfactory condition.

Dealers usually rent new or substantially reconditioned furniture. If you want reconditioned items, ask whether the dealer reduces the rental fee. This is most often the case.

Almost all rental showrooms let you buy the furniture you rent. Read your contract carefully and understand how this provision will work in your case. If you want to buy your pieces at the end of the rental period, your payments usually will be deducted from the purchase price. But, before you buy, check that the price is what you would pay at a retail furniture store. Rental showrooms often charge more for furniture sales.

As a renter, you can expect faster and more convenient delivery than as a buyer. Your entire shipment can arrive within forty-eight hours.

MEET YOUR METERS: GAS AND ELECTRICITY

Utility bills quickly become such a fact of life that it may not occur to you to look at anything other than the bottom line. But when energy costs rise, your monthly utility bills grow ever larger. In addition to learning ways to cut back on energy costs, get in the habit of reading your bills. You can then judge whether your attempts at conservation actually work, while you ferret out other energy-saving methods.

To help you read your bill, a few basic definitions follow:

• *Cubic foot* (cu.ft.) The quantity of natural gas is measured by its volume, hence, in cubic feet.
• *Watt:* The unit of electric power, which indicates the electrical demand or rate of energy delivery.

- *Kilowatt* (kW): 1,000 watts
- *Kilowatt-hour* (kWh): Utilities measure your consumption of electricity by the kilowatt-hour, which is the amount of energy delivered by an hour-long flow of 1 kilowatt of electric power. For example, a 100-watt bulb burning for 10 hours uses 1 kilowatt-hour of electric energy: 100 watts times 10 hours equals 1,000 watt-hours, or 1 kilowatt-hour. Your bill is based on the number of kilowatt-hours you used the previous month.

Locate your electric meter. This device keeps tabs on your use of kilowatt-hours. Here's how to read it:

- Observe that the meter has four dials. Start with the one on the left and read each dial, from left to right. (Note that numbers run clockwise on some dials and counterclockwise on others. The hand always moves in the direction of the higher numbers.)
- The figures above each dial show how many kilowatt-hours are recorded each time the pointer, or hand, makes a complete circle, in units of 10,000, 1,000, 100, and 10 kilowatt-hours.
- Start with the first dial. If the pointer lies between numbers, read the smaller figure; that is, if it is between 7 and 8, read 7. When the pointer lies squarely on a number, look to the dial on the right. If that pointer has not yet passed 0, record the lower number on the preceding dial; if it has passed 0, read the number at which the pointer is aimed. Continue until you have read all four dials.

To estimate your monthly use of electricity, take two readings a month apart and subtract the earlier one from the later one. Monthly readings are based on a cumulative total of kilowatt-hours—or since the meter was last set on zero.

A gas meter tallies the number of cubic feet of natural gas used the previous month. It is read in the same manner as an electric meter. You will note, though, that some gas meters have fewer than four dials and others have more, depending on the local utility. If you have questions about this, call the customer services office at the utility and ask for help.

Start with the dial on the left and read off the number passed by the pointer. Read the remaining dials in the same way, remembering that when a hand points straight at a number, move to the next dial and see whether that pointer has passed zero. After you arrive at a reading, multiply it by 100, since gas is measured in units of 100 cubic feet.

Many rental housing units do not come equipped with gas or electric meters. The landlord has a master meter, or series of meters, that registers the amount of gas and electricity used by all tenants. Your rent covers your percentage of these costs.

You can use your newfound knowledge to estimate how much gas and electricity you use each month. The federal government has suggested that you read the meter right before you go to bed one night and check it first thing in the morning, before you switch on lights and appliances, other than those that are "on" all the time, such as refrigerators and clocks. Subtract the earlier from the later reading to see how much energy was consumed overnight in your house or apartment.

Similarly, if you have air conditioning, take two readings an hour apart while the unit is working. Subtract the earlier reading from the later and measure how much total electricity was used. Then, repeat the process with the air-conditioner turned off and subtract that number from the bigger one. The difference reveals the amount of electricity your air-conditioner uses.

You can repeat this process for any major appliance—dishwasher, washing machine, kiln.

These calculations provide you with very rough figures, but they do indicate your energy consumption and can help stimulate ideas to modify your energy-eating habits.

If you're still befuddled by the process, or would like further guidelines and suggestions, request these pamphlets: *How to Understand Your Utility Bill* and *Tips for Energy Savers* (Energy, P.O. Box 62, Oak Ridge, TN 37830).

Also, your local utility's public affairs office has its own brochure, available on request, that should unravel the mysteries of its particular bill and explain each charge.

THE TELEPHONE

Buying a Telephone

Every month, you pay a rental charge to the phone company for your telephone. In exchange, you receive the instrument and a replacement if it should break or need repair. If you desire a pastel shade or push-button model, or more than one phone, your fees increase. These charges amount to a tidy sum as the months and years roll by. Sooner or later, you may ask yourself whether you can save money by purchasing your phone and, if so, whether you lose any convenience or services.

Customer-owned telephones accounted early in the decade for a small number of residential phones. Among the reasons: many people didn't know whether or how to buy telephones, and many of them didn't know how much rent was embedded in their monthly service charges. In New York State, for example, the phone company explains its charges once each year in an insert to the phone bill, yet a statewide survey showed that an estimated 62 percent of families had no idea what they paid to rent a phone.

A number of companies manufacture phones that are clones of the Bell System models: International Telephone and Telegraph, General Telephone and Electronics, Northern Telecom, and Radio Shack are among the brand names. Each makes the standard model, Princess and Trimline copies, wall and desktop units, with push-button or rotary dials, and in a rainbow of colors. If you plan to buy a phone, or are intrigued by the idea, be alert:

• When you rent from the phone company, you pay for customer service. This includes repair and replacement of phones that break down after months or years of use.

• Determine that you can easily install a new phone. You may have to change the jack first; check with an electronics store or the phone company. All phones manufactured now come with a standard modular jack.

• Compare the prices and warranties of competing manufacturers and stores. It pays to look—different stores charge widely varying prices for identical models.

• Investigate each manufacturer's warranty and ask about the store's repair policy. Can you get a phone on loan while yours is repaired? Who does the actual work? How long does the warranty last, and does the store have its own warranty that exceeds the one given by the manufacturer? Once a warranty expires, you can still have your phone repaired, only now it will be at your expense, so be clear on the different policies.

• Examine your new phone for the Federal Communications

Commission registration number, the ringer equivalence number, and the date of manufacture. These should be stamped on the bottom of the telephone. Report the first two numbers to the phone company; the date assures you that your phone is really new and not a reconditioned antique.

Once you have your new phone at home, unplug the old and return it to the phone company or ask to have it removed. Make sure that the rental charge is deleted from your monthly bill. You won't save a dime if you keep Ma Bell's property stashed in the closet and fail to report that you no longer rent.

To find out where to buy a telephone, check the Yellow Pages under "Telephone Equipment." You can purchase telephones at electronics stores, discount and department stores, and by mail order. Perhaps nearby you have a branch of AT&T's "Phone Center" stores.

Investigate costs thoroughly and match them against what you pay now to see when, and how much, you can save. Compare your current rental charges with the cost of a new phone. Add the cost of a special outlet or kit to convert to a standard modular jack if you need one. Will you need any assistance? Include that expense, too. Look for hidden charges from the phone company and with your new phone, too. When you finish your calculations, you should be able to estimate how much you can save, and know how many months will elapse before your phone starts to pay for itself.

If you have additional questions about buying a phone, call your local consumer affairs council and the Public Service Commission.

Slice Long-Distance Phone Bills

Here you are in your very first apartment or dormitory, and all your family and close friends are hundreds of miles away. You want to talk to them—all of them—often. But, as you learn the day your first phone bill arrives, long-distance charges mount up quickly and contribute to budget overload. It's time to look for alternatives.

Millions of people who like to chat with distant friends have switched to one of the four companies offering long-distance rates that are cheaper than those charged by local phone companies. Depending on where you call, you can save up to 50 percent by using one of the local telephone company's competitors. In the early 1980s, the four companies aggressively competing for residential long-distance calls are MCI Communications, International Telephone and Telegraph, Western Union, and Southern Pacific.

Here's how they work.

You phone the company's computer and enter your personal authorization code (a series of numbers) that has been assigned to you. Next, you punch in the area code and telephone number you are calling.

You've already encountered a potential drawback: to use these services, you must rent or own a push-button telephone. Factor in the rental or purchase cost when you calculate whether to try an alternative service. You can also buy an adaptor, a small push-button panel that attaches to a dial phone, at a ''Phone Center'' store or local electronics shop.

You've completed dialing, or punching in, the numbers. Your call proceeds to AT&T's central switching office, where it's transferred to the competitor's microwave system. From there, it is beamed to a satellite or is transmitted via a network of sending and receiving dishes and satellites. When it reaches its destination, the call is transferred back to the local phone company and, finally, the phone rings in the recipient's house. The whole process takes half a second or less.

These additional facts will help you weigh the pros and cons of buying an alternate long-distance service:

- Currently, all four can be used only in the United States.
- Each company offers a different range of services and rates.
- The competitors do not yet cover all area codes. As a would-be subscriber, make sure that the area codes you call most frequently are hooked into the system, and ask for sample rates.
- To realize any savings, industry specialists say, your long-distance phone bills should total $25 or more each month, since you have to pay either a monthly service charge or spend a minimum amount on calls. The competitors claim that you can save up to 40 or 50 percent on your current bills, depending on the time of day and the places you call.
- Ask about sales gimmicks and holiday rates. Each company

has a toll-free number to call and request information; for the numbers, dial the toll-free operator (1-800-555-1212) or check your phone directory.

- If you plan to try one of these systems, consider buying more than one for a couple of months. Compare the speed with which calls go through, quality of voice transmission, and rates. After a brief trial period, choose the service with features that suit you better.

- When you buy a competitive long-distance service, you don't pay installation or equipment charges. You do continue to pay the phone company for local service and the usual rental fees, taxes, and charges for any long-distance calls you can't dial on the alternate service.

- If you travel regularly, find out whether you can punch in your code from any push-button phone. If so, you will realize big savings on calls made while you're on the road, since hotel phone rates are notoriously high, and collect calls are costly.

If you decide not to switch to an alternate service, learn your local company's long-distance rates. Ask for a rate schedule or read through your bill to see if one is enclosed. Generally, calls are divided into day, evening, and night rates. Night rates are the cheapest. Low rates prevail on weekends and holidays, but each phone company defines these according to its own concept. Rates are calculated from where you place the call. Find out what the different rates are and time your calls accordingly. You might be able to talk for longer than you think, even without an alternate long-distance service. Collect calls (reversing the charges), operator-assisted calls, and charging calls to your home phone from a pay phone are the most costly forms of long-distance service. Avoid making these calls if you want to economize on your phone bills.

SECURITY AT HOME

You might not have given much thought to security while you lived with your folks. Now, though, you must: you are responsible for your own safety and that of your home. Tips:

- Change the locks on your door when you move in. Install a

deadbolt and security chain. (More about security equipment in a moment.)

• Don't keep your car keys and apartment keys on the same keyring. Parking lot attendants can copy any or all of your keys, for example.

• Ask to have a see-through viewer installed in your front door. In many areas, landlords are required by law to provide one.

• Never leave keys in the mailbox or under a doormat. Everyone in the world knows these are common hiding places—burglars, too. If you must, leave keys with a trusted neighbor or friend.

• Keep your door locked, even when you're at home.

• Do not admit delivery people or repair service people until they show you their identification. If in doubt, call the company for verification.

• Become acquainted with your neighbors.

• Install a smoke detector. Many areas require these by law.

• If you go away, arrange to have your mail delivery canceled, or have a friend empty your mailbox daily. Unplug your telephone and use a plug-in electric timer to activate a lamp or radio.

• If you receive strange or obscene phone calls, hang up. If they continue, try blowing a police whistle through the receiver. Report harassing calls to the phone company at once.

There is no such thing as total security against burglars. But use your head! Don't leave doors unlocked, even for a visit of a few minutes' duration. Don't invite the criminal to break in. Make it harder instead, so that he is more likely to give up and look for an easier target than your home.

What, though, should you do if a burglary occurs while you're away, and you return to find a door forced open or a window ajar or broken?

Don't enter the house! Quietly and quickly go to the nearest neighbor and call the police. Only after the police have examined and found your home safe should you enter.

If you do enter a seemingly intact home or apartment and suddenly confront a burglar, back off, extend your empty hands, tell him to take what he wants, assure him you will not try to interfere. Try, though, to remember what he looks like.

And what do you do if you're sitting at the dinner table and you hear a burglar inside your home?

- Rule 1: Avoid confronting him if possible. If there's a phone where you are, quietly call the police. Lock your door, if you can.
- Rule 2: Get help. Throw the window open and yell "Help! Police!" or "Help! Fire!" The "fire" call may be best. The burglar probably will leave as fast as he can when he hears the yell.
- Rule 3: Don't try to capture the burglar, for he'll do whatever he can to escape and avoid arrest—and that means using fists, club, knife, or gun.
- Rule 4: If the burglar confronts you, don't resist. Without obviously staring, study him so you can give a good description to the police and can pick him out in a lineup. After he leaves, try to determine in which direction he ran.
- Rule 5: Forget about guns unless you are an expert. A seldom-used weapon might not work, and there is nothing worse than trying to corner a felon with a useless weapon. That will invite his deadly force.

Now, turn back. What might you sensibly do, while this warning is still in your mind, to reduce the chances of an unauthorized entry into your home?

The most effective door lock is the mortise type, where each mechanism is contained inside the door. Be sure the lock has a separately activated deadlatch or deadbolt that cannot be pried. Even better, install an auxiliary lock with a bolt an inch long that goes into a metal slot in the jamb, or vertical bolt which interlocks with the strike on the jamb.

To prevent the cylinder from being pulled out of the lock, install a cylinder guard. This is a metal plate placed over the cylinder and bolted through the door. It has a small opening which gives access to the keyhole but is too small to permit the cylinder to be yanked out.

Install a key-operated lock on each window. The conventional windowsash fastener is useless.

Also install an electronic alarm system. These range from the familiar break-sensitive tape or wiring on windows and doors to sophisticated sensors that are activated by the body heat of the intruder. The response can be as simple as a local alarm to alert your neighbors or as complicated as sending a message to a central station, which notifies the police or dispatches its own patrols to investigate. Some even dial the police and play a recorded message that a burglary is under way at your address. Check with your police department, and ask for other suggestions from them. The police will be happy to oblige.

LIVING WITH YOUR FAMILY: HOW TO COPE

Dreams of moving out and setting up your own home may shatter before harsh economic truths. Perhaps you lack the money right now, or housing costs in your community have soared out of reach. Despite your long-cherished fantasies, you may find yourself living with your parents, grandparents, nephews, and nieces in a multigenerational household. Living with so many generations (and so many people!) requires a lot of planning to work, and you will have to contribute your share.

For all of you:

• Conduct your household financial arrangements in a businesslike manner, so each family member knows what each bill represents and what his/her share of each expense is. It would be wise to hold regular family meetings to discuss finances, house rules, other problems.

• Plan ahead for changes in family lifestyle, which are inevitable. Learn how to deal with problems in specific ways. It's not necessarily the big philosophical differences that cause problems; it's the nitty-gritty details that trigger the blowups. Work out the routines and make house rules.

• Be creative in living arrangements. A key point is that each person must have some private space belonging to him/her alone.

• Encourage each family member to retain independent activities and by no means try to do all things together.

• Make sure that each family member has some symbols of independence, such as a key to the house, and that each retains some familiar possessions, such as articles of furniture, if possible.

There are many positive factors to this multigenerational era: a more important role for older persons, increased respect all around, and improving our skills in solving conflicts and disagreements. In a way, it's a return to one of the finest aspects of the world's ancient cultures.

SHARED-SPACE HOUSING: BE ON GUARD

By the year 2000, or within less than twenty years, an almost unbelievable one-half of all Americans will be living in some sort of shared-space housing—a cooperative, a condominium, or what's known as a "planned unit development." It's too soon for many of you to make a commitment to shared-space housing, but it is not too soon to be aware of the differences among the three types of shared-space housing:

In a co-op, you own stock or a membership certificate in a corporation that entitles you to a housing unit.

In a condo, you own your own dwelling plus an undivided interest in the condo's common facilities.

In a planned unit development, or PUD, you own a traditional home, usually on a tiny lot, plus a share in a larger, separate piece of land (perhaps a park) owned by a homeowner's association.

The hidden danger in all three types is that sense of "complacency," if not safety, that comes when you feel you're not alone in your risk-taking. But here comes the first of the warnings: you alone have taken on expenses and the responsibility for preferences that often will turn out beyond your personal control and means.

Of course, the condo, the co-op, and the PUD remove you from the rolls of the renters and, in this era, the virtual certainty of annual rent hikes. They do pull you into the desired sphere of building equity for your own benefit. But as you would do if buying a single-family dwelling on its own lot, so you must do when buying shared-space housing: hire an expert to check the soundness of the dwelling, an appraiser to give you an objective estimate of its worth, and a lawyer to study the deed and to make sure you have made no commitments that will come back to haunt you later.

Similarly, when you're contemplating shared-space housing, you must start out "suspecting" even a polite greeting from the developer or management operator who will handle the details of any arrangement you make. You well might consider paying any fee involved in hiring an expert in these plans (guidance counselor, social director, civic planner) to warn you of the pitfalls.

In addition:

• Demand every detail in writing and insist on copies of all total-disclosure documents.

• Don't accept extracts of budgets, agreements, bylaws, and other vital documents, or permit yourself to be rushed (''We have a line waiting to buy'') into simply reading statements in someone else's office.

• Don't sign anything before you have had it checked thoroughly with your attorney. Nor make a down payment until you're sure you can handle all the financing needs and your money will be refunded in full if the deal falls through.

• Make sure you understand all costs and obligations, such as assessments related to shared facilities, expenses of maintenance and desired improvements, essential repairs of plumbing, and roofing.

INDEX